ECONOMICS

ECONOMICS

An Introductory Analysis

BY PAUL A. SAMUELSON

Professor of Economics
Massachusetts Institute of Technology

FIRST EDITION

McGraw-Hill Book Company, Inc.
NEW YORK TORONTO LONDON : 1948

ECONOMICS

THE MAPLE PRESS COMPANY, YORK, PA.

FOREWORD

Chaucer, seeing three men at work in the Middle Ages, asked them what they were doing. The first replied: "I'm earning pay, pretty good pay." The second said: "I'm shaping together intricate patterns of stone and glass." The third proclaimed: "I am building a cathedral." When I wrote this first edition of *Economics*, I was doing all three of these things without knowing it. But it was not the case that I started out with any such grandiloquent goals in mind.

Just as the story has already been told, this 1948 introductory textbook to economics was first conceived when my department head came to me with an offer I could not refuse—and could not have refused even if he had not been a valued friend. "Paul," he said, "800 MIT engineers are made to take a full year of economics. And they hate it. We've tried every one of the prominent texts. We've even written an in-house text. And still they don't like economics.

"Please lighten teaching duties for a semester or two and write a book that will be both interesting and accurate. Take as much or as little time as you want. Leave out whatever you want to. With your background in research and teaching, I know it will be a landmark text."

Well, flattery always wins over the young and brash. I was just back from the war and overflowing with ideas and energy. Even the available good contemporary introductory textbooks—such as that of Frank Taussig which I had taught from at Harvard—were woefully out of date. I knew in my bones that a window of opportunity was at hand: beginners in economics would be excited to study the macroeconomics of great depressions and hyperinflations. (The word "macroeconomics" had not yet come into the dictionary; it was not in this first edition's index!) Even the *micro*economics of supply and demand—how competition determines the relative prices of tea, coffee, lemons, cream, and salt—was still mired at the 1890 level of the art and science of economics.

So the die was cast. And my life was never the same afterward. What I thought would take three months took most of the 1945–1948 years. Yes, as I had suspected, I woke up to a Byronic success as a bestselling author. But what I had never expected was the durability of the book's dominance. Authorized and pirated translations appeared in scores of languages, so that sales abroad dominated the field even more than sales at home did. The coin I lusted for was not so much gold as it was scientific influence. When asked to testify before Congress on copyright protection, I abdicated in favor of more specialized and disinterested authorities.

I truly felt that imitation was the sincerest form of flattery; so that when in the course of four of five passing decades some other texts began to rival or outsell mine, I was pleased to find in them good things that had first entered the public domain in the present commemorative volume. Once, when Author X sued Author Y for plagiarism and copyright infringement, the exasperated judge threw the suit out of court with the curt remark: "They all seem to be Samuelson clones anyway." I hasten to stress the many innovations in contemporary textbooks that trace to the invisible college of economic researchers.

If it is anything, science is *public* knowledge, contributed to by all and rebuttable by anyone. As I had dared hope from the beginning, the authors most successful in competing with this work have frequently been friends of mine and not a few have been cherished pupils.

It will be clear by now that I think economics is an interesting and exciting and useful subject. Nor it its usefulness primarily to students in the West where competitive market mechanisms are predominantly relied upon. Just last month, when asked to prepare a foreword for the new Russian translation of Samuelson and Nordhaus's sixteenth edition, I wrote, "An introduction to modern mainstream economics will be even more valuable to a Russia or an emerging-market country than to college students in a Switzerland, America, or other quasi-capitalistic mixed economies. What our children absorb, so to speak with their mother's milk, you out there must learn from university studies—not in order to be converted to our way of life, but so that you can choose and pick rationally to best achieve your own cultural goals and desired standard of living."

An old classic, by definition, captures the state of the art in its time of conception. No living science stands still. But, as I have turned these pages at random, it has been a pleasant surprise to discover how much of the original verve and relevance is still there, preserved forever in amber on the library shelf.

That is the only kind of immortality that an author could have or want. And the same goes for this author's brainchild.

Paul A. Samuelson
Cambridge, MA
October, 1997

Preface

THIS book is written primarily as a textbook for those who will never take more than one or two semesters of economics but are interested in the subject as part of a general education. It aims at an understanding of the economic institutions and problems of American civilization in the middle of the twentieth century. National income provides the central unifying theme of the book.

No previous knowledge of economics is assumed. Each topic is developed leisurely and at length in recognition of the principle: "Short writing makes long reading." No use is made of mathematical equations or symbols. Even the currently fashionable use of geometric diagrams has been subordinated to an unusually extensive application of arithmetical examples, supplemented by pictorial charts.

With the needs of the intelligent layman in mind, the author has been ruthless in omitting completely many of the usual textbook topics and in reducing to more appropriate emphasis the conventional "marginal" analysis of "value and distribution" theory. This has released space for an extended presentation of the rich array of quantitative material about economic institutions that has become available for the first time only within the past half-dozen years. It has also made possible an increased emphasis on governmental and sociological influences. A modified case method has been used in the treatment of labor problems, business organization, and personal finance.

The subjects finally included represent a compromise, as they cover both (1) those economic topics important for understanding the postwar economic world and (2) the topics people find most interesting. Somewhat to the author's surprise, these two categories turned out in practice to coincide almost perfectly. The instinct of the nonspecialist is nearly infallible. The topics that excite him and pique his curiosity—the public debt, unemployment, inflation, social security, and so forth—are also of primary economic significance. The subjects that he finds tedious—bills of exchange, time and place utility, the pre-1913 National Banking System, and so forth—are usually of secondary importance from the standpoint of political economy.

Today the nonspecialist in physics deserves and expects to learn about atomic energy and nuclear structure in his first year of study, rather than to remain bogged down in elementary experiments on falling bodies and heat calorimetry. Why then should teachers of economics withhold from the first-year course the really interesting and vital problems of over-all economic policy?

Two concrete examples may help to suggest the direction of the elementary eeconomics text of the future. The Committee for Economic Development is a middle-of-the-road business group that initiates fundamental research in economic policy. Its leaders include the president of the Studebaker Automobile Company, the publisher of the *Saturday Evening Post*, a Republican Senator from New England, and other public-spirited businessmen. Every intelligent citizen should be able to read critically the important reports of this group, ranging as they do from international trade to postwar reconversion. But do present-day economics texts, built on foundations laid down at about the time of World War I, with chapters on monopolistic competition and national income appended—even the best of them—help in the above task?

Or, to take a second example: Perhaps present-day Americans will have no more important civic duty than that of approaching critically the President's Economic Report to Congress. Is it too much to ask of the text of the future that it contribute toward the effective performance of this task?

Over the past few years, several thousand civilian and armed-forces students—largely studying engineering or business—have been introduced in the M.I.T. required beginning course to such topics as saving and investment and income determination. The tentative verdict of the more than two dozen instructors that have participated is that introductory analysis of income determination is easier and more interesting than introductory "value and distribution theory." For this reason, the latter subject is treated in Part Three, after the treatment of income determination in Part Two.

Obviously, the present approach cannot avoid controversial problems and would not if it could. What it can try to do is avoid indoctrination and propagandizing. The important thing is to provide the analytical machinery that will enable the reader to arrive at, and defend, his own opinion, and, what is hardly less important, to understand the position of those with whom he most disagrees. If an author succeeds in providing this analytical insight, he need not worry unduly over the fact that any lengthy work will inevitably reveal some of his own personal predilections to the discerning reader.

The present work should provide material enough for a full year's course. A suggested table of contents for a one-semester course (like the author's at

Massachusetts Institute of Technology) is also included. By itself, Part One can be used for economic readings in an integrated social science survey course. Part Two may be used as a self-contained unit by intermediate money and banking and business-cycle courses to help fill the long-felt gap in introductory textual material on the theory of employment.

Each chapter has been planned to constitute a unit of understanding and is provided with an analytical summary and with discussion questions. Where a chapter tends to become long from the standpoint of classroom assignment, it has been broken up into sections A, B, and so forth. At numerous places, material has been placed in the appendix to a chapter. Such material is not necessarily more difficult, but it is usually something that can be eliminated if time is short. It is hoped that the introduction to the fundamentals of accounting will be found a useful part of the elementary course.

In the unexpectedly pleasurable task of writing and rewriting the various earlier versions of the present work, the author has incurred stupendous intellectual obligations—more than can be acknowledged. His M.I.T. colleagues have been shamefully exploited for their specialized knowledge and judicious criticism; special indebtedness is acknowledged to Profs. Robert L. Bishop, Ralph E. Freeman, Douglass V. Brown, Charles A. Myers, and Richard M. Bissell, Jr.; and to Drs. John G. Turnbull, Arthur G. Ashbrook, Jr., and John T. Wheeler. Numerous other economists in academic, government, and business life have been helpful, especially Prof. Daniel C. Vandermeulen of the Claremont Men's College, and Prof. George N. Halm of Tufts College and the Fletcher School of Law and Diplomacy. It may be added that the author's frequent refusal to accept good advice limits completely the liability of his intellectual creditors for any inadequacies of the present work.

Finally, it is pleasant to acknowledge the editorial and secretarial aid of Mrs. Lucy C. Maisel, Mrs. Elizabeth Metzelaar, Ethel Downer, Helen Sahagian, Mrs. Olive Gibson, and Mrs. Eleanor Clemence.

PAUL A. SAMUELSON

CAMBRIDGE, MASS.
April, 1948

Contents

Preface. v

Suggested Outline for a One-Semester Course. xix

PART ONE: BASIC ECONOMIC CONCEPT
AND NATIONAL INCOME

Chapter 1. INTRODUCTION 3

For Whom the Bell Tolls; Poverty Midst Plenty; Economic Description and Analysis; Economic Policy; Common Sense and Nonsense; Theory versus Practice; The Whole and the Part; Through the Looking Glass.

Chapter 2. CENTRAL PROBLEMS OF EVERY ECONOMIC SOCIETY . 12

A. Problems of Economic Organization 12
Boundaries and Limits to Economics; The Law of Scarcity.

B. The Technological Choices Open to Any Society 17
The Production-possibility or Transformation Curve; Increasing Costs; Economies of Mass Production: Decreasing Costs; The Famous Law of Diminishing Returns.

C. The Underlying Population Basis of Any Economy: Past and Future Population Trends 24
The Malthus Theory of Population; America and Europe Face Depopulation; The Net Reproduction Rate.

Summary 31

Chapter 3. FUNCTIONING OF A "MIXED" CAPITALISTIC ENTERPRISE SYSTEM 34

A. How A Free-enterprise System Solves the Basic Economic Problems . . . 35
Not Chaos but Economic Order; The Price System; Imperfections of Competition; Economic Role of Government.

ix

B. The Capitalistic Character of Modern Society   42
Capital and Time; Fixed and Circulating Capital; Capital and Income; Interest and the Real Net Productivity of Capital; Capital and Private Property.

C. Exchange, Division of Labor, and Money   51
Barter versus the Use of Money; Commodity Money, Paper Money, and Bank
Money; Price Ratios and Money Prices; Money as a Medium of Exchange or
as a Unit of Account; Money and Time.

Summary   59

Chapter 4. INDIVIDUAL AND FAMILY INCOME   61

Distribution of Income in the United States; The Inequality of Income; The De-
cline of Poverty; War Prosperity and Incomes; The So-called "Class Struggle";
Income from Work and from Property; The Rentier Class in a Decade of Falling
Interest Rates; Incomes of Farmers; Wage Incomes from Work; The Position of
Minorities.

Summary   84

Chapter 5. INDIVIDUAL AND FAMILY INCOME: EARNINGS IN
DIFFERENT OCCUPATIONS   86

The Labor Market's Basement; The Unskilled and Semiskilled Workers; The
Skilled Craftsmen; The White-collar Class; Professional Incomes; Is College
Worth While?; Economic Stratification and Opportunity.

Summary 107

Chapter 6. BUSINESS ORGANIZATION AND INCOME. 108

A. The Forms of Business Organization 108
The Population of Business Enterprises; Big, Small, and Infinitesimal Business;
The Single Proprietorship; Business Growth and the Need for Short-term
Capital; The Partnership; Causes of Business Growth; New Needs and
Sources of Capital; Disadvantages of the Partnership Form.

B. The Modern Corporation 118
Advantages and Disadvantages of the Corporate Form; How a Corporation
Can Raise Capital; Bonds; Common Stocks; Preferred Stocks; Advantages of
Different Securities; The Giant Corporation; The Evil of Monopoly; Divorce
of Ownership and Control in the Large Corporation; Amplification of Control
by the Pyramiding of Holding Companies; Leadership and Control of the
Large Corporation; The Curse of Bigness? . . . .

Summary 132

Appendix to Chapter 6: Elements of Accounting 134

The Balance Sheet; The Statement of Profit and Loss; Depreciation; The Relation between the Income Statement and the Balance Sheet; Earnings, Dividends, and Purchasing Power; Summary of Elementary Accounting Relations; Reserves, Funds, and Intangible Assets; Intangible Assets; Good Will and Monopoly Power.

Summary to Appendix 149

Chapter 7. THE ECONOMIC ROLE OF GOVERNMENT: EXPENDITURE, REGULATION, AND FINANCE 150

The Growth of Government Expenditure; The Growth of Government Controls and Regulation; Federal, Local, and State Functions; Federal Expenditure; Efficiency and Waste in Government; Socialism and the New Deal; Government Transfer Expenditures; Three Ways to Finance Expenditure; Financing Government Expenditure by New Money; Financing Deficits by Loan Finance or Borrowing; War Finance; Fiscal Policy during Boom and Depression.

Summary 166

Chapter 8. THE ECONOMIC ROLE OF GOVERNMENT: FEDERAL TAXATION AND LOCAL FINANCE. 168

Federal Taxation; Sales and Excise Taxes; Social Security, Payroll, and Employment Taxes; Corporation Income Taxes; The Progressive Income Tax; State and Local Expenditures; State and Local Taxes; Property Tax; Highway User Taxes; Sales Taxes; Payroll and Business Taxes; Personal Income and Inheritance Taxes; Borrowing and Debt Repayment; Coordinating Different Levels of Government.

Summary 184

Chapter 9. LABOR ORGANIZATION AND PROBLEMS. 185

History of the American Labor Movement; Craft versus Industrial Unions; Structure of the Labor Movement; Case Study of an AFL Carpenter; Case Study of a CIO Industrial Unionist; Case Study of a Labor Lawyer; The Case of the Philanthropic Capitalist; A Congressman's View of the Taft-Hartley Act of 1947; An Expert Looks at the Labor Problem.

Summary 199

Chapter 10. PERSONAL FINANCE AND SOCIAL SECURITY . . . 201

Budgetary Expenditure Patterns; Regional Differences in Cost of Living; Family Differences in the Cost of Living; The Backward Art of Spending Money; Income Patterns of Saving and Consumption; Graphical Depiction of the Propensity to Consume and to Save; The Wartime Accumulation of Saving; How People Borrow Money; Government Bonds as a Form of Saving; Investing in Securities; Economics of Home Ownership; Buying Life Insurance; Term Insurance;

Straight Life Insurance; Limited Payment Insurance; Endowment Plan; Social
Security and Health; Growth of Social Security.

Summary   223

Chapter 11. NATIONAL INCOME   225

Two Views: Money Income or Money Output; First View of National Income:
Cost and Earnings of Factors of Production; Transfer Payments; Real versus
Money Income; Second View of National Income as Net National Product; Final
Goods versus Double Counting of Intermediate Goods; Two Problems Introduced
by Government; Capital Formation; Gross versus Net Investment; International
Aspects of Income; Quantitative Recapitulation of National Income and Product.

Summary   243

PART TWO: DETERMINATION OF NATIONAL INCOME
AND ITS FLUCTUATIONS

Chapter 12. SAVING AND INVESTMENT   253

A. The Theory of Income Determination   253
The Cleavage between Saving and Investment; The Variability of Investment;
The Community's Propensity to Consume and to Save Schedules; How Income is Determined at Level Where Saving and Investment Schedules Intersect; Income Determination by Consumption and Investment; Arithmetical
Demonstration of Income Determination: A Third Restatement; The Theory
of Income Determination Restated.

B. Applications and Limitations of Income Analysis   265
The "Multiplier"; A Digression on the Identity between Measurable Saving
and Measurable Investment; Induced Investment and the Paradox of Thrift;
Deflationary and Inflatory Gaps; Taxation and Government Expenditure in
Income Analysis; Qualifications to Saving and Investment Analysis.

Summary   277

Chapter 13. PRICES, MONEY, AND INTEREST RATES   280

A. Prices   280
Inflation, Deflation, and Redistribution of Income between Economic Classes;
Effects of Changing Prices on Output and Employment; Galloping Inflation;
Goals of Long-term Price Behavior.

B. Money and Prices   285
The Three Kinds of Money: Small Coins, Paper Currency, and Bank Deposits; Why Checking Deposits Are Considered to Be Money; The Meaning
of the Value of Money as the Reciprocal of the Price Level; How the Limitation of the Quantity of Money Preserves Its Value and Affects the Price
Level; The Quantity Theory of Money; Inadequacies of the Quantity Theory:

Prices Not Proportional to Total Spending; Inadequacies of the Quantity Theory: Total Spending Not Proportional to the Stock of Money; Relation of Money and Spending to Saving, Investment, and Prices; Conclusion to Money and Prices.

C. Money and Interest Rates 297
Three Demands for Money; Transaction Demand for Money; Precautionary Motive; Investment Demand for Money; Money as a Temporary Form of Holding Wealth; Short-term Investments as Near Substitutes for Cash; Money as a Long-term Asset; Money and the Determination of Interest Rates; History of the Capital Markets since 1932; Money and Interest Rate during and after World War II.

Summary 306

Chapter 14. FUNDAMENTALS OF THE BANKING SYSTEM AND DEPOSIT CREATION 310

A. Nature and Functioning of the Modern Banking System 310
The Present Status of Banking; Creation of the Federal Reserve System; Banking as a Business; How Banks Developed Out of Goldsmith Establishments; Modern Fractional Reserve Banking; The Difference between a Bank and Any Corporation; Paradoxes of Fractional Reserve Banking; Making Banks Safe.

B. The Creation of Bank Deposits 323
Can Banks Really Create Money?; How Deposits Are Created; A "Monopoly Bank"; Simultaneous Expansion or Contraction by All Banks; Three Qualifications; Leakage into Hand-to-hand Circulation; Leakage into Bank Vault Cash; Possible Excess Reserves.

Summary 333

Chapter 15. FEDERAL RESERVE AND CENTRAL BANK MONETARY POLICY 337

Controlling the Business Cycle by Controlling the Quantity of Money; Brief Preview of How the Reserve Banks Can Affect the Supply of Money; The Federal Reserve Banks' Balance Sheet; Gold Certificates; "Reserve Bank Credit"; Federal Reserve "Open-market" Operations; Loan and Rediscount Policy; Changing Reserve Requirements as a Weapon of Monetary Control; The Problem of "Excess Reserves"; Summary of Reserve Banks' Control over Money; The Pyramid of Credit; War Finance and the Banks; The Inadequacies of Monetary Control of the Business Cycle; Public Debt Management and Monetary Control.

Summary 355

Chapter 16. INTERNATIONAL FINANCE AND DOMESTIC EMPLOY-
MENT. 358

A. International Trade and Capital Movements 359
Foreign Exchange Rates; The International Balance of Payments; Stages of
a Country's Balance of Payments; Basic Significance of International Capital
Movements; Financial versus Real Aspects of Foreign Lending.

B. Postwar International Trade and Full Employment 370
Exports and Jobs; Beggar-my-neighbor Policies; Postwar International Co-
operation; Problems of Postwar International Finance; Full Employment at
Home; Marshall Plan for Europe; The British Balance of Payments Problem;
Foreign Lending and the International Bank; Stable Exchange Rates and the
International; Monetary Fund; Freer Multilateral Trade.

Summary 382

Appendix to Chapter 16. A Few Mechanics of International Finance . . . 385

Freely Flexible Exchange Rates; Determinants of Supply and Demand; Disadvantages of Flexible Exchange Rates; Stable Exchange Rates; Workings of
the Gold Standard; The Equilibrating Specie-flow-price Mechanism; Income
Effects and the "Foreign Trade Multiplier."

Chapter 17. THE BUSINESS CYCLE. 393

Prosperity and Depression; Measuring and Forecasting the Business Cycle; Sta-
tistical Correction for Seasonal Variation and for Trends; The Four Phases of the
Cycle; Long Waves?; A First Clue to the Business Cycle: Capital Formation; A
Few Theories of the Business Cycle; Sunspots and Related Purely External
Theories; Purely Internal Theories; Combining External and Internal Elements
into a Synthesis; The Acceleration Principle.

Summary 408

Chapter 18. FISCAL POLICY AND FULL EMPLOYMENT WITHOUT
INFLATION. 409

A. Short-run and Long-run Fiscal Policy 410
Countercyclical Compensation versus Long-range Fiscal Policy; Counter-
cyclical Compensatory Policy; Types of Countercyclical Policy; Public
Works; Welfare and Other Expenditure; Automatic Changes in Tax Re-
ceipts; Countercyclical Tax-rate Changes; Limitations on Countercyclical
Compensatory Policy; Effects on Private Investment; Fiscal Perversity of
Local Finance; The "Pump-priming" Confusion; Long-run Fiscal Policy;
Secular Stagnation?; Investment Prospects; Personal and Corporate Saving
Prospects; Stagnation a Bogey?; Secular Exhilatation, Long-run Surplus
Financing, and Debt Retirement.

B. The Public Debt and Postwar Fiscal Policy 424
Retiring Nonbank Debt; Retiring Bank Debt; The Debt and the Propensity to Consume; Debt Retirement and Interest; The Public Debt and Its Limitations; External versus Internal Debt; Borrowing and Shifting Economic Burdens through Time; "We All Owe It to Ourselves"; Debt Management and Monetary Policy; The True Indirect Burden of Interest Charges; The Quantitative Problem of the Debt; Useful versus Wasteful Fiscal Policy; A Fundamental Difficulty with full Employment; The Employment Act of 1946.

Summary 437

Appendix to Chapter 18: Four Quantitative Paths to Full Employment . . . 440
Model I: Private Enterprise, Full Employment; Model II: Deficit-spending Path to Full Employment; Model III: Tax-reduction Path to Full Employment; Model IV: Balanced-budget Path to Full Employment.

PART THREE: THE COMPOSITION AND PRICING OF NATIONAL OUTPUT

Chapter 19. DETERMINATION OF PRICE BY SUPPLY AND DEMAND

Chapter 19. DETERMINATION OF PRICE BY SUPPLY AND
DEMAND 447

A. Determination of Market Price 447
The Demand Schedule and the Demand Curve; Elastic and Inelastic Demands; The Supply Schedule; Equilibrium of Supply and Demand.

B. Applications of Supply and Demand 457
Effects of Changes in Supply or Demand; A common Fallacy; Is the Law of Supply and Demand Immutable? Prices Fixed by Law.

Summary 466

Appendix to Chapter 19: Questions and Problems on Supply and Demand . . 469
Case 1: Constant Cost; Case 2: Increasing Costs and Diminishing Returns; Case 3: Completely Inelastic Supply and Economic Rent; Case 4: A Backward Rising Supply Curve; Case 5: A Possible Exception: Decreasing Cost; Case 6. Shifts in Supply.

Chapter 20. THE THEORY OF CONSUMPTION AND DEMAND . . 477
Theory of Consumer's Choice; Price and Income Changes in Demand; Cross Relations of Demand; Response of Quantity to Own Price; A Fundamental Law of Diminishing Substitution; The Paradox of Value; Consumer's Surplus.

Summary 485

Appendix to Chapter 20: Geometrical Analysis of Consumer Equilibrium . . 487

Chapter 21. COST AND THE EQUILIBRIUM OF THE FIRM UNDER
PERFECT AND IMPERFECT COMPETITION 491

A. The Maximum Profit Equilibrium Position within the Firm 491
Monopolistic Competition; The Firm's Demand under Perfect and Monopo-

listic Competition; Price, Quantity, and Total Revenue; Total and Marginal
Costs; Fixed Costs; Variable Costs; Total Cost; Average Cost; Marginal
Cost; Marginal Revenue and Price; Maximizing Profits; Graphical Depiction
of Firm's Optimum Position.

B. Applications of the Profit Maximizing Principles to Perfect Competition and
Patterns of Monopolistic Competition   503
Price and Supply under Perfect Competition; Decreasing Costs and the Break-
down of Perfect Competition; Minimizing Losses and Deciding When to
Shut Down; Firm and Industry; Price and Cost under Monopolistic Competi-
tion; Illustrative Patterns of Price; Chronically Overcrowded Sick Industries;
The Case of Few Sellers of Identical Products; Monopolies Maintained by
Constant Research and Advertising; Publicly Regulated Monopolies.

Summary   516

Chapter 22. PRODUCTION EQUILIBRIUM OF THE FIRM AND THE PROBLEM OF DISTRIBUTION   518

A. Production Equilibrium of the Firm   519
Final Production Equilibrium: Direct Approach; The Indirect Approach to
the Production Equilibrium; The "Production Function"; The Law of Diminishing Returns Once Again; Combining Inputs Optimally in Order to
Produce a Given Output; Final Production Equilibrium: Indirect Approach.

B. The Marginal Productivity Theory and the "Problem of Distribution" . .   526
Classical Theories of Rent; The So-called "Marginal Productivity Theory of
Distribution"; Can Trade-unions Raise Wages? Keeping Down the Total
Number of Laborers; Pushing Up Money Wages in Particular Occupations.

Summary   532

Appendix to Chapter 22: Graphical Depiction of Production Equilibrium . . .   534

Chap. 23. INTERNATIONAL TRADE AND THE THEORY OF COM-PARATIVE ADVANTAGE   538

Diversity of Conditions between Regions or Countries; A Simple Case: Europe
and America; America without Trade; Europe without Trade; The Opening Up of
Trade; Exact Determination of the Final Price Ratio.

Summary   549

Appendix to Chapter 23. Some Qualifications to the Discussion of Comparative
Advantage   552
Many Commodities and Countries; Increasing Costs; International Commodity
Movements as a Partial Substitute for Labor and Factor Movements; Decreasing
Costs and International Trade; Differences in Tastes or Demand as a Reason
for Trade; Transportation Costs.

Chapter 24. THE ECONOMICS OF TARIFF PROTECTION AND FREE
TRADE   559

Noneconomic Goals; Grossly Fallacious Arguments for Tariff; Keeping Money
in the Country; A Tariff for Higher Money Wages; Tariffs for Special-interest
Groups; Some Less Obvious Fallacies; A Tariff for Revenue; Tariffs and the
Home Market; Competition from Cheap Foreign Labor; A Tariff for Retaliation; The "Scientific" Tariff; Arguments for Protection under Dynamic Conditions; Tariffs and Unemployment; Tariffs for "Infant Industries"; The "Young
Economy" Argument.

Summary   569

Chapter 25. THE DYNAMICS OF SPECULATION AND RISK . . .   570

Speculation and Price Behavior over Time; The Great Stock-market Crash;
Gambling and Diminishing Utility; Economics of Insurance; What Can be Insured?; Joint Public and Private Responsibilities.

Summary   582

Chapter 26. SOCIAL MOVEMENTS AND ECONOMIC WELFARE . .   584

A. Fascism, Communism, and Socialism   584
The Crisis of Capitalism; A Bouquet of Isms; Fascism; Marxian Communism
and Soviet Russia; Socialism; Political Freedom and Economic Control.
B. The Use of An Over-all Pricing System under Socialism and Capitalism .   590
Review of Free Competitive Pricing; The Concept of General Equilibrium;
Pricing in a Socialist State: Consumption Goods Prices; The Distribution of In-
come; Pricing of Nonhuman Productive Resources; The Example of Land
Rent; The Role of the Interest Rate in a Socialist State; Wage Rates and
Incentive Pricing; Summary of Socialist Pricing; Welfare Economics in a
Free-enterprise Economy.

Summary   603

Chapter 27. EPILOGUE   606

Index   609

SUGGESTED OUTLINE FOR
A ONE-SEMESTER COURSE

Chapter 1. INTRODUCTION

Chapter 2. THE CENTRAL PROBLEMS OF EVERY ECONOMIC SOCIETY

A. Problems of Economic Organization
B. The Technological Choices Open to Any Society
C. The Underlying Population Basis of Any Economy: Past and Future Population Trends

Chapter 3. FUNCTIONING OF A "MIXED" CAPITALISTIC ENTERPRISE SYSTEM

A. How a Free Enterprise System Solves the Basic Economic Problems
B. The Capitalistic Character of Modern Society
C. Exchange, Division of Labor, and Money

Chapter 4. INDIVIDUAL AND FAMILY INCOME

Chapter 5. INDIVIDUAL AND FAMILY INCOME, CONTINUED: EARNINGS IN DIFFERENT OCCUPATIONS

Chapter 6. BUSINESS ORGANIZATION AND INCOME

A. The Forms of Business Organization
B. The Modern Corporation

Appendix: Elements of Accounting:

Chapter 19. DETERMINATION OF PRICE BY SUPPLY AND DEMAND

A. Determination of Market Price
B. Applications of Supply and Demand

Chapter 21. COST AND EQUILIBRIUM OF THE FIRM UNDER PERFECT AND IMPERFECT COMPETITION

A. The Maximum Profit Equilibrium Position within the Firm
B. Applications of the Profit Maximizing Principles to Perfect Competition and Patterns of Monopolistic Competition.

Chapter 7. THE ECONOMIC ROLE OF GOVERNMENT: EXPENDITURE, REGULATION, AND FINANCE

Chapter 8. THE ECONOMIC ROLE OF GOVERNMENT, CONTINUED: FEDERAL TAXATION AND LOCAL FINANCE

Chapter 9. LABOR ORGANIZATION AND PROBLEMS

Chapter 10. PERSONAL FINANCE AND SOCIAL SECURITY

Chapter 11. NATIONAL INCOME

Chapter 12. SAVING AND INVESTMENT

    A. The Theory of Income Determination
    B. Applications and Limitations of Income Analysis

Chapter 13. PRICES, MONEY, AND INTEREST RATES

    A. Prices
    B. Money and Prices
    C. Money and Interest Rates

Chapter 14. FUNDAMENTALS OF THE BANKING SYSTEM AND DEPOSIT CREATION

    A. Nature and Functioning of the Modern Banking System
    B. The Creation of Bank Deposits

Chapter 15. FEDERAL RESERVE AND CENTRAL · BANK MONETARY POLICY (OPTIONAL)

Chapter 16. INTERNATIONAL FINANCE AND DOMESTIC EMPLOYMENT

    A. International Trade and Capital Movements
    B. Postwar International Trade and Full Employment

Chapter 18. FISCAL POLICY AND FULL EMPLOYMENT WITHOUT INFLATION

    A. Short-run and Long-run Fiscal Policy
    B. The Public Debt and Postwar Fiscal Policy

ECONOMICS

The quality of the materials used in the manufacture of this book is governed by continued postwar shortages.

PART ONE

Basic Economic

Concepts and

National Income

Chapter 1: INTRODUCTION

FOR WHOM THE BELL TOLLS

The Dean of the Harvard Law School used to address the entering class: "Take a good look at the man on your right, and the man at your left; because next year one of you won't be here." Much the same can be said of everyone's stake in the successful functioning of the economic system.

When, and if, the next great depression comes along, any one of us may be completely unemployed—without income or prospects. Or if not totally unemployed, only partially employed at reduced hours and pay in an uninteresting dead-end job, without hope of advancement or assurance of keeping even what little we have. There is no vaccination or advance immunity from this modern-day plague. It is no respecter of class or rank. Neither veteran's preference nor go-getter pep talks nor advanced degrees can guarantee a job when whole factories are shutting down and when every industry is contracting production and employment.

From a purely selfish point of view, then, it is desirable to gain understanding of the first problem of modern economics: the causes on the one hand of unemployment, overcapacity, and depression; and on the other of prosperity, full employment, and high standards of living. But no less important is the fact—clearly to be read from the history of the twentieth century—that the political health of a democracy is tied up in a crucial way with the successful maintenance of stable high employment and living opportunities. It is not too much to say that the widespread creation of dictatorships and the resulting World War II stemmed in no small measure from the world's failure to meet this basic economic problem adequately.

POVERTY MIDST PLENTY

Modern economics tries to explain, among other things, how it is that nations are alternately afflicted with the dizzy ups and downs of business activity. In the old days before science and the industrial revolution had

3

developed our tremendous mechanical, electrical, and technological inventions, there were often periodic famines. The statistics of marriages varied inversely with the price of bread. Thousands or millions would die as a result of floods, droughts, or other easily recognized natural catastrophes. Everyone knew the causes of disasters, but nobody could do much about them.

Today it is just the opposite. Now we know how to produce an abundance of goods, but we are subject to periodic depressions of obscure causation. Bread is cheap in depression, but present-day marriages follow job opportunities rather than the cost of food. Famine due to crop failure in one part of the world can now be relieved by shipments from elsewhere. People go hungry in modern slumps not because we can produce too little but seemingly because we can produce too much. A man from Mars or a Rip Van Winkle from an earlier century would have been at a loss had he returned to the world of the 1930's. He would have thought that everybody had lost his senses. Little pigs were plowed under while families did without meat. Because we had new efficient factories, we did without production. Because we had too many skilled and willing hands, unemployment prevailed. Everybody tried to save and hoard money, with the result that everyone got poorer and poorer.

The man from Mars would have been even more surprised to observe that the onset of history's most destructive and bloody war, instead of depressing American business conditions further, had just the opposite effects. Business boomed as never before. Prices had to be held in rather than supported. Family and business savings mounted. Despite shortages, the American civilian standard of living surpassed all previous levels.

ECONOMIC DESCRIPTION AND ANALYSIS

It is the first task of modern economic science to describe, to analyze, to explain, to correlate these fluctuations of national income. Both boom and slump, price inflation and deflation, are our concern. This is a difficult and complicated task. Because of the complexity of human and social behavior, we cannot hope to attain the precision of a few of the physical sciences. We cannot perform the controlled experiments of the chemist or biologist. Like the astronomer we must be content largely to "observe." But economic events and statistical data observed are unfortunately not so well behaved and orderly as the paths of the heavenly planets. Fortunately, however, our answers need not be accurate to several decimal places; on the contrary, if only the right general *direction* of cause and effect can be determined, we shall have made a tremendous step forward.

Knowledge and understanding of nature and society are worth while for their own sake. Just as it is interesting to know the paths of planets and the antics of atoms, it is worth while to know how banks create money, how inflations behave, how supply and demand help to determine prices. In addition to knowledge for its own sake—and to most people of far greater importance— there is the hope that the findings of physics may help engineers make useful technological improvements, that the study of physiology may promote medical advancement, and that the dispassionate analysis of how economic events happen will enable society to devise ways to keep some of the more unpleasant ones from happening.

ECONOMIC POLICY

This brings us to the important problem of economic policy. Ultimately, understanding should aid in control and improvement. How can the business cycle be diminished? How can economic progress be furthered? How can standards of living be made more equitable?

At every point of our analysis we shall be seeking to shed light on these policy problems. But to succeed in this, the student of economics must first cultivate an objective and detached ability to see things as they *are*, regardless of his likes or dislikes. The fact must be faced that economic subjects are close to everybody emotionally. Blood pressures rise and voices become shrill whenever deep-seated beliefs and prejudices are involved; many of these prejudices are thinly veiled rationalizations of special economic interest. A doctor passionately interested in stamping out disease must train himself to observe things as they are. His bacteriology cannot be a different one from that of a mad scientist out to destroy the human race by plague. Wishful thinking is bad thinking and leads to little wish fulfillment.

In the same way there is only one valid reality in a given economic situation, however hard it may be to recognize and isolate it. There is not one theory of economics for Republicans and one for Democrats; not one for workers and one for employers. It appears that careful students are coming into increasingly greater agreement on the broad analytical outline of the forces determining national income and full employment, such as is sketched in later chapters.

This does not mean that economists always agree in the *policy* field. One economist may be for full employment at any cost; another may not rank it of primary importance; still another may be of the opinion that the problem will take care of itself in the immediate years ahead. Ethical questions each citizen must decide for himself, and an expert is entitled to only one vote along with everyone else.

Economics is not an easy subject. True, it does not require the mental application of, say, mathematics. But there is a definiteness in mathematics despite its complexity, so that most people feel that, by gritting their teeth and applying themselves sufficiently, they can learn to solve such things as quadratic equations just as other ordinary mortals have done.

Economics at first seems less definite. The world of prices, wages, interest rates, stocks and bonds, banks and credit, taxes and expenditure is a complicated one. Every question seems to have two (or more!) sides, and often the right answer seems to be only that of the last man to buttonhole you.

Now no one can understand a complicated subject like chemistry prior to long and careful study. This is an advantage and a disadvantage. The man on the street or behind a newspaper desk cannot possibly consider himself a final authority on these subjects—which is all to the good. On the other hand, the new student must be made familiar with all the basic concepts for the first time, all of which takes a good deal of time.

From childhood days on, everyone knows something about economics. This is both helpful and deceptive: helpful, because much knowledge can be taken for granted; deceptive, because it is natural and human to accept uncritically the truth of superficially plausible views. Everyone of college age knows a good deal about money, perhaps even more than he realizes. Thus he rightly laughs at the child who prefers the large nickel to the small dime or the shiny quarter to the paper dollar bill; and at the Basque peasants who murdered the visiting artist for his book of blank checks.

But a little knowledge may be a dangerous thing. Because a union leader has successfully negotiated several labor contracts, he may feel that he is an expert on the economics of wages. A businessman who has "met a payroll" may feel that his views on price control are final. A banker who can balance his books may conclude that he knows all there is to know about the creation of money. And an economist who has studied the business cycle may be under the illusion that he can outguess the stock market.

Moreover, peculiarly in a field where such an everyday concept as "capital" may have 10 or more different meanings, we must watch out for the "tyranny of words." The world is complicated enough without introducing further confusions and ambiguities because two different names are unknowingly being used for the same thing, or because the same word is being applied to quite different phenomena. Jones may call Robinson a liar for holding that the cause of depression is oversaving, saying, "Underconsumption is really the cause." Schwartz may enter the argument with the assertion, "You are both wrong. The real trouble is underinvestment." They may continue to argue all night, when really if they stopped to analyze their language, they might find that there were absolutely no differences in their opinions about the facts and that only a verbal confusion was involved.

Similarly, words may be treacherous because we do not react in a neutral manner to them. Thus a man who approves of a government program to ration housing will call it a program of "social planning" while an unsympathetic opponent will describe the same activity as "totalitarian bureaucratic regimentation." Who can object to the former, and who could condone the latter? Yet they refer to the same thing. One does not have to be an expert in *semantics*—the study of language and its meaning—to realize that scientific discussion requires us to avoid such emotional terminology, wherever possible.

THEORY VERSUS PRACTICE

The economic world is extremely complicated. Furthermore, it is usually not possible to make economic observations under controlled experimental conditions characteristic of scientific laboratories. A physiologist who wishes to determine the effects of penicillin on pneumonia may be able to "hold other things equal" by using two test groups who differ only in the fact that they do and do not get penicillin injections. The economist is less fortunately placed. If he wishes to determine the effect of a gasoline tax on fuel consumption, he may be vexed by the fact that, in the same year when the tax was imposed, pipe lines were first introduced. Nevertheless, he must try—if only mentally—to isolate the effects of the tax, with "other things being equal." Otherwise, he will understand the economic effects neither of taxation, nor of transportation improvements, nor of both together. The difficulty of analyzing causes when controlled experimentation is impossible is well illustrated by the confusion of the savage medicine man who thinks that witchcraft and a little arsenic are both necessary to kill his enemy, or that only after he has put on a green robe in spring will the trees afterward do the same.[1] As a result of this limitation and many others, our quantitative economic knowledge is far from complete. This does not mean that we do not have great amounts of accurate statistical knowledge available. We do. Bales of census data, market information, and financial statistics have been collected by governments, trade associations, and business concerns.

Even if we had more and better data, it would still be necessary—as in every

[1] In logic this is sometimes called the *post hoc, ergo propter hoc* fallacy (after this, therefore because of this).

science—to *simplify*, to *abstract* from the infinite mass of detail. No mind can apprehend a bundle of unrelated facts. All analysis involves abstraction. It is always necessary to *idealize*, to omit detail, to set up simple hypotheses and patterns by which the mass of facts are to be related, to set up the right questions before we go out looking at the world as it is. Every theory, whether in the physical or biological or social sciences, distorts reality in that it over-simplifies. But if it is a good theory, what is omitted is greatly outweighed by the beam of illmuination and understanding that is thrown over the diverse empirical data.

Properly understood, therefore, theory and observation, deduction and induction cannot be in conflict. Like eggs, there are only two kinds of theories: good ones and bad ones. And the test of a theory's goodness is its usefulness in illuminating observational reality. Its logical elegance and fine-spun beauty are irrelevant. Consequently, when a student says, "That's all right in theory but not in practice," he really means "That's not all right in theory," or else he is talking nonsense.

THE WHOLE AND THE PART

The first lesson in economics is: things are often not what they seem. Some examples chosen at random may illustrate this:

1. If all farmers work hard and nature cooperates in producing a bumper crop, total farm income *falls*.

2. *One* man by great ingenuity in hunting a job or by a willingness to work for less may thereby solve his own unemployment problem, but *all* cannot solve their problems in this way.

3. Higher prices for one industry may benéfit its members but, if the prices of everything bought and sold increased in the same proportion, no one would be any better off.

4. It may pay the United States to reduce tariffs charged on goods imported even if other countries refuse to do likewise.

5. It may pay a business firm to take on some business at much *less than full costs*.

6. Attempts of individuals to save more in depression may *lessen the total* of the community's savings.

7. What is prudent behavior for an individual or a single business firm may at times be *folly* for a nation or a state.

In the course of this book, each of the above seeming paradoxes will be resolved. Once explained, each is so obvious that you will wonder how anyone could ever have failed to notice it. This again is typical of economics. There are no magic formulas or hidden tricks. Anything that is really correct will seem perfectly reasonable once the argument is carefully developed.

At this point it is just as well to mention that many of the above paradoxes hinge around one single confusion or fallacy, called by logicians the "fallacy of composition." What is true for each is not necessarily true for all; and conversely, what is true for all may be quite false for each individual. Especially where his own interests are at stake, an individual tends to look only at the immediate effects upon himself of an economic event. A worker thrown out of employment in the buggy industry cannot be expected to reflect that new jobs may have been created in the automobile industry. But we must be prepared to do so. The reader should try to give other examples of this fallacy; *e.g.*, standing on tiptoes at a parade, counterfeiting meat-ration coupons, cutting production in order to raise one's prices, etc.

In an introductory survey, the economist is interested in the workings of the economy as a whole rather than in the viewpoint of any one group or unit. Social and national policies rather than individual policy are his goals. Too often, everybody's business is nobody's business. It is just as well, therefore, to understand at the beginning that an elementary course in economics does not pretend to teach one how to run a business or a bank, how to spend one's money wisely, or how to get rich quick from the stock market. However, it is to be hoped that general economics will provide a useful background for many such activities.

Certainly the economist must know a good deal about how businessmen, consumers, and investors behave and think. This does not mean that those individuals must use the same language and methods in coming at their decisions as economists find useful in describing their behavior—any more than the planets need know that they are following the elliptical paths traced by the astronomer. Just as many of us have been speaking prose all out lives without knowing it, so many businessmen would be surprised to learn that their behavior is capable of systematic economic analysis. This unawareness is not necessarily to be deprecated. It does not help a baseball pitcher to know the laws of aerodynamics; in fact, if we become self-conscious about how to button our shirts, we may find it harder to do.

THROUGH THE LOOKING GLASS

Here at the beginning it is best to point out one further source of difficulty which runs through economic discussions. When there is substantially full employment, certain important economic principles are valid. When there is substantial unemployment, many things go exactly into reverse. We then move into a topsy-turvy wonderland where right seems left and left is right; up seems down; and black, white.

Mathematicians tell us that in addition to Euclidean geometry there exist non-Euclidean geometries. In these non-Euclidean worlds, two parallel lines may meet—just as on the spherical surface of the earth two "parallel" lines perpendicular to the equator meet at the pole. What is true of one kind of world may be false of another. Similarly, for the modern world of unemployment, the conclusions of the old classical or Euclidean economics may be not at all applicable.

This difference between what is true when there is full employment and when there is unemployment may be illustrated by three examples, all of which will be fully explained later and need not be understood at this point:

1. Men mine gold from the bowels of the earth only to have it go back to the earth in the vaults at Fort. Knox, Ky. How good or bad this strange procedure is depends in an important way upon whether or not there is full employment.

2. Nations try in the worst way to raise their standards of living by exporting goods and by *not* importing them from other countries. This anxiety to give away goods would be merely stupid under conditions of full employment, but it makes some sense in a world of unemployment.

3. Thriftiness and parsimony may be individual and social virtues during a war or boom period, while during a depression these individual virtues may be self-defeating social vices that intensify our ills and represent the height of folly.

After one has thoroughly mastered the analysis of national income determination, it is not hard to steer one's way with confidence in these seemingly difficult fields. The important hard kernel of truth in the older economics of full employment can then be separated from the chaff of misleading applications. Moreover, as we shall see later, if modern economics does its task well so that widespread unemployment is substantially banished from democratic societies, then its importance will wither away and the traditional economics (whose concern is *wise* allocation of fully employed resources) will really come into its own—almost for the first time.

A preview of the ground to be covered may be helpful. Here in Part One we deal with the facts, institutions, and analysis necessary to an understanding of national income or output. In Part Two we analyze the causes of prosperity and depression—how the processes of saving and investment interact to determine the level of monetary purchasing power, income, and employment all over the world. Part Three is concerned with the forces of competition and monopoly which determine the composition of the national income, both in terms of goods and services and in terms of its distribution among different workers and property owners.

QUESTIONS FOR DISCUSSION

1. How do you expect to fare in the next depression?

2. Why does the physicist often talk about a frictionless system, when there is no such thing? Is there any justification for this?

3. Discuss the emotional content of the following words: regimentation, planning, usury, monopolist, gambling, speculation, American way of life, free enterprise, cartels, thrift, hoarding.

4. Give an example of the fallacy of composition.

5. Give an example of an economic principle which is valid when there is full employment but misleading when there is unemployment.

Chapter 2: CENTRAL PROBLEMS

OF EVERY ECONOMIC SOCIETY

AT THE foundations of any community there will always be found a few universal economic conditions. Certain background problems hold as much for our present-day economy as they did in the days of Homer and Caesar. And they will continue to be relevant in the "brave new world" of the years ahead.

In this chapter we shall see what some of these universal conditions are: (A) how every society must meet a triplet of *basic problems of economic organization;* (B) how technological knowledge together with limited amounts of economic resources defines the available choices between goods and services open to a community, and how these *production possibilities* are subject to changing costs and to the law of diminishing returns; (C) finally, the *underlying population or human basis of any economy.*

The above topics form the three parts of this chapter. We leave to Chap. 3 those important special economic features characteristic of our own mixed system of private and public enterprise.

A. *PROBLEMS OF ECONOMIC ORGANIZATION*

Any society, whether it consists of a totally collectivized communistic state, a tribe of South Sea Islanders, a capitalistic industrial nation, a Swiss Family Robinson or Robinson Crusoe, and one might almost add, a colony of bees, must somehow meet three fundamental economic problems.

1. *What* commodities shall be produced and in what quantities? That is, how much and which of many alternative goods and services shall be produced?

2. *How* shall they be produced? That is, by whom and with what resources and in what technological manner are they to be produced?

3. *For whom* are they to be produced? That is, who is to enjoy and get the benefit of the goods and services provided? Or, to put the same thing in another way, how is the total of national product to be distributed among different individuals and families?

These three questions[1] are fundamental and common to all economies. In a primitive civilization, custom may rule every facet of behavior. What, how, and for whom may be decided by reference to traditional ways of doing things. To members of another culture, the practices followed may seem bizarre and unreasonable, but the members of the tribe or clan may be so familiar with existing practices as to be surprised, and perhaps offended, if asked the reason for things. Thus, some tribes consider it desirable not to accumulate wealth but to give it away in the *potlatch*—a roisterous celebration. But this deviation from the acquisitive behavior of competition will not surprise anthropologists who know from their studies that what is correct behavior in one culture is often the greatest crime in another.

In the bee colony, all such problems, even those involving an extraordinarily elaborate cooperative division of labor, are solved automatically by means of so-called "biological instincts."

At the other extreme we can imagine an omnipotent, benevolent or malevolent, dictator who by arbitrary decree and fiat decides just what, how, and for whom economic activity is to be carried on. Or we might still have organization by decree, but with decrees drawn up by democratic vote; or what is more likely in view of the multiplicity and complexity of economic decisions, with decrees drawn up by selected legislative or planning authorities.

.Finally, as Chap. 3 develops at length, in a so-called "capitalist free-enterprise economy," a system of prices, of markets, of profits and losses primarily[2] determines what the methods of production and costs of goods shall be; and finally, how much different people shall get of the total national product or income as their share (for services performed and property supplied, or through government legislation) out of which to buy goods and services.

[1] Some economists would list a fourth fundamental question. *When* are goods to be consumed? That is, how much of present consumption shall we give up in order that resources may be devoted to producing capital goods that will increase future consumption. However, this may be treated as a special case under the problem of deciding *what* goods and services— present consumption goods versus capital goods—shall be produced.

[2] There never has been a 100 per cent purely automatic enterprise system. Even in our capitalistic system, the government has an important role in modifying the workings of the price system.

BOUNDARIES AND LIMITS TO ECONOMICS

The study of economics can provide part of the material necessary in answering these questions. Many specialists other than economists could also help in providing relevant facts and analysis bearing on them. Thus, psychology (the study of mental behavior), sociology (the study of group behavior), anthropology (the study of races and cultures), and even physiology (the biological study of how organisms function) might cast light on *what* people want in the way of goods and services: why they sometimes like nourishing food and sometimes do not; why people often find it as necessary to have a shiny automobile as a wife or a baby, and so forth.

Then, too, such noneconomic studies as the physical sciences and engineering provide much of the basis for the second question of *how* goods are to be produced. It is not the task of the economist to deal with the precise technological laws that determine how certain resource *inputs* are *transformed* into output of goods and services. By a division of labor common to all sciences, he takes much of the technological groundwork for granted, just as he must often take psychological tastes and social institutions for granted. Moreover, even in the technological sphere, his interests are not those of the physicist. The economist may regard a certain process as more efficient than another even though the first law of thermodynamics asserts that no energy can be created or lost in any process. And he may choose to disregard the physical fact that one process has a greater ratio of useful work (less useless heat and energy dissipation according to the second law of thermodynamics) than a second, provided the second is using up a cheaper source of energy. We must also guard against the muddled thinking that results from an attempt to reduce all values to ergs or energy units, as retired engineers (*viz.*, the short-lived technocrat movement of the early 1930's) are so often tempted to do.

When we come to the third question of the desirable distribution of wealth and income between individuals, we leave the field of science altogether. *De gustibus non est disputandum:* there is no disputing (scientifically!) tastes; and the same goes for ethics. We must leave the definition of social *ends* to the philosopher, the theologian, the statesman, and to public opinion.

To summarize the results of this section:

Economics cannot try to cover every fact of the universe. It must take certain things for granted as having been established by workers in other scientific fields. The institutional framework of society, the tastes of individuals, the ends for which they strive—all these must be taken as being given. These and more. For the character and quantity of resources and the technological facts about their combinations and productive transformations must also be taken as given.

Economics can, then, pursue the positive task of describing, analyzing, and understanding the processes that take place within the above framework. More than that, economics—and here it becomes "political economy"—can hope to appraise, and improve, the efficiency with which a community mobilizes its *means* to achieve the prescribed *ends*.

Fortunately, there is some underlying agreement with respect to social ends. Most western peoples profess to prefer (1) a measure of individual freedom of choice and action, (2) a high and improving standard of living, (3) an equitable distribution of income between classes so that gross inequalities are to be tolerated only if there is some strong and compelling reason.[1]

It is easy to see, therefore, that full employment, which we have taken to be the central problem of modern economics in the Introduction, must be viewed against the backdrop of two broader goals characteristic of *any* economy—past, present, or future. It is not enough simply to get men and machines employed at any old job, such as digging holes and then filling them. Rather must the goals be (1) *useful* or wise employment of resources, *i.e.*, a better, larger, and more stable level of production and consumption; and (2) an equitable distribution of that output between individuals.

From this point of view, unemployment is seen to be such an important evil precisely because it does represent one very unwise use of resources (in fact complete wastage!) and because it falls so heavily on those who already have been most adversely treated in distribution of income. The appendix is not the most important organ in the body, nor is the wisdom tooth anything but the least important. Yet each of these requires a great deal of attention. Similarly, full employment would not be characterized as such an important problem were it not for the fact that it is the one which has been "acting up" most in our generation and that it therefore is first on the social agenda calling for action. As the problem of unemployment is solved, other problems of wrong What, How, and For Whom, such as are created by monopolistic trade practices, excess corporate profits, international barriers, or wrong location of labor, will move up to first place on the program.

Solving the problem of unemployment and low income is particularly important because our failure here aggravates almost every other economic prob-

---

[1] The careful reader will note that some of these ends may be in partial conflict. Thus, shall a man be free to water milk? Or to exploit "his" patented invention so as to earn more in a year than most men can earn in a century? Freedom and equality may come into partial conflict. In itself "equality of opportunity" is an ambiguous slogan. What does it mean to treat equally people who have different amounts of property and different abilities? Moreover, a lottery or sweepstake provides equality of opportunity but a very bad distribution of income.

lem, such as that of old-age security, regional maladjustments of the labor force, or public and private health. The attainment of full employment will certainly itself create new problems, but these are intrinsic and must be squarely faced.

THE LAW OF SCARCITY

What to produce, how, and for whom would not be problems if resources were unlimited, if an infinite amount of every good could be produced, or if human wants were fully satisfied. Then it would not matter if too much of any particular good were produced. It would not matter if labor and materials were combined unwisely. Since everyone could have as much as he pleased, it would not matter how goods and income were divided among different individuals and families. There would be no *economic goods*, i.e., no goods that are relatively scarce, and there would hardly be any need for a study of economics or "economizing." All goods would be *free goods*, like water or air.

In the world as it is, even little children are supposed to learn in growing up that "both" is not an admissible answer to a choice of "which." Compared to backward nations or compared to previous centuries, modern industrial societies seem very wealthy indeed. But even the richest of such nations, the United States, would have to be hundreds of times more productive than it now is to give everybody as comfortable a standard of living as is enjoyed by our most fortunate few. Higher production levels always seem to bring in their train higher consumption standards. People feel that they want and "need" steam heat, indoor plumbing, education, movies, books, automobiles, travel, music (one kind or the other), fashionable clothes, etc. The biological scientist may tell them that they can be well nourished on a thin porridge for a few cents a day, but that leaves them as cold as the information that the chemicals in their bodies are worth less than a dollar. Anyone who has kept a family budget knows that the necessities of life, the absolute musts, have little to do with the minimum physiological needs of food, clothing, and shelter necessary to keep life flickering.

During the Great Depression that followed the stock-market crash of 1929, it was fashionable for popular writers to announce the repeal of the "law of scarcity" saying that we had moved into a new scientific era in which the economic system knew how to produce more than could be consumed. This was quite wrong. Such observers were perfectly right in pointing out that the system could produce more than we were then consuming, that nobody knew quite how to correct this, and that the problem of *technological unemployment* could not be shrugged off lightly. They were also right in pointing out that "freedom from (physical) want" could be achieved for the more productive parts of the globe if only unemployment could be banished. But they should also have realized, as the war period has since helped to confirm, that even with all resources working at top efficiency the average standard of living would be a quite moderate one compared to what we please to call the "American way of life," as revealed, for example, in rosy magazine advertisements. It is shown in Chap. 4 that dividing up equally the 1929 full-employment income among every man, woman, and child would still yield only an average of $15 per person per week. Even today, the figure would not exceed $25. Smashing the atom to liberate its internal energy would still not bring us near to the state of "bliss." There can be no shortage of useful work to be done. An infinite number of tunes are still to be written. If ever consumption needs should be sated—which is unlikely—there would always remain the alternative of leisure, recreation, and the other elements that go to make up the good life.

Today one hears the expression "secular stagnation" applied to our economy, and we shall discuss this concept at some length in later chapters. But whatever this means, it does *not* mean that our productive *potentialities* are ceasing to grow or that human and social wants and needs are becoming satiated. Nevertheless, there is a real possibility to be faced that it is as hard for wealthy nations to avoid unemployment without drastic action as it is for a camel to pass through the eye of a needle. But more of this anon.

B. *THE TECHNOLOGICAL CHOICES OPEN TO ANY SOCIETY*

THE PRODUCTION-POSSIBILITY OR TRANSFORMATION CURVE

We have discussed the basic economic fact that *limitation* of the total resources capable of producing different commodities necessitates a choice between relatively scarce commodities. This can be illustrated quantitatively by simple arithmetic examples and by means of geometrical diagrams. It has been found that diagrams and graphs are important visual aids in many parts of economics, so that a little care at the beginning in understanding them will be rewarded manyfold later on.

Consider an economy with only so many people, only so much technical knowledge, only so many factories and tools, only so much land, water power, and natural resources. In deciding what shall be produced and how, the economy must really decide just how these resources are to be allocated among the thousands of different possible commodities: how much land shall go into wheat cultivation or into pasturage, how many factories will produce hairpins, how much skilled labor shall go into machine shops, etc.

This is very complicated even to discuss, much less to do. Let us, therefore, simplify (idealize, abstract) and assume that there are *only two* different goods or classes of goods to be produced. For dramatic purposes, let us consider the famous pair, butter and guns, two commodities popularly used to illustrate the wartime problem of choosing between civilian and military production. Those who are war-weary may substitute any other two commodities such as bread and wine, or if they are teetotalers, bread and hyacinths, or for prosaic souls, food and clothing.

Now, if all resources are thrown into the production of civilian goods or butter, there will still be at most some maximum amount that can be produced per year. The exact amount depends upon the quantitative and qualitative resources of the economy in question and the technological efficiency with which they are used. Let us suppose that 5 (million) pounds of butter is this maximum amount that can then be produced in the existing state of the technological arts.

At the other extreme, let us imagine that 100 per cent of society's resources were to be devoted to the production of guns.[1] Only some maximum number of guns could be produced, say, 15 (thousand) guns of a certain description can be produced if we are willing to produce no butter.

TABLE 1. *Alternative Possibilities in the Production of Butter and Guns*

	A	B	C	D	E	F
Butter, millions of pounds............	0	1	2	3	4	5
Guns, thousands....................	15	14	12	9	5	0

These are the extreme possibilities. In between there are still others. If we are willing to give up some butter, we can have some guns; if we are willing to give up some guns, we can have some butter. A schedule of a number of possibilities is given in Table 1, with F being the extreme where all butter

[1] Of course, this could not really happen because without some civilian production the society could not live. But we are considering possibilities: the subjunctive mood not the indicative.

and no guns are produced, and *A* being the opposite extreme where all resources go into guns. In between, at *E*, *D*, *C*, and *B*, butter is increasingly

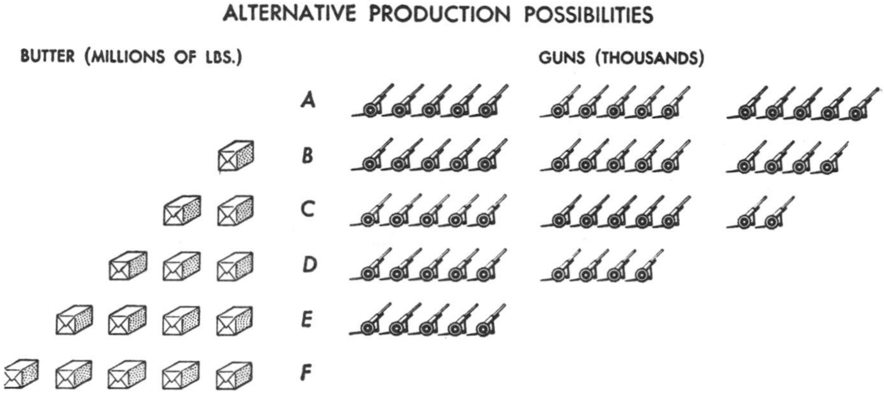

ALTERNATIVE PRODUCTION POSSIBILITIES

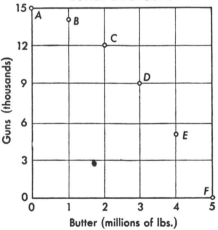

FIG. 1.

being given up in return for more guns. Butter is "transformed" into guns, not physically but by diverting resources from one use to the other.

Our numerical schedule can also be represented diagrammatically by Fig. 1, which should be self-explanatory.

It may be even more illuminating to represent this same production-possibility or production-transformation schedule by measuring butter along the horizontal axis and guns along the vertical, as in Fig. 2.

The student should, of course, be able to go directly from the numerical table to the final diagram; by counting over 5 butter units to the right in *F* and going up 0 gun units; in *E*, by counting over 4 butter units to the right and going up 5 gun units; and finally in *A* by going to the right 0 butter units and up 15 gun units.

POSSIBILITIES OF TRANSFORMING BUTTER INTO GUNS

FIG. 2. Each point shows the maximum amount of guns obtainable at full employment when different amounts of butter are to be produced.

We may fill in all intermediate positions, even those involving fractions of a million pounds, or of a thousand guns, as in Fig. 3.

The curve that we now have represents the fundamental fact that a full-employment economy must always in producing one good be giving up something of another. This assumes, of course, that at least some resources can be transferred from one good to another; *e.g.*, steel is used for guns and also enters into the production of butter via farm machinery.

THE "PRODUCTION - POSSIBILITY" OR "TRANSFORMATION" CURVE

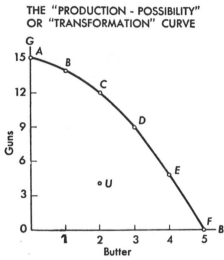

FIG. 3. This shows how society can choose to substitute "guns" for "butter," assuming a given state of technology and a given total of resources. Any point inside the curve, such as *U*, indicates that resources are not being fully employed in the best known way. SOURCE: Table 2. A smooth curve has been passed through the points of the previous figure.

Substitution is the law of life in a full-employment economy. But what if there had been widespread unemployment of resources: idle men, idle land, idle factories? We have already warned that our economic laws may then be quite different. And this is one such instance.

With unemployment we are not on the transformation or Production-possibility curve at all, but somewhere *inside* it; say at *U*, producing only 2 (million) pounds of butter and 4 (thousand) guns. If resources are idle, by putting them to work, we can have more butter *and* more guns. We can move from *U* to *D* or *E*, thereby getting more butter and more guns.

This throws light on the different important historical wartime experience of three countries: the United States, Germany, and Russia.

After 1940, the United States was able to become the "arsenal of democracy" and to enjoy civilian living standards higher than ever before, largely by taking up the slack of unemployment. Hitler Germany's war effort began in 1933, long before any formal declaration. It stemmed from a period of unemployment acute enough to win him the votes necessary to get into power peacefully. But the total extra output made possible by taking up unemployed workers and plants was almost completely siphoned into war goods rather than into higher civilian consumption. The Russians, having no unemployment before the war, were already on their Production-possibility curve. They had no choice but to substitute war goods for civilian production—with consequent privation.

INCREASING COSTS

Our transformation curve, sloping as it does rightward and downward (*i.e.*, from northwest to southeast), summarizes the fact of substitution and choice between commodities at full employment. But curving out as it does, a further important economic principle is illustrated: *as we want more of a good, we must usually pay a higher cost for it; we must give up more and more.*

The reader should verify that, in reversing the picture and thinking of giving up guns and taking on butter, costs of butter in terms of guns will be ever increasing. Thus the relationship is perfectly symmetrical.

The plausibility of the above general results may be increased if we consider that the first few guns can be produced in part with the kind of resources that are no good for butter anyway. If more guns are wanted, we must use resources that are quite valuable for butter production. And if we insist upon having all guns, we must be prepared to take farm land and farmers, which are very efficient in the production of butter, and transform them to the production of guns even though they can produce only very little in this sphere. Thus, increasing costs are to be expected.[1]

ECONOMIES OF MASS PRODUCTION: DECREASING COSTS

The above figure and reasoning assume that increasing costs set in from the very beginning. Actually, at first, there will be a countertendency that must be overcome before increasing costs will set in. This is the widely appreciated technological fact that many processes *increase in efficiency as their scale increases.* Among the causes of such "economies of mass production," to which we owe the great productivity of modern industries are (1) use of nonhuman and non-animal power sources (water and wind power, steam, electricity, turbines and internal-combustion engines, internal atomic energy); (2) automatic self-adjusting mechanisms (lathes, jigs, servomechanisms); (3) use of standardized, interchangeable parts; (4) breakdown of complex processes into simple repetitive operations; (5) specialization of function and division of labor; and many other technological factors. The automobile production assembly line or

[1] Even if resources could be divided into two uniform classes, such as homogeneous land and homogeneous labor, increasing costs would still result from the fact that guns and butter do not require the same proportion of these resources. Butter takes more land, and guns require relatively more labor. As we give up butter and substitute guns, the law of increasing costs sets in because there is released too little labor from butter production relative to land released. The result is a dilution of the amount of labor per unit of land in gun production (and, paradoxically, in butter production too). The next section shows that a change in the proportion of factors is responsible for diminishing returns to the abundant factor. It could also be shown that it will cause diminishing returns of one good in terms of the other.

the historical development of modern textile spinning and weaving typify these diverse factors.

Upon thought it will be obvious that each of these economies or savings comes into full play only if a large enough number of units is being produced to make it worth while to set up a fairly elaborate productive organization. If only a few guns are to be produced, they might just as well be produced by hand; but if resources are available to produce many thousands, it will pay to make certain elaborate initial preparations which need not be repeated when still more units are to be produced. Thus, it might come about that, unlike our simplified picture above, we would have to pay two butter units for our first gun unit; but to get still another gun unit we would have to pay only one butter unit because of the efficiency of mass production, which is a case of decreasing rather than increasing costs.

Thus, at first there might not be increasing costs. But finally, when the largest and most efficient gun factory size had been built, so that no further economies of scale could be realized, then the law of increasing costs might again come into its own. So if we are to be careful, we must say: *beyond some point*, the law of increasing costs is likely to become operative.

Actually in the postwar period it appears that the great production performance of the American economy was due not only to putting idle resources to work and to working overtime hours and multiple shifts, but also in an important measure to the economies of large-scale production that we have been discussing.

THE FAMOUS LAW OF DIMINISHING RETURNS

Underlying the previous discussion of increasing costs is a well-known technological economic relationship—the so-called "law of diminishing returns." The validity of this law is twice blessed: by the theorists who think they have proved it deductively on a priori grounds, and by the empiricists who regard it as a universally observed technological fact!

The law of diminishing returns refers to the amount of extra *output* obtained when we add more and more of some one input, or class of inputs. Thus, suppose food is produced by the cooperation of two resources: labor and land. If we add 1 man-year of labor to 100 acres of land, we may get a number of thousands of bushels of corn at harvest time. But if, on the same plot of land, we add still another man-year of labor, we shall probably get not quite so many extra bushels of corn. Adding a third man-year of labor to the same land will result in a still smaller increase in production.

Table 2 provides an arithmetical illustration of the law of diminishing returns.

TABLE 2. *Showing How Returns in Terms of Output Diminish When Successive Units of Labor Are Added to 100 Acres of Land*

No. of man-years of labor	Amount of product, bu.	Extra output added by additional unit of labor
0	0	
		2,000
1	2,000	
		1,000
2	3,000	
		500
3	3,500	
		300
4	3,800	
		100
5	3,900	

Why have diminishing returns set in? Primarily, of course, because if more workers are added, each has less and less acres of land to work with. The fixed factor of production, land, has decreased in proportion to the variable input, labor. If we crowd the land even further, we may by intensive cultivation of the soil still get some extra corn; but the amount of extra corn will become less and less.

We may summarize the law of diminishing returns as follows:

An increase in some inputs relative to other comparatively fixed inputs will cause output to increase; but after a point[1] the extra output resulting from the same additions of input will become less and less; this falling off of extra returns is a consequence of the fact that the new "doses" of the varying resources have to work with less and less of the constant resources.

[1] At first the countertendency of increasing mass-production efficiencies may outweigh the tendency toward diminishing returns. But ultimately diminishing returns will win out.

C. *THE UNDERLYING POPULATION BASIS OF ANY ECONOMY: PAST AND FUTURE POPULATION TRENDS*

THE MALTHUS THEORY OF POPULATION

There is an important and interesting application of this law in the field of population. Around 1800, Thomas Robert Malthus, a young English clergyman, used to argue at breakfast against his father's view that "Every day in every way, the human race is getting better and better." Finally the younger Malthus became so agitated that he wrote a book about it. His famous "Essay on the Principle of Population" (1st ed., 1798) was an instantaneous best seller, going through several editions and for a century influencing the thinking of people all over the world (including Charles Darwin, the expositor of the famous doctrine of biological evolution). It is still a living influence today. Malthus' views are based directly on the law of diminishing returns, and they continue to have relevance.

Malthus first took the observation of Benjamin Franklin and others that, in the American colonies or in other places where resources are abundant, populations tend to double every 25 years or so. This is less surprising than it seems since, except for early deaths, an average of only four or five children per family would be required to maintain this "compound interest" rate of growth. Malthus postulated, therefore, *a universal tendency for population— unless checked by food supply!—to grow at a geometric progression.* Now anyone who lets his imagination roam knows how rapidly geometric progressions grow—how soon 1, 2, 4, 8, 16, 32, 64, 128, 256, 512, 1,024, . . . , becomes so large that there is not space in the world for all the resulting offspring to stand.[1]

Malthus, Sr., would to all this only say, "So what?" Consequently, at this point Malthus unleashed the devil of the law of diminishing returns. As population doubles and redoubles, it is exactly as if the globe were halving in size, until finally it had shrunk so much that food and subsistence fall below that

---

[1] At 6 per cent compound interest, money doubles in value every 12 years. It has been estimated that the $24 received by the Indians for the island of Manhattan would, if deposited at compound interest, be today worth at least as much as all real property on the island.

necessary for life. Because of the law of diminishing returns, food cannot keep up the geometric progression rate of growth of population.

Mind you, Malthus did not say that population *would* increase at these rates. This was only its *tendency* if unchecked. He considered it an important part of his argument to demonstrate that, in all countries in all times, checks were operating holding population in. In the first edition of his work he put emphasis on *positive* checks that operate to increase the death rate: pestilence, famine, war, etc. Later he relented from this gloomy doctrine to hold out hope for the human race through *preventive* checks operating on the birth rate. Although the birth-control movement is often called Neo-Malthusianism, Malthus himself, being an early nineteenth-century clergyman, advocated only *moral restraint* with prudential postponement of early marriages until a family could be supported. In fact, he had enough of his father in him to think the struggle for existence an illustration of the wisdom of the Creator, and we can picture Malthus, Jr., discussing over a hearty breakfast with his own daughter how diminishing returns keeps poor people from getting soft and lazy and how great are the advantages of "virtuous celibacy."

This important application of diminishing returns illustrates what profound effects a simple theory can have. Malthus significantly altered thinking for a century, providing the basis for the nineteenth-century English poor laws, whereby destitution was considered a result of laziness and unemployment a state to be made as uncomfortable as possible; also he bolstered the argument that a trade-union could not improve the welfare of workers since any increase in their wages would only cause them to reproduce until there was again barely enough to go around.

Despite the tons of statistics in later editions covering many countries, it is today recognized that his views were oversimplifications. In his discussion of diminishing returns, he never anticipated the miracles of the industrial revolution which in the next century were to *shift* production-transformation curves *outward* and make possible better standards of living for more people. At the same time medical advances were prolonging human life and further lessening the positive checks to population. Nor did he realize that after 1870 in most Western nations, including the United States, family *fertility* as measured by actual number of children would begin to fall far short of family *fecundity*, or biological reproductive capacity. The average student need only consider the difference in size of his own family and that of his grandparents or parents to realize that for modern nations the problem in the years ahead is that of under- rather than overpopulation. Nevertheless, the germs of truth in his doctrines are important still for understanding the population behavior of India, China, and other parts of the globe where the balance of numbers and food supply is a vital factor.

TABLE 3. *Estimated Population of the World and Its Distribution*

Sections of the world	Population, millions	
	1800	1939
Europe....................................	188	542
North, South, and Central America............	29	273
Asia, Africa, and Oceania....................	702	1,265
World.................................	919	2,080

SOURCE: W. S. THOMPSON, "Plenty of People," Jacques Cattell, Lancaster, Pa., 1944.

Table 3 shows how the population of the world has more than doubled since 1800, while the population of the New World has increased almost tenfold. This increase was made possibly mainly through the declining death rate resulting from scientific advances in medicine and from the improved living standards made possible by the industrial revolution. Life expectancy has increased from 18 years in 1800 to about 68 years at present;[1] and standards of living far exceed that of any previous century. Moreover, the parts of the world where population is held in by food supply are shown in the table to have been of declining percentage importance. But will this last?

AMERICA AND EUROPE FACE DEPOPULATION

At the end of World War I men still feared the Malthusian curse of over-population. They wrote books with such alarming titles as "The World Faces Over-population" and "Standing Room Only!" But just as these books were coming wet off the presses, western Europe and the United States were undergoing a profound revolution in population.

Only now, a generation later, is this beginning to be understood. Today the pendulum has swung to the other extreme, with the best sellers bearing such flashy titles as "The Twilight of Parenthood" and "England Without People."

How can we account for this sudden change of tune? Are not births still in

[1] L. I. DUBLIN and A. J. LOTKA, "Length of Life," The Ronald Press Company, New York, 1936.

excess of deaths in England, France, Sweden, Germany, and the United States? Why then this fear of an impending decline in population?

The answer is not hard to find. Since 1870—even earlier in France—birth rates have begun to drop in most countries of western European civilization. After World War I, and especially after the Great Depression of the 1930's, the drop became precipitous. The alarming nature of the crisis in births was hidden for a time by two factors that are irrelevant for the long-run trend: First, the miracle of scientific medicine has been reducing the death rate, especially in connection with the infectious diseases responsible for deaths prior to the middle and old ages.[1]

The second and more important factor explaining the failure of people to realize the population crisis comes from the distortion of crude birth rates and death rates resulting from the fact that *the United States and western Europe temporarily have an unusually large number of women (and men) in the child-bearing age groups.*[2] Because so many women are at the ages of motherhood, the number of births appears disarmingly high. But so low has the number of children per mother become, that in the future, when the temporarily swollen number of young adults has disappeared, the populations of England, France, Sweden, Germany, and perhaps the United States will go downhill. At least this is inevitable unless there is a fundamental change in family psychology and social behavior.

Figure 4 shows the progressive shifts in our population toward more and more old people and toward a lower percentage of children, and eventually of young adults. The problems that this trend will create for the financing of old-age security will be touched upon later.

THE NET REPRODUCTION RATE

The true state of affairs as to population trends was revealed to us by a little arithmetical trick. Instead of concentrating on crude births and deaths, someone got the bright idea of asking, What is the total number of girl babies that will have been born to 1,000 newborn girl babies by the time they have all completed their life spans? If this total of daughters is exactly 1,000, then

---

[1] Despite the outlook for further progress in medicine, this first factor is not of vital importance for the long-run population trend, because once the death rate prior to the age fifty is brought to very low levels, there is little room for further improvement. Moreover, as will be shown in the discussion of the net reproduction rate, keeping old people alive longer has only temporary effects on population trends.

[2] These age groups are swollen because of the past high fertility of the parents and grandparents of present adults.

we say that the *net reproduction rate* is 1.0, and the population will just hold its own in the long run.

If only 900 girl babies are born to each 1,000 girl babies throughout their lives, then the net reproduction rate is only 0.9—and ultimately the population will begin to decrease at the rate of 10 per cent per generation. On the other hand, if each 1,000 women leave 2,000 daughters behind them (who will leave

PROPORTION OF POPULATION IN EACH AGE
DISTRIBUTION OF TOTAL POPULATION
1850-1980

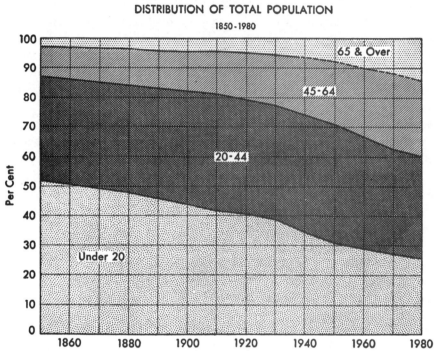

FIG. 4. This shows clearly the decreasing proportion of children in the population and the present-day swollen numbers of adults. It also indicates the growing importance of older people. SOURCE: "The Problems of a Changing Population," National Resources Committee, 1938.

4,000 daughters behind them, etc.), then the net reproduction rate is equal to 2.0 and the population will ultimately grow at a rate of 100 per cent increase per generation.

The exact computation of the net reproduction rate for a given group is not too difficult if the necessary statistical data are available. From past mortality data collected by insurance companies, we know what fraction of the original 1,000 women are likely still to be alive at the ages of 15, 20, 25, . . . , and 50 years. From data on the number of likely births to women of each of these ages—data that this country has often neglected to collect—we are able to calculate just how many babies our group of women will have throughout their entire lives. A little less than half of these will be girls, and this number of girls divided by 1,000 is the net reproduction rate.[1]

A few sample recent net reproduction rates are: United States (1939–1941), 1.01; Sweden (1941), 0.84; Germany (1936), 0.93; France (1939), 0.9; Italy (1935–1937), 1.13; Soviet Union (1935), 1.4 or over; United Kingdom (1944), 0.99; Japan (1937), 1.44.

The population crisis of our age may be summarized in the statement that the net reproduction rate is beginning to drop below unity in England, France, Germany, Sweden, and many other countries. The United States is balanced just around unity, and if it were not for the fact that our rural and Southern areas still have high net reproduction rates, we would be below the level necessary for population replacement, much less growth. Eastern Europe and Russia still have very high net reproduction rates. India and the Orient tend to have high fertility rates, but so few girls survive to adulthood and through the years of childbearing that their net reproduction rate does not greatly exceed unity.

An economics textbook is not the place to analyze the causes underlying these fundamental trends. In a sense, they are noneconomic. For as everybody knows, poor people have on the average many more children than wealthy. Harvard and Vassar students are not reproducing themselves. Nor are Michigan State and Oberlin students, nor most city dwellers who have gone only to high school.[2]

On the other hand, the ups and downs of the business cycle do affect marriages and births. Not all of the recent war and postwar crop of babies can be attributed to the war and the Selective Service Act. In considerable measure, they reflect the depression backlog of deferred marriages and births. The same

[1] The net reproduction rate can increase only if the birth rate per woman of each age rises or if fewer women die in infancy and prior to the completion of the child-bearing ages. Keeping older people alive, or having the same number of babies at an earlier age, will increase the population only in the short run, but will have no effect on whether the population will ultimately be declining.

[2] Most authorities believe that the decline is to be explained by social rather than biological factors. Thus, the French Canadians, who have high birth rates, came from just those rural regions of France with the lowest rates. Second-generation Italians and Jewish city dwellers show greatly reduced rates, as do Negroes who move from the South to the North. Some of the highest net reproduction rates are among the white people in the Southern hillbilly regions of the Appalachian Plateau. Ironically, the highest rates of all are to be found among—of all peoples—the American Indians, suggesting that we may yet give the country back to the Indians.

effect of prosperity on births has been seen in neutral countries like Sweden, in England, in Nazi Germany, and less comprehensibly, even in occupied countries like France and Norway.

Statistical experts warn us that the recent bumper crop of babies gives us no grounds for complacency with respect to the future maintenance of population. *Most of the upswing appears to have been in first and second children!* This proves nothing, since most of these would have been born anyway and were simply born earlier than otherwise. Unless a substantial number of families follow through with third, fourth, and fifth children, the net reproduction rate will fall below unity. A society in which parents think that "a boy and a girl would be nice" is doomed to ultimate extinction, since two children per family are not enough to make up for those who die at young ages, who never marry, or who have childless marriages. Governments are bestirring themselves to do something about the situation. Canada, for example, has introduced a system of family allowance payments depending on the number of children. Although not much has been done yet, we shall undoubtedly see more drastic government population policies in the next decades.

Table 4 shows the best present estimates of future populations for certain countries. Note the high estimate for the Soviet Union, where net reproduction rates have a long way to fall until they reach unity; and note the remarkably low figures for France and England.

TABLE 4. *Estimated Future Population of Different Countries in 1970 (All data in millions)*

Country	1940	1970
United States.............................	132	160
England and Wales........................	41	37
France....................................	41	37
Soviet Union.............................	174	251
Sweden....................................	6.3	5.8
Italy.....................................	44	49
Europe and U.S.S.R.......................	572	668

SOURCE: All data except those for the United States taken from Frank W. Notestein, "The Future Population of Europe and the Soviet Union: Population Projections 1940–1970," League of Nations, 1944. United States estimate made with the help of Warren S. Thompson, "Estimates of Future Population of the U.S. 1940–2000," National Resources Planning Board, 1943, but taking into account the wartime experience. All data rounded off to nearest million.

A military strategist might be interested in these figures from a power standpoint. We shall later be concerned with their bearing on demand for the products of wheel-chair factories rather than those producing baby buggies, on the number of our old folks in need of social security, upon the level and growth of investment in our economy, and upon our chances of maintaining full employment.[1]

SUMMARY

A. PROBLEMS OF ECONOMIC ORGANIZATION

1. Every economy must somehow solve the three fundamental economic problems: *what* and how much shall be produced of all possible goods and services; *how* shall economic resources be used in producing these goods; *for whom* the goods are produced; *i.e.*, what is the distribution of income among different individuals and classes.

2. Different societies meet these problems in different ways—by custom, instinct, fiat and decree, and in our own system partially through a price and market system. Other subjects than economics are involved in each of these questions: psychology and sociology, science and engineering, ethics, and even theology.

3. The basic problems are important because of the fundamental fact of all economic life: with limited resources and technology, standards of living are limited. Economic goods are scarce rather than free; society must choose between them because not all needs and desires can be fulfilled.

B. TECHNOLOGICAL CHOICES OPEN TO SOCIETY

4. With given resources and technology, the production choices open to a nation between two such goods as butter and guns can be summarized in the Production-possibility curve or schedule. This indicates how butter can be transformed into guns by transferring resources from butter to gun production.

5. Usually there will be increasing costs (in terms of sacrificing one good)

[1] The interested reader may consult the following books: T. R. Malthus, "Essay on the Principle of Population," 1798; R. R. Kuczynski, "The Balance of Births and Deaths," Vol. 1, The Macmillan Company, New York, 1928, a short readable explanation of the causes of the future underpopulation crisis; W. S. Thompson, "Plenty of People," Jacques Cattell, Lancaster, Pa., 1944, a recent popular survey.

of getting more of another good; but at first, economies of mass production may reverse this tendency.

6. The law of diminishing returns asserts that, after a point, as we add more and more of a variable input (like labor) to a fixed input (like capital), the amount of extra product will fall off. This law is really just a matter of proportions—the varying input has less and less of the fixed input to work with.

C. UNDERLYING POPULATION BASIS OF ANY ECONOMY

7. The Malthus theory of population rests on the law of diminishing returns. He thought that a population—if unchecked!—would tend to grow in geometric rate, doubling every generation or so. However, each member of the growing population would have less resources to work with. Therefore, because of diminishing returns, income would fall so low as to lead to starvation and pestilence.

8. For a century and a half after Malthus, populations grew by leaps and bounds everywhere. But so successful were the improvements of technology and in medicine that improved death rates are responsible for most of the increase.

9. Since 1870, birth rates have begun to fall. Today, western European nations and the United States are at a population crisis: unless social habits change and net reproduction rates are brought up to 1.0 or more, each of these countries faces ultimate population decrease in the near or distant future.

QUESTIONS FOR DISCUSSION

1. Without looking at the next chapter, can you anticipate how our price system through supply and demand solves the three problems of economic organization?

2. Attack or defend the social creed: "From each according to his ability. To each according to his need." What is your philosophy on the third question of For Whom?

3. Instead of choosing between war goods and peace goods, society may choose between *present consumption* and *production of future* capital goods. Draw a hypothetical Production-possibility curve indicating this choice.

4. What would happen to the transformation curve if all services (population, land, etc.) increased in amount? What would happen to it if scientific inventions increased the productivity of given resources? What if these improvements were only in butter production and not in guns?

5. If land were increased in a number of steps and labor were held constant, would the law of diminishing returns hold? Illustrate and tell why.

6. How many were there in your grandparents' family? in your parents' family? How many do you think there will be in your own family?

7. "Population pressure doesn't cause war as is commonly believed. Careful study suggests that cause and effect are just the reverse. Nations which want to expand try to persuade their citizens to grow in numbers so that the nation will be militarily strong and will have a pretext for expansion. Examples are Italy, Germany, and Japan." Discuss.

Chapter 3: FUNCTIONING

OF A "MIXED" CAPITALISTIC

ENTERPRISE SYSTEM

A MIXED ENTERPRISE SYSTEM

Most of our attention will be devoted to the special features of economic life found in twentieth-century industrial nations (with the exception of Soviet Russia). In most of these countries, there was a trend in the past few centuries toward less and less direct governmental control of economic activity as feudal and preindustrial conditions were replaced by greater emphasis on what is loosely called "free private enterprise" or "competitive capitalism." Long before this trend had approached a condition of *laissez faire* (*i.e.*, of complete governmental noninterference with business), the tide began to turn the other way.

Since some time in the nineteenth century, in almost all the countries under consideration there has been a steady increase in the economic functions of government. We may leave to historians the task of delineating the important factors underlying this significant and all-pervasive development. Suffice it to say here that ours is a mixed free-enterprise economic system in which both public and private institutions exercise economic control.

The first part of this chapter shows how our mixed system tackles the three problems of economic organization which we have seen must be answered by all societies. The last sections of this chapter deal with some fundamental characteristics of the present economic order.

A. *HOW A FREE-ENTERPRISE SYSTEM SOLVES THE BASIC ECONOMIC PROBLEMS*

NOT CHAOS BUT ECONOMIC ORDER

Now the remarkable fact is not how much the government does to control economic activity—tariff legislation, pure-food laws, utility and railroad regulations, minimum-wage regulations, fair-labor-practice acts, social security, price ceilings and floors, public works, national defense, national and local taxation, police protection and judicial redress, zoning ordinances, municipal water or gas works, etc.—but how much it does *not* do, even in time of war when controls multiply. Hundreds of thousands of commodities are produced by millions of people more or less at their own volition without central direction or master plan.

In a system of free private enterprise no individual or organization is consciously concerned with the triad of economic problems discussed in Chap. 2. This is really remarkable. To paraphrase a famous economic example, consider the city of New York. Without a constant flow of goods in and out of the city, in a week it would be on the verge of starvation. More than a variety of the right kinds and amounts of food is involved; from the surrounding hinterland, from 48 states, and from the far corners of the world, goods have been traveling for days and months with New York City as their destination. All this is undertaken without coercion or centralized direction by any conscious body!

How is it that 7 million people are able to sleep easy at night without living in mortal terror of a breakdown in the elaborate economic processes upon which the city's existence depends?

This alone is convincing proof that a competitive system of markets and prices—whatever else it may be, however imperfectly it may function—is not a system of chaos and anarchy. There is in it a certain order and orderliness. It works. It functions. Without intelligence it solves one of the most complex problems imaginable, involving thousands of unknown variables and relations. Nobody designed it. Like Topsy it just grew, and like human nature, it is changing; but at least it meets the first test of any social organization—it is able to survive.

Enough of these oh's and ah's. We shall have plenty of occasion to analyze further the nature and functioning of a price system. Right here in the beginning it is just as well to slip the antidote to those who, in reacting away from the extreme view of the economic system as chaos, go to the opposite extreme and regard it as perfection itself, the essence of providential harmony.

Even Adam Smith, the canny Scot whose monumental book, "The Wealth of Nations" (1776), represents the beginning of modern economics or political economy—even he was so thrilled by the recognition of an order in the economic system that he proclaimed the mystical principle of the "invisible hand": that each individual in pursuing only his own selfish good was led, as if by an invisible hand, to achieve the best good of all, so that any interference with free competition by government was almost certain to be injurious. This unguarded conclusion has done almost as much harm as good in the past century and a half, especially since too often it is all that some of our leading citizens remember, 30 years later, of their college course in economics. Actually much of the praise of perfect competition is beside the mark. As has been discussed earlier, ours is a mixed system of government and private enterprise; as will be discussed later, it is also a mixed system of monopoly and competition. It is neither black nor white, but gray and polka-dotted.

A cynic might say of free competition what Bernard Shaw once said of Christianity: the only trouble with it is that it has never been tried. There never was a golden age of free competition, and competition is not now perfect in the economist's sense; probably it is becoming less so every day, in large part because of the fundamental nature of large-scale production and technology, consumers' tastes, and business organization.

This does not mean that we must accept as inevitable the trend toward big business, mergers, trusts, and cartels that began to swell in the 1890's. We may not believe ourselves captains of our souls, but at least we can try to be first mates. Vigorous and intelligent administration of antitrust legislation may stem the tide; but it is like the dog baying at the moon to expect universal creation of the atomistic conditions that we shall see are necessary for perfect or pure competition. It will not be easy, but our imperfectly competitive system can be helped to work better. By itself, this will not solve the problem of unemployment or purchasing power, as is developed at length in the saving-investment analysis in Part Two.

THE PRICE SYSTEM

Just how does the unconscious automatic price mechanism operate? The bare outlines of a competitive profit-and-loss system are simple to describe.

Everything has a price: each commodity and each service. Even the different kinds of human labor have prices, usually called "wage rates."

Everybody receives money for what he sells, and uses this money to buy what he wishes. If more is wanted of any one good, say automobiles, a flood of new orders will be given for it. This will cause its price to rise and more to be produced. Similarly, if more is available of a good like tea than people want, its price will be marked down as a result of competition. At the lower price people will drink more tea, and producers will no longer produce so much. Thus equilibrium of supply and demand will be restored.

What is true of the markets for consumers' goods is also true of markets for *factors of production* such as labor, land, and capital goods. If welders rather than glass blowers are needed, job opportunities will be more favorable in the former field. The price of welders, their hourly wage, will tend to rise while that of glass blowers will tend to fall. Other things being equal, this will cause a shift into the desired occupation. Likewise an acre of Puerto Rican bottom land will go into sugar cultivation if the sugar producers bid the most for its use. In the same way, machine-tool production will be determined by supply and demand. Even the flow of money capital funds, between, say, Chicago and New York, will depend upon the relative interest rates or security prices prevailing in these two centers.

In other words, we have a vast system of trial and error, of successive approximation to an equilibrium system of prices and production. When supply everywhere matches demand and prices match costs, our three economic problems have been simultaneously solved.

For whom things are produced is determined by supply and demand in the markets for productive services: by wage rates, land rents, and capital profits which go to make up everybody's income—relative to everyone else and relative to the whole. The character of the resulting distribution of income is highly dependent upon the somewhat arbitrary distribution of property ownership.

How things are produced is determined by the competition of different producers. The method that is cheapest at any one time, because of both physical efficiency and cost efficiency, will displace a more costly method. The only way for producers to meet price competition and maximize profits is to keep costs at a minimum by adopting the most efficient methods. For example, synthetic rubber will be made from petroleum rather than from grain alcohol if the price of the one is in a certain relation to the price of the other; or electric power will be generated by steam rather than water power if the price of coal is below some critical level.

What things will be produced is determined by the votes of consumers—not every two years at the polls but every day in their decisions to purchase this item and not that. Of course, the money that they pay into business cash registers ultimately provides the payrolls, rents, and dividends that they receive in weekly income. Thus, the circle is a complete one.

A competitive system is impersonal but not completely so. The consuming families face business enterprises on two fronts, with only prices in between. One front is the widely dispersed one on which consumers buy thousands of small items from a score of different retail establishments: grocery, drug, and department stores; movie theaters, gasoline stations, and electric-power companies, government post offices, landlords, railroad lines, and insurance companies.

On the other front relations are not always so peaceful. To the family breadwinner his wage is not simply one other price. It is the difference between luxury and comfort, between comfort and privation. The large corporation can afford to close down for a week or month if necessary, whereas the laborer feels inferior in bargaining power, and he may turn to collective bargaining by means of trade-unions. By doing this he may at times be helping to restore competition, while at other times he may be causing conditions to deviate still further from competition.

The above picture of competition tending toward lowest costs is a highly oversimplified one. Even if the system worked as described above—which everybody knows to be far from the case—it could not be considered ideal. In the first place, goods go where there are the most votes or dollars. John D. Rockefeller's dog may receive the milk that a poor child needs to avoid rickets. Why? Because supply and demand are working badly? No. Because they are doing what they are designed to do, putting goods in the hands of those who can pay the most.

Or, to take another example, suppose the invention of automatic machines should cause the competitive price of labor to fall and thereby reduce incomes of the poor. Is there anything necessarily right in that? On the other hand, should the fact that a man inherited 500 square miles of range land, for which oil companies offer a million dollars per year, necessarily justify so large an income?

IMPERFECTIONS OF COMPETITION

As we said earlier, an equally serious drawback to the picture of the price system as described above is the fact that, in the real world, competition is nowhere near perfect. Firms do not know when consumer tastes will change;

therefore, they overproduce in one field and underproduce in another. By the time they are ready to learn from experience, the situation has again changed. Often nothing can be done about such mistakes because, like the weather, they are relatively unpredictable. But some of the mistakes that a flock of independent competitors make—for example, in all overbuilding as in 1929, or in continually entering the already overcrowded grocery-store business—would be lessened in an economy characterized by planning. (Of course, fallible bureaucrats might perpetrate a series of planning errors of their own, and new problems of individual liberty would be introduced.) Also, in a competitive system many producers simply do not know the methods of other producers, and costs do not fall to a minimum. One can sometimes succeed in the competitive struggle as much by keeping knowledge scarce as by keeping production high.

An even more serious deviation from perfect competition results from *monopoly elements*. These result in wrong pricing, distorted profit uses, incorrect and wasteful resource allocation. A monopolist is not a fat, greedy man with a big moustache and cigar who goes around violating the law. If he were, we could put him in jail. *He is anyone important enough to affect the prices of the things that he sells and buys.* To some degree that means almost every businessman, except possibly the millions of farmers who individually produce a negligible fraction of the total crop. All economic life is a blend of competitive and monopoly elements. Imperfect, or monopolistic, competition is the prevailing mode, not perfect competition.

Of course, as we shall later see, a businessman cannot set his prices completely as he pleases and still make profits. He must take into account the prices of goods that are substitutes for his own. Even if he produces a trade-marked coal with unique properties, he must reckon with the prices charged for other coals, for oil and gas, and for house insulation. But he is not compelled, as, we shall learn later, is a farmer in a perfect competitive market, to keep his price from rising above the prevailing market price for fear of selling nothing. The fact that the ordinary businessman can set his own price, instead of having to leave it up to an organized auction market, shows that he has some control over price and is not a perfect competitor in the economist's sense. The further fact that he will gladly take on extra new business at his prevailing price is, as we shall see, clear evidence that he is not like a perfectly competitive farm producer.

The businessman both likes and dislikes competition. He likes it when it enables him to expand his market. But he is the first to label it as "chiseling," "unfair," or "ruinous" when the knife cuts the other way. Occasionally he will try to use the mechanism of competition to drive out rivals and create a monopoly. At other times he will help to form a trade association to play down the effects of vigorous competition. Of course, the worker whose livelihood depends on how the market prices his labor is also the first to howl when competition threatens to depress wages.

Some of the basic factors responsible for monopoly are inherent in the economies of large-scale production. This is especially true in a dynamic world of technological change. Atomistic competition by numerous producers would simply not be efficient in many fields and could not last. Trade-marks, patents, and advertising are often responsible for still other monopoly elements. It would be humanly impossible, therefore, to attempt to create perfect competition by law. But we can hope to shape, regulate, and influence our world of monopolistic competition in order to create a more tolerable and workable competitive regime.

We shall return in Part Three to a more microscopic examination of supply and demand. After that discussion we shall be in a position to appraise the workings of the price system more judiciously. We have seen enough already to avoid the errors of both extremes. A competitive price system is one way of organizing an economy, but it is not the only way. Still it is of interest that some socialists plan to continue to use a price mechanism as one part of their new society.

ECONOMIC ROLE OF GOVERNMENT

It was said earlier that ours is not a pure price economy but a mixed system in which elements of government control are intermingled with market elements in organizing production and consumption. The economic role of government is so important now and will be so increasingly important in the years ahead that Chaps. 7 and 8 are devoted to it.

The broad outlines of its influence can be briefly indicated here. Democratic countries are not satisfied with the answers to the three questions, What, How, and For Whom given by a perfectly unrestrained market system. Such a system might dictate that certain people starve from lack of income and that others receive inadequate or excessive incomes. Therefore the government steps in with its own expenditure to supplement the real or money incomes of some individuals; e.g., it may provide hospital beds for its citizens or may present the more needy of them with monthly allowances in time of unemployment or old age.

More than this, it provides certain indispensable *collective* services without which community life would not be thinkable, and which by their nature cannot appropriately be left to private enterprises. Included in these are the maintenance of national defense, of internal law and order, and the administration of justice. By and large in its expenditure of money, it is behaving exactly like any other large spender. By casting sufficient votes in the form of dollar bids in certain directions, it causes resources to flow there. The price system works just as if these were individual rather than collective needs.

If governments financed all their expenditure by printing paper money or by endless borrowing, that would be almost the whole story. Actually most government expenditure is paid for out of taxes collected. It is here that an important element of *coercion* enters in. Of course the citizenry as a whole imposes the tax burden upon itself; also each citizen is sharing in the collective benefits of government. But there is not the same close connection between benefits and tax payments as holds when the individual citizen puts a quarter into a cigarette machine or makes an ordinary purchase. I must pay a tax whether or not I choose to. I need not smoke Luckies or buy Nylon stockings if I do not wish to.

Moreover, a second important form of coercion is involved in the universal custom of passing governmental laws: thou shalt not smoke opium, thou shalt not sell false weight, thou shalt not employ child labor, thou shalt not set a house on fire, thou shalt not charge more than the ceiling price for food, and so forth. This set of rules provides the framework within which private enterprise functions; it also modifies the direction of that functioning. Together with government expenditure and taxation, the decrees of government are hardly less important than the price system itself in determining the economic fate of the nation. It would be fruitless to try to decide whether public enterprise or private enterprise is the more important—as fruitless as to debate heredity versus environment. Without either our economic world would be an entirely different one.

Finally, as we shall see in Part Two, it is part of the government's function to alleviate one of the most important causes of acute and chronic cycles in unemployment. Especially in wealthy communities like our own, individuals as a whole may try to save much more or much less than the private enterprise can profitably or usefully invest in new real capital goods. We shall see that this will result in deflation or inflation and a distortion of the economy's long-run rate of progress. Clearly the government must try to use its full fiscal and monetary powers to enable private enterprise to maintain a steady level of high employment and rising productivity.

B. *THE CAPITALISTIC CHARACTER OF MODERN SOCIETY*

There are three further important features of modern economic society:

1. Modern advanced industrial technology rests upon the use of vast amounts of capital: elaborate machine equipment, large-scale factories and plants, stores and stocks of finished and unfinished materials. Our economy receives the name "capitalism" because this capital or "wealth" is primarily the private property of somebody—the capitalist.

2. The present-day economic system is characterized by an almost incredibly elaborate degree of *specialization* and intricate *division of labor*.

3. Finally, ours is a system that makes extensive use of *money*. The flow of money is the lifeblood of our system. It also provides the measuring rod of values.

All these features are interrelated—with each other and with the price mechanism previously described. Thus we shall see that an elaborate division of labor is possible only with the great facility for trade and exchange that money provides. Money and capital become related through the credit activities of the banking system and through the organized capital markets upon which securities can be transformed into money by sale or vice versa. And of course the relationship between the price mechanism and money is immediate and obvious.

CAPITAL AND TIME

First, let us survey the important economic role of capital. If men had to work with their hands on barren soil, productivity and consumption would be very low indeed. But gradually over time our economic system has been able to amass together a tremendous stock of instruments of production, of factories and housing, of goods in process. Each such capital good adds to national output, of course; but more important, throughout its lifetime it adds to national output more than it costs to have built it in the first place or to replace it after it is gone; it has a *net productivity* over and above all necessary "depreciation" costs.

Men learned very early, therefore, that the simple direct methods of production could be improved upon by using indirect methods. We who are inside the economic system are not conscious of how roundabout modern productive processes are. An outside observer would be struck with the fact that almost no one in our system is producing *finished* goods. Almost everyone is doing work of a preparatory nature, with final consumption a distant future goal. The farmer spends his time in fattening hogs, the truck driver in carrying them toward market, the packer in advancing them further toward the last stage of consumption. A steel worker prepares pig iron, part of which will become a hammer to build a house; another bit will become part of a pig-iron furnace, which in turn will prepare pig iron to be used in making further hammers and more pig-iron furnaces, and so forth.

And so the economic process goes—around and around like air inside the pipes of a French horn, or like the egg-chicken-egg-chicken-egg sequence of biological evolution.

Each person is unconscious of the roundabout character of production because all he has to do is to perform his own job and not worry himself as to where his output will ultimately go or whence come the raw materials to which his activity has added value. Even an outside observer of the system might not notice its complexity, once all the circular paths had become established and activity became synchronized. In such a steady state each day would look like the previous one, and it would appear that the work of each day was producing the output of that same day.

But this is an optical illusion. Time was required to get the process going in the first place. Human and nonhuman resources had to be put to work for a long time before any output came out from each new process. It is as if one had to blow into a huge French horn for some time to get the air pressure up before the note could be sounded. Gradually a steady state is reached when one is pumping air constantly in and receiving out a constant tone. Finally, if one stopped pumping air in, one would not incur the penalty of losing the note for some time. So in the economic world, we can stop replacing capital and begin to loaf for a while and still can hope to leave output undiminished for a spell while "milking capital."

The fact that it takes time to get things started and synchronized is important. It explains why society does not automatically replace all direct processes by more productive indirect ones; and all indirect processes by still more indirect processes. The advantage in doing so is balanced by the initial disadvantage of having *to forego present consumption goods* by directing resources from current production to uses that will bear fruit only after some time.

To the extent that people are willing to save—to abstain from present consumption and wait for future consumption—to that extent society can devote resources to new capital formation.[1] And to the extent that people are irresponsible as to the future, they may at any time try to "dissave"—to snatch present pleasures at the expense of the future. How? By diverting resources from the endless task of replacing and maintaining capital to the job of producing extra present-day consumption goods. There is an old Chinese proverb: "He who cannot see beyond the dawn will have much good wine to drink at noon, much green wine to cure his headache at dusk, and only rain water to drink for the rest of his days."

We may summarize as follows: The bulk of all economic activity is directed toward the future. By the same token, the bulk of current economic consumption is the consequence of past efforts. *It is the primary role of current productive efforts to produce for the future, so as to repay the past for present consumption.* Also, in progressive societies some fraction of current productive efforts is devoted to the new or net capital formation, in which current consumption is sacrificed to increase future production.

FIXED AND CIRCULATING CAPITAL

Even the cave man used some capital in the form of primitive hunting axes; his cave dwelling was also a form of capital and wealth, whether he dug it out himself or whether he had acquired possession of it by discovery or conquest. These two items of capital are precursors of factory productive equipment and residential housing. Both would come under the heading of what is called "fixed capital."

When primitive man reached the stage of domesticating animals and cultivating the growth of plants, a new form of capital came into existence: goods in process or so-called "circulating capital." A grain of wheat in the spring is the progenitor of a cup of wheat in the fall and of a loaf of bread in the following winter; a litter of squealing pigs represents to the knowing eye a bundle of pork chops, hams, salt pork, and lard.

The names "fixed and circulating capital" are not very aptly chosen. Certainly fixity in space is not their distinguishing criterion, because a locomotive represents fixed capital and a crop in the field represents circulating capital. The exact differentiation in borderline cases requires rather fine-spun and arbitrary distinction. An apple tree is treated as fixed capital, a stalk of corn as circulating capital; a milch cow is treated as fixed capital while a beef steer is treated as circulating capital. The distinction lies in the fact that the apple tree, like the

[1] We shall later see that, sometimes in our modern monetary economy, the more people try to save, the less capital goods are produced and, paradoxically, the more people spend on consumption, the greater the incentive for businessmen to build new factories and equipment.

cow and the locomotive, gives up its economic services over a long period of time; while the cornstalk, or the steer, or the raw cotton in a textile mill gives up its economic services all at once or in a short time. Usually in doing so, these change their form, while the fixed capital appears to keep its form.

However, to a careful observer it is obvious that the cow and locomotive are really *depreciating* and getting nearer to the day when their economically useful life is over.

Just how long is a "long time"? how short a "short time"? Obviously, one could split hairs indefinitely on such a problem. The modern financial community, very rightly, has no patience with such trifles. As we shall see, modern accountants simply apply a rough rule of thumb: any asset that is to be liquidated within a year is considered as part of working capital; any that requires more than a year is part of fixed capital.

CAPITAL AND INCOME

Capital is essentially something in existence at a moment of time. It would be revealed, so to speak, by an instantaneous flash photo or still picture of the economy at some instant of time. Its various components—machines, houses, warehouse stocks—could be listed on a balance sheet as of a given time, say Jan. 1, 1949.

Income, on the other hand, is by its nature a flow over time: a flow of dollars received per week or year, a flow of goods produced per day or month, a flow of satisfactions enjoyed over time. A moving-picture camera would be necessary to register its amount.

The change between at least two different still pictures would have to be recorded. All this is recognized by the accountant, who, as we shall see, supplements the static capital balance sheet by an income statement (of profit and loss) that reports flows over time.

Capital and income are dimensionally incommensurable. The rent income of a piece of land cannot be said to be greater or less than its capital value, any more than the length of a ship can be said to be greater than its speed. A ship $\frac{1}{4}$ mile long has a speed of $\frac{1}{2}$ mile per minute, 30 miles per hour, $\frac{1}{120}$ mile per second. How can we compare length and speed since one is measured in distance and the other in terms of distance per unit time?

Similarly, an acre of land that yields a rent income of $100 per month or $1,200 per year may have a capital value of $30,000. Before the reader jumps to the conclusion that its capital value exceeds its rate of flow of income, let him remember that its income is equivalent to a rate of $120,000 per century.[1] Under no circumstances can one add capital value, which has the dimension of dollars, to income, which has the dimensions of *dollars per unit time*.

But the market place does relate capital and income. The factor that does so is the *interest rate*. Thus a permanent source of income of $1,200 per year, from a corner lot or perhaps from a goose that never grows too old to lay golden eggs, can be bought at any one time for a fixed capital sum—say $30,000. This is called the "capitalized value" of such a "permanent income."

Looking at the same thing from the opposite point of view, a capital sum of $30,000 may earn, by being lent out or being invested in a security, a permanent income of $1,200 per year. At the end of a quarter of a century such earning will have amounted to $30,000 (25 × $1,200), but the investor will have already spent them and *still have* his original $30,000.

There must be a magic factor relating income and capital. The magic factor is nothing but the interest rate. Any one of the following three formulations is valid:

1. Annual income = interest rate (per annum) × capital value

or,

$$I = i \times C$$

2. Interest rate (per annum) = annual income ÷ capital value

or,

$$i = \frac{I}{C}$$

3. Capital value = annual income ÷ interest rate (per annum)

or,

$$C = \frac{I}{i}$$

Let us illustrate the meaning of these three different expressions for exactly the same relation:

1. A widow has $30,000. Her adviser tells her she can earn 4 per cent per annum on her money. How much income will she receive each year?

Obviously, C = $30,000 and i = 0.04; therefore,

$$I = 0.04 \times \$30,000 = \$1,200$$

[1] It would only confuse the issue to point out that income would not remain constant over a century, or that rents are usually paid by the month and not by the year. These are as irrelevant as the reply of Little Audrey, who when arrested for driving 75 miles an hour "just laughed and laughed, because she knew she had only been out riding for 15 minutes."

Ans. Her yearly income is $1,200.

2. Velvet Brown is granted a divorce from P. J. Brown. He makes a settlement upon her of a corner lot with a market value of $30,000. Its income, over and above all expenses, is $1,200. (In the Middle Ages this would have been called "25-year purchase" because the land can be sold for a sum equal to 25 years' annual rent.) What interest rate or yield is she earning on her investment?

Obviously, C and I are known and i is the unknown given by

$$i = \frac{\$1,200}{\$30,000} = \frac{4}{100}$$

Ans. The interest rate earned per annum is 4 per cent.

3. A life-insurance company offers Oxford University $1,200 per year to be paid forever. The interest rate expected to prevail indefinitely is 4 per cent. How much should Oxford pay for such a policy?

Here, I and i are known, and the capitalized value of the income is the unknown, given by

$$C = \frac{\$1,200}{0.04} = \$30,000$$

Ans. The policy should sell for $30,000.

The reader should work out for himself how the above examples must be modified if the interest rate falls to 3 per cent or rises to 10 per cent. He should also notice that doubling (halving) all the dollar sums will not change the rate of interest.

Of these three formulations, the first is of primary significance to the ordinary investor who buys a bond, stock, or mortgage investment.

The second formula is of primary interest to the economist who wishes to understand and describe the capital market. It can be thought of as a formula defining what is meant by the interest rate. But its importance is greater than that. Why? *Because competition in the capital market makes sure that every (equally safe) investment asset earns the same interest rate.* If $30,000 spent on land does not bring in so large a return as a similar sum spent on golden geese, land will be sold and not bought, geese will be bought and not sold—until finally their prices and earnings have been adjusted to yield the same return. It should hardly be necessary to add the warning that in real life no two securities are equally safe, so that some yield a very low rate of interest and others must have a very high yield in order to serve as a premium or compensation for their greater riskiness.

The third formulation is of greatest interest to those active investors who are appraising the economic value of different income-producing properties: real estate, an annuity, the good will of a trade-mark business, a medical or legal training, etc. To them interest appears as a *discount* factor. Suppose they estimate the rent return on a piece of land to be permanent; by waiting enough years, the receipts from the land will be infinite. But they will not pay an infinite price for the land. If the rate of interest is 4 per cent, they will only offer 25 times the annual income—or "25-year purchase." This is because they must discount future income if it accrues a long time in the future. So long as money can be invested at 4 per cent interest, $1 paid me next year is worth *less* than $1 paid me today; it is worth only about 96 cents. A dollar paid to me 2 years from today is worth even less today; $1 of rent collected 18 years from now is worth only about 50 cents today if the interest rate is 4 per cent. Every holder of war bonds knows that $100 ten years from now can be bought for $75 today, the average rate of compound interest on war bonds being 2.9 per cent per annum.

To the shrewd appraiser the piece of land is only a bundle of future dollars of rent payable in yearly installments. Each of these installments is discounted by an interest factor for its distance in the future to arrive at its *present value*. The final *total present value* of the property is equal to the sum of all these parts. The third formula above short-circuits all this work and gives us the simple correct relation between a permanent income and its capitalized value.[1]

Most securities, such as bonds, do not give a permanent income but only an income for a finite number of years. Halving the rate of interest will not, therefore, quite double their price. But still, the price of a bond and its interest yield will tend to move in the opposite direction. If investors bid up the price of New York Central bonds from $105 to $110, their interest yield will drop. The importance of this will be seen later in connection with money and interest.

---

[1] The mathematically inclined student can verify that discounting leads to this same relationship if, and only if, income is permanent and the interest rate constant over time. The land in the above example is a bundle of income dollars paid over the future: an installment of $1,200 one year hence, another of $1,200 two years hence, . . . , $1,200 a hundred years hence, . . . , and so forth. Discounted at 4 per cent the first installment has a present value today of $1,200/1.04; the second year installment has a present value of $1,200/(1.04)^2, . . . , the hundredth year's installment $1,200/(1.04)^{100}. Calculate the total by arithmetic or by the high-school algebra of geometric progressions and see if the final sum does not give a *total present capitalized* value of $30,000 or $1,200 ÷ 0.04. Fortunately investors need common sense rather than algebra; bond and compound-interest tables make such arithmetical virtuosity unnecessary.

INTEREST AND THE REAL NET PRODUCTIVITY OF CAPITAL

Lying behind the dollar relationships of capital and interest, there are certain fundamental real relationships. Capital goods contribute toward the production of a flow of current goods and services. Not only do capital goods have the productivity just described; in addition they must have over their lifetime a greater cumulative productivity than the resources that went to produce them. In other words, capital goods have a real net productivity (over and above replacement costs)—and this net productivity, when expressed as a percentage, constitutes the real aspect of the rate of interest.

When we increase the quantity of all capital goods relative to fixed land or labor, the law of diminishing returns will set in. The interest rate or net productivity of capital may decline from 10 to 5, to 1 per cent, until either capital stops growing or some technological improvement comes along and raises capital's interest yield.

In addition to manpower, natural resources, and know-how, a nation needs a large quantity of the best capital equipment if it is to enjoy a high standard of living. Our own industrial society is very fortunate in this respect. So efficient are our tools at producing new tools that we are likely to forget the plight of those backward nations that cannot get their heads above water because their production is so low that they can spare nothing for capital formation by which their standard of living could be raised.

The scarcity of capital among primitive communities is well illustrated by a story of a famous anthropologist. While traveling through a village, he noted the deep air of mourning and despondency. Upon inquiring as to whether a death had occurred, he received the reply, "Death, what is that? We have lost the needle!"

CAPITAL AND PRIVATE PROPERTY

Physical capital goods are important in any economy because they help to increase productivity. This is as true of a communistic system, like that of the Soviet Union, as it is of our own system. But there is one important difference. By and large, private individuals own the tools of production in our capitalistic system.

What is the exception in our system—government ownership of the means of production—is the rule in a socialized state where productive property is collectively owned. The returns from such real capital goods accrue to the government and not to individuals directly. The government then decides how such income is to be distributed among individuals. The communist government also decides how rapidly resources are to be invested in new capital formation: by how much *present* consumption should be curtailed in order to add to the total of factories, equipment, and productive stocks of goods which are necessary if *future* consumption is to rise.

In our system individual capitalists earn interest, dividends, and profits, or rents and royalties on the capital goods that they supply. Every patch of land and every bit of equipment has a deed or "title of ownership" that belongs to somebody directly—or if it belongs to a corporation, then indirectly it belongs to the individual stockholders who "own" the corporation. Moreover, each kind of capital good has a money market value. Hence each claim or title to ownership of a capital good also has a market value. A share of common stock of General Electric is quoted at some certain price, a New York Central bond at another price, a mortgage on a house is valued at some amount, the deed to a house and lot is appraised by the real-estate market at some given level, etc.

Clearly, in taking a census of the nation's total capital, we must avoid fallacious double counting. Nobody could be so foolish as to declare that his total capital was $20,000 if he owned a $10,000 house on Main Street and also had under his mattress a $10,000 deed to that house. Nor would three brothers who owned a small corporation manufacturing electric toasters ever be under the illusion that the million dollars of stock of the company could be *added* to the million dollars' worth of capital goods (factory, machines, wire, etc.) held by the corporation.

These cases are too simple to give rise to confusion. But the unwary statistical census taker would have to guard against more complicated cases. If A. T. & T. (American Telephone and Telegraph Company) is a holding company owning the stock of the New England Telephone and Telegraph Company, he must not count the same values in twice. Nor should we count in the national capital the value of all houses and also the value of all residential mortgages.

This need not be discussed further at this point. It is enough to point out that the everyday term "capital" has many different meanings. It may refer to a capital good; it may refer to a bond, stock, security or deed, or any document that represents a claim to an income-producing capital good. Often in everyday parlance, it is thought of as a sum of money. We say, "Jones is in need of $100,000 of capital which he hopes to raise from the bank." Actually, of course, when Jones borrows that sum from the bank, he will not continue to hold it in the form of a liquid cash asset. He will convert his assets into tangible capital assets, such as tools, or into intangible capital assets, such as an important patent.

It should be pointed out that the government does own a good deal of the national real capital; *e.g.*, Hoover Dam. In addition, its agencies, such as the RFC (Reconstruction Finance Corporation) and the Defense Plant Corporation, are important sources of capital loans for private business.

Also the legal property rights of an individual are relative and limited. Society determines how much of his property a man may bequeath to his heirs and how much must go in inheritance and estate taxes to the public treasury. Society determines how much the owners of public-utility companies—such as electric-light and gas companies—can earn and how they shall run their business.

Even a man's home is not his castle. He must obey zoning laws and, if necessary, make way for a railroad or slum-clearance project. Interestingly enough, two-thirds of society's economic income cannot be capitalized into private property. Since slavery was abolished, human earning power is forbidden by law to be capitalized. A man is not free to sell even himself.

C. *EXCHANGE, DIVISION OF LABOR, AND MONEY*

We turn now to the second of the three characteristic features of the present-day economy. The economies of mass production upon which modern standards of living are based would not be possible if production still took place in self-sufficient farm households or self-sufficient provinces. *Specialization* of function permits each person and each region to use to best advantage any peculiar differences in skill and resources. Even in a primitive economy men learn that, rather than have everyone do everything in a mediocre way, it is better to institute a *division of labor*: for fat men to do the fishing, lean men to do the hunting, and smart men to make the medicine.

Besides resting upon any interpersonal differences in ability, specialization accentuates and creates differences. Hunting makes a man thin and good at stalking prey; a region that has no resources especially adapted to hat making may nevertheless develop skills and know-how which give it advantages in this trade.

Finally, even with no natural or acquired differences in skills, specialization will sometimes pay if only in this way can a large enough volume of activity be reached to realize all the economies of large-scale production mentioned in the preceding chapter.[1] Two identical Indian twins might find it better for one to make all bows and the other all arrows—even if they had to draw lots to see which would make which—because only in this way could each be making enough of each item to warrant introducing improved techniques.

The classical example illustrating the increased productivity of specialization is provided by the making of pins. A single man could at best make a few dozen imperfect ones per day. But when a small group of men are subdivided with respect to function so that each performs simple repetitive operations, they can turn out hundreds of thousands of perfect pins in the same period of time.[2] Moreover, the simplification of function made possible by specialization lends itself to mechanization and the use of laborsaving capital. At the same time it avoids the wasteful duplication of tools that would be necessary if every man had to be a Jack-of-all-trades, and it also saves time lost in going from one job to another. The modern conveyer system of automobile assembly illustrates the efficiency of specialization. In the years after World War II, we may see an advance in the art of automatic self-controlling electronic servo-mechanisms that may revolutionize modern industry.

[1] In his famous work Adam Smith recognized that specialization and division of labor were limited by the extent of the market, *i.e.*, by the volume that can be sold.

[2] The following passage describing the extent of specialization in meat slaughtering has often been quoted: "It would be difficult to find another industry where division of labor has been so ingeniously and microscopically worked out. The animal has been surveyed and laid off like a map; and the men have been classified in over thirty specialties and twenty rates of pay, from 16 cents to 50 cents an hour. The 50-cent man is restricted to using the knife on the most delicate parts of the hide (floorman) or to using the ax in splitting the backbone (splitter); and, wherever a less skilled man can be slipped in at 18 cents, $18\frac{1}{2}$ cents, 20 cents, 21 cents, $22\frac{1}{2}$ cents, 24 cents, and so on, a place is made for him, and an occupation mapped out. In working on the hide alone there are nine positions, at eight different rates of pay. A 20-cent man pulls off the tail, a $22\frac{1}{2}$-cent man pounds off another part where good leather is not found, and the knife of the 40-cent man cuts a different texture and has a different 'feel' from that of the 50-cent man. Skill has become specialized to fit the anatomy. . . .

"The division of labor grew with the industry, following the introduction of the refrigerator car and the marketing of dressed beef, in the decade of the seventies. Before the market was widened by these revolutionizing inventions, the killing gangs were small, since only the local demands were supplied. But when the number of cattle to be killed each day increased to a thousand or more, an increasing gang or crew of men was put together; and the best men were kept at the most exacting work." From J. R. COMMONS. *Quarterly Journal of Economics*, vol. XIX, 1904, pp. 3, 6.

Clearly, however, specialization and division of labor involve one serious problem—that of *interdependence*. A single-celled low form of life such as the amoeba or paramecium is not particularly efficient; but it can live alone and like it. In higher animals such as man, every cell will die if once the heart cells fail. When all goes well, the extreme specialization of cells is very efficient, but at the cost of extreme interdependence.

In modern economic society this process is carried to the nth degree. No one manufacturer makes the smallest fraction of the commodities that he consumes. In medieval times the artisan made one article and exchanged it for many others. Today a worker produces not even a single good; he may make only shoe tongues or simply turn bolt 999 on the Chevrolet assembly line. Such may be his whole lifework. For performing this he will receive an income adequate to buy goods from all over the world; but a hidden cost is paid in the form of his complete dependence upon the rest of the world.

A bank in Austria fails and the natives in Fiji, who carry water in empty Standard Oil cans and clothe their infants in Pillsbury flour bags, lose their livelihood—yes, and may even starve. In the backwash of a war a breakdown in transportation and the economic fabric of exchange reveals how perilously modern economic life depends upon exchange. Would we, if we could, turn the clock back to a simpler and poorer life? Or should we keep the advantages of division of labor and seek policies that will prevent breakdowns?

BARTER VERSUS THE USE OF MONEY

The simplest imaginable way of making the exchanges necessary if there is to be division of labor involves *barter* or trade of one kind of merchandise for another. In primitive cultures it is not uncommon for food to be traded for weapons, or aid in the building of a house for aid in clearing a field. Even in the most advanced industrial economies, if we strip down exchange to its barest essentials, peeling off the obscuring layer of money, we find that trade between individuals or nations really boils down to barter—transforming one good into another by exchange rather than by physical production.

Barter represents a great improvement over a state of affairs in which every man had to be a Jack-of-all-trades and master of none, and a great debt of gratitude is owed to the first two ape men who suddenly perceived that each could be made better off by giving up some of one good in exchange for some of another. Nevertheless, simple barter operates under such great disadvantages that a highly elaborate division of labor would be unthinkable without the introduction of a second great improvement—the use of money.

In all but the most primitive cultures men do not trade one good against another, but instead sell one good for money, and then use money to buy the goods they wish. At first glance this seems to complicate rather than simplify matters, to replace a single transaction by two transactions. Thus, if I have 50 shares of duPont chemical stock and wish instead to have 100 shares of GM (General Motors), would it not be simpler to trade one for the other rather than to incur a brokerage charge in selling the duPont stock for money and another charge in converting the money into GM stock?

Actually the reverse is the case. The two transactions are simpler than one. Ordinarily there are always people ready to buy duPont stock and always some willing to sell—at a price—GM stock. But it would be an unusual coincidence to find a person with tastes just opposite to one's own, with an eager desire to sell GM and buy duPont. Such a coincidence would be as unlikely as the chance of picking two winning horses in a row. Even if the unusual should occasionally happen—as it occasionally must—there is no guarantee that the desires of the two parties with respect to the quantities and terms of the exchange would coincide.

To use a classical economic phrase: instead of there being a double coincidence of wants, there is likely to be a want of coincidence; so that, unless a hungry tailor happens to find a farmer who has enough wheat and a rough desire for a pair of pants, neither can make a trade.

COMMODITY MONEY, PAPER MONEY, AND BANK MONEY

If we were to reconstruct history along hypothetical, logical lines, we would naturally have the age of barter followed by the age of commodity money. Historically a great variety of commodities have served at one time or another as a medium of exchange: cattle (from which comes the Latin stem of "pecuniary" and also the words "capital" and "chattel"), tobacco, leather and hides, furs, olive oil, beer or spirits, slaves or wives, copper, iron, gold, silver, rings, diamonds, wampum beads or shells, huge rocks and landmarks, and cigarette butts.

Each of the above has some advantages and disadvantages. Cattle are not divisible into small change, but while it is being hoarded such money is likely to increase by reproduction, giving the lie to the doctrine of Aristotle that "money is barren." Wives and beer do not improve with keeping, although wine may. Olive oil provides a nice liquid currency which is as minutely divisible as one wishes. Iron will rust and is of so little value that one would need a cart instead of a pocketbook. The value of a diamond is not proportional to weight but varies with its square; therefore, if cut up into pieces it loses value. The yearly additions to (by mining) or subtractions from (by use in teeth or jewelry) the world's accumulated stock of precious metals is small in percentage terms; so that the total amounts and value of these substances do not fluctuate wildly. Silver has luster but will tarnish in air. Gold keeps its attractive sheen, but unless mixed with an alloy is very soft. However, its high specific gravity makes detection of counterfeiting and admixture easy; but through most of historical time, gold's scarcity value has been so great per ounce as to require inordinately minute coins for small purchases.

Most kinds of money tended once to be of some value or use for their own sake. Thus, even wampum had decorative uses, and paper money began as warehouse or mint receipts for so much metal. But the intrinsic usefulness of the money medium is the least important thing about it. The age of commodity money gives way to the age of paper money. The essence of money, its intrinsic nature, is typified by a card chip, a shell, or a paper bill. *Money, as money rather than a commodity, is wanted not for its own sake but for the things it will buy!* We do not wish to use money up; but rather to use it by getting rid of it; even when we choose to use it by holding it, its value comes from the fact that we can spend it later on.

Money is an artificial, social convention. If for any reason a given substance begins to be used as money, all people will begin to value it even if they happen to be teetotalers or vegetarians or disbelievers in its intrinsic usefulness. As long as things can be bought and sold for a given substance, people will be content to sell and buy with it. Paradoxically, money is accepted because it is accepted.

The use of paper currency (dollar bills, fives, tens, etc.) has become widespread except for small change because it has many conveniences as a medium of exchange. Currency is easily carried and stored away. By the printing of more or fewer zeros on the face value of the bill a great or small amount of value can be embodied in a light, transportable medium of little bulk. By the use of decimal points it can be made as divisible as we wish. By careful engraving, the value of the money can be made easily recognizable and can be protected from counterfeiting and adulteration. The fact that private individuals cannot create it at will in unlimited amounts keeps it scarce, *i.e.*, an economic rather than a free good.

Given this limitation in supply, modern currencies have value—*i.e.*, can buy things—independently of any gold, silver, or governmental backing. The public neither knows nor cares—and needs not know or care—whether its currency is in the form of so-called "silver certificates," Federal reserve notes, or in copper, silver, or nickel coin. So long as each form of money can be converted into any other form at fixed terms, the best is as good as the worst.[1]

Along with the age of paper money there is finally also the age of bank money, or bank checking deposits. Today at least nine-tenths of all transactions, by value if not number, take place by checks, which are canceled off between banks of a city and region. An executive will have his salary paid directly into his bank account, after income and social security taxes have already been withheld at the source by his employer. His rent or dentist bills will be paid by check, which his wife may not even give him the privilege of signing. Except then for a little petty cash for lunches, tobacco, and carfare, he may hardly handle any cash at all in the course of a year's time.

PRICE RATIOS AND MONEY PRICES

In every transaction, whether for barter or money, each person gives something up and receives something in exchange. If 5 apples are traded for 25 nuts, the price of apples in terms of nuts is 25 to 5 or, briefly, 5 to 1; the price of nuts in terms of apples is 5 to 25 or 1 to 5, or $\frac{1}{5}$, or in terms of decimals 0.2. Similarly, if 5 apples sell for 25 cents, then the price of apples in terms of money is 5 cents. It would be equally true, but not very customary or familiar, to say that a penny costs $\frac{1}{5}$ or 0.2 of an apple.

Every price is really a price ratio involving a numerator and a denominator. Each depends upon the way in which the two quantities are measured; thus, eggs are quoted at 5 cents apiece, 60 cents a dozen, or $7.20 a gross; likewise we may say that eggs sell for $\frac{1}{20}$ dollar, "get-away automobiles" for $1\frac{1}{2}$ "G's," and haircuts for "6 bits."

If we relied completely on barter, we should have to keep in mind a great number of price ratios—as many as the number of pairs that could be formed

[1] A century ago it was the exception rather than the rule for bank notes and coins to exchange for each other at par. Each had different prices which varied from day to day so that it was necessary for storekeepers to keep daily lists of values, and it became a profession in itself to change money, buying and selling it at a profit. For three centuries it has been known that bad money often tends to drive good money out of circulation; i.e., (1) coins made of metals that rise in price tend to be melted down and sold as bullion; also (2) individuals will try to pass on the kinds of money that are going down in value and hold those which are tending to appreciate in value. The tendency for bad money to drive out good is known as "Gresham's Law." There have however been inflationary periods where the reverse was true; where good money drove bad out of circulation because sellers refused to let buyers pass the bad on to them. This was especially true in North Africa during World War II, as a Princeton study by Richard A. Lester has shown. R. A. LESTER, "International Aspects of Wartime Monetary Experience," Princeton University Press, Princeton, N. J., 1944.

mathematically from the number of commodities. Thus, for only 5 different goods there would be 10 different price ratios to remember, just as there are 10 different tennis matches which must be played in a round robin of 5 different individuals. For 1,000 commodities, there would be almost 500,000 price ratios to remember.[1]

A little reflection will convince us that many of these price ratios are unnecessary, being deducible from a much smaller number. For example, if the price of apples in terms of nuts is 5 and the price of oranges in terms of nuts is 10, then it is not necessary for us to be told what the price of oranges is in terms of apples. Because 10 nuts is twice 5 nuts, we know already that 2 apples must be paid for 1 orange.

By use of the elementary axiom that things equal to the same thing are equal to each other, the reader can convince himself that, once he knows the price ratios of all goods in terms of any *one* good, he can easily get the price ratio between *any two goods* by division. For 5 commodities we need only remember 4 price ratios, not 10; 6 price ratios are redundant, being deducible from the others. For 1,000 commodities, only 999 price ratios are needed, not 500,000.[2]

MONEY AS A MEDIUM OF EXCHANGE OR AS A UNIT OF ACCOUNT

There are two distinct functions of money: as a medium of exchange and as a standard unit of value. This distinction is illustrated by a perfect clearing system, where careful record of all transactions is kept and where finally what each person has coming to him is canceled against what he owes with the balance credited to his account. In such a system no medium of exchange whatever is needed! But a common denominator of value, telling us how to compare and weigh such diverse items as a stick of gum and an automobile,

[1] By elementary algebra, the number of pairs that can be selected from n different objects is no less than $n(n - 1)/2$, or about $\frac{1}{2}n^2$ all together.

[2] This is only one illustration of a general principle applying to all price ratios. When we come to examine the exchange rate at which the moneys of different countries can be converted into each other, we find the same principle applies. If 4 dollars make 1 British pound sterling and $\frac{1}{50}$ of a dollar equals 1 Italian lira, then the number of lira in a pound is perfectly determinate (equal to 4 ÷ $\frac{1}{50}$ or 200). When the Allied military authorities first took over Italy in World War II, they overlooked this fundamental economic truth and set three independent rates. The result was what one might expect: by using currency A one could buy currency B which could then be exchanged for an amount of currency C—an amount that would buy more than the initial amount of A. This is just what happened. *Arbitragers* (*i.e.*, people who speculate on a sure thing) went 'round and 'round the circuit making a profit at each whirl. Of course, the military authorities suffered a corresponding loss. Finally they noticed what was happening and did what they should have done in the first place—set the third price ratio in proper relation to the other two.

would certainly still be necessary. Actually there once existed an African tribe which used as its unit of money the so-called "macute." This was not a shell or commodity; it had no corporeal existence but represented simply a money of *account* not a medium of exchange. Until recently the Paraguayan unit of money was based upon a long obsolete, extinct Argentine coin.

Similarly, fashionable London shops quote prices in terms of "guineas" even though that coin no longer exists. I buy a 1-guinea hat by actually paying 21 shillings because guineas no longer exist, although it is still fashionable to pretend they do. Americans can thank Franklin and Jefferson that the decimal system was adopted for our money. Imagine doing arithmetic problems with heterogeneous English small coins such as the farthing, penny, shilling, half-crown, etc. This is almost but not quite so bad as having to do long division with Roman rather than Arabic numerals.

Of course, any system of reckoning which a child has been taught seems easiest to him, and it is natural for provincial people to think their own methods best. But the real test is whether it would be easier for us to learn their system than for them to learn ours. The decimal system is an obvious winner in such a contest. To be really logical, we should perhaps have a 1-cent piece, a 2-cent piece, a 5-cent piece, a 50-cent piece, a $1 bill, a $2 bill, a $5 bill, a $10 bill, a $20 bill, etc., always repeating the octave 1, 2, 5, 10, or possibly 1, 2.5 5, 10.

In earliest schooling, we are taught never to add apples to oranges nor to combine dimensionally heterogeneous quantities. In economics it is the function of money prices to make all values commensurable. We cannot add apples to oranges. But if we multiply the number of apples by their price per apple, we get a dollar quantity. If we do the corresponding thing with respect to oranges and their price, we again get a dollar sum. And of course two dollar sums can be added together. Aesthetically bread and flowers may be incommensurable, but from an economic standpoint money reduces them to comparability.

MONEY AND TIME

We may summarize our analysis of the use of money by listing its two essential functions: (1) as a *medium of exchange* and (2) as a standard *unit of account* or common denominator of values. But before leaving the matter, it is well to point out how much each of these functions is tied up with the passage of time.

First, and least important, a man may choose to hold part of his wealth in the form of cash. In such a case money is the medium by which present purchasing power is held into the future. A demented miser like King Midas might always prefer to hold his wealth in the form of hoarded cash. But in normal times a man can earn a return on his savings if he puts them into a savings account, or invests them in a bond or stock. Thus it is not normal for money to serve as a "store of value." But in abnormal times, when uncertainty and lack of confidence are all pervasive, or when depressed financial conditions prevent most investments from yielding a positive rate of interest, then people develop a panicky desire for "liquidity" and try to use hoards of money as such a store of value. Needless to say, as the interest rate has fallen in recent years, such behavior has become increasingly important.

Also the use of money will always play an important role in serving as a *standard unit of reckoning* between financial transactions over time. When a man borrows $10,000 for 5 years, he is of course getting present money and agreeing to pay back future money. But suppose all prices have doubled in the meantime, or what is another way of saying the same thing, suppose the value of money has halved? Is it not unfair that the lender should receive much less in real purchasing power than he has given to the borrower?

Obviously, when prices are very unstable over time, when there is extreme inflation or deflation, money serves very badly as a "standard of deferred payment" (over time). Inflation favors debtors at the expense of the creditors; in deflation, when prices fall, debtors are hurt and creditors are benefited—if they can collect!

This completes the discussion of the way in which money performs its two essential functions between points in time. In Part Two, we shall examine in detail the monetary and credit operations of banks and the government to see how they bear on fluctuations in prices and production.

SUMMARY

Even though it deals with facts subconsciously familiar to every person, this is one of the most difficult chapters in the whole field of economics. We are too near to our own system to appreciate how it works.

1. In our mixed private enterprise system, the price mechanism, working through supply and demand in competitive markets, operates to answer the three fundamental problems of economic organization. The system is not perfect, but it works.

2. Our system is mixed in at least two senses: government action modifies private initiative, and monopolistic elements condition the working of competition.

3. Emphasis is to be placed upon three further important aspects of modern economic society: extensive use of privately owned capital, extreme specialization of function and division of labor, all-pervasive use of money in one or another of its functions. All three are fairly obvious once the spotlight of attention and analysis has been focused upon them.

QUESTIONS FOR DISCUSSION

1. During World War II did we let consumers' dollar demand determine their sugar consumption? Why not? What did?

2. Could supply and demand for labor work so as to distribute to salesmen with a "gift of gab" ten times as much income as to competent surgeons? At other times could it operate so as to give surgeons ten times the income of accountants?

3. Do you think that an "instinct of craftsmanship" and a "sense of social responsibility" could ever replace the "profit motive"?

4. List a number of cases where the government modifies the working of an automatic price system. Also list a number of cases where monopoly elements modify the workings of the price system.

5. Assuming that she cannot borrow abroad, what must China do if she wishes to become an efficient industrialized nation within the next few generations?

6. Which is fixed and which circulating capital: pen and ink; safety razor and blade; bow and arrow; cup and saucer; flashlight case, bulb, and battery? Try to think of a difficult borderline case between the two categories.

7. At 2.9 per cent interest per annum, a victory bond paying $25 ten years from now costs $18.75 today. If the rate of interest doubled, would it cost more or less than $18.75? Why? What if the interest rate went down to 1 per cent?

8. Cross out the incorrect words in the following sentence: "When the rate of interest rises, bond prices go (up, down). The price of 20-year bonds will change (more, less) than the price of 5-year bonds."

9. "In 1862 Lincoln freed the slaves. With one stroke of the pen he destroyed a large fraction of the capital which the South had been able to accumulate over the years." Comment.

10. Would ice cubes make a good unit of money? Why not? What about radium? How would people's spending habits be changed if every dollar bill decreased 10 per cent in value with each month that has elapsed since its date of printing?

11. What are some of the advantages of using bank checks rather than paper or metal money? List some of the disadvantages.

12. Late in 1947, Russia called in old rubles and issued one new one for ten old ones. How do such actions affect people's desire to hold wealth in the form of money?

Chapter 4: INDIVIDUAL

AND FAMILY INCOME

ONE does not have to know anything about the laws of economics to have a lively appreciation of the importance of income. The expression "Clothes make the man" would be more nearly right if it were "Income makes the man." That is to say, if one can know but one fact about a man, knowledge of his income will prove to be most revealing. Then a rough guess can be made as to his political opinions, his tastes and education, his age, and even his life expectancy. Furthermore, unless a steady stream of money comes into the family's hands every week, every month, and every year, even though it be made up of saints, that family is sick. Not only its materialistic activities, but its nonmaterialistic activities—the things that convert existence into living—must suffer: education, travel, health, recreation, and charity to say nothing of food, warmth, and shelter.

It is a commonplace to state that the American standard of living and level of family income are the highest in all the world. But few people have more than a hazy conception of just how small the average American income really is, or how great is the range between the highest and the lowest incomes, or even how great are the fluctuations over time in the levels of income.

DISTRIBUTION OF INCOME IN THE UNITED STATES

As a matter of fact any poll of students will show that they are not very certain as to what their own family incomes really are. Usually it turns out that students have a slightly exaggerated notion as to how much their father earns. And despite the recent (quite justified) claim of a prominent clubwoman that "women spend 70 per cent of the national income, and we soon hope to get hold of the rest"—nevertheless, an astonishing number of wives have no conception of their husbands' pay checks. In addition there are some people so inept at keeping records and with such variable earnings that they do not themselves know how much they make. Even where income is known within the family, there is a quite natural reticence to reveal it to outsiders, so much so that investigators who made a recent survey of the birth-control habits of native white protestants of a Middle Western city often found it harder to get financial data than intimate personal information.

In the absence of statistical knowledge, it is understandable that one should form an impression of the American standard of living from the full-page magazine advertisements that portray a jolly American family in an air-conditioned home with a Buick and a station wagon and all the other good things that go to make up comfortable living. Actually, of course, this sort of life is immeasurably beyond the grasp of 95 per cent of the American public, and even far beyond the means of most families from which the selected group of college students come.

In 1929, at the pinnacle of American prosperity, when complacency was also at its height, the amount of per capita income in the United States was around $750 per year per person, or less than $15 per week. Such an average figure has not very much meaning inasmuch as it is derived by pretending that all the income in the United States is divided up equally among every man, woman, and child. Of course, in real life income is distributed anything but equally as we shall see presently; furthermore, there is no guarantee that the attempt to divide up income in this way would leave the total unchanged.

If the members of a classroom, or of the whole country, write down their family income on a card, these cards may be sorted into different income classes; i.e., some cards will go into the $0 to $500 class, some into the $500 to $1,000 class, and so forth. In this way we get the *statistical frequency* distribution of income. At one extreme will be the very poor, who have drawn a blank in life; at the other extreme, the very rich who have hit the jack pot. In between will fall the vast majority of the population.

Table 1 summarizes the most complete statistics on this subject.[1] Column (1) gives the income class interval. Column (2) shows the number of families and individuals in each income class. Column (3) shows the percentage of all families with incomes at least that of the upper limit of the class interval in question. Column (4) shows the percentage of the total income belonging to people in the class in question and to all poorer classes.

[1] Several government agencies cooperated in two monumental studies: "Consumer Incomes in the United States, Their Distribution in 1935–36," National Resources Committee, U.S. Government Printing Office, Washington, D. C., 1938, and "Consumer Expenditures in the United States, Estimates for 1935–36," *ibid.*, 1939.

TABLE 1. *Distribution of Incomes of American Families and Individuals,*
1935–1936

Income class	No. of families and individuals	Percentage of families and individuals in stated income class or below	Percentage of total income belonging to families in stated income class or below
(1)	(2)	(3)	(4)
$ 0–$ 500	6,710,911	17.01	3.48
500– 1,000	11,648,038	46.54	18.23
1,000– 1,500	8,734,423	68.68	36.27
1,500– 2,000	5,185,926	81.82	51.25
2,000– 3,000	4,434,085	93.06	69.10
3,000– 4,000	1,354,078	96.49	76.86
4,000– 5,000	464,191	97.66	80.31
5,000– 7,500	380,266	98.62	84.10
7,500– 10,000	215,642	99.17	87.22
10,000– 20,000	220,605	99.73	92.15
20,000– 50,000	91,707	99.96	96.61
50,000– 100,000	13,041	99.99	98.14
Over $100,000	5,387	100.00	100.00
Total income, $59,258,628,000	Total families, etc., 39,458,300	. . . .	. . . .

SOURCE: Adapted from Table 2, "Consumer Incomes in the United States," National Resources Committee, p. 6.

It would be a great mistake to think that the poor and the rich are equally distributed around the middle. The biblical statement, "The poor you shall always have with you," gives no inkling of their vast numbers. Abraham Lincoln pointed up this fact more picturesquely in his statement, "God must have loved the common man, he made so many of them." A glance at the distribution of income in the United States shows how pointed is the income pyramid and how broad its base. The statement, "There's always room at the top," is certainly true, but it is so because it is hard to get there, not because it is easy. If we made such an income pyramid out of a child's play blocks with each layer portraying $1,000 of income, the peak would be far higher than the Eiffel Tower, but almost all of us would be within a yard of the ground.

Moreover, the middle or "median" income class around which most people fall and which divides the upper from the lower half, corresponds to *extremely low incomes*. Our best statistics of this are taken from the 1935–1936 study referred to earlier. At this time the worst of the Great Depression had been left behind. The median income class, for an average American family of two adults and a number of children, was only about $1,100. Such an income falls far short of the average income per family in 1929 or 1935–1936. This is primarily because the unequal distribution of income gives so much more to the families lying above the median.

Let us see how pitifully inadequate was the income level enjoyed by the typical American family in this prewar year. Social-service workers have made careful estimates of certain minimum budgets as follows:

1. Bare subsistence—no movies, practically no meat, no dental care, no newspapers, little clothing, etc.

2. Minimum health and decency—occasional movie or recreation expenditure, cheap cuts of meat at intervals, some medical and dental care, etc.

3. Minimum comfort—simple but adequate diet, occasional vacation, some tobacco and books, etc.

We may roughly estimate the cost of the first of these at $900 in 1935–1936 prices. Now, if we examine the actual 1935–1936 statistics rearranged in Table 1, it appears that 40 per cent of the population did not even reach this level of income, and 60 per cent earned less than the $1,250 needed for the second budget. Even allowing for the fact that it costs less to live in the country than in the city, we see how justified was the late President Roosevelt's concern with the "lower third" of the population.

From the same table, we find that only 30 per cent have incomes above the level of the $1,500 needed for the minimum comfort budget. If we revert to our typical American family of the slick-paper magazine ads, even after stripping them of their station wagons and mink coats, we still find that only 2 per cent of the population have the $5,000 of income, which we can conservatively estimate was the minimum necessary in 1935–1936 to rough it out at such an existence. And the less said the better about the number of American families who have as much as the $15,000 per year which *Fortune* magazine once estimated was absolutely necessary in order to make ends meet just east of Fifth Avenue in New York City.

THE INEQUALITY OF INCOME

The above sketch of the extent to which incomes fall short of popular notions and adequate standards must now be supplemented by a detailed consideration of the extent of inequality of income prevailing in our society.

It will be noted that the table of the 1935–1936 income distribution was not plotted for equal class intervals: at first each income class was for $500 intervals but the later class intervals cover a range several hundred times as large. This is no accident. An attempt to make all the class intervals equal with a reasonable scale of $1,000 per ¼ inch would require a chart wide enough for a 100-yard dash because of the *tremendous range* between the highest and lowest incomes. That is why the income scale must always be compressed in graphical charts, either by a logarithmic scale or by some other mathematical device.

A second way of describing inequality is to ascertain what per cent of the total income goes to the lowest 5 per cent of the population; what per cent goes to the lowest 50 per cent; what per cent goes to the lowest 95 per cent; and so forth. Such data can be easily derived from the data of Table 1.

If incomes were perfectly distributed, the lowest 5 per cent of the population would receive exactly 5 per cent of the total income; the lowest 95 per cent would receive 95 per cent of the income; and the highest 5 per cent would also get only 5 per cent of the income. This is typified by Table 2. In a so-called

TABLE 2. *Perfect Equality in Distribution of Income*

Per cent of the population..............	0	5	10	25	50	75	95	100
Per cent of income received..............	0	5	10	25	50	75	95	100

"Lorenz curve" we plot these data with the percentage of the population on the horizontal axis, and the percentage of income on the vertical axis. From the data for equal distribution of income, we get the diagonal straight line shown in Fig. 1.

So much for the case of perfect equality. At the other extreme, we have the hypothetical case of perfect inequality, where everybody (say 99 out of 100 people) has no income, except for one person who has all the income. This is shown in Table 3.

TABLE 3. *Perfect Inequality in the Distribution of Income*

Per cent of people............	0	5	10	50	90	95	100
Per cent of income............	0	0	0	0	0	0	100

Why? Because the lowest 0, 5, and 99 people have no income at all. But the lowest 100 people, or all the people, of course have all of the income. The lowest curve on the Lorenz diagram represents the case of perfect inequality.

Any actual income distribution such as that of the 1935–1936 case is of course in between these extremes. The student can verify from Cols. (3) and (4) of Table 1 that its table of values is given roughly by the numbers in Table 4. Its Lorenz curve is given by the indicated intermediate curve with the shaded area indicating the deviation from perfect equality, *i.e.*, the degree of inequality of income distribution.

TABLE 4. *Inequality in the Actual Distribution of Income, 1935–1936*

Per cent of people............	0	10	25	50	75	100
Per cent of income............	0	1.7	6.8	20.5	43.1	100

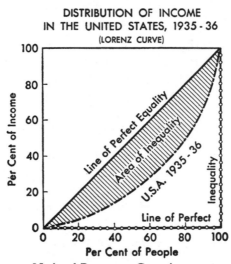

FIG. 1. SOURCE: National Resources Committee, 1935–1936 study.

There are still other ways of measuring the degree of inequality of income. One of the most interesting of these will be mentioned but not discussed in detail here. The Italian-born Swiss professor of economics, Vilfredo Pareto, was often called, with somewhat questionable accuracy, the ideological precursor of fascism. By using a certain logarithmic chart[1] called the "Pareto chart," he found that the "upper tail" of the income data of many different countries and many different times fell along straight lines of almost the same slopes. He came to believe this to be a fundamental natural law. According to Pareto's Law, *there is an inevitable tendency for income to be distributed in the*

[1] VILFREDO PARETO, *Cours d'économie politique*, Tome 2, Livre 3, Chap. I, Lausanne, 1897. A critical account in English of Pareto's Law is given by F. R. Macaulay, "Income in the United States—Its Amount and Distribution," pp. 341–425, National Bureau of Economic Research, New York, 1922.

same way—regardless of social and political institutions and regardless of taxation. In the past 50 years, more careful studies have cast doubt on the universality of Pareto's Law, and upon its inevitability.[1]

THE DECLINE OF POVERTY

It is now almost a century since Karl Marx and Friedrich Engels "in 1848" issued the notorious Communist Manifesto containing the lines: "Workers of the world, unite! You have nothing to lose but your chains." A number of the Marx predictions as to the future of industrial capitalism were proved to be only too correct in the intervening years, but one of the most famous has proved to be quite wrong. Careful historical and statistical research shows that the belief that "the poor are becoming poorer" cannot be sustained. In western Europe and in North America there has definitely been a steady improvement in minimum standards of living whether measured by food consumption, clothing, housing, or length of life. This is clear from statistics to be presented shortly. It is also obvious from a comparison with more backward nations, two-thirds of whose inhabitants are badly undernourished.

Not very long ago it was fashionable for economic historians to dwell on the evils of the industrial revolution and the poverty-ridden condition of the masses in the disease-producing cities. In point of fact no Dickens novel ever did justice to the conditions of child labor, length of the working day, and conditions of safety and sanitation in early nineteenth-century factories. A work week of 84 hours was the prevailing rule, with time out for breakfast and sometimes supper, as well as lunch. A good deal of work could be got out of a six-year-old boy or girl, so long as one didn't care about his health or existence beyond the age of twelve. If a man lost two fingers in a machine, he still had eight left.

However true their lurid picture of industrial factory towns, the earlier historians erred in thinking that conditions were worse than in the preindustrial era. The earlier "putting-out" or domestic system in which wool or yarn was provided to workers for them to spin or weave in their homes brought the worst conditions of the sweatshop into the home. Sleep and need battled for the week's 168 hours. The whole family, not just the breadwinner, was figuratively forced to run on the treadmill to keep alive. For these reasons labor unions have always opposed this system of production, even more than the factory with all its evils.

Furthermore, poverty is never so obvious in the country as in the industrial cities where it forces itself on the observer. The idyllic picture of the healthful

[1] In Great Britain in the immediate postwar period, progressive taxation had gone so far as to leave only 45 people with incomes of more than $24,000, after taxes were paid.

happy countryside peopled by stout yeoman and happy peasantry is a mirage in most parts of the world. Even today, nothing in New York's Hell's Kitchen or east side, nothing in Boston's south or north end, nothing "behind the Yards" in Chicago or in its black belt can overshadow the poverty and squalor of our rural problem areas: the Tobacco Road of the deep South, the hillbilly regions of the Appalachian Plateau, the two dust bowls, the ghost mining towns of Pennsylvania, and the cutover region of the upper Michigan peninsula.

Modern historians therefore emphasize that the inadequate conditions of the industrial present are nevertheless great improvements over the previous periods of commercial enterprise and agarian feudalism. How far we have come is illustrated by the following quotation describing a period that some men can still remember:

In the middle of the nineteenth century there lived in the parish of Marsham, Norfolk, a couple of poor people by the name of Thomas and Mary Edwards. It was on October 5th, 1850, that Mary Edwards bore her last baby boy. At the time of my birth my father was a bullock feeder, working seven days a week, leaving home in the morning before it was light, and not returning in the evening until it was dark. He never saw his children, at this time, except for a little while on the Sunday, as they were always put to bed during the winter months before his return from work. At this time my father's wage had been reduced to 7s. [about $1.40] per week, and had it not been that my mother was able to add a little to her husband's wages by hand-loom weaving the family would have absolutely starved. I have known my mother to be at the loom sixteen hours of the twenty-four, and for those long hours she would not average more than 4s. [80¢] a week, and very often less than that.

The cottage in which the child was born was a miserable one of but two bedrooms, in which had to sleep father, mother, and six children. The family at this time was in abject poverty. When lying in bed with the infant the mother's only food was onion gruel. As a result of the bad food, or, properly speaking, the want of food, she was only able to feed the child at her breast for a week. After the first week he had to be fed on bread soaked in very poor skimmed milk. As soon as my mother was able to get about again, she had to take herself again to the loom. . . . Food rose to famine prices. . . . The only article which did not rise to such a proportionately high figure was meat, but that was an article of food which rarely entered a poor man's home, except a little piece of pork occasionally which would weigh about 1½ lb., and would have to last a family of nine for a week! At the time of the Crimean War meat never entered my father's house more than once or twice a year! . . .

In order to save the family from actual starvation, my father, night by night, took a few turnips from his master's field. My father used to keep our little boots in the best state of repair he could. My sister and I went to bed early on Saturday nights so that my mother might be able to wash and mend our clothes, and we have them clean and tidy for the Sunday. We had no change of clothes in those days. This work kept my mother up nearly all the Saturday night, but she would be up early on the Sunday morning to get our scanty breakfast ready in time for us to go to Sunday School.

This was the only schooling I ever had![1]

Figure 2 shows the great increase in real national product per capita during most of the history of the United States.

If the poor are not getting poorer, are the rich getting richer? Here, the answer is not so simple. Probably for half a century Marx was correct. Huge fortunes were wrested from the earth's resources by such individuals as

HISTORICAL GROWTH OF AMERICAN OUTPUT
1800-1945

FIG. 2. This shows the growth of American output after adjustments have been made for changes in the cost of living and level of population. SOURCE: National Industrial Conference Board; and, for the most recent years, estimates based on data furnished by the Department of Commerce.

Astor (furs); Vanderbilt, Gould, Morgan, Drew, and Harriman (railroads); Carnegie, Mellon, Rockefeller, Rhodes, Hearst (mining, metals, and oil). The "finance capitalism" of the twentieth century added to the wealth of those who by ability, luck, or aggression were able to enter the millionaire class.

Up until 1929 in the United States the rich were certainly getting richer; and in England up until World War I. But following the great stock-market crash, bankruptcy and depression took their toll of many of the established American fortunes. Heavy income and inheritance taxes further reduced the incomes that the wealthy had at their disposal. Along with everyone else the rich have gained in income during the years since the bottom of the great slump, but they have not yet recovered to the dizzy heights of the pre-1929

[1] From the autobiography of George Edwards (1850–1934), quoted in Colin Clark, "National Income Outlay," pp. 262–264, Macmillan & Co., Ltd., London, 1938.

period. As we shall see presently, there have been some interesting shifts within the ranks of the relatively well-to-do classes.

WAR PROSPERITY AND INCOMES

The importance of having a high level of total demand and employment is dramatically revealed by a comparison of income data for the 1935–1936 period of mild depression and the 1945 year of wartime prosperity. Even allowing for a 30 per cent increase in living costs in the intervening decade, we see in Table 5 how much every economic class benefits from the abolition of depressions. In particular, the percentage of the population unlucky enough to have less than $2,500 (of 1945 purchasing power) was halved; and the median income increased from about $1,100 to $2,400 per family.

TABLE 5. *Incomes in 1945 Compared with 1935–1936*

Income	Percentage of all families and individuals	
	1945	1935–1936
Less than $ 1,000	18	47
Less than 2,000	41	82
Less than 3,500	74	95
Less than 5,000	88	98
More than 10,000	1.3	0.3

SOURCE: Census sample, 1945; National Resources Committee, 1935–1936.

THE SO-CALLED "CLASS STRUGGLE"

In his *economic or materialistic* determination of history theory, Karl Marx (1818–1883) placed great emphasis on the *class composition of society*. According to this doctrine the job makes the man, and a man's economic interests determine his political opinions. The well-paid college professor of economics writes textbooks that are apologies for capitalism; the newspaper editor, supported indirectly by advertisers' contributions, inevitably takes on a conservative slant.

Although he would have denied being a "vulgar political economist," Marx spent a good deal of his life in the library of the British Museum burrowing away at the classical economic writings of Adam Smith (1723–1790) and David Ricardo (1772–1823). Like them he came to attach importance to the nature of a man's income. The important thing according to Marx was not simply whether a man was rich or poor but whether his income came from land, capital, or labor.

In feudal times the landowners formed the dominant economic class. The industrial revolution caused the bourgeoisie (a 2-bit word for the business-man-capitalist) to become "the ruling class." As capitalism became more and more monopolistic, as business crises and imperialistic wars became more and more intense, as the lower middle class were ground down into the proletariat (working classes), as the owners of the tools of production increasingly exploited the laboring man, and as the "reserve army of the unemployed" grew, Marx believed the "internal contradictions of capitalism" would finally culminate in a "bloody revolution" which would bring the proletariat into power.

He thought that for a short time a "dictatorship of the proletariat" might be necessary. But once a "classless" or "one-class" society became firmly established, the class struggle would end once and for all, and the state and dictatorship would "wither away." Utopia would be established with "production for use and not for profit," with each "contributing to society according to his ability" and "receiving according to his need," and with "all values being determined by labor alone."

This is an oversimplified version of an oversimple doctrine. Marxists do not themselves agree on its details or even on its fundamentals. Non-Marxist scholars, and they form the vast majority, usually grant a grain of truth to the economic interpretation of history, provided it is not taken too literally and is swallowed down along with several grains of salt.

An economics textbook cannot hope to pass judgment on such questions as whether *evolutionary* rather than *revolutionary* improvement in society is more likely in the American future; whether the Russian experiment does not indicate the folly rather than the wisdom of communism. It is interesting, however, that a recent public-opinion poll showed that 9 out of 10 Americans fancy themselves as part of the "middle" class and resist being included with the proletariat. Some of the individuals so designating themselves were obviously pitifully poor or on relief, and many were members of trade-unions.

Furthermore, until recently challenged by the more militant CIO (Congress of Industrial Organizations), the AFL (American Federation of Labor) largely pursued the nonpartisan "business unionism" tactics established by its long-time leader Samuel Gompers, instead of seeking revolutionary change or political power. The same has been true of the British trade-unions, except that they have taken a more active part in politics, and with the coming to power of the Labor Party, the British, like the Swedes, have been in a position to push on with their program of modified socialism. It is perhaps not without significance that communist revolutions have broken out in countries disorganized by military defeat or depression, in which conservatives have failed to yield to the changing needs of the times and in which there has been little history of liberal, reformist, democratic movements.

INCOME FROM WORK AND FROM PROPERTY

Turning from these controversial political matters, let us consider the different economic sources of individual and family income. Obviously, the income of the cosmopolitan Woolworth heiress, Barbara Hutton, and that of the clerk at the local five-and-ten differ in amount. Although both incomes come indirectly from the same retail business, they differ in character. The clerk is paid for her *personal effort or labor:* for standing on her feet all day, for desisting from robbing the cash register, and for waiting on infallible customers.

Miss Hutton receives her income from *property*. A personal inventory of her total assets might reveal no land to speak of and no tools of production. But somewhere in her lockbox we should expect to find some rather handsomely engraved bits of paper. These securities, whether in the form of stocks, bonds, mortgages, deeds, or annuity policies represent claims or titles to property and income.

A naïve and uninspired physician in examining the two women in question might find little to choose from with respect to physique, I.Q., or temperament. But, although each was equally endowed by her parents as far as arms and legs, one was not so generously treated with respect to lockboxes and property. Under our common and statute law, any owner of private property has the right to give, bequeath, or sell it to whomever he pleases (subject only to taxation), and few will criticize *père* Hutton if he felt that "blood is thicker than water." But everyone will be curious about the workings of an economic society that enables a few individuals to amass such large accumulations of wealth and power and to perpetuate them by inheritance.

The distinction between income from personal work and from property was long recognized in the Federal Income Tax Statute. Until 1943 extra credit was allowed for earned as distinct from unearned income, *i.e.*, for income from work rather than from property income. Undoubtedly this mirrors a prevailing ethical belief in our democratic society that, however important property rights are in our society, they are secondary to human rights and needs.

This was not always the case. When Thomas Jefferson composed the Declaration of Independence, he was criticized for not having made "life, liberty, and the pursuit of happiness" read instead as "life, liberty, and property," the latter being considered a "natural right." Today, all historians recognize that the exceedingly able Constitutional founders drafted a document reflecting their prevailing fear that, if the unpropertied classes were given the suffrage, by their numbers and economic interests they would come into power and impair property rights. Not until after the Jacksonian era a century ago did apologists for the wealthier classes begin to play down class differences.

It is only too easy to stack the cards in favor of unearned income by a cleverly contrived example. Consider on the other hand the case of an opera singer who receives $100,000 a year for doing what he loves best to do and what it is natural for him to do well. And consider a widow whose late husband was able by scrimping and abstinence, by self-denial and waiting, to accumulate just enough property to yield her a minimum of comfort. We may leave to the reader to debate whether the "earned" income of the singer is socially more defensible than the small property income of the dependent woman.

Let us now turn briefly to the problem of subdividing and classifying kinds of income. The old-fashioned economist liked to work with the classifications land, labor, and capital. Consequently, he divided property incomes into land and capital, or into rent and interest. But it does not seem crucially important to us today that the Astor fortune is invested in New York real estate while the Marshall Field fortune comes from capital holdings.[1]

A more significant breakdown of property income is in terms of (1) relatively fixed income receivers who get a fixed interest rate on government or private bonds, mortgages, preferred stocks, and life-insurance annuity contracts, or relatively fixed incomes from real estate; and (2) those who receive a variable profit upon their investments depending upon whether business is good or bad. They are the residual claimants.

As a third great category of income we have wages and salaries—the earnings of skill and effort. Within the classification of earned incomes, we can distinguish a number of different ranks: the unskilled laborer, the semiskilled or skilled laborer, the white-collar or clerical worker, the business executive or manager, and the professional man. The rest of this chapter will be concerned with the three categories of income.

---

[1] Also, it is important to note that "rent" had a special meaning to the older economists. To them it did not mean what you paid your landlord for lodgings, but rather that part of the earnings of land which was attributable to the "initial, unchangeable, and indestructible creation of nature." Also, we should realize that land rent can be regarded as interest or as capital return on its (capitalized) value.

THE RENTIER CLASS IN A DECADE OF FALLING INTEREST RATES

These fixed-income receivers constitute the so-called *rentier* (rhymes with "gay") class. They clip bond coupons or live on the interest of mortgages and other types of securities. An inflation in the cost of living hurts this group because they receive no compensatory increase in income; contrariwise, when depressions strike the land and prices are falling, the *rentier* class would tend to benefit, if bonds did not go into default and if preferred stock dividends were not cut off.

Moreover, for the past decade there has been a steady fall in the interest rate. A man who retired in 1925 with a million dollars might count on earning 5 or 6 per cent on his portfolio. This would give him an income of $50,000 or $60,000 per year, enough to support a town and country home and a retinue of maids, chauffeurs, cooks, and gardeners. But gradually the high-yielding bonds in his portfolio would have come due or have been called in, and he would have been unable to replace them by equally high-yielding securities. His loss was American industry's gain; railroads, public utilities, and manufacturing concerns throughout the last decade have been able to reduce their fixed charges by refunding their bonded indebtedness at lower rates of interest.

Even if the retired millionaire were able to avoid capital loss in the stock-market crash, he would be lucky in the 1940's to average 3 per cent on his portfolio. This gives him an income of $30,000 or less, of which the steeply increased Federal income taxes would take over $10,000. Thus he is left with about $20,000 to live on. This is six times what the average family gets, but it is certainly not enough to keep two large homes, or very many servants these days.

When he considers that about one-third of his million dollars will go to the state and Federal governments in estate and inheritance taxes, it would not be surprising if our retired man should be tempted to buy an annuity with his money. The amount he would then receive each year naturally depends upon his age and life expectancy. Because each yearly payment would involve using up part of his original capital in addition to interest (on a dwindling amount), the annuity would give him a much larger amount to spend. In fact, if his life expectancy were about 10 years, he could get about four times as much money per year, *i.e.*, about $120,000 per year, of which the largest part would be nontaxable since it involves the eating up of capital rather than interest income. Of course, at his death he would have nothing left to pass on to his heirs.

The above example is rather unrealistic in that it refers to a millionaire. But the same applies to some extent to people of more moderate means. With declining rates of interest, it is becoming increasingly difficult for any family head to set aside enough savings to provide for his old age and dependents—or at least to provide for them from interest earnings on capital kept intact.

We are perhaps returning to the conditions of an earlier age. When the poet Pope's father retired to Italy to live, he took with him a chest of gold coins from which all family expenditures were subsequently made. Such a chest could not, of course, be bottomless. In a later day, however, it became possible with the development of financial markets for a wealthy man to have his cake and eat it too; *i.e.*, one could live off the interest income of his capital in perpetuity. In fact, some men had such large fortunes that they could, so to speak, live on the income of their income and permit their fortunes to increase at compound interest. To him who hath shall be given!

Today at 3 per cent it is not so easy to accumulate a fortune out of interest earnings. According to a rough rule of thumb, to find out how long it takes for money to double at compound interest, divide 72 by the interest rate. Instead of having to wait 12 years, as at 6 per cent, today one must wait a quarter of a century! In making his life plans, every citizen must therefore reckon with the fact that his savings earn only a moderate yield. Few can hope to live in retirement without depleting their capital. And because men marry wives younger than themselves, and because women live longer on the average than men, the same problem must be faced in providing for one's widow.

A visitor to a small New England town in the past century once observed that a certain harmless looking citizen was treated as a social pariah by all the other townfolks. After much importunate questioning as to what was wrong with the man, he was told in a shuddering whisper, "He dipped into his capital!" Such attitudes are perforce going out of date. And perhaps there is poetic justice that an epoch which no longer considers itself responsible for the care of its retired parents should at the same time be the one which can no longer afford to preserve and bequeath family inheritances.

Two important reservations to the above gloomy picture must be noted. First, the prophets of gloom who predict the gradual "euthanasia or extinction of the *rentier* class" should reserve their tears or gloating. Partly as a result of the government's "easy-money" policy—but more importantly as a result of the Great Depression which lies behind that policy—the interest earned on each dollar invested has been declining. True enough. But the number of dollars that the American people have been able to accumulate as savings has increased more than the decline in yield. Much of these savings are in the form of war bonds. In any case, even in the prewar years, total interest income going to the *rentier* class was not declining. For the postwar period, it will be about 10 billion dollars per year as compared to the prewar figure of 5 billions, or about double the previous amount.

The second reservation involves the fact that within the past decade a more or less comprehensive social security system has been set up to cover most of the population. This will provide more generously for the old age of the bulk of our people than individual savings and interest earnings ever were able to in the past. In fact we shall see in our later discussion of social security that one of the most crushing indictments of the capitalistic system has been the well-authenticated charge that the vast majority of citizens have been unable—even after a lifetime of effort—to provide adequately for their old age. "Cradle-to-grave" security has great popularity; if the private economy cannot supply it naturally, people will insist upon getting it artificially from governments.

Despite the above reservations, the importance of a declining rate of interest deserves emphasis. Low rate of yield may be with us, not for a year or a decade, but for the rest of our lives. The gilt-edged bonds we buy will not yield 6 per cent. Our new insurance policies will guarantee a return of only $2\frac{1}{2}$ per cent. Our universities and endowed institutions will have to look for new sources of funds or for expanded endowments if they are to offset the decline in the yield on their security portfolios.

INCOMES OF FARMERS

The real economic world is not so simple as textbook writers would like it to be. All people cannot be assigned into one of two pews depending upon whether their income is from work or from property. The ordinary working-man may have a share or two of A.T.&T. or some accrued interest on war bonds. The scion of an old Bostonian family may supplement his harvest of clipped bond coupons by producing an occasional landscape painting.

An especially important kind of income which contains both property and work elements is that from farming. Although today only 40-odd per cent of our population lives in the country as compared to 95 per cent in colonial days, some 30 million people still depend on farming for a living, making it our number one industry in size. On the typical family farm, still our dominant form of rural organization, the farmer himself cannot tell you what part of his income comes to him in his capacity as a worker, what in his capacity as a capitalist who has provided tools and implements, or finally what is his in his capacity as owner of land. In fact, he is not able to tell you how much of his total income stems from his own labors and how much comes from the varied, but important, efforts of his wife and children.

The paid farm laborer has no such problem of determining the different sources of his income. He has little but his sweat to contribute. The only problem that causes him any difficulty is to know how much his "keep"— room and board—is worth in addition to his cash income. Before the war, he was one of the lowest paid of all workers. It is estimated that two-fifths of the 2½ million farm laborers received less than $250 per year including keep! And only one-fifth received more than $500. During the war, the drafting of farm hands and the upswing in farm earnings sent farm wages up. By 1947, farm wages had increased almost fourfold in comparison with the average before World War I but still averaged less than $100 a month plus board. Even if this should not prove to be temporary, this still represents heart-breakingly low wages, considering the length of the working day and the exertions involved.

The Southern white or Negro *sharecropper*, who owns neither land nor tools and who lives during the year on credit and goods advanced from the company store, is a more complex case. In ordinary years, he is lucky if the cotton crop brings him enough cash to pay off the I.O.U's that he has incurred. Often he is chained to risking everything on a single crop—cotton—because it cannot be eaten or easily stolen. A week after the harvest, he is again in debt, again on the interminable annual treadmill. In exceptional years when the crop sells for a high value, he may make a profit high enough to pay back past debts and still have something left over. He is therefore a capitalist in a certain sense; but undoubtedly he would gladly change this status for decent steady wages. This explains the influx of Southern Negroes and poor whites into the Northern cities during the two wars and throughout the prosperous 1920's.

The *tenant farmer* represents another intermediate case typical of all parts of the United States. Ordinarily, he will rent land for a fixed price or on some sort of sharing basis. He may live on the farm, provide all of the labor, occasionally own half the equipment and half the livestock, and quite commonly share 50-50 in the annual return. Under the most favorable circumstances, tenant farming represents the stepladder by means of which a young farmer is able to climb to ownership of his own establishment. But when agriculture is depressed for many years, as in the period between the two world wars, even independent farmers may be losing their holdings through widespread mortgage foreclosure, and the traffic on the ladder may be predominantly downward. Heavy farm-mortgage indebtedness, based upon the land boom following World War I, proved one of the greatest burdens on agriculture between the two wars. It remains to be seen whether we shall avoid this difficulty this time, since farm real-estate prices boomed during World War II and its aftermath.

Agriculture has always been an up-and-down industry. Not only is the farmer dependent on the vagaries of the weather but also he is at the mercy of the market, so that a good cotton crop may bring in less than a poor one. Farm employment and production do not drop during the depression. They may even rise as people go back to or stay on the farms, and because of the farmer's frantic effort to maintain his income in the face of falling prices. Of course, this all serves simply to send prices down still farther.

Aside from its instability of income, the long-run trend is moving more and more against farm income relative to industrial income. Under these circumstances one would expect a movement of population from country to city. And so there has been for most of our history. With higher birth rates in the country and with intermittent depressions in the cities, the cityward migration has never been sufficiently rapid to result in any sort of an equilibrium between industrial and agricultural earnings.

Moreover, there are great differences between the levels of prosperity of different parts of the agricultural population. The rich farm lands of Iowa, where cultivation is mechanized, will yield a satisfactory income to their owners in all but the worst of times. The farmers out there drive Buicks and the villagers drive Fords. Although the relatively prosperous farms produce more than one-half of the total United States crop value, they include less than one-tenth of the total number of people engaged in agriculture. The bulk of the remaining people live on "marginal" farms and eke out a bare existence except in artificial periods of war prosperity. The attempts by the farm lobbies to secure Federal legislation to aid farm incomes were successful even before the New Deal. This is not surprising, in view of the number of farm votes. But too often, even today, these programs help the already relatively prosperous farmers, who dominate the lobbies, rather than those who need help most.

In one form or another, such legislation usually succeeds in raising farm income by *making farm products more scarce, thereby raising their prices*. Farmers are paid in one way or another to restrict production. A great hullabaloo was raised during the 1933 Depression because some little pigs were plowed under. But this was not nearly so important as the number of pigs and ears of corn that never came into being because of *restrictive acreage quotas* established at farmers' requests by the AAA (Agricultural Adjustment Act, declared unconstitutional in 1936), the soil conservation and ever-normal granary programs, the policy of guaranteeing prices by means of government crop loans.

These various programs can be summarized by the quest for farm parity.

The period 1910–1914 is looked upon as a golden age for farmers, as a norm toward which they aspire. Congress has agreed to restore the price and income relations which then prevailed. Unfortunately, different people define the word "parity" differently, as indicated by the title of a recent book, "Parity, Parity, Parity,"[1] to which might have been added, "And still more parity." At the least, parity means a restoration of 1910–1914 farm price levels. At the next level it means that farm prices should be as much higher than 1910-1914 as industrial prices are. Still another interpretation of parity is in terms of 1910–1914 *incomes* and *real purchasing power* for farmers. Finally, after all the other goals have been passed, the adherents of parity will aspire for the same relative share of today's much larger national income as farmers received in the glorious ante bellum period.

Farming is a way of life, not simply a business. That is why it is being discussed here and not in the chapter on business enterprise. For the same reason, the economist cannot say that the American people are wrong in establishing production-control programs to help the farmer. But economics can tell us (1) why and how such a program works (covered in the later sections of Part Three on supply and demand), (2) what other means than a tax on consumers might be used to aid needy farmers, and (3) in which direction lies the only satisfactory solution to the problem. Without anticipating later discussion, it may be noted here that *the farmer's solution is indissolubly linked with full employment and industrial prosperity.* Fortunately, or unfortunately, the reverse cannot be said.

WAGE INCOMES FROM WORK[2]

Most families receive their income from jobs. Out of the 60-odd million people in the labor force, probably 80 out of every 100 persons work for somebody else. The remaining 20 are bosses: either on farms, in self-owned businesses, or in such professional activities as medicine, law, and dentistry. Of course, as will be seen in the chapter on business, the largest part of the self-employed group boss only themselves or one or two other employees at most.

The weekly or monthly pay check—the so-called "take-home"—is the sensitive barometer of family well-being. As a matter of fact, many families,

[1] J. D. BLACK, "Parity, Parity, Parity," Harvard University Press, Cambridge, 1942.

[2] The social security system has had as one by-product a great amount of interesting statistical data. The author has relied heavily on the analyses of such data given in W. S. Woytinsky, "Earnings and Social Security in the United States," Social Science Research Council, New York, 1943.

through choice or necessity, have more than one pay check coming in. For each eight principal family breadwinners—usually men—there are two additional supplementary family earners, one being a woman. (This was true even before the war brought women, youths, and aged into the labor market in swollen numbers.) Of course not all these extra family earners wish to work throughout the year. Still others wish to but are unable to get steady jobs, the same being true as well for the principal breadwinners.

The outstanding fact about the labor market is the great difference in the pay for different jobs. Some of these we take for granted. A foreman receives more than a worker, an accountant more than a ditchdigger, a dress designer more than a cook. But some of the patterns are changing. A ditchdigger may today be getting as much as a bank teller, a waitress as much as a school teacher, an automobile worker more than twice as much as a minister. Some of the patterns are arbitrary and capricious: in one life-insurance company the switchboard operators may receive more than the filing clerks, while in another company the reverse may prevail.

Suppose that an intelligent person without much previous experience of the economic world sat down on his haunches in a closed library (ivory-paneled) and began to reflect on these differences in pay. His first conclusion might be that the dirty, strenuous, unattractive jobs must surely call for the highest pay. Because people are not easily enticed into them, wages must be high there. Likewise the easy and pleasant jobs must attract so many people that their wages fall. Even with wages low, there will be so much "psychic income" from the job itself that people will continue to be available for such jobs.

This first conclusion would be quite wrong, as our philosopher would find when he went out into the world to check his theory. The skilled surgeon who enjoys every minute of his work pulls down fifty times the pay of the ditchdigger who cusses at every shovelful. He would find it the same in almost every occupation. *The best jobs also have the best pay.* It is true that window washers for the hundredth floor of the Empire State building may receive twice the pay of similar people lower down, but their lifetime earnings are still probably not nearly so great.

After scurrying back to his study to recover from the paradoxical discovery that higher wages do not seem to serve the purpose of compensating for the greater irksomeness of certain jobs, he might try a second tack: *people are different.* Not everyone can become a good surgeon—or at least not so many as can become good ditchdiggers. Moreover, it takes 15 years to produce an expert doctor, whereas one should be able to tell at the end of 6 months whether or not a man has a brilliant career ahead of him as a ditchdigger.

These differences in people may be physical, mental, temperamental, or even moral. They may be associated with biological inheritance through the genetic cells, or with social and economic environment. They may be permanent—like being a man or a woman—or acquired, like educational advantage. These differences may even involve artificial conventionalities as the possession or nonpossession of a union card and one's propensity to drop "(h) aitches" in speaking or to pronounce "oil" with an "r" and "girl" without one.

Our observer can now turn back to the world with at least the beginning of an answer. But only a beginning. For he will find that most physical traits, such as height or hip girth, and most mental traits, such as intelligence quotient or tone perception, are not so different between people as are the differences in

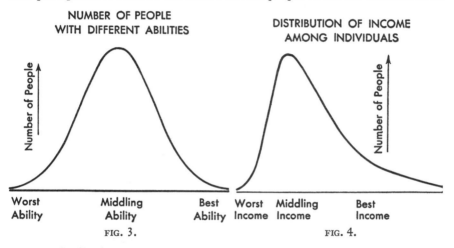

FIG. 3.   FIG. 4.

income distribution. Usually, by hook or crook, the scientist who measures these traits finds that they are "normally" distributed, with most people in the middle and fewer people at each end, as represented in Fig. 3. Whereas incomes—even those from work rather than property— are distributed *askew*, with a very long tail off in the direction of the highest paid, as in Fig. 4.

One could go on speculating on these fundamental questions. Probably it would be more scientific, and more fruitful at this point, to take a bird's-eye look at the facts about the earnings of different groups in different occupations. However, it may be as well to mention at this point that a recent careful study of wage inequalities in the Russian communistic economy[1] showed inequalities and dispersions between the best paid and the poorest paid workers which were surprisingly like those of our own society. Of course these were not accom-

[1] ABRAM BERGSON, "The Structure of Soviet Wages," Harvard University Press, Cambridge, 1944.

panied by further inequalities resulting from unequal property incomes. Perhaps a warning is in order at this point against jumping to the conclusion, as Pareto did, that there is something *necessary* and *inevitable* about this dispersion of income. Within the framework of our free competitive society fundamental changes in education have already made significant changes in inequality. Moreover, as no one knows better than the man at the top, our system of progressive income taxation has already greatly changed the relative take-home and—what is more important—the "keep-at-home" of the high and lowly paid; and there is every indication that this will continue to be an abiding feature of American life.

THE POSITION OF MINORITIES

No discussion of the inequality of incomes would be complete without mention of the position of economic minorities. In a real sense this is the concern of everyone because we all belong to some minority. Yes, even the Smiths.

Of course the economically most important minorities consist of Negroes, women, and old people. Careful, competent observers have asserted again and again that outright sexual discrimination in the sense of paying men higher rates for the same kind and volume of work is not a common practice. Similarly it has been asserted that racial discrimination in the sense of unequal pay for the same work is not prevailing practice.

How can we reconcile these statements with the economic inequalities which every sophisticated person knows prevail between the sexes and races and which are shown in Table 6? The answer to the paradox lies partly in the

TABLE 6. *Comparative 1940 Per Capita Earnings of Men and Women and of Negroes and Whites*

	Male	Female
White..................................	$1,401	$734
Negro..................................	$ 663	$396

SOURCE: W. S. WOYTINSKY, "Earnings and Social Security in the United States," Social Science Research Council, New York, 1943. Data refer only to occupations covered by social security.

fact that discrimination usually takes the more subtle and more effective form of *not admitting men and women to the same jobs and in barring Negroes from many of the higher paid jobs.*

Undoubtedly this explains much of the story. However, other competent observers maintain that women and Negroes on exactly the same job do often receive less pay. Women grade-school teachers often receive lower pay than men on the grounds that their *needs are less and their classroom authority not so great*. Where Negro and white dishwashers work side by side, it is not impossible that the former should receive lower pay. In a General Electric plant, job-evaluation experts divide all factory work into two parts: women's jobs and men's jobs. The pay of the lowest men begins about where the highest women's pay leaves off. Yet both management and the union will admit, off the record, that in many borderline jobs the productivity of women is greater than that of the men.

Now it cannot be denied that there are physical and temperamental differences between men and women. For example, a woman could not win the heavyweight wrestling championship nor set a record for the 100-yard dash. On the other hand, the female sex is the stronger sex in the sense of life expectancy and also, perhaps, in being capable of sustained, painstaking effort. It is equally obvious that there are differences of skin color and hair texture between colored and white races.

Whatever one's views as to the biological and environmental differences between the races and sexes—and the views of the scientists who have studied the question most are very different from those of the man on the street—it is absolutely clear to any observer that there are numerous jobs which either sex or race can do equally well and is prevented from doing. This is shown by the experience of wartime and boom when the usual barriers are lowered.

Similarly the older worker in ordinary times finds himself at a disadvantage in our society. A man may be thrown on the scrap heap by the age of forty when many of his best years are still ahead of him. It is not true that an older worker is the first to be fired; usually his experience or seniority helps to protect him. But once he is fired, it is much harder for him to become reemployed. Paradoxically, the humanitarian measures adopted by corporations to aid older workers (retirement pension schemes, etc.) are one of the reasons for corporations' refusing to hire older men, since it then becomes more expensive to hire them.

Again, from the horror of war a few salutary lessons have been snatched. Women, Negroes, and older workers have shown that they are capable of holding down better jobs and earning more money than was thought possible before the war. The experience of the Federal and state Fair Employment Practice Commissions has not been that prejudice can be legislated out of existence overnight, but that steady improvement is possible if the people really want it.

Nor can all of the blame be placed upon bigoted employers. Organized labor, particularly many unions of the AFL, must incur much of the blame or credit for Jim Crow legislation.[1]

The position of women shows steady improvement. In fact there is evidence that they are burrowing into those overhead white-collar jobs and service industries which are least sensitive to the ups and downs of the business cycle and which have more favorable long-run trends than the heavy capital goods sector of the economy in which men predominate. But except for the war, there are indications that the problem of Negro inequality, far from straightening itself out, is becoming worse. In times of prosperity, the Negro is last to be hired; when depression comes, the Negro is first to be fired and thrown on relief; when jobs become scarce, whites invade even the fields of domestic service usually abandoned to the Negro.

Still once again we are faced with the challenge of providing full employment. For it is in the wake of layoffs and economic insecurity that the disruptive cry against minorities—against Negro, Jew, Catholic, "Okie"—gathers the force to cause our democratic institutions to tremble.

SUMMARY

Among the most important economic problems is the continued growth of the average level of real income. Equally important both for politics and economics is the question of the degree to which income is unequally distributed around the average.

The facts concerning the distribution of income can be presented in terms of the statistics of the relative number of families in each income bracket. In addition, we can study the incomes of different economic classes—farmers, *rentiers*, etc—and also of different social and racial groups. From either point of view, the paramount importance of high and growing national product becomes indisputably apparent.

[1] See H. R. NORTHROP, "Organized Labor and the Negro," Harper & Brothers, New York, 1944. Also GUNNAR MYRDAL, *et al.*, "An American Dilemma," Vols. I and II, Harper & Brothers, New York, 1944.

QUESTIONS FOR DISCUSSION

1. Let each member of the class write down an estimate of his own family's income on a slip of paper. From these, draw up a frequency table showing the distribution of incomes. What is the median income? the average income?

2. How much do you think it takes for a childless married couple to live comfortably in your community? How would the money be spent?

3. Were your parents better off than their parents? What does this suggest with respect to the advantages and disadvantages of capitalism?

4. "Different economic groups and classes have interests very much in common. But they also have opposing interests." Discuss. Give illustrations.

5. Make an outline classifying the possible kinds of income. What has been happening to each kind in the past few years? What are some of the reasons?

6. Formulate some of your own ethical beliefs concerning how unequal incomes should be for people of different abilities and needs. How do you justify these beliefs? Would a nineteenty-century American agree? Would a present-day Russian? a South Sea Islander?

Chapter 5: INDIVIDUAL AND

FAMILY INCOME: EARNINGS IN

DIFFERENT OCCUPATIONS

THE LABOR MARKET'S BASEMENT

It is an old American custom to start in at the bottom and work one's way up. It is fitting therefore that we first examine the economic status of domestic servants. Not all the economic facts are available on this subject because few records are kept and so many establishments are involved. For these reasons primarily, this occupation is not now covered by the social security laws; presumably when it is covered, recourse will be had to a stamp system like that in England, where the employer fills out no records but simply buys a monthly stamp to put in the maid's book.

But enough facts are available to make it amply clear to all but irate and desperately harassed suburban matrons, that the great American sweatshop is to be found in the American home. A factory worker grumbles if she is made to work 8 hours a day 5 days a week for $20 per week or $1,000 a year. Yet two-thirds of the household workers in such representative prosperous states as Connecticut and Michigan before the war earned less than $500; one-third earned less than $250 per year! During this period, a servant who lived off the premises was lucky if she finished the supper dishes within a 12-hour day. If she was unfortunate enough to live on the premises, only the sleeping hours were her own, and she was lucky to get off Thursday evening and every other Sunday. Nor were there many of the alleged comforts of a cozy home, as she had long since lost the old Yankee privilege extended to the "help" of eating with and being one of the family. Finally, but not least important, a maid's chance of meeting a marriageable prospect has always been at rock bottom.

86

She needed no "Eleanor" club to tell her that. By 1945 wages had improved, but three-quarters of domestic servants still earned less than $500 of yearly cash income.

It is no wonder then that, when the war opened up jobs in stores, offices, factories, and beauty parlors, women left domestic service, never to return voluntarily. Moreover, if reasonably high levels of employment opportunities are maintained in the years ahead, middle-class families must resign themselves to the new order. Unless a family is willing to give up a significant fraction of its own income, it will not be able to find a reasonably intelligent person who will dedicate her life to raising other people's children. The moral: sell that big house and buy an automatic washing machine.

Scarcely higher in the economic scale are the miscellaneous dead-end jobs such as messenger, elevator operator, hat-check girl, bus boy, and dime-store clerk. Comparatively little experience, training, or ability is required for these jobs and the pay is correspondingly low. For a girl who hopes to be married in a few years, the economic waste in taking such a job before finishing high school may not be nearly so important as the social waste involved. But it is nothing less than an economic crime for a boy to terminate the schooling that can get him a higher skilled and better rewarded job for the few dollars and feeling of independence that come from such a futureless position. Five years later he is little better off than at the beginning, and the pay no longer seems munificent to him, or even adequate.

This does not mean that everyone should aspire to or achieve a high-paid job at the top or that everyone ought to go on to take the highest college degree possible. Somebody must perform the humble tasks of hewing wood and drawing water. But, as the artificial war period has shown, it is possible for these jobs to command better than substandard wages if (1) the supply of workers going into them is kept down by virtue of the fact that all those who can benefit from higher training do so and (2) the general demand for labor is brisk enough to provide better job opportunities elsewhere. Earnings in the more skilled jobs need not then necessarily fall; even if they should, total earnings of all labor would presumably be higher after equalization, because the average person is working more productively.

Finally, the enthusiastic student must not think that preaching the gospel of better training will have much influence on poor families. These feel desperately the need of every bit of extra income. Only when general family incomes are adequate and vocational or academic training is conveniently available along with part-time jobs, will there be much effect on those who are most in need of improvement.

THE UNSKILLED AND SEMISKILLED WORKERS

Perhaps next in the working scale come relatively *unskilled* or *semiskilled* factory jobs. No other group in the economy has shown such remarkable improvements in earnings since the days prior to World War I. When Henry Ford announced in 1914 his policy of paying $5 for an 8-hour day, it was considered revolutionary. Today, earnings of $2 per hour or $16 per day are above the average, but they are not uncommon. The sweatshop so characteristic of highly competitive industries like the garment trade is, in its worst forms, pretty much a thing of the past.

Two factors help to account for the improved status of factory labor. The first, and by far the more important, is the *steady increase in productivity and efficiency of labor resulting from technological improvements and large-scale production*. As a result, $1 spent on labor working in efficient American factories may be twice as worth while as $0.60 spent in England and Germany, and may be worth more than ten times $0.10 spent on Chinese coolie labor.

A secondary, but by no means negligible, factor has been the *growth of trade-union collective bargaining and government legislation*. Since 1933 the unskilled and semiskilled workers have become increasingly unionized in such fields as automobiles, textiles, and electricity. Unions have zealously—sometimes too zealously—made sure that the increases in productivity were shared by management with labor. We shall return to this field of labor relations many times in the course of our later discussions.

A factory worker will ordinarily be paid in one of two ways: by *the hour* or by *piece rates*. Under provisions of the Fair Labor Standards Act the hourly rate cannot be less than 40 cents for factories engaged in interstate commerce. It may of course be much greater than this. As of 1947, average standard hourly rates were around $1.70 in bituminous coal mining, $1.45 in automobile manufacturing, $1 in Northern textiles, $0.90 in Southern textiles, $1.47 in the steel industry, and $1.10 in the men's clothing industry.

The general geographic pattern of industrial wage rates is well summarized in the following quotation:

Considerable variation in both hourly and weekly earnings is found not only among the various major geographic regions, but also among states within the same region. Highest wages are noted in the Far West and lowest in the South. The differences in earnings between the East and Middle West are not marked. In large communities wages tend to be higher than in small communities, and in large companies wages are generally above those of small companies.[1]

[1] M. ADA BENEY, "Differentials in Industrial Wages and Hours in the United States," p. 1, National Industrial Conference Board, Inc., New York, 1938.

For work in excess of 40 hours per week, or 8 hours per day, it is customary to pay 1½ times the standard rate. Thus, when workers used to put in a 48-hour week during the war, they were paid not for 40 + 8, but for 40 + 12, or 52 hours, an increase of 30 per cent. After the war the return to 40 hours cut their take-home incomes by exactly the 30 per cent increase; and to prevent this, organized labor asked for a 30 per cent increase in standard hourly rates. After the strikes of 1945–1946 in steel and automobiles, labor and management compromised on about one-half of this demand.

When a worker is on piece rates, he is paid according to how many units of product he is able to turn out: a woman who wraps 10,000 candy bars per hour will receive one-third more than one who wraps only 7,500, and so forth. Such a method of pay has an element of fairness in it since those who work harder and more skillfully receive more. It also pleases the employer because it goads the workers into increasing production. On the other hand, workers claim that it leads to a fatiguing speed-up.

Moreover, it gives rise to endless debate concerning the fair piece rate. As workers are given better machines, their productivity increases even without increased effort and their earnings may become very great at the old rates. The employer not unnaturally, therefore, wishes to cut the piece rate. He may send a time-and-motion efficiency engineer (a modern disciple of Frederick Taylor's scientific management) around with a stop watch to clock the worker and set a new fair rate. Often the worker feels aggrieved and tries to slow down and magnify the difficulty of the new job. He feels that the incentive pay for increasing the number of pieces of output is an illusion; that whenever workers increase their speed, the rate is cut, and they end up by getting no more than before, while working harder and with a number of their unluckier buddies being laid off.

The natural consequence is for unions and unorganized workers to discourage their more energetic comrades from working too hard, and to reject the suggestions of the time-and-motion expert which would often result in miraculous saving of effort and fatigue, and stupendous increases in productivity. Thus part of the increases in efficiency, which come in after unions have forced management to pay workers well and use them more efficiently, may be lost by union "featherbedding" tactics.

THE SKILLED CRAFTSMEN

Formerly at the top of the manual-labor pyramid, but now seriously challenged by the rise in earnings of the class just described, is the skilled craftsman, such as the plumber, carpenter, bricklayer, machinist, and printer. In many cases these activities stem in an unbroken line from the journeymen artisans of the preindustrial period. The characteristic union organization by craft or skill, rather than by industry, with its elaborate set of rules concerning apprenticeship and training is highly reminiscent of the medieval guild system. It comes as no surprise, therefore, to learn that the first successful permanent American unionization movement—that of the AFL in the last part of the nineteenth century—involved such highly specialized trades.

Although hourly rates are still high in many of these activities, they no longer seem so very much beyond earnings in the large mechanized industries such as steel and automobiles. The reason for the relative, but not absolute, decline in the economic status of the skilled craftsman lies in the fact that the onward rush of invention and technological development has not tended to raise his productivity and strategic position commensurate with its effects on mass-production industries. Indeed, laborsaving and labor-simplifying inventions have almost completely wiped out such highly skilled occupations as the cigar makers, glass blowers, and movie-theater musicians. The printers on the other hand have been able to weather the storm threat of the linotype invention by taking over the new technique, rather than leaving it to low-paid female typists.

The high hourly rates referred to above are partly illusory because of the highly seasonal and uncertain employment prospects in many of these lines. Notable among these is the building trade in which the long winter layoff causes *annual* as distinct from *hourly* earnings to be quite low. We must leave to our later discussion this serious problem of stabilizing employment and earnings.

THE WHITE-COLLAR CLASS

As far as economic earnings go, clerks, salesmen, stenographers, bookkeepers, mailmen, bank tellers, and other members of the so-called "white-collar" class cannot be said to be better off than a substantial fraction of the manual-labor group. Perhaps once they were, in the days when literacy and a secondary-school education were not so prevalent as they now are. The presence of a substantial number of women in these fields and the fact that a high-school graduate with a few months of commercial-school training can qualify for most jobs helps to explain the failure of such earnings to rise along with increases in the cost of living and the upward trend in factory wages.

Contrary to the predictions of Karl Marx, these members of the so-called "petty bourgeoisie" have resisted sinking into the working class and have seldom offered fertile ground for unionization. On the contrary, observers of the rise of fascism in Europe have often claimed that the malcontentment of white-collar workers, together with that of displaced small businessmen and shopkeepers, provided a fertile and receptive field for fascist agitation and propaganda.

The more successful members of this group win the prize dangled before every American school child; *i.e.*, they are admitted over the bridge into the exclusive ranks of business managers and executives. This class constitutes the real aristocracy of our industrial society. As we shall see in the next chapter, corporation executives do not typically own any significant part of the corporation capital that they manage. In short, they are *bureaucrats* even though in ordinary times they have no connection with government. This is not used as a word of reproach or belittlement, for it has been claimed with some cogency that ours is essentially an age of bureaucracy.

During the decade of the prosperous 1920's, the prestige of the businessman was at an all-time high—much to the disgust and contempt of litterateurs isolated in Greenwich Village or expatriated in Paris. But despite the lampooning of Sinclair Lewis's "Babbitt" and H. L. Mencken's "Boobus Americanus," the businessman's go-getter philosophy was in the ascendancy. Even religion was promoted as good business and explained in accounting terms. With Calvin Coolidge in the White House and Andrew Mellon the Secretary of the Treasury, the businessman felt, quite rightly, that his was the dominant class.

It is now history how Calvin Coolidge sowed the wind, and poor Herbert Hoover reaped the whirlwind. The fickle public, terrified by unemployment and resentful of depression, drove out its old idols from the temple. Like savages who must blame even the breaking of a fish line on some evil spirit, the American people began a great witch hunt for the crooked businessmen who had caused the Great Depression. As if honest concerns had not failed with the dishonest, and as if ignorance and stupidity were not infinitely more important than fraud!

The businessman has never returned to his previous position of prestige. Shaken of self-confidence by a decade of considerable losses, harassed by government and labor, pounced upon by the courts for violation of antitrust laws he had forgotten existed, it is little wonder that he was dyspeptic before the war. But like the unemployed, he experienced during the emergency a feeling of being wanted and needed. With the return of strength, humility and inarticulateness are ebbing away. In the persons of Eric Johnston (former president of the U.S. Chamber of Commerce and now czar of the movie industry), Paul Hoffman (president of Studebaker Corporation), Ralph

Flanders, Beardsley Ruml (R. H. Macy's department store), and other businessmen of the Committee for Economic Development, there are clear indications of a more realistic and humanitarian business philosophy.

Although the large corporation executive, like the Soviet commissar, wields
infinitely more economic power than his own income would suggest, it would
be a mistake to dismiss his earnings as negligible. Each year the SEC (Securities
and Exchange Commission) requires corporations to list the amounts that
they pay their top employees. Usually the list is headed by Louis B. Mayer
of Metro-Goldwyn-Mayer movies, Thomas J. Watson of International
Business Machines, Charles Luckman of the Lever Brothers soap company,
Alfred P. Sloan of GM, E. G. Grace of Bethlehem Steel, and a number of
movie executives. Mixed in with these luminaries are usually such stars from
Hollywood as Bing Crosby, Ginger Rogers, Fred MacMurray, Cary Grant,
Greer Garson, and Bob Hope.

Part of the reward of top executives comes in the form of bonuses, retirement pensions, and capital stock. Bonuses, in particular, go up sharply with
improvements in business so it is hard to say just how much the top executives
of large companies can hope to get. Par may be set at somewhere below
$1,000 a day or around $300,000 a year. Of course, few people can hope to
shoot par; but during good times and wars, a few earn "birdies" and even
"eagles."

Of course, these very highest salaries do not apply to all senior corporation
executives, but only to those at the top of the largest companies. Presidents
of railroads, who usually come up from the ranks, rarely receive much more
than $60,000 a year or $1,200 a week. This is even less than the $75,000 per
year paid to the president of the United States and is not more than a United
States Senator receives in his 6 years of office, or than Generals Eisenhower
and MacArthur together received during the war.

As a matter of fact, a more detailed study[1] of good-sized companies (60 to
200 million dollars of assets) shows that in 1941, under favorable circumstances, the top executive might earn $195,000, the second in command
$122,000, the third $100,000, the tenth executive only $44,000, and the
twentieth $28,000. In the middling generous companies, the top man received
only $75,000, the fifth man $33,000, the tenth man $25,000, and the twelfth
man only $16,000.

[1] JOHN C. BAKER, Payments to Senior Corporation Executives, *Quarterly Journal of
Economics*, Vol. LIX, February, 1945, pp. 170–185. See also the discussion in Chap. XII of
R. A. Gordon, "Business Leadership in the Large Corporation," The Brookings Institution,
Washington, D.C., 1945, where further references are given.

Among smaller companies with assets from 5 to 50 million dollars, salaries were $75,000 at the top of the generous companies, $25,000 for the fifth man, and $11,000 for the fourteenth man on the totem pole. In the small companies of only medium generosity, the top man received $50,000 but the fourteenth man is down to only $8,000.

We may summarize the study by saying that, aside from differences in the generosity of companies, a medium executive in a medium large company earns about $25,000 a year before taxes and a similar man in the small company field receives about $12,000 a year. All the figures cited are *before* Federal personal income tax; such taxes are considerable and must be subtracted in arriving at the executive's *disposable income*.[1]

Some may think these figures low; some, reasonable. The late President Franklin Delano Roosevelt seemed to think them high. During the depression emergency and again during the war, he tried to limit salaries. His executive order put a wartime top on salaries of $67,000 per year *before* taxes, or $25,000 of yearly disposable income after taxes, but it was later overruled by Congress. One of the many reasons advanced was the fact that people with property income were under no similar ceiling so that the order was discriminatory. However, a quite opposite corollary might have been deduced from this. In any case, more than one shrewd observer of New York social life and café society has commented on the revolutionary change in the composition of the better heeled classes: those with property income are being displaced relatively by those with earned income. Rather few people have the million necessary to yield $30,000 at 3 per cent interest, but numerous individuals have salaries in excess of this amount.

PROFESSIONAL INCOMES

The various professions do not have a great deal in common except that they all tend to require a great deal of education and training. In addition to undergraduate college training of 3 or 4 years, a doctor requires 4 years of medical-school training and 1 or more years of hospital interneship. This is a far cry from the days when the new apprentice simply accompanied a doctor as he made his horse-and-buggy rounds. In lesser degree, the same trends are observable in the nonmedical professions: law, dentistry, veterinary service, accounting, engineering, teaching, nursing, pharmacy, and so forth. The chiropractor and osteopath as well as the preacher of the Gospel all require increased training.

[1] Since 1941, both executive salaries and living costs have continued to rise.

The professions differ, too, in the extent to which their members are self-employed or employed for wages by others. About four out of five doctors "hang out their shingles," but only seven out of ten lawyers do. The engineer, on the other hand, although he started out as a private consultant, is today almost completely in the regular employ of somebody else. The same is true of about three-fourths of the registered nurses, almost one-half of the certified public accountants, and practically all teachers. Dentists, chiropodists, chiropractors, and osteopaths, on the other hand, are self-employed in 95 per cent of the cases.

In one respect all the professions are alike. They all think that they are underpaid. This is understandable since nobody gets enough of the good things in life. What is strange is the fact that the spokesmen for each—intelligent deans, editors, and heads of professional societies—all seem honestly to believe that other professions receive more money or that in some past golden age their own professions earned more. Harold F. Clark's work on life earnings[1] gives a number of amusing quotations showing how the doctors think that they make less than lawyers, engineers, and plumbers, how the dentists think that they are slipping behind in the financial race, and so forth.

This would be merely comical, were it not for its serious side: the tendency for each profession to try to lessen competition by restricting its numbers. Not that such august bodies as the American Medical Association put matters in this way, or think cynically in these terms. Rather an appeal is made to raise minimum standards, in itself a commendable thing. But carried to its logical extreme, this could provide an excuse for any amount of cutting down of numbers, until we reach the *reductio ad absurdum* of having only the single best doctor left in the profession.

According to competent observers, whose testimony went unheard before the war emergency, the medical needs of the American people could not adequately be met by the existing number of doctors. Few experienced college deans would quarrel with Clark's statement,

There is good reason to think that there are perhaps two or three million people in skilled and unskilled labor who have ability equal to that of the average individual in medicine. . . . The average salary in engineering, for instance, is some five and a half times the average income in unskilled labor and three times the average income in skilled trades. There seems to be no reason for such large differences except lack of information in regard to average incomes and lack of opportunity to enter engineering. . . . Much as . . . professional groups dislike to have larger numbers of people

[1] H. F. CLARK, *et al.*, "Life Earnings in Selected Occupations in the United States," Harper & Brothers, New York, 1937.

entering, on grounds of social welfare there seems to be no other alternative. If income data are any adequate test, the country needs far more people in all these professional groups.[1]

Two different points of view should be clearly kept apart. One is that represented by President Conant of Harvard University. By means of a generous number of scholarships he would encourage the best to go into professions independently of their family income. But he is still for keeping numbers small and standards high. The second group of reformers would go with him on the recruitment of talent from all income strata, but would argue that an expansion of numbers is needed. They admit that average ability might be lowered but consider that measure of quality misleading. Instead they argue that quality at the top will still be there, and in addition there will be practitioners who are highly useful even if they are not geniuses or specialists.

It is somewhat ironical that, during the war, for the first time the expense of higher education was no bar to the poor student. The progressive activities of the Army and Navy in this regard have been supplemented by the G.I. Bill of Rights which gives financial aid up to and beyond $1,000 per academic year (depending upon marital status) to pay the schooling costs and living expenses of veterans. This is just one of the many examples that caused one wise, but realistic, observer to say, "It is too bad that everyone wasn't drafted into the armed forces! Then we should all be veterans. Then no one's illness or unemployment would be a matter of social indifference."

Let us turn now to the facts on professional earnings. In Table 1, comparative data are given for many different occupations. Column (2) gives estimated median annual earnings. (By the median man is meant the one just in the middle, with half the people above him and half below.) Column (3) gives average annual earnings; these exceed the medians because the extremely large earnings of the lucky few are divided equally among all members and swell the average. Column (4) gives the present (discounted) values of lifetime earnings. Thus, suppose the average doctor works from the ages of twenty-seven to sixty-nine, or 42 years in all. Forty-two years at $4,850 per year would give a total of lifetime earnings of about $203,700. But a dollar 10 years from now is not worth a dollar today. In fact, if the rate of interest is 2.9 per cent as in government victory bonds, $1 payable 10 years from now is worth only $0.75 today. At 4 per cent interest, as used by Clark in Table 1, even more would have to be deducted or "discounted" for interest. Now to a

[1] *Ibid.*, pp. 16, 24.

young student debating whether to be a doctor or not, part of his earnings in that profession will be even more than 10 or even 40 years away. This has been allowed for in the present (discounted) value of lifetime *earnings*, Col. (4). Column (5) gives the age span of those who remain in the occupation in question.

TABLE 1. *Income Data for Selected Occupations, 1920–1936*

Occupation (1)	Median annual earnings (2)	Average annual earnings (3)	Present (discounted) value of lifetime earnings (4)	Age span of occupation, years (5)
Medicine...............	$4,250	$4,850	$108,000	27–69
Law..................	3,600	4,730	105,000	
Dentistry..............	3,760	4,170	95,400	24–69
Engineering............	3,700	4,410	95,300	22–65
Architecture...........	3,190	3,820	82,500	22–65
College teaching........	2,470	3,050	69,300	25–69
Social work...........	1,517	1,650	51,000	30–65
Journalism.............	1,600	2,120	41,500	23–69
Ministry..............	1,780	1,980	41,000	25–69
Library work..........	.....	2,020	35,000	23–69
Public-school teaching....	1,220	1,350	29,700	20–69
Skilled trades..........	.....	1,430	28,600	18–62
Nursing...............	.....	1,310	23,300	21–51
Unskilled labor.........	.....	795	15,200	18–62
Farming...............	.....	580	12,500	51
Farm labor............	.....	485	10,400	51

SOURCE: H. F. CLARK, *et al.*, "Life Earnings in Selected Occupations in the United States," p. 5, and later chapters, Harper & Brothers, New York, 1937.

A number of interesting relations appear from the tables. Of all the "genteel" professions, that of the ministry is by far the worst paid, even though its members must maintain a relatively expensive standard of living. Obviously, no one enters the ministry for its financial rewards in this life, and a surprising number of ministers leave the profession for other activities. It is especially tragic that ministers are not covered by the old-age retirement pensions of the Social Security Act, since the sects that make adequate pension provisions are the exception rather than the rule. All observers have commented upon the revolutionary decline in the percentage of college students aiming at the ministry today as compared to 75 or 40 years ago.

To supplement the above estimates, which Clark is the first to admit are only roughly accurate, we are fortunate in having some rather elaborate questionnaire surveys by the Department of Commerce of earnings in a number of professions consisting primarily of independent practitioners.[1] Most of these records go right up to 1941 when the wartime prosperity was

TABLE 2. *Average and Median Net Income of Nonsalaried Practitioners in Stated Professions, Selected Years, 1929–1941*

Professional group	Net income					
	1929		1933		1941	
	Median	Average	Median	Average	Median	Average
Certified public accountants..............	......	$7,300	......	$4,200		
Lawyers..............	......	5,500	......	3,900	$3,000	$4,800
Physicians..............	......	5,200	......	2,900	3,800	5,000
Dentists..............	$3,700	4,300	$1,900	2,200	3,300	3,800
Osteopathic physicians..	3,100	3,600	1,500	1,900		
Veterinarians..........	......	......	......	......	2,300	2,700
Chiropractors..........	2,100	2,500	1,100	1,300		
Chiropodists..........	......	......	1,200	1,500		
Nurses..............	......	1,200	......	......	1,200	1,200

SOURCE: *Survey of Current Business*, May, 1944, p. 15. All data rounded off to nearest $100.

already beginning to be felt. In every case before arriving at net income we subtract from the professional man's gross income or cash intake all his expenses of doing business (rent, assistants' salaries, materials, etc.).

Both median and average incomes are given for the 1929 boom year, the 1933 depression year, and for the latest available year, 1941. From the comparison let us eliminate certified public accountants as being a select sample of the best accountants and as being more comparable to members of the

[1] These are reported in six articles entitled Incomes in Selected Professions, *Survey of Current Business*, 1943 and 1944. The last article (May, 1944, pp. 15–19) gives a useful summary.

College of Surgeons than to the rank and file of physicians. It then appears that lawyers and doctors lead the list in earnings. Actually in the last year the physicians were beginning to forge ahead of the attorneys in earnings. Dentists fall substantially below both of the above groups, but well ahead of veterinarians and registered nurses.

The more detailed yearly figures from which the table is taken show clearly that all professions are hard hit by depression. Aside from consulting engineers, whose earnings are cut to the bone, dentists are most affected by the business cycle, probably because many people consider their treatments as postponable. Doctors are next hardest hit, presumably because they, like dentists, cannot collect all their bills during depression nor cut down on their overhead expenses. Registered nurses, on the other hand, having no fixed expenses to speak of and working largely for cash, show rather steadier earnings over the cycle. However, if we allow for their unemployment for many days of the month as Clark does, we may estimate that their earnings fall 50 per cent in depression, which is a much less rosy picture.

What differences are there in professional earnings in cities of different sizes? The answer given by the Department of Commerce study is as follows: in all professions earnings increase as we go to larger towns and cities until we reach cities of about a ¼ or ½ million population. Then earnings seem to drop in all professions except law. Possibly because most successful corporation lawyers are to be found in large metropolitan centers, *average* legal earnings continue to rise; but interestingly enough, median earnings—the more significant measure—do fall off in the large cities as in the case of the other professions.

Also, there are characteristic income differences according to regions of the country. The Pacific Coast states lead in every case. Usually the Middle Eastern states come next. Almost invariably the Southern and Mountain states are near the bottom, and New England seems to be below the country-wide average. The moral seems to be to go to a good-sized West Coast town, but not to the largest ones. However, quite a number of people have been doing just that during the war. So before you pack the family into the automobile, you had better check with the latest statistics on earnings.

These average earnings figures must now be supplemented by data showing the dispersion around the average. Every one of the professions is characterized by considerable inequality of income. The spread between highest and lowest incomes is most marked in the case of law. This is in line with common-sense expectations, since experienced lawyers with wide contacts are known to have very high earnings. The least inequality holds in the case of nursing.

Again this is in line with the ordinary observation that rates of pay do not vary much with the experience or ability of the registered nurse in question.

To show graphically the amount of inequality in the professions as of 1941, we use our old friend the Lorenz curve. It will be recalled that the heavy diagonal line represents perfect equality. The curve for nursing is therefore nearest to this line. Law, being most unequal of all, naturally has a curve

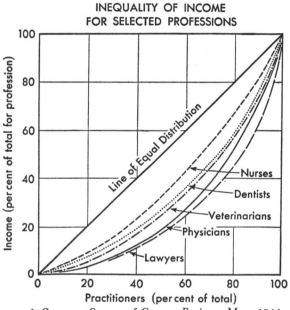

FIG. 1. SOURCE: *Survey of Current Business*, May, 1944.

farthest from this line. Since the spread in physicians' earnings is rather large, its curve comes near to that of lawyers. Dentistry, being by and large more of a routine profession, has its curve nearer to that of nursing, *i.e.*, with relatively little inequality.

Let us translate these inequality figures into concrete dollar terms. Because $3,300 is the median for dentists, half of them get less than that and half more. Twenty per cent get more than $6,000 per year; and only 3 per cent earn more than $10,000 per year. Most of these would be specialists (in teeth straightening, extractions, dental surgery), but a few might be "society dentists" with a good barber-chair manner.

With the growth of hospital care, private-duty nursing by both registered and practical nurses has been on the decline. Earnings in this field are about comparable to those of general staff nurses, counting in the latters' maintenance (food and lodging), but less than that of nurses engaged in public-health work. In other words, governments (state, local, and Federal) are good employers. A nurse contemplating free lancing should be warned that only 1 in 20 private-duty nurses can hope to earn more than $2,000 a year. Even fewer can hope to win a rich and elderly husband.

Of all physicians out on their own, about one-fourth earned less than $4,000 in 1941. A little more than one-fifth earned more than $7,000, and one in eight surpassed $10,000. Interestingly enough, physicians who worked for a salary averaged about $500 more per year than those on their own; while those part on salary and part on their own averaged almost $1,000 more. Moreover, those completely on salary hardly ever fell below the $2,000 level. They were grouped much more around the median. In view of the move toward clinical and socialized medicine, it is interesting to note that the best paid people seemed usually to lie in the category of being attached to some clinic or hospital and of receiving at least part of their income from that source.

Before leaving the independent professional practitioners, we must observe that all of them possess the pleasing quality of having earnings that rise with age and experience. A ditchdigger at twenty-five has passed his prime, but a physician or lawyer continues to improve economically until past middle age. Table 3 gives in Col. (2) the age at which earnings are at their peak. Column (3) gives the span of years in which earnings are within 10 per cent of the peak, or what has been called the "prime earning period."

TABLE 3. *Growth of Professional Earnings with Age*

Profession	Age of peak earnings	Prime earning period
(1)	(2)	(3)
Medicine........................	Low 50's	35–54
Law............................	Late 40's	45–59
Dentistry.......................	Around 40	35–49
Veterinary practice..............	Late 30's	35–39

SOURCE: *Survey of Current Business*, May, 1944, p. 16.

On the whole, lawyers seem to do best at the older ages. (In fact, the indicated peak around 50 years is followed by a long plateau in which earnings drop very little.) Physicians' earnings hold up well until the mid-fifties, and then drop rather rapidly. Presumably the strenuous character of a doctor's duties is the main reason. Dentists seem to reach their peak at the quite early age of forty. But veterinarians show even stranger behavior since the young men do better than the old. Probably this is misleading. Because of a virtual revolution in educational requirements in recent years in this field, the younger men—many of whom have a profitable pet practice rather than a farm practice—receive more money. Such a revolution will not be repeated presumably; therefore, in time, the well-trained older men will show more normal earnings.

Incidentally, it is not true, as many people believe, that doctors do badly in their early years of practice. Once their training is really completed, their earnings greatly exceed those of most workers. However, there is a possible joker in all the above statistics. They refer to the earnings of *active* practitioners. They do not relate to all the people who were *trained* for this profession. Thus, they do not indicate how many lawyers become discouraged by low earnings and quit to go into other businesses with their fathers-in-law.

Let us turn very briefly to teaching. Increasingly a college bachelor's degree rather than a couple of years of normal school is becoming the prerequisite for grade-school teaching; for high-school teaching in city schools, a master's degree. In the college field, only the large colleges can afford to buck the universal trend by taking on a man who does not have the doctor of philosophy degree.

There is a clear tendency for increases in teachers' salaries at all levels to be sticky and to fall behind the cost of living and wage increases elsewhere. This means that the quality and quantity of people going into the teaching field may fall. This was the case in World War I, in the 1920's, and during the recent war. At the college level the situation is most acute in the natural sciences and other fields (such as economics, surprisingly enough) where higher paid competitive offers from business and government threaten to drain off the best men.

We may close our discussion of professional incomes with a brief examination of engineering, a relatively new profession. Even today many of the older men designated as engineers have never had formal full-time college training. According to the 1940 Census about $\frac{1}{4}$ million individuals are classified as engineers. Civil engineers are the largest single group (about 90,000), mechanical engineers are almost as large a group, then electrical engineers (between 50,000 and 60,000). The relatively newer branch of chemical engineering had about the same number as that of mining and metallurgical engineering, (around 10,000) but the former was growing relatively to the latter.

We shall later see why construction activity falls off so much in depression, and even some evidence of a long-time decline in its importance. This explains the relatively difficult times experienced by civil engineers in the Great Depression (almost 40 per cent not employed at their normal types of job in March, 1933!). It also helps to explain why so many of them are anxious to work for the government. Moreover, even those who work for private companies often find that most of their jobs are concerned with public works (bridges, dams, etc.) that involve the government's dollar indirectly.

IS COLLEGE WORTH WHILE?

The answer to this question depends in only small measure upon economics. The social and cultural value of 4 years of collegiate life cannot be translated into exact dollar terms. If we consider the cost of a professional education and compare its earnings with less trained occupations, we should be able to reach some general conclusions about its purely economic advantages.

TABLE 4. *Illustrative Figures on the Cost and Value of Professional Training*

Kind of professional training	Cost*	Value†	Profit‡
(1)	(2)	(3)	(4)
High school only......................	0	0	0
College bachelor degree..................	$ 6,000	$25,000	+$19,000
Master's degree.......................	8,000	25,000	+ 17,000
Engineering degree.....................	7,000	55,000	+ 48,000
Ph.D. degree..........................	13,000	40,000	+ 27,000
Medical training.......................	16,000	70,000	+ 54,000
Legal training.........................	11,000	70,000	+ 59,000
Dental degree.........................	12,000	55,000	+ 43,000

SOURCE: In arriving at these estimates, consideration was given to the figures of Clark, *op. cit.* Walsh (J. R. Walsh, The Capital Concept Applied to Man, *Quarterly Journal of Economics*, 1935, pp. 225–285), and the Department of Commerce, *op. cit.* The quantitative results are very rough and should not be taken too seriously.

* Discounted at 4 per cent interest back to day of high-school graduation and inclusive of expenditures for books, tuition, board and room, recreation, as well as foregone earnings.

† Present discounted value of (median) lifetime earnings minus discounted value of a high-school graduate's earnings during the same years.

‡ How much of this algebraic difference between value and cost is due to training rather than ability or other factors cannot be said with confidence. Probably the figures for similar professions can be compared with the greatest accuracy.

To evaluate each profession, imagine a number of members of a high-school graduating class. A hard-boiled accountant with a crystal ball gazes into the future and draws up a balance sheet showing the present value *as of that moment* of all future costs of each occupation's training. These figures are given in Col. (2). Thus a boy without any resources who wished to have a medical education would have to borrow $16,000 on the day he graduated from high school to pay for a medical education and to cover the income he foregoes while in school. A boy who desires only a college bachelor's degree would need $6,000 in the bank to be free of worries. One who quits at high school needs zero dollars by definition. A similar procedure of estimating extra costs must be followed for each profession or for a college education itself.

With what shall we compare the extra costs of professional training? With the *present discounted value of lifetime earnings* in that profession? No. Instead, we should compare the extra training costs with the extra value of lifetime earnings over and above lifetime earnings without professional training. Column (3) gives a rough estimate of the average extra value of professional lifetime earnings over and above nonprofessional work. This must be compared with the extra cost.

Column (4) shows whether or not the professional training was worth while. It gives the difference between Cols. (3) and (2), or the algebraic profit or loss of an average individual going into the profession. As we should expect, it is very profitable to go into most of the professions with the possible exception of college teaching. Whether or not the nonpecuniary advantages of academic life overrule the money calculation will depend upon the individual in question. Certainly in all vocational decisions the net advantages of pleasantness, seniority rights, and continuity of employment must be given full weight.

Why does not competition wipe out the profit or loss from any profession? For example, why don't more people go into medicine and dentistry? In fact, why don't more individuals go into medicine instead of dentistry, since the returns are better and the prestige is greater? If competition does not set the right price for a spool of thread, the social loss is not catastrophic. But here in the most important aspect of getting a living we see that competition works very far from perfectly. A number of obvious reasons suggest themselves:

1. Families have not the necessary knowledge to make wise plans for their children. In part this ignorance can be dispelled by vocational guidance and factual information. In part it stems from the fact that the choice of a profession involves a decision that will cover a half century in the future. Who can be sure of any forecast over such a period?

2. Many families have not the necessary capital to invest in their children even though the return in money, happiness, and national service would be

very large. If people were property like horses or slaves and if a man could legally sell himself, shrewd speculators might invest in promising young people and share part of the return with them. But, quite properly, our laws do not permit this. Of course, the same desirable effect can be achieved in part if students of poor families can borrow from somebody and repay out of later earnings. Actually there is a good deal of this, often on a semiphilanthropic basis. But it is primarily of importance in enabling students to finish their college training; it does not bring very many people to college who would not otherwise go. The same is true, but in lesser degree, of undergraduate scholarships. These rarely cover the full expenses of schooling and rarely enable really poor boys and girls to go to school.

3. There is considerable evidence from the statistics of medical school and dentistry applications[1] that a considerable number of people *do* try to get such advanced training. Unlike a law student, a medical student does not cover most of his training costs when he pays tuition. With gifts and endowment earnings being limited, there are not new places in medical schools for more students even if they were willing to pay tuition. This fact plus the natural desire of the profession to limit numbers by raising standards has caused the American economy to have too few trained doctors as measured by three criteria: (1) national needs, (2) doctors' earnings, (3) the nation's stock of talented young people who are eager to be doctors or who would be eager if their economic situation didn't make that out of the question.

Thus a case can be made for Federal or state aid on a large scale to education, both for tuition and extra capital facilities. Moreover, since the government can borrow at 2 per cent or less, the above use of 4 per cent interest in the figures underestimates the nation's profit from providing greater educational opportunities. A Federal education program, going beyond the G.I. Bill of Rights, would be a continuation of what has always been peculiarly an American trend at the state and local levels.

In conclusion, the individual must keep two important qualifications in mind before applying our figures to his own case: (1) The fact that those with, say, a Harvard Business School degree earn some per cent more than those without does not necessarily mean that *anyone* who gets such a degree will secure similar increased earnings. Perhaps such Harvard students are already a select group with respect to wealth, influence, and ability; no one can tell how much of their extra earnings were due to the degree. The same

[1] See S. KUZNETS and MILTON FRIEDMAN, Incomes from Independent Professional Practice, 1929–1936, *Bull.* 72–73, pp. 15–17, National Bureau of Economic Research, Inc., New York, 1939.

point holds for all professions. (2) An individual choosing a profession is not interested just in average figures, but in the spread. If two professions have equal average earnings but one has greater extremes at the top and the bottom, which will be chosen by the individual? This depends. Some people who value certainty will prefer dentistry to medicine even though its average earnings are less, because there is less chance that a dentist will earn starvation wages than a doctor. However, there is also less chance that he will hit the jack pot of very high earnings. Other individuals like to take a chance, particularly since they and their families are often biased in favor of their own capabilities and chances of coming out on top. Certain it is that in professions like law and movie acting, the few rich plums held out at the top constitute an attraction for aspirants far beyond what is justified by any reasonable probability calculation. It is one of the more engaging traits of human nature to feel, "I am different!" Alas, there result vast social wastage and endless heartbreak to would-be artists, musicians, and inventors. To these fields as to the Kingdom of Heaven—many are called but few are chosen.

ECONOMIC STRATIFICATION AND OPPORTUNITY

America has always been considered the land of opportunity where anyone with ability might get ahead in the world. The success legend of the Horatio Alger, Jr., "poor but proud" hero who worked his way to the top and married the boss's daughter—or vice versa—has no doubt been overdrawn. But it did have elements of truth as compared to the situation in older European countries, where an aristocratic tradition lingered on, and where free schooling beyond the primary grades was never established.

For example, the "old school tie" and, more important, the Oxford accent were until recently almost indispensable to political and social advancement in Britain; even with the free scholarship system, few members of the lower or middle class could jump this hurdle. Whereas here in this country, few people outside the State Department even know how to recognize a "prep school" accent, and variations in speech are geographical rather than social. The American stenographer is almost indistinguishable in appearance from the blueblood debutante.

Moreover, ours has been rather a materialistic civilization in which success is interpreted in business terms. Because "money talks," it is easier for outsiders to break into the upper crust than it would be in a culture that puts greater emphasis upon tradition. The *nouveaux riches* of one generation, such as the Vanderbilts, become the social dictators of the next.

Nevertheless, a careful questionnaire investigation of the social origins of successful businessmen, namely, the directors and officers of corporations, turned up some surprising facts. The typical American business executive did not come off a farm or out of a workingman's home, but more likely his father was also a businessman or possibly in one of the professions. Table 5 summarizes the social origins of a large sample of businessmen as observed by Taussig and Joslyn. For comparison, the social origins of millionaires and of those listed in "Who's Who" are also presented.

TABLE 5. *Per Cent Distribution, by Occupation of Fathers of American Business Leaders, of Millionaires, and of Persons Listed in "Who's Who"*

Occupation of father	American business leaders, 1928	American millionaires, living in 1925	Persons listed in "Who's Who," 1912
Businessman.........	60.0	75.0	35.3
Professional man......	13.4	10.5	34.3
Farmer.............	12.4	7.3	23.4
Laborer.............	12.5	1.6	6.7
Other..............	1.7	5.6	0.3
Total.............	100.0	100.0	100.0

SOURCE: F. W. TAUSSIG and C. S. JOSLYN, "American Business Leaders," Chap. XII, The Macmillan Company, New York, 1932.

It is not surprising that millionaires come from well-to-do business backgrounds because here we should expect inherited wealth to be an important element. But it is rather unexpected to learn that there is a hundred times greater probability[1] of a businessman's son becoming a successful businessman than a laborer's son, and twenty times greater probability than for a farmer's son. Moreover, the trend was even more pronounced for the younger generation of businessmen studied.

Does this mean that American economic society is hardening along caste lines? Taussig and Joslyn are not sure. They point out that two diametrically opposite explanations are possible: (1) In the past there was high social mobility in America: all the cream rose to the top, leaving naturally less gifted people at the bottom. (2) There are strong, and perhaps growing, barriers to circulation between the economic classes.

Taussig and Joslyn incline rather to the first view, feeling that "You can't keep a good man down." Most sociologists would disagree. They would

[1] The reader should be sure that he realizes why this statement is not inconsistent with Table 5: there are more than twenty times as many sons of laborers as of businessmen.

emphasize the thousand and one subtle psychological, social, economic, and educational disadvantages of the children of less fortunate families; that equal ability is not always able to give rise to equal achievement; that

"Full many a flower is born to blush unseen,
And waste its sweetness on the desert air."

Whichever view is right, the implications for policy are the same. Human beings are a nation's most important form of social capital—a form, moreover, in which we have invested too little in the past. Talent, wherever it may be, is worth being sought out and nurtured.

SUMMARY

Annual and lifetime earnings differ considerably among occupations and professions. However, patterns of some regularity and persistence are discernible, and the differentials can be partially explained in terms of economic analysis.

The problem of changes in the pattern of earnings and the circulation of individuals up and down the ladders of economic success have been of peculiar interest in our American cultural scene, and much remains to be learned about the patterns of economic and social stratification.

QUESTIONS FOR DISCUSSION

1. List a number of business concerns in your vicinity. About how much do they pay for different kinds of work?

2. What vocation are you aiming for? What are its economic advantages and disadvantages? What about the noneconomic factors?

3. How much do you expect to be making (a) 3 months out of college, (b) 5 years later, (c) 15 years later, (d) 30 years later?

4. Express in words the statistical facts shown in Tables 1, 2, and 3.

5. Is America still the "land of opportunity"? How important are heredity, environment, "pull," zeal, utility, training, wealth, in getting ahead in different professions?

6. What does Table 5 suggest to you? How do you account for such results? What new data would you want to enable you to draw more definite conclusions?

Chapter 6: BUSINESS

ORGANIZATION AND INCOME

OURS is a business civilization. To understand it at all, we must first understand the organization and functioning of business enterprise. The first part of this chapter leads up to the analysis of the modern corporation, primarily by an extensive case study; the last half is concerned with the financial structure of corporations, particularly the modern large-scale or "giant" corporation. In an appendix there is presented a brief introduction to the fundamentals of accounting, without a comprehension of which there can be no real understanding of the economics of enterprise.

A. THE FORMS OF BUSINESS ORGANIZATION

THE POPULATION OF BUSINESS ENTERPRISES

There were some three million American business units in the period immediately following World War II, and all except a very small fraction of these enterprises consisted of very small-scale units owned by a single person. Most businesses are here today and gone tomorrow, the average life expectancy of a business being only about half a dozen years. Some will terminate in bankruptcy; many more will be voluntarily brought to a close with sighs of regret for dashed hopes and an expensive lesson learned; still others will come to a joyous end when their "self-employed" owner finally lands a good, steady job or takes up a new line of endeavor.

As fast as old businesses die, others are born. The present population of business concerns grew up as a result of the cumulated excess of business births over business deaths during previous years. As the American economy grows, we may expect a steady further increase in the number of firms from a normal excess of business births over deaths. Indeed, during the years of transition from war to postwar, there is taking place an acceleration in the blossoming of new businesses. This is in part because so many returning servicemen wish to launch new ventures with their own, their friends', or their grateful government's capital. But the great increase can also be attributed to the fact that wartime scarcities and restrictions kept down the formation of new enterprises, especially in the retail and services trades.

It had been predicted that the war would cause a tremendous shrinkage in the number of businesses, particularly as a result of many organizations' going bankrupt. Actually, the decrease in number was quite moderate and resulted to a considerable degree from the wartime decline in new business births. Failures and shutdowns were at a surprisingly low level during the war period; in some weeks hardly a single bankruptcy was listed for the whole United States, something that had scarcely ever occurred before in all our history since Columbus first sighted land.

In the two years prior to Jan. 1, 1946, some 700,000 new businesses were started, and only 300,000 were discontinued. As a result there was a net increase during the period of some 400,000—carrying the total number of enterprises to slightly over $3\frac{1}{4}$ million units. The causes are obvious: the end of the war, increasing supplies of civilian goods, business optimism, and the wartime accumulation of savings on the part of would-be entrepreneurs. A considerable excess of firms, as compared to prewar levels, became noticeable at an early date in the fields of radio and appliance stores, auto accessories, home furnishings, liquor, hardware, and farm stores. As the trends toward overexpansion and inflated capitalizations continue, the number of small-business failures and the magnitude of losses will undoubtedly mount.

BIG, SMALL, AND INFINITESIMAL BUSINESS

By number, the tiny, transient, self-owned "individual proprietorship" is overwhelmingly the dominant form of American business. But in terms of dollar value, political and economic power, payrolls and employment, some few hundred "giant corporations" occupy a strategically dominant position in the modern American economy.

Let us glance briefly at the role in our economy of "infinitesimal businesses." There are almost 400,000 grocery-store owners in the United States, all trying to make a living. There are almost a quarter of a million automobile service stations; more than 50,000 drugstores; and so it goes through all types of retailing and service establishments.[1]

Although some of these ventures are highly successful, it is still true to say that most do not earn much more for their owners than they could get with less effort and risk by working for somebody else. Thus, a few chain stores do about 35 per cent of all the grocery business, the rest being divided up among all the independents. Most of these independents consist of the so-called "Ma and Pa" stores, doing less than $30 of business every day. These are often started by people who have only a couple of thousand dollars of initial capital—less than half the amount necessary for an adequate grocery store that will do the $100 a day business necessary if the owner is to earn even minimum wages for his effort. Such small-scale efforts are doomed from their very beginning; they are finished when the owner's initial capital is used up. They help to illustrate why one-third to one-half of all retail businesses are discontinued before they are 2 years old.

Of course, different fields differ in the amount of capital that is required. To build a modern service station costs around $40,000; but to lease one from a gasoline company brings the initial capital requirement down to around $3,000 or $5,000. In this line, only 40 per cent of the stations have the $10,000 a year sales volume necessary to break even. (Three-quarters of all sales are

[1] Out of every 1,000 business establishments in the United States, approximately

170 are retail food stores

90 are eating and drinking establishments

90 are in the real-estate, insurance, or finance fields

70 are filling stations

60 are motor-truck or taxicab owners

60 are contractors, etc.

60 are beauty or barber shops

45 are wholesalers of various kinds

35 are automobile dealers, repair shops, or garages

35 are clothing or general-merchandise stores

30 are laundries, etc.

20 are shops for shoe repair, shoeshines, etc.

15 are food-manufacturing plants

15 are drugstores

15 are printing shops or publishing plants, etc.

All the data referred to thus far are from Department of Commerce and Census sources. In addition, reliance is placed throughout this chapter on data from The National Industrial Conference Board; The National Resources Planning Board; R. A. Gordon, "Business Leadership in the Large Corporation," Brookings Institution, Washington, D.C., 1945; *T.N.E.C. Report*, Temporary National Economic Committee, 1938–1940; W. L. Crum, "Corporate Size and Earning Power," Harvard University Press, Cambridge, 1939.

for gasoline upon which the profit is very much lower than it is for lubrication and other services.) A profit margin of 10 per cent of sales is the most that the operator can hope to get, not only as a capital return but also in personal wages.

Occupations with a high rate of turnover of inventory—like vegetable stores—obviously require less initial capital than drugstores, hardware, or jewelry stores where many items of stock will stay on the shelves for 3 to 5 years and where the average ratio of annual sales to stock of inventory may be less than one.

Aside from the capital necessary to open a business, there is the tremendous amount of personal effort that is required. Self-employed farmers usually work from 60 to 70 hours per week as compared to about 58 for farm hands. Similarly, it has been estimated that the people in other fields who are their own bosses put in at least 8 hours more per week than wage earners. Who, on his Sunday ride in the country, has not had pity for some self-employed drudge, whose own efforts and those of all his family hardly suffice to cause him to break even?

Still, people will always want to start out on their own. Theirs may be the successful venture. Even if they never do succeed in earning more than a couple of thousand a year, there is something attractive about being able to make your own plans and in performing the variety of tasks that a small enter-priser must tend to every day.

Economically, big business and infinitesimal business are almost as different as day and night. In between comes the category of small business, by which is usually meant corporate enterprises employing less than, say, a couple of hundred workers and having sales of less than a million dollars per year. When the heart of a Congressman or editor bleeds for small business, as when advocating the repeal of some tax legislation, it is usually to corporations of this considerable size that his remarks apply rather than to infinitesimal business.

THE SINGLE PROPRIETORSHIP

We may gain insight into the principal forms of business organization—the single proprietorship, the partnership, and the corporation—by following the history of a particular business venture as it grows from a small beginning into a good-sized corporation. In the last part of this chapter, we shall turn to the subject of the giant corporation and its modern economic role.

Let us suppose that you decide to start a business to produce tooth paste. You may have hit upon a good preparation in your chemistry class, or you may simply have looked up an old formula in the Encyclopaedia Britannica or the U.S. Pharmacopoeia. To be a single proprietor you need not get anybody's permission; you simply wake up one morning and say "Today, I am in business!" And you are.

You may hire as few or as many laborers as you wish, borrow whatever capital you can. At the end of the day or month whatever is left over as profits, after all costs have been met, is yours to do with as you like. And there is nothing to stop you at any time from going to the cash register, taking out $800, and giving it to your wife to buy a fur coat or a piece of Chippendale furniture. You must pay income taxes as an individual on all the earnings of the business.

The losses of the business also are all yours. If your sales fail to cover the costs you have incurred, your creditors can ask you to dig deep into your personal assets: the war bonds put aside for junior's education, the old farmstead, and all the rest. In legal terms an individual proprietor has "unlimited liability" for all debts contracted by the business. All of his property, beyond a small minimum, is legally attachable to meet those debts.[1]

BUSINESS GROWTH AND THE NEED FOR SHORT-TERM CAPITAL

Let us suppose that the business is prospering tremendously because a chain of five-and-ten-cent stores has been induced by your low price to place a large order for tubes of paste to be marketed under their name. Although you are now making more money than you expected to, you find yourself harder pressed for cash than ever before. Why? Because you are not paid in advance for your sales, whereas you must pay your workers and suppliers promptly on the receipt of their services. For the moment you are putting out money and getting nothing for it; *i.e.*, nothing except the certainty of future payment on the sales orders which you have booked, nothing but a miscellaneous batch of "goods in process"—unfinished tooth paste, empty tubing, and so forth.

To some extent, the stringency of "working capital" can be relieved by your not paying for supplies until the end of the month or even longer. However, there is a limit to which your suppliers will let you run up bills. Furthermore, letting your so-called "accounts payable liabilities" pile up is an expensive way of raising capital since goods are often billed 2 per cent discount if paid within 30 days. When you do not take advantage of such discounts, you are in effect paying so high an interest rate that borrowing at any reasonable rate of interest would be better.

---

[1] An economics textbook cannot go into the legal details, which vary from state to state, concerning the minimum amount of household furniture and property that bankrupt proprietors or partners are allowed to keep.

Where is such a single proprietor to borrow? A personal finance company will probably charge you something like 3 per cent per month or 40 per cent per year for a small personal loan, and even such a company will prefer to lend to a man with a steady wage, which can be legally "attached" or "garnisheed" in case of nonpayment. If you own a home without a mortgage, a loan at 4, 5, or 6 per cent might be raised upon it. To borrow in this way is clearly to risk your family's future well-being, but probably if you are sufficiently convinced of your business future you might assume the risk.

Someone will naturally ask why the local banker cannot be called upon for a commercial loan at 6 per cent or less. The answer is that, ordinarily, a commercial bank will not provide "venture capital" for an unproven enterprise. The bank's vice-president looks at your checking balance and naturally finds that it has always been near the vanishing point, because as fast as payments have come in, you have had to write checks to stave off the ever-insistent claims of your creditors. Ordinarily, the bank likes to make 3-month loans to be used for peak-season needs and to be canceled during the rest of the year. It is idle to pretend that 3 months from now your growing business will be any more flooded with cash than now, and that you will not at that time be applying for continuous renewal of the loan.

Even if the bank were emancipated from the old-fashioned prejudice against "term loans" of some years' duration, it could not conscientiously provide the capital to a business like yours. However certain and glorious the future of the business appears to you, to the banker you are only one of numerous would-be entrepreneurs, most of whom are destined for failure even in the best of times, and almost all of whom will certainly be wiped out when the first big depression comes along. For the bank really to protect the sums entrusted to it by its depositors, it would have to charge you an extra risk premium, in addition to, say, 4 per cent interest, of perhaps 10 per cent or more.[1] Otherwise, the successful ventures would not be meeting the losses of the unsuccessful ones.

There is probably only one possibility of your getting a loan from the bank. If you are a veteran, one of the provisions of the G.I. Bill of Rights provides that the government, after surveying your business prospects, may "guarantee" one-half of your bank loan, up to a guarantee by the government of

---

[1] Another alternative, which has been used extensively in Germany but not in the United States or Great Britain, would be for the bank to buy part ownership in your business and share in the jack pot of profits. Such participation in ownership inevitably leads to management responsibilities by the banks and often to monopoly control of business by banking interests. For this reason, and others, such activity is legally forbidden to our banks.

$2,000. Since the banker's risk has been reduced, he is usually glad to lend you the money at the specified 4 per cent. It is to be emphasized that the whole transaction is a loan and not a gift, a loan that the veteran will have to make good out of his private assets. Furthermore, if a veteran has used up his borrowing provisions on a foolish venture, he is out of luck as far as future loans are concerned.

Despite your makeshift attempts to borrow capital, the business is still suffering from a bad case of growing pains. You have exhausted all possibilities of raising further loan capital. There is nothing for you to do but look around for a partner.

THE PARTNERSHIP

Any two or more people can get together and form a partnership. Each party will agree to provide some fraction of the work and capital, to share some percentage of the profits, and of course to share some percentage of any losses or debts. A purely oral agreement will do, but it will be more business-like and make for less misunderstanding if some sort of formal partnership agreement is drawn up by a lawyer.

In the case of the tooth-paste business, let us suppose that your brother-in-law is given a half ownership in the business in return for putting up $21,000 of capital. Like you, he is to work for the company, receiving, let us say, a salary of $4,000 per year as compared to your $7,000. You are to receive two-thirds of all profits or losses and he one-third.

Your partner has put up $21,000 in cold cash. What have you brought into the venture? In the first place, you have, of course, some unfinished barrels of tooth paste to contribute, along with some unpaid accounts payable for goods already delivered. This does not seem like much.

Actually, what you bring to the partnership is an intangible but valuable asset: the profitable sales orders, the know-how, or what is called "good will." In short, you are bringing with you a potential profit-earning power over all costs of, say, $9,000 a year. You are letting your partner have a $4,000 a year job—which we shall assume is about equal to what he can get elsewhere—and in addition for $21,000 he is purchasing a one-third slice of $9,000 every year.

From the earlier discussion in Chap. 3 on capitalization of an income stream by means of the interest rate, it will be obvious that such a $3,000 annual income—if it were certain and permanent—would be worth at 5 per cent interest some $60,000 ($3,000 ÷ 0.05). Aside from the risk element, your brother-in-law is getting a good buy for his $21,000, since he will be collecting some 14 per cent on his investment every year. Clearly, therefore, your two-thirds share is justified by the more than $42,000 of good will (defined to be "capitalized excess earning power") which you are supplying.[1]

CAUSES OF BUSINESS GROWTH

So your business continues to prosper and grow. Each year both partners agree to take out of the business only their salaries and about a fifth of their profits, ploughing back the rest of the profits into the business.

The only reason that you decide to take out any profits from the business at all is because you both need the cash to pay your Federal personal income taxes, which are levied not only on your salaries but also upon your respective shares of the partnership's earnings. The government is a silent partner, sharing about 35 cents out of every extra dollar that you receive, and about 30 cents out of every extra dollar of your partner's slightly lower income.

The business has grown because (1) more orders for tooth paste have come in as a result of your trade name becoming advertised and better known, and as a result of your sending out more salesmen. (2) As more tooth paste is produced, economies of large-scale production are realized so that you are able to cut your price. (3) A new factor of growth results from "vertical integration": you decide to buy a chemical factory so as to be sure of a cheap source of supply, and in addition you become your own wholesaler, thus operating three rather than only one "stage of production." (4) In addition, the company begins to grow by "horizontal integration"; you take advantage of a profitable opportunity to buy out a number of competitors producing similar tooth pastes in this and other areas. (5) New "complementary products," such as soap and lipstick are added, because you feel that bringing in the new lines under the same roof will help to spread the overhead expenses and because your salesmen feel that they might just as well get many orders when making a call as only a few orders. (6) Finally, and it comes as something of an anticlimax, your business may even grow because you are producing a better tooth paste.

NEW NEEDS AND SOURCES OF CAPITAL

Once again the enterprise finds itself in the paradoxical situation of being still harder up for capital, the faster it grows. The $21,000 of new "equity capital" brought into the business did not stay in the form of cash very long. It was quickly transformed in part into circulating capital assets such as goods in process and office supplies. In part it was used to pay off the most pressing

[1] The problem of good will and capitalized earning power is discussed further in the accounting appendix to this chapter.

liabilities of the concern, particularly the highly costly, undiscounted, accounts payable liabilities.

The remainder was used as a down payment on a factory building and equipment, which the government's Surplus Property Administration had offered for sale. The building, formerly used as a wartime chemical factory, had been built at government expense for a chemical corporation. This corporation had operated the factory as "agent" for the government and was given the first option to buy it at the original cost minus an allowance for the fact that it had been depreciating through age and use. The corporation had decided, however, not to take up the option, and so your partnership had put in a bid and had been able to purchase it. Despite your shortage of cash, this was too good a bargain to pass up in view of the high rent that you had been paying for factory space and considering the high postwar cost of building.

The difference between the down payment and the purchase price of the factory was secured by a mortgage loan on the property. The mortgage money was advanced by a near-by life-insurance company and was to be amortized or paid off in installments over a period of 20 years along with $3\frac{1}{2}$ per cent interest per year on the actual principal still unpaid at any time. In case the loan should not be paid, the holder of the mortgage of course has the right to foreclose the mortgage, *i.e.*, to take over the ownership of the building and sell it for what it will bring. Since the down payment on the factory came to about one-fourth of its price, and since this price was a bargain price to begin with, and since each year the insurance company will be getting back part of its principal, the risk taken by the company is not very great. The only way it could lose would be if there were a disastrous real-estate crash within the first few years of the making of the contract.

Despite the continuous plowing of profits back into the business, the growth of the enterprise still leaves you in need of further capital. But now, having established your reputation, so to speak, some new avenues of borrowing are open to you. Your banker will be glad to lend you money to tide you over the busy pre-Christmas period. An industrial finance company, like the Commercial Credit Corporation, will lend you money on the basis of your safe, but as yet uncollected, "accounts receivable" (meaning by these two words the sums owed you for goods that you have sold and delivered but have not yet been paid for). Finally, your bank, which was leary of lending you money for venture capital, becomes willing to make a "term loan" for 5 years once the Federal government's RFC has agreed to guarantee the loan. Or if the bank should still be unwilling, the RFC can advance you the money on its own if it considers your activity to be in the national interest and to be a good risk.

Let us suppose that, when all is said and done, you still need more capital than you can raise by any kind of borrowing. The painful necessity arises of getting more "equity" capital by letting some new people share in the profits and losses of the business. As a matter of fact, even if you could still find some institutions to borrow from, it would be unwise to do so. You have already superimposed too many liabilities and fixed charges on a narrow equity base. As long as things go well, it is lovely to earn 10 per cent profit on capital that costs you only 5. But if losses should occur, they will fall all the more heavily on the two partners who are the residual owners.

DISADVANTAGES OF THE PARTNERSHIP FORM

One possibility of getting more ownership capital is to admit new partners. If your wife does not have a large family, you may of course go farther afield. There is no limit to the number of partners that you can admit; there have been partnerships in the brokerage and banking fields involving more than 100 people. However, every time a new partner is admitted, or one dies or resigns, a whole new partnership must be formed.

Moreover, as the number of partners increases, there comes to the fore a factor that has been soft-pedaled in our discussion up to now. Each partner is liable *without limit* to the full extent of his personal fortune for all debts contracted by the partnership. If he owns 1 per cent of the partnership and the business fails, then he will be called upon to foot 1 per cent of the bills, and the other partners will be assessed their 99 per cent. Should they be unable to pay any part of their assessment, then the 1 per cent partner may be called upon to pay for all, even if it means selling his fine etchings at auction or disposing of his home.

This feature of *unlimited liability* reveals why partnerships tend to be confined to small, homogeneous, personal enterprises. When it becomes a question of placing their personal fortunes in jeopardy, people are ordinarily very reluctant to put their capital into complex ventures over which they can exercise little control. According to the doctrine of "mutual agency" involved in the law of partnerships, each partner has rather broad powers to act as an agent to commit the whole partnership.

This explains why agriculture and retail trade are the only sectors of our economy where more than half of the business done is done by single proprietors and partnerships. Even in the field of investment banking, where concerns like J. P. Morgan & Company used to advertise proudly "not incorporated" so that their creditors could have the comfortable assurance that every Morgan yacht and Whitney greenhouse was standing squarely behind the company, even these concerns have transmuted themselves into such corporate entitles as Morgan, Stanley and Company, Inc., and J. P. Morgan, Inc.

Two further disadvantages—in addition to unlimited liability—are often said to characterize the partnership. First, and much less important than most textbooks would have us believe, there is the need to start a new partnership every time somebody new enters or when somebody dies. The trouble and nuisance of such reorganizations are rather trifling, as is well known in the investment banking field.

More weighty is the real disadvantage stemming from the fact that a partnership can be dissolved whenever any party finds the existing arrangement unsatisfactory and wishes to withdraw.[1] In any case, the law of partnerships makes it impossible for any partner to sell his share to a new party without the consent of his partners. If agreement cannot be secured, a costly liquidation of the assets of the partnership may be inevitable.

B. *THE MODERN CORPORATION*

At this point, therefore—or even long before—you will probably decide to form a corporation rather than a partnership. Usually you will incorporate in the state in which you live and operate. However, if the corporation is of any size, you may prefer to establish token headquarters in some state like Delaware or New Jersey, where the regulations governing corporations are made much lighter than in other states in order to attract corporations.

Some centuries ago, corporation charters were awarded by governments very rarely and only by special acts of the king and legislature. Parliament or

---

[1] Perhaps the reader will remember how the novelist William Dean Howells has his famous title character, Silas Lapham, a rising self-made paint tycoon, present his partner with the ultimatum: "You buy me out or I'll buy you out." Silas' two excuses, that his were the real brains and energy responsible for the success of the business and that the proffered price exceeded his partner's original investment, were cleverly seen through by Mrs. Lapham. She pointed out that, without the partner's money at the critical time, the business could never have succeeded and that Silas' offer to sell was premised upon the knowledge that his partner was not in a position to buy the whole of the business.

Congress would graciously permit a public-utility enterprise or railroad to form a corporation to do specific things and perform specific functions. The East India Company was such a privileged corporation. The early railroads here and abroad often had to spend as much money in getting a charter through the legislature as in preparing their roadbeds. Gradually within the past century, this procedure began to seem unfair and it became the practice to pass general incorporation laws granting almost anyone the privilege of forming a corporation for almost any purpose, without having to get a special vote of approval from Congress or Parliament.

Today, for a very small fee a lawyer will draw up the necessary papers of incorporation and will write into the charter almost as wide powers and purposes as you could wish. Automatically and at small expense the state will grant the corporate charter.

Let us see how the incorporating procedure works in the case of your tooth-paste company. You decide to issue 20,000 shares of common stock in the corporation, 6,600 going to you, 3,300 to your partner, 100 to your wife, and the other 10,000 to be sold to outside interests. Although each share is to have an initial stated value of $10, your lawyer has advised you to make them no-par-value shares, since "par value" has no particular significance anyway.

The 10,000 shares to be sold to the public are to be marketed through a local investment banking firm. They are simply merchandisers of securities; and like any merchant, their profit comes from the difference between their buying and selling prices. Because yours is such a small business, they can drive a hard bargain, especially since they can claim that the costs of selling the securities are likely to be high. Thus the investment brokers may offer you $10 per share and plan to resell at a price of $12.50 per share. Had you been a large company, you might have held out for as much as $12.40, or even in some cases $12.45, out of the $12.50 selling price, because of the eager competitive bidding of the different investment banking syndicates.

Moreover, for a large company the investment banker would probably have agreed to underwrite the new issue of 10,000 shares. This means that he would have guaranteed the full purchase of the full 10,000 shares at a set price. If the market then refused to buy all these shares from the investment banker at his announced price, he would have to absorb the loss, not you. But he probably regards you as too small and untried a business to justify his assuming the underwriting risk. Consequently, if it should have been impossible for him to sell all the shares, you would have had to do with less capital.

Fortunately, all goes well and he pays you $100,000 in cash for the securities that he has sold. Unlike the case of the partnership, you need not concern yourself with the people to whom he has sold the shares, nor with the fact that they may resell their shares to still someone else. The names of the owners of the shares are registered with the company just in case they get lost and so that you will know where to send the dividend checks or the announcements of stockholders' meetings. Ordinarily, each share's owner is thereby given one vote, and a proportionate share in the earnings of the corporation. Someone with 10 shares has 10 votes and will receive proportionally higher dividends.

The outside owners of 10,000 shares have paid in $100,000 of cash to the company. What have you and your partner paid in? Obviously not cash, but rather an equivalent amount of earning assets: plant, equipment, goods in process, and perhaps good will which is, as we have already seen, the capitalized value of the presumed "excess earning power" of the business, resulting from its trade-marks, patents, know-how, and so forth.

Back in the good old days before 1929, you and your investment banker might have evaluated the good will pretty much as liberally as you wished, possibly giving yourself 20,000 shares rather than 10,000 shares. This practice has been called "watering the stock." But today, you would have to submit your new issue to the SEC. They would have to satisfy themselves that the public is not being invited to pay good cash for "useless water" before they would approve the new flotation. Moreover, they would try to make sure that there was no phony advertising or inspired false rumors, and that the salesman who peddles the shares leans over backward in providing advice and authentic accounting information. However, they do not pretend to pass judgment on or certify as to the value of the stock.

ADVANTAGES AND DISADVANTAGES OF THE CORPORATE FORM

The corporation has solved most of the problems that bothered you about the partnership. It is an almost perfect device for the raising of large sums of capital. Most important, every stockholder now has limited liability. After paying $12.50 for a share of stock, the investor need not worry about his personal estate's being in jeopardy. If worse comes to worst and the business becomes bankrupt, the most that each shareholder could lose would be his original $12.50 per share. He cannot be assessed further.

Of secondary importance is the fact that the corporation is a fictitious legal person created by the state. It exists not by "natural right" but only at the pleasure of the state. The corporation, as distinct from its owners, can be sued in court and can sue. Any officer of the company, unlike any partner, is strictly limited in his legal ability to act as agent for the other owners and to commit them financially. Also, the corporation may have "perpetual succession" or existence, regardless of how many times the shares of stock change hands by sale or bequest, and regardless of whether there are 10,000 different stockholders. No group of shareholders can force any other group to sell or retain their holdings, and only a majority vote rather than unanimity is needed to reach any legitimate business discussion. Usually the stockholders will be too numerous to meet for every decision; they will prefer to elect a board of directors consisting of a dozen or so members to represent them between annual meetings, in much the same way that democratic electorates select legislative representatives to act for them. However, as we shall see in a moment, the problem of keeping large corporations truly democratic is almost an insuperable one.

There is one disadvantage to incorporation that has become increasingly serious in recent years. The Federal government, and many states, tax corporate income and regulate corporate activities. Thus, during the war a small and profitable corporation might have had to pay as much as 80 per cent of its income to the government in excess-profit taxation. Even today, it might have to pay almost 38 per cent. These corporate taxes are in addition to the personal income taxes which must later be paid on all dividends distributed to the share owners.

A number of intelligent businessmen are beginning to realize that this is a rather high price for a small business to pay for limited liability and greater ease of raising capital; they are deciding to continue business in the partnership form. However, their decision is complicated by the existence of tax *advantages* offered by the corporation form. There is a loophole in our present law whereby all *undistributed* corporate profits escape *personal* income taxes, only paid-out dividends being taxed by the personal income tax law. A very rich man who is taxed at about 85 cents on every dollar of personal income says to himself: "It would be better to invest in a corporation which distributes little of its earnings than to invest in a partnership and be taxed 85 per cent of all earnings whether they are plowed back into the business or paid out to me. Of course, the corporation has to pay 38 per cent on its earnings, and I must pay an additional 85 per cent on what they pay out to me in dividends. But if they don't pay out much in dividends, my effective tax rate is 38 rather than 85 per cent."

To some degree he is only putting off the evil day. For, when he does come to collect his future dividends, they will be taxable. As we saw in Chap. 3, in a world of compound interest, time is money, and tax lawyers earn their living by cooking up legal schemes of putting off the evil day for their clients.

The forgotten man who "gets it in the neck" is the relatively poor stockholder who is taxed personally perhaps 30 per cent on his dividend receipts and who already has indirectly paid a 38 per cent corporate tax. This is sometimes called "double taxation."[1]

Problems of taxation properly belong in the chapters on governmental finance and cannot be discussed further here.

HOW A CORPORATION CAN RAISE CAPITAL

Let us suppose that the corporation continues to grow as a result of vertical and horizontal combination, addition of new products, economies of mass production, advertising promotion, and so forth. What new forms of financing are available to it in addition to borrowing on promissory notes or mortgages or buying on credit?

Bonds. First it may issue bonds. These are nothing but special kinds of promissory notes printed on fancy paper and issued in $100 or other denominations so as to be readily marketable for resale. A bond is a security promising to pay a certain number of dollars every 6 months for a number of years until it matures. At that time the borrowing company promises to pay off the principal of the bond at its face value. (Often the company has the right to call in the bond a few years before its maturity date by paying the bondholders some previously agreed upon price.) The dollar installments paid every 6 months, which represent the interest earnings of the bond, are usually called the "coupon payments," because the owner of the bond cuts off a certain little corner of the bond each 6 months, which little coupon he then mails and receives his interest payment.

Ordinarily, the coupons and principal must be paid on time regardless of whether the company has been making earnings or not. Otherwise the company is in default of its obligations and can be taken to court like any debtor. (Occasionally the bonds are also covered by a mortgage on the corporation's factories or equipment so as to give the lenders extra security.) Of course, there is no particular reason why a partnership could not borrow by the use of bonds; but ordinarily it would not be well enough known to succeed in interesting any lenders. For that matter a small corporation is rarely in a position to raise capital by issuing bonds.

---

[1] Another loophole used to avoid the disadvantages of double taxation under the corporate form is for the owners of a closely held corporation to vote most of its earnings to themselves and their relatives in the form of high salaries. The Treasury Department tries to check up on such ways of avoiding taxes by puffing up expenses; but it is always hard to know whether a given second cousin is or is not really worth $15,000 a year.

Common Stocks. It will be clear that issuing bonds and issuing common stocks are exactly opposite methods of financing. The common stockholder is providing "equity" capital. He shares in all profits and in control of business decisions, but he must also share in all losses. His is a more risky venture, because he can never receive any dividends until the fixed charges owed to the bondholder are paid off. The bondholder gets a nominally lower but steadier income. Needless to say, unless the corporation is bankrupt or in danger of being so, the bondholder has ordinarily no control over the decisions of the business.

Preferred Stocks. Intermediate between bonds and common stocks are so-called "preferred stocks." These are like bonds in that the buyer who puts up capital for them is limited in the percentage return that he can get from them—say, to a stipulated 4 per cent of the face value per share—no matter how profitable is the business in any year. However, he is more sure of getting his fixed preferred stock dividend than is the common stockholder, because his legal claim stands next in line after that of the bondholder and before that of the common stockholder.

If the tooth-paste company owes $2,000 per year in bond interest and has issued $50,000 worth of 4 per cent preferred stock, then the common stockholders will receive no earnings until the company's net profits (after all taxes!) are about $2,000 + $2,000. If net earnings are $5,000, then only $1,000 will be available for the common stockholders or only about $\frac{1}{2}$ per cent return on their $200,000 capital investment. Should the company have a good year and earn $40,000, then no less than $36,000 would be available for the common stockholders.

Often "cumulative" preferred stock is issued rather than "noncumulative." The former term means that if for 5 years of depression there hasn't been enough in the way of earnings to pay any of the 4 per cent dividends on the preferred stock, then when good times come back again the "cumulated" $20 (5 × $4) of unpaid preferred stock dividends must be made good before the common stockholders can begin to share in the earnings. Often, too, preferred stock is "callable" or "convertible." The first term means that at some previously stated value, say $103, the company can buy back its outstanding preferred stock. The second term refers to the right given the preferred stockholder of converting each share into shares of common stock at some stipulated ratio.[1]

---

[1] Also some preferred stocks are made more attractive by being made "participating." This means that once profits exceed some agreed upon figure, they share with the common stockholder in any further profits.

ADVANTAGES OF DIFFERENT SECURITIES

From the standpoint of the investor, bonds, preferred stocks, and common stock obviously form a sequence of increasing risk and decreasing security—balanced by an increased chance of making high earnings. Thus, today, a "gilt-edge" bond may yield about 3 per cent, a good preferred stock about 4 per cent, and a good common stock anywhere from 8 to 10 per cent.

To test his understanding of these three forms of securities, the reader should make sure that he understands why common stocks are better investments in time of inflation than the other two.

It would be a mistake to leave the reader with the impression that bonds are perfectly safe investments. On the contrary, during depressions many companies have gone bankrupt and their bonds have gone into default, paying off only a few cents on the dollar. Often a company will undergo reorganization in which the stockholders may be squeezed out completely; the courts may appoint a "receiver" or trustee to run the business and the bondholders may be given bonds (or even stocks!) equal only to some fraction of their original investments. Moreover, certain bondholders may have prior claims over holders of other issues, depending upon whether the bonds were backed by so-called "first," "second," or even "third" mortgages, etc. Many railroad investors have learned of the above possibilities in the hard way.

From the standpoint of the corporation, bond borrowing creates low but inflexible fixed charges. These fixed charges may be highly embarrassing in bad times. Preferred stock is slightly better with respect to flexibility, and equity capital best of all.[1]

THE GIANT CORPORATION

We have now carried our successful tooth-paste enterprise far enough up the ladder of success. It has done well for itself, but the chances are literally a million to one against its breaking into the upper crust of corporate enterprise. The rest of this chapter will be concerned with the economic position and power of the very large modern corporation, and the problems that they create for the American economy.

A list of the 200 largest nonfinancial corporations reads like an honor roll of American business, almost every name being a familiar household word. Among the 107 industrial companies will be found United States Steel,

---

[1] Bond interest charges can also be deducted from the corporation earnings for tax purposes. There is an incentive, therefore, other things being equal, to use this method of financing rather than either kind of stock financing. However, other things have not been equal, and the great trend in the past 20 years has been away from fixed charges, or loan financing, and toward stock financing.

Bethlehem Steel, and the Aluminum Company of America; Standard Oil of New Jersey, of California, of Indiana, and several other Rockefeller "subsidiaries"; General Motors, Chrysler, and Ford; Swift, Armour, and Cudahy meat packing; American Tobacco (Luckies), R. J. Reynolds (Camels), and Ligget and Myers Tobacco (Chesterfields); The Great Atlantic & Pacific Tea Company, Sears Roebuck, Montgomery Ward, F. W. Woolworth, and J. C. Penney; National Dairy Company (Kraft's), Borden's, Procter & Gamble, and Lever Brothers, and so it goes.

Among the 39 railroads are such old stand-bys as Pennsylvania, New York Central, Southern Pacific, and many others. The public-utility list of 54 companies is headed by A.T.&T. and Commonwealth & Southern. This completes the three divisions of the 200 largest nonfinancial corporations. But if we go on to include in addition the 60 largest financial organizations, we bring in such giants as the Chase National Bank (New York City), the Bank of America (California), and National City Bank (New York City), the Continental Illinois National Bank (Chicago), and the First National Bank of Boston; the Metropolitan Life Insurance Company, the Prudential Life, New York Life, and so forth. Altogether there were in 1947 more than 35 companies whose assets had passed the billion dollar mark.

The tremendous concentration of economic power involved in these giant corporations may be gauged from the following facts: they alone own more than half of the total assets of all nonfinancial corporations, more than a third of all banking assets, and four-fifths of all life-insurance assets. In manufacturing alone, the 100 most important companies employed more than one-fifth of all manufacturing labor and accounted for one-third of the total value of all manufactured products.

Their power did not grow overnight. Up until the New Deal of 1933, their percentage importance steadily mounted. Throughout the 1930's and up to World War II, they grew some but just about held their own, relatively speaking. There is evidence that the war brought about some reshuffling as to the membership in the first 200; but by and large these same companies managed to operate more than half of all new war-plant facilities, and to have a slightly higher profit to sales ratio than the next smaller group of 800 companies. Large size breeds success, and success breeds further success.[1]

[1] The statistical evidence on profits suggests that profits increase with size, but that the very biggest firms in an industry sometimes seem to show a slight dropping off of relative profits compared with the next to the largest. A larger percentage of small firms than of large firms falls in the class of firms making losses. However, as W. L. Crum's study, "Corporate Size and Earning Power" (Harvard University Press, Cambridge, 1939) has shown, within the class of firms that make profits, size and percentage profitability are negatively rather than positively correlated.

However, the story of concentration is not yet told. If we examine "interlocking directorates" among these companies we find that in 1935 all but 4 per cent of their assets are owned by companies that share one or more directors with other companies; Western Union, for example, interlocked with no less than 35 other companies, and one busy banker served on the board of directors of no less than 9 different giant companies.

Furthermore, according to a careful qualitative study by the National Resources Planning Board,[1] about half of these companies, owning some two-thirds of all their total assets, can be assigned to one of eight loose "interest groups": (1) Morgan-First National, (2) The Kuhn, Loeb & Company, (3) Rockefeller, (4) duPont, (5) Mellon, (6) Chicago, (7) Boston, and (8) Cleveland.

Thus, the first and largest Morgan-First National group is in a position to exercise rough control over 13 industrial corporations (U.S. Steel, General Electric, etc.), 12 utility corporations, 11 major railroad systems, and 5 major financial institutions. Together, the total assets associated with this empire were about 30 billion dollars in the years before World War II. Or, to take another example, the Rockefeller family interests, besides controlling one of the world's two largest banks, the Chase, also have extensive interests in all the various Standard Oil companies created out of the Supreme Court's dissolution of the old Standard Oil monopoly.

THE EVIL OF MONOPOLY

In view of the above facts, it is not surprising to find that most important American industries are characterized by a few large corporations whose share of the particular total industry's output is vastly greater than their numerical importance would warrant. Figure 1 gives a list of the large American industries and depicts their degree of concentration by showing the relative proportion of total output controlled by the first four dominant corporations, and by the next four. Thus, the biggest automobile companies sell more than 85 per cent of the total output of that industry, while women's clothing presents an opposite industrial setup made up of many small firms.

Later in Part Three, we shall analyze some of the problems raised by monopoly and imperfect competition. Within the past 60 years, particularly since the 1890 Sherman Antitrust Act, there has been great concern over the breaking down of free competitive markets under the encroachment of large-scale enterprise. The Federal courts and the lawyers in the Department of

[1] "The Structure of the American Economy," pp. 100–103, and Appendix, 13 pp., 306–317, Washington, 1939.

Justice are greatly concerned over the exact way in which the monopoly came into existence as much as they are with its economic incidence, and over the motives of people rather than the effects of their action. Thus it makes a difference to the legal mind whether a man creates a monopoly by a deliberate act of buying up rivals or whether he simply is made a wedding present of his rivals' plants by his fiancée's father—although to the economist, only the final suppression of competition and raising of price count.

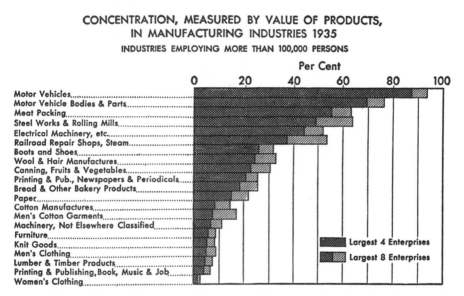

CONCENTRATION, MEASURED BY VALUE OF PRODUCTS,
IN MANUFACTURING INDUSTRIES 1935
INDUSTRIES EMPLOYING MORE THAN 100,000 PERSONS

FIG. 1. SOURCE: National Resources Committee, "Structure of the American Economy."

From an economic point of view it doesn't matter a great deal whether price is too high because of various of the following monopolistic devices: (1) cooperative "pools" or "cartel agreements," (2) so-called "trusts" (involving selected "trustees" who "coordinate" pricing policy), (3) interlocking directorates, (4) "holding company" control, (5) tacit collusion and trade association action, (6) government "fair price" legislation (Robinson-Patman Act, etc.) and government sponsored "commodity agreements" (wheat, rubber, cotton, etc.), or finally (7) because a company comes to dominate an industry simply because it is actually most efficient. Too high a price, wastage of resources, and creation of monopoly profits are economic evils, however they are brought about and whatever the legal technicalities of the matter.

DIVORCE OF OWNERSHIP AND CONTROL IN THE LARGE CORPORATION

Let us begin to examine the internal workings of one of these giant corporations. *The most striking feature is the tremendous diversification of ownership among thousands and thousands of small stockholders.* In the postwar period, almost 700,000 different people had shares in A.T.&T., with one-quarter of the shares being held in blocks of less than 100 shares, and with no single owner possessing as much as 1 per cent of the total outstanding shares.

Berle and Means in a path-breaking study[1] pointed out that this wide diversification of stockholding has resulted in a *separation of ownership and control.* Recent studies have confirmed the fact that in the typical giant corporation, all management together—officers and directors—hold only about 3 per cent of the outstanding common stock. The largest single minority ownership groups typically hold only about a fifth of all outstanding voting stock. Such a small fraction is considered more than enough to maintain "working control."[2]

AMPLIFICATION OF CONTROL BY THE PYRAMIDING OF HOLDING COMPANIES

Even the figure of 5 to 1 amplification of the control exercised by minority stockholders is a gross understatement. In addition to the common stock outstanding, the corporation may have the use of as much capital again in the form of bond borrowing or preferred-stock issues. Moreover, there grew up during the 1920's the practice of selling nonvoting common stock to the public while retaining control of the voting stock for the insiders. Therefore a figure of 10 to 1 of assets controlled to assets owned is not at all unrealistic.

Nor is this all. With $100,000 I can hope to control a million-dollar company. But what if the million-dollar corporation is a holding company whose sole function is to control a 10-million-dollar company through its ownership of 10 per cent of that company's stock? And the latter is a holding company controlling a 100-million-dollar company in a similar way? A small amount of money at the apex of the inverted pyramid can be given tremendous leverage of control simply by adding more layers to the structure—the result being 1,000 to 1 amplification of control, or even more.

This use of holding companies is not a mere theoretical possibility. During the 1920's, vast and complex public-utility empires were built up by their use. Just to chart the organizational structure of such corporations as the

[1] A. A. BERLE, JR., and GARDNER C. MEANS, "The Modern Corporation and Private Property," Commerce Clearing House, Inc., New York, 1932.

[2] See R. A. GORDON, "Business Leadership in the Large Corporation," Chap. II, The Brookings Institution, Washington, D.C., 1945.

Associated Gas & Electric· system would take a number of ordinary sized book pages. The greatest losses to investors after the great 1929 stock-market crash came from such holding-company securities. The small and large investors who were cajoled into buying Middle Western Utilities by the highly respectable Chicago tycoon, Samuel Insull, lost every penny of their investments. It is for this and other reasons that Congress and the SEC have, by the Public Utility Holding Company Act (1935), passed a "death sentence" on such holding-company systems, and that they are in a gradual state of dissolving themselves.

A less dramatic case of pyramiding of control may be mentioned. The duPont family owns most of the shares of a holding company, Christiana Securities Company. This company in turn owns about one-quarter of the voting stock of the great chemical concern E. I. duPont de Nemours, which in turn owns about one-quarter interest in GM. Although the direct participation by the duPonts in GM affairs appears to be lessening in recent years, it is clear that no management actually opposed to their interests and wishes would be able to get into office or maintain itself.

It should be added that in connection with neither GM nor the United States Rubber Company have the duPonts exercised their influence in a manner detrimental to the earnings of the other stockholders. On the contrary, anyone who put $1,000 into GM stock in 1920 would find himself with many, many times that wealth as a result of the repeated dividends of new shares of common stocks and the repeated split-ups of the common-stock shares.

LEADERSHIP AND CONTROL OF THE LARGE CORPORATION

The problem of keeping a large corporation truly democratic is a difficult one. Until recent years, less than a dozen stockholders would turn up for the annual meeting. More recently, a few hundred have been attending such meetings, often drawn by free chicken salad and, it must be confessed, by the chance to heckle management.

Decisions at the annual meeting are really settled by the use of "proxies." Each stockholder is asked to mail in a proxy permitting the management to exercise his votes. Many do not reply. But enough usually do to establish a quorum and a comfortable plurality for management. The SEC has tried to improve the democratic structure of corporations by insisting that motions to be decided at the annual meeting be indicated on the proxy statement so that stockholders can indicate their preferences; also rival groups must be permitted mailing access to the stockholders, and so forth.

However, it still remains true there is no fully effective democratic control of management by the stockholders. Political parties may go in and out of office, but most corporation managements are self-perpetuating. Occasionally there is a battle among giants, and one minority group is able to defeat another one. In 1929 John D. Rockefeller, Jr., led a spirited fight to oust from office Col. Robert W. Stewart, who had been allegedly engaged in some financial irregularities at the expense of Standard Oil of Indiana. After a titanic battle, Rockefeller won the day—only proving that it takes the initiative and the power of a Rockefeller to turn out a well-intrenched management.

If not the stockholders, who do make corporate decisions? Primarily, the increasingly important class of *professional managers*. The old-time captain of industry, for all his creativeness and ability to calculate the risks necessary to build up a great enterprise, often had something of the buccaneer in his make-up and an irresponsible "the-public-be-damned" attitude. In company after company, the original founder has been replaced by a new type of executive, usually having a different surname; if, as is increasingly unlikely, he should be a completely self-made man, he will nevertheless probably have acquired special training and management skills. The new professional executive is more adept at public relations and in the handling of people. He is necessarily more the bureaucrat, interested as much in preserving the *status quo* as in taking extreme risks.

Typically, the dominant spirit will be the president of the corporation. As he begins to feel his years, he may have himself made chairman of the board of directors, while still serving as the chief executive officer (*e.g.*, Alfred Sloan in GM until 1946, or Sewell Avery in Montgomery Ward & Co., Inc.). More often, the chairman of the board is an elder statesman, who, together with a small executive or steering committee of the board of directors, gives advice and approval to the actions of the president and his many vice-presidents.

The exact role of the board of directors varies from company to company, and from group to group. Many directors are simply well-known men selected to give the company prestige. Others possess special knowledge and take an active part in determining policy. On the whole, it would be going too far to say that most boards of directors simply act as rubber stamps to approve the decisions already taken by the officers of the company. But it is true that, so long as management possesses the confidence of the board, that body will usually not actively intervene to dictate specific policies. This is the same sound administrative procedure usually followed by the board of trustees of a philanthropic foundation or college, and is not too unlike the parliamentary system of ministerial responsibility.

Generally speaking, there will be no clash of goals between the management and stockholders. Both will be interested in maximizing the profits of the firm. However, in two important situations, there may be a divergence of interests, not infrequently settled in favor of management. First, insiders may legally or illegally vote themselves and their friends or relatives large salaries, expense accounts, bonuses, and retirement pensions at the stockholders' expense. (We saw in Chap. 5 the approximate level of top executive salaries in large and small corporations.) When many corporations do this, a vicious circle is introduced: every other corporation must follow suit under penalty of losing its better executives, and there is hardly any limit to the process. The wonder is not that executives' salaries are so high but that they are not higher. Also, insiders may throw the company's patronage to other concerns in which they, themselves, have a personal interest.

A second conflict of interest may arise in connection with undistributed profits. The managers of every organization have an innate tendency to try to make it grow and perpetuate itself. The psychological reasons are subtle and by no means always selfish ones. There is reason to question whether profits are not plowed back into a company in many cases when the same capital could better be invested by the stockholders elsewhere, or be spent upon consumption. The stockholders in effect are never really consulted in any effective way in the matter. Indeed, the case arises not infrequently when a company would be well advised to wind itself up and pay back its capital. But one need not be a cynic to doubt that management is likely to vote itself out of existence and out of jobs.

THE CURSE OF BIGNESS?

If the problem of full employment is solved reasonably satisfactorily in the years ahead, then one of our most important economic problems will become that of channeling the tremendously efficient and creative abilities of the modern large-scale corporation to the general public, good. Nobody wants the large corporation to appear in the role of a Frankenstein monster.[1] Whether, in the view of the technological trends toward large-scale production, a renewed program of trust busting can restore a greater degree of effective and workable competition, is a problem that we cannot begin to tackle until after an analysis of prices and cost under competition, monopoly, and monopolistic competition in Part Three.

[1] It would take us too far afield away from economics and into politics to discuss business as a system of power: how special-interest groups have occasionally lobbied, bribed, and agitated in order to influence public policy. Of course, the same has been known to be true of farmers and labor unions.

Lest it be thought that the present chapter emphasizes too strongly the defects of the big business, the following statement by a world-famous economist is presented:[1]

. . . the modern standard of life of the masses evolved during the period of relatively unfettered "big business." If we list the items that enter the modern workman's budget and from 1899 on observe the course of their prices not in terms of money but in terms of the hours of labor that will buy them—*i.e.*, each year's money prices divided by each year's hourly wage rates, we cannot fail to be struck by the rate of the advance which, considering the spectacular improvement in qualities, seems to have been greater and not smaller than it ever was before. . . . Nor is this all. As soon as we go into details and inquire into the individual items in which progress was most conspicuous, the trail leads not to the doors of those firms that work under conditions of comparatively free competition but precisely to the doors of the large concerns—which, as in the case of agricultural machinery, also account for much of the progress in the competitive sector—and a shocking suspicion dawns upon us that big business may have had more to do with creating that standard of life than keeping it down.

This suggests that the future problem may not be one of choosing between large monopolistic corporations and small-scale competitors, but rather that of devising ways to improve the social and economic performance of large corporate aggregates.

SUMMARY

A. FORMS OF BUSINESS ORGANIZATION

1. The present population of American businesses, which has grown up as a result of a cumulative excess of business births over business deaths, consists in the greater number of infinitesimal single proprietorships, largely in retail and service establishments. Their turnover is rapid.

2. The reader should understand how a small-scale enterprise grows, what are its needs and avenues for short-term or long-term capital, and what are the advantages and disadvantages of the corporate form over the single proprietorship and partnership.

[1] J. A. SCHUMPETER, "Capitalism, Socialism, and Democracy," Harper & Brothers, New York, 1942.

B. THE MODERN CORPORATION

1. He should also be acquainted with the fundamental legal rights involved in the corporation, and with the general features of bonds, preferred- and common-stock corporate securities.

2. The problems created by the separation of ownership and control and by the great concentration of economic wealth and monopoly power in the modern giant corporation, and in powerful interest groups and holding-company structures deserve serious study.

The best possible review of the economic principles discussed in this chapter is provided by a study of the fundamental principles of accounting presented briefly in the Appendix to this chapter. Accounting is an indispensable prerequisite to the understanding of economics.

QUESTIONS FOR DISCUSSION

1. Imagine that you are going to start a business of your own. Write a case history of its development.

2. Compare the advantages and disadvantages of (a) the single proprietorship, (b) the partnership, and (c) the corporation form of business organization.

3. What are the reasons underlying the growth of a business to large size?

4. Make a list of the ways of raising capital for small, medium, and large businesses.

5. What are the advantages and disadvantages of different kinds of securities?

6. Discuss the structure of the modern large corporation.

7. List a typical Balance Sheet, showing Assets, Liability, and Net Worth. Contrast its meaning with that of the Income Statement.

8. How does depreciation estimation affect stated earnings? Are depreciation reserves cash?

9. Exactly what is involved in plowing back earnings into surplus? Discuss common fallacies.

APPENDIX TO CHAPTER 6

ELEMENTS OF ACCOUNTING

THE BALANCE SHEET

It is necessary for every student of economics to have some understanding of the two fundamental accounting statements: the Balance Sheet and the Statement of Profit and Loss (or, as it is sometimes called, the Income Statement).

The Balance Sheet is presented in a report annually, or oftener. It represents an instantaneous "still picture" of the conditions of the enterprise as of some particular day, perhaps the last day of the year. Corresponding to the dollar value of every asset—tangible or intangible—there must of course be an exactly equal total amount of claims or ownership. The value of a $10,000 house is exactly matched by somebody's claim to ownership of that house, consisting, for example, of $7,000 owed to a creditor and $3,000 owned by its possessor.

This is the fundamental identity underlying every balance sheet:

$$\text{Value of assets} = \text{value of claims or ownership}$$
$$= \text{value of liabilities (owed)} + \text{value}$$
$$\text{of proprietorship (owned)}$$

or

Assets = Liabilities + Net Worth

Let us illustrate this by considering a simple balance sheet as shown on page 135.

A question mark has been deliberately placed next to the Common Stock Net Worth item because the reader should realize for himself that the only correct entry compatible with our fundamental balance sheet truism is the number $200,000. A balance sheet must always balance—because Net Worth, *i.e.*, the ownership of the "residual claimants," always adjusts itself to make things balance.

To illustrate this, let us suppose that a thief steals all the cash, and a fire burns up one-fourth of the inventory. The accountant will learn of this sad news without turning a hair. "Total Assets are down $40,000 all told. Liabilities remain unchanged. Very well, I must write down Capital by $40,000, to the level of only $160,000." Such is the accountant's method of keeping score.

TABLE 1. *Balance Sheet of Pepto-Glitter Co., Inc., as of Dec. 31, 1949*

ASSETS		LIABILITIES AND NET WORTH	
		Liabilities	
Current Assets:		*Current Liabilities:*	
Cash.....................	$ 20,000	Accounts payable..........	$ 20,000
Inventory................	80,000	Notes payable.............	30,000
Fixed Assets:		*Long-term Liabilities:*	
Equipment...............	130,000	RFC note.................	50,000
Buildings................	170,000	Bonds payable.............	50,000
		Net Worth	
		Capital:	
		Preferred stock	50,000
		Common stock	?.....
Total....................	$400,000	Total	$400,000

A number of interesting facts are revealed even by this simple Balance Sheet. First, it is customary to divide up assets according to whether they will be convertible into cash by normal operations within a year or not, the first category being called Current Assets and the second Fixed Assets. The liabilities can also be subdivided into Current and Long-term Liabilities depending upon whether they come due in less than a year. The difference between total Current Assets and total Current Liabilities,

$$\$50,000 = \$100,000 - \$50,000,$$

is usually termed "working capital"; also in more advanced discussions some attention is paid to the

"Working-capital ratio" = Current Assets ÷ Current Liabilities
$$= \$100,000 \div \$50,000, \text{ or } 2 \text{ to } 1.$$

Another thing to be noticed about our balance sheet is that, although its two sides must balance *in total*, yet no single item on one side is matched by an item on the other side. Thus, the Bonds do not correspond in value to the Equipment or Buildings, nor do the Capital items correspond to the Cash. The only correct statement about a balance sheet is that the creditors have a general claim against the enterprise of a definite value, and the owners have a residual claim against the rest.

Most of the specific items listed are more or less self-explanatory. Cash consists of coins, currency, and money on deposit in the bank. This is the only asset whose value is exact rather than an estimate. All other valuations involve some guesswork, albeit careful guesswork. Moreover, all accounting valuations must be made relative to the actual intended purpose or use of the asset in question. If a business is a going concern and not in the process of liquidation, the accountant will be careful not to value the assets at the low figure that they would bring at a forced sale, but he will rather value them at their worth to the company in its normal operation.

Inventory, consisting in the case of our tooth-paste company of sugar, chemicals, tubing, raw materials, and other goods in process, can be valued in many different ways. Many conservative companies use original cost of the inventories or present market value, whichever is lower. Especially difficult problems arise when the prices of materials vary from month to month. Should we figure the chemical cost of the tooth paste at the original price of the ingredients actually used, which of course were bought some time ago when prices were different? Or should we figure, as our cost, the price that must *now* be paid for the chemicals to replace those being used up? An elementary discussion cannot go into these two possible methods, which are respectively called by the puzzling names "First-in—first-out" (FIFO) and "Last-in—first-out" (LIFO). Obviously, it will make a great difference in stated profits during a time of inflation or deflation which of these two methods is used. It also will make a difference in income taxes. Therefore, the government is compelled to say, "Use whichever method you wish, but having made up your mind, stick to it." So much for inventories.

If we assume that the Equipment and Buildings items were just bought at the end of 1949, then their balance sheet values will be listed equal to their purchase price. This follows a fundamental accounting rule or convention: "At time of purchase a thing is presumed worth what the enterprise pays for it." However, as we shall see in connection with the Income Statement and the next year's Balance Sheet, almost insuperable problems are involved in deciding how to evaluate exactly equipment and buildings that have depreciated through use and age.

On the liability side, Accounts Payable are, as their name implies, the sums owed for goods bought and charged. Notes Payable represent promissory notes owed to the banks or to a finance company. The RFC Note listed under the Long-term Liabilities is a 5-year loan advanced by, or guaranteed by, the RFC of the Federal government. The Bonds Payable represent a long-term loan, floated at a 3 per cent coupon rate, and not due or callable for 15 years.

Turning now to the Net Worth items, we find that 500 shares of $100,

4 per cent, cumulative (nonparticipating) preferred stock have been issued. And finally 20,000 shares of no-par common stock were issued at $10 each. This completes our first glance at a simple balance sheet.

THE STATEMENT OF PROFIT AND LOSS

Now let time march on. During the following months, the firm is engaged in producing and selling tooth paste. This being a boom period when prices are soaring and sales are expanding, the firm can hardly fail to make some profits. To show its flow of income over the 12 months of the year, we must turn to its Income Statement, or as many companies prefer to call it, the Statement of Profit and Loss.

TABLE 2. *Income Statement Pepto-Glitter Co., Inc., from Jan. 1, 1950, to Dec. 31, 1950*

Net Sales (after all discounts and rebates)		$240,000
Less: manufacturing cost of goods sold		
Materials	$ 50,000	
Labor cost	100,000	
Depreciation charges	20,000	
Miscellaneous operating expense	5,000	
Total cost of goods *manufactured*	$175,000	
Add: beginning inventory	80,000	
	$255,000	
Less: final closing inventory	85,000	
Equals: manufacturing cost of goods *sold*	$170,000	170,000
Gross profits		$ 70,000
Less: selling costs		14,000
Net operating profits		$ 56,000
Less: fixed interest charges and state taxes		6,000
Net earnings before taxes		$ 50,000
Less: corporation income taxes		13,000
Net earnings after taxes		$ 37,000
Less: dividends on preferred stock		2,000
Net profits of common stockholders		$ 35,000
Less: dividends paid on common stock		5,000
Addition to surplus		$ 30,000

This is a rather straightforward statement showing what happens to the money that the company receives in the form of sales. It lists all the various costs that have to be subtracted in order to arrive at various net earnings or profits. At the end, after all operating costs have been met, all selling costs, all fixed charges, all taxes, and all preferred-stock dividends, there is left out of the original $240,000 of Net Sales only some $35,000 of Net Profits for the common-stock shareholders. Of this amount only $5,000 was paid to the common-stock shareholders as dividends, the remainder being an addition to Surplus.

However, before examining exactly how profits are plowed back into an enterprise, let us examine the various items in the Income Statement. The meaning of Net Sales is obvious, as are most of the components of Manufacturing Cost of Goods Sold. Material costs are the sums paid to other businesses for chemical supplies, tin, and so forth. When we come later to discuss national income in detail, we shall see that these are payments for production actually performed by other business units. Unlike labor costs they are not part of the "value added" by this particular stage of the productive process.

The Miscellaneous Operating Expense items include plant overhead costs, power, and other such expenses. A more difficult item to understand is the Depreciation Charges entry. In fact, the whole problem of depreciation is worth a small section to itself. But first, it should be clear that not all of our manufacturing cost outlay could be charged off to the present year's output if we were building up the amount of our inventory. In this event, the Cost of Goods Manufactured would be greater than the Cost of Goods Sold, greater by the increase in inventory of finished and unfinished goods. Contrariwise, if more inventory were being used up than was being replaced, the true Cost of Goods Sold would have to exceed the actual Cost of Goods Manufactured.

That is why to get Cost of Goods Sold from Cost of Goods Manufactured, we must first add in the value of Inventory at the beginning of the period and subtract the value of Inventory at the end of the period. In our example, the company built up its Inventory during the year from $80,000 to $85,000. Therefore, $5,000 of its costs could not fairly be counted in as part of the Cost of Goods *Sold*. By subtracting a Closing Inventory item larger than Beginning Inventory, we automatically make the correct adjustment for changing inventory.

DEPRECIATION

At first, one may wonder why any Depreciation Charges have been made for 1950. The buildings and equipment were newly bought at the beginning of the year, and surely they will not have been worn out already. (There will of course be need to spend money on men to maintain the equipment and keep the factories painted. But their wages are already included in Labor Cost or Miscellaneous Expense and are not included in Depreciation.)

Here is where the farseeing wisdom of the accountant comes to the fore. He points out that not a cent may have to be spent upon replacement of equipment for 10 years, at which time suddenly all the machines may have to be bought anew. It would be nonsense, he claims, to charge nothing to depreciation for 9 years and kid yourself into thinking you are making a nice profit, and then suddenly in the tenth year to have to charge off all the value of the machines at once and think you have made a tremendous loss in that year.

Actually, he points out, the equipment is being used up all the time. A truer, undistorted picture of net income or profit will be learned if the costs of the equipment are spread more evenly over its lifetime. The value of equipment declines as a result of age and use from its price when new to its final scrap value. In recognition of this, the accountant depreciates the value of fixed capital items by some *gradual* formula. Here, we have not the space to go into the various methods that have been used. Suffice it to mention two widely used ones.

The first is called "straight-line depreciation." Suppose that you have a truck whose cost when new is $10,100, and whose economic life is 10 years, after which its physical life may continue but its economic life will be over because of its unreliability and maintenance costs. Suppose that its scrap value at the end of 10 years is $100. According to the straight-line method you will charge off in depreciation to each year one-tenth of the lifetime decline in its total value, $10,000 (new price minus scrap value). Thus, $1,000 will be charged in depreciation every year.

A second general method called the "service unit method"—or "unit of production method"—can be mentioned only briefly here. According to this we would estimate the number of miles, or loads, or service units that the truck will perform in its life. Thus, if the truck goes a million miles in 10 years and its loss of value during that time is $10,000, then each mile used up represents about 1 cent. This method has the virtue that during the first year of life of the truck, when presumably it will be used proportionately more than toward the end of its life, depreciation charges may be reckoned at perhaps $1,500 (for 150,000 miles) rather than at only $1,000 as in the straight-line method. A second great advantage of this method is that, during periods of depression when trucks are idle a good deal of the time, the calculated depreciation charges are less, and so the businessman may not be prevented from reducing prices by an erroneous overestimate of his money costs.[1]

[1] Many accounting books also describe a still different method which permits of greater depreciation when an asset is new than when it is old. This is the constant percentage depreciation method, whereby the truck would be depreciated a constant percentage of

Although depreciation is usually figured by some apparently exact formula, every accountant knows that the estimates are really very rough, being subject to large and unpredictable errors, and involving arbitrary corrections and assumptions. He comforts himself with two thoughts: (1) A rough method of depreciation, like an imperfect watch, is often better than none at all. (2) Any mistakes in depreciation will ultimately "come out in the wash" anyway.

Let us see why a mistake in depreciation ultimately tends to correct itself. Suppose that the truck lasts 15 years rather than the predicted 10. We have been then overstating our depreciation expenses during the first 10 years. But in the eleventh and later years there will be no depreciation charged on the truck at all, since it has already been written off of its scrap value. Our profits in these later years tend, therefore, to be overstated by about as much as they were understated in the earlier years. After 15 years, everything is pretty much the same after all.

Except for taxes. Different methods of depreciation result in a different apparent distribution of earnings over time, and therefore in a different pattern over time of corporation income taxes. Naturally a businessman prefers a method of depreciation that will make his income average out more steadily over time—so as to keep his effective tax rate as low as possible and permit him to cancel off losses against profits; and also a method that will enable him to put off the evil day of taxes as far as possible.

This explains why so many corporations took advantage of the government's wartime offer to let them amortize (or depreciate) their newly built war plants and equipment over 5 years. They were glad to be able, by charging high depreciation expenses, to reduce their stated profits during the war years when their profits were enormous. They much preferred to take advantage of this "accelerated depreciation" plan so as to shift their profits from war years to postwar years when corporation tax rates were expected to be much lower.

In ordinary times, the Treasury will not let a corporation manipulate its depreciation charges so as to avoid taxes. The company may select any reasonable method; but having once made its choice, it must stick to it. Mention may be made of the fact that many economists are today worried about the harmful effects of taxation on "venture capital." They argue that we shall get

---

remaining value each year, until it reached its final scrap value. During the first year, the depreciation charged would be largest because of the truck's high initial value; during the last year, a constant percentage of the greatly reduced remaining value would result in low depreciation charged.

more investment in new tools and create more jobs, if the Treasury is a little more liberal in letting companies depreciate their equipment more rapidly, thereby saving on their taxes.

For the moment no more will be said of depreciation. However, one aspect of the problem needs final stressing. Depreciation is an *expense* and not necessarily an *expenditure*. Thus it differs from labor expense, which is an accounting cost and at one and the same time a flow of purchasing power from business to the public. We shall return to this problem of purchasing power in a moment.

THE RELATION BETWEEN THE INCOME STATEMENT AND THE BALANCE SHEET

The algebraic difference between available net earnings and actual dividend payments is added to a Net Worth account called Surplus. Table 3 shows the Balance Sheet of our tooth-paste corporation at the end of its first year of operation. It has prospered. Net Worth, the difference between Total Assets and Total Liabilities, has increased between the beginning and end of the accounting period by $30,000—from $250,000 to $280,000. The amount of this increase, as shown by a comparison of balance sheets, is of course just equal to the amount of earnings or profits *available* to the common stockholders but not paid out to them in dividends; or as we saw at the bottom of the Income Statement, just equal to $35,000 − $5,000.

Some Net Worth item must be written up by $30,000. It would clearly never do to increase the Preferred Stock Capital Account, because such stockholders are not the residual claimants to the profits of the corporation. Theoretically, one could add the $30,000 to the Common Stock Capital Account. However, this is not done. Instead the Common Stock Capital Account is left at its original par value or value when issued.

It is more informative to create a new account called Surplus—or sometimes Earned Surplus—to show how much of the increase in "book value" or Net Worth has resulted from accumulated undistributed earnings plowed back through the years.

In many ways Surplus is a misleading word. It sounds like something extra or unnecessary; or too often like a nice spare chunk of cash which the company's workers or stockholders might hope to stage a raid against. Actually, Surplus is distinctly not an asset account, much less a pool of liquid cash. It simply indicates a part of the ownership—over and above liabilities to creditors and original subscribed capital ownership—in the polyglot assets of the corporation. A glance at Table 3 will convince us that the $30,000 of Surplus is not matched by an equivalent amount of cash on the asset side.

We must once again issue a warning against trying to link up specific items on the two sides of the Balance Sheet. Only the totals correspond. That is all. It is not even possible to say exactly how the $30,000 plowed back into the business, or added to Surplus, has been used. Part of it was used to pay off some of the liabilities of the business, part to enable the corporation to add to its assets (patents, etc.).

TABLE 3. *Balance Sheet of Pepto-Glitter, Inc., as of Dec. 31, 1950*

ASSETS			LIABILITIES AND NET WORTH	
			Liabilities	
Current Assets:			*Current Liabilities:*	
Cash............		$ 20,000	Accounts payable.........	$ 10,000
Inventory.........		85,000	Notes payable...........	17,000
Sinking Fund to Replace Equip-			Reserve for taxes.........	13,000
ment............		5,000		
(U.S. Government Bonds)				
Fixed Assets:			*Long-term Liabilities:*	
Equipment......	$130,000		RFC note.............	50,000
Less allowance (or reserve) for deprecia-			Bonds payable.........	50,000
tion........	15,000			
		115,000	**Net Worth**	
Buildings........	$170,000		*Capital:*	
Less allowance (or reserve) for			Preferred stock..........	50,000
			Common stock..........	200,000
depreciation....	5,000		Surplus...............	30,000
		165,000		
Intangible Assets:				
Patents............		10,000		
Good will..........		20,000		
Total............		$420,000	Total...............	$420,000

It would be an equal mistake to think that the profits of a corporation accrue in the form of cash; so that on the last day of the year, just before the board of directors decided upon its dividend rate, there was some $35,000 of cash on hand, available either for the stockholder or to be invested back in the business. When we later come to discuss the important process of saving and investment in Part Two, we shall have reason to emphasize that a business makes profits in part by selling for cash more than it pays out as costs; but also in part by getting, in return for its cost outlays, an increase in its noncash asset items. Or as we shall say later: net capital formation is a part of national income in addition to consumption sales.

In the case of our tooth-paste company, the very handsome profit earned was largely embodied in the form of new assets and lowered liabilities; not very much more than $5,000 could have been paid out as cash dividends without forcing serious changes in the financial decisions of the company—decisions such as to borrow more, to sell off some of the equipment and inventory at a loss, or to operate with a ludicrously low cash balance.

Only very rarely can a company contemplate declaring a dividend in kind, rather than cash. One such famous example of this was the case of the American Distillery Company which gave each shareholder a barrel of whisky during the war, sending the price of the stock up from $15 to more than $100 after the news got around. Even in that case, the dividend was paid out of an Asset, Inventory; Surplus was simultaneously diminished to show a decrease in ownership in total of the company's assets.

EARNINGS, DIVIDENDS, AND PURCHASING POWER

As we have seen, earnings and declared dividends need not be equal. In bad years like 1932, companies like A.T.&T. may continue to pay out in dividends more than they have earned (for A.T.&T., $9 per share). In good years, companies will often pay out only part of their earnings in dividends, plowing back the rest in order to provide for growth of the enterprise. The Ford Motor Company is a wonderful example of a closely held company which rarely turned to the banks or to the securities markets for its capital. Instead it grew primarily from internal corporate savings out of profits.

In the case of our tooth-paste company, the board of directors decide that only $5,000 out of the $35,000 of available earnings should be paid out in common-stock dividends. Why are the stockholders satisfied to realize only this measly $2.50 per share or $2\frac{1}{2}$ per cent on their investment? In the first place, there is not much they can do to make their wishes felt, since the management needs only a few shares and the proxies of the rest of indifferent shareholders to get its own way.

In the second place, it would be a great mistake to think that the stockholders are unwilling to invest earnings back in the company. Such investments can be presumed to increase future earnings and dividends. And from the short-run point of view, more important yet is the fact that the stock market can be counted upon to take notice that each share of the corporation now has a claim to more valuable assets and earnings. The market value of the shares may even be bid up in price by as much or more than has been plowed back into the company, giving the stockholders a chance to realize immediate (lightly taxed!) capital gains.

This explains why investors are eager to buy the shares of such "growth" companies as duPont and Monsanto Chemical, whose present dividends are a low percentage of their market value, but whose future looks bright.

It would be a mistake, however, to think that any excess of dividend payments over earnings represents an expansion of purchasing power, and that any excess of earnings over dividend payments represents a contraction of total spending. As discussed earlier in connection with depreciation, earnings are reckoned by counting in many expenses that may not involve expenditures. We have only to look at the 1950 expenses of our tooth-paste company to see the difference.

Because the equipment and buildings were new at the beginning of the year, not a penny had to be spent during the year toward the production cost of new equipment and buildings. That is, 1950 *replacement expenditure* and *net additional capital expenditure* was zero—even though *depreciation charged* (in the Income Statement) was $15,000 all together. Even if the company had been paying out all its stated earnings in dividends—so that its intake of revenue on sales gave the appearance of being matched by an equal total of costs and earnings—even then, the fact that depreciation expense is not an expenditure but only a paper accounting charge could mean that the *company was not passing on in purchasing power as much as it was receiving.*[1]

SUMMARY OF ELEMENTARY ACCOUNTING RELATIONS

Before taking a last look at the new complexities introduced in the 1950 Balance Sheet over that of 1949, we may briefly summarize the relationship between balance sheets and income statements: (1) The Balance Sheet indicates an instantaneous financial picture. (2) The Income Statement shows the flow of sales, cost, and revenue over time. (3) The change in total Net Worth between the beginning and the end of the accountancy period—as shown by comparing the new and old balance sheets—is also to be understood from an examination of the changes in Surplus as shown at the end of most modern income statements. This assumes no recapitalization of the corporation.

There do remain, however, certain shifts in the balance sheet items from their previous levels in the earlier period to which the intervening Income Statement gives us no clue. A closer look at the Dec. 31, 1950 Balance Sheet

[1] Many economic experts overlooked this possibility during the early depression years. They mistakenly thought that American industry was splashing the community with extra purchasing power in 1932, just because dividends paid out were in excess of actual corporate earnings. In reality, because of the great excess in that year of depreciation charged over actual capital replacement *expenditure*, there was little such creation of purchasing power.

will therefore prove instructive, although enough has been said already to introduce the reader to the fundamentals of accounting.

The new Balance Sheet looks much like the old for the most part, but with some new items present for the first time. The last of these new items, Surplus, we have already explained. Among the Liabilities there is a new item called Reserve for Taxes of $13,000. It is not hard to understand. The taxes that the corporation will have to pay the government on Mar. 15, 1951 and succeeding quarterly dates are as much short-term liabilities as the Accounts Payable or Notes Payable.

Taxes Payable might have been a better title since the word "Reserve" suggests a pool of cash, which it decidedly is not. Instead the Reserve for Taxes is simply an earmarking of part of the total assets of the company for a special creditor, and a reminder that the Net Worth of the owners is less by the amount of owed taxes. In a moment we shall see that there are three main kinds of "reserves," and no one of them represents a pool of cash or liquid assets.

Let us turn to the Asset sides for new items.[1] The first stranger, entitled "Sinking Fund to Replace Equipment" is listed midway between the Current and Fixed Assets. It is an asset consisting of, say, 2 per cent government bonds which are to be held for the purpose of ultimately providing part of the money to buy new machines when the old ones are to be replaced. Although the corporation could change its mind and use the Sinking Fund bonds for some other purpose, it presumably will not choose to do so. The nature of this Sinking Fund is very understandable; it is simply a pool of liquid assets set aside for a specific future purpose.

Turning to the Fixed Assets, we find ourselves in for a surprise. From our previous discussion of the depreciation charges of the Income Statement, we should have expected the Building and Equipment items to total $280,000. Why? Because at the beginning of the year they added up to $300,000, because no new equipment was bought during the year, and because the Income Statement told us that $20,000 of depreciation accrued during the period as part of the necessary costs of production.

Why then are these Fixed Assets carried on the new Balance Sheet at the

[1] Neither this Balance Sheet nor the previous one contains a frequently met current asset item called Prepaid Expenses. Often an enterprise will pay its rent or for some of its supplies a number of months in advance. Very properly, the enterprise is regarded as possessing on its Balance Sheet an equivalent asset.

old $130,000 and $170,000 figure? Looking more closely we see that they are not really. From the $130,000 nominal Equipment valuation, there is subtracted an Allowance (or reserve) for Depreciation, so that really only $115,000 is carried for Equipment. Similarly from the $170,000 original value of the Buildings, there is subtracted some $5,000 of Depreciation. Our faith in the accountant's sanity is restored; but we may still wonder why he goes through this roundabout procedure of stating "two" as "four minus two" instead of simply as "two."

Actually, he has his good reasons. An honest accountant knows that his Depreciation charges are only the roughest of guesses. If he were simply to make his guess and put down the final figure of $115,000 for equipment, the public would not be able to know how much reliance to place upon the figure. But if he puts down $130,000 of original value which is firmly rooted in the solid fact of original cost, and if he then carefully isolates his own guessed-at Allowance for Depreciation, then the public is in a better position to evaluate the reliability of the final $115,000 figure. The roundabout procedure does no harm, and may do good.

Now we know the precise meaning of Depreciation Allowances or Reserves. They are not sums of money; they are not sinking funds of liquid assets that can be spent on replacement. They are simply *subtractions from overstated asset figures*. Thus, the Allowance for Depreciation of Buildings of $5,000 is simply an explicit correction to the overstated original value of the Buildings. This correction must be made to keep Assets and Net Worth from both being artificially inflated.

It must be made regardless of whether at the same time any money is or is not being set aside into sinking funds to replace the Depreciation asset. Note that there is no Sinking Fund for Buildings, and that the Sinking Fund for Equipment is only one-third as large as the estimated depreciation of equipment. As a matter of fact, American businesses rarely set aside any considerable sums of money in replacement Sinking Funds. This is because liquid gilt-edge bonds earn at most only a few per cent interest, whereas capital invested in the firm's own activities usually brings in much more.[1]

---

[1] Where then will the money be coming from to replace any particular machine or building if no sinking funds have been set aside? Ordinarily, the equipment can be purchased with sales dollars earned by other equipment that is not currently calling for replacement expenditure. The selling price of the output of such other equipment contains an accounting allowance for depreciation expense, and this sum of money is available for investment elsewhere in the business. Speaking somewhat loosely, we may say that each asset not needing replacement lends its depreciation charges to those which need replacement, knowing that it too will be taken care of when the need arises.

We have met two kinds of reserves: (1) A Liability Reserve, like that for taxes, which is really simply a liability of fairly certain value, and (2) an Asset Valuation Reserve like that for Depreciation (or allowance for estimated uncollectible bills), which is really simply a subtraction from an overstated asset. A third so-called "Surplus Reserve," which is also not to be confused with a sum of money, may be briefly mentioned: Sometimes a firm takes part of its Surplus and sets it aside under a different name so that the stockholders will not be tempted to lobby for higher dividend payments. For example, our tooth-paste company might earmark one-third of its $30,000 Surplus account into a Reserve for Research and Development. This $10,000 Reserve would no more consist of cash or liquid funds than does Surplus itself, or than does any other kind of Reserve. It should never be confused with a fund.[1]

Never was it more important to emphasize these accounting fundamentals. Time and again a trade-union will claim higher wages to be paid out of the Surplus or Reserves of some big company. Except in terms of demagoguery, it is often weakening its own case when falling into such egregious and transparent errors.

INTANGIBLE ASSETS

Only one further new category of Assets can still be found on the Dec. 31, 1950, Balance Sheet. To illustrate that an asset need not be a tangible commodity, a piece of equipment, or a sum of money, a Patent has been introduced into the picture. Let us suppose that it is a patent on a profitable new chemical process, which gives the company the exclusive production rights for 17 years.

Such a patent is obviously worth money. How much money? The sum of the present or discounted values of all its future net profits over the next 17 years—with the more distant years' profits being more heavily discounted by compound interest. Of course, as 5, 10, 12, and 16 years pass, the patent will be coming near to the end of its life and will be declining in value. Therefore, some depreciation formula will be applied to it just as if it were a truck. Probably the ideal formula would be to recalculate each year its *present discounted value*, and charge to Depreciation the decline from the previous year; it should be remembered however, that in practice this theoretical refinement is impossible to carry out.

---

[1] The problem of reserves becomes even more complicated in connection with contingencies that may or may not occur. Thus Reserve for Postwar Contingencies or for Renegotiation would fall halfway between true Liability and Surplus Reserves.

GOOD WILL AND MONOPOLY POWER

So much for the Patent as an illustration of an intangible asset. Let us suppose that, at the same time we bought the patent, we also took over a rival tooth-paste company. This horizontal combination will presumably add to our monopoly position and earning power. Therefore, we were willing to buy the company for more than its trifling assets—which happened to consist solely of a little inventory—were worth. Perhaps part of the purchase price went as profits to the promoters who engineered this little monopolistic merger.

Here we have a small-scale example of what J. P. Morgan did on a large scale in forming the giant United States Steel Company at the turn of the century. He bought out the Andrew Carnegie steel plants and combined them with half a dozen other holdings. But in economics, as in certain branches of atomic physics, the whole is equal to more than the sum of its parts. After Morgan had put the pieces together, he found himself with some 130 million dollars of extra capital value—which of course like a generous man he proceeded to share with his associates.

Who was hurt by this transaction? Certainly not Carnegie or Morgan. Even the people who bought the stock had no right to complain that it had been "watered," since for many years they continued to get more than a fair return on their investments. To have sold them the stock for its actual cost (without water) would be (1) to make them a free gift of the monopoly profits of the concern and (2) to give them the privilege of reselling the stock at the higher price that its earning power could earn for it in a competitive stock market.

If there is a real victim it is the consuming public, which perhaps had to overpay for its steel for the next quarter of a century because of the formation of the monopoly. To argue about who should share in the profits from a newly created monopoly is as pointless as to try to decide fair principles upon which pirates' plunder should be distributed.

However, our practical-minded accountant is not concerned with such matters of public policy and political economy. He will tell our tooth-paste company or J. P. Morgan the same thing: "If you paid a certain sum of money for some assets, they must presumably be worth that much to you. If the assets don't exist, they must be created. 'Good Will' is their name." But since this term has come into bad repute in recent years, it is often lumped in with some other assets.

This explains our last intangible asset. Good Will is the difference between what a company pays in buying out another company and what it gets in the way of identifiable assets.

One final point should be stressed. An accountant is a practical man who must make a living without concerning himself unduly over social welfare. That doesn't mean he is without principles, professional standards, and a code of ethics. A reputable accountant would no more think of approving an audit that didn't balance than he would of committing murder. Nor would such an accountant permit a firm suddenly to create a Good Will asset on its own Balance Sheet—even if its excess earning power had presumably increased! He knows that the future is uncertain, and that it is easy for management to dupe its stockholders and itself with wishful thinking.

Although he is unwilling to let a firm write up its own Good Will, he is usually willing to give his stamp of approval to any Good Will that is created as a result of the sale of one business to another. Thus the GM Balance Sheet contains some Good Will elements as a result of purchases at inflated prices of other companies made years and years ago by W. C. Durant in forming GM; but paradoxically, its really profitable operations since 1920 have not been substantially capitalized into Good Will. In accounting, as in economics, things are not always what they seem.

SUMMARY TO APPENDIX

Instead of a lengthy recapitulation, this section presents only a check list of the accounting concepts that the student should understand:

1. The fundamental balance sheet relationship between Assets, Liabilities, and Net Worth; and the breakdown of each of these categories into Current and Fixed Assets, Current and Long-term Liabilities, Capital and Surplus.

2. The character of the Income Statement (or Profit-and-loss Statement), and the relationship between its final undistributed profits and the changes in Surplus on the new Balance Sheet.

3. The whole problem of Depreciation, both in its income statement aspect as a necessary expense, which need not be an expenditure, and in its balance sheet treatment as a deduction from a purposely overstated asset; also the logic of the two principal depreciation methods.

4. The difference between a Fund or a pool of liquid assets and the three kinds of so-called Reserves; also the meaning of such intangible assets as Patents or Good Will.

Chapter 7: THE ECONOMIC ROLE

OF GOVERNMENT: EXPENDITURE,

REGULATION, AND FINANCE

THE activities of the state are becoming an increasingly important part of the study of modern economics. This is reflected in the quantitative growth of government expenditure and in the great expansion of direct regulation of economic life.

After discussing these topics, the present chapter goes on to survey the salient features of Federal expenditure and the economic characteristics of three alternative methods of financing public expenditure. The discussion is continued in Chap. 8 with special reference to Federal taxation and local public finance.

THE GROWTH OF GOVERNMENT EXPENDITURE

Before World War I, Federal, state, and local government expenditure amounted to little more than one-twelfth of our whole national income. During World War II, it became necessary for the government to consume about half of the nation's greatly expanded total output. Within the space of a third of a century, the cost of all government in the United States had risen from a paltry 3 billion dollars spent in 1913 to a temporary peak of around 110 billion dollars in 1945.

If this remarkable contrast were only the result of a temporary wartime condition, it could be shrugged off as being of but passing significance. Actually, the exact reverse is the case. For more than a century, national income and production have been rising; at the same time the trend of governmental expenditure has been rising even faster in almost all countries and all cultures.

Each period of emergency—each war, each depression—expands the activity of government. After each emergency has passed, expenditures never seem to go back to their previous levels.

Nor is the end in sight. With all-out total war over, government expenditure has receded from its wartime peak level, but by no means back down to

NATIONAL DEBT, ANNUAL NATIONAL INCOME AND
TOTAL ANNUAL GOVERNMENT EXPENDITURES 1900-1945

FIG. 1. Government expenditure includes Federal, state, and local expenditures. Note that the vertical scale is "logarithmic," so that equal vertical distances represent equal percentage changes. SOURCE: National Industrial Conference Board, *The Economic Almanac.*

those prewar levels which we used to consider so alarmingly high only a few short years ago. Before World War II, the annual Federal budget never reached the 10-billion-dollar mark. In the years ahead, regardless of whether the Republican party or the Democratic party holds office, probably no man now alive will ever live to see the year when there is a Federal budget of less than 20 billion dollars, or a combined Federal-state-local expenditure of much less than one-fifth of the national income.

Figure 1 indicates the historical trend of total government expenditure and Federal debt relative to the growth of national income. The vertical scale of this so-called "ratio chart" is graduated in logarithmic fashion so that equal distances correspond to equal percentage changes, rather than to equal absolute changes as in the usual chart. Such ratio charts are often used to show rates of growth of business and economic statistics.

The above are the hard cold facts about public finance. Some may deplore them. Some may like them. But there they are. They make clear the increasingly important economic role of government. They explain why no modern economic textbook can relegate to an obscure corner the vitally important problems of public finance.

THE GROWTH OF GOVERNMENT CONTROLS AND REGULATION

The increase in collective expenditure is only part of the story. In addition to increased direct participation by government in national production there has been a vast expansion in its laws and executive orders regulating economic activity.

No longer is modern man able to believe "that government governs best which governs least." In a frontier society, when a man moved farther west as soon as he could hear the bark of his neighbor's dog, there was some validity to the view "let every man paddle his own canoe." But today, in our vast interdependent society, the waters are too crowded to make unadulterated "rugged individualism" tolerable. The emphasis is increasingly on "we're all in the same boat," "don't rock the craft," "don't spit into the wind," and "don't disregard the traffic signals."

Perhaps nineteenth-century America came as close as any economy ever has to that state of *laissez faire* which Carlyle called "anarchy plus the constable." The result was a century of rapid material progress and an environment of individual freedom. Also there resulted periodic business crises, wasteful exhaustion of irreplaceable material resources, extremes of poverty and wealth, corruption of government by vested interest groups, and too often the supplanting of self-regulating competition in favor of all-consuming monopoly.

Gradually, and in the face of continuing opposition, the methods of Alexander Hamilton began to be applied toward the objectives of Thomas Jefferson: the constitutional powers of central and local government were interpreted broadly and were used to "secure the public interest" and to "police" the economic system. Utilities and railroads were brought under state regulation; after 1887, the Federal ICC (Interstate Commerce Commission) was set up to regulate rail traffic across state boundaries. The Sherman Antitrust Act and other laws were invoked after 1890 against monopolistic combinations in "restraint of trade." Regulation of banking became thoroughgoing; after 1913, the Federal reserve system was set up to serve as a central bank, aiding and controlling member commercial banks; and since 1933 most bank deposits have been insured by the Federal Deposit Insurance Corporation or in the case of Federal saving banks, by the Federal Savings and Loan Insurance Corporation.

Pure food and drug acts were passed following the revelations of the "muck-raking era" of the early 1900's. Loan sharks came under regulation in many states. The abuses of high finance, before and after 1929, gave rise to ever more stringent regulation of the financial markets by the SEC and other bodies.

Humanitarian legislation to better factory conditions for children and women won at first only a grudging acceptance by the courts. But with the passage of time, as the radical doctrines of one era became the accepted and even reactionary beliefs of a later era, state and Federal legislation was expanded to include minimum-wage legislation, compulsory workmen's accident compensation insurance, compulsory unemployment insurance and old-age pensions, maximum-hour laws for children, women, and men, regulation of factory conditions of work, compulsory collective bargaining, fair labor relations acts, and so forth.

To understand this trend toward greater governmental authority one must maintain a sense of historical perspective. Each new step generated strong political feelings on both sides. Thus the "square deal" doctrines of the Republican Theodore Roosevelt, which today would cause no raising of eyebrows or fluttering of pulses, were considered dangerous and radical in their time. Similarly many of the most controversial aspects of Franklin Roosevelt's Democratic New Deal are, for better or worse, here to stay.

Our democracy cannot, and would not if it could, turn the clock back to the conditions of the nineteenth century as represented by Henry Ford's Greenfield Village and McGuffey's Reader. Nevertheless, it would be wrong to regard these historical processes as inevitable, to join Omar in his mournful chant:

> "The Moving Finger writes; and having writ,
> Moves on: nor all your Piety nor Wit
> Shall lure it back to cancel half a Line,
> Nor all your Tears wash out a word of it."

No immutable "wave of the future" washes us down "the road to serfdom," or to utopia. Where the complex economic conditions of life necessitate social coordination and planning, there can sensible men of good will be expected to invoke the authority and creative activity of government. But expansion of centralized power as a worthy end for its sake is quite another matter—an end alien to the typical American citizen's credo. (Unfortunately, not until long after the event will history tell us—and perhaps not then—whether or not a given expansion of governmental authority was a good or bad policy; whether or not it should have the approval of all those genuinely interested in conserving and improving the good elements in our system.)

But this, past history does seem to suggest. Unyielding conservatism defeats its own purpose. Steel without "give" will rupture suddenly under strain. Brittle economic systems without the flexibility to accommodate themselves in an evolutionary manner to accumulating tensions and social changes— however strong such systems may appear in the short run—are in the greatest peril of extinction. For science and technology are constantly changing the natural lines of economic life. If the system is to continue to function well, our social institutions and beliefs must be capable of adjusting themselves to these changes.

To a world living in the shadow of the atomic bomb, these are hackneyed truisms. They were no less true before World War II. And their disregard perhaps helps to explain the breakdown of democracy abroad and our need to participate in the most costly war in all history.

These remarks are not intended to imply that we should all rush out and vote for every crackpot or sensible reform currently being proposed. Each measure must be considered on its merits—not only in light of its probable economic worth but also in its relation to our fundamental social and personal beliefs concerning freedom. Nevertheless, without a sense of historical perspective neither radicals nor conservatives nor middle-of-the-roaders can effectively advance their own true long-run interests.

FEDERAL, LOCAL, AND STATE FUNCTIONS

If we return now to the over-all figures of expenditure, we find that they become more meaningful when we break them down to see just what activities they represent and by which branch of government they are administered.

Primarily, each American is faced with three levels of government: Federal, state, and local. It will surprise most people to learn that, of the three, the states have always been the least important with respect to government expenditure. This is still true although, as we shall see, it is becoming less so.

Prior to World War I, local government was by far the most important of the three. The Federal government did little more than pay for national defense, meet pensions and interest on past wars, finance a few public works, and pay the salaries of judges, congressmen, and other government officials. Almost all its tax collections came from liquor and tobacco excises and from tariff duties levied on imports. Life was simple in those days; local governments performed most functions and collected the most revenue, primarily from taxes on property owners.

In Fig. 2, we see how different everything has been since World War I. The Federal government now leads in total expenditure. The states are still

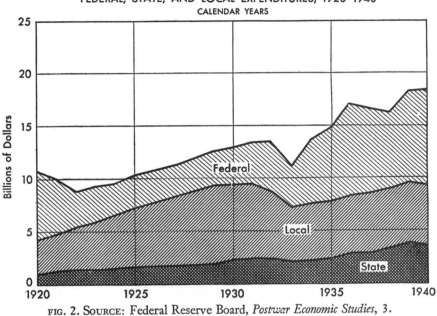

FEDERAL, STATE, AND LOCAL EXPENDITURES, 1920-1940
CALENDAR YEARS

FIG. 2. SOURCE: Federal Reserve Board, *Postwar Economic Studies*, 3.

last but are gradually gaining on the local governments. The recent abnormal war years are not shown in Fig. 2.

Let us turn now to Federal finance.

FEDERAL EXPENDITURE

The United States government is the biggest business on earth. It buys more typewriters and more cement, meets a bigger payroll, and handles more money than any other organization anywhere. Many a temporary "dollar-a-year" government executive, recruited for the war period from the top ranks of private industry, found himself working harder and making bigger decisions than ever he had dreamed of in private business life.

The numbers involved in Federal finance are astronomical: not millions, or hundreds of millions, but literally billions (*i.e.*, thousands of millions). At the peak of the war effort, the Federal government was spending about 100 billion dollars annually. The 1948 public debt was slightly more than 250 billion dollars, or more than a quarter of a trillion dollars.

Obviously, such magnitudes convey no meaning to the human mind. We all know what it means to be a mile from school, but assertions that the sun is 93 million miles from the earth or that there are enough molecules in a glass of water to make a string of pearls from here to kingdom come always leave us unimpressed and somewhat cold. Perhaps public expenditure will have more meaning if we remember that each billion dollars amounts to about $7 per American man, woman, and child. A postwar Federal annual budget of about 30 billion dollars would be equivalent then to about $210 per capita, or around one-sixth of the total national income.

As this is written (1948), it is still too soon to know the exact level toward which the postwar Federal budget will tend or the exact quantitative breakdown of expenditure. Figures could be given for the war years, but they would be too distorted to be of interest to anyone but an economic historian. Similarly, figures for the last prewar normal year, 1941 or earlier, would give a misleading impression of the postwar Federal budget, because the war has left its heritage of heavy defense expenditures, heavy expenditures on veterans, and interest on the vast war debt.

Table 1 illustrates, therefore, only a provisional and hypothetical estimate of the importance of different categories of Federal expenditure in the fiscal year 1949; *i.e.*, from July 1, 1948, to June 30, 1949.

The first four items represent the costs of past and future wars. Together they account for three-fourths of all Federal expenditure, and for most of the increase in Federal expenditure over prewar levels. Naturally, these are only rough estimates. If the international situation is troubled, we may expend larger sums on the Army, Navy, and Air Force; and the pressure of politics may force Congress to vote larger expenditures for the needs of veterans.

On the other hand, if there is great prosperity, social security expenditures for the aged, unemployed, sick, and handicapped may amount to less than the indicated figure. In any case it should be pointed out that a substantial part of these funds will be given to the states and localities to administer.

The same is true of the next category of public works and development projects, many of which will be constructed by local governments with partial financial aid from the national government. If unemployment grows in the years ahead, we may expect this particular item to exceed the estimated figure by a great deal.

The final category includes the costs of running Congress, the courts, and the general expenses of the executive branch of the government. In conclusion, it is to be emphasized that the bulk of postwar Federal expenditure and debt are the consequences of war and not the depression.

TABLE 1. *Federal Postwar Expenditure in Fiscal Year 1949*

Items	Budget estimate, billions	Percentage
1. International affairs (European Recovery Program, etc.)	$ 7.0	19
2. National defense (Army, Navy, Air, atomic energy, etc.)	11.0	29
3. Veterans (G.I. Bill of Rights, hospitals, pensions, etc.)	6.1	16
4. Interest on debt	5.3	14
5. Social security, welfare and educational expenditures (Old age, unemployment, public health, etc.)	2.4	7
6. National resources (Conservation, public works, etc.)	1.6	4
7. Other expenditures	3.1	8
8. General government expenditures	1.2	3
Total	37.7	100
9. Surplus (Available for debt retirement out of estimated receipts—over and above tax refunds—of $42.5 billions for fiscal year)	4.8	
Net total	42.5	

SOURCE: President's Budget Message to Congress, January, 1948.

EFFICIENCY AND WASTE IN GOVERNMENT

Even if the above estimates should be 10 per cent too high or low, they would still represent large sums of money. Undoubtedly, we should all be better off if the government were to increase its efficiency so as to give us the same services for lower costs; or what is equally important, if it were able to give us more and better services for the same dollar of expense.

Every effort should be made toward these ends. Having said this, one must go on to add: it is easier to preach economy than to practice it; easy to speak of cutting public expenditure to the bone, but when it becomes a matter of slashing aeronautical research, skimping on a veteran's hospital, denying aid to farmers, and so forth—then it is not so easy to carry out. The result: our legislators are forced to talk one way and act another; to content themselves with occasional outbursts of penny wisdom mixed with dollar foolishness. A case in point is the present absurd practice of paying congressmen only $12,500 a year.

Every student of public administration and history knows that, if our government expenditures are too high, it is not primarily because of personal corruption or technical incompetence on the part of civil servants and legislators. As far as standards of intelligence, training, and personal financial accountability are concerned, the present Federal government ranks far better than that of earlier times, or for that matter than similar establishments at the state and local levels.

The trouble, if there is a trouble, goes much deeper. It lies within ourselves as citizens. We want government economy, and at the same time we want the governmental services that cost money!

To put the matter in a more sophisticated way: Government expenditure is a way of utilizing national output so as to meet human wants and needs. When national income rises, people want more and better schooling and other forms of government services, just as they want to spend more on personal clothing, housing, and recreation. Our social conscience and humanitarian standards have completely changed, so that today we insist upon providing certain minimum standards of existence for those who are unable to provide for themselves. Often we speak loosely of government expenditure in the abstract, as if it were simply a subtraction from national production. Actually, the statistical definition of national product is drawn up so that government expenditure on goods and services becomes a way of using and producing economic output. It is not always an ideal way, any more than is production by the "private sector" of the economy. But it is a way which we could not do without, one which will probably continue to grow and—we all hope—to improve in the future.

SOCIALISM AND THE NEW DEAL

We are now perhaps far enough away from the controversial New Deal days to appraise the charge that the Federal government is replacing capitalism by socialism. This question can be tackled by considering government activity under four headings:

First, as we have already noted, there has been a great increase in the amount of government control. Nevertheless, much of this body of regulation can hardly be dignified by the title of "planning," and despite its bulk we are still a long way from a planned state.

Second, as we have also seen, the increase in government expenditure means that as a nation we are consuming more of our national product *collectively* rather than individually through private money purchases. Rather than pay to ride on the public roads as we do to ride on railroads, we pay for such valuable services by taxes.

But note that such collectively consumed goods and services are still *largely produced by free private enterprise*. The government may pay for a hospital or a typewriter, but each of these items is produced by free private enterprise. And so it is with most government expenditure on productive goods. This is hardly what the socialists mean by socialism—"government ownership and operation of factories, etc."[1]

If we analyze the third kind of government activity, direct government production, we find that throughout recent decades there has been but little expansion in this direction. Historically, our government has performed certain direct economic production functions, and not others. The post office and parcel post have long been a function of government, while private management has operated our telegraph service and railway express. Airports, but not railway terminal facilities, are usually governmentally owned. Governments now provide water, gas, and electric utilities, but not telephone service. The reasons for drawing the line at any one place rather than another are partly historical, partly arbitrary, and to some degree changing.

The courts have held that, in the special case of "public utilities affected with public interest," there is no possibility of effective competition between many independent producers; and it does not seem possible to decide which mode of operation would be the more successful except by a careful factual study which would transcend the field of economics.

Whatever the merits of the arguments on either side, it is important to realize that during the New Deal of the 1930's there was no vast expansion of government into such fields—except in one direction.[2] We did not nationalize our railroads as Sweden and many other countries have done, nor our coal industry, nor our banks, nor our radio broadcasting system, nor our insurance companies, nor our air lines. The New Deal differed in this important respect from the present (1948) Labor government in England, which has definite socialistic aspirations.

[1] See Chap. 26, which discusses certain differences between a socialized state and our own.

[2] The TVA (Tennessee Valley Authority) and other vast hydroelectric public-utility projects (Bonneville Dam in the Northwest, Hoover Dam in the Southwest, etc.) represent true cases where the government has taken over new active producing functions. It is noteworthy that the war plants built by the government are, almost without exception, being sold and leased to private industry or are being shut down.

Before leaving this third category, which involves the use of human and other resources directly by the government, we should recognize that there has been a substantial rise of the Federal payroll and in the number of government employees. Many of the latter are in the Washington executive offices, in regional laboratories, in the armed services, and so forth. Even if they are not directly producing private goods and services in competition with private industry, such resources are being used by the government; and it behooves us all as citizens that they be used wisely and in the right amounts relative to the importance of our different national needs.

Finally, we turn to a fourth activity of government which did expand tremendously in the 1930's and which will continue to loom large in the decades ahead—namely, government *welfare expenditures* which transfer purchasing power to the needy or worthy without regard to their providing any service in return. Thus, payments are made to veterans, old people, blind and handicapped, orphans, and the unemployed. This fourth category of transfer expenditure deserves further detailed discussion.

GOVERNMENT TRANSFER EXPENDITURES

A government check received by any of the above veterans or needy persons differs economically from that received by a postal clerk or from that paid to a man who produces typewriters. It is important that we understand why, because our later discussion of national income will involve this same distinction between items that are "transfers" and items that we can truly count as parts of national production or income.

The payments to a postal clerk or typewriter producer are counted as parts of national income and output because they do cover services rendered, they do use up resources and production, and they do provide collective direct or indirect consumption to the citizens of the United States. This is true whether they are financed by taxes, by the sale of postage stamps, or by any other means. The government collects dollars from the public and uses those dollars to provide services for the public. Such dollars are as much part of national income as the dollars collected by a railroad company and used to provide transportation services for its customers.

A blind widow's pension is something else again. Socially, it may be one of our most desirable expenditures, but nevertheless it is not part of national output or national income. Why? Because the widow does not render any services to the government or its citizens in exchange for the pension. She does not provide any labor, land, or capital. The pension increases her purchasing power. It permits her to live more adequately and to buy goods and services from other individuals. These goods and services that she buys are part of the national income and output; but they are attributable to the people and factories that have produced them, and they are not attributable to her.

Such transfer expenditures grew greatly in the years before World War II, partly as a result of the depression, which made relief expenditures necessary, but also because new minimum standards of health, nutrition, and security have been set up by the collective conscience of the American people. Society now rules that children should not have rickets because of the bad luck or weakness of their parents, that poor people should not die at the age of thirty because of insufficient money for operations and needed care, that the old should be able to live out their years with some minimum of income.

Such expenditures are not really anticapitalistic. "On the first round," these expenditures do not directly consume goods and services; but by swelling the purchasing power of their recipients, they do, "on the second round," create orders and jobs for free private enterprise. However, the thing to note is that the production induced by this process is both privately produced and privately consumed.

Unless these expenditures are financed by the printing of money or by government bond borrowing, larger taxes will have to be levied on the public, and it is for this reason that they are usually called "transfer expenditures." Often the more furtunate citizens are paying for the consumption of the less fortunate; and probably within reasonable limits, most people will feel that this is only as it should be.

Moreover to the extent that taxes come out of the income of the more well to do and thrifty and are used to make payments to the needy and ready-to-spend—to that extent the total of purchasing power is increased. In time of depression this is a good thing since, as we shall see, it expands production and jobs. But in times of inflationary pressure, it aggravates the upward spiral of prices and makes the shortages of goods worse.

THREE WAYS TO FINANCE EXPENDITURE

Where does the money come from to meet government expenditures? Primarily from three sources: (1) taxes,[1] (2) interest-paying loans, and (3) the issue of noninterest-bearing currency. Normally, taxes are the most important of these; during World War II borrowing was just as important, and during the Revolutionary War paper money was of greater importance.

---

[1] Governments also receive some revenue from miscellaneous sources: sale of surplus equipment, sale of stamps, water, and gas, sale of public land, gifts from the appreciative citizenry, etc.

Let us examine the precise differences among these three methods of finance. Suppose that the government has spent or is about to spend an extra billion dollars on some project that the American people and their legislative representatives deem necessary and desirable.

As a first alternative, the government can use its coercive powers and collect 1 billion dollars from its citizens in the form of one tax or another. Not all citizens would pay the same amount of taxes. Not all citizens would have received the same benefit from the government's expenditure. Some will have received more benefit than they have paid for. Others will have received less benefit than they have paid for, but Congress will have felt that they are better able to afford the tax burden than other groups in the community.

The tax has provided the money for government expenditure. But it has done something else in addition, something that is especially important at a time when there are no idle men or factories. Superficially, the government needs only dollars for its expenditure program. Actually, and much more important, it needs land, capital, and labor resources to carry out its project. Where are these resources to come from if there is full employment everywhere?

Here is where the taxes step in to perform their second, much more important, function in addition to the provision of money. The individuals who are taxed find that their incomes are reduced. Because they cannot spend their receipted tax bills, they are no longer able to buy as much as previously of private consumption goods. These goods were being produced by land, labor, and capital. By contracting the production of such goods (or shifting goods directly to government use), we are releasing resources from the community's private consumption activities and shifting them to its collective governmental activities.

In a full-employment economy, scarcity and choice are all prevailing. The more resources the people consume collectively, the less there is left for them to consume individually, and vice versa. They must choose carefully between the worth to the community on the one hand of more and better hospitals, post offices, agricultural laboratories, and on the other hand, of greater disposable family incomes to be spent individually on more and better clothing, food, shelter, tobacco, and recreation.

FINANCING GOVERNMENT EXPENDITURE BY NEW MONEY

So much for the economic effects of tax finance under full employment. Let us examine the effects under the same conditions of full employment of the opposite method of financing our billion dollars of expenditure—namely, by the third method of printing new money. The government exercises its constitutional powers over the currency to print off one billion nice, new, crisp dollar bills. It finds that people are just as eager to work for these as for any other kind of money since they are all legal tender, interchangeable, and all the rest.

The American people have, therefore, succeeded in getting their billion-dollar collective project completed. The result has been completely painless, hasn't it? Why then ever levy taxes? Death may be inevitable but why must taxes be?

The fallacy in the above arguments applied to a full-employment economy should not be hard to isolate. And make no mistake about it, the arguments are then completely fallacious.

The government needs resources for its project—not primarily money. Where are the resources to come from in a full-employment world? Obviously only from the sacrifices of private individuals. By printing enough money, the government can outbid the present users of land, labor, and capital; it can suck resources into its own use. But in doing so, it will bid up wages, rents, and prices.

Now we see who really foots the bill. Because of the reduction in the supply of goods available for individuals' use, the cost of living will rise beyond the increase in people's money incomes. True, the government has not taken money away from them, but who can eat money or wear it on his back?

Such an increase in government expenditure in a full-employment world will necessarily cause some degree of inflation, and inflation is a mighty tax collector—albeit an indirect and often unobserved one. The hidden tax of higher prices tends to fall most heavily on the poor and on the relatively low-paid white-collar workers whose wages are sticky. There can be no doubt that inflation is a method of taxing, and a highly arbitrary and inequitable one.

FINANCING DEFICITS BY LOAN FINANCE OR BORROWING

We have now analyzed the difference between tax financing and new-money financing in a full-employment world. There remains the intermediate case of loan financing by the sale of government bonds. The government uses the services of land, labor, and capital as before. But it does not pay for these by giving people receipted tax bills as in the first mode of finance. Nor does it simply present them with currency that they can then spend as they please. Instead it gives them I.O.U.'s, payable with compound interest in 1, 5, or 25 years.

There is nothing compulsory about the process. People with savings are glad to subscribe for government bonds rather than have to hold their wealth all idle or in the form of private securities. Government bonds are a particularly attractive investment because they can always be sold on the market or redeemed in case the need should arise. Equally important, there is never any possibility that the government—which has complete powers to issue new currency—would ever be unable to pay off the holders of government bonds in full.

A European might hesitate to hold our bonds under some circumstances because he could only be sure of being paid off in *dollars*, and he would be most concerned about francs or pounds. But an American, whose concern will naturally be with dollars, can always rest easily even though his fortune is invested 99.9 per cent in government bonds, knowing that the dollar value of his principal is perfectly safe. As we shall later see, he cannot be so sure that 5 or 20 years from now the dollars that he gets back will purchase as much goods as they do now. But that is a risk which is not peculiar to government bonds; if he were to buy railroad bonds, he would still run such a risk, along with the additional risk that the principal of his bonds may go into default when the day for collection arrives.

The economic effects of financing a deficit by loans are more nearly like those resulting from the issue of new money than like those resulting from taxation (as is shown in Part Two). Loan financing does not ordinarily cause a significant curtailment of individual consumption and subsequent release of resources for government use. At times of full employment, the result of such deficit financing is likely to be inflationary because prices have to be bid up by the government in order to win resources away from existing users.

If an excess of government expenditure over taxation increases inflationary pressure, then by reversing the process we should have a mechanism for reducing inflationary pressure. Actually this is what was done on a small scale in the postwar period, and should have been done even more intensively. Congress should have (1) cut down on government expenditure and (2) raised taxes in order to convert a deficit into a budgetary surplus. The resulting excess of tax revenue over government expenditure could have been used to retire or pay off part of the public debt; but in any case the heavy tax collections would have reduced the excessive spending of the public and helped to moderate the inflationary pressures. However, it is always easier for us American people and our politicians to vote increases in expenditure and decreases in taxes than the reverse.

WAR FINANCE

As an illustration of the importance of the above remarks, we need only recall that a large part of the costs of World War I were paid for by "inflation taxes" in the United States, Great Britain, France, and Germany.

In this war, we had full employment and heavy new government expenditures. Only by reducing people's incomes through very heavy taxing, could the government have got the resources necessary to fit out and operate our costly military machine. Congress did vote some new taxes: on the incomes of both rich and poor, on the excess profits of corporations, on purchases of furs, cosmetics, liquors, tobacco, and so forth.

Nevertheless, it did not vote new taxes equal to the incredible costs of modern warfare. It was forced, therefore, to finance almost half of its war expenditures by the second method: by selling government bonds to cover its budgetary deficit. To some extent people did cut down their consumption expenditures in order to buy savings bonds. Such bond sales would tend to have the same effects as taxes in releasing resources to the government without a bidding up of prices.

But chiefly, bonds were bought (1) by the banks out of "newly created bank money"—a process that will be described in Part Two, or (2) by individuals and insurance companies out of funds that they were going to save anyway. By and large, therefore, we had every right to expect a tremendous, cataclysmic inflation during the war.

Prices did gradually rise by about one-third, but not at all in the predicted explosive inflationary fashion. Why not? How did the government get its necessary resources without sending prices sky-high? The answer is to be found in the *direct controls* introduced by the government: resources were allocated by order from the civilian production to the war effort; prices were arbitrarily frozen; scarce goods were rationed according to social priorities rather than ability to pay. Without these direct controls, there might well have been chaos, inflation, and even defeat.

FISCAL POLICY DURING BOOM AND DEPRESSION

Our conclusions above concerning the different methods of finance can be summarized simply as they apply to a full-employment economy:

> *Any additional government expenditure which the people think necessary and desirable should be financed by taxes. The primary purposes of taxation are to spread the "real" costs of collective governmental activity fairly and equitably among individuals and to prevent inflation.*

But the economic world as we have known it for the last century and a half is not a stable system in full-employment equilibrium. Occasionally it is running an inflationary fever; often, and for long periods, it is in the frozen torpor of unemployment and slump. Policies that are economically unsound in a full-employment world may be the height of wisdom in a period of deep and prolonged unemployment: levying taxes may be proper when we want people to release resources; in time of depression when we want to increase the number of both private and public jobs, increasing taxes may be disastrous. Similarly, policies that would wreck a normal world may be just what the doctor would order for an economy suffering from a runaway inflation.

No more than a warning to this effect need be sounded at this point. After the analysis of saving and investment in Part Two, the reader will be in a better position to understand the importance and the limitations of government fiscal policy: why the government should run a surplus of taxes over expenditure in times of boom and the reverse in the depression and why it should plan its construction of dams, post offices, and other public works so that they will take place when men and machines are idle and cheap rather than when there is a universal shortage of resources.

In Chap. 8, our discussion of public finance as it relates to the tax systems of the Federal, state, and local governments will be continued. The expenditure of the states and localities, and their coordination with the Federal government and with each other, are also examined.

SUMMARY

1. The economic role of government has been a steadily expanding one. Not only are more and more activities in our complex, interdependent society coming under direct regulation and control, but in addition an ever larger fraction of the nation's output is being devoted to collective governmental consumption. And an increasingly large part of the national income is being "transferred" by taxation and government welfare expenditure from the relatively rich to the relatively poor.

2. Since World War I, Federal expenditure has far outstripped local and state expenditure. During the depression of the 1930's, expenditures on relief, public works, etc., lifted the Federal budget to a level of almost 10 billion dollars. At best, our postwar budget will be more than triple prewar levels because of increased defense outlays, interest on the public debt, and aid to veterans. Should the postwar boom explode in a panic or peter out into a slump, Federal expenditure on public works and development programs will certainly increase in magnitude, at the same time that welfare expenditure for the unemployed and needy will vastly expand.

3. Government expenditure is financed by three sources: taxes, interest-bearing loans, and issue of noninterest-bearing currency. In a full-employment world only the first method can be relied upon to secure an equitable distribution of the real costs of government. And in such a world, only the first will cause sufficient reduction in private individual consumption to release the necessary resources for governmental projects without inflation—that hidden tax collector. The proper fiscal policy for a period of unemployment and slump or for a period of inflation orgy will be discussed later in Part Two.

QUESTIONS FOR DISCUSSION

1. What are some things that the government does today that it didn't formerly do?

2. Between now and 1970, how would you expect the government's share in the national income to develop? Why? What factors would affect your answer?

3. Does the increasing economic cost of government reflect decreasing efficiency? How would you go about making a scientific study of this question?

4. "The radical doctrines of three decades ago are the conservative doctrines of today." Is this ever true? Is it always true? Give favorable illustrations and exceptions.

5. "Government expenditure on goods and services represents collective consumption rather than individualistic consumption, but nevertheless it does represent consumption." Would you always agree? Give your own qualifications.

6. "If the postwar Federal budget is to be brought anywhere near back to the prewar level, the veterans' program and national defense will have to be the main things reduced." Do you agree? Why or why not?

7. Compare the President's last budget message with Table 1. What are the principal differences?

8. What were some of the measures of the New Deal? Which have been abandoned, and which are still in effect?

9. Define and give examples of a transfer payment.

10. Contrast the effects of the three ways of financing government expenditure: (a) under full-employment conditions, and (b) under depressed conditions.

11. How was the war financed? How should it have been?

12. What should be current postwar tax policy?

Chapter 8: THE ECONOMIC ROLE

OF GOVERNMENT: FEDERAL

TAXATION AND LOCAL FINANCE

OUR discussion of public finance continues in this chapter with a survev of the Federal tax system, followed by a brief examination of expenditure and taxation at the state and local levels. It concludes with a short discussion of the problems of coordinating the activities of different levels of government.

FEDERAL TAXATION

The great variety of present Federal taxes is indicated by Table 1.[1] Of these, the first two, personal income and estate, are "equitable" in that they bear down "progressively" more on those people with higher incomes. The last two taxes on sales and payrolls are relatively "regressive" in that they take a larger fraction of the poor man's income than they do of the rich man's. The

[1] These totals may be compared with the more recently available tax estimates for the period July 1, 1948, to June 30, 1949, as presented in the President's Budget Message, January, 1948:

Federal Receipts (In billions of dollars)

Personal income taxes.	$22.5
Corporation taxes.	10.2
Excise taxes.	7.5
Employment taxes.	2.8
Other taxes.	1.5
Total.	$44.5
Minus	
Tax refunds.	2.0
Net total.	$42.5

corporation tax is intermediate in its effects; on balance, it is probably progressive, since the incomes of the well to do are more heavily made up of stock dividends than are poor incomes. Although it is true that many poor workers and orphans own some shares of stock, still the total that they own is not a large fraction of all stock shares. But to the extent that corporations can pass on the tax to the consumer in higher prices, a tax on business profits fails to

TABLE 1. *Tax Receipts of Federal Government, Calendar Year 1946 (In billions)*

1. Personal income:		
Withheld at source	$ 9.2	
Other	8.7	
		$17.9
2. Estate and gift		0.7
3. Corporation:		
Normal corporate and capital stock	$ 4.7	
Excess profits	6.4	
		11.1
4. Payroll and employment taxes		1.8
5. Sales or excise taxes:		
Tobacco (primarily cigarettes)	$ 1.2	
Liquor	2.7	
Retailers excise (cosmetic, furs, etc.)	1.7	
Customs, duties, or imports	0.5	
Miscellaneous taxes	1.6	
		7.7
Total		$39.2

be progressive. Our Federal tax system is immeasurably more progressive than it was 15 years ago or than are the tax systems of the states and localities today. A brief glance at the various taxes may be helpful.

Sales and Excise Taxes. In order of regressiveness, these would probably come first. So-called "liberals" usually oppose these taxes, while "conservatives" extol their virtues. As far as Federal finance is concerned there has resulted a compromise: no general sales tax has been passed, but there are taxes on cigarettes, liquors, amusements, cosmetics, etc. One does not have to be an expert economist to guess whether a tax on movie admissions or sport events is a tax on the rich man's luxury; to judge whether a lipstick tax is confined to Park Avenue rather than Main Street; to know whether a tax on cigarettes causes people to give up smoking or to reduce their consumption of tobacco substantially.

Social Security, Payroll, and Employment Taxes.   Most industries—with the exception of agriculture, nonprofit hospitals and schools, etc.—come under the Social Security Act. All employees are eligible to receive old-age retirement benefits of so much per month, depending upon their previous earnings and not upon any humiliating demonstration of poverty; even Henry Ford was eligible for a retirement pension.

To help pay for these benefits, the employee and employer each contribute 1 per cent of all wage income below $3,000 per year. No insurance company could possibly sell such liberal retirement and other benefits for so small a rate. Consequently, unless Congress follows the original plan of raising tax rates considerably in the near future, it will later have to add a government contribution to that of the employer and employee as the age distribution of the population gradually shifts toward the older ages of retirement.

Taken by itself, the payroll tax is regressive in its impact upon the poor and middle classes. But combined with social security benefit payments, the degree of regressiveness is materially less.[1]

Corporation Income Taxes.   After a corporation has paid all its expenses and reckoned its annual income, it must pay part of its income to the Federal government. The rate varies from year to year; for 1947, corporations were taxed 38 cents out of every dollar of earnings of $50,000 per year or more and slightly less when their earnings are less than that amount.[2]

Some people think that this tax rate is too high, that corporations are discouraged from venturing on worth-while, but risky, job-making investment projects. These people would also argue that a small corporation would be able to grow more rapidly if it could plow back into the business what the government takes in taxes. Proponents of these views say it is sinful "double taxation" for the government to tax corporate earnings and also to make the stockholders pay personal income taxes on the dividends received from corporations.

On the other side there are those who argue that corporations should be taxed heavily, with the bigger corporations taxed at progressively heavier rates. These people believe that, if the government must collect large sums of money, a tax on corporations is better than a sales tax or payroll tax. Moreover, they point out that corporations do not distribute all their earnings to the stock-

[1] Some people, like the author, would question the social wisdom of linking a particular tax to a particular expenditure benefiting those taxed. So long as social security legislation had to be (somewhat dishonestly) sold to the public as an extension of private insurance, this may have been tactically necessary, but surely that day is long past.

[2] During World War II, the excess profits tax on corporations, levied to prevent wartime profiteering, took 85 cents out of every dollar earned in excess of normal profits.

holders but save some to be plowed back in the business. The stockholder avoids personal income tax on these corporation savings, so that according to this viewpoint a corporation tax will at least partially remedy the situation.

The problem is too complex a one to be given a final evaluation here. It is fair to say that the general trend—with which the present writer is in only partial agreement—is to advocate a partial reduction of corporation tax rates in exchange for higher personal income taxes. This last tax is so important as to justify a section to itself.

THE PROGRESSIVE INCOME TAX

Before the war, March 15 was an unhappy day, in which wails of anguish were heard throughout the land as people wrestled with their income tax blanks. Moreover, they had then to pay for the previous year's income, which often had already been spent.

Now things are much better. All through the year every employer automatically withholds from each paycheck most of what the employee will have to pay to the government. This puts us all on a pay-as-you-go basis, so that by the end of the year we are more or less all paid up even if our pay checks have all been spent.

Anyone with an annual income of under $5,000, and no appreciable non-withheld earnings, can at the end of the year simply send in to the government his withholding tax receipt. The government will compute his true tax, compare that with what he has paid, and refund or bill him for the difference. In this way the Bureau of Internal Revenue of the Treasury Department currently computes the tax bills for some 25 million people.

Anyone with an income higher than $5,000, or with income from property of more than $100, or with exceptional contributions to charity, must file a more elaborate income tax return. In fact, early in any year he must make a simple, rough estimate of his income for the rest of the year and how much will be withheld; each 3 months he makes a quarterly payment of the difference between what his tax will probably be and what will be withheld. Thus at the end of the year, he is just about paid up on a true pay-as-you-go basis. On the following March 15, a final reckoning with the government is made, and any difference between earlier provisional payments and the true amount of the tax is settled by a bill or a refund.

This is a tremendous improvement over the previous method of always paying this year for last year's income. In fact, the old method was tolerable only so long as just a few million relatively well-to-do citizens paid income taxes. Before the depression, few family men with incomes of less than $5,000 had to pay a personal income tax or even file a return, because of the very liberal exemptions of income. Now, exemptions have been drastically reduced so that the majority of all wage earners come under the income tax. A single person earning around $500 per year, or as little as $10 per week, will pay some tax. A wife will give a man an extra $500 of exempted income, and each dependent child will exempt an extra $500 of annual income from taxation. (These figures all refer to the 1947 rates, which will undoubtedly undergo modification throughout the years.)

There is still some burning of the midnight oil around the Ides of March by those who are filling out income tax returns. However, many of those who are not permitted simply to sent in their withholding receipt find their work much simplified by using the so-called "short form." This automatically allows a deduction of about 10 per cent for charitable gifts, medical and interest expenses, etc. All you have to do is fill in your name, your current marital status, consult a table, and write in your income tax.

The real grief comes only for those with enough varied income to require the long-form return. They must worry about the depreciation of their trucks, about their capital gains and losses on the sale of land or securities, about filing a joint return by husband and wife so as to avoid higher taxes, about a self-financed trip to the medical convention, about tax-exempt interest from a state bond, etc.

However, even here the difficulties are commonly exaggerated. It is only a moderate intelligence test for any citizen to fill out his own tax form, with or without the aid of the many helpful pamphlets on the subject and with or without the aid of accountants and Bureau of Internal Revenue officials. Perhaps it should be a prerequisite for graduation from high school that the citizen be able to perform this important ritual.

Enough has been said about these details. The important thing is to know about how much a typical individual pays at different income levels, as shown by Table 2. Column (2) shows about how much people would have to pay in taxes for each of the incomes listed in Col. (1). Note that the tax starts at a low figure for poor people and rises very rapidly in relation to income. Indeed, beyond $200,000 of taxable income, about 86 cents of each extra dollar goes to the government and only 14 cents stays with the individual as part of his "disposable" or "spendable" income.

Column (3) shows just how progressive the personal income tax is. A $10,000-a-year man is made to bear a relatively heavier burden than a $3,000-a-year man—26 rather than 11 per cent; and a millionaire is made to bear a still heavier relative burden. Column (4) shows the amount of disposable income left after taxes. Note that it always pays to get more income even if you are as rich as Doris Duke. The government always takes *less* than 86 cents out of each extra dollar.

The income tax appears to be succeeding in its purpose of sharing the cost of government more "equitably or progressively" in relation to income. (The effects of death and gift taxes are in the same direction. They are discussed later in connection with state taxation.) It tends to reduce the inequality of disposable income. Thus, in Fig. 1, the hypothetical effect of progressive

TABLE 2. *Amount of Personal Income Tax to Be Paid at Different Income Levels by a Childless Married Man, 1947*

Income	Personal income tax	Proportion of tax to income	Disposable income left after taxes
(1)	(2)	(3)	(4)
$ 1,000 (or below)	$ 0	0	$ 1,000 (or below)
3,000	330	11	2,670
5,000	700	14	4,300
10,000	2,600	26	7,400
20,000	6,100	30	13,900
50,000	24,000	48	26,000
200,000	148,000	74	52,000
1,000,000	839,000	84	161,000

taxes on the inequality of income is indicated. Note how the area of inequality on the Lorenz diagram has been reduced; progressive taxation has shifted the solid line into the broken line, nearer to the 45° line of perfect equality.

Often, doubts are raised as to whether high income taxes do not discourage effort and risk taking. This is not an easy question to answer since taxation will cause some people to work harder in order to make their million; many doctors, scientists, artists, and businessmen who enjoy their jobs and the sense of power or accomplishment that they bring, will work the same amount for $30,000 as for $100,000; still others may prefer more leisure to work as a result of progressive taxes. The net result is hard to be dogmatic about. We must content ourselves with posing the problem.

The effects of progressive taxes on risky investment are easier to appraise. They are probably adverse. In part the government says to the taxpayer "heads I win, tails you lose." For example, suppose a man earns $200,000 in, one year and nothing in the next three years, while his brother earns $50,000 in each of the four years. Their average earnings before taxes over the period are the same, but the venturesome brother pays over the period $148,000 in taxes, leaving him with a total income after taxes of $52,000 (see Table 2). On the other hand, the steady brother pays a total of only $96,000 in taxes and is left with total income of $104,000 for the period after taxes. In this example, the progression in the tax system has penalized the venturesome brother to the tune of leaving him only half as well off as his conservative brother.

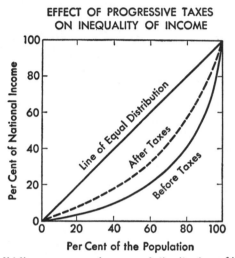

EFFECT OF PROGRESSIVE TAXES
ON INEQUALITY OF INCOME

FIG. 1. The heavy solid line represents the unequal distribution of income before taxes. The broken line shows how progressive taxes result in a more equal distribution of "disposable" income after taxes.

Opposing the unfavorable effect of progressive taxes on investment and jobs, there is an important favorable effect. To the extent that dollars are taken from frugal wealthy people rather than from poor ready spenders, progressive taxes tend to keep purchasing power and jobs at a high level— perhaps at too high a level if inflation is threatening.

Thus no one can be sure whether the unfavorable effects of the personal income tax on investment offset the opposite effects in cutting down potentially excessive savings. In the last analysis, therefore, every voter must decide largely on ethical grounds whether he favors a more or less equalitarian society, greater or smaller rewards to individual initiative.

STATE AND LOCAL EXPENDITURES

Let us now turn to finance other than Federal. Although quantitatively the Federal government's 40 billion dollars of expenditure is about triple that of the states and localities, still these are very important in their own right.

To see what the states and localities spend their money on, turn to Fig. 2 and to Table 3. All these items are more or less self-explanatory. Note that expenditure on schools—mostly by localities—is the biggest single item by

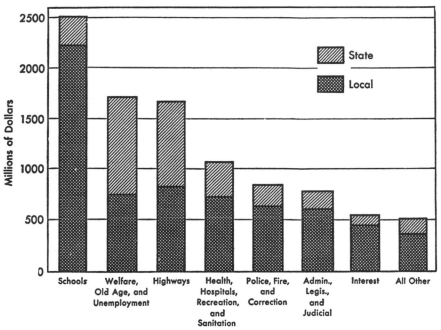

FIG. 2. SOURCE: Federal Reserve Board, *Postwar Economic Studies*, 3.

far. Note also that the salaries of judges, legislators, and so-called "bureaucrats" are only 8 per cent of the total.

STATE AND LOCAL TAXES

To see the main source of funds to finance such expenditure turn to Fig. 3 and Table 4, which show the tax collections of state and local governments. In terms of the previous discussion of kinds of taxes, it must be admitted that, on the whole, the principal taxes of the states and localities are so-called "regressive taxes." Let us discuss some of the more important ones.

Property Tax. It will be noted that the property tax still accounts for almost one-half of the total revenues of state and local finance and that the states have permitted the more needy localities to collect almost all property taxes, as Table 4 shows.

The property tax is levied primarily on real estate, land and buildings, but in some places also on personal property such as furniture and watches. Each

TABLE 3. *Expenditures of State and Local Governments, by Function, 1941 (Dollar items are in millions)*

Function	State	Local	Total	Percentage distribution of total
Cost payments—Total*...............	$3,072	$6,637	$9,709	100.0
Schools.........................	274	2,238	2,512	25.9
Highways.......................	848	823	1,671	17.2
Old-age and unemployment insurance..	486	3	489	5.0
Welfare.........................	485	740	1,225	12.6
Health and hospitals..............	315	284	599	6.2
Corrections.....................	86	65	151	1.6
Sanitation.......................	......	291	291	3.0
Police and fire....................	131	581	712	7.3
General administrative, legislative, and judicial.......................	190	601	791	8.2
Interest.........................	111	456	567	5.8
Recreation......................	15	171	186	1.9
All other.......................	131	384	515	5.3
Debt retirement†....................	238	615	853	

SOURCE: Federal Reserve Board, *Postwar Economic Studies*, 3, p. 104. U.S. Department of Commerce, Bureau of the Census, *Financing Federal, State and Local Governments*, 1941, p. 54. This table includes payments from funds received from other governments.

* Excludes net addition to reserves of 544 million dollars, for old-age and unemployment insurance, and 142 million for contributions to pension funds.

† Not included in the total.

locality sets an annual tax rate. Thus, in a large city $35 on each $1,000 of assessed valuation (3.5 per cent) may be the tax rate. This means that I must pay $350 of property taxes if my house has been assessed as being worth $10,000. However, in many places assessed valuations tend to be some fraction of true market value. Perhaps my house and all like it have a current market value of $15,000, but they may be assessed at about two-thirds that much.

Really therefore, my true property tax rate is a little less than 3.5 per cent, nearer to 2.4 per cent.

The property tax is very inflexible. Rates and assessments tend to be changed only slowly. In bad times when real-estate values fall, the tax is very burdensome and gives rise to bankruptcy, mortgage foreclosures, and forced sales.

In colonial times, a man's total income and wealth may have been all connected with real estate. Even then the property tax increased a rich man's taxes

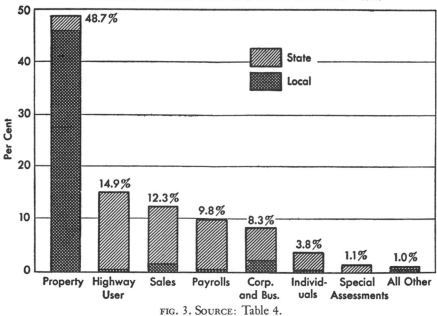

FIG. 3. SOURCE: Table 4.

only in proportion to his total property—instead of increasing his taxes in greater proportion than income, as do modern progressive taxes. Furthermore, today when so much of wealth and income is divorced from real estate, many well-to-do people are able to avoid state and local taxes almost completely. Also, it is well known that small properties tend to be assessed relatively higher than large. For these reasons the property tax is far from ideal.

Highway User Taxes. As the name suggests, these revenues come from two primary sources: from a tax of so many pennies per gallon of gasoline and from license fees on automobiles, trucks, and drivers. In many states, more dollars are collected in this way than are spent on roads and bridges. The extra revenues are used for schools, old-age pensions, and other needs, just as in some colleges extra revenue from football games is used to buy track equipment or even Greek manuscripts.

TABLE 4. *Tax Revenues of State and Local Governments, 1941* (Dollar items are in millions)*

Source and type of revenue	State†	Local	Total	Percentage distribution of total
Total............................	$4,507	$4,708	$9,215	100
Property..........................	268	4,224	4,492	49
Sales and gross receipts..............	1,033	98	1,131	12
General sales.....................	575	66	641	7
Alcoholic beverages.................	216	......	216	2
Tobacco products..................	107	‡	107	1
Public-utility receipts..............	90	......	90	1
Miscellaneous excises..............	45	32	77	1
Payrolls...........................	901	5	906	10
Corporation and business.............	586	181	767	8
Corporate net income..............	197	2	199	2
Corporate license and privilege.......	79	40	119	1
Insurance premiums................	98	......	98	1
Alcoholic beverages...............	58	35	93	1
Severance and other...............	154	104	258	3
Individuals........................	343	3	346	4
Net income......................	225	2	227	3
Inheritance, estate, and gift...........	118	1	119	1
Highway user......................	1,346	31	1,377	15
Motor-vehicle fuels................	913	7	920	10
Motor-vehicle licenses and operators...	433	24	457	5
Special assessments..................	......	102	102	1
All other..........................	30	64	94	1

SOURCE: Federal Reserve Board, *Postwar Economic Studies*, 3, p. 108.

* Adapted from U.S. Department of Commerce, Bureau of the Census, *Statistics of Sales*, 1941, and *Financing Federal, State, and Local Governments*, 1941.

† The amounts include local shares of state-collected taxes.

‡ Less than $500,000.

These highway taxes are usually justified on the ground that the taxpayer is simply paying for the *benefit* of using the roads in much the same way as he pays for a railroad ticket or for his use of water and electricity.

Sales Taxes. In the past few years many states have begun to rely more and more on excises levied on tobacco, alcohol, and even on general sales. Most people—including many cigarette smokers and moderate drinkers—have a vague feeling that there is something immoral about tobacco and alcohol. They feel as though two birds are being killed with one stone when these articles are taxed; the state gets revenue and vice is made more expensive.

The same rationalization is not possible for, say, a 5 per cent tax on everything that a consumer buys whether it is a pair of shoes, a cake of soap, or a church candle. Rich and poor are taxed alike on each dollar spent; and since the poor are forced to spend a larger portion of their total dollars, it is easy to see that the sales tax is a regressive tax; *i.e.*, it takes a larger portion of low incomes than of high ones. Most economists therefore regard it as an undesirable, inequitable tax which is only the child of necessity. Except as applied to clear-cut luxuries, they think it should be replaced by more progressive taxes, such as personal income or inheritance taxes.

Payroll and Business Taxes. States and localities often charge license fees for the privilege of acting as a corporation, running a tavern, and so forth. Some states tax the net income of a corporation as well, and collect miscellaneous other fees from business enterprises.

In addition, all states have been bribed by the Federal government into collecting a wage tax equal to about 3 per cent of payrolls in occupations covered by social security. The proceeds are used to provide "unemployment compensation benefits or insurance" when workers become unemployed. Before the Federal Social Security Act was passed (1935), the few pioneering states, like Wisconsin and Ohio, that had unemployment insurance schemes were at a disadvantage. Industries would threaten, and occasionally more than threaten, to leave the state for neighboring places where there were no such unemployment compensation taxes and where an employer could wash his hands of a discharged worker. Naturally, even the states with good intentions tended to be dragged down to the level of those which were most irresponsible.

The Social Security Act changed all that. Instead of passing a Federal act that many experts favored and many opposed, the national government accomplished the same thing by indirection. It passed a 3 per cent payroll tax on all states—but offered to rebate most of the proceeds to every state that set up a suitable unemployment compensation system. Of course, every one of the 48 states suddenly discovered within its legislatures a burning enthusiasm for the unemployed worker, since now this cost the state and its citizens nothing extra. The economics of social security as it concerns the individual and family will be discussed further in Chap. 10.

Personal Income and Inheritance Taxes.   More than half the states imitate the Federal government, but on a much smaller scale, by taxing individuals according to the size of their incomes. Such a method of taxation has already been discussed in connection with Federal finance. A few important states, such as Illinois, do not rely at all on this relatively progressive tax; moreover, almost all those states that have an income tax could increase rates and collect more revenue from this source. But the greatest difficulty in applying this equitable tax at the state level is the fact that the Federal government already makes such intensive use of the personal income tax as to leave relatively little.

Inheritance taxes on individuals who inherit bequests of property upon death of a relative or friend are self-explanatory. They differ only in minor detail from estates taxes that are levied on the dead giver's estate and not on the receivers. Also, it will be obvious that gifts must be taxed, or else wealthy people would have every incentive to distribute before death all their wealth to their heirs, so as to escape taxation then.

Both the Federal and the state governments share in estate and inheritance taxes. Once again, the Federal government had to act to prevent states like Florida from advertising to old folks, "Come here to die and avoid all inheritance taxes." The Federal Government gives up part of its revenues to any state that passes such a tax law, by accepting a state tax receipt in part payment of a citizen's taxes. However, it goes only a small part of the whole way in this respect.

The inheritance and estates tax is called a progressive and democratic tax. The poor widow's inheritance usually pays no tax at all because of liberal exemptions, while the rich man's estate pays at a progressive rate. Social reformers attach great importance to death taxes for the purpose of preventing the development in this country of a permanent moneyed caste, living not on its effort and intelligence, but on its property inherited from one generation to the next.

There are other miscellaneous revenues which need hardly be described. Some localities sell natural gas and electricity. Some tax slot machines and race-track betting. All collect some revenue from assessments on property owners who benefit from specific sewage and road improvements. A much more important revenue source, as we shall see in a moment, is the financial aid which the states receive from the Federal government and which localities receive from the states.

Borrowing and Debt Repayment.   When all is counted in, it is still not true that the total of state and local expenditures equals the total of their revenues.

The difference represents new borrowing or debt repayment. Since 1940, wartime prosperity has swelled their tax revenues (despite the rationing of gasoline). At the same time it became impossible to build new schools and highways, and unnecessary to support so many needy people on relief.

As a result, most states were able to run a surplus and retire part of their previously accumulated debt. This opportunity will continue in the postwar period for as long as the industrial boom holds out. A few foolish states are failing to prepare in this way for the time when it will again be necessary and desirable to build public works and finance relief; these states are cutting tax rates and in doing so are adding to people's purchasing power and thereby, feeding more fuel to the immediate postwar inflationary flames.

Such states are the exception today. However, between World War I and World War II, most state and local borrowing tended to behave perversely so as to accentuate rather than damp down the business cycle. During the prosperous 1920's when the Federal government was retiring part of its war debt, states and localities floated tremendous amounts of bonds, so as to build needed highways and schools at the high prices then prevailing. When the depression of the 1930's came, despite the publicity given to emergency borrowing of some cities, *state and local governments on balance reduced their debts!* They refused to build necessary public works even though costs were advantageous and jobs were desperately needed. Instead, they began to lean more and more on the Federal government in this matter of public works as well as in connection with unemployment relief.

It is perhaps too much to ask the states and localities to take an active part in moderating the business cycle. But a minimum goal would be for them, if they cannot do good, at least to do no harm. If they are too weak to increase their outlay in depression, at least they should endeavor to withstand the temptation of increasing their expenditures in boom times. If they follow this advice, their dollars will go farther and the problem of unemployment will not be quite such a great and difficult one.

COORDINATING DIFFERENT LEVELS OF GOVERNMENT

Existing state and local boundaries do not reflect true economic entities. Gary, Ind., is more truly a part of the Greater Chicago metropolitan region than it is of Indiana, and a similar relationship holds between Greenwich, Conn., and New York City. Relatively well-to-do people can commute from Wellesley, Mass., to Boston in order to avoid having to share the high tax burden of keeping up Boston streets and aiding the Boston poor; and New Jersey suburbs beckon the wealthy New Yorker with the assurance that there is no income tax across the Hudson.[1] To avoid taxes, wealthy cosmopolitans even tried a few years ago to leave the United States for legal residences in Bermuda and elsewhere, until the war sent them scurrying home to the protecting arms of the Statue of Liberty.

What can be done about all these problems of coordinating different levels of government? The answer must be faced primarily in terms of political science rather than economics. In part we can and have set up new units of government cutting across existing boundaries: the Port of New York Authority, the Cook County Sanitary Commission, etc. All these fill a function. But sometimes the result is a patchwork of confusion. Thus, within the Greater Chicago area alone, there are literally *hundreds* of different units of government: three or four states, innumerable counties, townships and municipalities, etc. Worse than that, any one citizen will be under the separate jurisdiction of a score of such overlapping agencies. It is not only that he doesn't know where to go when he gets a ticket for speeding; he is actually paying taxes to the city of Chicago, to Cook County, to a School District, etc., etc.

From an economic point of view, some of the worst aspects of the existing situation are partially corrected by having the states make grants of money to the localities. In 1941, out of 4.5 billion dollars of state tax revenues, about one-third was shared with the localities—primarily for schools, highways, and public assistance (relief, old-age pensions, aid to blind, etc.). Only in this way can the poorer parts of each state maintain certain minimum standards of schooling, roads, and living. Only in this way can well-to-do suburbanites be prevented from running out completely upon their fair share of public responsibility.

Just as there are differences in financial need and income within a state, so are there tremendous differences in income and needs in different parts of the country. The South in particular has such a low economic income as to penalize seriously its citizens in the pursuit of an adequate education and standard of living. The logical step has been for the Federal government, with its great taxing power all over the country, to share some of its revenues with the states —particularly since most modern economic problems (such as unemployment, good roads, etc.) are national in scope.

In 1941, the Federal government made "grants-in-aid" to the states of some three-quarters of a billion dollars, or of as much as one-sixth of their total tax revenues. These grants were primarily for highways, public assistance, and education (vocational and agricultural training, etc.). Moreover, in the depressed years in the 1930's, the Federal government made very large gifts

---

[1] The city of Philadelphia collects a 1 per cent tax on all wages earned by people working there, whether or not they live somewhere outside the city limits and commute.

to the states and localities in the form of hospitals, schools, and other public works constructed under the WPA (Works Progress Administration) and PWA (Public Works Administration).

To show how a typical grant-in-aid works, let us consider the Federal old-age program under the Social Security Act. This consists of two parts: a contributory old-age pension plan run completely by the Federal government, in which employees in most industries other than agriculture receive automatically—regardless of their needs—certain old-age benefits (pension, insurance, etc.) toward which they and their employers have helped to pay. This was discussed earlier in connection with the 3 per cent Federal payroll tax. It has nothing to do with the states and will not be discussed further at this point.

However, there is a second part of the Social Security Act requiring the Federal government to make "matching" grants-in-aid to the states to help them give assistance to the needy, aged, and handicapped. Thus, if New York State will vote $45 a month to its needy aged people, then the Federal government will pay two-thirds of the first $15 and match the rest dollar for dollar (up to a total pension of $45 a month), thereby making the cost to the state only $20. Such a matching grant is easy to administer because of its automatic character. Also, it obviously acts as an inducement to get the states to vote money for old-age assistance, since every dollar they provide does double duty.

On the other hand, such a grant partially fails in its purpose of equalizing standards between rich and poor states. Thus, the state of Mississippi which cannot, or thinks it cannot, afford to vote pensions of much more than $15 per month, will receive only about $10 from the Federal government. At the same time, wealthy New York is receiving $25 from the Federal government. Once more we are up against a case of "to him who hath shall be given." It remains to be seen whether some future Congress will pass a remedying law in which grants-in-aid to the states will be based upon, and vary inversely with, the level of per capita state incomes.

The atomic bomb has perhaps taught us that ours is One World. We have yet to learn the full significance of the fact that this is One Country.

SUMMARY

This chapter has examined the important taxes relied upon by the Federal and local governments and has shown how much these differ in progressiveness. In addition, the patterns of local and state expenditure have been surveyed, and the interrelation between different levels of government.

QUESTIONS FOR DISCUSSION

1. Make a list of different kinds of taxes in order of their progressiveness. What is the importance of each at the (a) Federal, (b) state, and (c) local level?

2. About how much would a childless married man pay in income tax at the present time if his total income was $2,000, $5,000, $20,000, or $1,000,000?

3. List different state and local expenditure categories in order of their quantitative importance.

4. How do you think different government functions should be allocated among the three levels of government? How about revenues and grants-in-aid?

5. What has been your own state's postwar fiscal policy? Do you approve? Why?

Chapter 9: LABOR

ORGANIZATION AND PROBLEMS

AT the end of World War II, 15 million workers, or about half of all the eligible employees in private industry, were members of trade-unions or worked under collective bargaining contracts. Among manufacturing wage earners, the proportions were even greater; and in many lines such as automobiles, men's clothing, basic steel, coal mining, railways, and construction, the fraction ranged well over 80 or 90 per cent. In fact, the only fields in which there were relatively few union members were agriculture, domestic service, retail and wholesale trade, and white-collar or professional occupations.[1]

Figure 1 shows the prodigious growth of union membership since 1900: the slow, steady advance up to World War I; the upsurge during that war and immediately thereafter; the rather sharp decline and leveling off during the 1920's; the explosive acquisition of new members during the New Deal years of recovery from the depths of the Great Depression; and finally the continued rapid growth since the beginning of World War II.

The bulk of organized labor belongs to unions that are affiliated either with the AFL or the CIO, each having about 6 million members. In addition there are a number of independent unions, the most important being the four great Railroad Brotherhoods (locomotive engineers, firemen, conductors, and trainmen).

HISTORY OF THE AMERICAN LABOR MOVEMENT

The history of trade-unions in this country goes back a long way. More than a century ago local and national unions of skilled craftsmen were formed;

[1] For a fuller account of organized labor, the reader may be referred to Florence Peterson, "American Labor Unions," Harper & Brothers, New York, 1945, upon which considerable reliance has been placed in writing this chapter.

in many ways—such as in their apprenticeship regulations—these craft unions were the vestigial outgrowth of the medieval guilds. In the half century after the Civil War, frequent attempts were made to organize American labor into one great union; but after 1886, the most successful attempt of this kind, the Knights of Labor, passed its peak of membership and became extinct.

During this same decade of the 1880's, the AFL was successfully launched. The philosophy of this organization, under the leadership of its long-time president, Samuel Gompers, was the antithesis of a revolutionary political

MEMBERSHIP IN AMERICAN LABOR UNIONS

FIG. 1. SOURCE: Florence Peterson, *American Labor Unions*, Harper and Brothers, New York, 1945.

movement. It did not sponsor a new political party, but confined its political activity to endorsing those candidates of either party who favored labor and humanitarian legislation. It was not one big union, but was simply a loose federation whose constituent autonomous parts consisted of the national (or if we include Canada, international) craft unions. Its goals were improved wages and conditions of work immediately rather than long-run reform, its outlook was evolutionary, and its motto was "More, more, and more—now."

CRAFT VERSUS INDUSTRIAL UNIONS

The CIO was formed in 1935 when John L. Lewis of the UMW (United Mine Workers), the late Sidney Hillman of the Amalgamated Clothing Workers Union, and a number of other leaders became dissatisfied with the craft union setup of the AFL that constantly gave rise to bitter jurisdictional disputes and made unionization of the mass-production industries difficult or impossible. Later after a whirlwind campaign, the CIO succeeded in organizing on an *industrial* rather than *craft* basis such basic industries as steel (United Steel Workers), automobiles (United Auto, Aircraft, & Equipment Workers), electrical and radio (United Electrical, Radio, & Machine Workers of America), textiles (Textile Workers Union of America), and many others.

The various advantages and disadvantages of industrial versus craft unions are each numerous. Modern technology has been gradually displacing the old craft skills. Cigars are now largely rolled by machine without the aid of highly skilled craftsmen; glass blowing has been largely replaced by machine technology. In a modern automobile plant, each person is performing a different function, and it would be difficult to get very far if two men working side by side had to belong to different unions. All this argues in favor of industrial unions, including all the workers in a given plant or industry regardless of their special skills.

Craft unionization, on the other hand, is most successful where there is a small group whose members, because of their strategic importance, are in a position to bargain for very high wages. Although there are some industrial unions in the AFL, it is still fair to say that, as compared to the CIO, the former consists largely of craft rather than industrial unions.[1]

STRUCTURE OF THE LABOR MOVEMENT

Despite its industrial union character, the CIO is organized along the same general lines as the AFL. Both are simply loose federations of autonomous national unions, with officers elected by the national unions and with strictly limited powers of authority over these national units. However, the CIO executive board in fact has more power and authority than the AFL central organization.

The national unions, whether organized largely on industrial lines as in the CIO, or largely on craft lines as in the AFL, have as their constituent parts the local unions. These locals, through business agents or shop stewards, help to bargain collectively with management, along with representatives of the national union. Figure 2 shows the organization charts of the AFL and the CIO, both being very nearly the same in form.

In addition to the national and local units, there are city and state federations or industrial councils, whose functions are simply those of cooperation in the production of radio programs, parades, and election or strike solidarity. Also, as will be seen from the chart, both the AFL and the CIO have a few local unions directly attached to them rather than to any national union. Usually, these locals are in new fields just in process of being organized or in fields that

[1] In recent years, John L. Lewis of the UMW and David Dubinsky (of the International Ladies' Garment Workers Union), leaders of two important industrial unions, left the CIO and rejoined the AFL. In 1947 the miners quit the AFL.

fall between the jurisdiction and territories of the constituent national unions. During the war, the CIO began to take an active role in political campaigning through its PAC (Political Action Committee).

CASE STUDY OF AN AFL CARPENTER

Let us seek to understand the nature of the modern American labor movement through an examination of the case histories of some important, typical participants.

STRUCTURE OF AMERICAN UNIONS

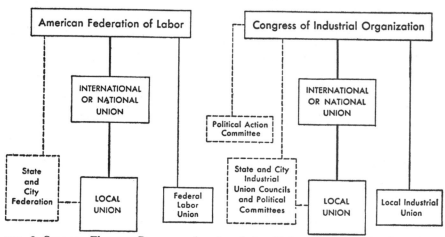

FIG. 2. SOURCE: Florence Peterson, *American Labor Unions*, Harper & Brothers, New York, 1945.

John Kennedy is a carpenter in a large American city. He is one of more than half a million members of the United Brotherhood of Carpenters and Joiners, affiliated with the AFL. Being just over sixty years old, he remembers back a long way to the years before World War I, when he used to make only 30 cents an hour as a nonunion man. He has been a union member for more than 40 years, and now is being paid about $2 an hour for a 5½-day week, with overtime pay for any work over 8 hours a day. However, he usually is laid off 20 weeks a year during the winter, and so his annual earnings are only about $2,500.

This hourly wage rate was set for him by a contract between the local carpenter's union and the employer. Today, he says he would "starve or go on relief" before working for less than this standard union rate, although back in 1931 he became so desperate for work that he secretly "kicked back" part of his pay to his boss, a small-scale contractor who might otherwise have had to go out of business.

It goes without saying that Kennedy would refuse to work on any job where there was a nonunion carpenter. In fact his employer has signed a "closed shop" contract obliging himself to hire only union men. Kennedy favors a closed shop because he happens to think it sinful not to belong to a union, and because he doesn't see why a nonunion worker, who pays no dues, should benefit from the pay increases won by the union. He is hot under the collar over the Taft-Hartley Labor Relations Act of 1947 which bans the closed shop. He calls this series of amendments to the Wagner National Labor Relations Act (1935) the "Slave Labor Act."

During the postwar housing boom, his employer has been having great difficulty in getting as many union men as he would like. Because of the long depression slump in building, many of the carpenters are elderly men like Kennedy. Theoretically, anyone can join the union by paying a $10 minimum initiation fee; but actually in Kennedy's local the fee is $100. Moreover, he must serve long years of apprenticeship. The situation is eased a little by the fact that the carpenter's union local gives temporary *work permits*, but not full union membership, to a number of returning war veterans. Kennedy's union dues are only about $2 a month, and part of this goes for a pension in his old age.

Back in the early 1920's, Kennedy's union had a tough time weathering the concerted attack made on all unions by business groups, who had taken their cue from the successful smashing of organized labor by the United States Steel Corporation after the unsuccessful 1919 strike. Kennedy's son, who went out to Southern California to work, was forced for a while in 1922 to sign a "yellow-dog" contract, in which in return for his job he swore away his freedom to join a union. Kennedy is rather profane on the subject: "They called it the 'American Plan.' Well, that's not my idea of Americanism!"

Usually Kennedy votes for the Democratic party, but in 1924 he followed the AFL in voting for "Old Bob" LaFollette's Progressive third party. In 1928, he was back voting for Al Smith. Although he was strong for Franklin Roosevelt, Kennedy wasn't so sure about Truman; and in 1946 he considered following the lead of the president of his international union who is a strong Republican. But Truman's unsuccessful veto of the Taft-Hartley Act put Kennedy back in the Democratic fold.

Kennedy has no use for communists and he has never met one face to face— fortunately for the communist. Although his father came from Ireland in 1870, Kennedy approved the AFL's efforts to keep wages up by stopping the flow of cheap immigrant labor. He also thinks that tariffs to keep down the competition of low-paid foreign labor—and for that matter if it could be arranged, of low-paid Southern labor—are good. Although no "Ku Kluxer," he approves of his union's policy of letting Negroes join only special locals, and of often not letting them work for white contractors.

Kennedy's local is run about as he thinks it should be; but he has heard more than rumors to the effect that liquor gangsters "muscled in" on the union of a near-by city back in 1929, and through violence have been extorting large sums of money from both union members and from employers. However, he is against any "antilabor racketeering" legislation; first because he is automatically against all antilabor legislation, and second because he thinks that the enemies of labor will use such laws to harm legitimate union activities.

CASE STUDY OF A CIO INDUSTRIAL UNIONIST

Shelby White works for a large auto company in Detroit. Although only 29, he has been pulling down top pay for 10 of the 12 years since he thumbed a ride north from the Tennessee mountain country where he was born. He belongs to the UAW (United Automobile, Aircraft, and Implement Workers of America, CIO). Unlike Kennedy's AFL craft union this is an *industrial* union comprising as members all workers in the plant, including helpers, maintenance workers, janitors, craftsmen, truckers, etc., and involving many different skills and no skills at all. White's UAW local was recognized as sole bargaining agent of the workers only after a titanic battle with the company, which refused to do so until ordered to under the 1935 National Labor Relations Act (the Wagner Act) by the Federal courts.

White doesn't have to read the report of a congressional committee to refresh his memory of how the company at first hired "finks" and "goons"—gunners and spies—from a strikebreaking agency, in order to beat up union organizers; or how men who joined the union were laid off on the pretext of inefficiency and then put on an employers' "black list" as far as getting a job elsewhere; or how a "company" or "stooge" union was encouraged by management when it began to see the handwriting on the wall. Finally, after a number of illegal "sit-down" and "slow-down" strikes, and after a dozen people on both sides were killed in violent picketing, the Federal government's NLRB (National Labor Relations Board) held an election in the plant to see whether the union should be recognized as "sole bargaining" agent, and the UAW won with a comfortable majority.

The company White works for is quite efficient and profitable, and he highly approves of his union leaders' periodic attempts to capture some of these earnings by hiking up their wage demands on the basis of the company's "ability to pay." White, like most of his coworkers, usually votes "yes" whenever there is a strike vote. In fact, there's nothing he likes better than a nice, brief, successful strike. It's almost like a short vacation, and with some added excitement. But when a strike drags on for a long time, as it did in the spring of 1946, so that his war savings began to go fast, White begins to share his wife's bitterness against the blankety-blank company, and the blankety-blank union leaders who should have known better.

Being a Southerner, White at first resented having Negroes in his union and working on the same jobs, but now he takes this fact for granted. There is a small, but vocal and well-organized, percentage of his union members who seem to follow the communist party line. White hasn't much use for them, but they occasionally outsmart him by shrewed tactics at union meetings, and also by coming out strong for many of the things that he, himself, is for. He'd just as soon they weren't in the union, but he still likes them better than "scabs" (people who work during a strike), "stool pigeons," or "eager beavers" who speed up the tempo of output in order to get more pay, without thinking what the effect may be on the number of jobs and on piece rates.

CASE STUDY OF A LABOR LAWYER

Sam Green is an old-time labor lawyer who works primarily for unions in the clothing trades. Before World War I he went to night school, learning law and English at the same time, and he's still better at the former than the latter. Today, he's pretty prosperous and also pretty busy. If you ask him, he'll tell you that it's a pleasanter business than it used to be because now he's not always on the losing end. If you get him started, he"ll tell you what "Big" and "Little" Steel used to get away with in the courts and with the help of the police and the militia, and how Tom Mooney was railroaded off to jail.

If you pin him down on details, he's less interesting but more informative. He'll tell you how the Sherman Antitrust Act (1890) was used against unions, until in 1914 Congress passed the Clayton Antitrust Act, declaring that labor is not a "commodity," and attempting to remove trade-union organizations from liability on the charge of monopolistic conspiracy and restraint of trade. But the Clayton Act never did really achieve its purpose. He'll tell you how judges used to use "court injunctions" to break up strikes and peaceful picketing, until the 1932 Norris-LaGuardia Act limited the use of Federal injunctions in labor disputes (and also prohibited the yellow-dog contract). Green will get red in the face recalling the famous Danbury Hatters case (1908) where the Court held every member of the Hatter's union responsible to the full extent of his personal property for damage done to the company as a result of a nation-wide economic boycott. He remembers too the legislative and judicial battles over minimum wage and maximum hour legislation for women, child-labor restriction, factory-safety conditions, and workmen's accident compensation.

But since the NRA (National Recovery Administration) days of Franklin Roosevelt's first term, and particularly since the 1935 Wagner Act, the pendulum was swinging his way. Too much so say the lawyers who oppose him in court. But to Green, who admits that he is not impartial, the Wagner Act only corrected the inequities and inequality of bargaining power as between labor and management that existed prior to that date.

In any case, the Wagner Act explicitly encouraged "collective bargaining" between workers and management with respect to wages and conditions of work. Under its provisions an employer could be found guilty of an "unfair labor practice" if he refused to bargain collectively with employee representatives; discriminated against or interfered with their rights to form and participate in union activities; and gave financial or other support to a union of the employer's choice. A clever lawyer like Green could have an employer hauled up before the NLRB—set up by the Wagner Act—if he made coercive speeches to his men during the lunch hour, or sent them post cards telling them that the company would have to close down and they would all lose their jobs unless the union desisted from its mad, exorbitant wage demands.

Green thinks that the Federal Fair Labor Standards Act of 1938, setting a minimum wage of 40 cents per hour (after 1945) and maximum standard hours of 40 per week for all producers of goods engaged in interstate commerce,[1] is one of the best things that ever happened to low-paid nonunion labor, particularly in the South. In 1948, he strongly backed the campaign in Congress to raise the minimum, in graduated steps, to 65 cents per hour.

Sam Green is not so glib when you press him on "unpeaceful picketing," or the "secondary boycott" in which labor not only boycotts the offending employer but also all other concerns who continue to do business with him. When you ask him whether a union should not be forced to make public financial reports and perhaps be accountable for breaches in its contract, he merely shrugs his shoulders and asserts his belief that such measures are proposed by those who want to kill unions.

The Taft-Hartley Act has changed everything for Green. Until the new

---

[1] Green is also delighted that, after a 30-year struggle with the courts and legislators, an effective curb on child labor in certain occupations was written into this law.

situation is clarified—which may take years—he is sure of only one thing: he and other lawyers on both sides are going to be kept awfully busy.

THE CASE OF THE PHILANTHROPIC CAPITALIST

Daniel Peterson is a self-made rich man. His metal-products plant hires 1,000 men, and until 10 years ago he knew every man by his first name. Peterson prides himself on his good employee relations, always paying higher than prevailing wages, giving his employees bonuses at Christmas, and during the 1920's letting them buy shares of stock in the company. Until the Great Depression, he had instituted a guaranteed wage and employment plan, by which every regular was sure of at least 48 weeks of work a year.

Back in the old days when the work force went out on a picnic, Peterson often went along, and provided a keg of beer for the occasion. He encouraged them to form a Worker's Association and Athletic Club, for paternalistic reasons and because management received many helpful suggestions from its members and learned of grievances that required correcting. When the association turned into a company union, he let them have the soft-drink concession in the plant. He opposed the attempts of outside organizers to form a CIO union, primarily because he was convinced that it would not help the workers and that they really didn't want it. Because of the principle of the thing, he fought the union even when it was costing him (and his stockholders) money. Except for the time when his small son died of scarlet fever, he never felt so bad as on the day when one of the two competing outside unions won the NLRB election and gained recognition as sole bargaining agent.

He had to admit that things were more peaceful, at first, after the union was finally recognized. The bitter three-way fight between the AFL, CIO, and company union had kept anybody from getting much work done; and in order to gain popularity the different unions had vied with each other in the unreasonableness of their demands. The new written contract with the union concerning wages, hours, and vacations was scrupulously adhered to by both sides, and the following year was renewed with little change, except for a 5 per cent wage increase right down the line.

But the next time the contract came up, the union demanded and won a "maintenance of union membership" clause and also the "automatic checkoff." Under the former clause (which in 1946 covered about one-third of all workers under collective agreements) a worker does not have to join the union, but once he becomes a member, he is limited in his freedom to quit it for the duration of the agreement. Under the automatic check-off, the company turns over a member's union dues directly out of his pay check. (Two-fifths of all workers under collective agreements in 1946 came under some sort of check-off arrangement.)

Peterson also had to swallow the union's rules concerning seniority, often having to lay off efficient and loyal younger men in favor of those who had been on the job longer. He later fought, but lost, the battle against a "union shop" clause, whereby he could hire whom he pleased, but after a certain period of time (usually 30 days) they had to join the union. He was still fighting the union's demand for a closed shop, whereby even new employees must be hired through the union or must at least be union members when hired, when his state legislature and a voters' referendum made it illegal. However, being engaged in interstate commerce, he feared that the Supreme Court would declare him to be out of state jurisdiction. His worries on this score are over now that the Taft-Hartley Act explicitly gives state legislatures the go-ahead signal to superimpose their own restrictions on union abuses on top of Federal controls.

At times Peterson feels almost friendly toward the union. During the war, they stuck to their no-strike pledge, and Peterson was kept from acceding to their demands for pay increases only by the War Labor Board's refusal to permit more than the 15 per cent increases in wages granted by the "Little Steel Formula" to compensate for wartime increases in the cost of living. Peterson did the next best thing, granting 2 weeks vacation with pay. He is also grateful to the union because it has raised wage rates in Southern industry, and reduced that region's competitive differential.

But just when he was feeling well disposed toward the union, after V-J day it asked for an "outrageous" 30 per cent increase in hourly pay so as to "preserve wartime take-home pay." He refused, offering a 13 per cent increase. After a lengthy strike—which would have been even more costly to Peterson's company were it not for its right to get a "carry-back tax rebate" from the government under the excess profits tax provision for losses—a "fact-finding" board recommended an 18½ per cent rate increase. This was finally agreed upon. In the postwar period, Peterson often dreams of the good old days—gone forever. In his reveries there is more lament for the loss of his freedom to run the business his own way, than for his loss of profits.

A CONGRESSMAN'S VIEW OF THE TAFT-HARTLEY ACT OF 1947

Roger M. Cabot is a Republican congressman from upstate New York. He is no reactionary, having broken with his party in 1935 to back the Wagner National Labor Relations Act. But in 1947 he not only voted to amend the

Wagner Act by the (Taft-Hartley) Labor-Management Relations Act of 1947; more than that, he voted to override President Truman's veto. The reason for this turnabout is simple: Cabot and many of his constituents back home feel that labor and its leaders are becoming too "uppity." He is sick and tired of having every spring bring robins and a coal strike as well. He is particularly incensed against work stoppages that tie up the whole country and create a national emergency.

The Taft-Hartley Act involves more than 20 pages of fine print. It contains hundreds of provisions that he doesn't pretend to understand. But primarily he and other congressmen aimed at a *two-edged* National Labor Relations Act that—unlike the Wagner Act—will prescribe standards of conduct for unions as well as for employers. It can accomplish this, Cabot has to admit, only by increasing the degree of government control over labor relations.

Some of the principal features of the Labor-Management Act of 1947 are briefly as follows:

1. *The closed shop is banned.* Employers do not have to hire union men. Even a union shop, where the employee must join the union within 30 days, is *permitted* only where a majority of all *eligible* workers (not of all those voting) insist upon this. State legislatures are given a free hand to impose stronger restrictions.

2. *Strikes in essential industries may be banned by Federal injunction.* In this reversal of earlier legislation, the U.S. Attorney General can ask for an 80-day court injunction in situations that would "imperil the national health or safety." (The powers and duties of the NLRB to secure court injunctions against unfair labor practices are also expanded.)

3. *Unfair labor practices on the part of unions are defined for the first time. Unions can be sued,* among other things for violation of a no-strike contract. Unions are now to be held responsible for acts of their agents. Their health and welfare funds are to be subject to strict supervision. Their exclusive right to handle grievances is curtailed. Their initiation fees cannot be unreasonable. They are forbidden to "featherbed" (*i.e.*, exact pay for services not performed). They must bargain collectively. Their right to an automatic checkoff of union dues is limited. Their right to discipline members for other activities than nonpayment of dues is restricted. Innumerable other restrictions on unions could also be listed. Employers can also be taken to court over violations of collective bargaining contracts.

4. *Unions are held strictly accountable.* They must file data giving names of officers, their pay, their manner of election, etc. Officers must swear that they are not communists. Financial data for the union must be reported.

5. *Political activity and financial contributions of unions to Federal election and primary campaigns are forbidden.* There is some question concerning the constitutionality of this and other limitations on free speech and free press of unions. The free-speech rights of the employer are reaffirmed and strengthened.

6. *Secondary boycotts and jurisdictional strikes are made illegal.*

7. *Supervisors ("foremen") are given no protection to bargain collectively; an employer may bargain with them collectively only if he wishes to.*

8. *A 60-day strikeless period is provided,* requiring that much advance notice if a collective bargaining contract is not to be renewed. The penalty on workers who strike during this period is loss of their Wagner Act rights. Arbitration is not to be compulsory, but new mediation and conciliation machinery—removed from the Department of Labor—has been provided for.

9. *The NLRB is expanded in size from three to five members and given new responsibilities.* It is also subject to new restrictions so that it becomes a quasi-judicial body. The General Counsel of the Board is given wide discretionary powers to prosecute cases.

A Senator friend of Congressmen Cabot has differed with him sharply on the Act, claiming (1) that it is administratively unworkable, (2) that strong unions will be tempted to by-pass the NLRB completely, just as the Teamsters Union has often done, (3) that weak unions can be harassed by employers under the Act, and finally (4) that the penalties upon labor are much heavier than those on employers (who often can be told only to "cease and desist" while unions can be subject to weighty damages and legal involvements).

Not for years will anyone know the full significance of the Taft-Hartley Act. Of its nine topics mentioned here, probably the most important will turn out to be (2) and (3); but only time will tell. To criticize the 1947 Act because it bears down on labor unions is beside the point; that is its purpose. Historical perspective suggests skepticism toward the belief that the Act is utterly ruinous, unworkable, and the death knell of labor's freedom. Probably it will occasion short-term industrial strife. But as wise old Adam Smith said, "There is a good deal of ruin in a nation."

AN EXPERT LOOKS AT THE LABOR PROBLEM

To conclude our discussion of the labor movement, let us examine some of the more important issues as they appear to a careful nonpartisan student of labor relations. Gordon Bruce, aged 45, is a professor of labor economics in a large Middle Western state university. He has written a research monograph and several articles on labor economics. A number of his former students work for the U.S. Department of Labor and the NLRB. A few have become personnel managers and counselors for large private concerns, and one has become director of research for a large CIO union.

Bruce himself has served as a public member on semijudicial panels set up by the War Labor Board to pass on wartime wage disputes. That he enjoys the confidence of both labor and management is shown by the fact that a number of industries have appointed him as arbitrator of disputes which both sides voluntarily agree to bring before him and to abide by his decisions.

For all of his knowledge, Bruce is a troubled and perplexed man. Of a few things he is sure: management is not a heartless octopus with a bottomless purse, and labor leaders are not malevolent spawn of the devil who have bewitched and enslaved the American worker. He knows that many of the excesses of the labor struggle will die out, once unions no longer need to battle for their very existence. He points to peaceful practices and reasonable attitudes of the older unions to bear this out, and to the relative peace that settled on the English and Swedish labor scenes as soon as almost all the workers had become unionized and management had recognized this fact once and for all. He is fond of quoting two similar statements: one by a successful business man, Cyrus S. Ching, vice-president of the United States Rubber Company, and the other by Philip Murray, head of CIO and the Steel Workers' Union:

Where we are dealing with organized labor, we are going to get about the type of leadership that we are ourselves.[1]

Employers generally get the kind of labor relations they ask for. If the unions indulge in "excesses," then the employer as a rule has no one but himself to blame for it. For instance, if he engages the services of labor espionage agencies such as the Railway Audit, Pinkerton's, or others, if he stocks up his plant with tear gas, hand grenades, submachine guns, blackjacks, rifles, and other implements of war, if he hires high-priced Wall Street lawyers to harass the union before the Labor Board and in the courts, if he distributes to his foremen anti-union literature and lets it be known to them that any harm they can do to the union would be forgiven by him, if he contributes to anti-labor organizations such as the notorious Johnstown Citizens' Committee, if he quibbles over words, if he refuses to consent to an election or to sign a contract when he knows the union has a majority, if after a contract has been forced from him he delays and hampers the settlements of grievances, if he continues to discriminate against union members, then labor will answer in kind and nine out of ten businessmen, viewing it from afar, will say, "Ah, another excess."[2]

Bruce knows that it takes two to make a strike and keep it going: the

[1] CYRUS S. CHING, Problems in Collective Bargaining, *Journal of Business*, January, 1938, Part 2, p. 40.

[2] M. L. COOKE and P. MURRAY, "Organized Labor and Production," pp. 259–260, Harper & Brothers, New York, 1940.

workers who make wage demands and the company officials who refuse them. He knows that the number of man-days lost from work stoppages and the production costs of strikes are often exaggerated by the public press. He also knows that, although a strike itself may be costly to labor as well as to management, the ever-present threat that labor can and will if necessary strike is one of labor's most powerful weapons to push up money wages.

However, he also knows that no human rights are absolute, and that the time may come when in certain key industries—such as power and light, milk, transportation, and strategic governmental functions—it may be necessary to limit the right to strike. To the charge that this is equivalent to instituting "slavery and involuntary servitude" he has no glib answer, except that during war and emergency breakdowns of the whole economy due to strikes, it may be necessary for social survival to limit individual freedoms.

Bruce is also worried over the possibility that labor may press its money-wage demands too high whenever there is a high level of purchasing power and a tendency in the economy toward full employment, and that as a result we may never get near to full employment but pass into an inflationary spiral. On the other hand, Bruce expects and hopes that average money wages will rise steadily over the years and decades ahead, more or less in step with the steady growth of labor productivity and technical progress. He is a little concerned that workers who have exceptional monopoly power over the labor market may tend to raise prices to the consumer unduly high, or to keep consumers from benefiting from falling prices in lines that have enjoyed an extraordinary amount of technological progress. One of his major concerns is with the increase of labor featherbedding tactics[1] designed to keep labor productivity low and so increase jobs and maintain money rates. He is, as yet, less concerned that wage demands will wipe out the profits of capital, especially of the bigger corporations.[2]

If he ever began to list his doubts and fears, Bruce could go on almost indefinitely. For example, he is concerned over the problem of keeping unions democratic, and he is beginning to wonder whether the trend of collective bargaining toward a wider and wider industrial and national scale will not intensify the danger from strikes and inevitably call forth strong, almost

---

[1] Examples of such tactics are as follows: Bricklayers will lay only so many bricks per day; painters refuse to use spray guns and sometimes limit the number of inches of the paint brush; Petrillo's Musicians' Union requires stand-by orchestras to be hired whenever "canned" music is being played. Also, unions often fight technological innovations: new machinery, new methods, and new materials.

[2] Chapter 22 discusses some of these economic problems in more detail.

totalitarian government action which will infringe on individual freedom. But that is his job, to worry over all matters connected with labor. When called upon to summarize his attitude toward the labor problem, he is still reasonably optimistic. It goes without saying that his viewpoint is condemned alike by the typical conservative farmer and the small-town editor, and by the left-wing agitator. That too he has come to expect as part of his job.

SUMMARY

In this chapter we have briefly surveyed the history, organization, and functioning of organized labor. More important still are the attitudes of craft and industrial unionists, of government officials, legislators, and judges, and of the public; for these attitudes will determine the future trends of labor relations in this country.

It is no longer accurate to regard organized labor as a weak underling. Trade unions, like other economic pressure groups, possess a vast amount of power. One of the great political problems of our time is the harnessing of that power to the constructive betterment of national productivity and living standards.

QUESTIONS FOR DISCUSSION

1. Do you think there would be equality of bargaining power between capital and labor without trade-unions?

2. What legislative and judicial policies would the government have to follow in order to be neutral in its influence on the power of labor and of management?

3. Should the worker have the right to sign a yellow-dog contract if he wants to? to refuse to work if he is an auto worker on strike? if he is a railroad engineer? if he is a policeman? Where would you draw the line?

4. List some of the pros and cons of craft versus industrial unions.

5. Make a list of featherbedding tactics practiced by some unions.

6.   "Whether you work by the piece or the day,
       The shorter the hours the higher the pay."

Comment on this slogan. What economic law is involved?

7. Should professional people who work on salaries organize in unions? In what way does the American Medical Association—or the various bar or engineering associations—resemble and differ from trade-unions?

8. What has been the development of government legislation relative to (a) the yellow-dog contract, (b) the injunction, (c) peaceful and boycott picketing, (d) conspiracy under the Sherman Antitrust Act, (e) financial responsibility of unions, (f) the rights of employers to refuse to bargain collectively and to hire whom they please, (g) labor racketeering, (h) minimum wages, maximum hours, and fair labor standards, (i) communist infiltration of unions, (j) union political activity, (k) conciliation, mediation, and arbitration?

9. Should a firm's ability to pay be taken into account in collective bargaining? Should labor's productivity? If a union jacks up money wages, what may happen to unemployment?

10. What is a typical union-management contract like? What is meant by union recognition, maintenance of union membership, the checkoff, a union shop, a closed shop, seniority?

Chapter 10: PERSONAL

FINANCE AND SOCIAL SECURITY

NOT everyone will come into first-hand contact with the workings of the gold standard or of Federal reserve banking policy; but everyone will encounter, each day of his life, the problem of acquiring income, spending it upon consumption goods, and investing his savings so as to afford maximum protection against the vicissitudes of life.

BUDGETARY EXPENDITURE PATTERNS

Although no two families spend their money in exactly the same way, statistics show that there is a predictable regularity—on the average—in the way people allocate their expenditures on such items as food and clothing. Literally thousands of budgetary investigations have been made of the ways in which people at different levels of income spend their money; and there is remarkable agreement as to the general, qualitative pattern of behavior.[1]

Poor families must, of course, spend their incomes largely on the necessities of life: food, shelter, and in lesser degree, clothing. As income increases, expenditure on many food items goes up. People eat more and better. There is a shift away from the cheap, bulky carbohydrates to the more expensive meats and proteins, and to milk, fruit, and vegetables. This increase in food purchases, and not consumption by the armed forces or foreign nations, explains why meats and dairy products appeared to be scarce during the war and in the years thereafter. The domestic per capita consumption of meat, in the "white" market, averaged much higher between 1941 and 1946 than it had from 1935 to 1939. But, of course, only in the latter period were the poorer classes getting their share.

---

[1] These behavior patterns have sometimes been called "laws"—Engel's Laws, after the nineteenth-century Prussian statistician (not to be confused with the Engels of Marx and Engels) who first enunciated them clearly.

However, there are limits to the extent of extra money that people will spend on food when their incomes rise. Consequently, the percentage importance of food expenditure declines as income increases. (As a matter of fact, there are even a few cheap, but filling, items such as potatoes or oleomargarine whose consumption decreases absolutely with income. These are called "inferior goods.")

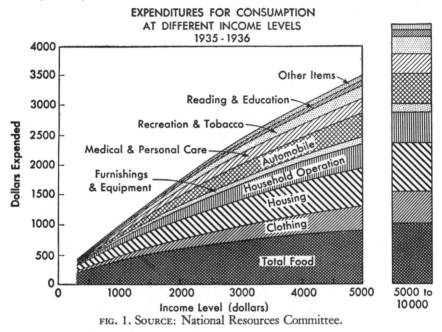

FIG. 1. SOURCE: National Resources Committee.

After one gets out of the very poorest income class, the proportion of income spent on shelter is pretty constant for a wide range and is expressed in the familiar rule of thumb: one week's salary should cover one month's expenditure on rent and household utilities. This will seem rather a quaint, outmoded rule to a veteran who is going to college on $105 per month under the G.I. Bill, or to a person not lucky enough to have found an apartment with a low-ceiling rental. But for the vast majority of people, who have not had to move since the war, it was still true late in 1947 that rent controls had held rental costs down better than in almost any other field of expenditure. However, with no price controls on real estate, the other rule of thumb—that one should pay for a house no more than 2 years' income—of course, began to seem somewhat comical and obsolete.

Expenditure on clothing, recreation, medical care, and automobiles increases more than in proportion to income, until the very high incomes are reached.

Of course, luxury items, almost by definition, increase in greater proportion than income; and in many ways, as we shall see in a moment, saving is the greatest luxury of all, particularly at very high incomes.

The above empirical generalizations are illustrated pictorially in Figs. 1 and 2. Of course, prices have risen since the monumental study, "Consumers' Income in the United States, 1935–36" was made by the combined efforts of

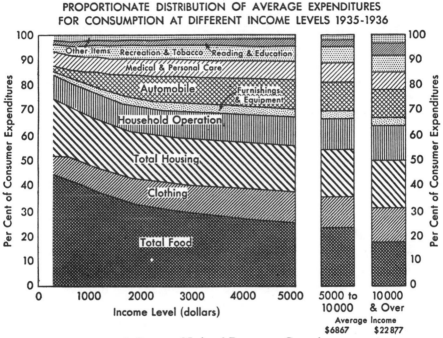

FIG. 2. SOURCE: National Resources Committee.

many government agencies (the National Resources Committee, the Bureau of Labor Statistics, the Bureau of Home Economics, and the WPA). However, further careful sampling surveys were made in 1941 and in 1944; and, except for the higher prices and taxes and for unavailable consumers' durable goods, they present a consistent corroborating picture.

REGIONAL DIFFERENCES IN COST OF LIVING

It should also be pointed out that prices and living conditions vary throughout the United States. House rents are cheaper in the country than in the city, and they used to be cheaper on the West Coast than in the East. The war has lessened the regional differentials in the cost of living, primarily by raising prices in the previously cheaper places more than in the large Northern cities—as many Southerners and Middle Westerners have learned to their sorrow.

However, even before the war people were prone to exaggerate the differences in the cost of living between North and South and between different cities. According to a careful study by the Labor Department, the differences between the cost of living in 33 large cities during the spring of 1945 were relatively minor, with the most expensive city, Seattle, only about 8 per cent above the average and the least expensive city, Houston, about the same per cent below the average. While many Southern cities tended to have a low cost of living, such cities as Kansas City, Scranton, and Buffalo had just as low or lower prices. On the other hand, Washington, which is fairly far south, was right up among the most expensive places along with Seattle, New York City, and San Francisco.

It may be well to speak a word on how these cost-of-living measurements are made, because the statistical difficulties in constructing an index number of prices are considerable. First, a careful study must furnish accurate reports on actual price quotations. Then if all prices in Houston were exactly 88 per cent of all prices in Washington, we could assert with confidence that the cost of living in Houston was 88, as compared to Washington as a base of 100. But some prices in Houston are only 65 per cent of the corresponding Washington price, and a few will be 150 per cent. The statistician, therefore, must take *weighted* averages of the different price comparisons. The Bureau of Labor Statistics does this by carefully compiling a list of items necessary in each community for a given, *equivalent standard of living*, and by then reckoning the total cost of such a market basket of goods.

Great care must be taken in doing this because for the South, where the climate is warmer, a special allowance must be made in estimating heating and building costs. Even more difficult, and almost insoluble, problems arise from the fact that there are differences in taste between South and North: pork versus beef, and bourbon versus rye. However, as best he can, the statistician tries to measure the different costs of an equivalent standard of living.

This is where the man in the street usually goes wrong. He says to his wife, "I think I'll take that job teaching physics at Dixie Polytech. Of course, it only pays what we're now getting, but $2,500 there is like $5,000 here." It is true that people live on less in the South, but that is primarily because many of them live less well.

However, to the extent that we are worried about the problem of "keeping up with the Joneses," it is quite possible that a family in the South with $2,500 a year will feel happier than a comparable family in the North; because in the South there will be relatively fewer families with income in excess of that figure. This probably helps to explain why farmers, small-town people, and Negroes are more thrifty at any given level of income than white city dwellers. A Negro with $4,000 a year income in Columbus, Ohio, will be as near the top of the income pyramid of his group as is a white person on Park Avenue in New York City with a $40,000 income; and both may save about the same percentage of their income.

FAMILY DIFFERENCES IN THE COST OF LIVING

The same statistical budgetary data throw some light on the age-old question: "Can two live as cheaply as one?" The answer is "no," not even if one works in the home. It costs a married couple about 10% times what it costs a single person to live, on the average. This is still less, however, than it costs two to live singly.

Each child in the family inevitably adds to the cost of living. Thus, if it costs 70 to live alone and 100 to live with a wife, it will cost about 130 with one child, 160 with two, and so forth for each additional child. (Of course, as the number of children increase, some "economies of scale and spreading the overhead" set in, but these may begin to be balanced by the operation of the law of diminishing returns. Or is it the other way around?) Studies of poor families with many children turn up a surprising fact: large families spend a smaller fraction of their income on housing than do small families. This is because they must spend so much for food, just to keep alive.

Moreover, as with an automobile, it is not the initial outlay that counts but the upkeep. Before the war, the Metropolitan Life Insurance Company estimated that it cost a family with an income of $2,500 a year about $10,000 to raise a child to the age of eighteen, or slightly more than $500 per year. A study of Army officers' families showed the prewar cost of raising a child to be at least 75 per cent more than this figure. It is not surprising, therefore, that studies made some years ago of college professors' families at the University of California and at Yale University elicited the frequent response, "The only real way we can save money is by not having another child."

Canada,[1] England, France, Sweden, and other governments have begun to give "family allowances" every month, the amount varying with the number of children in the family. This is done both for humanitarian reasons and to try to stimulate population growth. It is not hard to see why the government, rather than private industry, must make these payments; for if corporations had to pay higher wages to men with large families, they would soon begin to

---

[1] The Canadian government pays family allowances of $5 to $8 per month for each child, depending upon its age. After the fourth child, there is a slight reduction in these family-allowance payments.

discriminate in their hiring in favor of ancient bachelors and against the heads of large families.

THE BACKWARD ART OF SPENDING MONEY

In spending their money, people act with regularity but not always with rationality. For example, people with incomes of around $3,000 per year are known to spend less upon medical care than modern science and prudence would seem to suggest is necessary. Furthermore, what people consider to be absolute necessities consist to a large degree not of physiological necessities, but of conventional social desirabilities. Almost for a joke a Middle Western economist once estimated how much it would cost to buy most cheaply a yearly diet with all the health ingredients (vitamins A, B, C, D, etc., iron, calcium, etc., etc.) recommended by the National Research Council. The cost per year (!) was $39 in 1939 and $57 in 1944. But of course the diet consisted of nothing so expensive as bread or potatoes, but rather of wheat flour, cabbage, lima beans, kidneys, and not much else. Most people would rather starve than eat such an unpalatable and monotonous diet, just as dogs who have been conditioned to eat fish alone will almost starve before they will touch delicious beefsteaks.

A corporation buying a great quantity of a commodity tests it carefully for quality and makes sure that it is bought from the cheapest source. Not so the average consumer, who is an amateur when it comes to spending money. He pays 25 cents for 6 aspirin tablets when he could buy 100 equally good aspirin (monoaceticacidester of salicylic acid) tablets for 19 cents. More money is spent on advertising the cigarettes he buys than is spent upon their tobacco content. The cost of the ingredients in a $2 lipstick is exactly the same as that in a 25 cent one, and time and time again disinterested laboratory testers have been unable to detect any differences between them at all. A can of Campbell's soup sells for 9 cents in a chain grocery store and next door at a little "independent" for 12 cents. A large glass of Coca-Cola contains less than twice the amount of a small one. Until forbidden to by law, coffee companies would sell their "first-grade" coffees under a different label at lower prices; and a well-known brand-name tire used to be sold by Sears Roebuck under the All State name at a considerable reduction in price.

The consumer's health as well as his pocketbook is at stake.[1] When Upton

---

[1] The interested reader may be referred to the somewhat partisan views expressed in Stuart Chase and F. J. Schlink, "Your Money's Worth," The Macmillan Company, New York, 1931; and A. Kallet and F. J. Schlink, "One Hundred Million Guinea Pigs," Vanguard Press, New York, 1932.

Sinclair published the novel, "The Jungle," showing what conditions were like in the Chicago stockyards early in this century, many people stopped eating meat. Against the heavy opposition of business interests, Congress passed pure food and drug acts, but an American is still free to poison himself with hair dyes and to go to an early grave as a result of taking patent medicines and being his own doctor. The Federal Trade Commission prosecutes corporations indulging in extreme forms of misrepresentation in advertising, with the result that greater reliance is placed upon innuendo than upon direct statement. (For example, the label on a famous women's compound now says, "This preparation is recommended for those ailments to which it is adapted.") During World War II, a move by OPA (Office of Price Administration) to require canned groceries to contain a grade label stating their quality scores in letters as large as their brand names was hailed as the opening wedge in a campaign to undermine capitalism.

As far as national health and the number of people who die from consuming nationally advertised products are concerned, undoubtedly there is a slow but steady improvement going on. Even a patent-medicine corporation would rather make money from selling vitamins than selling arsenic. But as far as the magnitude of money and social resources spent upon wasteful advertising is concerned, any trend toward improvement is hazy, to say the least.

This is not to deny that advertising expenditure which brings information to the public and develops mass-production markets performs a desirable social function, or that as a by-product of advertising expense we have a free press and symphony orchestras on the radio. But along with the good points of advertising, we have the squandering of valuable brains on repetitious slogans, and for each minute of symphony, we have half an hour of "soap opera." The situation would be the more regrettable were it not for the apparent fact, surprising though it may seem, that many people seem to like advertising. They don't believe all they hear, but they can't help remembering it just the same.

INCOME PATTERNS OF SAVING AND CONSUMPTION

It is a matter of common observation that rich men save more than poor men, not only in absolute amounts but also in percentage amounts. The very poor are unable to save at all, but instead are dissaving each year; *i.e.*, they are spending more every year than they earn, the difference being covered by going into debt or using up previously accumulated savings. In 1944, the typical urban family with two children had to have $2,050 per year on the average in order to be able just to break even. Each dollar of income less than this amount sent the family into dissaving and debt, and each dollar of income above this amount went partially into saving.

Table 1 gives data on savings taken from a study of urban families in 1944, made by the Department of Labor. Column (2) shows the average amount of family saving (+) or dissaving (−) at each level of disposable income shown in Col. (1). Consumption is just the other side of the saving picture and is shown in Col. (3). Thus at the $2,000 "break-even" income where net saving is zero, consumption given in Col. (3) just exactly equals income. At the

TABLE 1. *Propensity of Urban Families to Save and Consume, 1944*

Disposable income, after taxes (1)	Net saving (+) or dissaving (−) (2)	Consumption (3)
$1,000	— $180	$1,180
2,000	0	2,000
3,000	+ 300	2,700
4,000	+ 600	3,400
5,000	+ 1,000	4,000
6,000	+ 1,500	4,500
7,000	+ 2,000	5,000

SOURCE: Department of Labor Survey, with data for all families smoothed and rounded off.

$1,000 income, the family spends $1,180 on consumption, the difference being financed out of dissaving or borrowing. Each extra $1,000 of family income is seen to be divided between extra consumption and extra saving. As we go from $1,000 to $2,000 of income, net (algebraic) saving increases by $180 and consumption increases by the rest of the $1,000 or by $820. (This $820 figure can also be derived and checked by taking the difference between the $1,180 spent by the poorest families on consumption and the $2,000 shown by Col. (3) to be spent by the next poorest families on consumption.)

What happens to each new dollar of income as we go from $2,000 to $3,000 family income? A comparison of the second and third rows in the table shows us that $700, or 70 cents of every new dollar, goes for extra consumption, and $300 or 30 cents of every new dollar goes for saving. As we should be inclined to expect from our knowledge of human behavior, as people get still richer a larger fraction of every dollar begins to go for saving rather than consumption. The reader should verify that, in 1944, families appeared to put

50 per cent of all income over $5,000 into saving and only 50 per cent into consumption. Such a high degree of thriftiness can hardly be normal and must have been due to the peculiar wartime conditions when goods were not available and when people were being urged to save.

Later when we come to the discussion in Part Two of how saving and investment determined the level of national income and employment, we shall see how crucially important is the Propensity-to-save schedule relating saving and income and its twin brother the Propensity-to-consume schedule relating consumption and income. Particularly important too is the fraction of every new dollar of income that the community devotes to new saving and new consumption—so important that new technical names have been given to these fractions. The fraction of every *extra* dollar of income that goes to *extra* consumption is called the "marginal propensity to consume," or MPC for short. The fraction of every dollar that does not go for consumption but goes to extra saving is called the "marginal propensity to save," MPS. The reader should verify from the table that for the very poorest people the MPC was about 0.82 (82 cents out of every dollar) in 1944, and the MPS was 0.18. As people became richer, the MPC and MPS became, respectively, about 0.70 and 0.30; then at still higher income levels they were each about 0.60 and 0.40; and finally for the wealthiest groups shown, about 0.50 and 0.50. (SUGGESTION: Fill in a fourth column in Table 1 showing how much consumption increases for each $1,000 increase in income.) Once again it is well to remember that the MPC was abnormally low and the MPS exceptionally high because of peculiar wartime conditions. As we shall see later, it is extremely fortunate that during the postwar period people can be expected to spend large amounts of their income upon consumption; otherwise the problem of avoiding a great depression would be very serious indeed.

GRAPHICAL DEPICTION OF THE PROPENSITY TO CONSUME AND TO SAVE

The data of Table 1 can be shown more vividly in diagrammatic form. Figure 3 shows the Propensity-to-consume schedule, with the total of consumption expenditure plotted against people's disposable incomes after taxes. A smooth curve has been drawn through the circles that represent the data of Col. (3) plotted against Col. (1). Except that there is no detailed breakdown of consumption into food, clothing, and other components, the curve in Fig. 3 is really very similar to the top curve already shown in Fig. 1. (Of course, Fig. 1 referred to 1935–1936 and not 1944, and there are other minor differences.)

The Propensity-to-consume schedule clearly rises as income increases. A 45° helping line is shown on the chart to indicate what would happen if people were always to spend 100 per cent of their income on consumption and to save nothing. At low levels of income, families spend more than their income and so the Propensity-to-consume curve begins above the 45° line. At the $2,000 break-even income, it crosses the 45° line, and thereafter, because something of every extra dollar goes into saving, the line of consumption keeps falling below the 45° helping line. In fact, by measuring the vertical difference be-

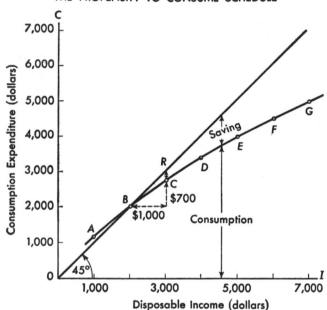

FIG. 3. This shows how consumption depends on family income. SOURCE: Table 1.

tween the Propensity-to-consume schedule and the 45° line, we get a picture of the exact amount of saving being done; at first negative, but beyond the break-even point increasingly positive.

Figure 4 shows the data on *saving* plotted explicitly against *income* to form the so-called Propensity-to-save curve. This is obviously the other side of the picture of the propensity to consume, since every dollar is divided between consumption and saving.

Our new concepts—the marginal propensity to consume and the marginal propensity to save—can also be represented on these diagrams. The MPC is given by the *numerical* slope[1] of the consumption curve. For example, as we

[1] By the numerical slope of the line XY, we always mean the numerical ratio of the length ZY to the length XZ.

go from the point *B* to *C*, the slope of the curve is less than that of the 45°
curve. In the little dotted triangle in Fig. 3, we go over to the right $1,000 and
go up only $700, indicating a numerical slope or MPC of $700 ÷ $1,000, or
0.7. The Propensity-to-consume curve is always flatter than the 45° line,
whose numerical slope is always exactly 1.0. This is because the MPC is
always less than 1.0, the differences being MPS, the extra amount saved. The
reader should verify that the numerical slope of the Propensity-to-save curve
is exactly the same thing as the MPS by drawing in a little dotted triangle be-

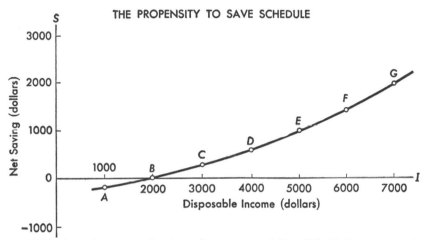

FIG. 4. This shows how some fraction of every extra dollar of family income goes into
saving. SOURCE: Table 1.

tween *B* and *C* in Fig. 4, and verifying that the ratio of its altitude to base is
$300 ÷ $1,000 or 0.3. He should also be able to calculate the approximate
MPC and MPS between any two other income levels on the charts.

THE WARTIME ACCUMULATION OF SAVING

Let us forget about tables and curves for a minute and investigate how
people go about spending more than their income. They may of course spend
out of previously hoarded cash. Or they may draw upon their balance at the
bank, either from their checking or savings accounts. Or they may cash in a
government saving bond. Or, if they are among the relatively few people with
marketable stocks and bonds, they may request their broker to sell enough of
their securities to finance a trip to California, a new automobile, or whatever
ends of the family budget fail to meet.

As a result of the war, the American people have accumulated more savings than ever before in our history. During the half decade of war most people had abnormally high incomes but were able to spend only at a normal rate on non-durable consumer goods, and at a very depressed rate on durable goods such as autos and radios. The difference between income and expenditure piled up in the form of war bonds, savings accounts, insurance policies, the paying off of previous debts, and finally in the holding of paper money and checking deposits. American individuals and businesses came out of the war with about 250 billion dollars (¼ trillion!) of liquid savings—about 100 billion dollars, or 40 cents of every savings dollar, in government bonds; another 75 billion dollars, or 30 cents of every dollar, in the form of checking accounts; 25 billion dollars, or 10 cents of each dollar, in the form of paper currency; and finally about 50 billion dollars, or 20 cents of every dollar, in the form of savings accounts.

This total of liquid wealth represents a threefold increase as compared to the prewar, so that Americans on the average now have a nest egg equal to about 20 months' income. This sum came into existence because of only one factor— the great wartime increase in the Federal government's public debt. These assets in the hands of the public are just the other side of the social balance sheet which shows the government's liability. If the public debt is a completely bad thing, then these family savings are a bad thing; if these family savings are a good thing, then the public debt cannot be as completely black as it is often painted.

In reality there is no such thing as the *average* family. The total of liquid assets is far from being divided equally among all families. A large family with many people working long hours in the shipyards might have been able to accumulate much saving during the war. So, too, might a speculator and a war profiteer; or a lieutenant commander in the Navy, who before the war made $2,200 a year and whose wife took a job and went to live with her family. On the other hand, a war worker with a large family who had to move to a new town and overpay on his automobile and house rent may have gone into debt during the war. Still other men and women may have squandered all they earned during the war—if not on silk shirts, then on night clubs and black-market nylons.

Fortunately, it is not necessary to rely on guesses concerning the distribution of war savings. At the request of the Federal Reserve Board, the Bureau of Agricultural Economics made a careful statistical survey of the distribution of savings. According to the "National Survey of Liquid Asset Holdings, Spending and Savings," a quarter of all families (or spending units) had no liquid savings at all in 1946: no savings accounts, no checking accounts, no government bonds. Half the families had less than $400 of savings. On the other hand, the 10 per cent of families with the highest savings averaged more than $10,000 of liquid assets apiece and had 60 per cent of the total liquid assets. Moreover, the statistics turned up one surprising result: within any one income class, it appears that a small proportion of very—what shall we say?—"thrifty" people tend to do most of the accumulating. These people are veritable sponges when it comes to saving.

However, it still remains true as a broad generalization that the American people will be better able to afford to make down payments on new houses and to buy new cars than ever before in history. Besides, as a result of the war, many people who succeeded in saving nothing at least got out of installment debt for the first time and can now begin all over again.

HOW PEOPLE BORROW MONEY

Let us briefly explore the channels open to people who must borrow. Up until the last 15 years or so, poor people as a rule fell into the hands of un-licensed loan sharks, and they still do in those states which have not passed a uniform small-loan act. These loan sharks charge interest at anywhere from a low of 120 per cent per year to above 1,200 per cent per year! Not 12 per cent, 12 *hundred* per cent! It is not uncommon to hear of cases where a man borrowed $20 in 1929 because of illness, and then paid $2.25 every week until 1938, or $1,053 in all and at a rate of 600 per cent interest per year. The curse of the poor is their poverty. They go into debt because of a lack of money, and they cannot get out for the same reason. Moreover, the last thing that a loan shark wants is to have his loan paid back. He will occasionally use violence, but more often he blackmails his victim by threatening to tell his boss or wife. The borrower never realizes that legally he need only refuse to pay, and the loan shark will never dare bring the matter to court.

There is only one way to remedy this despicable situation. Paradoxically, it is by passing a small-loan act which *raises* the legal interest rate that can be charged to far above the 6 per cent maximum set by the old-time usury laws. For honest personal-finance companies cannot stay in business unless they can charge much higher rates than this on small loans. Such loans involve an ele-ment of risk and much costly red tape and supervision. A few states, primarily in the South and in the Rocky Mountain region, still have not adopted such sensible uniform small-loan legislation—primarily because of a campaign by the loan sharks of legislative bribing, blackmail, and demagogic appeal to protect the public against paying more than 6 per cent interest. The Russell Sage Foundation and other disinterested groups have made a study of this problem and their reports of the true facts are as incredible as any melodramatic novel.[1]

In the better regulated states, a person can borrow from a licensed personal finance company such a small sum as $250 and hope to pay it off in 12 installments at a cost of about 36 per cent interest per year, with no other fees. He can borrow from a Morris Plan or Industrial Bank for about 15 per cent per annum or less. If the company he works for has a credit union, he can probably borrow there at about 12 per cent per annum. If he is willing to put up some article of jewelry, he can borrow about three-fourths of its auction sale value at a better pawn shop, paying about 36 per cent per year interest.

If his local bank will make him a small personal loan, repayable in installments, he will probably pay around 10 per cent per year for it, unless he is known to be a very good risk. If he buys his automobile or furniture on installment credit from a reliable concern, he will probably pay something like 12 per cent interest per year. If he borrows by putting a mortgage on his house, he will pay 4, 5, or 6 per cent per year. If he has a life-insurance policy with a paid-up value, he can borrow on it from the insurance company at 5 or 6 per cent per year or from many banks at 4 per cent or less. If he has listed securities or government bonds, he can make a collateral loan on them at 4 per cent or less.

These charges vary from region to region and from institution to institution, being generally lowest in Northeastern large cities and being lowest for large short-term loans. Thus, a wealthy man in New York City can borrow on his *marketable* government bonds at $1\frac{1}{2}$ per cent per year (per year not per month!) or less.

All the above interest rates are expressed in terms of the average *unpaid* balance. When a man is really paying 12 per cent per year on an installment loan, he probably thinks that he is only paying 6 per cent, or half as much. Let us see why. Suppose he is to pay $105 per month for 10 installments to pay off a $1,000 loan, the extra $5 being the monthly interest charge. Is he then paying an interest charge of $5 on a principal of $1,000 or only $\frac{1}{2}$ of 1 per cent per month? The answer is "no." He is really paying about 1 per cent per month or 12 per cent per year on his true *average unpaid balance*. The average amount of his indebtedness during the period is not $1,000 but only one-half that much, $500, because he is paying off the debt through the year. Interest of $5 per month on $500 is about 1 per cent per month or 12 per cent per year.

---

[1] The interested reader may be referred to Nos. 5 and 39 of the 25-cent Public Affairs Pamphlet Series, Public Affairs Committee, Inc., for an authoritative account of the loan-shark and consumer-credit problems. Almost all the subjects mentioned in this chapter are discussed interestingly and authoritatively in this valuable series of pamphlets.

Few people realize this and are often swindled by unethical dealers. Such a dealer would rather sell a car on credit than for cash, because the finance company gives him a commission. The dealer will quote a price for an automobile of $1,600, casually add on extra charges for bumpers, heater, and radio, and then slip in a "small finance charge" of $100, knowing that most people will not recognize that this represents more than 20 per cent interest per year. Moreover, some people will buy on installment credit, paying high rates of interest, at the same time that they have money in the bank earning only 1 per cent per year, or war bonds earning only 3 or 4 per cent per year. They do this either out of ignorance, or because they wish to make themselves save out of current income by having to make installment payments. Good advice for most people who must borrow or buy on installments is first to try a local bank.

GOVERNMENT BONDS AS A FORM OF SAVING

Let us turn now to the more cheerful question of what people should do with their savings. A few idiots, timid souls, or criminals will hold their money in the form of small bills kept in their stockings or rolled up in the window curtains. More normal people will put some into the savings bank or postal savings (at the local post office) so as to earn 1 or 2 per cent per year. Still others will put a large part of their savings into United States savings bonds, Series E. These earn about 3 per cent interest per year and can be bought directly out of one's pay check under the payroll saving plan, or at any bank.

They are issued in multiples of $25 and are registered in the name of one or two co-owners, or one owner and a beneficiary. As they are nontransferable, they can be neither sold nor borrowed upon. Each $25 face-value bond costs $18.75, and its face value is paid in full at the end of 10 years. It is redeemable at any bank upon proper identification within 60 days after issue in accordance with the abridged scale of redemption values given in Table 2. These values are arranged so that the longer one holds the bonds the higher their yield; therefore, if a person has to cash in part of his bonds prior to maturity, he should always cash in his *newest* ones first.

A 3 per cent yield for a perfectly safe, instantly redeemable bond is a very great bargain. In fact, insurance companies and banks would gladly trade all their 1, 1½, 2, and 2½ per cent marketable bonds for Series E bonds were it not for the fact that the government rigidly limits the amount that any one person or institution can buy per year.[1] No patriotism is necessary to make a

[1] Series F is a 12-year bond similar to Series E but yielding only about 2½ per cent; Series G is a nontransferable coupon bond yielding about the same percentage in yearly installments or coupons. In addition, there are marketable government bonds which mature after periods of time of 90 days, 1 year, or 20 years and more, and which bear interest yields of from ½ to 2½ per cent.

wise person take advantage up to his limit of what is almost literally a gift from the government. If a government bond is not thought to be perfectly safe, then neither is paper money nor a bank account.

TABLE 2. *Abridged Table of Redemption Values of Series E Bonds*

Issue price.................... $18.75   Maturity value................ $25.00

(Yield to maturity = 2.9 per cent per annum)*

Value after 1 year.............	$18.87	Value after 6 years...........	$21.00
Value after 2 years............	19.12	Value after 7 years...........	22.00
Value after 3 years............	19.50	Value after 8 years...........	23.00
Value after 4 years............	20.00	Value after 9 years...........	24.00
Value after 5 years............	20.25	Value after 10 years..........	25.00

* $25 is to $18.75 as 4 is to 3. Any compound-interest table will tell us that 3 multiplied by $(1.03)^{10}$ is about 4, showing that the savings bonds yield just under 3 per cent interest.

INVESTING IN SECURITIES

In Chap. 6 on Business Organization, the difference between bonds and common and preferred stocks was discussed. In Chap. 25, dealing with speculation, the workings of the stock market will be taken up. We need only say at this point, therefore, that people with a great deal of savings will not put all their eggs in one basket, but aim at a diversified portfolio of securities such as the following $100,000 holdings of a New England widow:

Security Holdings

Government Bonds, Series E.............................	$10,000
Government Bonds, Series G.............................	10,000
Government Bonds, 2½% marketable.....................	5,000
New York Central 4½% (due in 2013)..................	5,000
Total bonds...	$30,000
U.S. Gypsum 7% preferred.............................	$10,000
Marshall Field 4¼% preferred..........................	10,000
Total preferred stock.................................	$20,000
American Tel. & Tel. common..........................	$20,000
Firestone Tire common................................	10,000
General Motors common...............................	10,000
R. H. Macy & Co., common............................	5,000
Twentieth Century Fox common........................	5,000
Total common stock..................................	$50,000

On such a portfolio of securities, she would be lucky these days to earn much over $3,000 per year in total dividends and interest. If the widow is smart, she will seek reliable investment guidance.

ECONOMICS OF HOME OWNERSHIP

Because of the depression and the war, there is and will long be a great shortage of housing relative to population needs; and many people will wish to invest their savings in home ownership. More than a million dwellings per year will be built in the next decade. Because construction is a backward industry technologically, poorly organized and inefficient, and because the cost of labor and materials has risen substantially, the postwar prices of new and old homes will be too high for most families, probably averaging 50 to 100 per cent higher than the average level of the prewar 1930's.

TABLE 3. *Monthly Cost to Own a $10,000 House*

1. Initial cash payments:

10% down payment (90% mortgage)....................	$1,000
Closing fees, commissions, etc.........................	200
Total cash payments................................	$1,200

2. Monthly cost (over 25 years) for

Interest (5%)..	$ 23
Amortization (or paying back principal over 25 years)	30
Taxes (2½%)..	21
Hazard insurance (0.2 of 1%)........................	2
Maintenance ($200 per annum)........................	17
Loss of interest on cash payments (3%).................	3
Total monthly cost................................	$ 96

SOURCE: National Housing Agency, *Bull.* 2.

Owning one's own home is not necessarily always a good investment, although it is usually an interesting hobby. Moreover, multiple dwellings of two, four, or more units often work out cheaper on a cost basis than the more popular single dwelling. Aside from the upkeep of a house, the most important costs are not the physical wearing out of the house but rather the deterioration and obsolescence of the neighborhood. From the personal viewpoint, there is also the problem that the family may suddenly have to move and sell at a loss, or that family size and needs may change with time. These risks would not be so great were it not for the ever-present risk of a depression in real-estate values as a result of business slump, overspeculation, or overexpansion of building.

None of the above considerations should stop anyone, who really wants to, from buying or building a house in the price class that he can afford. But how much can he afford? The rule of twice one's annual income is a little on the conservative side these days; at least it errs in the right direction. It is consistent with the other rule that one ought not to spend more than 1 out of every 5 weeks' income on housing costs exclusive of electricity, gas, water, telephone, and heating, and not more than 1 out of every 4 weeks' income including these last elements.

Suppose that a man is sure of making $100 a week or $5,200 a year. Why can he afford only a $10,000 house (including cost of land)?[1] Table 3 shows how much it will cost per month to carry the $10,000 house; of course a $5,000 or $15,000 house will be proportionately lower or higher.

It will be seen from these figures that a veteran earning only half of $100 a week is most unwise to buy a $12,000 house, even if he is desperate for a place to live. He would be better off to pay $200 a month rent and live on his savings for a few years than to lose $2,000 or $3,000 on an unwise investment in property of inflated value.

BUYING LIFE INSURANCE

Aside from government bonds, bank accounts, and homes, the only savings of most people are in the form of life insurance. This comes in three main forms: *group insurance* (provided, as the name implies, for a whole group of employees of large companies or institutions), so-called *industrial life insurance*, and finally so-called *ordinary life insurance*.

The first kind is gaining in popularity and usually represents an advantageous form of insurance, especially when the employer pays for part of it.

Just as the Holy Roman Empire was neither holy, nor Roman, nor an empire, so industrial insurance is not industrial and it is hardly insurance. It has nothing to do with industry but is used to refer to the few hundred-dollar policies sold primarily to the very poor, usually for burial money. Generally, no health examination is required, and the agent calls at the house every week to collect the nickel or dime of insurance premium. Naturally a large part of this premium must go to the agent and to defray bookkeeping costs, so that industrial insurance is a very inefficient form of insurance, especially when the great number of policy lapses by the poor are taken into consideration. The Temporary National Economic Committee of Congress severely criticized industrial insurance; the best that can be said about it is that—except for social security—it is the only insurance that poor people ever do take out. Whether poor people, who can hardly make ends meet in this world, should be encouraged to pay undertakers large sums of money to mark their exit is not our business.

[1] About 7 per cent of this $10,000 will usually go for unimproved land, and another 6 per cent for pipes and other improvements on the land. About 45 per cent will go for building materials (including delivery), and the remaining 42 per cent will go for labor and contractor's profits.

The only insurance, then, that we need to consider is ordinary life insurance. This comes in a variety of different forms, the principal ones being (1) term insurance, (2) straight life, (3) limited payment, and (4) endowment plan.

Term Insurance. Term insurance, which is not very popular in practice, is the easiest to understand. Let us say that 100,000 men of age 35 each sign up for $1,000 of insurance for a term of 1 year. Mortality statistics show that a definite percentage of them will die within the year, say 1 per cent, or 1,000 men. The company will have to pay out to widows and beneficiaries, therefore, 1,000 × $1,000 or 1 million dollars. It must charge each thirty-five-year-old man, therefore, slightly more than $10 as his insurance premium. The next year it begins all over again, but of course as the men get older the cost of the insurance will gradually rise. Under term insurance, each year stands on its own legs, so to speak, and there is no need for the company to accumulate large saving reserves. In fact, anyone who buys term insurance is doing no saving for the future at all. On the other hand, while he is young and with a growing family, he is getting the maximum possible insurance protection in case of death.

Straight Life Insurance. Under straight life insurance, all the men who join at the age of 35 agree to pay a *constant* yearly premium until they die, a premium that is higher for people who join at 35 than for those joining at 34 or 30. This constant premium is set so that at first they are overpaying, on the average, for their insurance; *i.e.*, the company will begin by paying out to the whole group of thirty-five-year-olds less than it collects, the difference being invested at interest in a so-called "insurance reserve" which consists of stocks, bonds, and mortgages. Late in life, the steady constant premium is less than the true insurance cost for the group, the difference coming out of the previously accumulated reserve. By the time everyone in the group is 100 and dead, all the reserve will have been used up.

Figure 5 illustrates the difference between renewable-term and straight life insurance for a man who joins at 35 and lives to be 80.

Limited Payment Insurance. Limited payment is just like straight life except that after 20 or 30 years the insured person need not pay any more premiums. Of course, his constant premium during that time must be still greater than under straight life and will be much greater at the beginning than under term. Even larger reserves are built up under this plan, so that it will be seen to involve a larger element of saving and a slightly smaller element of insurance coverage.[1]

---

[1] Servicemen in World War II were sold 8-year term life insurance at favorable rates. This can be and, because of the favorable rates and disability provisions, should eventually be converted into either ordinary, 20-payment, 30-payment, or endowment life insurance.

Endowment Plan. Finally, an endowment plan policy provides a still larger element of saving than of insurance coverage. Under a 20-year endowment policy, the thirty-five-year-old man agrees to pay in a high constant premium for 20 years, after which time, at the age of 55, he will receive the whole face value of the policy even though he has not died. Thus endowment insurance is a combination of saving and insurance. Provided that it is not allowed to lapse prior to the end of the 20-year period, endowment insurance is a good thing for anyone who wants to make himself save regularly. How-

RENEWABLE TERM LIFE INSURANCE

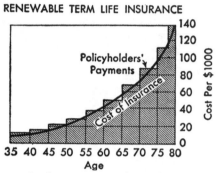

STRAIGHT LIFE

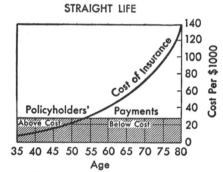

FIG. 5*a*. Insurance premiums always just cover each period's "actuarial" costs, with no savings reserves piling up. SOURCE: *Public Affairs Pamphlet*, No. 62.

FIG. 5*b*. Constant premiums at first exceed current actuarial costs, the difference being invested at compound interest in an actuarial reserve. Later, when the reverse is true, this reserve is used up. SOURCE: *Public Affairs Pamphlet*, No. 62.

ever, under it, he will not receive any higher rate of return than he could get for himself by doing what the insurance company primarily does anyway, *i.e.*, by investing his savings regularly in government bonds.

For more details the student may be referred to the readable pamphlet "How to Buy Life Insurance"[1] or to his local agent. He will find that in practice each company's policy differs slightly in some provision from that of other companies, so that he will hardly know how to decide which is the best buy. The problem is complicated further by the fact that most "mutual" companies deliberately err on the side of overconservatism and overcharge their policyholders; then at the end of the year they pay back part of the overcharge in so-called "dividends." Still, according to the experts, policies of the various companies differ considerably in their true net cost, so that a little study of the problem and shopping around are worth while. Furthermore, in states like Massachusetts or New York, there are definite cost advantages to buying Savings Bank Life Insurance at an accredited bank. However, because life

[1] Public Affairs Pamphlet 62.

insurance is mostly "sold to people and not bought," the majority of the people will continue to pay slightly more from commercial companies.

SOCIAL SECURITY AND HEALTH

In 1937, the Social Security Act went into effect to help protect the American people against economic want resulting from old age or unemployment. Despite dire warnings at the time, the system has worked very well, and now both the Republican and the Democratic parties are pledged to its support.

The system works simply and consists of three parts: (1) contributory old-age retirement and survivors benefits insurance, (2) unemployment compensation insurance, and (3) old-age assistance and public welfare. Under the first two plans, people, as a matter of right, automatically receive benefit payments when retired through old age or when unemployed, without having to go through a "needs test" to reveal whether they have any money of their own.[1] Social security taxes are levied against payrolls as described in Chap. 8, so that each person may be thought of as partially paying for his own benefits. However, social insurance or social security differs from private insurance in that a person may receive in benefits more than he is actuarially or mathematically entitled to on the basis of his payments, the difference being made up out of government taxes. A generation from now, when a larger fraction of the population will be above the retirement age, the contribution of the government will have to be considerably increased. Moreover, the system is placed on a pay-as-you-go basis, so that no actuarial reserves need pile up. The piling up of such reserves in a growing economy tends, as we shall see later, to increase saving and to aggravate the likelihood of deflation.

Under the unemployment compensation plans, set up by the states at the instigation of the Federal government, payments are made into an unemployment reserve fund every week that a worker is employed. If he should be laid off, then by meeting certain requirements—such as being willing to accept any suitable job offered him by the Public Employment Exchange Office and

---

[1] Anyone who has worked long enough in jobs covered by social security will receive upon retirement under the present law anywhere from $10 to $85 a month. The exact amount depends upon (1) his *average monthly earnings* (being reckoned at 40 per cent of monthly earnings up to $50 per month plus 10 per cent of additional average monthly earnings up to $250 per month), (2) his *length of service* in covered employment (a bonus of 1 per cent extra being paid for each year of service), (3) his *dependents* (a wife over 65 receives one-half of his benefits; a widow over 65, three-fourths of his benefits; and if there are any dependent children, each will receive one-half of his benefits; and the wife or widow will receive benefits even if less than 65. Also, there is provision for burial money payments at time of death, equal to 6 months' benefits). No private insurance company could afford to sell such a policy at these give-away rates.

having worked a minimum number of weeks in the period preceding his unemployment—he automatically receives a weekly unemployment compensation check whose magnitude depends upon his previous earnings and contributions. There is no humiliating "needs" test, nor are benefit payments set so high as to encourage people to remain idle. During prosperity, the unemployment reserve fund grows; during depression, when it is most needed, it is used to help support people and maintain general purchasing power.

The old-age assistance and public welfare part of the Social Security Act consists of grants-in-aid by the Federal government to be used by the states to support the needy aged, blind, widowed and orphaned, physically and mentally handicapped, who themselves could not possibly contribute to their own support.

GROWTH OF SOCIAL SECURITY

Not only is the social security system here to stay, but it is growing and being extended. Huge punch-card machines in Baltimore have made the administrative aspects of the program insignificant. Society today believes increasingly in the philosophy that the worst personal and social misfortunes result from contingencies over which the single individual has little control. In 1932 people walked the street without work; in 1929 and 1946 the same people had prosperous jobs. The answer is not in them.

Leaving all humanitarianism aside, a social security program is simply a cheap and sensible way of providing the individual care that would have to be provided or financed in some other way. Private insurance is not a subtraction from national output and income; neither is social insurance. The statement is sometimes encountered that "a poor country like England cannot afford a Beveridge Plan calling for cradle to grave security against the chief vicissitudes of life—against the expenses of unemployment, old age, sickness, pregnancy, and large families." Such a statement is just not good economics. These contingencies have to be met in any case, and the question is whether they should be budgeted in a systematic, efficient, and sensible way, or be left to fall upon the individual or upon haphazard charity.

Already annuities for widows and dependent children have been added to the social security benefits. It is not at all unlikely that in the next generation payments for sickness and disability, and a comprehensive public health and hospital program, will have been introduced. In 1931, many medical associations strongly disapproved and fought against the systems of private health and hospitalization insurance such as Blue Cross or Blue Shield. Today they are among the strongest supporters of these systems. Nobody advocates socialized medicine in this country, and nobody will admit, at least, that he wishes to impair the personal relationship between patient and physician. But as every careful official and unofficial survey of the American people has shown,

A large portion of the population receives insufficient and inadequate medical care, chiefly because people are unable to pay the costs of services on an individual basis when they are needed, or because the services are not available.[1]

SUMMARY

1. The patterns of family expenditure on different consumption items, such as food, clothing, shelter, and saving, are fairly regular and predictable after we make allowances for family size and regional differences in the cost of living.

2. The important Propensity-to-consume and Propensity-to-save schedules show how people spend on consumption more than their incomes at low incomes, the difference representing algebraically negative saving or dissaving. As income increases beyond the break-even point, some fraction of each new dollar of disposable income (after taxes) goes into consumption and the rest goes into saving. The fractions of extra dollars going into consumption and saving are called, respectively, the "marginal propensity to consume" (MPC) and the "marginal propensity to save" (MPS). They are depicted geometrically by the numerical slopes of the Propensity-to-consume and Propensity-to-save schedules.

3. There are various ways in which a family can borrow, each involving widely differing rates of interest. Similarly, the ways in which a family can invest its savings include bank accounts, government bonds, owning one's own home, marketable stocks and bonds, and the purchase of one of the different forms of life insurance.

4. There are important differences between private and social insurance. Our social security program now provides the majority of our citizens, for the first time, a measure of protection against old age, unemployment, and physical handicaps. The program is an expanding one, and proposals have been made to improve further the present, inadequate provision for American medical and health care.

[1] Public Affairs Pamphlets 10, 27, and especially 104 provide further material on the problem of medical care. The last also discusses the provisions of the controversial Murray-Dingle-Wagner Act long before Congress, which would greatly extend the scope of social security and public health.

QUESTIONS FOR DISCUSSION

1. Make up a budget for yourself or your family. What if your income were cut by 30 per cent, or increased by that amount?

2. If everybody saved about one-third of all extra incomes, how much would national income have to rise in order to bring forth 1 billion dollars of extra saving? If the MPS were 0.2, what would your answer be?

3. If the rich who have a MPS of 0.5 were taxed 10 billion dollars and this was given to the poor who have a MPS of only 0.1, how much would the total of saving be reduced? How much would the total of consumption be increased?

4. What are interest charges on loans in your community?

5. Make certain assumptions about your own earnings and expenditure over the next 30 years. Draw up an investment program for yourself.

6. What investments would you buy if you thought that inflation was ahead? what if you thought that the outlook was for deflation?

7. Recently, life-insurance companies began to draw up their policies assuming only a 2½ per cent interest yield on their investments instead of 3 and 3½ per cent as previously. What effect would this have on life-insurance premiums? Of the four kinds of ordinary life insurance described in the text, which would have the greatest and least increases in premium rates?

8. "I want to buy an annuity which will do more than pay me a given dollar income until I die. To hedge against inflation, I want one which will pay me a given *real* income every year. More than that, I know that technological progress will give everyone increased real incomes in the years ahead, so that two decades from now, anyone with my present real income will be surpassed by most of the population. What I really want is an annuity which guarantees that I will always remain at the same relative position in the income pyramid." Why can no private insurance company sell such an annuity policy? Could the government's social security program cover this man's need? Why would inflation, which might wipe out private insurance, leave social security protection undiminished?

9. The Metropolitan Life Insurance Company collects more money from New York citizens than the state government. What happens to this money? Is it a subtraction from the national income?

10. The statement "Only the very rich and the very poor receive adequate medical care," is only half true. Which half? Does the fact that there are three times as many doctors per capita in California as in South Carolina and five times as many dentists per capita in Oregon as in Mississippi prove that there are too many doctors and dentists on the West Coast?

Chapter 11: NATIONAL INCOME

THE whole of our discussion of Part One leads up to and can be summarized by the important concepts of national income or net national product. Most simply, these are nothing more nor less than the final sum total of all labor and property incomes earned in producing the national output.

Only in the last decade or so have we had any adequate statistical data on these important concepts; only in the dozen most advanced countries of the world are there yet readily available yearly data on changes in this all-important magnitude. Here in the United States we are fortunate in having national income estimates from the Department of Commerce (a branch of the Federal government), from the National Bureau of Economic Research (a nonprofit scientific institute), and the National Industrial Conference Board (a business-financed research organization). Their estimates are in very good quantitative agreement so long as they claim to be using the same definitions, so that we may have considerable confidence in national income statistics.[1]

By means of statistics of national income, we can chart the movements of a country from depression to prosperity, its steady long-term rate of economic growth and development, and finally its material standard of living in comparison with other nations. How then is national income defined and measured?

TWO VIEWS: MONEY INCOME OR MONEY OUTPUT

There are two different ways of looking at national income. Being essentially two aspects of the same thing, they each will have to add up to the same thing.

Approaching the problem from the first direction, we may say (1) that national income is the sum total of *income earned* by owners of the various productive factors: wages of workers, plus net interest on capital loans and

[1] The standard reference is to S. Kuznets, "National Income and Its Composition, 1919–1938," Vols. I and II, National Bureau of Economic Research, Inc., New York, 1941. See also "Survey of Current Business" of the Department of Commerce, particularly the July, 1947, Supplement; and the yearly "Economic Almanac" of the National Industrial Conference Board.

securities, plus net rents and royalties, plus corporate profits, plus net income of unincorporated enterprises.

Looked at from the other direction, we may say (2) that the incomes paid out to the various productive factors altogether go to make up the sum total of the costs or *net value* of all the *goods produced* by the community. (The careful reader will note that the "profit" of corporations must be carefully included in the value of output if the two sides of the picture are to add up to *exactly* the same thing; "undistributed profits" are to be included as well as profits paid out as dividends.)

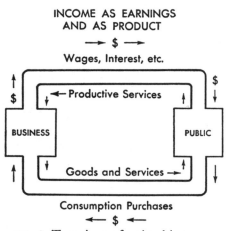

INCOME AS EARNINGS
AND AS PRODUCT

→ $ →

Wages, Interest, etc.

Productive Services

BUSINESS   PUBLIC

Goods and Services →

Consumption Purchases

← $ ←

FIG. 1. Two views of national income.

In the simplest case, we can imagine a circular flow of dollars going from business to the public in return for productive services of labor and property; this is just matched by a flow of consumption dollars going from the public to business to pay for the purchase of real consumption goods and services.

It doesn't matter—so long as there is a perfect circular flow—whether we measure the flow of national income in the upper loop where it appears in the form of people's earned incomes; or whether we measure it in the lower loop as the expenditure value of consumption goods and services. Either answer will be the same. (When we come to introduce saving and investment, and the government into the picture, the diagram will have to be made a little more complicated, but the two different ways of looking at national income will still be valid.)

FIRST VIEW OF NATIONAL INCOME: COST AND EARNINGS OF FACTORS OF PRODUCTION

To arrive at estimates of the total flow of income accruing to the public we must carefully collect data (from company and government reports, tax returns, etc.) on (1) wages, salaries, and supplements earned by all employees; (2) net income of unincorporated business, meaning by this the net returns to farmers, doctors, partners, single proprietors, etc.; (3) net interest, received from private bonds, mortgages, and other loans; (4) net rents of persons, including self-occupied homes; (5) net corporate earnings, whether (*a*) distributed to the common and preferred stockholders as dividends, or (*b*) plowed back into (the surplus of) the corporation, as undistributed corporate profits, or (c) payable to the government in corporate income taxes. Table 1 shows these data for the first postwar year, 1946.

TABLE 1. *National Income Earned by Factors, 1946*

Items	Billions of dollars	Percentage
Wages and other compensation of employees.............	$116.8	65
Income of unincorporated enterprises (adjusted).........	34.9	20
Rental income of persons...........................	6.9	4
Corporate profits before tax (adjusted)................	16.4	9
Dividends............................. $+5.6		
Undistributed profits...................... +6.9		
Corporate profits taxes.................... +8.6		
Inventory valuation adjustment............. −4.7		
$ 16.4		
Net interest......................................	3.2	2
National income..................................	$178.2	100

It is rather remarkable how nearly constant are the proportions of the various categories of income over long periods of time, between both good years and bad. The size of the total social pie may wax and wane, but total wages seem always to add up to about two-thirds of the total.

The proportions of the remainder do not remain perfectly constant. Interest and rent payments tend to be relatively fixed charges on business enterprises and do not at first decline so much in deep depression as the other items, with the result that corporate profits must show a greater relative decline. In fact profits may become negative for many firms and industries; and in still other lines net corporate profits (or earnings) may fall below actual dividend payments. Consequently in a deep depression year like 1932, undistributed corporate profits will become algebraically negative as businesses are paying out in dividends more than they earn, and as accounting balance sheets reveal that surplus and assets are being gradually liquidated.

Of course, one and the same person may receive income from several of these sources simultaneously. Probably this is true of almost any college student's own family; in any case, as an exercise, the reader should attempt to estimate the amount and source of his own family's income. If the members of the class are an average sample, it will be found that the higher the family income, the smaller the proportion of wage or salary income, and the larger the relative amount of dividend and interest income.

TRANSFER PAYMENTS

Not every sum of money that an individual receives in any period can be counted as personal income, or as part of the national income. If I sell an old painting for $1,000, I am simply exchanging one kind of asset for another and so is the purchaser. But if I am a painter who produces one picture a month and thereby earns $12,000 a year, then all of this (over and above my expenses for materials) will be counted as national income.

This is just another illustration of a transfer payment such as we met in the discussion of public finance in Chap. 7. There we pointed out why relief payments and pensions to disabled veterans or to the aged should not be counted in as income.

The decisive test as to whether a given item should be counted in national income is as follows: *Does it represent a cost payment to a factor of production for a contribution toward production?* This does not mean that the contribution to production by the income recipient must be rendered personally. Rent paid to him for the use of land that he has provided, or interest on his capital—all these must be counted (even if the charge seems to us exorbitant or undeserved) so long as they enter into the cost of production of some commodity.

The reader might amuse himself by trying to decide whether the following money transactions ought or ought not enter into national income: (1) an inheritance of a million dollars, (2) a yearly gift of $1,000 from a rich aunt to avoid inheritance tax when she dies, (3) a student's monthly allowance from his father or from the Veterans Administration, (4) the sale of an old house, (5) relief allowances to needy families, (6) interest received on government bonds, (7) work relief of the WPA kind, (8) monthly annuity payments, (9) the earnings of a housemaid, (10) the value of the housekeeping services of a wife, (11) sales of vegetables from a farmer's garden, (12) the value of vegetables from a farmer's garden consumed by the family, (13) the income of an advertising salesman, (14) the income of a brewer, (15) the income of a monopolist, (16) the value of food of a soldier. Some of these questions are very easy; some are very difficult borderline cases.[1]

---

[1] Those excluded from national income are 1–6, 10. The first six are transfer payments. A wife's housework services are not included simply because it is hard to find a market-price yardstick or any other to evaluate them. In all logic, they should be included, and national income should be increased by one-fifth or more. Part of the annuity is excluded because it is a transfer item representing the return of a person's capital; that part which is interest is to be counted in.

REAL VERSUS MONEY INCOME

While national income is expressed in money terms, its importance depends upon what each dollar will buy. If inflation raised all prices and wages tenfold but left everything else unchanged, national income would appear ten times as large but each new dollar would have only the same *real significance* as the old dime. If our money incomes all increase tenfold but we have to pay ten times as much for all goods, who would be so foolish as to think anyone better off?

To take an actual example, the drop of national income from 80-odd billion dollars in 1929 to 40 billion dollars in 1932 would seem to suggest that national income had been about halved. But the average level of prices current in 1932 was some 20 per cent lower than in 1929. Part of the halving in income is fictitious, representing merely paper changes in prices.

To compute the change in *real* national income (expressed in prices of constant purchasing power) as distinct from *money* national income (expressed in changing current prices), we must "deflate" the money figures by dividing them through by an index of the cost of living (or price level).[1] Thus, real

	Money national income, billions (1)	Price index 1929 as base (2)	Real national income in 1929 prices, billions (3)
1929	$80	100	$\frac{\$80}{100} \times 100 = \$80$
1932	$40	80	$\frac{\$40}{80} \times 100 = \$50$

national income is found to be about 50 billion dollars in 1932 if expressed in constant 1929 prices, rather than 40 billion dollars expressed in the then current dollars; *i.e.*, 40 billion dollars at 1932 prices would buy as much as 50 billion dollars at 1929 prices. Therefore, *real* national income had fallen by only about 40 rather than 50 per cent.

As an exercise, the student should recompute the above results, using 1932 prices as a base, and verify that we get the same percentage change in real national income by either the 1929 or the 1932 comparison. One result differs from the other only by a scale-proportionality factor reflecting the difference

[1] The accompanying table illustrates with approximate numbers how we go about deflating national income or any other monetary series. Suppose that money national income is given in Col. (1) and an index number of the cost of living (with 1929 prices = 100) in Col. (2). Then Col. (3) gives *real* national income, derived by dividing Col. (1) by Col. (2) and multiplying by 100.

between 1929 and 1932 prices. The student should also try to allow for the
fact that population increased from 122 to about 125 millions between the two

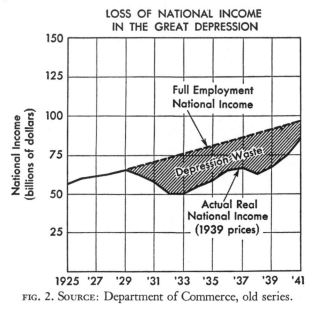

FIG. 2. SOURCE: Department of Commerce, old series.

dates. By what percentage would *per capita* real national income have fallen
between these two dates? Is this a greater or a less percentage than the fall in
total real national income?

TABLE 2. *U.S. Money and Real National Income (In billions of dollars)*

Year	National income (current prices)	Real national income (constant prices of) 1929 purchasing power
1929	$ 83	$ 83
1932	40	51
1937	71	86
1938	64	78
1939	71	87
1940	78	94
1941	97	113
1945	161	154
1946	178	157

SOURCE: Unrevised Department of Commerce data, deflated by cost of living index
of Bureau of Labor Statistics.

Table 2 presents data on money and real national income for selected years. The great and wasteful loss of real income during the 1930's because of depression unemployment can easily be seen in Fig. 2 to run to some 300 billion dollars—almost equal to the real economic cost of World War II.

Figure 3 shows how the wartime upswing in prices caused the money measure of national income to be artificially inflated relative to the increase in real income.

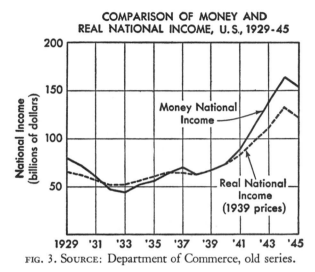

COMPARISON OF MONEY AND REAL NATIONAL INCOME, U.S., 1929-45

FIG. 3. SOURCE: Department of Commerce, old series.

SECOND VIEW OF NATIONAL INCOME AS NET NATIONAL PRODUCT

In deflating money income to get a measure of real income, we are beginning to approach the second way of looking at national income mentioned earlier: the net value of all goods and services produced. Let us explore this further.

The primary purpose of economic activity is the provision of consumption goods and services. A little thought will make it clear that the rendering of services must be included along with the production of tangible, national commodities. The pay of an opera singer or shoeshine boy enters into national income or net national product, and the service each renders is as important in net national product as the manufacture of a camera or for that matter a phonograph record. In fact it will be clear to the reader upon reflection that material objects are useful in the last analysis because of the services (or utilities) that they render.

But how can we add *diverse* goods and services to form a meaningful total? What is the meaning of 2 apples plus 3 oranges? At least two methods may be suggested of reducing the million and one different goods produced every year to a common denominator. The first method would apply some sort of psychological or welfare yardstick based on satisfactions enjoyed by people as a result of consuming different goods. It would not be theoretically inconceivable that some one might dream up a definition of "psychological utility" or "psychic income" whereby oranges and apples could be combined. The result would be somewhat arbitrary and might depend a great deal on how we weight different individuals' tastes; for example, a vegetarian and a cannibal might differ sharply in their estimate of people's psychic income.

For this and other reasons, economists prefer to use a second kind of yardstick or common denominator—namely, *money value*. Though we cannot add apples and oranges by themselves, once we know their relative prices, say, apples 4 cents apiece and oranges 5 cents, then we can speak of the value of 2 apples and 3 oranges as being 23 cents. Market price provides us with the factor that makes it possible to measure output in a common dimension.

To be sure, this is not a perfect solution. The total of money value is only a rough index of social welfare. Some of the best things in life cannot be measured in money. The Department of Commerce cannot always get hold of accurate estimates of the value of such items as a farmer's home-grown tomatoes, or of owner-occupied homes. But they do their best. Perfectly accurate market prices are hard even to define for such ambiguous services as a doctor's appointment. And finally, to cut the list short, we still have the problem of deflating our resulting money total for fictitious, paper changes in the price level. (The reader should think up further difficulties and pitfalls.)

FINAL GOODS VERSUS DOUBLE COUNTING OF INTERMEDIATE GOODS

Even after we have brushed aside some of the worries of a perfectionist, we must still face the problem of deciding what goods are to be included in net national product. There is always the danger of double counting. It would be wrong, for example, to count bread in the net national product and also at the same time to count in the flour that went into that bread, or to triple count by also counting in the wheat.

To avoid this pitfall, the words "*net* value of goods and services" were inserted into our definition. We must first be sure that each included item truly represents a *final* good or service. Thus, a 10-cent loaf of bread was made from wheat which sold for 2 cents, from flour worth 3 cents, and baked dough worth 5 cents; finally wrapped, it was sold to the ultimate customer for 10 cents. Its contribution to the national product is not 2 + 3 + 5 + 10 cents. That would involve considerable double counting, because the flour, dough, etc., are not *final* products. Only the 10-cent bread is a final product, not the 20-cent total of all intermediate products.

If we insist upon decomposing the 10 cents of final product represented by the bread into the contributions of the different states of production, we can always do so by concentrating on the so-called "value added" at each stage of production. This is nothing but a return to our first way of looking at net national product—from the standpoint of costs of production paid out at each stage as earned incomes to the owners of factors of production (wages, interest, etc.). Our final product equals the sum of value added at each stage of production:

TABLE 3. *Final Product, Value Added, and Intermediate Product*

Stage of production of a loaf of bread	Sales value, cents	Cost of material, cents	Value added, cents
On the farm.............................	2 —	0 =	2
At the mill and by transport.............	3 —	2 =	1
At the bakery...........................	5 —	3 =	2
By wholesaler and retail distributors......	10 —	5 =	5
Total value of final product.............	20 —	10 =	10, sum of value added

The reader should verify that there is no double counting because in calculating the value added at each stage, we first carefully subtract all the costs of materials and intermediate products not produced in that stage but bought from other business firms. (The numbers in the columns of Table 3 show that every intermediate product appears in two rows *with opposite* signs and can be canceled out.)

The value added at each stage can be broken down into wages, salaries, interest, and rents, and into all the other components that we have already discussed in connection with the first way of looking at national income. Again we see that the two methods are perfectly equivalent and self-checking.[1]

Usually there is no great difficulty in avoiding double counting by concentrating on value added and omitting all the intermediate goods that one business firm buys from another. It is easy to see that coal used in a baker's oven is not itself to be counted as part of national product if we have already counted in

[1] A failure to understand the relation between final product, value added, and intermediate goods lies at the basis of the mysterious "Type A and Type B payments" invented by a retired British engineer, Major Douglas, the founder of the Social Credit movement. This political party, which advocates the printing of new money, has followers in Canada, England, Australia, and California; and it has actually come into power in one of the western Canadian provinces.

the full value of final bread consumption. It is also equally obvious that the coal burned in a home and yielding a final utility to consumers is part of national income or product. And very clearly, the ovens and plows used up in making a finished loaf of bread are to be counted (once but not twice!) in the value of national product.

Occasionally we are confronted with more difficult decisions. Should the traveling-expense charge account of a salesman be counted in as income? No. Like the coal in the baker's oven, this is a necessary expense of producing final goods and has already been counted in the value of final output. On the other hand, it is equally obvious that, when a firm provides housing for one of its workers, his wages are really increased by the rental value of this house and such an item has to be treated as a final good. Between these two clear cases, there are more difficult ones to classify: for example, if a salesman takes a client to an enjoyable baseball game or night club, ought not we to consider the salesman's wages and consumption of final goods and services as including at least part of this item?[1]

TWO PROBLEMS INTRODUCED BY GOVERNMENT

Such borderline cases between final consumption and intermediate goods are not so important as long as we stick to the sphere of private production. When we come to consider the value of government services, the problem becomes acute. For example, when the government provides free roads for commercial trucks, the value of such services would seem to be intermediate goods like the baker's coal and would seem to be quite different from the case where the government provides final services to the consumer in the form of roads for joy riding.

The first problem raised by government may, therefore, be phrased as follows: How much of the total purchase of goods and services by the government should be treated as final (collective) output? How much should be treated as intermediate output designed to increase private production, and hence not itself to be counted into final net product?

This first problem is sometimes confused with a second problem introduced by government: How shall we treat *indirect taxes* collected by the government

---

[1] A philosophical case can be made out for treating a good deal of man's consumption expenditure as really a necessary business expense; for example, a carpenter's overalls or his carfare to work. The practical national income statistician insists upon counting these as final consumption rather than as intermediate goods because as soon as he begins to make one exception he must make another—and pretty soon there might be no national income left because all the food we eat would be counted as a necessary expense to keep up our working efficiency, and so forth.

from business? Obviously, a sales tax paid by a grocer is an expense, just like wages or interest; equally obviously, this expense is not paid out to any factor of production, such as labor and capital.

These two problems are not to be confused: the government may be providing much more or much less of intermediate services to a business than it is collecting in indirect taxes from that business.

The second of these problems—that of indirect taxes—is the easier to solve. Suppose we are interested in the net flow of output evaluated *at actual market price* or— in the case of a government service—evaluated at actual money cost. Then we must agree to include indirect business taxes in the total of net national product (at market prices). After all, a loaf of bread that sells for 11 cents—because of 10 cents of wages and profits and 1 cent of taxes—is selling for 10 + 1 cents and not for 10 cents alone.

As far as NNP (Net National Product) is concerned, our answer is plain: include *all* indirect business taxes. This, the Department of Commerce does. However, in order to keep the concept of national income more closely geared to the amount of factor earnings, the Department of Commerce chooses to define national income so that it falls short of NNP by the exclusion of all indirect business taxes other than corporate profits taxes. A case could be made out for excluding even corporate profits taxes, but since July, 1947, the Department of Commerce has decided to include them in national income.[1]

The earlier question, introduced by the problem of intermediate versus final government product, is not so easy to solve. In practice, the national income statistician throws up his hands and refuses to be the judge on this question. Therefore, he arbitrarily includes *all* government purchases of goods and services in NNP, warning the reader that there may be double counting involved.

We may summarize this section as follows: Government expenditure on goods and services is treated as part of net national product along with private consumption expenditure on goods and services. Let us now turn to the third and final output component of national product—investment or capital formation.

[1] Exactly where one draws the line in defining national income is not so important, especially if statistical data for two subsidiary concepts are available. One of these concepts, "disposable income," shows how much people have left to spend after paying all their taxes. In between this concept and national income falls the monthly series of personal income. This differs from national income by excluding undistributed profits, corporate taxes, and social security tax contributions, and by including transfer payments to individuals.

The tables and figure at the end of the chapter will help to make all this clear to the interested reader.

CAPITAL FORMATION

To get at net product, we must actually count in more than *final* goods and services. We must also allow for any capital formation that has taken place. For, if we were to neglect this factor, we would not be accurately measuring the true *net* product of the country.

Ordinarily, the value of goods consumed in most communities will fall short of the value of goods produced. On the other hand, in years of deep depression like 1932, the published statistics indicate that the national output *consumed* will exceed the national income *produced* by several billion dollars. Does this anomalous result mean that statisticians are blundering bureaucrats who are so ignorant of the laws of arithmetic and nature as to believe that people can consume things that have not been produced? We shall see not.

Where then does the difference between production and consumption go in the usual case when the community is not consuming all that it is producing? It takes the form of an increase in the real capital stock of the community: more and better machinery, new or enlarged factories; larger inventories and stocks of raw materials and finished goods; more homes, roads, public buildings; and so forth.[1]

Present consumption falls short of present production because part of the productive resources of society are diverted from current consumption efforts to the task of producing the extra capital that will make possible higher future production or consumption.

Thus, when a pioneer first settled on a farm in the West, he had little to show for his efforts in the first years. Or did he have so little to show? Little, as far as the current production of grain or meat, but much in the way of improvement of the land and farm: removal of boulders, clearing of trees, construction of buildings, and so forth. Like all capital formation designed at the expense of present consumption to increase future consumption, these activities are to be counted in national income or net national product.

The word "net" requires emphasis. To illustrate the opposite case of capital

---

[1] Note that in the stock of real capital we do not include bonds, mortgages, stock shares, and other paper titles to capital. Also, we must be careful to exclude from real capital formation, all capital gains or losses resulting from the writing up or down of prices. If last year my inventory of wheat was 100 bushels worth $2 per bushel, and this year I have 110 bushels at $3 per bushel, the value of my inventory has gone up by $130 or (330 − 200). But the value of my increase in real physical capital is much less than this, being not more than $30. All financial windfalls, acts of God, and nonrecurring capital gains are excluded from the reckoning of income: this is the meaning of the adjustments indicated in many of the following tables.

disinvestment, consider a farmer who begins in the spring with 10 bushels of seed corn and then harvests 110 bushels of corn in the fall. Has he produced 110 bushels *net?* No. If he were to eat or drink 110 bushels of corn, he would have consumed more than his true net production. The difference would be algebraically negative capital formation, *i.e.,* disinvestment and running down of capital (a reduction in his inventory of seed).

To summarize:

> *Consumption and net production are equal only in a stationary economy, where capital is just being replaced as fast as it is used up—where there is no growth or decay in the stock of capital.*

> *When capital is growing, national income consumed falls short of income produced, the difference being net capital formation; and the opposite is true when capital is declining.*

Figure 4*a* illustrates a growing economy. The pie represents the total of net national product or income. The lower left-hand rectangle represents the national stock of capital at the beginning of the year, and the lower right-hand shape represents the amount of capital at the end of the period. Note that the amount of product not consumed (saved) is equal to the increment in the stock of capital, or to the little triangle. (In measuring the increase in real capital, we must be careful to exclude purely fictitious "paper" revaluations of existing assets such as the capital gains in a stock market or land boom.)

Figure 4*b* illustrates the stationary case where consumption equals production and capital is just maintained intact. Figure 4*c* represents the case of retrogression when consumption exceeds net production.

CAPITAL FORMATION AND INCOME

a GROWING ECONOMY   b STATIONARY ECONOMY   c DISINVESTING ECONOMY

C = Consumption
CF = Capital Formation
Income = Algebraic Sum of Consumption and Capital Formation

CAPITAL STOCK

Initial Final   Initial Final   Initial Final
FIGS. 4*a*, 4*b*, 4*c*.

The reader will now be able to dispel the paradox of a nation consuming more than it produces. It can never consume what has not been produced; it is simply consuming more than it is *currently* producing, by drawing on *past* production. Even this is not the whole story.

Can a nation consume more than it produces only to the extent that it has supplies of previously produced *finished* goods (cans of food, etc.)? If this were the case, the difference between consumption and production could not be very large. For the stocks of finished goods in stores and warehouses do not amount to very much even in modern wealthy communities. Egypt may have lived for 7 years on its stores, but we would starve in much less than that time.

Actually a country can live in excess of its net production by "eating up" its physical capital other than finished goods. But good soup cannot be made by boiling lathes or generators. How then are such capital goods actually eaten?

They are consumed in the sense that workers and other factors of production ordinarily engaged in their *replacement and maintenance* are diverted to the production of digestible consumers' goods. In a modern economy, such a process can go on for some time, and it is immeasurably more important than the actual using up of inventories of finished goods.

During World War II, it was deliberate national policy to enhance our striking power at the enemy (*i.e.*, to increase current military consumption) by preventing nonessential civilian capital goods from being replaced as rapidly as they were used up. Our homes and automobiles grew older and lacked paint so that the diverted resources could be poured into the war effort.

As an opposite peacetime illustration, we may cite the case of the Soviet Union. In order to bring Russia quickly from a backward state of industry to a high level of technology, consumption was deliberately kept considerably below net production in the years between the two wars. The community was forced into a high level of saving and investment.

GROSS VERSUS NET INVESTMENT

One thing we must be clear about: A new addition to the community's stock of bread ovens is *net* capital formation and must be included in NNP. But an oven that is built to replace a currently used-up oven cannot be treated as part of NNP, any more than could the used-up flour and coal be counted along with the final bread. Such an oven, used to make good depreciation or capital consumption, is part of what is called "gross investment or capital formation," but is not part of net investment.

Gross investment is easier to reckon than net investment, because who is to tell which of two ovens off the assembly line is net and which is not? What accountant is so optimistic as to think that he can accurately measure depreciation?

For this reason, statisticians often add gross investment to consumption and government expenditure rather than adding net investment. The result is called "gross national product" rather than net national product, the two concepts differing only by allowances for depreciation or capital consumption.

The actual breakdown of gross investment is shown in Table 4.

TABLE 4. *Gross and Net Investment (In billions of dollars)*

	1929	1932	1946
New construction..........................	$ 7.8	$ 1.7	$ 8.5
Producers' durable equipment.................	6.4	1.8	12.4
Change in business inventory.................	1.6	−2.6	3.7
Gross private domestic investment...........	$ 15.8	$ 0.9	$ 24.6
Net foreign investment.....................	0.8	0.2	4.8
Gross private investment...................	$ 16.6	$ 1.1	$ 29.4
Allowances for depreciation or capital consumption................................	−8.8	−7.6	−11.0
Net private investment....................	$ 7.8	$ −6.5	$ 18.4

INTERNATIONAL ASPECTS OF INCOME

The distinction between domestic and foreign investment brings us to the last problem of defining national income. How do we allow for the fact that the United States is not self-sufficient but trades with the rest of the world?

In practice, we agree to measure the income or product accruing to all "permanent residents" of the United States. This includes American citizens temporarily abroad, and also unnaturalized immigrants who live permanently in the United States. It also includes dividends or interest going to our permanent residents because of capital that they own abroad. It excludes dividends and profits paid to permanent residents of other countries because of their ownership of capital located in America.

As we shall see in Chap. 16 on International Finance, a balance of international payments may be drawn up between the United States and the rest of the world. For national income purposes, we cancel exports of goods against imports, cancel dividends and other income received from abroad against income paid to foreigners, until finally we end up with our "net foreign investment" (which in any year might be negative instead of positive). Net foreign investment is treated as one component of net private investment, and hence of NNP.

QUANTITATIVE RECAPITULATION OF NATIONAL INCOME AND PRODUCT

The whole problem of national income and product is summarized in the fundamental Table 5. On the left-hand side, the cost or factor-earnings aspect

TABLE 5. *National Income and Product, 1946 (In billions of dollars)*

Wages and other employee supplements			$116.7	Personal consumption expenditure			$143.7
Unincorporated income (adjusted)			35.0	Government expenditure on goods and services			30.7
Rent income of persons			6.9				
Corporate profits (before taxes)			16.4	Net private investment			18.2
Dividends		$+5.6		Domestic		$13.4	
Undistributed profits		+6.9		Foreign		4.8	
Corporate-profits taxes		+8.6					$192.6
Inventory valuation adjustment		−4.7					
Net interest			3.2				
			$178.2				
NATIONAL INCOME			$178.2	NET NATIONAL PRODUCT			
Indirect business taxes and adjustments*			14.4	(at market prices)			$192.6
			192.6	Depreciation			11.1
NET NATIONAL PRODUCT			192.6				203.7
Depreciation or capital consumption allowances			11.1				
			203.7	GROSS NATIONAL PRODUCT			
GROSS NATIONAL PRODUCT			203.7	(at market prices)			203.7

* Includes business transfers, subsidies, and current surplus of government enterprises.

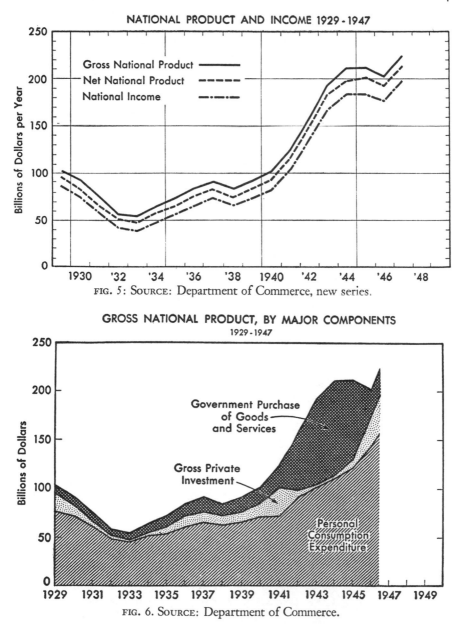

FIG. 5: SOURCE: Department of Commerce, new series.

FIG. 6. SOURCE: Department of Commerce.

is depicted. National income is the sum of earnings payable to the factors of production (wages, interest, profits, etc.). If we add indirect business taxes and adjustments to national income, we get net national product (at market prices).

But this NNP can also be thought of as a flow of three kinds of output: consumption, government, and net investment expenditure, as shown on the right-hand side of the table. Both sides add up to the same thing, by definition.

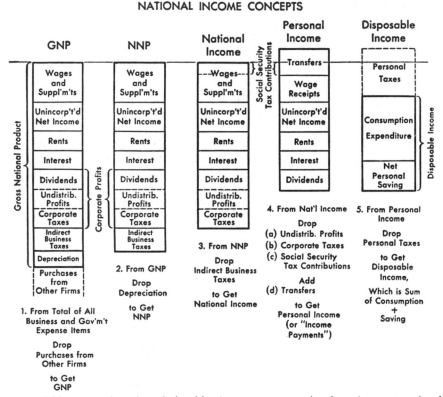

NATIONAL INCOME CONCEPTS

FIG. 7. This summarizes the relationships between gross national product, net national product, national income, personal income, and disposable income. (SOURCE: Department of Commerce revised concepts, adapted from Richard Ruggles, "*Harvard Econ A Syllabus*.")

If we add depreciation of capital to both sides, we get gross national product (at market prices). GNP (gross national product) can also be split up into three kinds of output, but now we must use gross investment rather than net.

In Tables 6 to 10 at the end of this chapter, the history from 1929 to 1946 of these and other important magnitudes is shown. Figures 5 and 6 show the same in pictorial form, while Fig. 7 shows the relationship between the five most important national income concepts.

SUMMARY

1. National income may first be looked at from the standpoint of the costs of output payable as earnings to the factors of production. It is thus equal to the sum: wages and supplements to employees + net income of unincorporated enterprise + net interest and rents + net corporate profits.

2. Or we may look at net national product as a flow of goods and services evaluated and made comparable by the use of market prices. Hence, NNP can be split into consumption expenditure on goods and services + government expenditure on goods and services + net private investment (domestic and foreign).

3. To eliminate fictitious changes in the price level, money income must be deflated by some index of changing prices. This gives a measure of real income, measured in terms of dollars of constant purchasing power.

4. Pure transfer items and windfall capital gains must be excluded from national income. Also, we must be careful not to double-count intermediate along with final product. Instead, we must concentrate on the value-added approach which cancels out at every stage all purchases of intermediate goods by one firm from another.

5. Net product is correctly reached only after we have taken account of net capital formation or net investment. Private and public consumption will fall short of net national product if resources are being used to build up the community's stock of capital goods.

6. Gross national product, which includes gross rather than net investment, involves some deliberate double counting in comparison with net national product. Because of the difficulty of evaluating capital consumption or depreciation, GNP is often used instead of—or along with—NNP.

7. All indirect business taxes must be included in NNP if goods are to be evaluated at their market prices and cost to government. But indirect business taxes are not included in national income, since this concept is to represent factor earnings (before personal and corporate income taxes).

8. The problem of indirect business taxes should not be confused with the thornier problem of what part of government expenditure on goods and services is to be treated as intermediate services rendered to business. The statistician refuses to judge this question. Instead, he warns his readers that all goods and services purchased by government have been arbitrarily included in the NNP figures.

9. International trade introduces one new problem of definition. National income is defined as income accruing to all permanent residents of a country. To arrive at this, we cancel off in the international balance of payments all purchases and sales of goods and services until we arrive at a figure for net foreign investment (+ or −). This is added algebraically into investment and into national income.

There are many philosophical problems of defining national income. Once a definition has been agreed upon, the statistical estimates do not differ by a great deal, and the resulting data give a pretty good picture of changes over time. Therefore, the analysis of business cycles and unemployment, as discussed in Part Two, is enormously aided by the improvements in the national income data of the past decades.

QUESTIONS FOR DISCUSSION

1. Make a list of items that are easy to classify as being included in or excluded from national income. Make a list of difficult items.

2. Give some examples showing that money is not always a good measuring rod of well-being.

3. The wartime increase in money incomes exceeded the increase in real incomes. How would you allow for this? Be specific.

4. List the items on a business statement of profit and loss. Which are part of value added? of NNP? of GNP?

5. Discuss the meaning of personal income and disposable income in Tables 8 and 9. How are they related to NNP and national income?

6. Discuss how people dispose of their personal incomes in Table 9. Are the results reasonable?

7. Discuss the changes in investment between 1929, 1932, and 1946. Are these changes important? Why?

8. Summarize some of the definitional problems raised by international trade.

9. What are some of the problems raised by capital formation?

TABLE 6. *National Income by Distributive Shares, 1929–1947* (*In millions of dollars*)

	1929	1932	1937	1938	1939	1941	1942	1943	1944	1945	1946	1947* 1st half
National income	87,355	41,690	73,627	67,375	72,532	103,834	136,486	168,262	182,260	182,808	178,204	199.0
Compensation of employees	50,786	30,826	47,696	44,747	47,820	64,280	84,689	109,102	121,184	122,872	116,763	125.3
Wages and salaries	50,165	30,284	45,948	42,812	45,745	61,708	81,681	105,537	116,944	117,551	111,113	
Private	45,206	25,297	38,432	34,564	37,519	51,537	65,628	78,671	83,317	82,085	90,237	
Military	312	295	358	370	398	1,862	6,285	14,478	20,782	22,438	8,010	
Government civilian‡	4,647	4,692	7,158	7,878	7,828	8,309	9,768	12,388	12,845	13,028	12,866	
Supplements to wages and salaries	621	542	1,748	1,935	2,075	2,572	3,008	3,565	4,240	5,321	5,650	
Employer contributions for social insurance	101	126	1,234	1,423	1,540	1,983	2,302	2,677	2,936	3,805	4,072	
Other labor income	520	416	514	512	535	589	706	888	1,304	1,516	1,578	
Income of unincorporated enterprises and inventory valuation adjustment	13,927	4,921	12,249	10,768	11,282	16,504	22,724	25,951	27,690	30,165	34,951	39.8
Business and professional	8,262	3,206	6,630	6,347	6,776	9,566	12,112	14,128	15,310	16,700	19,738	
Income of unincorporated enterprises	8,120	2,911	6,659	6,126	6,942	10,210	12,464	14,266	15,369	16,754	21,046	
Inventory valuation adjustment	142	295	−29	221	−166	−644	−352	−138	−59	−54	−1,308	
Farm‡	5,665	1,715	5,619	4,421	4,506	6,938	10,612	11,823	12,380	13,465	15,213	17.6
Rental income of persons	5,811	2,508	3,140	3,278	3,465	4,322	5,371	6,150	6,693	6,952	6,865	7.1
Corporate profits and inventory valuation adjustment	10,290	−1,995	6,166	4,292	5,753	14,615	19,824	23,692	23,486	19,689	16,451	23.5
Corporate profits before tax	9,818	−3,042	6,197	3,329	6,467	17,232	21,098	24,516	23,841	20,222	21,140	29.0
Corporate-profits tax liability	1,398	382	1,512	1,040	1,462	7,846	11,665	14,153	13,913	11,283	8,601	11.6
Corporate profits after tax	8,420	−3,424	4,685	2,289	5,005	9,386	9,433	10,363	9,928	8,939	12,539	17.4
Dividends	5,823	2,574	4,693	3,195	3,796	4,465	4,297	4,477	4,689	4,765	5,614	6.2
Undistributed profits	2,597	−5,998	−8	−906	1,209	4,921	5,136	5,886	5,239	4,174	6,925	11.2
Inventory valuation adjustment	472	1,047	−31	963	−714	−2,617	−1,274	−824	−355	−533	−4,689	−5.5
Net interest	6,541	5,430	4,376	4,290	4,212	4,113	3,878	3,367	3,207	3,130	3,174	3.3

* Estimated annual rates, in billions of dollars. Year-end data suggest that GNP, NNP, personal income, disposable income, and consumption were for the whole year slightly more than 6 billion dollars greater than the corresponding figures shown here; national income for the whole of 1947 was about 4 billion dollars higher than estimates in these tables.

† Includes the pay of employees of government enterprises and of permanent United States residents employed in the United States by foreign governments and international organizations.

‡ Inventory valuation adjustment data for farms are not available separately.

SOURCE: Department of Commerce.

TABLE 7. *Gross National Product or Expenditure, 1929–1947 (In millions of dollars)*

	1929	1932	1937	1938	1939	1941	1942	1943	1944	1945	1946	1947* 1st half
Gross national product	103,828	58,340	90,213	84,683	90,426	125,294	159,628	192,573	210,551	213,120	203,679	225.0
Personal consumption expenditures	78,761	49,208	67,121	64,513	67,466	82,255	90,835	101,626	110,417	121,698	143,670	158.0
Durable goods	9,362	3,694	7,005	5,754	6,729	9,750	6,845	6,515	6,755	7,977	14,917	
Nondurable goods	37,742	22,743	35,232	34,032	35,258	43,960	52,962	61,205	67,190	75,298	87,061	
Services	31,657	22,771	24,884	24,727	25,479	28,545	31,028	33,906	36,472	38,423	41,692	
Gross private domestic investment	15,824	886	11,440	6,311	9,004	17,211	9,330	4,591	5,658	9,058	24,582	29.5
New construction†	7,824	1,668	3,687	3,309	3,986	5,661	3,212	2,010	2,267	3,146	8,525	
Producers' durable equipment	6,438	1,781	5,444	3,975	4,577	7,676	4,702	3,761	5,348	7,134	12,393	
Change in business inventories	1,562	−2,563	2,309	−973	441	3,874	1,416	−1,180	−1,957	−1,222	3,664	
Net foreign investment	771	169	62	1,109	888	1,124	−207	−2,245	−2,099	−754	4,773	10.0
Government purchases of goods and services	8,472	8,077	11,590	12,750	13,068	24,704	59,670	88,601	96,575	83,118	30,654	27.5
Federal	1,311	1,480	4,552	5,280	5,157	16,923	52,027	81,223	89,029	74,963	20,671	
War‡	{ 1,344	1,484	4,557	5,286	{ 1,258	13,794	49,567	80,384	88,638	76,172	21,293	
Nonwar‡					3,908	3,173	2,664	1,480	1,552	1,011	2,383	
Less: Government sales§	33	4	5	6	9	44	204	641	1,161	2,220	3,005	
State and local	7,161	6,597	7,038	7,470	7,911	7,781	7,643	7,378	7,546	8,155	9,983	

* Estimated annual rates, in billions of dollars.

† Includes construction expenditures for crude petroleum and natural gas drilling.

‡ The classification of purchases of goods and services into war and nonwar conforms, in general, to the Daily Treasury Statement classification of general and special account expenditures. War purchases include also that part of the capital formation of government enterprises which is attributable to their war activities. Government contributions to the Nation Service Life Insurance Fund are classified as war; all other government contributions for social insurance, as nonwar.

§ Consists of sales to abroad and domestic sales of surplus consumption goods and materials.

SOURCE: Department of Commerce.

TABLE 8. *Relation of Gross National Product, National Income, and Personal Income, 1929–1947 (In millions of dollars)*

	1929	1932	1937	1938	1939	1941	1942	1943	1944	1945	1946	1947* 1st half
Gross national product	103,828	58,340	90,213	84,683	90,426	125,294	159,628	192,573	210,551	213,120	203,679	225.0
Less: Capital consumption allowances	8,816	7,663	7,972	7,992	8,101	9,294	9,935	10,585	11,773	12,085	11,040	11.8
Depreciation charges	7,553	6,950	6,838	6,894	7,082	7,878	8,666	9,409	10,456	10,557	8,875	
Accidental damage to fixed capital	413	329	304	387	222	273	484	399	374	384	404	
Capital outlays charged to current expense	850	384	830	711	797	1,143	785	777	943	1,144	1,761	
Equals: Net national product	95,012	50,677	82,241	76,691	82,325	116,000	149,693	181,988	198,778	201,035	192,639	213.2
Plus: Subsidies minus current surplus of government enterprises	−147	−45	60	176	485	102	150	183	659	775	843	+.1
Less: Indirect business tax and nontax liability	7,003	6,768	9,157	9,154	9,365	11,296	11,813	12,685	14,029	15,339	16,851	16.8
Business transfer payments	587	737	567	429	451	502	494	504	549	564	528	.5
Statistical discrepancy	−80	1,437	−1,050	−91	462	470	1,050	720	2,599	3,099	−2,101	−3.0
Equals: National income	87,355	41,690	73,627	67,375	72,532	103,834	136,486	168,262	182,260	182,808	178,204	199.0
Less: Undistributed corporate profits	2,597	−5,998	−8	−906	1,209	4,921	5,136	5,886	5,239	4,174	6,925	11.2
Corporate-profits tax liability	1,398	382	1,512	1,040	1,462	7,846	11,665	14,153	13,913	11,283	8,601	11.6
Corporate inventory valuation adjustment	472	1,047	−31	963	−714	−2,617	−1,274	−824	−355	−533	−4,689	5.5
Contributions for social insurance	243	278	1,800	1,977	2,136	2,784	3,468	4,516	5,172	6,140	5,990	5.9
Excess of wage accruals over disbursements	0	0	0	0	0	0	0	209	−193	14	−30	0.0
Plus: Net interest paid by government	983	1,141	1,204	1,192	1,205	1,289	1,517	2,140	2,800	3,675	4,491	4.5
Government transfer payments	912	1,415	1,851	2,405	2,512	2,617	2,657	2,466	3,082	5,621	10,791	10.3
Business transfer payments	587	737	567	429	451	502	494	504	549	564	528	.5
Equals: Personal income	85,127	49,274	73,976	68,327	72,607	95,308	122,159	149,432	164,915	171,590	177,217	191.1

* Estimated annual rates, in billions of dollars.
SOURCE: Department of Commerce.

TABLE 9. *Personal Income and Disposition of Income, 1929–1947 (In millions of dollars)*

	1929	1932	1937	1938	1939	1941	1942	1943	1944	1945	1946	1947* 1st half
Personal income	85,127	49,274	73,976	68,327	72,607	95,308	122,159	149,432	164,915	171,590	177,217	191.1
Wage and salary receipts	50,023	30,132	45,382	42,258	45,149	60,907	80,515	103,489	114,901	115,202	109,225	117.8
Total employer disbursements	50,165	30,284	45,948	42,812	45,745	61,708	81,681	105,328	117,137	117,537	111,143	
Less: Employee contributions for social insurance	142	152	566	554	596	801	1,166	1,839	2,236	2,335	1,918	1.7
Other labor income	520	416	514	512	535	589	706	888	1,304	1,516	1,578	
Proprietors' and rental income	19,738	7,429	15,389	14,046	14,747	20,826	28,095	32,101	34,383	37,117	41,816	46.9
Dividends	5,823	2,574	4,693	3,195	3,796	4,465	4,297	4,477	4,689	4,765	5,614	6.2
Personal interest income	7,524	6,571	5,580	5,482	5,417	5,402	5,395	5,507	6,007	6,805	7,665	7.7
Transfer payments	1,499	2,152	2,418	2,834	2,963	3,119	3,151	2,970	3,631	6,185	11,319	10.8
Less: Personal tax and nontax payments	2,643	1,455	2,921	2,862	2,440	3,293	5,962	17,815	18,904	20,878	18,789	21.5
Federal	1,263	331	1,723	1,635	1,235	2,016	4,668	16,517	17,536	19,379	17,211	
State and local	1,380	1,124	1,198	1,227	1,205	1,277	1,294	1,298	1,368	1,499	1,578	
Equals: Disposable personal income	82,484	47,819	71,055	65,465	70,167	92,015	116,197	131,617	146,011	150,712	158,428	169.6
Less: Personal consumption expenditures	78,761	49,208	67,121	64,513	67,466	82,255	90,835	101,626	110,417	121,698	143,670	158.0
Equals: Personal saving	3,723	−1,389	3,934	952	2,701	9,760	25,362	29,991	35,594	29,014	14,758	11.6

* Estimated annual rates, in billions of dollars.
SOURCE: Department of Commerce.

TABLE 10. *Labor Force, 1940–1947 (In thousands)*

Year or month	Total labor force (including armed forces)	Civilian labor force				
		Total civilian labor force	Employment			Unemployment
			Total	Nonagricultural	Agricultural	
1940 monthly average...	56,030	55,640	47,520	37,980	9,540	8,120
1941 monthly average...	57,380	55,910	50,350	41,250	9,100	5,560
1942 monthly average...	60,230	56,410	53,750	44,500	9,250	2,660
1943 monthly average...	64,410	55,540	54,470	45,390	9,080	1,070
1944 monthly average...	65,890	54,630	53,960	45,010	8,950	670
1945 monthly average...	65,140	53,860	52,820	44,240	8,580	1,040
1946 monthly average...	60,820	57,520	55,250	46,930	8,320	2,270
1946 June.............	62,000	58,930	56,360	46,350	10,010	2,570
1947 June............	64,007	62,609	60,055	49,678	10,377	2,555

NOTE: Detail will not necessarily add to totals because of rounding.
SOURCE: Department of Commerce.

PART TWO

Determination of
National Income and
Its Fluctuations

Chapter 12: SAVING AND

INVESTMENT

A. *THE THEORY OF INCOME DETERMINATION*

In Part One the groundwork was laid for an understanding of the concept of national income. Now we can go beyond the anatomy of the problem to see what causes national income to rise, to fall, to be what it is at any time and not something larger or smaller.

This chapter provides an introduction to what is called the "modern theory of income analysis." The principal stress is upon the *level of total spending as determined by the interplay of the forces of saving and investment.*

Although much of this analysis is due to an English economist, John Maynard Keynes (later made Lord Keynes, Baron of Tilton, before his death in 1946), today its broad fundamentals are increasingly accepted by economists of all schools of thought, including, it is important to notice, many writers who do not share Keynes' particular policy viewpoints and who differ on technical details of analysis.[1]

The income analysis here described is itself neutral: it can be used as well to defend private enterprise as to limit it, as well to attack as to defend government fiscal intervention. When business organizations such as the Committee

[1] Keynes himself was a many-sided genius who won eminence in the field of mathematics and philosophy and in the literary field. In addition he found time to run a large insurance company, to advise the British Treasury, to serve on the governing board of the Bank of England, to edit a world-famous economic journal, and to sponsor the ballet and the drama. He was also an economist who knew how to make money, both for himself and for King's College, Cambridge. His 1936 book, "The General Theory of Employment, Interest, and Money" created one of the greatest stirs in economic thinking of the century and is likely to live longer than his other works as a classic.

for Economic Development or the National City Bank use the terminology of saving and investment, it is absurd to think that this implies that they are "Keynesian" in the sense of belonging to that narrow band of zealots associated with some of the policy programs that Keynes himself espoused during the great depression.

THE CLEAVAGE BETWEEN SAVING AND INVESTMENT

The most important single fact about saving and investment is that in our industrial society they are largely done by different people and for different reasons.

This was not always so; even today, when a farmer devotes his time to draining a field instead of to planting and harvesting a crop, he is saving and at the same time investing. He is saving because he is abstaining from present consumption in order to provide for larger consumption in the future, the amount of his saving being measured by the difference between his net real income and his consumption. But he is also investing; *i.e.*, he is undertaking net capital formation, improving the productive capacity of his land and equipment.

Not only are saving and investment the same things for a primitive farmer, but his reasons for undertaking them are the same. He abstains from present consumption (saves) only because there is a possibility or need to drain the field (to invest). If there were no investment opportunity, it would never occur to him to save; nor would there be any way for him to save should he be so foolish as to wish to.

In our modern economy, net capital formation or investment is carried on by business enterprises, especially corporations. Although to some extent firms themselves save, saving is also done by an entirely different group: by individuals, by families, by households. An individual may wish to save for a great variety of reasons: because he wishes to provide for his old age or for a future expenditure (a vacation or an automobile). Or he may feel insecure and wish to guard against a rainy day. Or he may wish to leave an estate to his children or to his childrens' children. Or he may be an eighty-year-old miser with no heirs who enjoys the act of accumulating for its own sake. Or he may already have signed himself up to a savings program because an insurance salesman bought him a drink. Or he may desire the power that greater wealth brings. Or thrift may simply be a habit, a conditioned reflex whose origin he himself does not know. And so forth.

Whatever the individual's motivation to save, it has practically nothing to do with investment or investment opportunities. This truth is obscured by the fact that in everyday language "investment" does not always have the same meaning as in economic discussions. We have defined "net investment" or capital formation to be the net increase in the community's real capital (equipment, buildings, inventories, etc.). But the man on the street speaks of "investing" when he buys a piece of land, an old security, or any title to property. For economists these are clearly *transfer* items. What one man is investing, some one else is disinvesting. There is net investment only when new real capital is created.

Now, even if there are no investment opportunities that seem profitable, an individual will often still wish to save. He can always buy an existing security or asset. If necessary, he can accumulate, or try to accumulate, cash.

THE VARIABILITY OF INVESTMENT

Thus, we are left with our proposition that *saving and investing are done by different individuals and for largely independent reasons*. Net capital formation (with the exception of housing, automobiles, and other "consumers' durables") takes place largely in business enterprise. Its amount is highly variable from year to year and decade to decade. This capricious, volatile behavior is understandable when we realize that investment opportunities depend on *new* discoveries, *new* products, *new* territories and frontiers, *new* resources, *new* population, *higher* production and income. Note the emphasis on new and on higher. Investment depends on the *dynamic* and relatively unpredictable elements of *growth* in the system, on elements outside the economic system itself: technology, politics, optimistic and pessimistic expectations, governmental tax and expenditure, legislative policies, etc.

This extreme variability of investment is the next important fact to be emphasized. We shall see that a capitalistic free-enterprise system such as our own can do many wonderful things. It can mobilize men, equipment and know-how to respond to any given demand for goods and services. Over time it can improve upon its own response.

But there is one thing it cannot do. It cannot guarantee that there will be just exactly the required amount of investment to ensure full employment: not too little so as to cause unemployment, nor too much so as to cause inflation. So far as total investment or purchasing power is concerned, ours is a system without a steering wheel. For decades there may be too much investment, leading to periods of chronic inflation. For other years or decades, there may be too little investment, leading to deflation, losses, excess capacity, unemployment, and destitution.

Nor is there any "invisible hand" guaranteeing that the good years will equal the bad, or that our scientists will discover at just the right time precisely sufficient new products and processes to keep the system on an even keel. From the 1850's to the 1870's railroads were built all over the world. In the next two decades nothing quite took their place. The automobile and public utilities produced a similar revolution in the 1920's. In the 1930's plastics, air conditioning, radio, television, etc., were of trifling importance as contributing to total net investment.

Scientific progress was going on in the 1930's. Our wartime production shows that clearly. But some scientific discoveries can have a harmful effect on employment and purchasing power, both in the long run and in the short run, but especially in the latter. Again, there is no automatic principle of compensation which guarantees that technological change will produce a *sufficiently* favorable effect on purchasing power, or even any favorable effect.

This then is one of our most important economic lessons. As far as total investment is concerned, the system is in the lap of the gods. We may be lucky or unlucky, and the only thing we can say about luck is that it is going to change.

But we are running ahead of our story. We have not yet seen why investment is so important in determining the general level of national income and employment. To understand this we must first investigate the relation between Consumption, Saving, and Income.

THE COMMUNITY'S PROPENSITY TO CONSUME AND TO SAVE SCHEDULES

Income is the single most important determinant of consumption and saving. Poor families must spend much of their income on the necessities of life—food, shelter, and, in lesser degree, clothing. By and large, rich men can, and do, save more than poor men, not only more absolutely, but a larger percentage of their income.

In Chap. 10, we saw how people with different sized budgets spend their incomes on the various consumption items and on saving. In Table 1 and Figs. 3 and 4 of that chapter, the budgetary patterns of saving and consumption against income were summarized in the Propensity-to-save schedule and the Propensity-to-consume schedule, curves which showed how consumption and saving each vary with income. We also were introduced to the concept of the marginal propensity to consume (MPC), which was quite different from the average propensity to consume, which simply represents the ratio of total consumption to total income.

The MPC represents instead, the amount of *extra* expenditure on consumption out of each *extra* dollar of income. A family that spends all of its $2,000 income will have an average propensity to consume of 1.0 and an average propensity to save of 0.0. But if it spends only 67 cents out of every extra dollar upon consumption and saves the rest, then its MPC is ⅔ and its marginal propensity to save (MPS) is ⅓. (Note that MPC + MPS = 1.)

So far our Consumption and Saving schedules have referred only to the behavior of a typical family as it receives more or less income. Now we want to add up all the different family patterns to get the Propensity-to-consume schedule for the whole community. On the horizontal axis, we want to have national income, and on the vertical axis, total consumption.

To go from the family-budget patterns to the community schedules, we must make some assumptions about the *distribution of income:* If a national income of 200 billion dollars were exactly divided equally among 40 million families, then the level of total consumption would be higher than if a large proportion of the families fell far above and far below the average level of $5,000 per family. Why is this? Because giving dollars to rich people with low *marginal* propensities to consume will result in more saving and less consumption than if the income is divided more equally.

Taking the distribution of income as given, we can observe just how much consumption and saving there will be at *each* level of national income. Figures 1*b* and 1*a* show the community's Propensity-to-consume and Propensity-to-save schedules. If we agree to forget about government taxes and expenditure at first, Figs. 1*a* and 1*b* are closely related to each other. Note how the Consumption schedule crosses the 45° helping line at exactly the same national income level where the Saving schedule goes from minus to plus. To the left of this "break-even point," total consumption exceeds total income, and net saving is negative; to the right of the break-even point, income exceeds consumption by an amount of positive saving.

In fact, the Saving schedule is nothing else but the result of subtracting the Consumption schedule in Fig. 1*b* from the 45° line. This is because saving represents that part of total income *not spent* on consumption. Because the Consumption schedule's slope is less than 1 (*i.e.*, less than the slope of the 45° line), the Saving schedule is a rising one. Because the Consumption schedule has a slightly convex curvature, the Saving schedule must have a slightly concave curvature. This is because any drop in the MPC (say from ¾ to ⅔) must result in an increase in the MPS (from ¼ to ⅓). In both figures, the level of full-employment income is indicated by the broken vertical line.

We have now set the stage to demonstrate how national income is determined by saving and investment. First, the reader should pause to verify his understanding of the Consumption and Saving schedules. He should understand why an increase in the *inequality* of the distribution of income will lower the level of consumption at each and every level of total national income—below, above, and at full-employment income. What kind of shift of the Consumption schedule in Fig. 1*b* does this imply? What kind of shift in Fig. 1*a*? Similarly, the reader should pencil into Figs. 1*a* and 1*b* the result of everybody's becoming more *thrifty*, *i.e.*, wanting to consume less and save more at

THE CONSUMPTION AND SAVING SCHEDULES

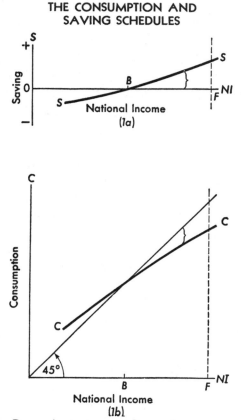

FIGS. 1*a* and 1*b*. The Propensity-to-save and Propensity-to-consume schedules for the community. The vertical distances shown by brackets are equal.

each income level. (One last caution: Taxes have not yet reared their ugly head and will not be permitted to do so until the first principles of income determination have been firmly grasped.)

HOW INCOME IS DETERMINED AT LEVEL WHERE SAVING AND INVESTMENT
SCHEDULES INTERSECT

We have seen that saving and investment are dependent on quite different factors: that saving tends to depend in a "passive" way upon income, while volatile investment depends upon "autonomous" factors of dynamic growth. For simplicity, let us first suppose that investment opportunities are such that net investment would be exactly 10 billion dollars per year regardless of the level of national income. This means that if we were to draw a schedule of investment against national income, it would have to be a *horizontal* line, always being the same distance above the lower axis. In Fig. 2, this simplified Investment schedule is labeled *I-I* to distinguish it from the *S-S* Saving schedule.

The Saving and Investment schedules intersect at a level of national income equal to the distance *OM*. This *intersection of the Saving and Investment schedules is the equilibrium toward which income will gravitate.* Under our assumed conditions, no other level of income can perpetuate itself.

**HOW SAVING AND INVESTMENT
DETERMINE INCOME**

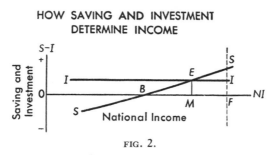

FIG. 2.

If income were higher than the intersection point, then investment spending would be less than what people would want to save: total spending on consumption plus investment would then add up to less than the cost of national output; businessmen would be unable to sell enough to justify their current level of output, so they would contract their production and lay workers off. Only by the time national income had dropped to the equilibrium level would people have such small incomes as to be finally willing to save exactly what businessmen are willing to invest. Income would not thereafter have to fall any further; no additional men would have to join the ranks of the unemployed.

Similarly, it can be shown that income will not permanently remain below the equilibrium level where the saving that people want to do is matched by continuing profitable investment opportunities. For example, suppose income were temporarily so small that businesses were wanting to invest more than people were willing to save. Then total spending on consumption and investment would be "tending" to exceed the amounts of national income being paid out to produce the national product. Profits would be buoyant, so that entrepreneurs would be hiring more men and causing national income to rise—up to the equilibrium intersection point, at which saving and investment would be just in balance, and income would be having a tendency neither to rise nor fall.

INCOME DETERMINATION BY CONSUMPTION AND INVESTMENT

There is a second way of showing how income is determined, other than by the intersection of the Saving and Investment schedules. Instead, if we wish, we may add the Investment schedule on top of the Consumption schedule. The resulting equilibrium level of income shown in Fig. 3 will be at the intersection of this new schedule (pushed upward everywhere by the 10 billion dollars of investment) with the 45° line. Why does this intersection determine the equilibrium level of national income? Because along a 45° line, the level of national income as recorded on the horizontal axis is exactly equal to the sum of the vertical distances representing the amount of consumption plus investment expenditure that people are willing to make. This shows that businesses are getting back just enough to justify their continuing that level of national product.

HOW CONSUMPTION AND INVESTMENT DETERMINE INCOME

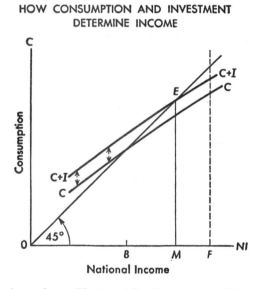

FIG. 3. This is an alternative to Fig. 2. Adding Investment to Consumption gives same result as Saving and Investment Analysis.

Needless to say, this must give us exactly the same income as will the intersection of saving and investment. The reader should compare Figs. 2 and 3 and satisfy himself that it is not an accident for these two different kinds of intersection to give exactly the same level of national income.

These two methods of showing national income determination are really identical, each being a different aspect of the same thing. Some people like to speak of income as determined by consumption plus investment expenditure; others like to state income determination in terms of saving and investment.

ARITHMETICAL DEMONSTRATION OF INCOME DETERMINATION: A THIRD RESTATEMENT

A thoughtful reader may still not be satisfied with his comprehension of *why* the equilibrium level of income will have to be at the intersection of the Saving and Investment schedules. What forces push income to that level and no other?

TABLE 1. *National Income Determination by Saving and Investment*
(In billions of dollars)

Possible levels of National income	Propensity to Consume	Propensity to save	Assumed level of maintainable investment	Paid out by businesses	Received back by businesses	Resulting tendency of of income
(1)	(2)	(3) = (1) − (2)	(4)	(5) = (1)	(6) = (2) + (4)	(7)
A. $230	$200	$ 30	$10	$230 >	$210	↓ Contraction
B. 200	180	20	10	200 >	190	↓ Contraction
C. 170	160	10	10	170 =	170	⸕ Equilibrium
D. 140	140	0	10	140 <	150	↑ Expansion
E. 110	120	− 10	10	110 <	130	↑ Expansion

An arithmetic example may help to clinch his grasp of this important matter. In Table 1, an especially simple pattern of the propensity to save against national income has been recorded. The break-even level of income where the nation is too poor to do any net saving on balance is assumed to be 140 billion dollars. Each change of national income of 30 billion dollars is assumed to lead to a 10-billion-dollar change in saving and a 20-billion-dollar change in consumption; in other words, the MPC is assumed to be constant and exactly equal to ⅔. For this reason, the Saving Propensity schedule, *S-S*, in Fig. 4 takes on the especially simple form of a perfectly straight line.

What shall we assume about investment? For simplicity, let us suppose again that the only level of investment that can be maintained indefinitely is exactly 10 billion dollars, as shown in Col. (4) of Table 1.

Now, Cols. (5) and (6) are the crucial ones. Column (5) shows how much money business firms are *paying out* in costs of production to wage earners, interest-, rent-, and profit-receivers. This is nothing but national income of

Col. (1) copied once again into Col. (5), because our repeated discussions of Chap. 11 showed that total cost payments represent one way of looking at income.

Column (6), on the other hand, shows what business firms would be *getting back* in the form of consumption sales plus investment (or net increase in their assets as shown on their consolidated balance sheets).

DEMONSTRATION THAT INCOME MOVES TOWARD EQUILIBRIUM

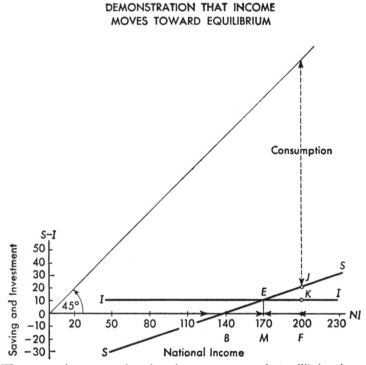

FIG. 4. The converging arrows show how income moves to the equilibrium intersection. SOURCE: Table 1.

When business firms as a whole are paying out more than they get back, they will then contract their operations and national income will tend to fall. When they are getting back more than they are paying out, they will increase their production, and national income will rise. Only when the level of scheduled saving is exactly equal to scheduled investment will business firms continue to be in aggregative equilibrium. Their sales will then be just enough to justify continuing their current level of aggregate output, so national income will neither expand nor contract.

This same story is shown in Fig. 4. National income can be read in either of two ways: on the horizontal axis, or (from the nature of a 45° line) as the equivalent vertical distance from that axis up to the helping 45° line. The line S-S represents the Saving schedule; the line I-I represents the scheduled level of investment that can be maintained over time. Consumption can also be seen on the figure: since income not consumed is saved, consumption is always the vertical distance between the Saving schedule and the 45° line.

Anywhere to the right of the intersection of the Saving and Investment schedules (which intersection takes place in this example at 170-billion-dollar national income), the *amount paid out* by businesses (the distance up to the 45° line) exceeds the amount received back by business (the distance up to the Investment schedule + the consumption distance between the Saving schedule and the 45° line). The size of these business losses is given by the distance from the Investment schedule up to the Saving schedule. Thus, in Fig. 4, a full-employment income level of 200 billion dollars cannot be maintained because of the vertical discrepancy between the Saving and Investment schedules, the distance K up to J. Therefore, the arrow on the income axis points toward contracting national income. (Now go back and reread this paragraph at least once.)

The reader should go through a similar argument to show why income will tend to rise from any place to the left of the equilibrium-intersection level. Indicate on the diagram the relation between what business pays out and what it receives back, and draw in the required arrow to show the resulting expansion of income.

THE THEORY OF INCOME DETERMINATION RESTATED

Figure 5 pulls together in a simplified way the main elements of income determination. Without saving and investment, there would be a circular flow of income between business and the public: business pays out (in the upper pipe) wages, interest, rents, and profits to the public in return for the services of labor and property; and the public pays consumption funds to business in return for goods and services.

To be realistic, we must recognize that the public will wish to save some of their income, as shown in the spigot at Z. Therefore, business firms cannot expect their consumption sales to be as large as the total of wages, interests, rents, and profits.

Some monetary cranks think that this saving necessaringly means unemployment and depression. Such a view is simply incorrect. If there happen to be profitable investment opportunities, business firms will be paying out wages, interest, and other costs in part for new capital formation. Hence, to continue to be happy, business will have to receive back in consumption sales only *part* of the total income paid out to the public—only that part which involves the cost of current consumption goods. The saving of the public will do no harm to national income so long as it is not greater than what business can profitably invest.

In Fig. 5, investment is shown being pumped into the income stream at A. The handle of the pump is being moved by (1) technological invention, (2)

HOW INVESTMENT DETERMINES INCOME

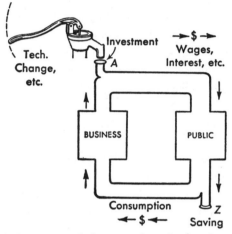

FIG. 5. Technological change, population growth, and other dynamic factors keep the investment pump handle going. Income rises and falls with changes in investment, its equilibrium level, at any time, being realized only when intended saving at Z matches intended investment at A.

population growth, and (3) other dynamic factors. When the investment pump is going at a rapid pace, national income is high and reaches its equilibrium rate when the saving at Z just balances the investment at A.

This demonstrates that the pessimistic monetary cranks who think that saving is always disastrous are plain wrong. But there is also a second school of monetary cranks: they go to the opposite extreme and insist that saving and investment can never cause income to be too high or too low. They make the fatal error of rigidly connecting up the pipe at Z with the pipe at A. Roomfuls of books have been written on this subject, but it is only in the last few decades that economists have learned how to separate out the truth and falsity of both extreme viewpoints.

B. *APPLICATIONS AND LIMITATIONS OF INCOME ANALYSIS*

THE "MULTIPLIER"

We have now completed the essentials of the modern theory of income determination. Naturally, we must go on to discuss a number of important qualifications: the effect of government finance on income analysis, and how you would go about measuring saving and investment statistically. But these are refinements and can wait.

Let us first show how *an increase in private investment will cause income to expand*, and a *decrease in investment will cause it to contract*. This is not a very surprising result. After all, we have learned that net capital formation is one part of net national product; when one of the parts increases in value, we would naturally expect the whole to increase in value.

That is only part of the story. Our theory of income determination gives us a much more striking result. Modern income analysis shows that an increase in net investment will increase national income by a multiplied amount—by an amount greater than itself! Investment dollars are high-powered, double-duty dollars, so to speak.

This amplified effect of investment on income is called the "multiplier" doctrine; the word "multiplier" itself is used for *the numerical coefficient showing how great an increase in income results from each increase in investment*. Some examples will make this terminology clear. If an increase of investment of 5 billion dollars causes an increase of income of 15 billion dollars, then the multiplier is 3. If the increase in income were 20 billion dollars, then the multiplier would be 4. The multiplier is the number by which the change in investment must be amplified (or multiplied) in order to get the resulting change in income.

No proof has yet been presented to show that the multiplier will be greater than 1. But using ordinary common sense, we can begin to see why, when I hire unemployed resources to build a $1,000 garage, there will be a secondary expansion of national income and production, over and above my primary investment. My carpenters and lumber producers will get an extra $1,000 of income. But that is not the end of the story. If they all have a marginal propensity to consume of $2/3$, they will now spend $666.67 on new consumption goods. The producers of these goods will now have an extra income of $2/3$ of $1,000.

If their MPC is also ⅔, they will create ⅔ of ⅔ of $1,000 of further spending (or ⅔ of $666.67 = $444.44), and so forth.

Thus a whole chain of secondary consumption responding is set up by my primary $1,000 of investment spending. But it is a dwindling chain, and it all adds up to a finite amount. Either by grade-school arithmetic or high-school geometric progression, we get

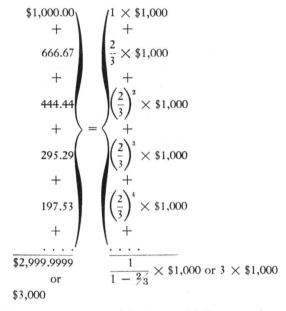

$$
\left.
\begin{array}{c}
\$1,000.00 \\
+ \\
666.67 \\
+ \\
444.44 \\
+ \\
295.29 \\
+ \\
197.53 \\
+ \\
\cdots
\end{array}
\right\}
=
\left\{
\begin{array}{c}
1 \times \$1,000 \\
+ \\
\frac{2}{3} \times \$1,000 \\
+ \\
\left(\frac{2}{3}\right)^2 \times \$1,000 \\
+ \\
\left(\frac{2}{3}\right)^3 \times \$1,000 \\
+ \\
\left(\frac{2}{3}\right)^4 \times \$1,000 \\
+ \\
\cdots
\end{array}
\right.
$$

$$
\$2,999.9999 \text{ or } \$3,000 \qquad \frac{1}{1 - \frac{2}{3}} \times \$1,000 \text{ or } 3 \times \$1,000
$$

This shows that, with an MPC of ⅔, the multiplier must be 3, consisting of the 1 of primary investment plus 2 extra of secondary consumption responding.

The same arithmetic would give a multiplier of 4 if the MPC were ¾. (HINT: What does $1 + \frac{3}{4} + (\frac{3}{4})^2 + (\frac{3}{4})^3 + \cdots$ finally add up to?) If the MPC were ½, the multiplier would be 2. If the MPS were ¼, the MPC would be ¾, and the multiplier would be 4. If the MPS were ⅓, the multiplier would be 3.

By this time the reader will guess that the multiplier is always the upside-down or "reciprocal" of the marginal propensity to save. Our general multiplier formula is always

$$
\textbf{Change in income} = \frac{1}{\textbf{MPS}} \times \textbf{change in investment}
$$

$$
= \frac{1}{1 - \textbf{MPC}} \times \textbf{change in investment}
$$

In other words, the greater the extra consumption spending, the greater the multiplier. The greater the "leakage" into extra saving at each round of spending, the smaller the final multiplier.

Up to this point, we have discussed the multiplier in terms of common sense and arithmetic. Will our saving-investment analysis of income give us the same result? The answer must of course be "yes." If a new series of inventions comes along and gives rise to an extra 10 billion dollars of continuing investment opportunities, over and above our previous 10 billion dollars, then the increase in national income should raise national income from 170 to 200 billion dollars.

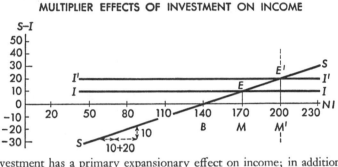

FIG. 6. Investment has a primary expansionary effect on income; in addition, because of consumption respending, it has a secondary effect as well.

In Fig. 6, our old Investment schedule, *I-I*, is shifted upward by 10 billion dollars to the new level *I'-I'*. The new intersection point is *E'*. Lo and behold, the increase in income is by exactly three times as much as the increase in investment. This is because a MPS of only $\frac{1}{3}$ means a relatively flat *S-S* Saving schedule. As the dotted arrows show, the horizontal income distance is always three times as great as the "primary" vertical saving-investment distance, the discrepancy being equal to the secondary "consumption respending."[1]

In short, income must rise enough to bring out a volume of voluntary saving equal to the new investment. With a MPS of $\frac{1}{3}$, income has to rise by 30 billion dollars to bring out 10 billion dollars of new saving.

A DIGRESSION ON THE IDENTITY BETWEEN MEASURABLE SAVING AND MEASURABLE INVESTMENT

National income is determined by the interplay of saving and investment. This should not be misunderstood to imply that during a depression a statisti-

[1] Table 1 will also verify this answer. In Col. (4), we now have 20 billion dollars instead of 10 billion dollars of investment. The new equilibrium level of income now shifts to row *B* (200 billion dollars income) from the old equilibrium level in row *C* (170 billion dollars).

cian can measure saving, then measure investment, and expect to find that the former is statistically greater than the latter.

The discussion of national income in Chap. 11 showed that—leaving government finance aside—the total of saving of any period is defined in such a way that it must be exactly equal to the total of net investment of that period. Saving is the difference between total income and total consumption; or in terms of the pie diagram of Fig. 4 in Chap. 11, saving equals ⟁ . Net investment or net capital formation was the difference between the capital stock at the end and the beginning of the period; or to ☐ minus ◺. By the very definition of national income or of net national product (which consists of consumption plus net investment), measurable saving and measurable investment are simply two different names for the same thing: namely, net income minus consumption.[1]

This identity of measurable saving and measurable investment at every income level is not the same thing as the *equality* of the *scheduled* amounts of saving and investment which takes place only at the equilibrium level of income.[2] If income is temporarily pulled away for some reason from the longer run equilibrium level, then the amount of investment that businesses will be willing to maintain will not be equal to the saving that people will want to continue to make. Despite the superficial identity of measured saving and investment, national income will not be able to remain away from the equilibrium level indefinitely—because in the next period, dissatisfied savers or investors will act so as to set in motion a return toward equilibrium.

Two examples, out of many possible ones, may be presented to illustrate how national income may temporarily be away from the equilibrium level with scheduled investment and saving unequal—but, of course, with measured investment and saving being always defined so as to come out equal.

In the first example, suppose that every family suddenly decides to have a higher propensity to consume and a lower propensity to save. This should finally lead to a higher equilibrium level of national income. But not necessarily all at once. On the first day of the new era, they will troop to the stores and

[1] This identity has an exact analogue: the amount bought must be identically equal to the amount sold in any transaction involving the exchange of goods for money.

[2] This may be applied to the pump diagram of Fig. 5. The flow of water at the saving pipe, Z, will equal the flow of water at the investment pump, A, only when national income is at its equilibrium level. But in real life, equilibrium is always changing, with the system avidly pursuing it. The statistician isn't able to measure saving at Z and investment at A. Instead, he always counts in unintended saving and unintended investment that may pile up in the pipes, so that no water goes uncounted, and the measure of saving is identical to that of investment.

increase their consumption purchases (by, let us say, 1 million dollars) out of their as yet unchanged incomes. Merchants had no reason to foresee this development; therefore they will find their inventory of goods reduced by 1 million dollars. National income has not risen to the new equilibrium level: indeed, it has not yet risen at all. This is because the reduction of consumers' intended saving was temporarily matched by an unintentional reduction in business inventory investment. But—and this is the crux of the matter— businessmen will not continue indefinitely to deplete their inventories. In subsequent periods when they increase their production orders, national income will rise to its equilibrium level, where everyone is content to maintain the *status quo*.

In our second example, suppose that corporations begin to take advantage of new investment opportunities. They borrow money from banks or spend their idle cash balances to give construction jobs to workers. According to our equilibrium analysis, secondary consumption respending should have a multiplier effect upon income beyond the original primary effect. But this respending process may take time to work itself out. There may be a long or short period of delay between the moment when people receive new income and the time when they are able to spend it. In the short run, therefore, the economic system may fall short of the equilibrium level because the new investment has been temporarily offset by increased saving: not yet having time to spend their higher incomes, people are temporarily forced *below* their Consumption schedule and *above* their Saving schedule. When national income finally ceases growing and settles down, then people will be back on their *S-S* schedule and income will be at the new equilibrium intersection.

What this section says can be boiled down to the following:

> *The equality of the saving and investment that people are willing to continue to make holds only at the equilibrium level of income. But the definitional identity of measured saving and investment holds all the time —even when income is away from the equilibrium level and is in process of being pushed by people's dissatisfaction with their actual realized saving and investment back toward equilibrium.*[1]

INDUCED INVESTMENT AND THE PARADOX OF THRIFT

Until now we have always treated net investment as an autonomous element, absolutely independent of national income. All our Investment schedules have

---

[1] Advanced students of economics will wish to go into the subject matter of this section in greater detail, comparing income-analysis at every stage with the supply and demand analysis of competitive market price. Readers wishing an introduction to economics need not worry themselves unduly over this problem.

been drawn as horizontal lines, their level being always the same regardless of income. This simplification can now be relaxed.

Any practical businessman will tell you that he is more likely to add to his plant or equipment if his sales are high relative to his plant capacity. In the short run (before businessmen have had time to adjust their capital stock to a changed plateau of income), it is reasonable for us to draw the *I-I* schedule in Fig. 7 (page 272) as a rising curve. *An increase in national income may induce a higher level of net investment.*

As before, the equilibrium level of (maintainable) national income is given by the intersection of the Investment and Saving schedules; or in the first instance by the point *E* in Fig. 7. So long as the *S-S* curve always cuts the *I-I* curve from below, businessmen's action will always bring the economic system back to the equilibrium level.[1]

Induced investment means that anything that increases national income is likely to be good for the capital goods industries; anything that hurts national income is likely to be bad for those industries. This throws a new spotlight on the age-old question of thrift versus consumption. It shows that an increased desire to consume—which is another way of looking at a decreased desire to save—is likely to boost business sales and increase investment. An increase in thriftiness, on the other hand, is likely to make a depression worse and reduce the amount of actual net capital formation in the community. *High consumption and high investment go hand in hand rather than being competing.*

This surprising result is sometimes called the "paradox of thrift." It is a paradox because in kindergarten we are all taught that thrift is *always* a good thing. Benjamin Franklin's "Poor Richard's Almanac" never tired of preaching the doctrine of saving. And now along comes a new generation of alleged financial experts who seem to be telling us that black is white and white is black, and that the old virtues may be modern sins.

Let us for the moment leave our cherished beliefs to the side, and try to disentangle the paradox in a dispassionate, scientific manner. Two considerations will help to clarify the whole matter.

The first is this. In economics, we must always be on guard against the logical fallacy of composition. What is good for each person separately need not be good for all; under some circumstances, private prudence may be social folly. Specifically, this means that the *attempt* of each and every person to

---

[1] If the two curves crossed in the opposite way, we would have unstable equilibrium, and the economy would rush away—in either direction—from the intersection neighborhood. A physical analogy may be suggestive: An egg on its side is in stable equilibrium; when given a slight disturbance, it returns to equilibrium. An egg on its tip is in unstable equilibrium; a light touch and it topples.

increase his saving may—under the conditions to be described—result in a reduction in *actual* saving by all the people in the community. Note the italicized words "attempt" and "actual"; between them there may be a world of difference if people find themselves thrown out of jobs and with lowered income payments.

The second clue to the paradox of thrift lies in the question of whether or not national income is at a depression level. If we were at full employment, then obviously the more of our national product that we devote to current consumption, the less is available for capital formation. If output could be assumed to be always at its maximum, then the old-fashioned doctrine of thrift would be absolutely correct—correct, be it noted, from both the individual and the social standpoints.

In primitive agricultural communities, such as the American colonies of Franklin's day, there was truth in Franklin's prescription. The same was true during World Wars I and II, and it becomes true during periods of inflation and boom: if people will become more thrifty, then less consumption will mean more investment.

But full employment and inflationary conditions have occurred only occasionally in our recent history. Much of the time there is some wastage of resources, some unemployment, some insufficiency of demand, investment, and purchasing power. When this is the case, everything goes into reverse. What once was a social virtue may become a social vice. What is true for the individual—that extra thriftiness means increased saving and wealth—may become completely untrue for the community as a whole.

Under conditions of unemployment, the *attempt to save* may result in *less*, not more, saving. The individual who saves cuts down on his consumption. He passes on less purchasing power than before. Therefore, someone else's income is reduced. For one man's outgo is another man's income. If one individual succeeds in saving more, it is because someone else is forced to dissave. If one individual succeeds in hoarding more money, someone else must do without. If all individuals try to hoard, they cannot all succeed in doing so, but they can force down the velocity of circulation of money—and national income.

Thus, when there is unemployment, consumption and investment are complementary, not competitive. What helps one helps the other. The attempt to cut down on consumption (to save) only results in a reduction of income until everyone feels poor enough no longer to try to save more than can be invested. Moreover, at lower levels of income, less and not more capital goods will be needed. Therefore, *investment will actually be less as a result of thriftiness.*

Let us clinch our common-sense understanding of this paradox by turning to the income analysis of Fig. 7. An increase in thriftiness or the desire to save will shift the SS curve upward to S'S'. Note that the new intersection, E', is now at a lower level of income. Because of induced *dis*investment, the drop in income will also mean smaller investment. Thus both income and investment have actually decreased. The attempt to save more has resulted in less actual saving!

If true, this is an important lesson. Never again can people be urged in time of depression to tighten their belts, to save more in order to restore prosperity. The result will be just the reverse—a worsening of the vicious deflationary spiral.

What becomes of the argument that wealthy people are needed to provide saving, that inequality of the distribution of income is needed to push up the Saving schedule? We see it then go into reverse. An economic lobbyist to the capital goods industries would, if he has their selfish interests at heart, advocate less thriftiness in depressed times, so that the Saving schedule will be pushed down, and so that attempts to save—which really only lead to decreases in income—will be discouraged. For only then will investment and sales of heavy capital goods flourish.[1]

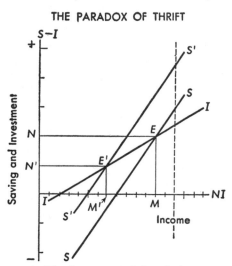

THE PARADOX OF THRIFT

FIG. 7. The Investment Schedule is now a rising one because of investment induced by income changes. An increase in the desire to save (from S-S to S'-S') results in less realized saving and investment because income is lowered.

DEFLATIONARY AND INFLATIONARY GAPS

The multiplier is a two-edged sword. It will cut for you or against you. It will amplify new investment as we have seen. But it will also amplify downward any *decrease* in investment. Thus, if investment opportunities had dropped from our original 10-billion-dollar level down to zero, national income would have to fall by three times as much—from 170 billion dollars down to the 140-

[1] We have seen that this line of argument does not apply in conditions of full employment. It also requires some slight modifications to allow for the fact that thriftiness, by lowering income, may also lower interest rates and promote investment. In the author's opinion, this qualification is unimportant in time of depression.

billion-dollar break-even point where the community is made poor enough to stop all net savings.

This shows that there is nothing particularly good about what we have called the equilibrium level of national income. If investment is low, the equilibrium level of income will involve much unemployment and wastage of national resources. The only level of national income that we are entitled to regard as a desirable goal is that near to full employment. But we will end up at such a level of high employment only if investment opportunities happen to be as large as full-employment saving.

Unless this full-employment saving is "offset" by private investment (or by governmental policies), the nation cannot continue to enjoy full employment. There is then said to be a "deflationary gap," the size of this gap being measured by the deficiency of investment compared to full-employment saving —or by the vertical distance along the dotted full-employment line between the Saving and Investment schedules.

Thus, if full-employment saving out of a 200-billion-dollar national income were 20 billion dollars, while investment was only 15 billion dollars, we would speak of a 5-billion-dollar deflationary gap. Income could not stay at the full-employment level but would have to drop by about 15 to 185 billion dollars.

Now stop for a moment. National income is 15 billion dollars short of the full-employment level. Does that mean that we need 15 billion dollars of private or public investment to give us full employment? You will have to answer "no," as soon as you recall that investment dollars are high-powered dollars which have a multiplier effect on national income. At most, we will need only 5 billion dollars of public or private investment to fill in for a deflationary gap of 5 billion dollars. The secondary consumption spending will do the rest, leading in the end to a full 15 billion dollar increase in national income.

Our theory explains depressions. It will be a much more useful and general theory if it also helps to explain inflations, when there is too much rather than too little total spending.

Suppose that the Saving and Investment schedules will intersect only to the right of the full-employment dotted line. In this case, full-employment saving is less than full-employment investment. Instead of having a deflationary gap, we have what is called an "inflationary gap." This inflationary gap is measured by the vertical excess of full-employment investment over full-employment saving; or what is numerically the same thing, by the money that the community tries to spend on consumption plus investment goods out of their full employment income *in excess* of the value of goods actually produced.

Although an inflationary gap is the opposite of a deflationary gap, its effects upon employment and production are of a slightly different qualitative nature. A deflationary gap can move production leftward, down to three-quarters or even one-half of a full-employment level. But an inflationary gap cannot possibly move employment rightward to 150 per cent of full or maximum employment. The economic system cannot move in real terms very far to the right of the dotted full-employment line.

The excess in purchasing power can only result in price increases and an inflationary spiral: money national income will rise because of "paper" price changes, but real national product cannot go above its maximum full-employment level. Unfortunately, the upward movement of prices will continue for as long as there is an inflationary gap, i.e., until we are lucky enough for investment or consumption demand to fall off, or smart enough as a nation to adopt corrective policies that will wipe out the inflationary gap.

One of the principal problems of Chap. 18 on Fiscal Policy will be that of trying to compensate by public taxes and expenditure for both inflationary and deflationary gaps, so that high employment can be maintained without inflation.

TAXATION AND GOVERNMENT EXPENDITURE IN INCOME ANALYSIS

Let us, therefore, push our analysis beyond the oversimplified case where government economic activity is ignored. To be realistic, we must examine the effects upon income determination of government expenditure and taxes.

The effect of government expenditure can best be analyzed if we first hold taxes constant. Because government expenditure on goods and services uses up labor and other productive resources, we learned in Chap. 11 that net national product consists of three, rather than two, parts; namely,

NNP = consumption expenditure + private net capital formation
              + government expenditure on goods and services

Therefore, on our 45°-line diagram in Fig. 8, we must superimpose upon the Consumption schedule not only private investment but also government expenditure, G. This is because public road building is financially no different from private railroad building; and collective consumption expenditure involved in maintaining a free public library has the same effect upon jobs as private consumption expenditure for movies or rental libraries.

We add government expenditure to private investment and go to the intersection with the 45° line to read off the equilibrium level of national income. Obviously, therefore, taken by itself and disregarding taxes, government expenditure has a multiplier effect upon income just like that of private investment. The reason is, of course, that the chain of consumption respending is set into motion by the road builders, librarians, and other people who receive primary income from the government.[1]

Let us now turn briefly to the effect of taxes on national income. If the government takes 20 billion dollars of our incomes in taxes, then out of a 200-billion-dollar national income, we have only 180 billion dollars left as disposable income to spend on consumption and saving. Similarly, out of a 180-billion-

**EFFECT OF GOVERNMENT
EXPENDITURE ON
INCOME DETERMINATION**

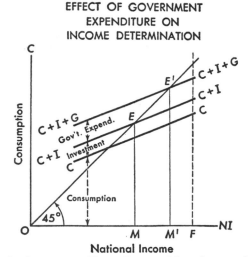

National Income

FIG. 8. An increase in Government Expenditure, with no increase in Taxes, has Multiplier effects on Income just like private Investment. On top of the Consumption Schedule, we must add the other two components of Net National Product, namely, Private Investment, *I*, and Government Expenditure on goods and services, *G*.

dollar national income, we have only 160 billion dollars of disposable income. Therefore, the greater are total taxes, the lower is the relation of disposable income to national income and the lower is consumption at any given level of national income. The Consumption schedule is shifted *rightward* by the amount of taxes—because national income must be increased by the full amount of taxes if consumption (and disposable income) is to be left the same. Such a *rightward* shift is also a downward shift.

Figure 9 shows how taxes shift the Consumption schedule rightward and downward. After 20 billion dollars of taxes have been introduced, national

[1] Our saving-investment diagram will give the same answer as the 45°-line diagram. The increase in government expenditure means an equivalent increase in the government deficit if taxes have not been increased. Net saving must always equal private investment + government deficit. Therefore, we add the deficit on top of the *I-I* curve and get our new greater equilibrium level of national income.

income must increase from M to M' in order to have the same disposable income and consumption as before.

Obviously, taxes reduce total purchasing power and decrease the equilibrium level of national income. The downward shift in the Consumption schedule pushes the equilibrium intersection downward and to the left. Reducing taxes, on the other hand, increases purchasing power and income.[1] If there is much unemployment, this is all to the good. If employment is full and prices are tending to rise, reducing taxes will add to the inflationary fuel and ultimately leave us all worse off.

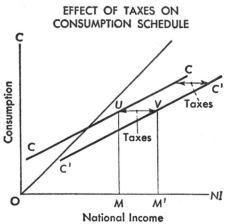

EFFECT OF TAXES ON CONSUMPTION SCHEDULE

FIG. 9. Following the imposition of Taxes, National Income must increase from M to M' in order to have the same Consumption (and Disposable Income) as before. Thus, the new Consumption Schedule is shifted to the right by the amount of Taxes. This rightward and downward shift will lower the equilibrium National Income level almost as much as an equivalent increase in Government Expenditure would have raised it.

QUALIFICATIONS TO SAVING AND INVESTMENT ANALYSIS

The theory of income determination sketched in this chapter is a powerful tool. It helps us to understand the ups and downs of the business cycle. It helps us to understand how foreign lending (which is one part of total net investment) affects domestic employment and income. It helps us to understand how governmental fiscal policy can be used to fight inflation and unemployment. All these topics are treated in later chapters of Part Two.

---

[1] On the saving and investment diagram, an increase in taxes shifts the S-S curve to the right: it now takes more national income for people to be able to break even. That part of each extra dollar of national income going for taxes is unavailable for saving, so the S-S curve will be flatter. If government expenditure just balances the taxes, there will be no deficit to add to the I-I curve, and the new equilibrium income level will have risen slightly. If government expenditure has not increased with taxes, then there will be a treasury surplus. This surplus must be subtracted from the I-I curve. The new intersection will give us a *lower* national income because the downward shift from the I-I schedule will always be greater than the downward shift in the S-S schedule, as can be seen if the figure is carefully drawn.

Corporate saving can be handled graphically in much the same way as taxes, but this may be left to more advanced discussions.

It would be a mistake to think that an economist can be made out of a parrot, simply by teaching him the magical words saving and investment. Behind the scenes of these schedules a great deal is taking place. Interest rates may go up, causing the Investment schedule to shift downward. (This is discussed further in Chap. 13.) Or an increase in the public's holding of government bonds and other wealth may shift the Consumption schedule upward. Or rising living standards (resulting from advertising and the invention of new products) may shift the Consumption schedule up just as it has in the past.

In short, it is an oversimplification to regard investment as always an autonomous factor, and consumption always a passive factor depending upon income. True, this is a fruitful oversimplification. But as we have already seen, some of net investment may be "induced" by income changes in the short run. Likewise, consumption will sometimes shift autonomously even though income has remained constant. And, as the reader can verify by experimenting with the saving-investment and the 45°-line diagrams, such shifts in the Consumption or Saving schedules have multiplier effects upon national income—just like the multiplier effects of changes in investment.

For this reason, there is at least one school of thought that favors fighting any future chronic depressions by policies aimed at making the United States a "high-consumption economy"; *i.e.*, an economy with a high Consumption schedule, whose corresponding level of full-employment saving is just equal to the level of net capital formation needed for progress.

SUMMARY

A. INCOME DETERMINATION

1. The motives that make people save are quite different from those that make businesses invest. Net investment tends to depend on such autonomous elements as new population, new territory, new inventions, new tastes, and other growth elements; consumption and saving tend to behave along passive schedules plotted against national income.

2. People's wishes to save and the willingness of corporations to invest are brought into line with each other by means of changes in national income. The equilibrium level of national income must be at the intersection of the Saving and Investment schedules; or what is exactly the same thing, at the intersection of the Consumption plus Investment schedule with the 45° line of total income.

To put the matter most simply: investment calls the tune. Investment and saving are equal because investment causes income to rise or fall until saving has adjusted itself.[1] The simplest sequence is

INVESTMENT ———————⟶ INCOME ———————⟶ SAVING

B. APPLICATIONS AND LIMITATIONS

3. Investment has a multiplier effect on income. When investment changes, there is an equal primary change in national income. But as these primary income-receivers in the capital goods industries get more or less income, they set into motion a whole chain of additional secondary consumption spending. If people always spend about $\frac{2}{3}$ of each extra dollar of income upon consumption, the total of the multiplier chain will be $1 + \frac{2}{3} + (\frac{2}{3})^2 + \ldots = 1/(1 - \frac{2}{3}) = 3$. The multiplier works backward or forward, amplifying either increases or decreases in investment. The multiplier is numerically equal to the reciprocal of the MPS; this is because it always takes more than a dollar's change in income to bring forth a dollar's change in saving.

4. The *attempt* to save more is quite different from the achievement of increased saving for society as a whole. The paradox of thrift shows how an increase in thriftiness may reduce income and, through induced effects on investment, actually result in less net investment. Only when employment remains full are consumption and investment competing; only then are private virtues always social virtues.

The moral is not for each individual to squander his money in trying to be patriotic. Instead, through proper national policies, we must recreate a high employment environment in which private virtues are no longer social follies.

5. In short, we must avoid both inflationary and deflationary gaps, so that full-employment saving and investment just match.

6. One weapon in the battle for stability is government fiscal policy: an increase in government expenditure, taken by itself, has expansionary effects on national income, much like those of private investment. An increase in taxes, taken by itself, tends to contract the equilibrium level of national income.

[1] The equality of the saving that people are willing to maintain with the investment that business firms are willing to maintain is the equilibrium condition that permits national income to remain steady. This equality should not be confused with the definitional identity of measured saving and investment at every income level. Such a confusion would be like the century-old fallacy that says, "Supply and demand cannot possibly determine competitive market price, because after all, the amount bought must necessarily be identically equal to the amount sold."

We must leave to Chap. 18 the analysis of government surpluses, deficits, debt, and fiscal policy. To the intervening chapters we must turn for an analysis of money, prices, and interest; of international finance; and the wild dance of the business cycle.

QUESTIONS FOR DISCUSSION

1. What are some of the reasons that cause people to save? What are some of the forms in which people are able to keep their saving?

2. Imagine that you are a businessman. What changes would make you invest more? less? Make a list of possible programs of real investment. Where do they fit into the list of different kinds of private net capital formation in Chap. 11?

3. The saving and investment diagram and the 45°-line (or consumption + investment) diagram are two different ways of showing how national income is determined. Describe each. Show that they are equivalent. Which do you prefer?

4. Reconstruct Table 1 assuming that net investment is equal to (a) 20 billion dollars, (b) 40 billion dollars. What is the resulting difference in national income? Is this greater or smaller than the change in investment? Why?

5. Describe in a few paragraphs (a) the common sense, (b) the arithmetic, and (c) the geometry of the multiplier.

6. "While no one *attempts* to save with any thought of investment outlets, yet the amount that all succeed in saving is brought into alignment with investment by the movements of National Income. But the alignment is performed on a cruel Procrustean bed with income and employment being lopped off if the desire to save is excessive in comparison with available investment, or with an inflationary straining of demand if investment is excessive." Do you agree? Is the final *equality* of saving and investment described here the same thing as the *identity* of measured saving and measured investment?

7. In Fig. 2, how would you measure the deflationary gap? in Figs. 3 and 4? in Table 1? How would you change the figures to show an inflationary gap?

8. Give arguments for and against thriftiness. Distinguish carefully (a) between the individual and the community viewpoint and (b) between different states of business activity.

9. Describe briefly the effects upon income of (a) government expenditure, (b) taxes, (c) our sale of less goods and services to foreigners than we buy from them.

10. Why will corporate saving have the same effect on the Consumption schedule as taxes?

11. What do you regard as some of the limitations on the saving and investment analysis of national income?

Chapter 13: PRICES, MONEY,

AND INTEREST RATES

THIS chapter falls naturally into three parts. In the first part the importance of price changes—of inflation and deflation—is discussed. In the second part there is a description of our money supply, and of the relationship between that supply and the price level. Then in the third section we shall see how money affects the level and structure of interest rates.

A. *PRICES*

INFLATION, DEFLATION, AND REDISTRIBUTION OF INCOME BETWEEN ECONOMIC CLASSES

By inflation we mean a period of generally rising prices. By deflation we mean a period in which most prices are falling. The root cause of inflation and deflation is a change in total money *spending* relative to the flow of goods offered for sale. If the total flow of purchasing power coming on to the market is not matched by a sufficient flow of goods, prices will tend to rise. On the other hand, when total spending declines, prices and the real flow of production tend to be depressed.

Neither in inflation nor in deflation do all prices move in the same direction or in exactly the same proportion. As a result of changes in *relative* prices and in total spending, the two processes of inflation and deflation cause definite and characteristic changes in (1) total output and (2) the distribution of income between economic classes.

Inflation tends to favor debtors and profit receivers at the expense of creditors and fixed-income receivers, while the effects of deflation are the opposite. Suppose a creditor lends $1,000 today and is paid back one year from now. If in the meantime prices have doubled, then the debtor will be paying back only about one-half as much real purchasing power as was given to him.

If prices were to increase a trillion-fold, as they did in the German inflation of 1920–1923, then the wealth of creditors would be completely wiped out. This actually happened to German university endowments and life-insurance assets. After World War II an American who earned 4 per cent yearly on a mortgage found that he was not even holding his own as far as the *real purchasing power* of the dollar was concerned. During and after World War I, American prices were still more inadequately controlled, with the result that white-collar workers like teachers, postmen, and bookkeepers found their relatively fixed incomes inadequate to maintain living standards in the face of the rising cost of living. Widows living on fixed pensions, on life-insurance annuities, or on bond interest found themselves in the same difficult straits because the postwar dollar would buy less than a prewar 50-cent piece.

On the other hand, anyone who invests his money in real estate, in common stocks, or in sacks of flour makes a great money profit during inflation. The volume of business sales shoots up. Prices rise between the time that the businessmen buy and sell their merchandise. Fixed or overhead costs remain the same. Other costs rise but not so rapidly as prices. For all these reasons profits increase—often faster than does the cost of living. In such periods of great inflation, every reckless fool can become a great financier. Some workers in highly organized occupations may, by militant collective bargaining, be able to keep up with the high cost of living, but many find their real wages shrinking.

In time of deflation, the shoe is on the other foot. Creditors and fixed-income receivers tend to gain at the expense of debtors and profit receivers. If prices fall between the time that a creditor lends money and is repaid, then he gets back more purchasing power than he lent. Between the time that a merchant buys and sells goods, he will have to take a loss.

The schoolteacher who keeps her job and whose pay is not cut too deeply finds that her real income has increased. The widow who withstood the temptation to buy common stock during the boom and instead put all her money into gilt-edge government bonds finds herself better off. At the same time the government finds that the real burden of its public debt has gone up relative to tax collections and national income. A hoarder who earns no money interest on his mattress cache finds that the real value of his wealth is increasing every day as prices fall. If prices fall at the rate of 10 per cent per year, he is being rewarded for his antisocial act of hoarding at a 10 per cent rate of interest in real terms, while the businessman who is foolish enough to give someone a job will probably find that he cannot even get back his original outlay, much less earn a profit.

EFFECTS OF CHANGING PRICES ON OUTPUT AND EMPLOYMENT

An increase in prices is usually associated with an increase in employment. In mild inflation the wheels of industry are well lubricated and total output goes up. Private investment is brisk, and jobs plentiful. Thus a little inflation is usually to be preferred to a little deflation. The losses to fixed-income groups are a good deal less than the gains to the rest of the community. Even workers with relatively fixed wages are often better off because of improved employment opportunities and greater take-home pay; and a rise in interest rates on new securities may partly make up any losses to creditors.

In deflation, on the other hand, the growing unemployment of labor and capital causes the total of the community's well-being to be less, so that those few who gain receive much less benefit than those who lose. As a matter of fact, in deep depression, almost everyone—including the creditor who is left with uncollectible debts—is likely to suffer.

The above remarks show conclusively why an increase in consumption or investment spending is a good thing in times of unemployment, even if there is some upward pressure on prices. If the economic system is suffering from acute deflation, it makes little sense to criticize public or private spending on the ground that this might be inflationary. Actually most of the increased spending will then go to increase production and create jobs. But the same reasoning shows that once full employment and full plant capacity have been reached, any further increases in spending must necessarily be completely wasted in "paper" price increases.

GALLOPING INFLATION

If price increases could be held down to, say, less than 5 per cent per year, such a mild steady inflation need not cause too great concern. If each increase in price becomes the signal for an increase in wages and costs, which again sends prices up still further, we may be in the midst of a malignant, galloping, hyperinflation. There is nothing good to be said for a rapid rise of prices such as took place in Germany in 1920–1923. Production and even the social order are then disorganized. The total wealth of large groups of the population is wiped out as money becomes worthless. Debtors ruthlessly pursue creditors in order to pay off their obligations in valueless money. Speculators profiteer. Housewives rush to spend their husbands' pay checks before prices rise still further, but in doing so only bid prices up even faster.

As a Southerner said during the Confederate inflation,

We used to go to the stores with money in our pockets and come back with food in our baskets. Now we go with money in baskets and return with food in our pockets. Everything is scarce except money! Prices are chaotic and production disorganized. A meal which used to cost the same amount as an opera ticket now costs twenty times as much. Business is often at a standstill because no one knows how much to charge. As a result, everybody tends to hoard "things" and to try to get rid of the "bad" paper money, which drives the "good" metal money out of circulation. A partial return to barter—with all its inconveniences—is the result.

Fortunately, there are few, if any, cases of hyperinflation except during war or in the backwash of war and revolution. There are some economists, however, who fear that our system is becoming jittery with a tendency to go into an explosive price rise whenever full employment comes into view. If workers, farmers, and businessmen become aware that their welfare depends as much on what their money can buy as upon their money earnings, perhaps this awareness may cause them in the future to moderate their demands for higher prices and money wages. This would tend to have a favorable result: for then all increases in purchasing power would go to create increases in employment and real output, rather than to dissipate themselves simply 'in higher prices.

If workers, farmers, and businessmen do not learn this lesson, our economic system may be in for a bad time. In that case, whenever there is enough purchasing power to bring the system near the full employment, there will tend to result a vicious upward spiral of prices and wages. Even more ominous is the possibility that prices may begin to shoot up *long before* full employment is reached.[1] As a result full employment may never be reached.

Such behavior would not alarm those who believe in direct control by government of prices and wages, *i.e.*, in a permanent OPA. But those who value freedom of enterprise and dislike unnecessary authoritative government controls, would be much disturbed. For unless the price behavior of a relatively free economy is consistent with the needs of a progressive high-employment society, many people will find themselves reluctantly joining the group in favor of permanent government controls.[2]

[1] This is what happened in the short-lived 1936–1937 boom, which was followed by the sharp, but brief, 1938 recession.

[2] The noted English economist, Sir William Beveridge, author of the comprehensive British plan for cradle-to-grave Social Security, has come out for price and wage controls—if necessary—in his recent book, "Full Employment in a Free Society," W. W. Norton & Company, New York, 1945. The dilemma of a price-wage policy for full employment is discussed again at the end of Chap. 18 on Fiscal Policy.

GOALS OF LONG-TERM PRICE BEHAVIOR

Ideally, we all want a progressive full-employment economy in which the excesses of the business cycle are moderated. We want to control the "mad dance of the dollar" as the business cycle passes from boom to crisis and slump. But as far as the long-run trend of prices is concerned, there are three possible programs espoused by different economists:

1. *Prices—on the average—are to be stable.* As output increases over time owing to population increase and technological progress, the total of spending rises. Money wages and real wages also rise as a result of increases in productivity over time.

2. *Prices are to be gently rising.* Because full-employment output is also increasing with productivity and growth, total spending rises even faster than prices. Money wages also rise rapidly; but the increase in real wages is not quite so great, because of the upward trend in the cost of living.

3. *Prices are to be falling steadily.* The total of money wages and property income remains almost constant. But the increase in output resulting from improved technological productivity is passed on to the consumer in lower prices. Real wages rise even though wages may remain constant. Such a fall in prices need not depress business activity unduly, provided that it results from previous reductions in cost.

All three solutions are tolerable if unemployment is kept at a low figure. But economic history and analysis suggest that high employment is least likely to be maintained under the third possibility, and the real burden of the public debt would be heaviest. Most of the vigorous periods of healthy capitalist development have been during periods of stable or gently rising prices. Capitalism, itself, developed during the centuries when Spanish New World gold was raising prices—not because anyone planned it that way, but simply because our monetary system used to consist of precious metals, and Columbus accidentally discovered the New World. The life expectancy of free private enterprise may well be lowered if there are to be deflation and falling prices in the decades ahead.

B. *MONEY AND PRICES*

Let us now turn to the second problem of this chapter: the supply of money and its possible relation to the price level.

THE THREE KINDS OF MONEY: SMALL COINS, PAPER CURRENCY, AND BANK DEPOSITS

Let us list the main categories of money with which we all have daily contact: small change, paper currency, and bank-deposit money.

First, there is small change: copper pennies, nickel five-cent pieces, silver dimes, quarters, half dollars, and (in the Far West) silver dollars. These all constitute our so-called "fractional currency." In total they do not add up to very much—in fact, to much less than one-twentieth of the community's cash. Because the metal in all these coins is worth far less than their face value, they are termed "token money." Obviously, these coins are valued far beyond their metallic worth only because they can be readily converted into other kinds of money—20 nickels to the dollar, etc. They are not forced upon anybody; their quantity is limited by the public's demand for them to buy cigarettes, newspapers, and so forth.

Far more important is the second kind of money: "folding money" or paper currency. Most of us know little more about a one-dollar or five-dollar bill than that each is inscribed with the picture of some American statesman, that each contains the signature of one or another government official, and—most important of all—each bears a number showing its face value.

If you look at a one-dollar bill more closely, you will find that it contains the words "Silver Certificate." This means that the U.S. Treasury is holding on deposit a silver dollar for you to claim if you wish. But as has been already mentioned, a silver dollar contains considerably less than a dollar's worth of silver. Obviously, if you really want silver, you will do much better to buy it on the open market with your paper dollar, rather than go to the Treasury. Anyone who knows much about American politics and history realizes that some paper bills are called "silver" certificates only because a few Western senators from mining states have been able to persuade Congress to give silver mining a continuing subsidy by buying up quantities of silver for monetary use. Otherwise, silver has absolutely no monetary significance; many foreign countries are abandoning it even for small coins, and silver is beginning to lose its hold on the Orient.

If you examine a ten-dollar bill, or some other paper bill, you will probably find that it says "Federal Reserve Note."[1] Like the dollar bill, this announces itself as "legal tender for all debts, public and private," but it contains the further nonsensical statement that it "is redeemable in *lawful money* at the United States Treasury or at any Federal Reserve Bank." The words "lawful money" have been italicized, *because there isn't any such thing* other than "legal tender" bills under discussion—namely, Federal reserve notes, silver certificates, etc. In other words, your old wrinkled ten-dollar bill is redeemable into a crisp new bill, into two fives, or into ten ones if you prefer. But that is all.

Back before 1933, when the present college generation was just beginning to have birthdays, it was not uncommon for good little boys and girls to be presented on anniversaries with five- or ten-dollar gold pieces. And gold certificates were often seen in circulation. But in 1933, when Congress raised the buying price of gold from about $21 to $35 an ounce, all gold—except that tied up in wedding rings and dental fillings—was called in. This was done so that holders or hoarders of gold could not make a 67 per cent profit as a result of the devaluation of the dollar. At the same time, all gold certificates—ten-dollar bills (or larger), printed in green on one side and goldish orange on the other—were called in. These certificates were warehouse receipts promising the bearer redemption in gold upon application to the U.S. Treasury. But in 1933 Congress ruled that these certificates were not to be exchanged for gold upon being called in, but simply for ordinary paper dollars. A few absent-minded people still have not turned in their gold certificates, but once these are brought to a bank, they will be retired from circulation forever and replaced by other bills.[2]

From the standpoint of understanding the nature of money, it is a good thing that these gold certificates no longer exist. The modern student need

---

[1] Two-dollar bills, considered to be bad luck in most parts of the country other than New England, are so-called United States Notes—remnants of the greenbacks used to finance the Civil War. Occasionally you may run into a bill that says "Federal Reserve Bank Note," or even a "National Bank Note" containing the name of some near-by national bank. These are being gradually retired from circulation.

[2] The courts also upheld a statute that invalidated contracts calling for payment in gold; only payment in terms of dollars was permitted. Otherwise, creditors would have made a 67 per cent profit on the revaluation and debtors would have lost 67 per cent. As we shall see in Chap. 15, the 12 Federal Reserve Banks hold gold certificates. In fact, they are required to hold at least 25 per cent as many certificates as their deposits and outstanding Federal reserve notes. But since they never reach this limit, it has little effect on their activity.

not be misled, as were earlier generations of students, by some mystical belief that "gold backing" is what gives money its value. We shall see in a moment what does determine the value of money, but certainly gold has little or nothing to do with the problem.

Every expert knows that the popular conception that money has more value if it is exchangeable into gold exactly reverses the true relation. If it were not that gold has some monetary uses, its value as a metal would be much less than it is today. We should have cheaper inlays and wedding rings. When a government requires itself to hold some fraction of gold reserves against its paper money, the gold affects prices only through its ability to limit or to expand the volume of paper money and total spending. This was overlooked by foolish European chancellors of the exchequer who, after World War I, tried to stop inflation by accumulating new gold reserves through the purchase with paper money of gold on the open market. Of course, the effect was just the opposite. Later they had to reverse the process and use their gold to buy up and burn outstanding paper money.

WHY CHECKING DEPOSITS ARE CONSIDERED TO BE MONEY

Before the question of the value of money is considered, it should be pointed out that there is a third category of what economists call money, in addition to metallic small change and paper currency. This is so-called "bank money"— made up of bank deposits subject to checking on demand. If I have $1,000 in my checking account at the Cambridge Trust Company, that deposit can be regarded as money because I can pay for purchases with checks drawn upon it. The deposit is like any other medium of exchange and, being payable on demand, it serves as a "standard of value" or "unit of account" in the same sense as $1,000 worth of silver quarters, *i.e.*, both the deposit and the quarters are convertible into standard money or cash at fixed terms, dollar for dollar.

Possessing the essential properties of money, bank demand deposits might just as well be counted as money. And they are.[1]

Actually, as was noted in the discussion of money in Chap. 3, bank money is quantitatively more important than currency because most transactions are consummated by check. The convenience of checks for mailing, for paying the exact sum of money due, for providing a receipt in the form of the canceled check voucher, for protecting against loss when stolen or misplaced (while

---

[1] My balance on deposit in the bank is usually considered to be money—not the checks that I write. These represent only the spending or transfer of money; the money itself, quantitatively, is the deposit.

unendorsed, or for that matter, endorsed)—all these advantages are obvious and explain the widespread use of bank money.

Table 1 illustrates the quantitative importance of the three kinds of money in 1947.

TABLE 1. *Total Quantity of U.S. Money in Circulation (In billions of dollars)*

	March, 1947	March, 1939
Small change:		
Minor coins...............................	$ 0.3	$0.2
Silver coins................................	1.0	0.4
	$ 1.3	$ 0.6
Paper currency:		
Federal reserve notes.........................	$24.1	$4.3
Silver certificates and U.S. notes...............	2.3	1.6
Other currency (largely in process of being retired).......................................	0.6	0.3
	27.0	6.2
Bank money:		
Demand deposits of all banks (adjusted to exclude government deposits, etc.)....................	80.4	26.1
	$108.7	$32.9

SOURCE: *Federal Reserve Bulletin.*

Because bank deposits are such an important part of our money supply, we shall have to discuss in later chapters what determines their total amount, *i.e.,* how bank money is allegedly "created." How and why did bank deposits more than triple during the war years, and why did Federal reserve notes increase by 20 billion dollars?

Before turning to this in Chaps. 14 and 15, we must first settle the question of why modern money, created all over the world by pure credit and government fiat and with no intrinsic commodity value, may still have value.

THE MEANING OF THE VALUE OF MONEY AS THE RECIPROCAL OF THE PRICE LEVEL

In the beginning, we must get fairly in mind what we mean by the value of money. If wheat costs $2 per bushel, then the value of $1 in terms of wheat is ½ bushel; if eggs sell for 5 cents apiece, then the value of $1 of money in terms of eggs is obviously 20. In other words, *the value of money is the re-*

ciprocal of a price: turn the price of any good upside down and you have the value of money in terms of that good.

It should be clear, therefore, that we cannot speak of *the* value of money. A dollar has as many different values as there are different commodities and prices. If prices should all double, we could then say that the value of money had been cut in half; if all prices decreased by 50 per cent, we could say that the value of money had doubled.

PRICE LEVEL CHANGES

FIG. 1. SOURCE: Leonard P. Ayres, *Our National Debt After Great Wars*, Committee on Public Debt Policy.

But we have earlier learned that all prices do not change by precisely the same percentage amount. Statisticians find it necessary, therefore, to compute some sort of composite or index of the *average price level*, made up by taking a weighted average of the different prices entering into the cost of living and expressed as 100 in some year selected as a base of comparison. Often, too, statisticians are as much interested in the average of all *wholesale* prices as they are in the cost of living.[1]

From now on, we shall mean by the value of money nothing more than the reciprocal or upside-down of an index of general prices. Figure 1 shows the

[1] There are many statistical and theoretical problems in computing an average index number. Not only is it difficult to get accurate price quotations for all commodities, but there is also the question of how to weight the different prices. The cost of living for a rich man may change differently from that for a poor man, just as the cost of living of a vegetarian may change differently from that of a steak addict. In view of these difficulties, it is surprising how much alike are the changes of different kinds of index numbers.

history of American wholesale prices, with 1910–1914 selected as the base period in which the price index is arbitrarily set at 100.

HOW THE LIMITATION OF THE QUANTITY OF MONEY PRESERVES ITS VALUE AND AFFECTS THE PRICE LEVEL

Let us return to the basic problem of this second section: Why does token money with no gold backing have value? Why isn't the price level infinitely high in terms of such worthless stuff?

Like any other question concerning value, this boils down into a simple question of *scarcity of supply in relation to demand.*

A money currency offers great convenience in facilitating exchanges. People demand money for what it will buy. It does not matter what kind of money (shells, chips, or paper) people decide to use as a medium of exchange, *provided they are all accustomed to the same thing.* Quite naturally, governments, whose courts must enforce contracts, everywhere establish the standard monetary unit; just as governments everywhere establish weights, measures, and daylight-saving time.

So long, therefore, as the government strictly limits its supply of issued money, just so long will that money have a high value. If the supply of money is indefinitely increased (as it was during the German inflation after World War I), so that everyone is able to spend ever-more money on relatively fixed amounts of goods, then prices will be bid up and the value of money will fall. We see, therefore,

> *Money is no exception to the general laws of supply and demand. Its value is derived from relative scarcity. To the extent that an increase in the money supply tends to increase the flow of total spending relative to the flow of goods, prices will rise and the value of money will fall.*

THE QUANTITY THEORY OF MONEY

So far money has obeyed the same laws as any commodity. But there is a further peculiarity about money emphasized by those economists who believe in the so-called "quantity theory of money." They say,

Money is like no other commodity. The demand for money, therefore, has a very special form: *double the value of money or halve the price level and you will exactly halve the amount of money which people will wish to hold.* Why? Because if everything now costs only one-half as much, people's cash requirements will be only half as great. In fact, when the prices of absolutely everything change in exactly the same proportion, money is the *only* commodity whose demand is changed—because as far as all *real* magnitudes are concerned, nothing has changed.

Consequently, these theorists arrive at the important conclusion (other things being equal) : *the price level is directly proportional to the amount of money in existence; vice versa, the amount of money that people will hold is directly proportional to the price level.* If the total amount of all three kinds of money is M and the price level is P, then according to the simplified quantity theory,

$$M = kP \qquad \text{or} \qquad P = \frac{1}{k} M$$

where k is a factor of proportionality which remains constant if "other things are equal."[1]

In bare essentials, this is the quantity theory. How valid is it? how useful? Obviously, it is a highly simplified theory; and most economists today would say it is a highly oversimplified theory. The "other things" do not always—or often—remain equal in real life, and so the quantity theory often breaks down.

The fact, however, that the quantity theory is a simplification of the truth and does not always hold with great precision should not be used to damn it utterly. If at least it indicates the general direction of economic behavior, that would be a great deal to be said in its favor. Unfortunately, even this limited claim cannot be made for the quantity theory. Its weaknesses have been particularly apparent in connection with attempts to interpret economic events of the past 15 years. Some of the reasons for this we shall see presently.

Mention should be made of some of its more valid applications. In times of great inflation when the printing presses are pouring out floods of paper money, the general direction of causation is so simple that even a simplified theory can throw much light on the facts. During the hyperinflations characteristic of some wars or periods of postwar breakdown, the quantity theory could aid in the interpretation of economic events. The recent Chinese and Hungarian inflations provide such examples; and so does the 1920–1923 German inflation. Still earlier examples occur in American history—during the Revolutionary War and at the time when the Southern Confederacy was forced to issue tremendous amounts of paper money.[2]

The quantity theory may also have a limited validity in interpreting some of the historical long swings in the price level: the rise in prices following

---

[1] For example, if k is equal to 5, then M is always 5 times the price level. Doubling prices would exactly double M. If k were 0.7, the same thing would be true. The important thing is that k remain a constant. Then prices and money will be proportional.

[2] Even in such times, the painstaking observer will be left with the feeling that the quantity theory does not get down to the fundamental reasons why money is being created at the rate it is being created. The true direction of causation is by no means in the one-way direction from M to P.

the Spanish discovery of New World gold, the rise in prices after the Californian and Australian gold discoveries of the middle of the nineteenth century, and the rise in prices around the turn of the century as a result of South African and Alaskan gold production.

INADEQUACIES OF THE QUANTITY THEORY: PRICES NOT PROPORTIONAL TO TOTAL SPENDING[1]

The truth of the quantity theory of prices depends upon two propositions, neither of which is universally valid: (1) *Prices* must be proportional to *total spending* and (2) *total spending* must be proportional to the amount of *total money* in existence. It would then follow that prices are proportional to the total quantity of money. If either or both (1) and (2) fail to be true, the quantity theory fails as a correct explanation of prices.[2]

That prices are not always proportional to total spending is clearly seen if we examine an upswing of business activity from a time of deep depression. If the output of goods increases along with the total of spending, *i.e.*, so long as there is still unemployment of labor and factories, there is no need for prices to increase much. In fact, economies of mass production may permit prices to fall as demand increases. Only if we were to make the highly unrealistic assumption of full employment and constant total output—only then would an increase in the total of spending[3] always send prices up proportionately. But if, on the contrary, total output should double, then spending could double without having *any* effect on prices!

In most cycles of business activity, the truth lies somewhere in between:

> *An increase from depression levels in total spending causes a considerable increase in output and a less than proportionate increase in average prices; on the downswing, the drop in spending results in a drop in output and employment with less than a proportionate fall in prices.*

[1] This and the next section on the inadequacies of the quantity theory of money and prices may be skipped by readers not interested in the relationship between modern and older viewpoints.

[2] There is a third serious drawback to the quantity theory which cannot be discussed in an elementary treatment of the subject. Even if it were valid, the quantity theory would be of limited usefulness because the quantity theorists had no theory—except an inadequate and superficial one—of what determines changes in the quantity of money. Certainly, in modern times, gold-mining production is only one relatively minor element in the problem, and banking policy cannot be validly interpreted in terms of one-way causation.

[3] Total spending can be thought of as the sum of the value or revenue from all commodities; *i.e.*, as $p_1q_1 + p_2q_2 + \cdots = $ sum $pq = PQ$, where Q is total output and P the general price level. Only if the effects of money on total output were "neutral"—which they decidedly are not—would prices be proportional to total spending.

INADEQUACIES OF THE QUANTITY THEORY: TOTAL SPENDING NOT PROPORTIONAL
TO THE STOCK OF MONEY

The quantity of money is a capital or wealth item. Like any asset, it exists at an instant of time. An instantaneous "still photo" or balance sheet would record its amount. But spending (excluding all "transfer" transactions) represents a *flow of income over time*, a rate of dollars per day, per month, or per year. Dimensionally speaking, spending bears the same relationship to the stock of money that a flow of water through a lake bears to the lake itself.

We saw in Chap. 3 that the interest rate relates the capital value of an asset and its flow of income. What is the factor relating the flow of income spending to the stock of money? It is easy to give a name to this factor; but, as we shall see, it is not very helpful to do so. In fact, scientists must constantly guard against a universal human weakness which makes us impute life and importance into a concept just because it has received a name and has been called to our attention.

The factor relating the volume of spending per unit time to the total stock of money is the *rate of turnover of money*, or the *income velocity of circulation of money*. The total stock of money in the United States during 1947 was about 100 billion dollars. (This includes coins, paper currency outside the banks, and checking deposits.) The total volume of spending on final products (including net capital formation) was, of course, equal to net national product or to about 200 billion dollars. Consequently, we can say that the average income velocity of money was about 2 times per year or about 0.17 times per month. This means that, although some coins, bills, and deposits were used many times during that year, other units of money were not even used once— as the *average rate of turnover* just indicated.[1]

We may summarize the definition of the average income velocity of circulation of money, V, as follows:

$$\text{Average income velocity per year} = \frac{\text{rate of income spending per year}}{\text{total volume of money}}$$

or in symbols:

$$V = \frac{p_1 q_1 + p_2 q_2 + \cdots}{M} = \frac{\text{sum } pq}{M} = \frac{PQ}{M}$$

[1] Of course, most transactions are not for final goods and services, but rather are transfers; e.g., when a baker pays a miller for flour, when an investor buys a stock or shares or real estate, etc. According to 1947 statistics of bank debits (checking transactions), urban bank deposits turn over some 18 times a year outside of New York City and 24 times a year in New York City. This velocity of circulation for all transaction purposes must be contrasted with the 2.0 income velocity rate of turnover against final goods and services.

where $\quad\quad\quad\quad M$ = total volume of all money

$\quad\quad\quad\quad\quad\quad p_1q_1$ = amount spent on the first good or service

$\quad\quad\quad\quad\quad\quad p_2q_2$ = amount spent on second good or service

$\quad\quad\quad\quad\quad\quad P$ = average price level of output

$\quad\quad\quad\quad\quad\quad Q$ = total quantity of output per unit time

Note that this equation is simply a definition of the velocity of circulation of money—nothing more and nothing less.

So much for the definition of the velocity of money. What good does it do us to have introduced the concept? The older economists, who were good quantity theorists through thick and thin, thought it did lots of good. Today, those of their ranks who are still alive are not so sure; and the new generation of economists tends to believe that the concept of velocity is not very useful and that in most circumstances of boom and depression, it may do more harm than good.

It puts off answering a question by asking another question. Thus, one of the reasons given for the Great Depression of the 1930's was the reduced velocity of circulation of money. But why was velocity reduced? To know that is already to know the answer to the riddle of the slump. Similarly, those who thought recovery could be ensured by increasing the quantity of money were disappointed by the unexpected decline in the velocity of the new money.

This takes us back to the heading of the present section; or to the fact that the quantity theory is invalidated by the failure of total spending to be proportional to the quantity of money. In terms of our new concept, this concept may be explained as follows: *the velocity of circulation of money is not even approximately constant.* It changes in boom and depression in a way that cannot be predicted except from fundamental factors such as savings and investment, trade-union policy, technological innovations, the total quantity of money, the composition of that quantity of money, the way that money came into existence, and finally—to bring the list to an end—the movement and structure of interest rates and security prices.[1] This we discuss further elsewhere.

---

[1] If correct, these statements illustrate the sterility of the so-called "quantity equation of exchange," according to which

$$MV = PQ \quad\quad \text{or} \quad\quad P = \frac{V}{Q}M$$

This is a truism based, as we have just seen, on the definition of V, and it should not be confused with the quantity theory, which has the merit of attempting to set up an explanatory hypothesis to fit facts. If, as the older writers thought, V were a constant, or if the movements of Q were such as to offset the movements of V, thereby leaving V/Q a constant, then

RELATION OF MONEY AND SPENDING TO SAVING, INVESTMENT, AND PRICES

The preceding remarks concerning the quantity theory represent, in a sense, a detour into the past. Let us conclude the second section of this chapter with a discussion relating money to the behavior of the savings and investment schedules that were shown in the previous chapter to determine the level of total money spending and income.

We saw that the community's saving schedule depends primarily on income; and that when private, public, and foreign investment are at low levels, then income and employment will also be at low levels. At such times the desire of the unemployed for jobs and the competition of producers to sell more goods tend to put downward pressure on wages and prices. Some flexible prices, like those of competitive agricultural products, fall a great deal. But many prices, particularly those subject to monopoly conditions, tend to be relatively sticky and do not fall very rapidly or very far. The same stickiness is true of wage rates and of commodities that involve much labor.

All this may be summarized as follows:

When national income falls fars below full-employment levels, there is downward pressure on prices and wages; but because of stickiness of money prices and wages, most of the reduction in purchasing power shows itself in reduced output and employment.

What will happen to prices when investment factors are so favorable in relation to the saving schedule that they push national incomes near to or in excess of full-employment levels? Prices will then be pushed up for two related reasons: wage increases and "bottlenecks."

When there are no more unemployed workers available to expand output, wages will begin to shoot up—thereby raising costs and prices, and also workers' money demand for goods. Second, as the increased spending by consumers and investors is unmatched by an expansion of goods because of "bottlenecks" in plant capacity, then prices will be bid up.

Unfortunately, the process does not end there. The new higher price level will not equilibrate total supply and demand once and for all. On the contrary, since the higher prices received by businesses become in turn somebody's income—that of worker or property owner—demand again shifts upward

---

the equation of exchange might be a useful truism. But if, as has been argued, V is a catchall which is as hard to understand as the business cycle itself, then the equation of exchange is a blind alley or possibly a red herring. Instead of setting out the important questions in a useful way, it diverts attention from the really interesting and important problems.

and prices must continue to rise. Attempts of labor to secure higher wages as compensation for the soaring cost of living, may only cause the inflationary spiral to zoom at a dizzier speed.

The process will come to an end only when private investment demand and net government spending are no longer so powerful as to push the system beyond full employment; and when labor keeps its monetary demands within the limits set by growing productivity.

This process of inflation is beautifully illustrated by the experience in World War II. The government found it necessary to spend almost one-half of our gross national product on war. Private civilian investment was cut down almost to nothing, taxes were raised, people were urged to buy war bonds and increase their savings. Nevertheless, the civilian economy still *tried* to spend more than one-half, perhaps two-thirds of its gross national income on civilian products. But less than one-half of gross product was left after the armed forces took what was necessary for the war.

As would be expected from such an excess of spending over available goods, there resulted a strong tendency for prices to rise. The inflation was curbed only by OPA price ceilings and rationing, by War Labor Board wage controls, and by the War Production Board's controlled allocation of scarce resources.

CONCLUSION TO MONEY AND PRICES

The above analysis of price increases is fairly straightforward. But what has it to do with the amount of *money?* The quantity of money does not seem to have figured at all in this discussion. In part this is as it should be since the quantity of money, per se, is only one of many factors impinging on saving and investment.

However, its effects are by no means negligible. To the extent that people's consumption and saving habits depend not only upon their current incomes but also on their past accumulated *wealth*—particularly their "liquid" wealth—the amount of money is important.

American families and corporations have accumulated almost 200 billion dollars of cash and liquid government securities during the war because their incomes exceeded what they were then able to spend. This financial "cushion" may very well encourage people to spend a larger proportion of their incomes in the immediate postwar years. To the extent that this does take place, the saving schedule will have shifted downward, and there will be a tendency for both national income and prices to rise.

Thus, the quantity of money does have an influence on prices. This is a far cry from the simple quantity theory. One of the weaknesses of that theory lies in its belief that an increased quantity of money will be spent upon consumption goods and services. Instead, people are likely to buy securities and life insurance, make savings bank deposits with their excessive liquid cash, or even invest in idle cash. All this will have certain definite effects on interest rates, and so we must now turn to the subject matter of the third major section of this chapter.

C. *MONEY AND INTEREST RATES*

THREE DEMANDS FOR MONEY

To understand the relation between money and interest we must first go back to the important problem of determining how much money people and business firms will decide to hold. There are three main motives for holding cash balances in the form of currency or checking deposits: the money may be desired for "transaction" purposes (*i.e.*, as a medium of exchange), for "precautionary" purposes (*i.e.*, for cash needs which may suddenly occur), or for "investment" purposes (*i.e.*, to serve as a store of value).

Transaction Demand for Money. Let us examine the transaction motive for holding money. A family or business firm is continually paying out money for the numerous things it buys; and intermittently it is receiving payments of money. If these inpayments and outpayments were perfectly synchronized, hardly any cash balance would ever have to be held. Actually, of course, such payments are not synchronized. Nor is it possible for any of us to foresee exactly when and in what amounts cash will be coming in and going out. Because of this unevenness and uncertainty, we must keep on hand a cash balance of some magnitude. When inpayments exceed outpayments, cash balances grow; when more is being paid out than is currently coming in, cash balances are decreasing.

An ordinary wage earner who gets paid $50 every week will find that his cash balance shows a characteristic weekly fluctuation. Just after Saturday payday it will be at a maximum, equaling $50 or more. If he spends his money evenly during the week, it will decrease at about the rate of $7 a day, until finally just before payday, his cash balance will again be at a minimum—perhaps around zero if he is not very well off. On the average, his cash balance is around $25, and each dollar lingers about half a week in his hands.

Actually, some people get income weekly; others every 2 weeks or every month; some, such as dividend receivers or bond coupon clippers, get paid every 3, 6, or 12 months. In addition, people rarely spend their money evenly over time. Within 24 hours after payday, one-third of the family earnings will often have been used to pay accrued rent or grocery bills. Each family and each company will work out for itself the most convenient pattern of cash holding and expenditure. The ratio between the average cash balance held to facilitate transactions and average income will vary with the interval between income payments, with the extent to which people buy on credit by "charging" purchases, with the rate of discount received by firms who pay their bills promptly, with one's distance from department stores, and even with such factors as the amount charged by banks for each check.

As a result of the complicated interplay of a thousand such factors, there will result at any time a certain minimum amount of cash which the community will wish to hold for transaction purposes. Such money is held for definitely predictable expenditures.

Precautionary Motive. In addition, there will always be some further money payments which may or may not have to be made. The grocer may insist on having his bill taken care of at once. The family car may break down and have to be fixed for cash. A C.O.D. package may suddenly arrive. A farmer may run into a bargain in a sow. A firm's note payable may be called in. A bank's customers may draw out their money.

Numerous other such reasons could be given for this second motive for holding a cash balance—in excess of what is held because of the ordinary transaction motive. It is not easy to decide rationally how much money should be held for this precautionary reason, because from the nature of the case the amount of money that will be needed is uncertain. Mr. Milquetoast will keep a large cash or checking balance on hand for every possible contingency, how-ever remote; whereas a more optimistic person will allow for only the most likely events. In depression, when everyone is feeling insecure and "on edge," people will be likely to hold relatively more precautionary money, at the same time that they hold less transaction money because of the decline in income, prices, and general business activity.

Investment Demand for Money. The demand for money as a liquid asset is the most complex of all to analyze. The transaction and precautionary motives tell us what is the minimum amount of money that individuals will want to hold. But why shouldn't they hold more than the minimum? The answer is simple: *A cash balance earns no interest or yield*, whereas using the money to buy stocks, bonds, mortgage loans, or promissory notes will in ordinary times bring in a yield in the form of interest payments or profit dividends. Liquid cash is a nonearning asset, and most investors will prefer not to be excessively liquid if this means surely foregoing some juicy interest or dividend earnings.

As we have seen, people will wish to hold some money for transaction purposes even when there is a large positive rate of interest to be earned on nonliquid assets. The convenience to a $3,500-a-year family of an average cash balance (mostly in a checking account) of, say, $500 costs only about $1.50 a month when there is a 3 per cent per annum interest rate. Even at 6 per cent interest, the cost would be only $3 per month. Doubtless at higher rates of interest a very calculating individual might hesitate to hold quite so much money idle simply as a precaution against rather unlikely needs for cash. But in view of the convenience of a cash balance, to most individuals the difference of a few dollars per month of interest would not be sufficiently great to worry about.[1]

MONEY AS A TEMPORARY FORM OF HOLDING WEALTH

There is still another reason why people will on the average hold cash in excess of income and expenditure needs. Savings pile up gradually. But it is only convenient to invest them in lump sums. To buy even so little as one share of A.T. & T. common stock costs almost $200; until that sum has been accumulated, cash will be the most convenient form in which to hold wealth. Wealthy people will wish to invest in still larger amounts, preferring to buy in 100-share lots rather than to pay an additional brokerage commission for so-called "odd-lot" purchases of less than 100 shares. (Large insurance companies, in order to keep supervisory responsibilities down to a minimum usually refuse to invest in less than $100,000 blocks.) Cash tends, therefore, to be accumulated until the minimum amounts necessary for investment have been reached.

Still another reason for holding cash is provided by the fact that a wise investor will carefully watch over the securities in his portfolio, dropping those which begin to seem less promising and adding others. In the transition from one asset to another he will necessarily hold some cash. Moreover, careful

---

[1] A further modern inducement to hold large cash balances is the fact that most banks set their charges for checks cashed and other services inversely to the size of the customer's bank balance. Thus, in spite of the Federal law prohibiting the payment of interest on demand deposits, my checking account in New England "implicitly" earns 0.1 of 1 per cent per month (or about 1.2 per cent per year), so long as its total earnings do not exceed the amount that the bank charges me every month for cashing checks and making book entries. Why? Because if I write about 20 checks a month, and if the bank charges me about $6\frac{1}{2}$ cents for each check drawn, then I can avoid paying the bank service charges only by keeping a large cash balance upon which they will allow me a credit of 0.1 of 1 per cent per month. It pays me, therefore, to keep in the bank not $300 or twice that much but actually more than $1,000! I need this large a cash balance if I am to get a bookkeeping credit sufficiently large to cover all service charges.

investors will always keep some cash on hand in order to avail themselves of any bargains that may suddenly appear on the market.

SHORT-TERM INVESTMENTS AS NEAR SUBSTITUTES FOR CASH

In the palmy days of the 1920's, it was not necessary to hold very much cash for the above temporary purposes because of the possibility of profitably lending out your money at short term. Thus in those days any individual could get 5 or 6 per cent per annum on all funds lent out "on call" to the stock market. These call loans were made to brokers who used the funds to finance "margin" purchases by stock-market speculators. Such speculators would put up in cash only 40 cents on the dollar or less, borrowing the rest by pledging as collateral the stocks bought. Being well secured by the pledging of securities as collateral, being callable on demand, and bearing a high rate of interest, such call loans were as liquid as cash and yet provided a good return.

Today the "call market" rate of interest is down almost to 1 per cent and only banks are permitted to lend in this market; moreover, speculators must now put up 75 per cent "cash margins." The rate of interest on government bonds of less than a year's duration (usually called notes, bills, or certificates) is only about 1 per cent per annum—hardly enough for small investors to bother with.

Thus, short-term securities do not today yield much more of a return than cash. Nor will it pay an investor to buy a long-term security to hold for only a few weeks, because the brokerage charges on its purchase and sale will more than eat up its yield during that time. Consequently, there is at the present time no profitable alternative to the *short-term* holding of cash. Even savings accounts, whose average rate of interest the country over is scarcely more than 1 per cent, usually pay interest only on funds that are left idle in the bank until the end of the 6-month interest period. Moreover, many—if not most—banks will refuse to pay much, if any, interest on deposits in savings accounts greatly in excess of the Federally insured $5,000 maximum. Often they will not even accept large sums of money, especially if there is no guarantee that the deposit will be left in the bank for an indefinite period. Also, the banker can always stand on his rights and demand 30 days' notice for withdrawal of a large time or savings deposit, even though he may waive this technicality for small withdrawals.

MONEY AS A LONG-TERM ASSET

For all the above reasons, it is clear that, under the conditions which have prevailed since 1930, there has been every inducement for an individual to invest his wealth in the form of cash for *short* periods of time. This is important. But far more important is the fact that under these same conditions many individuals and financial institutions will *permanently* invest part of their assets in the form of liquid cash. Money is for them a long-term store of value. How can we account for this?

Of course, a few pathological misers will hold money because of a love for the paper bills or the shiny coins. A few timid widows will be distrustful of all investments. A few black marketeers, anxious to leave no records for the income-tax collector, may hoard $1,000 bills in black suitcases or safety-deposit lockboxes.

But quantitatively, these cases are usually rather trifling. They do not explain why hard-headed, legitimate bankers held *excess cash reserves* throughout the 1930's, or why life-insurance companies and private investors did the same thing. Why did these individuals, knowing that they had no need for such funds, deliberately keep them in the form of nonearning liquid cash? And persist in keeping them in this form over a period of years?

To throw light on this question, let us ask it in another form: "Why shouldn't individuals keep a substantial fraction of their assets in the form of cash?"

By now, the reader should be able to supply an answer. "Because," he will say, "cash earns no income. How much better it will be to buy securities that do earn a positive yield. Although there are admittedly few opportunities to invest in short-run securities with an advantageous yield, surely the record shows that there have always been long-term securities yielding a positive rate of earnings."

To appraise this answer, let us turn to the historical record. During the decade of the 1930's, gilt-edge bonds did show some earnings. Whereas they had often yielded 5 and 6 per cent during the 1920's, their yields during the 1930's had dropped to 3 per cent or less. Therefore, the penalty for holding cash—*i.e.*, the foregone interest earnings—was not nearly so great in the 1930's as in the 1920's, particularly when brokerage fees and supervisory difficulties are taken into consideration.

Still, 3 per cent would seem to be better than nothing, even if not so good as 6 per cent. In view of this remark, only one factor can explain why individuals and financial institutions, nevertheless, continue to keep a substantial fraction of their wealth in the form of noninterest-earning liquid cash—not for a day or a month, but over the years. That factor is their *uncertainty* as to whether long-term securities will really give them a positive yield. It is not that they doubt the solvency of the United States government or its ability to pay bond interest and principal whenever due; or that they think that the A.T.&T. will default on its bonds or cease paying dividends. Rather it is the fact that they remember the higher interest rates of previous years. And remembering those golden days, they regard existing interest rates as abnormally low and temporary. Investors cannot and do not believe that such abnormal conditions will persist. They tend to believe that an increase in rates is just around the corner. Believing this, it would be folly for an investor to put his money into long-term securities at a lower yield than he thinks will be available soon. The next paragraph will show why.

These days the investor must pay about $120 for a safe long-term bond that pays $4 per year. Its price being high, its interest yield is low.[1] What if the investor has held the $120 bond a year, received his $4, and then the market long-term interest rate should rise? The bond could then only be sold for, say, $115. Has the investor been well advised to buy the bond rather than hold cash?

The answer is "no." Instead of earning 2 to 3 per cent on his capital, the investor has had negative earnings! His $4 coupon return was more than wiped out by his $5 capital loss. He would have been better off if he had stuck to cash; for even if he then wouldn't have earned anything, at least he could have kept his principal intact.

Now we see why people will hold cash as a long-term asset. Just as it is a good speculation to buy real estate if you think land will give you the best earnings, so it is a good speculation not to buy long-term stocks and bonds if you think that such securities may experience a capital loss. In the same sense it is a good speculation to invest in money, if in that way you will best maximize your capital wealth or minimize your losses.[2]

The speculative motive for holding cash as an investment may also come into play if investors fear that stock prices or real-estate values will collapse for reasons other than an increase in the interest rate, e.g., a depression in business activity, increased corporation taxes, or increased wages.

---

[1] Recall the discussion in Chap. 3 of capital value and interest. With a fixed permanent-income source, halving the interest rate would double its capital value. For a 5-, 10-, or 30-year bond, there is still an inverse relation between its price and interest yield, but not so strong a one as for a *perpetual* bond.

[2] Most people do not think of money holding as a speculation, because there is then no chance of making a capital loss or gain. But this is important only if we reckon gains and losses in terms of *money*, as most of us—because of indoctrination since childhood—have got into the habit of doing. By this fallacious reasoning, a widow who keeps her money in a stocking during the years when inflation is wiping out the value of her wealth is holding her own; when, actually, she is frittering away her inheritance.

Moreover, there is a wise old saying with respect to investment behavior: "Don't put all your eggs in one basket." Therefore, even if an investor doesn't really expect that interest rates will rise and that capital values will fall, or even if he has no particular opinion about these matters, still if he is farseeing, he will *fear* that this may happen. He may invest as much as half or three-quarters of his wealth in diversified long-term securities. But as a hedge against losses, a prudent long-term investor is likely to keep some minimum percentage of his assets in the form of safe cash. This is very important.

We may sum up the reasons why people will hold money as an investment as follows:

> *When the rate of interest promised by securities is low and when investors are uncertain as to whether interest rates will continue to be low and security prices continue to be high, then there will be a substantial investment motive for the holding of liquid cash.*

MONEY AND THE DETERMINATION OF INTEREST RATES

The above discussion gives us one clue to the determination of the interest rate, or the structure of interest rates. From one point of view, interest can be thought of as the "price of money." (More precisely, it is the price of the *use* of money. This should not be confused with our earlier usage of the concept, "the value of money," which was nothing more or less than the "general price level" turned upside down.)

The late Lord Keynes showed how a large supply of money will—other things being equal—tend to depress interest rates. Suppose gold mines or printing presses or the banking system have created a large amount of money some time in the past. This money has to be held by someone. If more money is given to people than they find convenient or necessary for their level of income and expenditure, what will they do? The simple quantity theory thought that they would spend it on consumers' goods. But this would pass the money on to someone else; and he, also being unwilling to hold the "hot brick," will spend it on consumers' goods. In the end, the prices of consumers' goods will be bid so high that people will finally need all the existing money just for transaction purposes. So argued the quantity theorists.

Keynes argued that people's consumption spending depends primarily on their income and total wealth, and only secondarily upon the composition of their wealth between cash and less liquid assets. Therefore, if the amount of total M tends to be too large, people and banks will try to use the excess to buy securities—not consumers' goods. This will gradually raise the price of stocks and bonds, or what is the same thing, reduce interest rates.

How long will this process go on? At first, one might be tempted to say until all the extra money is used up. But this would be wrong, since the money cannot be used up in this way. For every buyer of a bond, there is a seller and the money appears in his pockets. The only true end to the process is as follows:

An increase in total money tends—other things being equal—to lower the rate of interest, until finally the yield of stocks and bonds is so low that they have ceased any longer to be attractive alternatives to the holding of cash. *At a low enough rate of interest, people will finally develop a strong enough invest-ment motive for holding all the existing amount of money.*

This is an important clue to the determination of interest. As advanced discussions show, it is only one clue among a number. We must not forget the qualifying expression, "other things being equal." Other things do not remain perfectly equal: for example, the "net productivity of capital" of Chap. 3 may increase; so may the level of transactions and income; and people's expectations about the future profitability of noncash assets may change. All these can affect interest, even though M does not change.

HISTORY OF THE CAPITAL MARKETS SINCE 1932

The above analysis is often called the "theory of liquidity preference." It explains not only why people will hold idle money, but also why they will put so much of their money into short-term securities as to bid up their prices and bid down their interest yields almost to zero.

This is exactly what happened all through the 1930's. Remembering interest rates of 6 per cent, investors regarded rates of 3 or 4 per cent as only temporary. Therefore, they feared capital losses if they bought long-term securities. Instead they held cash, or bought short-term government bonds whose capital values are almost perfectly fixed because their maturity date is so near. The strong demand for such liquid short-term securities caused their prices to rise and their yield to go down to a fraction of a fraction of 1 per cent per annum.

Gradually as time passed and the long-expected return to high interest rates failed to materialize, banks and insurance companies found that they had been passing up 3 and 4 per cent on long-term securities because of their unfounded fears. Very slowly they began to buy long-term securities, thus bidding up their prices and bidding down their yields. But the process was remarkably slow.

Two distinct factors help to explain this slowness in the decline of long term rates: first, the fact that investors still kept fearing each year a future decline in capital values and an increase in interest rates, even though events had proved their last year's expectations to be wrong on this point.

Second, the Federal government was spending more than it taxed in those years, and borrowing the difference. The new supply of bonds coming on the market helped to keep security prices down and to keep interest yields up. Next to the 50-billion-dollar yearly deficits of World War II, the 3- or 4-billion-dollar annual deficits of the New Deal days may seem trifling; but they loomed larger in those days, and they did provide an important outlet for bank and insurance-company funds. Without this relatively safe investment outlet, the tremendous inflow of gold into this country during the 1930's would undoubtedly have depressed interest rates even more than it did.[1]

MONEY AND INTEREST RATE DURING AND AFTER WORLD WAR II

The history of the decade prior to our entrance into the war is one of slowly falling long-term rates of interest, with short-term rates down almost to zero, and with many financial institutions holding unprecedented amounts of idle cash.

The growing supply of capital funds was not matched by a growing demand for funds by business enterprises. Juicy and riskless investment opportunities were hard to find during the depressed 1930's especially since no strikingly noble and important industries rose to prominence.

Our vast governmental war expenditures changed all this. Congress failed to vote taxes sufficient to wage the war, and the public failed to buy enough war bonds out of voluntary savings to make up the difference.

But battles will not wait upon finances. The government's needs for funds had to be met by tremendous borrowing. Bonds were sold to commercial banks and to the Federal Reserve Banks. By the creation of bank money—described in Chaps. 14 and 15—the interest rate structure was maintained at low prewar levels.

By 1945 the notion that interest rates would stay low had finally percolated into the minds of investors. This helps to explain why they have been trying frantically to convert their cash into stocks and bonds. In doing so, they have bid up security prices and bid down their interest yields still further.

Old bonds of railroads, public utilities, and individual companies—issued at

---

[1] This illustrates how confused those writers are who think that "deficit spending" is the same thing as an "easy money" policy. In fact, the two policies are opposites *so far as their effects on the interest rate are concerned;* the easy money policy is in part adopted for the purpose of offsetting the effects of Treasury borrowing on the money market..

6, 5, 4, and even 3 per cent!—have been called in and refunded at as low as $2\frac{1}{2}$ per cent interest. This has made for a healthier structure of corporate debt and fixed charges. Moreover, investors have gained as common-stock shareholders most of what they have lost as *rentiers* (interest receivers). Still the anguish and cries of universities and investors have been pitiful to hear.

Early in 1948 it began to look as if the easy-money era might be rounding a corner. The Treasury and Federal Reserve authorities, because of their worry over postwar inflation, permitted short-term interest rates to rise a little. They also permitted long-term government bonds to fall in price from the high previous levels of 103–106 down to nearly 100, or par. This meant a rise of the long-term interest rate from $2\frac{1}{4}$ to $2\frac{1}{2}$ per cent, and an even greater rise of interest yield of industrial bonds.

Will the authorities push such monetary policies even farther? What is the effect on commercial banks and central banks? on the management of the Federal debt? The next two chapters will help in understanding these important questions.

SUMMARY

This chapter has covered much important ground. For this reason, a rather extensive listing of the points covered may be helpful.

A. PRICES

1. When prices change in periods of inflation or deflation, they do not all change in exactly the same degree. Instead of being neutral, such price changes have definite real effects on the economic system.

2. In times of inflation, debtors and profit receivers benefit at the expense of creditors and fixed-income groups. Deflation has opposite effects upon the distribution of income between economic classes.

3. Aside from causing transfers between economic groups, deflation acts to reduce the total of national production and employment. Until it becomes excessive, inflation tends to expand employment and output, because the lag of costs behind prices stimulates industrial expansion.

4. Ideally, therefore, we should aim for stable or slowly rising prices, with money wages rising even more rapidly as the growth of productivity makes higher real wages possible.

B. MONEY AND PRICES

5. There are three kinds of modern money: small token coins (or small change); fiat paper currency issued by the government and its Federal reserve system; and demand bank deposits subject to check. Being convertible into each other at par, all of these have the same value unit for unit, independently of the trifling paper, ink, and metal costs involved in each.

6. The value of money, which is nothing but the reciprocal of the average price level, is determined like the value of everything else: by scarcity of its supply in relation to the demand for it. If unlimited billions of $1,000 bills are issued and spent, they would bid prices up indefinitely, even if they are fully backed by gold. By contrast, even a purely paper currency will have high value, despite its lack of gold backing, so long as its supply is rigidly limited.

7. The quantity theory of money is a special, simplified doctrine, according to which prices and the quantity of money are directly proportional. The quantity theory would be valid only if prices were proportional to total spending, and if total spending were proportional to the amount of money.[1]

Today, while granting its occasional validity, most economists do not accept the quantity theory except with copious grains of salt. They remember long years during the 1930's when changes in *spending* resulted primarily in changes in output and not in prices. And they also remember how in those same years, increases in the amount of money resulted in no corresponding changes in spending because the velocity of circulation of money would not remain constant.

8. Instead of the quantity theory, emphasis is today placed upon the height of private, public, and foreign investment relative to full-employment savings. If these autonomous factors fall far short of full-employment savings, then income and employment will be low and there will be downward pressure on prices. If the investment factors are strong enough to push the system near to full employment or beyond, there is a tendency for prices and wages to rise—perhaps in a cumulative, vicious spiral of inflation.

9. The quantity of money is only one of many factors affecting the balance of saving and investment described in the previous paragraph. Only to the extent that the community's propensity to save out of a given income is shifted downward will there be any influence of money on prices and demand—or to the extent that increased supplies of money may lower interest rates slightly and thereby increase investment and income.

[1] Or if the error in one of these relationships just happened to cancel the error in the other.

C. MONEY AND INTEREST

10. The demand for money can be split into three components: a transaction demand, a precautionary demand, and finally an investment demand.

11. The last of these is the most complex, and depends most upon the rate of interest. *The higher the rate of interest, the less money will people be willing to hold as an investment.* Because of uncertainty concerning the safety and future prices of securities, investors will often wish to hold some idle cash even though this seems to involve giving up an interest return on their assets.

12. When money in a community is so scarce that it barely suffices to satisfy the transaction and precautionary motives, interest rates tend to be high and short-term interest rates are often as great as long-term rates. But suppose the supply of money is greatly increased—by government action, bank action, or because of gold mining and imports. Then instead of spending the surplus money on consumption, people tend to use it to purchase securities. Unless there is a brisk demand for investment funds, the new money will bid up security prices and lower interest yields.

Short-term rates fall first and farthest, often until their level is practically negligible. Long-term rates finally begin to decline; but they do so slowly because investors, remembering previous higher interest levels, fear (or hope) that the decrease in rates is only temporary.

13. The theory of liquidity preference explains how—with other things being equal!—an increase in total money tends to depress interest rates.

14. Today the long-term rate on safe investments is down to $2\frac{1}{2}$ per cent or below, but it took more than a decade to get it there. The interest return on each dollar is at an all-time low, but the war has so swollen the total number of bonds that interest receivers are getting more total income than ever before in all history.

QUESTIONS FOR DISCUSSION

1. If you were sure of inflation ahead, what are some of the things you might do to protect yourself against it?

2. List some of the dramatic happenings that go with galloping hyperinflation.

3. "A depression is really a great time of opportunity, for him who will recognize it." Comment.

4. Distinguish carefully between inflation, prosperity, deflation, depression, hyperinflation, technological cost-price reduction, etc.

5. Sometimes wages or loan contracts are expressed in terms of a sliding scale rather than in terms of fixed money. How would you use an index of the cost of living to protect workers against a change in real wages due to price level changes? How would you do the same thing with respect to an I.O.U.?

6. Take inventory of the different kinds of money in the pockets of the class members. Make up a table. What about checking deposits? Estimate the velocity of circulation of money from the average class quantity of money and average weekly expenditure.

7. Why are checks used as often as they are? Why not more often? Trace the history of a check that you send to your broker when you buy one share of A.T.&T. stock at $175 per share. Suppose that your broker is 1,000 miles away.

8. Twenty-five years from now when national income may be 400 billion dollars, what do you think our money supply will look like? What about the value of a dollar, or the price level?

9. A man spends half his income on one loaf of bread, half on one dozen hyacinths. The price of bread doubles, while the price of hyacinths halves. Compute an index of the cost of living: (a) using the "before" situation as 100, (b) using the "after" situation as 100. Why is there a difference? If so, which—if either—is right?

10. "The quantity theory is highly oversimplified. But in times of inflation it comes into its own; and in these times it is so important that we should preach the quantity theory in season and out of season." Discuss.

11. Two identical twins have identical incomes and wealth. One has half of his wealth in cash and half in liquid government bonds. The other has nine-tenths in cash and one-tenth in bonds. Will their propensities to consume be significantly different? their respective velocities of circulation of money?

12. Make an outline showing the motives for holding money. When the rate of interest is near zero, why does the demand for money become indefinitely large?

13. Lord Keynes believed that the decision to consume or not consume (save) is quite different from the decision to hold cash or other forms of wealth. Do you agree? Which of these decisions depends primarily on the interest rate?

Chapter 14: FUNDAMENTALS OF

THE BANKING SYSTEM AND

DEPOSIT CREATION

THE outstanding importance of bank deposits as part of the community's money supply has already been discussed. This chapter continues the discussion in two distinct parts. In the first, we must examine briefly the important facts and functionings of the modern banking system, showing how the present-day commercial bank gradually began to keep only fractional cash reserves against its deposits; in the second part, an attempt is made to describe simply and clearly how the banking system "manufactures" bank deposits.

A. *NATURE AND FUNCTIONING OF THE MODERN BANKING SYSTEM*

THE PRESENT STATUS OF BANKING

Today there are about 14,000 banks in the United States that accept checking deposits. Only about a third of these banks are national banks, the rest being under state supervision. All national banks are automatically members of the Federal reserve system, and in addition most of the larger state institutions are Federal reserve members. Although this still leaves more than half of all the banks which are not members of the Federal reserve system, they are sufficiently small in size so that their total deposits are only about one-fifth of the total.[1] Moreover, since 1933 almost all commercial banks, state or national, have had their deposits (up to $5,000) insured by the FDIC (Federal Deposit Insurance Corporation).

Unlike England or Canada where a few large banks with hundreds of branches are dominant, the United States has tended to rely upon many independent, relatively small, localized units.[2] Until fairly recently, almost anyone could open a bank with relatively limited capital. It is not surprising, therefore, that the American history of bank failures and losses to depositors has been a grievous one. Indeed, only about one-half the banks in existence in 1915 are still solvent; even in prosperous 1929, long before the Great Depression, no less than 659 banks with estimated total deposits of 200 million dollars failed.

Although the primary business of commercial banks is to receive demand deposits and to honor checks drawn upon them, we shall see that they usually branch out and perform a variety of other functions in competition with other financial institutions. Thus, they usually accept savings or time deposits—theoretically withdrawable only after 30 days' notice—but in fact usually withdrawn (by their owners) on demand. In taking on such a function, the commercial banks are, in parts of the country like New England, competing with the so-called "mutual savings banks" which accept only time deposits; almost anywhere in the country they are competing with cooperative building and loan societies and postal savings. In selling money orders or travelers' checks, the banks are competing with the post office and with Western Union. In handling "trusts" and estates, they overlap with investment counselors, executors, and other fiduciaries.

Furthermore, even in lending money to individuals and businessmen, the banks are competing with finance companies, and with so-called "factors," who provide corporations with working capital (e.g., the Commercial Credit Corporation). In buying bonds, mortgages, and other securities, the banks are in competition with insurance companies and other investors.[3]

The commercial banks are by no means, therefore, our only financial insti-

[1] Many of these state banks that are not full-fledged members nevertheless do belong to the Federal reserve clearinghouse system and are able to use this service in handling checks on other banks.

[2] In California, the Bank of America has numerous branches all over the state, just as the Chase National Bank has branches all over New York City, and just as a few holding companies control many banks in Minnesota and Wisconsin. But by and large, the old American distrust of "big finance" has caused legislatures to restrict multiple-branch banking.

[3] Massachusetts and New York State savings banks actually sell life insurance, and at such low rates and favorable terms as to compete seriously with commercial insurance companies.

tutions. But, by definition, they are the only organizations able to provide "bank money," *i.e.*, checkable demand deposits which can be conveniently used as a medium of exchange. Therein lies their primary importance and chief economic interest. For, except with respect to this unique function, the modern American commercial bank seemed at the war's end to be gradually becoming hardly more than a holder of government bonds—an indirect agency by means of which business and the public hold the great public debt.[1]

Since V-E and V-J days, bank loans have had a considerable increase, largely to help business, farmers, and the public finance the large volume of postwar activity, carried on at high postwar price levels. Interestingly enough, in recent years commercial banks have begun increasingly to make "term loans" of more than a year's duration, thus refuting the belief of those theorists who believe that banks shall provide only short-term, 90-day seasonal credit.

CREATION OF THE FEDERAL RESERVE SYSTEM

Two days prior to the last Christmas preceding the outbreak of World War I, the Federal Reserve Act was passed by Congress and signed by President Wilson. The panic of 1907, with its more than usual epidemic of bank failures, was the straw that broke the camel's back: the country was fed up once and for all with the anarchy of unstable private banking. After half a dozen years' agitation and discussion by both the Republican and Democratic parties, the Federal reserve system was formed—in face of the opposition of the large banks and of bankers' associations.

The country was divided into 12 Federal reserve districts, each with its own Federal Reserve Bank. The initial capital of each bank was subscribed by the commercial bank members of the Federal reserve system; and so *nominally* they are each corporations owned by the "Member Banks." All are coordinated by the 7-member Board of Governors of the Federal reserve system in Washington.[2]

When the system was first established, numerous petty "checks and balances" were written into the law, largely on the basis of a number of now

[1] By the beginning of 1947, bank holdings of government securities were more than three times as great as their loans, and interest on these securities covered practically all their running expenses. Whereas loans formed more than half of bank assets in the 1920's, by the late 1940's, they were down to only about a sixth, of which only about one-half represented agricultural or industrial loans.

[2] There is also a 12-man Federal Open Market Committee, consisting of 5 representatives of the 12 districts as well as the 7-man Board of Governors. In addition a Federal Advisory Council, consisting of a representative selected by each of the 12 banks, can make suggestions but is without legal powers.

obsolete theories about money and because of the then prevailing fear of centralized banking authority. It was another example of what is so common in our history: the desire of the American people to go swimming without going near the water. We wanted, we desperately needed a central bank; yet we were afraid of the concept. Therefore, a compromise bill was passed—dividing the country up into 12 separate districts; providing for six directors of each bank to be appointed by the vote of the Member Banks and three to be appointed by the Board of Governors; requiring three of the local six directors to be bankers and the other three to represent business, industry, and agriculture, respectively; providing 14-year terms for governors; limiting the Reserve Banks to certain special types of loans, and preventing them from buying bonds directly from the government; etc.

Today none of these restrictions is of primary importance. Again and again Congress has modified the original act whenever one of these restrictions stood in the way of the needs of the time. Let us examine, therefore, the effective realities and present status of the Federal reserve system.

It consists of a Board of Governors with wide powers who work very closely with the President and the Treasury, and who have in effect 12 branch offices throughout the land. Although the Member Banks nominally own the Reserve Banks, in fact no profits over 6 per cent of the original capital may be paid out to Member Banks; and almost all excess earnings are paid into the U.S. Treasury. Although the Reserve Banks have been enormously profitable, the public interest and not profit is their goal, and many of their most important activities are deliberately adopted in the full knowledge that they will involve losses.[1]

The detailed functionings of the Federal Reserve Banks is reserved for discussion in the next chapter. Here it is only necessary to know that they are banks for bankers and for the government. Most of the Federal taxes and expenditures pass through the Reserve Banks. The Member Banks hold their cash reserves on deposit in the nearest Reserve Bank, and look to it for help in time of crisis and for leadership at all times.

BANKING AS A BUSINESS

The ordinary commercial bank is a relatively simple and unexciting business concern. Banking is a business much like any other business. A bank provides

[1] That the details of ownership of a Central Bank are not vital is indicated by the history of the Bank of England. For two and a half centuries prior to its being nationalized by the present Labor government, it was a private corporation; but for the latter part of that period it acted (except for a few slips) pretty much the same as it would have if officially part of the government.

certain services for its customers and in return receives payments from them in one form or another. If possible, it tries to earn a capital yield for its stockholders or owners.

A bank's balance sheet shows certain assets, certain liabilities, and certain capital ownership. Except that its liabilities usually follow rather than precede capital items, the bank's published balance sheet looks, on the whole, much like the balance sheet of any other business, and rather simpler than most.

The only peculiar feature about the consolidated balance sheet of all national banks shown in Table 1 is the fact that such a large portion of the banks' liabilities are payable on demand; *i.e.*, they are deposits subject to checking. This fact is intriguing to the economist because he chooses to call such demand liabilities money; but to the banker it is a familiar condition which has long since been taken for granted. He knows full well that, although it would be

TABLE 1. *Consolidated Balance Sheet of All National Banks, Jan. 1, 1946*
(In billions of dollars)

Assets		Liabilities	
Cash and balances with Reserve Banks and other banks	$20.2	Capital accounts	$ 4.6
Loans and discounts	13.9	Time deposits	15.9
U.S. government obligations	51.5	Demand deposits	69.4
Other securities	4.1	Other liabilities	0.6
Other assets	0.8		
Total assets	$90.5	Total liabilities	$90.5

SOURCE: U.S. Treasury.

possible for every depositor suddenly to decide to withdraw all his money from the bank on the same day, nevertheless the probability of this happening is infinitely remote. Each day as some people are withdrawing their money, others are normally making deposits that tend to cancel the withdrawals. As a matter of fact, in our growing economy the new depositings more than offset the withdrawals.

This, however, need not be strictly true at any one moment, in any one day, or in any one week. By chance alone the amount of withdrawals might exceed depositings for some period of time, just as a coin may land with heads turned up rather than tails for a consecutive number of tosses. For this reason, the banker keeps a little cash handy in his cash vaults and a "reserve deposit" at the near-by Federal Reserve Bank. *Normally the till money in the bank's own vaults and its reserves at the Reserve Bank need be only a small fraction of the bank's total deposits;* and the same mathematical law of large numbers which makes life insurance possible assures the banker that the larger his bank and the more numerous his independent depositors, the smaller need this fraction be.

All these facts are so much taken for granted by every modern banker that he is hardly aware of them. But it was not always so. Commercial banking is usually assumed to have begun with the ancient goldsmiths who developed the practice of storing people's gold and valuables for safekeeping. At first such establishments were simply like parcel checkrooms or warehouses. The depositor left his gold for safekeeping, was given a receipt, later presented that receipt, paid a small fee for safekeeping, and got back his gold.

Quite obviously, however, money is wanted only for what it will buy, not for its own sake. Money has an anonymous quality, so that one dollar is just as good as another, and one piece of pure gold as good as another. The goldsmiths soon found it more convenient *not* to have to tag the gold belonging to any one individual so as to be able to give to him upon request exactly the same piece of gold that he had left. Instead, the customer was quite willing to accept a receipt for an amount of gold or money *of a given value*, even though it was not the identical particle of matter that he had actually left.

This is important. Therein lies a significant difference between today's bank and a checkroom or warehouse. If I check my bag at Grand Central Station and later see someone walking down the street with that same suitcase, there is nothing for me to do but call my lawyer and sue the railroad company. If I mark my initials on a $10 bill, deposit it in my bank account, and later notice it in the hands of a stranger, I have no grievance against the bank management. They have agreed only to pay me on demand any old $10 of legal tender.

But let us return to the goldsmith establishments which are supposed to typify the first embryonic commercial banks. What would balance sheets of a typical establishment look like? Perhaps like Table 2.

TABLE 2. *Balance Sheet of Early Bank*

Assets		Liabilities and Net Worth	
Cash	$1,000,000	Capital and surplus	$ 50,000
Loans and investments	50,000	Demand deposit liability	1,000,000
Total	$1,050,000	Total	$1,050,000

We have assumed that the company has long since dropped its activities as a smith and is principally occupied with storing people's money for safekeeping. Over past time, 1 million dollars has been deposited in its vaults, and this whole sum it holds as a cash asset. To balance this asset, there is a current deposit liability of the same amount. Actually such a business need have no other assets (except the negligible value of its office space and vaults). But there is no reason why its owners should not have—on the side, so to speak—subscribed $50,000 of capital to be lent out at interest or to buy securities such as stocks or bonds. On the asset side this amount is shown under the heading Loans and Investments; this is balanced on the right-hand side by a similar sum in the Capital account.

At this primitive stage, the bank would be of no particular interest to the economist. The investment and capital items have nothing to do with the bank's deposits; if all the loans and investments should go sour and become worthless, the loss would fall completely on the stockholders who have agreed to take that risk in the hope of making a profit. Every depositor could still be paid off in full out of the 100 per cent cash reserves held by the bank. The bank would still cover its overhead and clerical expenses by making its customers pay storage charges. (These charges would presumably vary with the length of time the customer left his money for safekeeping, the average amount of his money that required safekeeping, and the number of times the turnover of his account made it necessary for a clerk to wait on him and keep records.)

The economist would have little interest in the bank's operations because the bank money[1]—the demand deposits created jointly by the bank's willingness to accept a demand obligation and the customer's willingness to hold a deposit—would just offset the amount of ordinary money (currency or gold) placed in the bank's safe and withdrawn from active circulation. The whole process would be of no more interest than if the public decided to convert some of its dollar bills into an equivalent amount of quarters and dimes. In the language of the simple quantity theory of money, we would say that the banking system is having a *neutral* effect on prices since it is neither adding nor subtracting from the total of ("active") money.

Before leaving this simple first stage of banking, we must point out that there is a substantial group of economic experts who today advocate as a thoroughgoing reform of our banking system the return to a system of 100 per cent cash reserves against all demand deposits. This, they say, is the only safe system of banking, in which depositors can really all get their money out of the bank any time they all want it together. It is the only honest system of banking, in which the banks are not "creating" new money for their own

[1] The economist would consider the demand deposit as money just as soon as the custom grew up for depositors to pay for the goods they bought by giving the storekeeper a little note to the bank saying, "Mr. Goldsmith, pay to the order of Sears, Roebuck $2.99, (signed) John Q. Doe." In other words, as soon as the use of checks became customary.

profit, and in so doing usurping the constitutional monetary prerogatives of the government. Finally, it is the only system of banking in which the banking system is neutral, neither creating money in time of boom and thereby adding to inflation, nor contracting the money supply in times of panic and depression and thereby adding to deflation, bankruptcy, and unemployment.

We cannot appraise the value of this reform until we have examined the nature of modern banks operating with only fractional legal reserve ratios.

MODERN FRACTIONAL RESERVE BANKING

Let us return to our early goldsmith-banker to see how modern banks gradually evolved. If he were an alert fellow, he would soon notice that, although his deposits are payable on demand, they are not all withdrawn together. He would soon learn that, although 100 per cent reserves are necessary if the bank is to be liquidated and all depositors to be paid off in full, they are not at all necessary if his bank is a "going concern." New deposits tend to balance withdrawals. Only a little till money, perhaps less than 2 per cent, will ever be needed in the form of vault cash.[1]

At first he probably thought this discovery too good to be true. Then perhaps he recalled the story of a rival bank in which a dishonest clerk ran off with 95 per cent of the bank's cash reserve—and the fact was never discovered for 50 years. No one ever had occasion to go to the back rooms of the vault because all withdrawals were financed by recently deposited money held in the front vaults!

We can imagine our intelligent banker—at first cautiously—beginning to acquire earning assets with some of the cash entrusted to his care. Everything works out all right; depositors are still paid off on demand, and the bank has made some extra earnings. Gradually the banker no longer feels it necessary to conceal from his depositors what he is doing. If a depositor complains, the banker retorts, "Your money is safe. If you don't like my way of doing business, you are at liberty to withdraw your funds. Besides, haven't you noticed that the new method of fractional cash reserves has enabled me to lower my service charges to you? Also, it has enabled me to give a helping hand to our

---

[1] If the bank could pay off its depositors with one of its own checks (or as in former times with one of its paper bank notes), it might not have to keep any till money at all! By judiciously limiting the rate at which it was making investments, the bank could ensure that the checks it received from other banks plus the cash deposited in it were just matched by its outpayments. An occasional, temporary outward drain of funds could be met by permitting the bank to pay by check what it owed to other banks for the few hours or days until some part of its asset portfolio was able to be liquidated or until it contracted its operations so as to get in a surplus of inpayments over outpayments.

local businessmen who need more capital to buy new tools, buildings, and inventories. Such capital formation benefits consumers because they get better goods for lower prices. It also creates jobs for workers."

Little wonder, therefore, that all banks should have begun to invest most of the money deposited with them in earning assets and to keep only fractional cash reserves against deposits. Indeed, as long as business confidence remains high, and provided the managers of the bank are judicious in their choice of loans and investments, *there is no reason why the bank should keep much more than 2 per cent cash reserves against deposits.*

What if the banker makes a mistake in his investments? Since nobody's judgment is perfect and since all investments involve some element of speculative risk, this is certainly a possibility that must be reckoned with. To lessen the possibility of extreme losses, the banker can try to diversify his investments as much as possible, so as not to put all his eggs in one basket. More than that, a conservative bank will have a considerable amount of capital put up by the stockholders. For example, capital stock may have been issued equal to 10 per cent of demand deposits. Then, even if all the bank's assets are in earning investments rather than in nonearning cash, the depositors are protected against all capital losses that do not exceed 10 per cent of the bank's investment portfolio. In ordinary times, this would be quite sufficient so long as the bank confines its activities to gilt-edge bonds, well-investigated mortgages, and conservative business loans.

There is only one last requirement that the bank would have to meet if we are to give it an A+ in deportment. The management must watch the general trend in the growth of its deposits to make sure that the city in which it is located is not becoming a "ghost town" and that the bank is not losing deposits steadily over a long period of time. If this were the case, the bank's investment portfolio would have to be arranged so that it consisted of securities and loans that could be gradually liquidated over time and converted into cash to meet depositors' withdrawals.

Even if the bank is not a declining business, prudent managers must still protect themselves against a temporary surge of withdrawals. To hold cash against such a contingency would be costly, since cash earns no yield. They will usually decide, therefore, to hold in their portfolios as secondary reserves some securities that always have a ready market and can be liquidated at short notice. Government bonds serve this purpose admirably. Short-term bonds (called notes, bills, or certificates) vary little in value and can be liquidated simply by not buying new ones as the old ones come due every 90 days or

12 months. But even long-term government bonds, with 30 years of life before they mature, can serve as secondary reserves in normal times, because they can always be transferred to some other buyer at the quoted market price.[1] The important thing in this connection is not the *date of maturity* of the bond or loan, but rather how "shiftable" the asset is to some other investment institution. Thus, a 90-day loan to a local merchant, which is nonshiftable, is intrinsically less appropriate as secondary reserves than a 90-year gilt-edge bond traded on an organized securities exchange.

THE DIFFERENCE BETWEEN A BANK AND ANY CORPORATION

The above precepts of sound banking practice are quite simple and understandable. They are a little harder to carry out in practice than to state in principle; but the same is true of most sage prescriptions concerning sound investing and wise living.

We have seen what the differences are between a bank and a checkroom. What, if any, are the differences between a bank and any corporation? To say that economists like to call bank demand liabilities money is not to say very much—after one has abandoned the strict quantity theory. To say that bank operations affect the totals of investment, purchasing power, and employment is nothing that cannot be said equally of public-utility companies, of manufacturing enterprise, and of the stock market. That the lifetime savings of widows, orphans, and the public depend upon the solvency of the banks can with almost equal truth be said of insurance companies, of government bond borrowings, and of trust and holding companies.

If we compare a "going and growing" bank with any corporation, the surprising thing is not how little cash reserves the banks keep, but that they keep any at all (in excess of till-money requirements). *As long as financial skies are sunny, the same logic that compels the abandonment of a system of 100 per cent reserves argues in favor of negligible reserves!*

Yet, if we turn to the facts, we find that a modern prudent bank is expected—and required by law!—to keep a substantial portion of its assets in nonearning cash. These "legal reserves" are in addition to the till money in the bank's vaults and are kept on deposit with the local Federal Reserve Bank. They are never to be used up so long as the bank is solvent. At the present time American commercial banks belonging to the Federal reserve system are, on the average, legally required to keep in the form of nonearning cash reserves deposited with the Federal Reserve Bank a little less than 20 per cent of their demand de-

[1] There is a saying that "You can sell government bonds even on Sunday."

posits.[1] More precisely, Table 3 gives the present-day legal reserve requirements of all member banks of the Federal reserve system.

TABLE 3. *Legal Reserve Rates for Federal Reserve Member Banks,** *March, 1948*

	Reserve rates against demand deposits, per cent	Reserve rates against time deposits, per cent
Central Reserve City Banks (New York and Chicago)...	22	6
Reserve City Banks (large and medium cities)	20	6
Other Member Banks (small town or country). . . .	14	6

* Before 1936, reserve requirements were for a long time 13, 10, 7, and 3 per cent instead of the present 22, 20, 14, and 6 per cent. Early in 1948 the Reserve authorities had power from Congress to set maximum reserve requirements of 26, 20, 14, and 6 per cent—or twice the predepression levels. In Chap. 15, we shall see how the Federal reserve authorities can vary reserve requirements as a weapon of monetary control.

If, as has just been argued, reserves seem to be largely unnecessary, why are there such legal requirements? And why, in all logic, should the so-called "time" or "saving" deposits of banks only require a 6 per cent reserve ratio? Although these are theoretically withdrawable only on 30 days' notice, they are in fact paid on personal demand. Surely no bank that can be solvent in 30 days can really be bankrupt today. Moreover, more than any other form of investment, savings deposits embody the wealth of the very poor, and their safety is of primary social importance.

PARADOXES OF FRACTIONAL RESERVE BANKING

A partial answer to our paradox arises from the fundamental fact that *fractional reserve banking* is essentially an unstable, "fair-weather" business. So long as all depositors do not want to withdraw all their deposits at one and the same time, they are free to have their money on demand. But as soon as they all care to exercise this right simultaneously, no one can have his money!

[1] English banks are required by force of custom rather than law to keep about 8 to 10 per cent cash reserves, and, if possible, another 20 per cent in the secondary form of short-term government and private "bills" (highly endorsed, secured, and negotiable, short-term promissory notes).

A single bank can weather a bank run by shifting its assets on to some other financial institution and thereby converting them into cash.

Especially in time of financial panic, all banks together cannot meet a general run by liquidating their portfolios. There is then no one—except the government—to whom their earning assets can be shifted; no way of transposing them into cash to meet depositors' withdrawals; no way to keep even the strongest and most conservative bank from becoming bankrupt.

This perverse situation is made all the worse because of a similar perversity on the part of depositors. As long as they know they can have their money from the bank, the depositors don't want it. As soon as they know (or suspect) that they can't withdraw their money, they insist on having it! But when all act upon this fear or suspicion, they unwittingly transform it from an unfounded rumor into actual reality.

This is borne out by the history of private banking. Both here and in England it is a history of periodic crisis, panic, and bankruptcy.[1] When the foul storm blows, all banks are bowled over, and, afterward only the strongest institutions are able to get back on their feet. The weaker ones are gone forever and with them part of the depositors' money.

It is against such financial contingencies that the custom of requiring legal reserves against deposits grew up. *As a result, modern private banking is an uneasy compromise of elements which are unnecessary if the sun is shining and insufficient if it is not.* In time of financial panic, no private banking system with less than 100 per cent cash reserves will do, certainly not one with 10 or 20 per cent reserves—as the bank crisis of 1933 shows. In normal times when money can be safely invested at a profit, there is no good reason for requiring nonearning cash reserves of anywhere near the legal amounts.

Actually legal reserve requirements can conceivably cause more banks to fail than otherwise. Because banks had little excess reserves prior to the crisis of the early 1930's, the first drain of deposits caused some banks to fall below their legal reserve ratios. Thus, technically, they became insolvent and were shut down, thus intensifying the panic. Some of the closed banks might possibly have been able to weather the crisis but for their being declared insolvent. After all, most insurance companies, whose assets declined in market value and marketability along with bank assets in the years following 1929, were able to weather the storm just because their policy contracts did not require them to *appear* to be able to liquidate all their liabilities at an instant's

---

[1] Some 8,000 banks with more than 5 billion dollars of deposits became insolvent in 1930–1933.

notice. Except for loans on policies, they were largely able to meet all demands for cash from the new business coming in.

Even a bank with cash reserves far in excess of legal requirements can be in a very bad condition if the true value of its earning assets has fallen far enough below their cost. The extra cash reserve may enable it to put up a bold, false front and best a psychological bank run. (For this purpose the best strategy is always to maintain a cheerful countenance and to pay out money gladly and freely to all comers in the hope that this will allay their doubts and fears and end the panic.) But still from a long-run standpoint, the bank may be completely insolvent.

Making the bank hold extra dollars of cash is a very indirect and somewhat ineffective way of protecting depositors from suffering when banks experience losses on their earning assets. All that can be said for this method is that each dollar held in cash is at least safe from loss. Sound principles of bank management and bank regulation imply infinitely more—and possibly less—than this.

MAKING BANKS SAFE

Perhaps this is a rather gloomy picture. Certainly if one reviews the history of private, small-scale nineteenth-century banking, there is plenty of gloom to be found in it. However, the above remarks are not still fully applicable because today we no longer have a purely *private* banking system. All countries have long recognized that banking is one of those activities "affected with public interest" and in need of government control. They have created central banks, like the Federal reserve system and the Bank of England, to correct the intrinsic instability of laissez-faire banking. All the monetary and fiscal powers of the government's Treasury Department are used to keep financial panics from developing and to stem them when they do. In addition, through bank examinations and by enforceable rules, the freedom of behavior of bank management is narrowly limited.

The successive steps taken by government to modify the instability of laissez-faire banking can be briefly described:

1. *Regulation of Bank Formation and Activity.* For decades, either the state or Federal authorities have set down the conditions under which banks could be formed—the minimum amount of capital they must have, etc. Bank examiners periodically scrutinize the composition of bank assets and pass on the bank's solvency, always keeping in mind that an ounce of prevention is worth a pound of cure.

2. *Formation of Federal Reserve System.* The next great forward step was the establishment of central banks, whose primary function is to stand as a

Rock of Gibraltar in time of panic, to be ready to use the full monetary powers of the government to stem collapse of the banking system. The other subsidiary, but important, functions of a central bank will be discussed later.

3. *Government Insurance of Bank Deposits.* One of the most important government bank reforms is also one of the most recent. Following the bank crisis of 1933, the FDIC was set up to insure the safety of all bank deposits up to $5,000. All banks which are members of the Federal reserve system *must* belong, and most state banks also do belong. In return for a yearly payment by the banks, which varies with their total deposits, all their customers are completely protected against any loss (up to $5,000) even if the bank should go bankrupt.

The importance of this measure can hardly be exaggerated. It would be absolutely wrong to say that bank bankruptcy is no longer a danger. But, certainly, there need never again be universal bank runs. From now on banks will be closed up by bank examiners and government authorities, and not by the panicky behavior of depositors whose fears bring on the very contingency they are most afraid of. A single bank need no longer fear that its reputation, like that of a good woman, is compromised simply by being accused, regardless of the truth of the charge.

How is government action able to bring about this important change, without which our system of small unit banking would remain perilously unsafe? First, by relying on the comforting basic principle underlying all insurance; *i.e.*, by being able to average out and cancel off large-scale probabilities. Second, and most important in view of our many earlier warnings that depressions cannot be insured against by ordinary actuarial methods, is the fact that the government can (and must!) use its *boundless emergency monetary powers* to avert collapse whenever a real financial crisis should arise.

B. *THE CREATION OF BANK DEPOSITS*

CAN BANKS REALLY CREATE MONEY?

We now turn to one of the most interesting aspects of money and credit, the process called "multiple expansion of bank deposits." This is little understood. Most people have heard that in some mysterious manner banks are able to create money out of thin air, but too few really understand how the process works.

Actually, there is nothing magical or incomprehensible about the creation of bank deposits. At every step of the way, any intelligent person can follow what is happening to the banks' accounts. The true explanation of deposit creation is simple. What is difficult to grasp are the false explanations still in wide circulation.

According to these false explanations, the managers of an ordinary bank are able, by some use of their fountain pens, to lend several dollars for each dollar left on deposit with them. No wonder practical bankers see red when such behavior is attributed to them. They only wish they could do so. As every banker well knows, he cannot invest money that he does not have; and any money that he does invest in buying a security or making a loan will soon leave his bank.

Bankers, therefore, often go to the opposite extreme. Because each small bank is limited in the way it can "create money," they sometimes argue that the whole banking system cannot create money. "After all," they say, "we can invest only what is left with us. We don't create anything. We only put the communities' savings to work." Bankers who argue in this way are quite wrong. They have become enmeshed in our old friend, the fallacy of composition: what is true for each is not true for all. The banking system as a whole can do what each small bank cannot do!

Our answer then to the question of this section is in the affirmative. Yes, the banking system and the public do, between them, create about $5 of bank deposits for every dollar taken out of circulation and left in the banks. Let us see how.

HOW DEPOSITS ARE CREATED

We begin with a brand-new deposit of $1,000 which is brought to a bank. Now, if banks were to keep 100 per cent cash reserves, like the old goldsmiths,

TABLE 4*a*. *Original Bank in Initial Position*

Assets		Liabilities	
Cash reserves	+$1,000	Deposits	+$1,000
Total	+$1,000	Total	+$1,000

they could not create any extra money out of a new deposit of $1,000 left with them. The depositor would be simply giving up $1,000 of currency for a $1,000 checking deposit whenever he brought his money to the bank.

The change in the bank's balance sheet, as far as the new demand deposit is concerned, would be as shown in Table 4*a*.

The bank has not created this deposit *alone*. The customer had to be willing to make the deposit. Once he took the initiative, the bank was also willing to accept a checking account from the customer. Together the bank and the public have "created" $1,000 of bank money or deposit. But there is no multiple expansion, no 5 for 1 or anything else. So long as the banks keep 100 per cent reserves, the growth of bank money is just offset by the decline of currency in circulation.

Suppose now that the bank does not have to keep 100 per cent reserves. Suppose that the law requires it to keep only 20 per cent legal reserves. (It can always keep larger reserves if it wishes to; but if there are many outstanding, relatively safe, interest-yielding government bonds or numerous profitable lending opportunities, the bank will not find it profitable to keep much more reserves than the law requires.)

What can the bank now do? Can it expand its loans and investments by $4,000 so that the change in its balance sheet looks as shown in Table 4b?

TABLE 4b. *Impossible Situation for Single Small Bank*

Assets		Liabilities	
Cash reserves	+$1,000	Deposits	+$5,000
Loans and investments	+ 4,000		
Total	+$5,000	Total	+$5,000

The answer is definitely "no." Why not? Total assets equal total liabilities. Cash reserves meet the legal requirement of being 20 per cent of total deposits.

True enough. But how does the bank pay for the investments or earning assets that it buys? Like everyone else it writes out a check—to the man who sells the bond or signs the promissory note. If all such people would promise not to cash the bank's check—or what is the same thing, to hold all such money frozen on deposit in the bank—then, of course, the bank could buy all it wants to without losing any cash.

In fact, no one borrows money at 6 per cent just to hold it all in the bank. The borrower spends the money on labor, on materials, or perhaps on an automobile. The money will very soon, therefore, have to be paid out of the bank. And if the bank is only one of many serving that city, county, state, and country, only a fraction of the sums withdrawn will ever come back to the original bank in another customer's deposit.

This loss of cash by a bank expanding its investments is even more clearly seen if the bank buys a bond rather than makes a local loan. The man who sells to a New England bank a United States government bond through a New York brokerage house may himself live in Columbus, Ohio. He puts the check that he receives in his own bank. This Columbus bank, of course, presents the check—through the Federal reserve clearing system—to the New England bank for payment. The New England bank loses cash, or what is the same thing, loses part of its legal reserve deposit at the (Boston) Federal Reserve Bank. (Go back and read this paragraph over again until you are sure you can follow the various steps.)

A bank cannot eat its cake and have it too. The New England bank cannot buy a bond and keep its cash at the same time. Table 4b gives, therefore, a completely false picture of what an individual bank can do.

Must the bank, therefore, behave like the 100 per cent reserve goldsmith bankers? Of course not. Although the bank cannot jack its deposits up to five times its cash reserve, it certainly can *reduce its cash down* to one-fifth of its deposits. Nothing is easier. For, as we have just seen, all it has to do is buy $800 worth of earning assets—bonds, loans, or mortgages. In a day or so it will lose practically all this cash as its checks come back for payment. Now its balance sheet will be as shown in Table 4c.

TABLE 4c. *Original Bank in Final Position*

Assets		Liabilities	
Cash	+$ 200	Deposits	+$1,000
Loans and investments	+ 800		
Total	+$1,000	Total	+$1,000

As far as this first bank is concerned, we are through. Its legal reserves are just enough to match its deposits. There is nothing more it can do until the public decides to bring in some more money on deposit.

But the banking system cannot yet settle down. The people who originally sold the bonds or borrowed from the bank will presumably deposit the proceeds in some other bank or pay them out to someone else who will make such a deposit. Our original bank has thus lost $800 to some other banks in the system. If we lump these all together and call these "second-generation banks," their balance sheets now appear as shown in Table 4d.

TABLE 4d. *Second-generation Banks in Initial Position*

Assets		Liabilities	
Cash	+$800	Deposits	+$800
Total	+$800	Total	+$800

Of course, these banks are scattered all over the country. (Our original bank might even constitute a small part of the second generation as a few of its checks fell into the hands of its own depositors.) To these banks the dollars deposited are just like any other dollars, just like our original deposit; these banks don't know and don't care, that they are second in a chain of deposits. They do know, and they do care, that they are now holding too much non-earning cash. Only one-fifth of $800, or $160, is legally needed against $800 deposits. Therefore, they can, and will, use the other four-fifths to buy $640 worth of loans and investments; so that in a few days, their balance sheet will have reached equilibrium as shown in Table 4e. So much for the second-genera-

TABLE 4e. *Final Position of Second-generation Banks*

Assets		Liabilities	
Cash.........................	+$160	Deposits.....................	+$800
Loans and investments.........	+ 640		
Total.....................	+$800	Total.....................	+$800

tion banks.

Thus far, the original $1,000 taken out of hand-to-hand circulation and put into the banking system has given rise to $1,000 (first-generation deposits) plus $800 (second-generation deposits). The total of money has increased, and the end is not yet in sight.

For the $640 lost by the second-generation banks will go to a new set of banks called the "third-generation banks." The reader should by now be able to fill in their balance sheets as they look initially (see Table 4f). Clearly they

TABLE 4f. *Initial Position of Third-generation Banks*

Assets		Liabilities	
Cash.........................	+....	Deposits.....................	+....
Loans and investments.........	....		
Total.....................	+....	Total.....................	+$640

will at first have *excess* cash *reserves* of an amount equal to four-fifths of $640, or $512. After this sum has been spent on loans and investments—and only then—the third-generation banks will reach equilibrium with the balance sheet as shown in Table 4g.

TABLE 4g. *Final Equilibrium of Third-generation Banks*

Assets		Liabilities	
Cash.........................	+$128	Deposits.....................	+$640
Loans and investments........	+ 512		
Total.....................	+$640	Total.....................	+$640

The total of bank money is now $1,000 plus $800 plus $640, or $2,440. This is already almost 2½ to 1 expansion. But a fourth generation of banks will clearly end up with four-fifths of $640 in deposits, or $512; and the fifth generation will get four-fifths of $512, or $409.60; and the sixth generation four-fifths of $409.60; and so on; until finally by the twenty-fifth round, we shall have got all but $1 of the total sum of the infinitely many series of generations.

What will be the final sum: $1,000 + $800 + $640 + $512 + $409.60 + · · · ? If we patiently do out the sum by arithmetic, we shall find that it gets to $4999.999 . . . and "finally" to $5,000. Table 4h shows the complete effects of the chain of deposit creation.

TABLE 4h. *Multiple Expansion of Bank Deposits through the Banking System*

	New Deposits	New loans and investments	Cash reserves
Original bank..........................	$1,000.00	$ 800.00	$ 200.00
2d-generation banks....................	800.00	640.00	160.00
3d-generation banks....................	640.00	512.00	128.00
4th-generation banks..................	512.00	409.60	102.40
5th-generation banks..................	409.60	327.68	81.92
6th-generation banks..................	327.68	262.14*	65.54*
7th-generation banks..................	262.14*	209.72*	52.42*
8th-generation banks..................	209.72*	167.77*	41.95*
9th-generation banks..................	167.77*	134.22*	33.55*
10th-generation banks.................	134.22*	107.37*	26.85*
Sum of first 10 generation banks........	$4,463.13*	$3,570.50*	$ 892.63*
Sum of remaining generation banks......	536.87*	429.50*	107.37*
Total for banking system as a whole....	$5,000.00	$4,000.00	$1,000.00

* Rounded off to two decimal places.

We can also get the same answer in two other ways—by common sense and by elementary algebra.

Common sense[1] tells us that the process of deposit creation can come to an end only when no bank *anywhere in the system* has cash reserves in excess of the

[1] This can be proved algebraically as follows:

$$\$1,000 + \$800 + \$640 + \cdot\cdot\cdot = \$1,000[1 + \tfrac{4}{5} + (\tfrac{4}{5})^2 + (\tfrac{4}{5})^3 + \cdot\cdot\cdot]$$
$$= \$1,000\left(\frac{1}{1 - \tfrac{4}{5}}\right) = \$1,000\,(5)$$
$$= \$5,000$$

20 per cent reserve ratio to deposits. In all our previous examples no cash has ever leaked out of the banking system, but has simply gone out, as a result of security purchases, from one set of banks into another set of banks' vaults. Everyone will be at equilibrium only when, for all the banks together—the first, the second, and the hundredth generation—a consolidated balance sheet would look as shown in Table 4*i*. For if deposits were less than $5,000, the 20 per cent ratio would not yet be reached and equilibrium would not yet have been achieved.

TABLE 4*i. Consolidated Balance Sheet Showing Final Position of All Banks Together*

Assets		Liabilities	
Cash......................	+$1,000	Deposits....................	+$5,000
Loans and investments........	+$4,000		
Total....................	+$5,000	Total....................	+$5,000

If the reader will turn to Table 4*b* previously marked *impossible*, he will see that the whole banking system can do what no one bank can do by itself. Bank money has been created 5 for 1—and all the while each bank has only invested and lent a fraction of what it has received as deposits!

Who creates the multiple expansion of deposits? Three parties do so jointly: the public by always keeping their money in the bank on deposit; the banks by keeping only a fraction of their deposits in the form of cash; the public and private borrowers who make it possible for the banks to find earning assets to buy with their excess cash. There is also a fourth party, the Central Bank, which by its activities makes it possible for new reserves to come to the banking system, as the next chapter will show.

There is nothing paradoxical in the fact that total bank deposits are several times as great as the amount of paper cash in existence anywhere. The same is true of the total government bonds and real-estate values. Deposits are something that banks owe their customers; cash is *left* in a bank, but it does not *remain* in that bank. Throughout its lifetime a dollar may have been *left* in many banks, just as it may be used over a long period of time to buy hundreds of dollars of merchandise. The thing to keep firmly in mind is that bank deposits are one of the three forms of modern money, and quantitatively the most important.

Before leaving this section, the student should test his knowledge of credit creation by tracing through in detail what happens when a nervous widow permanently *withdraws* $1,000 from a single bank and hides it in her attic. (1) The bank loses $1,000 of cash and $1,000 of deposits. But it previously held only 20 per cent cash reserves or $200 against her deposit. Clearly it must have given up to her some of the legally necessary cash reserves held against its other demand deposits. Its total reserves are now below the legal minimum. (2) Therefore, it must sell $800 worth of investments or call in that many loans. The first-generation bank will be in equilibrium only when its balance sheet finally looks as shown in Table 5a.

TABLE 5a. *Equilibrium Position of Original Bank Losing a Deposit*

Assets		Liabilities	
Cash.....................	−$ 200	Deposits....................	−$1,000
Loans and investments........	− 800		
Total....................	−$1,000	Total....................	−$1,000

But in selling its securities, our original bank has drained $800 from a second generation of banks; and they in turn by liquidating securities, drain reserves from a third generation. And so it goes—until the widow's withdrawal of $1,000 has produced a chain "killing off" $5,000 worth of deposits throughout the whole system and $4,000 of bank-earning assets. The student should trace through each stage: Table 5b, Table 5c, . . . , etc.

The reader should also be able to show how an initial deposit of $1,000 can result in $10,000 of bank deposits if banks keep only 10 per cent reserve ratios, as they used to until about 10 years ago.

A "MONOPOLY BANK"

In all of the above processes, it was assumed that no cash leaked out of the banking system into someone's mattress or into permanent hand-to-hand circulation. The banking system was then in the enviable position of finding that its checks were always deposited somewhere within itself.

This being so, it is easy to see that a single "monopoly bank" (with many branches), serving the whole nation, would be able to do at once what we have said each small bank cannot do. Its balance sheet could quickly go to the condition shown in Table 4b or 4i. It could write checks freely to pay for securities or loans, knowing that the people to whom they are paid would always deposit their proceeds in the one and only monopoly bank. In countries like England, where there is a "big 5" group of branch banks, or like Canada where there are a few large banks, or in states like California where there are a few great multiple-branch banks—in such cases a bank may be able to lend out more than its legal excess reserves, knowing that part of the money will come back to itself in later generations. However, these so-called "derivative" or "self-returning" deposits are not important for the United States, and calling attention to them often only confuses the beginning student.

In the previous section we have seen how the banking system can reach the limits of its expansion through many successive rounds or generations. If we allow half a week for checks to clear at each stage and for decisions to be made, 5 to 8 weeks would be required for the process to have substantially worked itself out through more than a dozen rounds.

As a practical matter, it is usually not necessary to follow the chain of each dollar deposited through its successive rounds. For example, a decrease in hoarding by the public will affect almost all the banks at the same time. They will all receive some new deposits at pretty much the same time. They will all have excess reserves in the first instance, and so they will all together begin to buy securities or make loans.

When a single bank, all by itself, writes checks to acquire securities, these checks go to other banks and it loses cash. But when all are writing checks simultaneously and in balance, there will tend to be a cancellation of new checks deposited in each bank against those paid out. No one bank need lose cash reserves. Consequently, without going through the successive generations of the previous section, all banks together can simply and blithely expand their loans and investments—so long as they do not jeopardize their reserve position —until deposits are finally brought into a 5:1 relation to cash. When this state has been reached, the banking system has reached the limit of its ability to create money.

The student should work through the similar process by which all banks simultaneously contract money 5:1 for each dollar of reserve withdrawn from the banking system, and also how a monopoly bank would contract.

THREE QUALIFICATIONS

Finally, a few qualifications must be made, only the last of which is of very great significance. We have shown that $1,000 taken out of hand-to-hand circulation and put into a bank can result in an increase of $5,000 of bank deposits. This assumed that all the new money remained somewhere in the banking system, in one bank or another at every stage of the process, and that all banks were able to keep "loaned up" with no "excess reserves."

Leakage into Hand-to-hand Circulation. It is quite possible, however, and even likely, that somewhere along the chain of deposit expansion some individual who receives a check will not leave the proceeds in a bank, but will withdraw it into circulation or into hoarding outside the banking system. As a matter of fact, in boom times when bank deposits are expanding, there is usually at the same time an increased need for pennies, dimes, and paper currency to transact the increased volume of petty transactions.

The effects of such withdrawals on our analysis are simple. When $1,000 stayed in the banking system, $5,000 of new deposits were created. If $200 were to leak out into circulation outside the banks, and only $800 of new reserves were to remain in the banking system, then the new deposits created would be $4,000 ($800 × 5). The banking system can always amplify in a 5:1 ratio whatever amount of new reserves are permanently left with it.

Leakage into Bank Vault Cash.   Similar to the leakage of cash into circulation outside the banks is the fact that banks will have to keep some of their new cash in the form of till money, or vault cash. This is in addition to their legally required 20 per cent reserves left on deposit with the local Federal Reserve Bank. Such cash cannot be counted as part of the bank's 20 per cent legal reserve because all legal reserves must be on deposit with the Federal Reserve Bank in the bank's district. In 1947, something like 2 per cent of their deposits were kept by banks as till money. Such vault cash acts rather like a leakage of cash into hand-to-hand circulation. Instead of having new deposits equal to 5 × $1,000, we have them equal to about 5 × ($1,000 − $100) or $4,500. This is because $100—more or less 2 per cent of $5,000—is the amount of vault cash which the bank cannot use as its legal reserve.[1]

Possible Excess Reserves.   Our description of multiple deposit creation has proceeded on the assumption that the commercial banks stick fairly closely to their legal reserve ratios. Of course there is no reason why a bank cannot choose to keep more than the legally required amount of reserves. Thus, if the original bank receiving a new $1,000 deposit were satisfied to hold $800 of it in excess reserves, then the whole process would end right there. Or if banks always kept 5 per cent excess reserves, in addition to the 20 per cent legal requirement, we should have a chain of expansion of deposits of the form $[1 + \frac{3}{4} + (\frac{3}{4})^2 + \cdots]$ rather than $[1 + \frac{4}{5} + (\frac{4}{5})^2 + \cdots]$ with only a 4:1 rather than a 5:1 expansion of deposits.

Hence there is nothing automatic about deposit creation. Four factors are necessary: The banks must somehow receive new reserves; they must be willing to make loans or buy securities; someone must be willing to borrow or to sell securities; and finally, the public must choose to leave their money on deposit

---

[1] Another way of expressing this relation, and one that is slightly more exact, is as follows: The new $1,000 will give rise not to $1,000 × 1/0.20, but to

$$\$1,000 \times \frac{1}{(0.20 + 0.02)}.$$

This gives $4,545.45 of new deposits.

with the banks. We shall return to the problem of excess and legal reserves in Chap. 15.

SUMMARY

A. THE MODERN BANKING SYSTEM

1. The American banking system consists primarily of relatively small-scale unit banks, chartered by the national government or by the states. Although less than half are members of the Federal reserve system, their deposits include four-fifths of the total of all deposits.

2. The functions of commercial banks are numerous and overlap with those of such other financial institutions as mutual savings banks, cooperative building and loan societies, finance companies, trusteeships, and insurance companies. But in their function of collecting and honoring bank checks, the commercial banks perform a unique and important economic role. Their demand deposits constitute the single most important component of our money supply or medium of exchange.

3. The Federal reserve system consists primarily of (a) Member Banks, (b) the 12 Federal Reserve Banks spread over the country, (c) the Board of Governors of the Federal reserve system in Washington.

Although nominally corporations owned by the member banks, the Federal Reserve Banks are, in fact, almost branches of the Federal government, possessing wide powers and being concerned with the public interest rather than with bank profits. In practice, their activities are not independent of Treasury and Administration policy. It is the primary responsibility of the Reserve Banks to use their powers in time of panic so as to prevent a collapse of the banking system.

4. Modern banks gradually evolved from the old goldsmith establishments in which money and valuables were stored. The practice finally became general of holding far less than 100 per cent reserves against deposits, the rest being invested in securities and loans for an interest yield.

5. The resulting laissez-faire fractional reserve system would be a fair-weather system with great instability, were it not for government control and assistance. If depositors all try to withdraw their money, they can ruin the banking system despite the existence of legal reserves. On the other hand, when financial skies are clear, cash reserves far less than the legal requirements will enable a bank to meet all calls upon it.

6. Without government regulation and examination, without the Federal reserve system, and without the guaranteeing of bank deposits (up to $5,000) by the FDIC, our system of small unit banking would be intolerable. Indeed, a few economists think that a return to a 100 per cent reserve banking system is desirable and necessary, not only for safety, but also to prevent banks from creating bank deposits.

B. THE CREATION OF BANK DEPOSITS

This leads us to the subject matter of the second half of the chapter.

7. Bank demand deposits serve as a medium of exchange and a store of value; they are considered, therefore, to be money.

8. If banks kept 100 per cent cash reserves against all deposits, there would be no creation of money when currency was taken out of circulation and deposited in the banking system. There would be only a 1:1 exchange of one kind of money for another kind of money.

9. Modern banks do not keep 100 per cent cash reserves against deposits. In the United States large-city members of the Federal reserve system are required to keep on deposit with the regional Federal Reserve Bank legal reserves equal to 20 or 22 per cent of demand deposits; small-town Member Banks need keep only 14 per cent.

10. Consequently, the banking system as a whole—together with public or private borrowers and the depositing public—does create deposit money about 5:1 for each new dollar taken out of circulation and left on deposit somewhere in the system.

11. Each small bank is limited in its ability to create deposits. It cannot lend or invest more than it has received from depositors, but only about four-fifths as much. Its deposits are five times its cash only because it spends away cash every time it buys earning assets—only because its cash decreases and not because its deposits increase.

12. But the system as a whole can do what each small bank cannot do. This can be seen if we examine a monopoly bank in a closed community. The checks written by such a bank always come back to it; therefore the only restriction upon its ability to expand its investments and deposits (its assets *and* its liabilities in double-entry bookkeeping) is the requirement that it keep one-fifth cash reserve ratios against deposits. When deposits have expanded until they are five times the increase of reserves, the monopoly bank is "loaned up" and can create no further deposits until given more cash reserves.

13. In present-day America, there is no monopoly bank. Nevertheless, the same 5:1 expansion of bank deposits takes place. The first individual bank

receiving a new $1,000 of deposits spends four-fifths of its newly acquired cash on loans and investments. This gives a second group of banks four-fifths of $1,000 in new deposits. They, in turn, keep one-fifth in cash and spend the other four-fifths for new earning assets; this causes them to lose cash to a third set of banks, whose deposits have gone up by four-fifths of four-fifths of $1,000. Obviously, if we follow through the successive groups of banks in the dwindling, never-ending chain, we find for the system as a whole that new deposits created are

$$\$1,000 + \$800 + \$640 + \$512 + \cdots$$
$$= \$1,000 \times \left(1 + \frac{4}{5} + \left(\frac{4}{5}\right)^2 + \left(\frac{4}{5}\right)^3 + \cdots\right)$$
$$= \$1,000 \left(\frac{1}{1 - 4/5}\right) = \$1,000 \left(\frac{1}{1/5}\right) = \$5,000$$

Only when every one of the thousand dollars of new reserves supports $5 of deposits somewhere in the system, will the limits to deposit expansion be reached. Then the system is loaned up; it can create no new deposits until it is given more reserves.

14. In practice, it is not necessary to wait for the successive rounds in the chain of $1,000, $800, $640, etc., to work themselves out. Usually, many banks tend to get new reserves at about the same time. If they all expand their loans and investments pretty much in balance, their outpayments will tend to cancel each other. Consequently, they won't lose cash. And so, all together can rather quickly expand their earning assets and deposits to the 5:1 limit.

15. As a minor qualification to the above discussion, we must admit that there will be some leakage of the new cash reserves of the banking system into circulation outside the banks. Therefore, instead of $5 \times \$1,000$ of new deposits created as in the previous examples, we may have $5 \times$ something less than $1,000—the difference being what is withdrawn out of the system. It is still correct to say that the new deposits created will be 5 times whatever is the amount of the new legal reserves left with the banks.

A second minor qualification must take account of the need of banks to use a little of their new reserves for vault cash or till money. Recently this has been about 2 per cent of deposits. This reduces our true ratio of expansion from about 5/1 to about 4.5/1 or more exactly 1/(0.20 + 0.02).

A third and more important qualification results from the fact that a timid bank may keep *excess reserves* in addition to legally required reserves.

In this chapter we have seen how bank deposits are kept at about five times the legal reserves of the banking system. In the next chapter, we shall learn how the Federal Reserve Banks cause bank reserves to go up when an expansion of the total money supply is desired. When a contraction of·the quantity of money is in order, the Federal Reserve authorities pull the brakes. Instead of pumping new reserves into the banking system, they kill off some of the reserves. We shall see that in doing so they are able to reduce the quantity of money not 1 for 1, but, as we have shown, almost 5 for 1.

QUESTIONS FOR DISCUSSION

1. Describe the banking setup in your area. Make a list of the services rendered by banks. Who else renders such services? Examine the balance sheet of local banks. What is the meaning of the different items? Can you find out how local checks are cleared?

2. Suppose that all banks kept 100 per cent reserves. How different would they be?

3. Assume a 10 per cent reserve ratio. Trace through the process of multiple bank expansion, duplicating Tables 4a through 4i. Reverse the process.

4. Do bankers create deposits? Who does? If a banker receives a new deposit and new reserves, is he always able to expand his loans? What can he do beyond lowering his interest charges in order to increase his loans? Can he always expand his holdings of government securities? How does he go about it?

5. In terms of the discussion in Chap. 13, show why a banker will be willing to hold huge excess reserves whenever the interest rate drops close to zero; or whenever he expects future interest rates to be higher than present.

6. How would you invest a bank's money? Give a typical portfolio of investments.

7. Comment on the following 1939 statement of the Board of Governors of the Federal reserve system: "The Federal Reserve System can see to it that banks have enough reserves to make money available to commerce, industry, and agriculture at low rates; but it cannot make the people borrow, and it cannot make the public spend the deposits that result when the banks do make loans and investments."

8. How would your answer to Question 3 be changed if banks always kept 2 per cent of their deposits in the form of vault cash?

9. Suppose that a single bank always found that one-tenth of the money that it spends on bonds or loans comes back to roost among its own deposits. Assuming a 20 per cent reserve ratio, what would be the amount of expansion of its own deposits as a result of 1,000 new dollars brought to it?

Chapter 15: FEDERAL

RESERVE AND CENTRAL BANK

MONETARY POLICY

ALTHOUGH nominally a corporation owned by its Member Banks, the Federal Reserve Banks are in fact, as we have seen, equivalent to a branch of the government. Like the Bank of England or the Bank of France, they constitute a Central Bank—a bank for bankers. Instead of seeking profits, the Federal Reserve authorities have for their sole purpose the promotion of the public interest.

The Federal Reserve Banks, together with the U.S. Treasury, provide us with our supply of currency. Almost more important, the Reserve Banks are *the ultimate creators of the reserves of the Member Banks;* and as we have seen in the previous chapters, each $1 change in bank reserves may have a fivefold effect upon the volume of bank money or demand deposits.

CONTROLLING THE BUSINESS CYCLE BY CONTROLLING THE QUANTITY OF MONEY

The activities of the Reserve Banks (1) in connection with the clearings of checks and (2) as fiscal agent for the U.S. Treasury are important, but they are of a routine character and have already been briefly discussed. Here we shall be concerned with the vital function of the Federal Reserve Banks *as creator and controller of the community's supply of money, and as a vital factor determining the level of interest yields on government and private securities.*

Left to itself, our economic system is subject to alternate spells of boom and slump, prosperity and depression, inflation and deflation. Associated with boom times are upswings in the community's total stock of cash and deposit money; and associated with years of depression is a reduction in the total quantity of money.

Our earlier discussion of saving and investment has taught us that the primary cause of fluctuation in business activity is the fluctuation in *public and private investment*. Older economists did not realize this. They tended to attach primary causal importance to fluctuations in M, the total quantity of money. According to them, when M goes up—either because mines are spitting out gold, or because governments are printing new money, or because banks are expanding their investments and deposits, or for all these reasons—then prices rise and there will be a boom. When limits to the further creation of new money have been reached, prices can no longer rise, and the system will probably go into a downward spiral of depression and deflation. Loans will be called in or paid off, banks will go bankrupt, the total of M will decrease, and depression will stalk the land. A favorable upturn can come only when M stops decreasing and begins to rise. Then we are off on another complete cycle.

This is an oversimplified version of the monetary theory of the business cycle, but not an unfair account of its essential beliefs. Since believers in this theory diagnosed the causes of the boom in terms of fluctuations in M, their prescription of monetary stabilization to cure the system of its business cycle jitters followed very logically.[1] The primary duty of the Federal Reserve Board authorities, according to this theory, should be (1) to increase M in bad times, (2) to decrease M in good times when business activity is too high, or in short (3) to stabilize the cyclical fluctuations in the supply of money. According to the quantity theory, this would stabilize prices.

Today, after our experiences in two world wars, after the relatively prosperous decade of the 1920's and the relatively depressed decade of the 1930's, we no longer hold out high hopes for effectively maintaining full employment and high production by means of Federal reserve monetary policy. To see why this should be so, we must first analyze the exact steps by which the Reserve Banks are able to influence and control the supply of money.

BRIEF PREVIEW OF HOW THE RESERVE BANKS CAN AFFECT THE SUPPLY OF MONEY

To state the matter most briefly, the 12 Reserve Banks are able to increase the amount of outstanding money, M, by paying out (1) Federal reserve notes or (2) checks to the public, to the Treasury, or to the commercial banks. Either of these two kinds of payment results in an expansion of reserve Bank liabilities: Federal reserve note liabilities, or deposit liabilities which the Reserve Banks owe to the commercial Member Banks. In return for

---

[1] Some of the more cautious members of this school admitted that the origin of the cycle might be nonmonetary. But they still believed that monetary measures can offset other destabilizing influences.

this expansion of their liabilities, the Reserve Banks must acquire an equal amount of assets: government securities, loans ("rediscounts," "acceptances," or "advances"), or gold certificates.

To contract the supply of money, the Reserve Banks must do just the reverse. They must give up security assets, loan assets, or gold certificate assets and take back an equivalent amount of their Federal reserve notes or deposit liabilities.

Contracting Federal reserve notes will reduce the currency in the hands of the public and the banks. Even more powerful is the contraction brought about by a reduction in the deposits held by the Member Banks with the 12 Reserve Banks. For we have seen that these deposits constitute the "reserve balances" of the Member Banks; and if these fall $1 below the legal requirement of 20 per cent of commercial bank demand deposits, *then the Member Banks as a whole must contract demand deposits by* $5. Thus, changes in the deposit liabilities of the 12 Reserve Banks may have a 5:1 leverage on the total supply of money —upward or downward.

This briefly is the essence of Central Bank control of the supply of money. Let us examine the process in greater detail.

THE FEDERAL RESERVE BANKS' BALANCE SHEET

The role of the Federal Reserve Banks can best be understood from an examination of their combined balance sheet. Table 1 indicates the principal assets and liabilities of the 12 Reserve Banks. In appearance, it is not unlike the balance sheet of any ordinary bank, containing as it does on the asset side cash, loans, and securities; and on the liability side capital accounts, deposit obligations and a new large item, Federal reserve notes outstanding.

TABLE 1. *Combined Balance Sheet of Twelve Federal Reserve Banks, June 26, 1946 (In millions of dollars)*

Assets		Liabilities	
Gold certificates and other cash.	$18,383	Capital accounts.	$ 636
U.S. government securities.	23,385	Federal reserve notes.	24,091
Loans and acceptances.	251	Deposits:	
Miscellaneous other assets (primarily "uncollected items")	2,388	Member Banks.	15,910
		U.S. Treasury.	969
		Foreign and other.	951
		Miscellaneous liabilities.	1,850
Total.	$44,407	Total.	$44,407

Any Central Bank has a crucial influence on the supply of money because of the character of its two main liabilities. The first of these liabilities is the paper money which it has issued: in this country Federal reserve notes (and in Britain, Bank of England notes). These Federal reserve notes are held either by the public directly or as vault cash by the commercial banks.[1]

The second main liability of the Reserve Banks consists of the sums of money which the Member Banks hold on deposit with them and which constitute the reserves of the Member Banks. These balances are vitally important, because when they increase by $1, demand bank deposits can increase by $5; when they decrease by $1, bank demand deposits may shrink by $5; and without a change in the total of Member Bank reserves, bank deposits cannot increase.[2]

GOLD CERTIFICATES

To understand how these Reserve Bank liabilities, which constitute such an important part of the nation's money supply, come into existence, we need only inquire how the Reserve Bank's assets come into existence, since assets and liabilities must always balance. The assets are of two main kinds, gold certificates and the total of government securities and loans.

The gold certificates come into existence more or less independently of any policy decisions on the part of the Reserve Bank authorities. So long as a country makes a practice of being on the gold standard, the process is fairly straightforward and automatic. Our government agrees to buy all gold brought to it at $35 an ounce. Since 1933, no American residents have been permitted to hold monetary gold. Today a gold-mining company will sell its newly produced gold in small part to jewelers and dentists, but in the larger part to the U.S. Treasury. The same will happen to any gold that is imported into the United States from abroad, either to pay for our export of goods or to buy some of our long- or short-term capital securities.

In either case, we may suppose that the gold is sold to the U.S. Treasury in return for a check drawn upon the government's deposit account at the Federal Reserve Bank. The gold seller might cash this check and take the proceeds in Federal reserve notes or other paper currency. More likely, he will deposit the

[1] A century ago, before checking deposits had acquired their present dominant importance, these paper units of money were the most important part of a nation's money supply. Formerly, private banks could and did issue bank notes, or paper money. These liabilities, payable on demand, circulated and provided an important part of the community's money supply, just as they still do in Scotland and some other countries. But the growth of checking accounts and the difficulties of public control of private note issue have caused most countries to restrict the issue of new currency to the Central Bank and Treasury.

[2] This assumes that the banks do not hold considerable "excess reserves" above their legal requirements.

government check in his own bank account. His bank will deposit the check in its account at the Federal Reserve Bank. The total of Member Bank balances is thereby swelled by as much as the reduction in the government deposit balance. The total of Reserve Bank assets and liabilities is still unchanged.

But unless the U.S. Treasury is deliberately trying to "sterilize" the gold inflow (as it has done on a few occasions in the past to fight inflation), it will not let the process end there. It will wish to replenish its depleted deposit account at the Reserve Banks. To do this, it will issue gold certificates against its newly acquired gold, and put these certificates into the Reserve Bank in exchange for a deposit as large as it was originally holding.

At the end of the whole process, the Reserve Bank has an increase in its assets (gold certificates) and an increase in its liabilities over the previous situation (new Member Bank reserve deposits). The Member Banks have increased assets (new reserve balances) and also increased deposit liabilities. The public—importers or gold miners—have less gold and more bank deposits. The government has the same amount of deposits as before; but now it has more gold in its vaults at Fort Knox, Ky., against which it has issued new gold certificates.

This completes the discussion of how gold certificates come into being. In addition, the Reserve Banks hold a few silver certificates and coins that have been deposited with it in the past, but these are not important enough to discuss. Also mention should be made that its holdings of printed but unissued Federal reserve notes are never listed as assets.

"RESERVE BANK CREDIT"

The part of our money supply that has arisen from Reserve Bank acquisition of gold certificates is the passive part. Its magnitude depends upon the happenstance of gold discoveries, of withdrawals in and out of the industrial uses of gold, and of gold flows from abroad in and out of the United States. If this were the whole story, our money supply would be a very haphazard quantity, having little to do with our economic needs and leading in some periods toward inflationary expansion and in other periods toward deflation and monetary stringency.

Fortunately, a Central Bank can adopt policies that deliberately cause its assets other than gold to expand or contract; in this way it can cause its liabilities to grow when the community needs more money or to contract when less money is called for. These other noncash assets (or as they are sometimes called, "earning assets") consist primarily of government securities and to a lesser degree, of loans. The total of investment and loans is often called the amount of "Reserve Bank Credit." By causing the total to grow, the Reserve authorities are able to expand the total of demand deposits and Federal reserve notes in circulation. By engineering a contraction of Reserve Bank Credit, the authorities can cause our money supply to shrink.

FEDERAL RESERVE "OPEN-MARKET" OPERATIONS

Let us follow the process of deliberately expanding Reserve Bank Credit and the money supply. By far the most important way of doing this is through what is called an "open-market purchase." The 12 Reserve Banks could buy a bushel of wheat, a man's services for a year, or anything else, and the mechanics of the process would be the same. But actually, they almost always confine their open-market purchases and sales to government securities: long-term or short-term government bonds, especially short terms of a year or less maturity.[1]

The Reserve Bank goes to the market and buys, let us say, a million dollars' worth of government bonds. It pays its check to the sellers, who may be private individuals or a bank. If the sellers want to cash this check in for currency, the Federal Reserve Bank will present them with Federal reserve notes; and the process ends right there, with the community's money supply up by 1 million dollars.

It is more likely that the sellers will wish to hold most of their proceeds in the form of a deposit. If the seller was a bank, it will then simply deposit the check (that it received for the bonds) in its account at the Federal Reserve Bank.

If the seller was a private individual, the same thing will happen, but with one intermediate step. The private seller will deposit the Reserve Bank's check in his own account. His bank will then deposit the check in its account at the Reserve Bank.

In either case, the open-market purchase of 1 million dollars has resulted in an equivalent expansion of the Reserve Bank's assets (investments) and in its deposit liabilities.

But this is hardly more than a beginning. The commercial Member Banks will now have at least four-fifths of 1 million dollars of *excess reserves*, since their extra million dollars of reserve balances with the Reserve Bank are only

[1] Usually the Treasury does not sell government bonds directly to the Federal Reserve Banks. This is only because of a belief that the Government is not to be trusted. But since the Federal Reserve Banks may buy bonds from the market on the next day after the government has issued them, the ineffectiveness of this curb is clearly revealed. Moreover, for the last few war years even this pretense was dropped, and some government obligations were sold directly to the Reserve Banks; in the postwar, refundings are handled directly with the government.

legally necessary against an extra 5 million dollars of demand deposits. (This is because of the 20 per cent legal reserve ratio required against deposits.) Therefore, the commercial banks will have an incentive to go out and acquire new earning assets (loans and investments). On the basis of the discussion in Chap. 14, the reader will realize that the whole process can give rise to a chain of multiple deposit creation—which need come to an end only when the commercial banks as a whole have experienced a 5 million dollar expansion in bank deposits.

TABLE 2a. *Effect of a Million-dollar Open-market Purchase on Reserve Bank's Balance Sheet*

Assets		Liabilities	
Investments..............	+$1 million	(Legal) Reserve deposits..	+$1 million
Total................	+$1 million	Total................	+$1 million

Tables 2a and 2b summarize the possible 5:1 leverage on the money supply resulting from Federal Reserve open-market purchases. After this has caused a 5:1 expansion of Member Bank deposits, the final effect on Member Banks' balance sheets is as shown in Table 2b.

TABLE 2b. *Final Effect on Member Banks of a Million-dollar Open-market Purchase*

Assets		Liabilities	
Legal reserves............	+$1 million	Deposits................	+$5 million
Loans and investments.....	+$4 million		
Total................	+$5 million	Total................	+$5 million

As will be discussed again in a moment, we must qualify this discussion to take account of the possibility that there may actually result less than the maximum 5:1 expansion possible. Before worrying about this, the reader should clinch his understanding of the mechanism of open-market operations by working through the details of the reverse operation whereby the Reserve Bank engages in an open-market sale of 1 million dollars of government securities in order to engineer a multiple contraction of the money supply.

LOAN AND REDISCOUNT POLICY

If the Reserve authorities acquire some other asset than government bonds— for example, a loan—the mechanical expansionary effects are exactly the same; and if they contract their loans, then the contractionary effect is just like that of an open-market sale. Originally, the founders of the Federal reserve system thought that the loan operations of the Reserve Banks would be by far their most powerful weapon. But when we glance back at the Combined Balance Sheet of the Reserve Banks (Table 1), we see how wrong these expectations have turned out to be. The total of loans and acceptances is of absolutely negligible quantitative importance and has been for more than a dozen years.

When the original Federal Reserve Act was passed in 1913, the experts all attached great importance to providing short-term working capital for industry, trade, and agriculture. The commercial banks were to be encouraged to make 90-day loans to businessmen and farmers on the basis of crops, inventories, and shipments of goods. To make sure that the banks always had money for these worthy purposes, the Federal Reserve Bank stood ready to "rediscount" all such advances: *i.e.*, the Member Bank could take the customer's I.O.U., endorse it, and then turn it over to the Federal Reserve Bank, which would advance the face value of the note minus a published interest charge—known as the "rediscount rate." (This rediscount rate was normally below the interest rate charge by banks on their loans.)

In other words, the commercial bank would get a check from the Federal Reserve Bank, or what is the same thing, its legal reserve deposit would be increased. This increase in reserve balances of the banking system enables that system—but not the single bank in question—to expand total deposits five times as much, and total loans and investments four times as much. Thus, by rediscounting one customer's I.O.U. out of every five, the banks could theoretically create any amount of new loans and deposits—so long as the Federal Reserve Banks continue to expand their rediscounts.

Some of the founders of the Federal reserve system thought that this process would work automatically. The Reserve authorities would not need to exercise any intelligence or make any decisions. So long as the banks confined themselves to "bona fide, short-term, self-liquidating working capital loans meeting the legitimate needs of trade," the system would take care of itself. But the short-lived inflation of 1919–1920 after World War I put an end to this simple notion. It showed plainly that such a theory implied an expansion of M during inflationary boom times, just when there was already too much spending; and a contraction of M in depression when borrowers were few but spending was desperately needed.

After this period of disillusionment, there grew up in the 1920's the theory that the rediscount rate might be a powerful weapon of monetary control. By raising the rediscount rate, the Reserve authorities were supposed to be able to engineer a contraction of the money supply and to tighten interest rates all along the line. By lowering the rediscount rate, they were supposed to be able to increase capital availability and lower interest rates.

In view of the infinitesimal use of rediscounting, this cannot now be regarded as an important weapon of monetary control. The real importance of the Reserve Bank's lending powers probably lies in the firm support that it can always give to our banking system in time of financial crisis.

Since 1933, the Federal Reserve Act has been drastically amended. The Reserve Banks can lend to almost anybody, not just to banks. Also, they can lend to banks and can issue notes, not only against short-term industrial and agricultural promissory notes, but also against government bonds put up by the banks as collateral, or in some cases, against *any* agreed-upon collateral. Since 1933, despite the reduction of the rediscount rate to 1¼ per cent, banks have preferred to borrow on government bonds rather than on customers' promissory notes, which have been profitable but scarce. Most often, today, when banks need more cash, they simply sell some of their government bonds on the open market, or occasionally some of their highest grade promissory notes known as "bankers' acceptances."[1]

In addition to rediscounts, the Reserve Banks can lend directly to private industry, but this they rarely do. Primarily, they leave this function to the commercial banks, to the Home Owners' Loan Corporation, to the RFC, and the various farm credit agencies. Also, the Reserve Banks stand ready to buy up all bankers' acceptances at some published interest rate. Thus, the market rather than the Reserve Banks takes the initiative in determining how many acceptances the Reserve Banks will hold; but the Reserve Banks by changing the interest rate that they charge for holding acceptances, relative to market rates of interest, can indirectly influence the level of their assets held in the form of acceptances.

CHANGING RESERVE REQUIREMENTS AS A WEAPON OF MONETARY CONTROL

In addition to selling off its earning assets—bonds or loans—and thereby reducing the Reserve Bank Credit basis underlying the legal reserves of the banking system, the Reserve authorities and Congress can engineer a contraction of the supply of money in one other important way. They might raise the legal reserve requirements of the Member Banks from 1948 22:20:14 levels to some higher levels, say 40:40:40.[2] Banks would then find that their

---

[1] For our purpose bankers' acceptances may be considered simply to be highly negotiable promissory notes, well secured by merchandise and by the endorsement of a reliable bank. Acceptances usually run for 90 days or short periods and have a very low rate of interest yield. Quantitatively they are of minor importance today.

[2] In 1947 when inflation seemed inevitable, the Reserve Board asked Congress for the power to raise reserve requirements, at any future date that it desired, beyond the present limits permitted it, namely, beyond 26: 20: 14.

legal reserves were inadequate in comparison with their deposits. They would have to sell many of their securities to the public—probably at some loss. The public would use up its bank accounts buying the bonds, and the process would only come to an end when about one-half of all deposits had been destroyed. Then and only then would the banks find that their old unchanged dollar reserves were large enough in relation to their deposits to meet the new legal requirements. The depressed price of bonds would be equivalent to higher interest rates or "dearer money."

It would make for great confusion if the legal reserve ratios of banks were constantly being changed. Consequently, this weapon would probably be used only at infrequent intervals. Moreover, such an extreme increase of reserve requirements as that mentioned above would take place only at a time when banks already had large excess reserves over and above their legal requirements. Fearing a possible inflationary expansion of bank deposits at some future date, the Reserve authorities might then decide to convert the potentially "hot" excess reserves into relatively stable legal reserves by raising legal reserve ratios. This is exactly what was done in 1936–1937, when reserve ratios were raised in a number of steps from 13:10:7 to 26:20:14. However, after 1942 the need to finance the war caused the 26 per cent legal reserve ratio to be lowered in New York and Chicago to 20 and later to 22 per cent.[1]

THE PROBLEM OF "EXCESS RESERVES"

During the Great Depression, there was a great decrease of bank deposits, of at least a third. How was this brought about? Was it because gold left our shores, thereby causing gold certificates to disappear from the Reserve Banks, and at the same time causing a reduction in reserve deposits and a 5:1 or 10:1 contraction of bank deposits? The answer is "no." Gold was coming into this country during much of the period.

Was it because of open-market operations of the Reserve authorities? Were they perhaps selling government bonds to the public and to the Member Banks, and thereby destroying Member Bank reserves and causing a multiple destruction of deposits? The answer is again "no." Throughout most of the early 1930's, the Reserve Banks were buying government bonds on the open market in an attempt to increase bank reserves and lower interest rates. (They

[1] In the decades ahead, we may see a further *reduction* of reserve ratios if the government ever has to sell more bonds to the banks. But since the government receives back in excess profits almost all that it pays to the Reserve Banks for bond interest, the Treasury is more likely to prefer to expand Reserve Bank Credit and Member Bank reserves by having the Reserve Banks buy more bonds.

also tried, but with little success, to get commercial banks to expand their loans and discounts.)

How then can we explain the great decline in bank deposits? The answer lies partially in the fact that the banks began to keep a much higher proportion of reserves to deposits than they had formerly or than they were *legally* required to keep by law. Banks were fearful of making loans during the depression, and they didn't even find government bonds too attractive. In other words, all of the discussion in Chap. 13 of why people hold idle, nonyielding money applies with full force to the behavior of bankers during the 1930's.

Now we have seen that the Federal Reserve authorities can kill off M by raising legal reserve ratios from say 10 to 20 per cent, or from 20 to 30 per cent. The Member Bankers can do the same thing without any laws being passed at all. Suppose they suddenly decide to hold 30 per cent reserves against deposits even though only 20 per cent are legally required, the extra 10 per cent constituting what is called "excess reserves?" Then bank deposits will have to be greatly contracted.

The Federal Reserve Board was disturbed at the destruction of bank deposits during the depression as a result of bankers holding excess reserves. But more than that, they were disturbed because excess reserves act as a buffer which protects the Member Banks against control by the Federal Reserve Banks. If the Member Banks have excess reserves, then open-market sales of government bonds by the Reserve Banks will not necessarily force the Member Banks into a multiple contraction of demand deposits.

The open-market sales kill off some Member Bank reserves. True enough. But the banks have more than enough reserves already and need not call in a single loan or sell to the public a single security. Consequently, there is no 5:1 change in demand deposits, nor even a 2:1, or 1:1. The Member Banks have simply traded some of their excess reserves for old government bonds.

The existence of excess reserves helps to explain why monetary policy by a Central Bank may be relatively ineffective in contracting deposits and curtailing inflation. It also explains why the Central Bank is relatively powerless to initiate an expansion from depressed conditions. Open-market purchases may serve only to increase the amount of excess reserves, with the process ending there.

SUMMARY OF RESERVE BANKS' CONTROL OVER MONEY

This is a good place to outline the Reserve authorities' power over the money supply. First, there is a part of our money supply which arises passively from gold production and gold imports, regardless of the direct volition of the Reserve authorities.

This can be countered or supplemented, however, by deliberate Central Bank policies. If the Reserve authorities wish to contract the money supply and tighten interest rates, they may take the following steps:

1. Most important is the *open-market operation*. By selling government securities, they can reduce Federal reserve notes and Member Bank reserves, and through the latter engineer as much as a fivefold contraction of demand deposits.

2. Next to open-market operations in importance is a policy of *raising reserve requirements*.

3. Less important is *loan policy:* raising the rediscount rate, raising the discount or interest rate on acceptances, etc.

4. They may also try to use *moral suasion*, putting public and private pressure on the banks to contract their operations.

5. Finally, the Board of Governors has the power to *raise margin requirements* for stock-market purchasing, if necessary up to 100 per cent. During World War II it also exercised direct control over the terms of installment and charge-account purchasing, specifying minimum down payments and maximum periods of payment.

The reader may work out the various steps to be followed if an expansion, rather than a contraction, of the money supply is desired.

THE PYRAMID OF CREDIT

Figure 1 summarizes the relation between the commercial or Member Banks and the public, between the banks and the Federal Reserve Banks, and between the Reserve Banks and the Treasury. At the bottom of the pyramid is a relatively small amount of gold held by the U.S. Treasury; about 21 billion dollars' worth in early 1947. A little of this is held as nominal "backing" against the relatively minor amount of coins and paper money issued by the Treasury, and a little is held by the Exchange Equalization Fund for use in connection with the United States quota in the International Monetary Fund. But by far the largest part is matched by gold certificates in the coffers of the Federal Reserve Banks—some 19 billion dollars in all.

Moving up the pyramid from the Treasury to the Federal Reserve Banks, we find their total liabilities and total assets to be over 40 billion dollars, so that Reserve Bank cash reserves are about 40 per cent of their total liabilities. Just as the commercial banks have a legal minimum reserve ratio against deposit liabilities, so the Federal Reserve Banks have a legal minimum reserve ratio of required cash to be held against their deposits and currency liabilities. In 1948, 25 per cent was the legal ratio; until recently, the ratios were 35 and 40 per cent, respectively.

THE CREDIT PYRAMID U.S.A. 1947
(Billions of $)

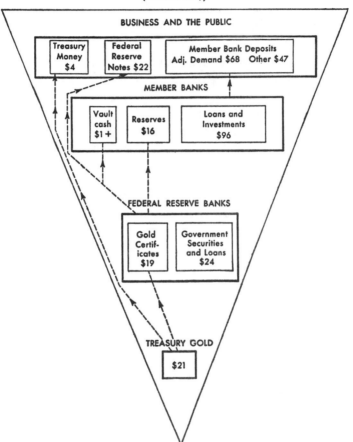

FIG. 1. This shows how our money supply adds up to several times the gold base underlying the Federal reserve system. (SOURCE: data from *Federal Reserve Bulletin*.)

However, the Federal Reserve legal reserve ratio does *not* have the significance of the Member Banks' legal ratios. Often the Member Banks *in fact* operate near their legal ratios; to the extent that they do so, they must react mechanically and lose their autonomy of action. They are not free, at any given time, to increase their earning assets and their customers' deposits. But it is the essence of central banking to pursue deliberate, discretionary policies in the public interest. This can be done only if the Reserve authorities resist the temptation to earn profits by always buying earning assets right up to their legal reserve limit. The Reserve Banks are normally operating at far higher reserve ratios than are required. In fact, when their actual reserve ratio approaches the legal ratio so that an impairment of their power and freedom is in sight, Congress very properly passes a new law lowering their legal ratio.

Theoretically, therefore, each new dollar of gold at the base of the pyramid could expand ultimate bank deposits not simply by $5:1$ ($1 \div \frac{1}{5}$), but by $20:1 = 5 \times 4 = 1 \div (\frac{1}{5} \times \frac{1}{4})$. Each dollar of gold in the Reserve Banks can theoretically expand the legal reserve deposits of the Member Banks 4 times; and each dollar of these reserves can further expand ordinary bank demand deposits 5 times, or $20:1$ in all.

Actually, the Reserve authorities do not mechanically expand $4:1$ for each extra dollar of cash received by them. Therefore, $5:1$ is more realistic for the system as a whole than $20:1$. Before the present generation of college students hold their twenty-fifth reunion, it is not at all impossible that the Federal Reserve legal ratio will be changed to $10:1$, and that the total of money in the community will be much more than twenty times our gold holdings. A legal limit, which like the limit on the Federal debt can be constantly changed, is no real economic limitation.[1]

Let us return to the pyramid of credit. In addition to cash assets, the Reserve Banks hold about 24 billion dollars of loans and investments, almost all in short-term government bonds. Matching their total assets, the Reserve Banks' first principal liability consists of Federal reserve note currency. This is held largely by the public as indicated, but in small degree also by the banks as till money or vault cash.

The other principal liability of the Reserve Banks consists of the legal reserve deposits of the Member Banks. Pyramided upon this 16 billion dollars of reserves is the volume of bank checking deposits or bank money held by the public.

To test his grasp of these important financial institutions, the reader should perform the following review in terms of the different parts of the pyramid: (1) Show what happens eventually to 1 billion dollars of newly mined or newly imported gold. Show how this will give rise to new Member Bank reserves and to new checking deposits, and possibly to a little new paper money in circulation. (2) Show what happens if the Reserve Banks make 1 billion dollars of open-market purchases of government bonds from the public.

[1] Today this is taken for granted. But one of the contributing reasons for the severity of the 1920–1921 price collapse was the failure of anyone to think of this easy solution to the Federal Reserve Bank's shortage of legal reserves.

WAR FINANCE AND THE BANKS

We may supplement this still picture of our credit pyramid by showing how World War II caused most of our money to come into existence. In Chap. 13, page 288, we saw how greatly our money supply increased from 1939 to 1947: from a total of 33 to 109 billion dollars. Most of this took the form of demand deposits and Federal reserve notes. Now we are in a position to explain how this all came about.

During World War II, the government found it necessary to spend more than half the gross national product on guns, ships, men, and so forth. At first this resulted in increased output and reduced unemployment. Finally output reached its peak. Congress was unwilling to raise taxes sufficiently to get people to stop consuming the resources necessary for the war effort. Patriotic exhortations to save more were also not strong enough. Therefore, price controls, rationing, and deliberate making of goods unavailable had to step in to cut down on private consumption and increase private saving.

We financed the war by a huge excess of government expenditure over taxes. Corresponding to this huge deficit, direct controls forced an abnormally high rate of saving on people. They were free to save their extra income in whatever form they liked: payroll war bonds, life insurance, savings accounts, paper currency, demand deposits, etc. People chose to put about half their savings in government bonds; another portion went indirectly into government bonds via insurance companies and savings banks; the rest they chose to hold in the form of currency or demand deposits. In fact, because so many men were away from home, because of black markets, because of the great increase in incomes of the poor—for all these reasons there was an astonishingly large increase in the amount of paper currency, largely Federal reserve notes, that people wished to hold.

To all this, the government raised no objections; it urged thrift and war bonds on people, but let them do finally as they liked. Regardless of the form in which the public chose to hold its wealth, the same gigantic deficit had to be covered by loan financing. The Treasury simply sold to the banking system whatever bonds the public would not take. To the extent that people chose to hold demand deposits, bonds were sold to the commercial banks. To make sure that these banks did not run out of legal reserves, the Treasury sold about 20 per cent of all bonds to the 12 Reserve Banks—thereby expanding Reserve Bank Credit and Member Bank reserves. In addition, of course, some further bonds had to be sold to the Reserve Banks so as to enable them to issue the required amount of Federal reserve notes.

Figure 2 is a well-known chart which appears monthly in the *Federal Reserve*

Bulletin. It shows conclusively that the increase in our money supply from 1939 to 1947 had nothing to do with gold, but followed from the expansion of Reserve Bank Credit, made necessary by our unwillingness to finance the war by taxation.

MEMBER BANK RESERVES, RESERVE BANK CREDIT, AND RELATED ITEMS
WEDNESDAY FIGURES

FIG. 2. This shows how our money supply was expanded as a result of government bond sales to Member Banks and to the 12 Reserve Banks. (SOURCE: Federal Reserve Board.)

In this way, interest rates were kept at a low level, and money proved no bottleneck to the successful prosecution of the war. Unlike past wars, the Treasury was able to make this one a "2 per cent war."[1]

[1] The process described in the preceding paragraph is sometimes described as "monetization of the public debt." Reversing the process in the postwar period, or "demonetizing the public debt," would take place if the public decided to use their demand deposits and currency to take over the government bonds held by the banking system. The total of liquid wealth (salable and redeemable government bonds plus money) would remain exactly the same. Unless one believes in a simple quantity theory of money and prices, it is hard to see how this, by itself, would be any less (or more) inflationary.

THE INADEQUACIES OF MONETARY CONTROL OF THE BUSINESS CYCLE

Today few economists regard Federal Reserve monetary policy as a panacea for controlling the business cycle. Purely monetary factors are considered to be as much symptoms as causes, albeit often symptoms with aggravating effects that should not be completely neglected.

By increasing the volume of their government securities and loans and by lowering Member Bank legal reserve requirements, the Reserve Banks can encourage an increase in the supply of money and bank deposits. They can encourage but, without taking drastic action, they cannot *compel*. For in the middle of a deep depression just when we most want Reserve policy to be effective, the Member Banks are likely to be timid about buying new investments or making loans. If the Reserve authorities buy government bonds in the open market and thereby swell bank reserves, the banks will not put these funds to work but will simply hold reserves. Result: no 5 for 1, "no nothing," simply a substitution on the bank's balance sheet of idle cash for old government bonds. If banks and the public are quite indifferent between gilt-edged bonds—whose yields are already very low—and idle cash, then the Reserve authorities may not even succeed in bidding up the price of old government bonds; or what is the same thing, in bidding down the interest rate.

Even if the authorities should succeed in forcing down short-term interest rates, they may find it impossible to convince investors that long-term rates will stay low. If by superhuman efforts, they do get interest rates down on high-grade gilt-edged government and private securities, the interest rates charged on more risky new investments financed by mortgage or commercial loans or stock-market flotations may remain sticky. In other words, *an expansionary monetary policy may not lower effective interest rates very much but may simply spend itself in making everybody more liquid.*

What if interest rates are finally lowered? A number of questionnaire studies of businessmen's behavior suggest that the level of the interest rate is not an important factor in their investment decisions. Particularly in deep depression when there is widespread excess capacity, *investment is likely to be inelastic with respect to the interest rate.* The same is even more true about people's decisions on how much of their incomes to spend on consumption.

In terms of the quantity theory of money, we may say that the velocity of circulation of money does not remain constant. "You can lead a horse to water, but you can't make him drink." You can force money on the system in exchange for government bonds, its close money substitute; but you can't make the money circulate against new goods and new jobs. You can get some interest rates down, but not all to the same degree. You can tempt businessmen with cheap rates of borrowing, but you can't make them borrow and spend on new investment goods.[1]

The Reserve authorities may be a little more successful in putting on the brakes of monetary contraction, but even this is not certain. Most investment is today relatively independent of the short-term capital market and of banking rates of interest. Moreover, if the authorities rely simply on over-all quantitative control as they did in 1929, they may find it necessary, in order to choke off a speculative stock-market boom, to raise rates of interest so high for "legitimate" industrial borrowers as to create a depression. It is not good medical practice to put a tourniquet around the patient's neck in order to check a little bleeding at the ear. Recent legislation has relied partially on the greater use of specific qualitative controls: changing "margin" requirements on brokers' loans, charging special RFC rates for investment activities to be encouraged, placing special curbs and limitations on installment selling and other consumer credit, etc. But, in part, the answer must be found outside of monetary policy.

PUBLIC DEBT MANAGEMENT AND MONETARY CONTROL

The possibility of using effective monetary controls to hold down inflation is further weakened in the period after World War II by the fact that some quarter of a trillion dollars of public debt is outstanding. If the Federal Reserve authorities were to try to break away from the Treasury's influence and really to force up bond interest rates, then the prices of bonds would fall as precipitously as they did after World War I. If bonds fell from 5 points above par down some 25 points to 80 or below, our whole banking system might be technically bankrupt. Moreover, the interest charges on the public debt would increase greatly in amount and burden, as the government would have to pay higher rates on its borrowing.

For what purpose would this increase in interest rates from present levels of 2 to 4 per cent to higher levels of 5 to 7 per cent be instituted? In order to induce people to cut down on their department-store purchases by a couple of per cent? In order to discourage a billion dollars of private investment, primarily on the part of less fortunate smaller businesses? These questions explain why only a minority of present-day economic experts hold out very high hopes for monetary policy to control a postwar boom. Yet if the postwar inflation

---

[1] The banking authorities—unlike the fiscal authorities—deal only in secondhand assets, in transfer items. They are powerless to act directly on people's incomes and on production!

persists for a long time, the authorities will be faced with the problem of letting interest rates increase and permitting marketable war bonds to fall below par.

SUMMARY

1. In Chap. 14 it was shown that demand deposits of the commercial banking system can fluctuate in a 5:1 amplification of changes in bank reserves. In this chapter, it is shown that the Federal Reserve Banks—or any Central Bank—are able to control and influence the direction and quantity of bank reserves. These Member Bank reserves (together with outstanding paper Federal reserve notes) constitute the principal liabilities of the Reserve Banks. By understanding the process by which Federal Reserve Bank assets come into existence, we have the key to the behavior of these liabilities.

2. The first principal asset of the Reserve Banks consists of gold certificates. For a country on the gold standard, whose Treasury agrees to buy and sell all gold brought to it, the process by which these gold certificates change in amount is more or less automatic, depending primarily upon gold mining and the importing or exporting of gold. Each dollar of new gold adds about a dollar to gold certificates and to Member Bank reserves, and indirectly several dollars in multiplied commercial bank demand deposits.

3. Far from automatic, however, is the process by which the Reserve authorities increase the volume of Federal Reserve Credit by expanding their holdings of *earning assets:* primarily short-term government securities, but also a few longer term bonds and loans, acceptances, or rediscounts. When the total of these earning assets—often called Reserve Bank Credit—expands, then Member Bank reserves are increased, interest rates are eased, and demand deposits may rise fivefold. When the total of Reserve Bank Credit contracts, then bank reserves and deposits must shrink and interest rates tend to rise. These changes are supposed to induce the desired changes in investment and consumption spending.

4. During the 1920's, the Federal Reserve authorities used to be able to control the volume of their earning assets to some degree by means of the rediscount rate, the raising of which decreased its loans and put upward pressure on market interest rates in general. But in recent years the volume of Federal Reserve loans of all kinds has diminished to a mere trickle, so that primary reliance must be placed upon open-market purchases and sales of government securities. When the Reserve Banks buy securities on the open market, they

depress interest rates and increase bank reserves, thereby paving the way for an expansion of bank deposits and investment expenditure. When they sell, the opposite tends to happen.

5. However, in the past 15 years, the Member Banks have often tended to hold excess reserves, so that the power of the Reserve authorities to engineer a contraction or expansion of the total money supply has been seriously limited. Moreover, interest rates have often tended to be sticky, and investment spending to be unresponsive to changes in the interest rate.

6. To some degree, the power of Congress and the Reserve Board to raise or lower legal reserve requirements helps to plug up these loopholes to monetary control, but only in part. Other supplementary methods of affecting business conditions involve the use of moral suasion to persuade the banks to expand or contract their operations, the regulation of margin requirements for buying securities, and the regulation of installment selling and other consumers' credit.

7. War and postwar finance provide a convenient exercise illustrating the principles of modern central banking. Partly as a result of the need of the Treasury and the banking system to keep up government bond prices and keep down interest rates, and partly as a result of the demonstrated weaknesses of monetary control policies from 1929 to 1941, the trend of modern thinking seems to be away from central banking money and interest rate policy toward the fiscal policies discussed at the end of Part Two.

QUESTIONS FOR DISCUSSION

1. In what Federal Reserve district is your locality? Where is the nearest branch? Can you open up an account there? Why not? Have you ever seen the *Monthly Newsletter* for your reserve district?

2. There is an excellent little descriptive book on the Federal reserve system called "The Federal Reserve System, Its Purposes and Functions." If you are interested, look up in it the details of how your check to someone in another part of the country is cleared.

3. Try to interpret the various items on the latest combined balance sheet of the Reserve Banks.

4. You find an ounce of gold in a cave. Describe the steps in the process set up by your selling it to the Treasury.

5. You buy $1,000 in gold from the Treasury to ship to South America. Describe all the effects on the banking system and the supply of American money.

6. "Gold movements affected prices only because we followed the practice of

using them as a barometer, signalling us to expand or contract the total of money supply. Of course, the gold standard was a stupid system. But it was wiser to tie ourselves to such an imperfect system than to trust corrupt legislatures whose tendency is always to print inflationary paper money." Discuss.

7. Trace through the effects of a 1-billion-dollar open-market sale.

8. Trace the effects of a doubling of reserve requirements.

9. List the weapons of monetary control of the Reserve authorities. How powerful are they (a) to control M, (b) to control interest rates, (c) to control prices, (d) to control employment and unemployment? Justify your answer.

10. How would postwar debt retirement out of a surplus of taxes affect the banking system? Trace the steps.

11. Discuss once again the statement of the Reserve Board given in Question 7 of Chap. 14.

12. Comment on the following 1939 Reserve Board pronouncements:

"[The Board] recognizes the importance of making every effort to achieve the underlying objective, which, broadly speaking, is the fullest practicable utilization of the country's human and material resources . . . stability in production and employment is a more satisfactory objective of public policy than price stability alone."

" . . . experience has shown the prices do not depend prmarily on the volume or the cost of money."

" . . . that the Board's control over the volume of money is not and cannot be made complete."

" . . . and that steady average prices, even if obtainable by official action, would not assure lasting prosperity."

" . . . the powers over [the supply and cost of money] possessed by the Treasury now outweigh those of the [Federal Reserve] System."

Chapter 16: INTERNATIONAL

FINANCE AND DOMESTIC

EMPLOYMENT

IN the preceding chapters we have seen how the balance of saving and investment affects—and is affected by—national income and employment, prices, money, and banking. Now we must add a new factor: international trade. How do we pay for goods that we import from abroad? How do foreigners pay for our exports? What determines the "balance of international payments" and foreign exchange rates? How does international trade affect our jobs and economic standards of living? Finally, what are the significant postwar problems of international trade and lending that the International Monetary Fund, the International Bank for Reconstruction and Development, the European Recovery Program, and the United Nations hope to solve?

In answering such questions, this chapter is divided into two parts. Section A gives a description of some of the basic facts and concepts of international finance: foreign exchange rates, the balance of international payments and its various components, and the nature of foreign capital movements. Section B shows how these concepts can be applied to the postwar world: to the problem of full employment and international cooperation. A few of the more important technical aspects of the international finance mechanism (gold standard mechanism, etc.) are discussed in an appendix, which may be omitted completely or may profitably be read in between the two main sections.

A. *INTERNATIONAL TRADE AND CAPITAL MOVEMENTS*

FOREIGN EXCHANGE RATES

If I buy maple sugar from Vermont or pig iron from Pittsburgh, I naturally want to pay in dollars. Also, the farmers and steel producers in question expect to be paid in dollars, because their expenses are all in dollars and because their living costs are all in dollars. Within a country, economic transactions are simple.

But if I wish to buy an English bicycle, matters are more complicated. I must pay in British money, or what is called "pounds sterling," rather than in dollars. Similarly, an Englishman must somehow get dollars to an American producer if he wants our merchandise. Most Americans have never seen a British pound note. Certainly they would accept pounds only if they could be sure of converting them into American dollars—dollars to spend or save.

Clearly, therefore, exports and imports of goods between nations with different units of money introduce a new economic factor: the foreign exchange rate, giving the price of the foreigner's unit of money in terms of our own.

Thus, the price of a British pound is about $4; or, what is the same thing, the foreign exchange rate between pounds and dollars is $\frac{1}{4}$ pound to each dollar. There is, of course, a foreign exchange rate between American money and the currencies of each and every country: 50 cents for a Philippine peso, less than 1 cent for a French franc, etc.[1]

Given the foreign exchange rates, it is now simple for me to buy my English bicycle. Suppose its quoted price is £10 (*i.e.*, 10 British pounds). All I have to do is look up in the newspaper the foreign exchange rate for pounds. If this is $4 per pound, I simply go to a bank or post office with $40 and ask that the money be used to pay the English bicycle exporter. Pay him what? Pounds, of course, the only kind of money he needs.

Whether I use the post office or a bank or a broker is of no particular importance. In fact it is all the same if the English exporter sends me a bill request-

---

[1] There are also foreign exchange rates between the pound and the French franc, etc. But these rates between other countries need not interest us much, particularly since in a free competitive market the pound-franc rate can be simply calculated from the pound-dollar and franc-dollar rate, because sharp-eyed international arbitragers see to it that relative rates do not get out of line.

ing payment in dollars. In any case, he ultimately wants pounds, not dollars, and will soon trade the $40 for £10. (Needless to say, we are neglecting commission charges and the cost of money orders.)

The reader should be able to show what a British importer of American grains or automobiles has to do if he wants to buy, say, an $800 shipment from an American exporter. In this case pounds must be converted into dollars. Why? How?

THE INTERNATIONAL BALANCE OF PAYMENTS

So much at present for foreign exchange rates. Unless you are an expert, you need not worry further about mechanical details. Still your knowledge will be incomplete unless you understand the basic economic forces working behind the scenes. How are banks, post offices, and brokers always able, here and abroad, to exchange pounds for dollars and dollars for pounds?

The answer lies in the fact that international trade is largely a two-way street. Goods are being traded for goods, just as in a horse swap. When we import, we offer dollars for pounds. When we export, the English offer pounds for dollars. Let us see why this is all so by examining the balance of international payments.

Official records are kept of all international transactions during a year: of merchandise exported and imported, of money lent abroad or borrowed, of gold movements, of tourist expenditures, of interest and dividends received or paid abroad, of shipping services, etc. They all go to make up the balance of international payments, which is simply a double-entry listing of all items, drawn up in such a way that it must always show a balance.[1]

Within the balance of international payments, there are two narrower categories: (1) the balance of (merchandise) trade and (2) the balance of current items. The balance of trade is simply the difference between goods exported and goods imported. When exports exceed imports, *i.e.*, when we are giving away more goods than we are receiving, we use the rather misleading expression, a "favorable balance of trade." When there is an import surplus, we use the term "unfavorable balance of trade."

The balance of current items differs from the balance of trade by including, in addition to purely merchandise exports or imports, certain so-called "invisible" items, such as tourist expenditures and shipping services.

Thus, expenditures of American travelers abroad operate just like an import

[1] Smuggling and some other items elude the record keepers, so it is almost always necessary to introduce a miscellaneous category of omitted items just large enough to show a formal balance.

into the United States. As far as international trade is concerned, it doesn't matter whether Americans consume French brandy in Paris or Seattle; in both cases we must trade dollars for foreign currency in order to consume foreign goods or services. Gifts of funds abroad by immigrants or by the government are also invisible items exactly like imports. Shipping services which we provide for foreigners affect foreign exchange and the balance of international payments just like an export of American goods; but shipping services that we buy from abroad are invisible items just like imports.

The last important invisible item is interests and dividends. When Americans receive interest and dividends from abroad, this acts just like an export in making foreign currencies available to us. In short, just as a present-day export enables us to import from abroad, so does a present-day dividend on capital, which we formerly lent abroad, permit us to pay for imports.

Merchandise exports or imports plus invisible items go to make up the balance of current items. The only items not included in the current items are (1) all short- or long-term capital loans and (2) all gold or specie movements. As far as the supply and demand for dollars and foreign currency are concerned, gold flowing into a country can be treated like the import of any chemical element or commodity. But when we import capital by borrowing from a country like England, the effect on the market for dollars and pounds is just the opposite of a commodity import. Instead of having to pay pounds to foreigners, we are in effect receiving pounds—just as if we had been exporting goods. For this reason, it is always least confusing to speak of a capital import into the United States as being an "export of United States securities or I.O.U.'s." Following this method of speech, we can treat all imports or exports alike regardless of whether they are of gold, merchandise, or capital securities.

The balance of international payments is usually presented in three sections:

1. Current items:
   Merchandise (or trade balance)
   Invisibles
     Shipping
     Tourist expenditures
     Immigrants' remittances
     Interest and dividends
     Government gifts and transactions
2. Gold (or "specie") movements (in and out)
3. Capital movements (in and out):
   Long-term
   Short-term

The balance of trade is, of course, but one part of the first, or current, section. It is to be stressed that the balance of trade and the balance of current items do not necessarily have to be in perfect balance. Only the *total* balance of international payments must be always in balance. This is because any lack of balance of current items must be exactly matched by an opposite balance of the capital and gold items. Why? Because whichever of our sales abroad are not matched by swaps against goods must be paid for by gold or must be owed to us.

It should be noted that our balance of payments is with all the rest of the world and not with just one country. Our total balance of payments must always be in balance, but there is no reason why there must be a balance with any one country, such as Britain. On the contrary, it is usual and desirable for us to sell more to Britain than we buy from her; for Britain to sell more to the East Indies than she buys from them; and for the East Indies to sell more to us than we sell to them. This example of triangular trade is just one instance of the profitability of multilateral trade. As discussed in a later chapter, standards of living all over the world would deteriorate if international trade were pressed into the mold of bilateralism, with a perfect balance being insisted upon between every pair of countries.

Table 1 presents the official Balance of International Payments of the United States for the last prewar year. In Col. (1) the various current items (merchandise and invisibles), gold, silver, or specie items, and capital items are listed by name. In the three remaining columns, the quantitative figures are listed for each item. Column (2) lists all the "credit items"; *i.e.*, all the international transactions that are just like exports and enable us to get hold of foreign currencies. Column (3) lists all so-called "debit items," *i.e.*, all transactions that are just like imports and require us to give up dollars for foreign currencies. Column (4) gives the net difference between credits and debits.

This is well illustrated by the merchandise item. Our exports were 3,241 million dollars in 1939; because foreigners had to pay ultimately for these in dollars, foreign currencies were made available to us in this amount. Therefore, this is listed as a credit item in Col. (2). Our imports were 2,362 million dollars, and since we had to pay for these in foreign currencies, this is listed in the debit column. With our exports in excess of imports, we had a favorable balance of trade of 879 million dollars (3,241 − 2,362). This is listed as a + item in the net credits. The reader should go through all the remaining items one by one to be sure he understands their true nature and prewar role.

Note that in the last prewar year, we had a so-called "favorable" balance of

TABLE .1. *Balance of International Payments of the United States, 1939*
(In millions of dollars)

Items (1)	Credits (items—like exports— providing America with foreign currencies) (2)	Debits (items—like imports— using up foreign currencies) (3)	Net Credits (+) or Debits (−) (4)
Current merchandise and service:			
Merchandise......................	$3,241	$2,362	$+879
Freight and shipping...............	125	249	−124
Travel expenditures................	170	469	−299
Remittances and charitable contributions........................	45	187	−142
Interest and dividends..............	531	211	+320
Government transactions and miscellaneous.......................	179	155	+24
Total current items...............	$4,291	$3,633	$ +658
Gold and silver:			
Gold movements (net, including "earmarking").....................	—	—	$−3,040
Silver exports and imports..........	$ 14	$ 85	−71
Total gold and silver movements (net).	—	—	$−3,111
Capital: exports of our I.O.U.'s (+) or imports (−):			
Long-term......................	$1,624	$1,510	$ +114
Short-term and miscellaneous (net) (includes paper currency movements).......................	—	—	+1,302
Total capital items (net)..........	—	—	$+1,416
Omissions and unrecorded transactions..	—	—	$+1,037

trade: we were exporting more goods than we were importing. The difference was covered in part by such invisible items as travel expenditure and shipping, but more importantly by the gold that was being sent to us.

On balance, we were *not* importing I.O.U.'s and lending abroad. On the contrary, there was "capital flight" to the United States in 1939: so many jittery foreigners wanted to get their money safely invested in the United States that we were exporting I.O.U.'s and becoming less of a creditor nation. Of course, our I.O.U.'s were not being exported to pay for any surplus of our imports. Reading the table closely will show they were necessary to acknowledge the receipt of so much gold that foreigners were anxiously sending to us for safe keeping. Our short-term I.O.U.'s were primarily nothing but acknowledgments of the deposits that foreigners placed in our banks.

We may summarize our discussion of the balance of international payments as follows:

1. If exports and imports produce a perfect balance of trade, then although individuals are going through the motions of exchanging dollars for pounds and vice versa, international trade is really taking place by a swap of goods for goods.

2. A favorable or unfavorable balance of merchandise trade may be taken care of by invisible current items. Thus, we may import more than we export if we are providing shipping services to foreigners or are receiving interest and dividends or immigrants' remittances from abroad.

3. There may still be an unfavorable balance of all current items. This may be met in part or in full by our shipping gold abroad. Similarly, at other times gold may flow into the United States.

4. Instead of gold flowing in or out to meet a lack of balance of current items, I.O.U.'s (i.e., "I-owe-you's") may flow in or out.[1] Such capital movements are extremely important and deserve considerable attention.

Suppose that we have an export surplus which is to be balanced by our importing foreign I.O.U.'s. There are various ways in which this capital movement can take place: Foreigners or their government might (1) borrow from a New York bank, or (2) sell bonds in the New York market, or (3) borrow from the U.S. government's Export-Import bank, or (4) sell some of their shares of stock in American or foreign companies, or (5) fail to renew an old loan that they made to us years ago, or (6) use up a deposit that they hold in an American bank, etc. The reader should go through the opposite steps when we borrow from abroad and describe some of the ways that this might take place.

STAGES OF A COUNTRY'S BALANCE OF PAYMENTS

Historically, the United States has gone through four stages typical of the growth of a young agricultural nation into a well-developed industrialized one.

[1] Capital or gold movements are often causes, as well as effects, of trade movements.

1. *Young and Growing Debtor Nation.* From the Revolutionary War era until just after the Civil War, we imported more than we exported. England and Europe lent us the difference in order to build up our capital structure. We were a typical young and growing debtor nation.

2. *Mature Debtor Nation.* From about 1873 to World War I, our balance of trade appears to have become favorable. Aside from tourists' and immigrants' items, this was made necessary by the growth of the dividends and interest that we had to pay abroad on our past borrowing. These invisible items kept our balance on current account more or less in balance. Capital movements were also about in balance, our new lending just about canceling off our borrowing.

3. *New Creditor Nation.* In World War I, we expanded our exports tremendously. At first, private American citizens made loans to the warring Allied powers. After we got in the war, our government lent money to England and France for war equipment and postwar relief needs. We emerged from the war a creditor nation. But our psychological frame of mind had not adjusted itself to our new creditor position. We passed high tariff laws in the early 1920's and again in 1930. Because America refused to import, foreigners found it difficult to get the dollars to pay us interest and dividends, much less repay the principal.

So long as we remained in this third stage of being a new creditor country; so long, that is, as we kept making *new* private foreign loans all through the 1920's, everything momentarily appeared all right on the surface. We could continue to sell more than we were buying, by putting most of it "on the cuff." The rest of the world met our export surplus by sending us gold, and by sending us I.O.U.'s. As long as Wall Street bankers could interest Main Street in foreign bonds, everything seemed rosy. But by 1928 and later, when Americans would no longer lend abroad, the crash finally came. International trade broke down. Debts were defaulted. America, as much as the rest of the world, was to blame.

4. *Mature Creditor Nation.* America has not yet succeeded in moving into the fourth stage of being a mature creditor nation. England reached this stage some years ago. As is usual in such cases, her imports exceeded her exports. Before we feel sorry for her because of her so-called "unfavorable" balance of trade, let us note what this really means.

Her citizens were living better because they were able to import much cheap food, and in return did not have to part with much in the way of valuable export goods. The English were paying for their import surplus by the interest and dividend receipts they were receiving from past foreign lending.

Fine for the English. But what about the rest of the world? Weren't they worse off having to send exports to England in excess of imports? Not necessarily. Normally, the capital goods that England had previously lent them permitted them to add to their domestic production—to add *more* than had to be paid out to England in interest and dividends. Both parties were better off. Nineteenth-century foreign lending was twice blessed: it blessed him who gave and him who received. Of course, things were not always quite so smooth. Some investments proved unwise. Political problems of colonies and nationalism complicated the situation. And as we shall see, after World War I, the whole process broke down.

BASIC SIGNIFICANCE OF INTERNATIONAL CAPITAL MOVEMENTS

Let us return now to the problem of capital movements. If political problems of nationality and domestic problems of unemployment did not enter the picture, then the fundaments of international lending would be easy to understand. We could easily cut through the fog of money and finance and concentrate upon the real aspects in terms of goods and resources.

How does capital grow within a country? By our diverting labor, land, machinery, and other resources away from the production of current consumption goods. Instead, we plant trees, drain rivers, build new machinery and buildings. All these add to our future national income and levels of future consumption.

We are postponing present consumption for future consumption; in fact, for an even *greater* amount of future consumption. Where does the increase in future consumption come from? From the fact that *capital goods have a "net" productivity*. This net productivity of capital is the real side of the interest rate, whose monetary side we discussed earlier.

As an example of the net productivity of capital, imagine a farmer who plants 100 seeds instead of eating them. After a year, they have grown into more than 100 seeds. Some of this harvest he must feed his horse, some he must give to his hired man. Perhaps only 106 are left. Of course, the first 100 are used to replace him in the situation in which he started. But the 6 extra represent the net productivity of capital. Expressed as an interest rate, we say that he is earning 6 per cent per year on his real capital. What is true of seeds or rabbits is also true of inorganic capital such as hammers or machine tools. It takes tools to make tools! If we are willing to forego the use of tools for present consumption pleasures, we can use them to make more tools. The new tools made cannot all be considered the net productivity of capital. Only the increase or surplus over and above the used-up tools represents a real return on our capital. In other words, the net productivity is reached after depreciation or replacement has been allowed for. All capital goods tend to have a net productivity; and of course, people always tend to invest only in those projects with the highest interest return.

In countries with much labor and many inventions, the rate of interest tends to be high. But as more and more capital is produced—as more seeds are added to the same acres of land and more tools are given to a limited number of people—the law of diminishing returns sets in. The rate of interest drops from 6 to 5 to 4 and even below 1 per cent. Now that businessmen can borrow at a lower rate of interest, projects that were before unprofitable do become profitable. Investors wish for inventions or for new labor and resources.

Different parts of the world have different amounts of resources: labor, minerals, climate, know-how, etc. Were it not for ignorance or political boundaries, no one would push investment in North America down to the point of 3 per cent returns *if elsewhere there still existed 6 per cent opportunities.* Some capital would certainly be invested abroad. This would give foreign labor higher wages, because now the foreign worker has more and better tools to work with. It would increase foreign production. By how much? Not only by enough to pay for the constant replacement of used-up capital goods, but in addition by enough to pay us an interest or dividend return on our investment. This interest return would take the form of goods and services which we receive from abroad and which add to our standard of living. An all-wise scientist would probably approve of the process. It would make sense to him because capital is going into the regions where its productivity is highest.

When would we be repaid our principal? So long as we are earning a good return, there is no reason why we should ever wish to have it repaid. However, the once backward country may finally become rather prosperous. It may wish to pull in its belt as far as consumption is concerned, and to use its savings to buy out our ownership in its factories, farms, and mines. But suppose that we are rich, with plenty of savings and with so much capital at home that our rate of interest is low. We will not particularly wish to sell out or be repaid. We will raise the selling price of our farm and factory holdings abroad. Or in other words, we will be content with a smaller percentage interest return. Thus, there is no necessary reason why a country should ever be paid off for its past lending, unless it has become older and poorer than the rest of the world.

When nationalism rears its ugly (or beautiful) head, matters change. Within the United States, interest and dividends may stream from South to North and West to East until doomsday. A few people may grumble about absentee ownership; but the courts and police are there to see that property rights are respected. Not so between nations. When a country is poor, it may be anxious to borrow. After it has become richer, it becomes unhappy to have to pay dividends and interest abroad. It chooses not to remember that its prosperity stemmed in part from its past borrowing. More than an economic burden is involved; politically, countries don't like the principle of absentee ownership by "furriners." Therefore, they are prone to insist upon getting rid of their international liabilities: paying them off at a fair price, at an unfair price, or often by outright default.

Economics and politics mix in ways too complicated to discuss in this book. Some say "trade follows the flag." Others say the flag follows trade. Some say the pursuit of economic gain is the primary motive behind the imperialistic search for colonies. Others claim that national power (offensive and defensive) is an end in itself; that economic well-being is sacrificed to this end; and that economic resources are sought for their contribution to military strength (offensive and defensive) rather than for their contribution to economic well-being. According to this view, without wars and nationalism, anyone could invest and trade anywhere; all sensible people would prefer to live in small countries unhindered by costly military establishments and colonial administration. At the opposite extreme is the view that victory in battle, rather than comfortable living, is the only worthy end in life; the foreigner is of no importance compared with the fatherland; he can be stripped of his goods and land, and he can be made to work for the "superrace," so that the latter can have its cake and cannons too. The world of the last few centuries lies somewhere in between these extreme cases.

FINANCIAL VERSUS REAL ASPECTS OF FOREIGN LENDING

Let us turn from politics back to economics, to see how these processes take place in financial terms. Money throws a veil over the real aspects of capital movements. Usually a foreigner borrows *money* from us rather than capital goods directly. He gives us an I.O.U. in the form of a bond, note, or stock certificate. We give him dollars. If he simply holds the dollars or puts them in an American bank or invests them in an American security, then there has been no net capital movement at all. We have some form of his I.O.U.; he has some form of ours. In the capital movements section of the balance of international payments, the difference just cancels out. Only when he uses the receipts of the loan to import goods and services (or gold) in excess of his exports to us, only then has a real and a financial capital movement taken place.

When the time comes for interest payment, the foreigners must sell us more goods than they buy in order to get the extra dollars to remit to us. Our balance of international payments then will show an import surplus, balanced by the invisible credit item, interest and dividends.

Should we feel glad or sorry when we are exporting more than we are importing? If we never had to worry about unemployment, we would certainly regret having to give away goods that might better serve our own well-being. Only the consolation of later receiving goods in return could serve to compensate us for this present loss. If we could look into a crystal ball and see that the investment were sure to go sour later and never be repaid either in principal or interest, then we should certainly conclude that the capital movement was a bad and not a good thing.

Why then do people seem to become so happy over a so-called "favorable" balance of trade when they are giving away more goods than they get? Why does a congressman's heart bleed when we have an "unfavorable" balance of trade and are receiving more in goods than we give? The answer is partly stupidity. The congressman has not thought the matter through. But that is only the smallest part of the story.

The answer is also partly selfishness. Particular businessmen and laborers may benefit by our shutting out imports and encouraging exports—even though the country as a whole is worse off. Suppose that the 60 million workers in the United States are always fully employed. Then it will be to our greatest advantage to put our resources to work in those industries where we have the greatest *relative* advantage. This may mean that it is better for us to produce automobiles and trade them for watches rather than to produce watches; better to produce machine tools and import wool rather than produce both; better to take advantage of all possibilities to get goods cheaply from abroad.

But that is looking at the matter from the standpoint of all the country and of all consumers, from the standpoint of real wages of American labor as a whole. But what about the watchmakers and the wool growers? The tariff may be subsidizing them, and they will put pressure on their congressmen not to lose that subsidy. If it were a question of a sudden removal of all tariffs or of national defense, arguments could be made on both sides. But certainly there is no strong *economic* argument against a gradual reduction of protective tariffs, so that as workers died off and transferred from relatively inefficient industries, there would be a shift to American industries with greater long-run efficiency.

The above all holds, assuming that total spending is always just sufficient to keep us at full employment. When investment outlets are so brisk as to lead to inflation, the argument that a country should want to import rather than export is even more powerful. When total spending tends to be higher than the value of goods that can be produced, people who leave watchmaking and wool growing can find new jobs with relative ease. The more we import of goods and the less we export, the greater is the stock of goods available for our money to purchase. Also, the more efficiently we allocate our resources, the more goods will we be producing. The greater the flow of goods compared to the total of spending, then the better our ability to control inflation. The time, therefore, to reduce tariffs gradually is during booms—such as the years immediately following World War II. Special interests will still squawk. But they need not then be given excessive attention.

It is when we drop the assumption of full employment that we find that there is something more than ignorance or special pleading to explain the mad frenzy of nations to give away rather than receive goods. We then begin to move in a never-never land of non-Euclidean axioms, where black appears white and parallel lines meet, where individual wisdom appears as social folly, and where even social folly seems to have some of the aspects of social wisdom. The remaining section deals with international trade and jobs in the years ahead.[1]

B. *POSTWAR INTERNATIONAL TRADE AND FULL EMPLOYMENT*

EXPORTS AND JOBS

Talk to a businessman whose memory goes back 40 years. He will point out that exports have always been a stimulating factor along with domestic private or public investment. He will recall the years 1915 and 1916, before we entered World War I, when France, Russia, and England suddenly became avid customers for our exports. We sent them goods in return for barren gold and fancy gilt-edged certificates. The result: a shift from American depression to great prosperity. Or in the period after we entered the first war, when our shipments of useless shot and shell increased, again there resulted all the apparent trappings of prosperity-booms, *i.e.*, high prices and plentiful jobs.

During the 1920's when we were making many foolish private loans to the

---

[1] Some readers may wish to read the Appendix to this chapter before going on to the next section.

rest of the world and whooping it up for tariffs allegedly to "protect the American workers' standard of living," one of the contributing factors to our favorable balance of saving and investment seemed to be heavy foreign lending. Like domestic private investment or government deficit expenditure, the foreign trade balance was adding more to total money spending than it was subtracting. The hard-boiled businessman sums it up: "Of course, many of our foreign loans later turned sour and investors lost their money. But while we are shipping goods abroad, jobs are created. It doesn't matter as far as *current* jobs and prices in the twenties are concerned whether the loans 10 years later will turn out good or bad, or whether they represent public or private gifts." Or, as the late president of the First National Bank put it: "It is better to have lent and lost than never to have lent at all."

This teaches us a lesson: as far as present total purchasing power and employment are concerned, wise domestic investment is no more powerful than ultimately foolish investment; wasteful public expenditure is as inflationary as useful expenditure; giving away goods rather than accepting them from abroad helps the current job situation for as long as you can get away with it.

What is the true cost to the American people of the goods we are throwing away? If unemployment were always at a minimum, the answer would be clear. The cost of devoting resources to unwise domestic investment, to public leaf raking, and to throwing goods abroad would be the useful goods and services that we could be producing by applying those same economic resources to useful lines. This is the fundamental real cost to keep in mind—not some confusing financial figure.

What happens to this cost analysis if there is unemployment? if the alternative to shipping goods abroad is idle factories and idle men? If we accept this hopeless assumption, then everything is changed. The extra production seems to cost us nothing, since it is produced with resources that would otherwise be rusting and champing in wasteful idleness. The lucky (or shall we say unlucky?) foreigners get our goods; but that doesn't mean that we are forced to consume any less than before. Drawing up our national score card, we might state that (1) our production has gone up by, say a million dollars, (2) we ship one million dollars of exports abroad receiving no worthwhile goods in return; (3) our jobs and sweat have increased, and the evils of idleness have slightly decreased; (4) our total consumption seems to have remained the same.

Now if we believe that the proper end of economic activity is the consumption of goods and services, our verdict would have to be, "We are neither better off than before nor worse off." Actually, this is wrong. We have for-gotten something very important.

When workers and capitalists in Lynn, Mass., receive extra income from producing generators for export, they will spend part of that income upon new American consumption goods. When export producers have received an extra million dollars of income, they will respend perhaps two-thirds of it upon consumers goods produced in Pennsylvania or Iowa. Now there is an extra $666,667 of production, jobs, and income in those states. Two-thirds of this will be spent upon other American consumers' goods. And so it goes. The "multiplier" analysis of earlier chapters applies just as much to inter-national investment as to anything else. By the time the process has worked itself out, American production and employment have gone up by 3 million dollars: 1 million of primary exports plus another 2 millions of secondary consumption.

Our national score card reads as follows: (1) total production and employ-ment up by 3 million dollars; (2) total domestic consumption up by 2 million dollars. Thus, even those interested only in consumption as an end of activity must admit that, as compared to twiddling our thumbs in depression idleness, throwing away goods has made us better off rather than costing us something! To this our businessmen will say, "See, I told you so, even though I didn't know the economists' fancy language and couldn't spell out all the details."

So far so good, even though the whole process reminds us of the first savages who had to burn down a house to roast a pig. International "boondoggling"—for that's just what it is—is no better or worse than scattering leaves and raking them, but it may be better than nothing.

But why assume that the only alternative is doing nothing? Surely, a third alternative, other than (1) inaction or (2) international boondoggling can be found, so that we shall not only get the 3 million dollars' worth of jobs and the 2 million dollars of second-round consumption but also will get something useful for our 1 million dollars of work on the first round. Instead of throwing useful goods into the ocean, so to speak, why not use them for domestic consumption or domestic capital formation? Or if we feel that it is to our national interest and preference to help out the consumption and development of foreign nations, let us make sure that it does really help them out. This is just common sense; just as it is clearly better for the government to build useful dams and hospitals rather than to rake leaves or construct pyramids. Both policies may lead to extra jobs and extra induced private consumption, but one leads to a greater total of useful production than the other.

BEGGAR-MY-NEIGHBOR POLICIES

In an earlier chapter we learned the paradox of thrift: the attempt of individuals to increase their saving will, in a world of unemployment, often result in *less* actual saving and investment because of the harmful effects on income and employment. Here we have just come to understand what might be called the "paradox of international charity": *As compared to doing nothing toward curing depression unemployment, it may be better to increase exports and refuse imports; better not just from the standpoint of jobs, but from the standpoint of domestic consumption.*

A little knowledge is a dangerous thing. Suppose that you are a congressman who has grasped this possibility. You might immediately set about to create a favorable balance of trade for the United States. You might begin to do one or all of the following beggar-my-neighbor policies:

1. Increase protective *tariffs* on our imports and promote "Buy American" campaigns.

2. Better still, pass a law setting low *import quotas*, so that not more than a specified amount of each good can be shipped to us.

3. Or, taking a leaf from Hitler's Nazi book, introduce comprehensive *exchange control:* so that every import must receive a special license; exports are to be subsidized; bilateral trade agreements are made with each country, limiting the direction and degree of trade and serving as a political weapon of intimidation or bribery. An elaborate system of regulations is set up, according to which foreigners have to pay different prices for the dollars they need for each different kind of good—depending upon what you think the "traffic will bear," etc. (As this is written, in 1948, most nations still have extensive exchange control.)

4. *Depreciate the dollar* as much as possible, so that foreigners can buy our imports very cheaply, while pounds and francs are made so expensive as to discourage our importing. In other words, the more we succeed in depreciating the dollar compared to all foreign currencies, the greater the exports we are able to give away and the fewer are the imports we are willing to take. One way to depreciate the dollar is to raise our buying price for gold. If other countries do not retaliate, this "devaluation of the dollar" will cheapen the dollar relative to foreign currencies and will enable us to give away exports in return for useless gold imports.

(A fifth way that a country can expand its exports relative to its imports is to offer foreigners sound or unsound *international loans* at low rates of interest;

or even more, to make them huge gifts—financed by the Treasury or by gullible private investors. But unlike the previous four devices, the foreign country is not necessarily beggared as a result.)

A good congressman should be able to think up a few more devices, but these are the most important policies to be followed by a country that hopes to solve its unemployment problem at the expense of its neighbors: *i.e.*, by a country whose motto is "A short life and a merry one. Export and be happy, even though an international financial crash is brewing."

Any intelligent person who agrees that the United States must play an important role in the postwar international world will strongly oppose the above policies, because they all attempt to snatch prosperity for ourselves at the expense of the rest of the world. Such a person would think it unfair of us to try to export our unemployment, so to speak, on to our neighbors.

But suppose we are hard-boiled; or to put it crudely, selfish. We must still regard these beggar-my-neighbor policies as rather foolish. Why?

One does not need much intelligence to see that foreign nations will not stand idly by while we attempt these policies. They too have economics textbooks, and legislators. They, too, during a great depression will be following beggar-my-neighbor tactics; they too will be raising tariffs and introducing import quotas and exchange control; they will be trying to depreciate the pound (or the franc as the case may be) so that the dollar will appreciate in value. In short, they will be trying to increase their exports and reduce their imports.

What is the result when all countries try to beggar their neighbors in this way—when all try to climb on each other's shoulders to see the parade? Obviously, we cannot succeed in exporting to England more than she is importing to us, while *at the same time* England is succeeding in exporting to us more than she is importing. Our mutual attempts to develop favorable balances of trade are worse than canceling. International trade drops to the lowest level of exports and imports. Both nations are worse off.

Again, how can we succeed in getting the pound-dollar foreign exchange rate up to $6 per pound (a "depreciation" of the dollar) at the same time that the English are succeeding in depreciating their pound down to way below $4 per pound? We both can't succeed. Because depreciation and appreciation are relative things, no one is better off. To elaborate the obvious further, how can we lend to Britain (net) in the next depression at the same time that she is lending (net) to us? In fact, if the legislators of both countries are on their toes, we cannot even succeed in giving away goods to each other. For, if free supplies began to come in from abroad, more American workers would be thrown out of jobs—a condition that no red-blooded American could ever permit to happen.

What is the final moral? Obviously, that a strong, important country like the United States cannot sensibly regard international trade as a way of solving its unemployment program. We cannot and should not, if we could. But we cannot. Other countries will retaliate to our beggar-my-neighbor tactics, with the result that we shall all be much worse off. Between 1950 and 1970, our choice should not be between (1) doing nothing about unemployment or (2) trying to export our unemployment abroad by restrictive trade policies in the hope of getting favorable secondary multiplier effects. Instead we must aim at a superior third choice (3) whereby we conquer the problem of unemployment by domestic policies and use international trade only to increase our present and future standards of consumption, or to serve our political aspirations and responsibilities.

POSTWAR INTERNATIONAL COOPERATION

Economic isolation will not work. On this, if on no other proposition $99^{44}\!/_{100}$ per cent of all economists are agreed. Nevertheless, economic isolation may again rear its head, because nations who ignore history are condemned to repeat it. Let us turn to the problems that the United States must face in the postwar world.

Let us assume that we all want to aim at the twin goals: full and efficient employment at home, with a rising standard of living and productivity; and peaceful, profitable trade relations with our neighbors on a durable basis. To achieve these goals we must face and solve the following half-dozen main problems.

PROBLEMS OF POSTWAR INTERNATIONAL FINANCE

1. *Full Employment at Home.* The United States can make its greatest single contribution to sound postwar economic relations by adopting such domestic public and private policies as will keep its real national income high and growing. In the past, America has long been the important plague center of unemployment. By letting our national income slump off, we permit our imports to fall to low levels, while still striving to export. As a result of trying to solve our unemployment problem through a favorable balance of trade, we deflate and impoverish the rest of the world. This invites retaliatory foreign restrictions; and all nations lose in the mad game of beggar-my-neighbor.

If we do a pretty fair job in the postwar of keeping American employment and income high—by means of *domestically created* purchasing power!—other nations will be able to pay us for our exports by their exports. With reasonably full employment at home, we shall be in a position to welcome goods sent to us as dividends and interest on our past investments and as repayment of principal. With full employment, we can welcome anything that enables us to raise our living standards by importing more *cheaply* and fully. With full employment, we can gradually reduce our artificial protective barriers and subsidies to relatively inefficient American industries.

2. *Marshall Plan for Europe.*   We have come out of the war with more resources than ever before. Other nations—such as Holland, France, England, Czechoslovakia—suffered extensive war damage. If the peace is to be durable and if democracy is to flourish, we ought to send these countries food and goods for relief and rehabilitation purposes. We must do this because of our generosity—or some will argue, because of our power politics—but not because gifts make jobs on our farms and in our export industries.

Because of the painful lesson learned from the World War I debts, we have been smart enough to cancel off immediately our lend-lease debts with England, France, and other allied powers. By having their men fight the enemy with our guns, planes, and ships, we saved American lives. Let us leave the matter there, and not let interallied war debts lead to the bad feeling and economic collapse of the previous postwar period.

Even though UNRRA (United Nations Relief and Rehabilitation Administration) ended with 1946, America is still finding it necessary and desirable to send further relief supplies abroad. Relief, as such, should be recognized as a gift, not as a loan.

Communism thrives on economic chaos abroad. Disorganization and privation in Europe constitute a threat to the peace and security of the United States. For this reason President Truman and Secretary of State Marshall asked the countries of Europe to get together and draw up plans for helping themselves to economic recovery, so that we could intelligently aid them in this task. Sixteen nations—excluding the satellites of the Soviet Union, who all declined to participate—met at Paris in the summer of 1947 and drew up an important economic report pointing out the roads to cooperative recovery over the following 4 years and indicating how American financial aid would be necessary to help them help themselves in becoming again self-supporting. They pointed out the great and universal "shortage of dollars," which is the financial counterpart of the great need in Europe for the food, fertilizer, and capital equipment that only America can provide.

Despite the fact that high postwar spending in the United States kept goods scarce and prices high, both political parties pledged their support to the

European recovery program: for reasons of charity, for reasons of political security, and to head off the spread of European communism. The exact size and form of the aid program will determine themselves only over a period of years; but it is certain to be large enough to affect appreciably the level of United States purchasing power and consumable output.

3. *The British Balance of Payments Problem.* In addition to relief, countries such as Britain and France have been given reconstruction loans. The British loan is for 3½ billion dollars to be spread over 1946–1951 and to be repaid with interest in yearly installments thereafter. Aside from her bombed cities and factories, Britain suffered tremendous losses of her foreign investments as a result of the war. Before lend-lease and Pearl Harbor, she had to sell almost all her holdings of American stocks and bonds; we sent her guns in exchange for her giving us back our old I.O.U.'s. The same thing happened with respect to England's relations to Canada, Australia, India, and the Empire. England now owes them, instead of being their creditor. Not being able to pay them on demand, she has "blocked" or frozen their right to receive payment. They can use these balances only to buy goods in Britain. Our loan and Marshall Plan aid may eventually help toward unfreezing the so-called "blocked sterling balances" owed by England abroad.

More directly, our loan will enable Britain to pay for the food imports that used to be paid for by her interest and dividends from abroad. The war has revolutionized Britain's creditor position—her net interest and dividends have been greatly reduced. If her standard of living and her food imports are to be maintained, she must greatly expand her volume of physical export trade, to 175 per cent of prewar levels. Our loan to Britain is to tide her over the transitional postwar period and enable her to improve her technology so as to be able to expand her production. Note that Britain's exports must expand, not to make jobs but rather to make imports. "We must export or die" really means for her "We must import or die. No longer enjoying extensive returns on foreign investments, we must export in order to import." In the meantime, England and almost all the other countries of the world—except the United States—must still ration imports by exchange control.

4. *Foreign Lending and the International Bank.* The United States is more developed industrially than the rest of the world. South America, the Orient, and other regions of the world could profitably use our capital for their industrial development. Such capital could be expected to increase their production by more than enough to pay generous interest and repay the principal.

But private American citizens are not willing to lend. Substantial private lending died some time in 1929, perhaps forever. Yet American citizens have savings which they would be glad to lend if such capital transactions could be made safe; and the American nation would benefit by a higher future standard of living from such sound foreign lending, provided we arrange our affairs so as not to have to worry about extensive future unemployment.

Therefore, the leading nations of the world (except Soviet Russia) have come together to form the International Bank for Reconstruction and Development and its sister institution, the International Monetary Fund. As its name implies the International Bank is formed to provide sound long-term loans for reconstruction and development. (The International Fund is concerned, as we shall see shortly, with short-term credit and the cooperative stabilization of foreign exchange rates.)

The International Bank is easy to understand. The leading nations subscribe to its initial 9 billion dollars of capital stock in proportion to their economic importance. The United States quota is about one-third, or 3 billion dollars. The bank can use its capital to make sound international loans—to people or countries whose projects seem economically sound but who cannot get private loans at reasonably low interest rates.

So far, each country has been called upon to put up only 20 per cent of its full quota, and it is not planned that the members will have to put up the remaining 80 per cent. Obviously this is not much money on international standards. The International Bank's true importance arises from something greater than the loans that it can make out of its own capital. More important is the fact that it can float bonds and use the proceeds to make loans. The bonds are safe because they are backed by the credit of all the nations (up to their 100 per cent of quotas). Also, the International Bank can *insure* loans in return for a ½ or 1 per cent premium; private parties can then put up the money knowing that the Bank's credit is behind the loan.

As a result of these three ways of extending long-term credits, we can expect to see goods in the years ahead flowing out of the United States whose ultimate purpose will be international reconstruction and development. If sound, these loans will be repaid in full. If some go sour, the loss will be paid out of the Bank's interest or premium earnings. If still more go sour, the loss will be spread over all the member nations—not on Uncle Sam alone. While the loans are being made, Uncle Sam will be getting jobs (and if spending is already too great, some increase in its inflation problems). When the loans are being "serviced" or repaid, America will be experiencing an import surplus of useful goods.

In addition to the International Bank to which many nations belong, the Federal government has set up its own Export-Import Bank. This also makes foreign loans: *e.g.*, an American exporter who wants to sell machine tools to Brazil may be helped to do so by the Export-Import Bank. Many of these loans are "tied loans"; *i.e.*, our Congress has insisted that the proceeds all be spent *directly* in this country. We criticize this sort of restrictive practice in others but, obsessed by the job aspects of international trade, we practice it ourselves.[1] Table 2 indicates the main postwar loans of the United States.

TABLE 2. *Known United States Postwar Foreign Aid and Lending as of 1947 (In millions of dollars)*

UNNRA and occupied areas relief	$ 4,000
Loan to the United Kingdom	3,750
Export-Import Bank loans	2,300
Surplus-property credits and postwar lend-lease credits (approximate)	2,500
U.S. Maritime Commission ship sales credits	200
Private lending (including "new financing" through dollar bond issues)	100
Federal reserve system credit to the Netherlands	100
Philippine Aid Program	695
Greek-Turkish political loans	400
Total (approximate)	$14,000
Europe recovery program (estimated cost of Marshall Plan, 1948–1952)	$12–19 billion

In addition to these governmental loans, we are also engaged in exporting our "know-how" abroad. Many of our largest companies are establishing branch factories abroad; often the capital is largely raised abroad, with Americans supplying the technical knowledge. Some shortsighted people raise their hands in horror at the thought of our helping foreign nations to become our industrial competitors. They seem to forget the statistical fact that international trade is largest between developed industrial nations, not between us and backward countries.

5. Stable Exchange Rates and the International Monetary Fund. When exchange rates vary from day to day, the risks of international trading become so great that its volume is greatly reduced. World specialization and productivity is reduced. Also, when every nation tries to engage in a race for com-

---

[1] Not only do tied loans distort the direction of international trade, but in many cases they are quite unnecessary. If part of our loan is used abroad, say in England, rather than here in the United States, then the extra dollars put in the hands of the British will probably cause them to take some of our exports. International trade is multilateral rather than bilateral.

petitive exchange depreciation, all end up worse and world trade ends up on its back.

The gold standard, while it operated, kept exchange rates constant. But (as is shown in the Appendix to this chapter) it made each country a slave rather than a master of its own economic destiny. As long as we stuck to its rules, we had to inflate ourselves whenever the rest of the world said inflate; and deflate ourselves when the rest of the world had a depression. Of course it had some advantages, but alas, poor gold standard! It was a casualty of World War I, and since then all the king's horses and all the king's men couldn't put it together again, and many wouldn't want to if they could.

The International Monetary Fund along with the International Bank grew out of some international conferences held in Bretton Woods, N. H., in 1944. The Fund hopes to secure the advantages of the gold standard without its disadvantages; *i.e.*, exchange rates are to be relatively stable, but international cooperation is to replace the previous automatic mechanism; also, countries are to be spared the need for making adjustments by deflating themselves into unemployment.

Early in 1947, the Fund set initial postwar exchange rates for most of its members. (Thus the dollar was set equal to 0.889 gram of gold and the British pound to 3.581 grams, with a resulting dollar-pound exchange rate of $4.03 per pound.) But king gold is tolerated only as a constitutional, rather than an absolute, monarch.

It is too much to expect that there will be a perfect balance of international transactions in the troubled postwar period. Quite clearly, some countries, such as the United States, will for a while sell more abroad than they buy—even after taking into account long-term foreign lending and aid programs. Other countries will be running into adverse trade balances and debt. How then can stable exchange rates be maintained?

Here is where the International Fund comes in. It provides short-term credits for the debtor countries. The Fund tries to set up rules and procedures to keep a country from going on year after year, getting deeper into debt. After a country has been piling up debts for a considerable period, certain financial penalties are applied. More important, the Fund's directors consult with the country and make recommendations for remedying the disequilibrium. However, they do not tell a country that it must create a depression for itself in order to cut down its national income to such a low level that its imports will finally fall to within its means. Instead, the country is permitted on its own hook first to depreciate its currency by 10 per cent. This will tend to restore equilibrium in its international trade by expanding its exports and contracting its imports.

If this is still not enough to correct the so-called "overvaluation" of the debtor country's currency, the Fund authorities may, after proper consultation, permit still further depreciation of the debtor country's exchange rate. But note this: all changes in rates take place in an orderly way. Most of the time, we have international stability. But there is also provision for flexibility when needed—which is better by far than waiting for a big international blowup or breakdown.

Let us discuss briefly and without going into the mechanical details how the International Fund is able to extend short-term credits. First, all the member nations must pay in certain initial quotas, which are set in proportion to national income and the volume of international trade. The United States quota is about one-third of the total and equals $2\frac{3}{4}$ billion dollars. At least 75 per cent of each country's quota is payable in its own currency; the rest is payable in gold, but not beyond 10 per cent of a country's official holding of gold and American dollars.

Ordinarily a country will go along paying for its imports by means of its exports or long-term borrowing. But suppose these are not large enough, and the country—say, England—is in need of short-term credit from the Fund. How does the Fund enable such a debtor country to get hold of, say, dollars? It does this by extending "purchasing rights." It simply permits the British to buy with British currency some of the Fund's own holdings of dollars. To keep the Fund from getting loaded up with pounds and stripped of its dollars, in any 12-month period, the British are not permitted to buy an amount greater than one-fourth of their original quota. And the Fund will never hold more than twice the original quota number of British pounds.

After the British balance of payments has improved, they are expected to buy back with gold (or with dollars) the pounds they have sold to the Fund. Thus, the Fund need never run out of dollars or any other currency; especially if it leads to corrective action to prevent continuing disequilibrium.

No more need be said here of the technical mechanics of the Fund. It is enough to emphasize that the Fund helps to establish stable—but flexible— exchange rates; that it provides short-term credits toward this end; and that it works toward international equilibrium by cooperation, coordination, and consultation and attempts to work against trade restrictions.

6. *Freer Multilateral Trade.* We have already discussed the postwar problems of (1) domestic full employment in America, (2) European Recovery Pro-

gram, (3) British balance of payments, (4) foreign lending and the International Bank, and (5) stable exchange rates via the International Fund. To the extent that these problems are successfully met—and only after they have been met— can we push toward the final goal of freer international trade. Only then can the Roosevelt-Hull program of reciprocal trade agreements be successful in reducing (1) tariffs, (2) import quotas, and (3) exchange control, (4) monopolistic international "cartels," (5) restrictive international commodity agreements by governments, and other forms of protectionism. Only then can the newly created ITO (International Trade Organization) and the Economic and Social Council of the United Nations succeed in combatting bilateralism in favor of mutually beneficial multilateral trade. Because World War II was so vast and devastating, we must expect and be patient with slow progress toward these goals.

SUMMARY

A. INTERNATIONAL TRADE AND CAPITAL MOVEMENTS

1. The balance of international payments (credit and debit items) should be understood, including invisibles, gold, and capital movements.

2. Also, the student should know the stages that the balance of trade and balance of current items go through as a nation passes from a young debtor stage to the position of a mature creditor.

3. No problem in international finance is more important than that of understanding the real and the monetary aspects of capital movements, in their effects both upon the industrial development of nations and upon the problem of unemployment.

B. POSTWAR INTERNATIONAL TRADE AND FULL EMPLOYMENT

4. Beggar-my-neighbor tactics, such as tariff protection and competitive exchange depreciation, are attempts to gain favorable multiplier effects on domestic employment and consumption. When successful, these policies may be better than nothing from our selfish view—but they are always inferior to intelligent antidepression policies which create useful production as well as favorable secondary effects on employment. Moreover, beggar-my-neighbor protectionist policies cannot be universally successful; they almost certainly invite retaliation and become "beggar-myself" tactics, which invite international financial breakdowns.

5. All this analysis is useless if it cannot be intelligently applied to the half-dozen crucial problems of postwar international finance.

QUESTIONS FOR DISCUSSION

1. Draw up a list of items that belong on the credit side of the balance of international payments; that belong on the debit side. Divide the statement into three parts: current, specie, and capital movements.

2. What is meant by a favorable balance of trade? How does the trade balance differ from the balance on current account? Why the term "invisible items"? What is the difference between short-term and long-term capital movements?

3. Construct hypothetical balance sheets for (a) a young debtor country, (b) a mature debtor country, (c) a new creditor country, (d) a mature creditor country.

4. America buys from the East Indies; England buys from America; England sells to the East Indies. How might the balance of payments between any two of these countries look? between any country and all the rest of the world? (HINT: Instead of having a single column of credits, of debits, and of net credits, introduce new columns for each country traded with.)

5. A Canadian railroad company floats bonds in England and uses the proceeds to buy tracks and locomotives. How would the English balance of payments be affected by this capital movement? Later the loan is repaid with interest. How would the balance of payments be affected?

6. "Foreign lending causes war. Foreign giving postpones war. Free foreign trading prevents war." Comment.

7. Comment on Stuart Chase's "common-sense formula":

> "The stuff we produce, as a nation,
> Plus the stuff we import,
> Less the stuff we export,
> Is a measure of our standard of living."

8. Comment on his description of international finance in the 1920's:

> "American investors loaned dollars abroad.
> Foreigners used the dollars to pay for
> American exports.
> The exports stimulated production and
> employment in America."

But,

> "Foreigners got the goods, while
> American investors lost their shirts."

9. "In 1935 it was better to export goods in exchange for useless gold than to do nothing." Discuss critically. Would your answer be different in 1942 or 1948?

10. How does the multiplier analysis apply to international trade?

11. Define, describe, and criticize beggar-my-neighbor policies.

12. Contrast and compare the International Bank and the International Fund.

13. Draw up a list of what you consider our most important postwar economic problems. If you were in Congress, what would you do about them?

APPENDIX TO CHAPTER 16
A FEW MECHANICS OF INTERNATIONAL
FINANCE

Without going into details, we may briefly survey how exchange rates, prices, and trade are determined (1) under *freely flexible* exchange rates and (2) under the *gold standard* or some other regime of stable exchange rates.

FREELY FLEXIBLE EXCHANGE RATES

From 1919 to 1925, the price of the pound fluctuated from day to day, going from almost $5 down to $3. Such a rate is determined by the interplay of competitive supply and demand for foreign exchange. When Americans wish to import or travel, their demand for pounds tends to push up the rate—say from $4 to $4.10. Any other American debit item, such as our desire to lend abroad, has the same effect.

Any credit item, on the other hand, such as our exporting to Britain, adds to the supply of pounds, because foreigners then need dollars. This tends to depress the price of foreign exchange or pounds. Brokers and bankers keep their ears glued to the telephone in order to follow the tug of war of supply and demand acting on flexible exchange rates.

We need not go into details of the exact mechanism, except to note one important tendency: When the price of foreign exchange rises, there are usually strong forces making for self-correction and helping to keep it from rising indefinitely. Similarly, there are self-correcting forces tending to limit a decline in the exchange rate.

Thus, if our imports become too large, we bid up the price of pounds. But at $5 per pound rather than $4, Americans find that British dishes and cloth have greatly increased in cost. Our imports are discouraged, which tends to correct the situation or at least to keep the exchange rate from rising further. More than that. Now an Englishman can get more dollars for his pounds. Consequently, even if American industries do not change their dollar price tags, the British will be encouraged to take more of our exports once the dollar has depreciated. This is an additional factor operating toward restoring the equilibrium of exports and imports and limiting the magnitude of the exchange-rate variation.

The reader should show that, just as a depreciation of the dollar tended to create an American export surplus and to correct an import surplus, so will an appreciation of the dollar tend to encourage American imports and dis-courage American exports and to be self-correcting and self-limiting. (HINT: Let the pound fall to $3.50. Why will it not fall farther?)

DETERMINANTS OF SUPPLY AND DEMAND

It is all very well to say, as we have just been saying, that supply and demand determine a flexible exchange rate. But if we want to probe deeper behind the scenes to ascertain what makes supply and demand act as they do, we shall find that the level of the exchange rate depends upon at least the following four fundamental factors.

1. The *strength of our desires* for foreign goods and services relative to their desires for our goods and services: the greater our desire for their goods, the higher will the price of foreign exchange be bid. The dollar will depreciate in value; the pound will tend to appreciate.

2. *The more our national income rises*, the greater will be our demand for imports. This will tend to make the dollar depreciate. On the other hand, high foreign national income makes the dollar appreciate, or what is the same thing, makes the price of foreign exchange cheaper for Americans. All this comes about because a country's "propensity to import" increases with national income in much the same way that its willingness to consume does.

3. The higher our *prices* and *costs* are, relative to the foreigners, the greater will be our imports, relative to exports. Therefore, high American prices and low foreign prices usually means a high price for foreign exchange. After World War I this third factor, considered to be most important of all, was called the "purchasing power parity" theory of exchange rates. According to this theory, the relative change in exchange rate between two countries will—other things being equal!—be proportional to the relative change in our prices compared to those abroad. Or,

$$\text{Foreign exchange rate} = \frac{\text{American prices}}{\text{foreign prices}}$$

This theory is most important when one of the two countries has had a tremendous inflation which has tended to raise most of its prices by almost the same percentage. If now everything else is exactly the same, except that it takes one hundred times as much foreign money to buy things, then we should expect that the exchange rate (the price of a unit of foreign currency) would probably have to find its level at about one one-hundredth of the previous rate.[1]

---

[1] The fall during inflation of the German mark, the Greek drachma, the Italian lira, the French franc, and the Chinese dollar, and other foreign exchange rates are all good examples.

4. Finally, the foreign exchange rate will be higher, the more Americans wish to lend abroad, the greater the payments we have to make on past debts or on war-punishment reparation payments, and the less willing foreigners are to hold dollars. When our investors develop a desire to hold foreign I.O.U.'s, bonds, stocks, bank deposits, or currency—then they will bid up the foreign exchange rate. The reader can work out the reverse case, where payments into the United States tend to lower the foreign exchange rate.

This last factor of capital movements is intimately tied up with *speculation* in foreign exchange. If only merchandise exports or current items were involved, the foreign exchange rate might be sluggish and change very little. Unfortunately, when the price of the pound drops from $4 to $3.96, many people begin to be afraid that it may fall still farther. Therefore, they try to get out of dollars and into pounds. But the increased sale of pounds and reduced demand for dollars, resulting from jittery short-term speculative capital movements, tends to push the pound down farther. Thus, small movements of the exchange rate are often amplified in a self-aggravating way by "hot money," which rushes from country to country with every rumor of war, politics, and exchange rate fluctuation. When such "capital flight" gets started in one direction on a large scale, the exchange rate may move chaotically and in extreme degree.

DISADVANTAGES OF FLEXIBLE EXCHANGE RATES

There is much to be said for flexible exchanges. Each country is free to pursue its own internal economic policies, leaving the exchange rate to take care of itself. However, there are also important disadvantages. With the exchange rate varying wildly from month to month, the volume of international trade and lending is greatly discouraged. A producer of goods would naturally prefer to sell and buy at home rather than to be betting continually upon the foreign exchange rate.[1]

A further disadvantage of fluctuating exchange rates results from the fact that each change in rates disturbs the existing situation in export and import markets. When suddenly the dollar depreciates, our exporters are helped and our importers are hurt. When the dollar appreciates, the reverse happens. This contributes toward unemployment, windfall profits and losses, and general instability.

[1] In Chap 25 on Speculation, the possibility of reducing risks by "hedging" in a "futures market" is discussed. Unfortunately, foreign-exchange markets have not been well enough organized to make this very helpful.

STABLE EXCHANGE RATES

For these reasons, nations usually try to introduce some stability into the exchange rate. The simplest way to do this is, not to pass a law or edict, but rather to come into the market with a big enough supply or demand for foreign exchange to keep the rate stable. Usually governments do this through so-called "exchange stabilization funds." There is no reason why a wealthy eccentric private citizen might not attempt to stabilize, say, the dollar price of Belgian francs. He, or any governmental fund, would have to start out with a huge pile of both dollars and Belgian francs (or with commodities like gold or wheat which could be converted by sale into either currency). Then to stabilize the price of the franc, he would simply instruct his brokers to bid dollars for francs whenever the price tended to fall, and to sell francs for dollars whenever the price tended to rise. So long as he did not run out of either francs or dollars, and so long as he stood ready both to buy and to sell francs at a given dollar price, then the franc-dollar exchange rate would be perfectly stable at that level.

Of course, even a multimillionaire might not be rich enough to do this for very long. A government, or the International Monetary Fund, is in a more powerful position. However, even the most powerful government will not be able to stand up against the ocean's tide and maintain any given exchange rate—unless it is able to influence prices, costs, and other conditions *so as to make private supply and demand for foreign exchange just about balance at the "pegged" rate.* Otherwise it will eventually be drained of all its holdings of one of the currencies—and then bingo! the rate can no longer be held steady.

Historically, the so-called "quasi-automatic gold standard" was a still more important method of stabilizing exchange rates and of thereby facilitating international trade. Let us turn to it.

WORKINGS OF THE GOLD STANDARD

To go on the gold standard a country need consult no one. Its Treasury must do two simple things: (1) agree to buy all gold brought to it at a given price—say $35 an ounce for the American Treasury (or £8¾ per ounce for the British) and (2) offer to sell gold freely to all comers at the same price. The result: the dollar price of gold becomes perfectly fixed, at a level called "mint parity."

As far as a single country is concerned, that is all there is to it. But where does the foreign exchange rate enter the picture? As soon as a second country (say Britain in addition to the United States) goes on the gold standard, then the *price of gold in terms of pounds* is also stabilized.

Of course, things equal to the same thing must be equal to each other. If a dollar is $\frac{1}{35}$ ounce of gold, and a pound is $\frac{4}{35}$ ounce of gold $(1 \div 8\frac{3}{4})$, then the price of a pound in terms of dollars must be $4(\frac{4}{35} \div \frac{1}{35})$. This is not simply a question of arithmetic, but of hard practical business sense. If I want to buy pounds in order to import from Britain, I will never pay more than $4 for them. Why? Because I can take four crisp American bills and get from the U.S. Treasury $\frac{4}{35}$ ounce of gold. I ship this gold to London, where the English Treasury gives me a crisp pound note. The reader should be able to work out the reason why an Englishman will never supply pounds for less than $4.

Thus, with each currency tied to gold, they become tied to each other at a fixed exchange rate. But with one minor qualification. There is approximately a 2-cent shipping, insurance, and interest charge involved in transporting gold between New York and London. Therefore, supply and demand can bid the pound price up to $4.02 before it becomes profitable for Americans to export gold. This is called the American gold-export point (or the British gold-import point). As an exercise, the reader may show that the British gold-export point is at about $3.98, and that the exchange rate is free to wobble around the $4 mint parity point within the range set by the two gold points.

THE EQUILIBRATING SPECIE-FLOW-PRICE MECHANISM

Up to this point the process has been completely mechanical. But the thoughtful reader will worry, as the "mercantilist" writers of the seventeenth and eighteenth centuries did, over what is to prevent the exchange rate from always being forced to the gold-export point of one of the countries until the one-way drain finally uses up all its gold reserves and forces it off the gold standard? The answer was first discovered just two centuries ago by the Scotch philosopher, David Hume. He claimed there was an automatic self-correcting "specie-flow-price" mechanism at work. According to him, Americans need not worry if they are importing more than they are exporting and are losing gold or specie. (1) The gold pouring into England will proportionately increase the amount of English money. (2) The increase in English money will (via the quantity theory of money and prices) cause a proportionate inflationary increase in British prices. Also, (3) the gold flowing out of America will cause a proportionate contraction of our money supply. (4) Again, via the quantity theory, this will cause a proportionate deflationary fall in American prices.

As a result of these four steps, there will be a double-edged tendency toward correcting the outflow of gold. (5) With British prices high relative to our own, Britons will begin to buy more of our exports. (6) Similarly, with our low prices, it will now pay us to buy less of their imports. Thus, the situation will finally correct itself. The changes in relative price levels caused by the flow of gold will restore the adverse trade balance and choke off the one-way flow of gold before it has gone very far. Therefore, said Hume, there is nothing to worry about.

Today we are not so sure. England may not want to have an inflation, and America may not like the idea of having a deflation just because the impersonal gods of the gold standard dictate it.

Besides, since Hume's time, banking and finance have become more elaborate. Now that gold coins are no longer the important part of our money supply, the process is not automatic. Instead the Treasury and the Central Bank are supposed to "follow the rules of the gold-standard game." When gold flows out, this is to be a signal for us to put on the deflationary brakes. For example, we should (1) increase tax collections relative to expenditure; (2) discourage private investment by raising the "rediscount" and other interest rates; (3) tighten up on bank reserves by Federal reserve open-market sales of securities or by raising legal reserve rates; (4) put downward pressure on wages and prices. In short, we should deliberately create a depression and deflation.

The reader should be able to list the inflationary steps that the rules of the game would impose on the country receiving gold. He will then be in a position to understand how, and why, countries refused to play the rules of the gold-standard game in the years after World War I. They did this to avoid inflation or deflation. But, as a further result, the one-way drains of gold were not corrected, and finally the gold standard broke down.

However, the breakdown was due not simply to the willful disregard by nations of the rules of the game, but also to the fact that the gold standard is a "fair-weather system" that works best only when small strains are placed upon it. In the jittery, troubled period between the two wars, with erratic capital movements, the strains were anything but small.

Finally, from a technical economic viewpoint, we are no longer so optimistic as Hume was about the efficacy of the specie-flow-price mechanism. The weaknesses of the quantity theory have already been pointed out in earlier chapters. Also we have seen that prices and costs are often sticky in capitalistic countries. Still worse, there is a possibility that the Hume price changes could make the situation worse rather than better if international demands turn out to be inelastic rather than elastic. In such cases, lowering the prices of American export goods will not expand our sales much; therefore, Englishmen will actually offer fewer pounds for dollars rather than more pounds. Similarly, if the American demand for British goods should be very urgent and inelastic, raising British prices may force us to demand more pounds rather than less. Thus, the price reaction to a depreciation of the dollar may be a perverse rather than an equilibrating one: the dollar would have to depreciate still further.

INCOME EFFECTS AND THE "FOREIGN TRADE MULTIPLIER"

For all these reasons, it is probable that the gold standard would have broken down and been abandoned long ago, were it not for an important equilibrating process not dreamed of in Hume's specie-flow-price philosophy. In recent years economists have emphasized that *income changes in the two countries help to restore equilibrium*. If our exports go up, then even without any price changes, we now have a higher national income. Part of this higher income we shall want to use to buy more imported goods. Thus, to some degree, an increase in exports will directly induce an increase in imports via income, no matter what happens to prices. (When we come to analyze in detail the full multiplier effects of our increased income, we shall see that the induced increase in imports is only *partial* rather than being equal to the original increase in exports. There is still some need for prices or exchange rate changes to restore equilibrium.)

Let us turn then to the multiplier analysis of foreign trade. We have seen that new domestic investment creates primary jobs and income and that the spending and respending of this new income give rise to a chain of secondary multiplier effects. New exports have exactly the same multiplier effects. They raise incomes directly, but in addition they set up a chain of further spending and respending.

Thus, a billion dollars' worth of new export orders to New England machine-tool factories will create 1 billion dollars of primary jobs and income. Then workers and owners may respend perhaps two-third of their new income on the consumption products of Indiana and California; two-thirds of this extra income is in turn respent, etc. The process comes to a halt only when the total adds up to $1 + \frac{2}{3} + (\frac{2}{3})^2 + \cdots = 1/(1 - \frac{2}{3})$ times 1 billion dollars, or to 2 billion dollars of secondary consumption expenditure in addition to the 1 billion dollars of primary expenditure.

Besides introducing a multiplier effect of exports into the picture, international trade has a second important effect. Higher American national income will increase our imports, let us say by one-twelfth out of every extra dollar.

This means that our chain of induced domestic purchasing power will peter out quicker than in the above example. At each step, these imports act as "leakages," just like the marginal propensity to save.[1]

Therefore, out of the original 1 billion dollars of income in the export industries, perhaps only $\frac{7}{12}(= \frac{2}{3} - \frac{1}{12})$ rather than $\frac{8}{12}$ will be respent on *American* consumption goods (in Indiana, California, and so forth). And so it will go at each stage. The whole multiplier will now add up only to

$$1 + \frac{7}{12} + (\frac{7}{12})^2 + \cdots,$$

or only to $2\frac{2}{5} = 1 \div (1 - \frac{7}{12}) = 1 \div \frac{5}{12}$ instead of to 3. This is because $\frac{1}{12}$ of our extra $2\frac{2}{5}$ billion dollars of generated income—or $\frac{1}{5}$ of a billion dollars in this case—tends to go abroad for extra imports.

It would be wrong to look upon this leakage of purchasing power abroad as simply a nuisance. Disregarding unemployment and looking at matters from the standpoint of stable international finance, we must rather regret that 1 billion dollars of new exports has only induced $\frac{1}{5}$ of a billion dollars of imports.

If we look at our multiplier formulas we find that this is a general rule:

> *So long as some fraction of income at every stage is leaking into domestic savings, a new dollar of exports will never be able to lift income by enough to call forth a full dollar of new imports.*[2]

Many recent economic writers have overlooked this fact and have exaggerated the importance of income effects in achieving smooth international adjustments. But these multiplied income effects do help to explain why nations pursue beggar-my-neighbor policies.

---

[1] If the reader applies the foreign trade multiplier analysis to a small city or country, he will find that the secondary multiplier effects upon the workers of that region are almost negligible, since almost all of extra income leaks out to other regions.

[2] Suppose that each extra dollar of income is always split up into the three fractions: a for American consumption goods, b for America's propensity to import goods from abroad, c for the remaining amount going into saving. Then let exports go up by one unit. The multiplier tells us that our income will go up by $1/(1 - c) = 1/(b + a)$. Multiplying this extra income by the fraction b, we get induced imports of $b/(b + a)$, which is certainly less than our original one of new exports—to the extent that the marginal propensity to save, a, is positive.

Chapter 17: THE BUSINESS CYCLE

WE have now examined the economic forces operating to determine the level of national income—the balance of saving and investment; and how money, banks, and international finance affect this balance. We must turn in this chapter to the problem of how and why the level of national income fluctuates. We may leave to Chap. 18 on Fiscal Policy the question of what can be done to keep national income relatively stable and employment relatively high.

PROSPERITY AND DEPRESSION

Business conditions never stand still. Prosperity is followed by a panic or a crash. National income, employment, and production fall. Price and profits decline and men are thrown out of work. Eventually the bottom is reached, and revival begins. The recovery may be slow or fast. It may be incomplete, or it may be so strong as to lead to a new boom. The new prosperity may represent a long, sustained plateau of brisk demand, plentiful jobs, buoyant ·prices, and increased living standards. Or it may represent a quick, inflationary flaring up of prices and speculation, to be followed by another disastrous slump.

Such in brief is the so-called "business cycle" that has characterized the industrialized nations of the world for the last century and a half at least, ever since an elaborate, interdependent, *money economy* began to replace a relatively self-sufficient, precommercial society.

No two business cycles are quite the same; yet they all have much in common. They are not identical twins, but they are recognizable as belonging to the same family. No exact formula, such as might apply to the motions of the moon or of a simple pendulum, can be used to predict the timing of future (or past) business cycles. Rather do they resemble, in their rough appearance and irregularities, the fluctuations of disease epidemics, the vagaries of the weather, or the variations in a child's temperature.

To democratic nations, the business cycle presents a challenge—almost an ultimatum. Either we learn to control depressions and inflationary booms better than we did before World War II, or the political structure of our society will hang in jeopardy. For the ups and downs in business do not cancel out. At the top of the boom—if we are lucky!—there may be relatively favorable job opportunities for all who wish to work. Throughout the rest of the business cycle, men's lives are being wasted, and the progress of our economic society falls short of our true economic possibilities. If, as before the war, America marks time for another decade, the collectivized nations of the world, who need have no fear of the business cycle as we know it, will forge that much nearer or beyond us. Worse than that, peace-loving people who do not pretend to know very much advanced economics will begin to wonder why it is that during two World Wars individuals were freed for the first time from the insecurity of losing their jobs and livelihoods.

From these introductory remarks, it will be clear that the business cycle is simply one further aspect of the economic problem of achieving and maintaining high levels of jobs and production, and a healthy progressive economy.

MEASURING AND FORECASTING THE BUSINESS CYCLE

Figure 1 shows how the economic system has been plagued with the business cycle throughout our history as a nation, although never with so sustained and costly a slump as in the post-1929 Great Depression. The same pattern of cyclical fluctuations is repeated in England, Germany, and other foreign nations with surprisingly few variations. But it is a strange fact that the United States, supposedly one of the youngest and most vigorous of nations, tends always to have greater average amounts of unemployment and greater variation in unemployment than any other country. Not only was this true in 1933, when our percentage of unemployment surpassed even that of Germany, but it appears to have been the case for almost as far back as we have any records or indications.

Figure 2 shows a number of diverse recent economic "time series," presented next to each other for comparison. Note the all-pervasive common pulse of the business cycle: in production, in employment, in incomes, and even in such particular series as stock-market prices and imports. Moreover, if we had included data on such noneconomic matters as marriages, births, and malnutrition, we would also be able to see in them the heavy hand of the business cycle. Even political party elections follow the business cycle; in depressions, the ins go out.

Of course, as economists and citizens, we are primarily interested in the fluctuations in total jobs, total production, and total (real) national income. But for many countries and for many earlier decades, such data are very hard to come by. Moreover, certain specialists are often interested in various secondary series: in stock prices, in wholesale prices, in profits, in steel production, and so forth. Often, therefore, statisticians use such a time series as pig-iron production as an index of the business cycle. Or better still, they may take some sort of a weighted average of many series—such as freight-

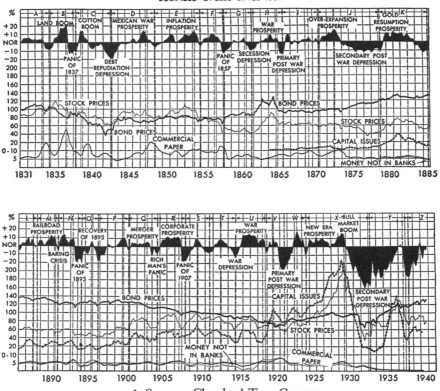

FIG. 1. Source: Cleveland Trust Company.

car loadings, electric-power production, or bank clearings (value of checks cashed)—and combine them into a barometer of the business cycle. Figure 1 illustrated such an index of business activity.

Many grown men, who should perhaps know better, ruin their eyesight peering at charts like those shown in Fig. 2, in the hope of finding a magic forecaster which always moves up or down a few months *before* business conditions, and by its movements signals the coming trend of events. Alas, they might almost as well consult a fortuneteller. For example, in 1937 the stock market began to turn down early in the year as though in anticipation of the sharp mid-year recession of 1937–1938. But if we go back to 1929, we find that the stock market continued to climb until late in October, whereas business conditions—we now know!—began to turn down some months

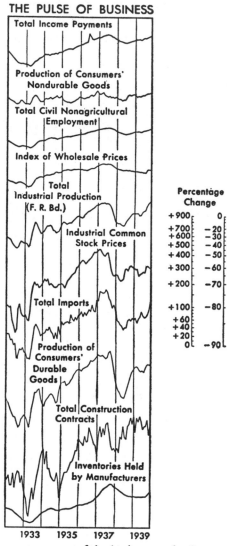

THE PULSE OF BUSINESS

Total Income Payments

Production of Consumers' Nondurable Goods

Total Civil Nonagricultural Employment

Index of Wholesale Prices

Total Industrial Production (F. R. Bd.)

Industrial Common Stock Prices

Total Imports

Production of Consumers' Durable Goods

Total Construction Contracts

Inventories Held by Manufacturers

Percentage Change

+900	0
+700	−20
+600	−30
+500	−40
+400	−50
+300	−60
+200	−70
+100	−80
+60	
+40	
+20	
0	−90

1933   1935   1937   1939

FIG. 2. Note the common pattern of the business cycle. SOURCE: National Bureau of Economic Research.

earlier. Many brave souls have been led to believe in one system or another for "calling the turns" of the cycle, but usually the next boom or depression kills off their hopes and—it may be added—their clients.

Let us for the moment, therefore, stick to the facts and statistics. Later we shall attempt to devise hypotheses and explanatory theories to account for the broad factual patterns, but not for the month-to-month happenings.

STATISTICAL CORRECTION FOR SEASONAL VARIATION AND FOR TRENDS

First, of course, we must remove from our statistical data irrelevant, disturbing factors such as seasonal patterns, and also certain so-called long-term "trends." If Sears Roebuck's sales go up from November to December, 1937, we cannot conclude from this that the 1937 recession is over. Retail trade goes up every Christmas, just as New Hampshire hotels tend to be crowded in summer. The statistician attempts to remove the "seasonal influence" by carefully studying previous yearly patterns. If he finds that every December tends to involve about 150 per cent as much business as the average month of the year, and every January only 90 per cent, then he will take the actual raw monthly data and divide all the December figures by 1.5 and all the January figures by 0.9, and so forth, for each month. After this has been done, the statistician will end up with a time series of monthly department-store sales which have been "seasonally adjusted." These will show what we expected all along, that business was really still declining throughout all the last months of 1937, because December's increase of business over November's was less than the seasonal normal.

A similar problem arises when we examine the fluctuations over time of such a rapidly growing time series as electric-power consumption. Electric-power production did not decline much in the depression. But the depression is to be seen in that series, nevertheless. It rears its ugly head in the form of a *slowing down of the rate of growth* of the time series as compared to its normal or long-term "secular trend." If we draw a smooth trend line or curve, either by eye or by some statistical formula, through the *electric-power production* chart, we shall discover the business cycle in the twistings of the data above and below the trend line. If we measure the vertical deviations up and down from the trend line and plot them on a separate diagram, we shall get a pretty clear picture of the business cycle.[1] Let us take a look at it.

THE FOUR PHASES OF THE CYCLE

Early writers on the business cycle, possessing little quantitative information, tended to attach disproportionate attention to *panics* and *crises* such as the

[1] The reader may be referred to any standard textbook on statistics for these technical procedures. Let it be said, however, that cautious judgment must be exercised in using the mechanical tools of statistics. A beginner, who is carelessly "eliminating a trend," may throw out the baby along with the bath water if he is not careful, or at least distort the true appearance of the infant.

collapse of the South Sea Bubble in 1720, the panic of 1837, the Jay Cooke panic of 1873, the Cleveland panic of 1893, the "rich man's panic" of 1907, and of course, the superduper stock-market crash of "black Tuesday," Oct. 29, 1929. Later writers began soon to speak of two phases of business: prosperity and depression, or boom and slump—with peaks and troughs marking the turning points in between.

Today, it is recognized that not every period of improving business need necessarily take us all the way to full employment. For example, throughout the decade of the 1930's there was a measure of recovery from the 1932–1933 trough levels, but we could by no means speak of the period as being one of true

FOUR PHASES OF THE CYCLE

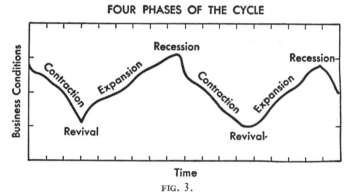

FIG. 3.

prosperity. The prevailing fashion, therefore, is to follow the terminology of Wesley C. Mitchell, long-time director of the nonprofit National Bureau of Economic Research and assiduous student of business cycles.[1]

The cycle is broken up by Mitchell and many other economists into four phases, the two most important ones being called the periods of "expansion" and "contraction." The expansion phase comes to an end and goes into the contraction phase at the so-called upper turning point (peak) called "recession." Similarly, the contraction phase gives way to that of expansion at the lower turning point (trough) or "revival." Thus, the four phases keep repeating themselves in the oversimplified picture as shown in Fig. 3. Note that the emphasis now is not so much on *high* or *low* business activity, but on the dynamic aspects of *rising* or *falling* business activity.

Each phase of the cycle passes into the next. Each phase is characterized by different economic conditions,[2] and each requires special explanatory princi-

[1] W. C. MITCHELL, "Business Cycles: The Problem and Its Setting." National Bureau of Economic Research, New York, 1927

[2] For example, during expansion, we find that employment, production, prices, money, wages, interest rates, and profits are usually rising, while the reverse is true during contraction.

ples. But let us continue a little while more with the facts before attempting analysis and theorizing.

How long are the usual economic cycles? This depends upon how many minor cycles you wish to count. Most observers have no trouble in agreeing on the major cycles, which run somewhere around 8 to 10 years in length. Everyone agrees that the late 1920's represent a period of prosperity and the early 1930's one of depression, and similarly with the past major business cycles. But not all economists attach much importance to the shorter minor cycles which are often to be seen in economic charts. In 1924 and 1927, there were small dips in business activity. Shall we call the 1920's, therefore, three different (minor) cycles or one major prosperity period? In an elementary introduction of this type, it is perhaps best to stick primarily to major business cycles. For our purposes we may accept Prof. Alvin H. Hansen's brief summary:[1]

The American experience indicates that the major business cycle has had an average duration of a little over eight years. Thus, from 1795 to 1937 there were seventeen cycles of an average duration of 8.35 years. . . .

Since one to two minor peaks regularly occur between the major peaks, it is clear that the minor cycle is something less than half the duration of the major cycle. In the one hundred and thirty-year period 1807 to 1937 there were thirty-seven minor cycles with an average duration of 3.51 years.

. . . it appears that the building cycle averages somewhere between seventeen and eighteen years in length, or almost precisely twice the length of the major business cycle. . . .

. . . American experience indicates that with a high degree of regularity every other major business boom coincides roughly with a boom in building construction, while the succeeding major cycle recovery is forced to buck up against a building slump. . . .

. . . the depressions which have fallen in the interval of the construction down-swing are typically deep and long. And the succeeding recovery is held back and retarded by the unfavorable depressional influence from the slump in the building industry.

LONG WAVES?

Some economists, taking a broad historical view, like to speak of very "long waves," whose complete cycle length is about half a century. Thus from the end of the Napoleonic Wars in 1815 to the middle of the nineteenth century, prices tended to fall and times tended to be unusually hard, on the average. After the Californian and Australian gold discoveries following 1850, and as a partial result of the Civil and Crimean Wars, prices tended to rise. A new

[1] ALVIN H. HANSEN, "Fiscal Policy and Business Cycles," pp. 18–19, 20, 23–24, W. W. Norton & Company, New York, 1941.

long cycle of falling prices followed the 1873 depression, tending to last until the 1890's when there was a great increase in gold production following the South African and Alaskan discoveries and improvements in gold refining. McKinley and the Republican party swam to prosperity and power on the crest of the new long wave.

Whether these long waves are simply historical accidents due to chance gold discoveries, political wars, and chance inventions, it is still too soon to say.[1]

A FIRST CLUE TO THE BUSINESS CYCLE: CAPITAL FORMATION

Professor Hansen's emphasis on construction gives us our first clue as to the causation of the business cycle. Certain economic variables always show greater fluctuations than others in the business cycle. Thus, if it were to plot pig-iron production and anthracite-coal consumption side by side, we would hardly see the business cycle in the latter, whereas in the pig-iron series there would be little else to see but the business cycle. Why? Because anthracite is used largely for heating people's houses, and in both good and bad times most people are going to manage to keep reasonably warm. Pig iron, on the other hand, is one of the principal ingredients of capital and durable goods of all kinds: of plant equipment and durable machinery, of industrial and residential construction, of automobiles, washing machines, and other durable consumers' goods.

By their nature, such durable goods are subject to violently erratic patterns of demand. In bad times their new purchase can be indefinitely postponed; in a good year, everyone may suddenly decide to stock up on a 10-year supply of the services of such durable goods. *Our first clue to the nature of the business cycle lies then in the fact that it is the durable or capital goods sectors of the economy which show by far the greatest cyclical fluctuations.*[2]

If the reader will now turn to Fig. 2 on page 396 he will see the contrast between capital and nondurable goods fluctuations clearly brought out. The last time series all represent various categories of durable or capital-goods formation. Note how wide their swings all are, as compared to those of the second time series which represents nondurable consumers' goods. Except for

[1] The interested reader may be referred to J. A. Schumpeter, "Business Cycles," Chaps. 6, 7, McGraw-Hill Book Company, Inc., New York, 1939.

[2] Lord Beveridge in his "Full Employment in a Free Society" (W. W. Norton & Company, New York, 1945) made a careful calculation of the degree of variability of the capital-goods industries in Great Britain ever since 1785 and found it to be twice as great as for other industries. Some economists and statisticians also think that they can detect a tendency for *construction* and other capital-goods series to "lead" general business activity by some interval at both the upturn and the downturn of business, but this is less certain.

a few short, choppy surface disturbances in this latter series, it will be seen to follow the general flow of income in rather a passive fashion. Consumption movements seem the effect rather than cause of the business cycle, while there is good reason to believe that the movements of durable goods represent key causes in a more fundamental sense.

It is comforting to find that our statistical analysis supports and confirms the emphasis in previous chapters on the crucial importance of the capital investment process.

A FEW THEORIES OF THE BUSINESS CYCLE

An industrious student could easily compile a list of separate theories of the business cycle which would run into the dozens.[1] Each theory seems to be quite different; but when we examine them closely and throw out those which obviously contradict the facts or the rules of logic, or which just appear to be conveying an explanation when really they are not saying anything at all— when we do all this, we are left with a relatively few different explanations. Most of them differ from each other only in emphasis. One man believes the cycle to be primarily the result of fluctuations in total net investment, while another prefers to attribute the cycle to fluctuations in the rate of technological inventions and innovations, which act on business *through* net investment. A third man says that the root of the cycle is to be found in the fact that the creation of deposit money by our banking system causes investment spending to expand and contract so as to create boom and bust.

These sound like three different theories, and in most advanced textbooks they might be given the names of three different writers, but from our standpoint they are but three different aspects of the same process. (This does not mean that there is perfect agreement among all theories of the cycle or that there are not some important differences in emphasis between different writers.)

[1] We may just mention a few of the better known theories: (1) the *monetary* theory, which attributes the cycle to the expansion and contraction of bank credit (Hawtrey, *et al.*); (2) the *innovation* theory, which attributes the cycle to the clustering of important inventions such as the railroad (Schumpeter, Hansen, *et al.*); (3) the *psychological* theory, which treats the cycle as a case of people's infecting each other with pessimistic and optimistic expectations (Pigou, Bagehot, *et al.*); (4) the *underconsumption* theory, which claims that too much income goes to wealthy or thrifty people compared to what can be invested (Hobson, Foster, and Catchings, *et al.*); (5) the *overinvestment* theory, which claims that too much rather than too little investment causes recessions (Hayek, Mises, *et al.*); (6) the *sunspot-weather-crop* theories (Jevons, Moore). The interested reader should consult G. Haberler, "Prosperity and Depression," 3d ed. (League of Nations, Geneva, 1944) or some other business-cycles text for further information on this subject.

To classify the different theories, we may first divide them into the two categories of primarily external and primarily internal theories. The external theories find the root cause of the business cycle in the fluctuations of something *outside* the economic system—in sunspot cycles, in wars, revolutions, and political events, in gold discoveries, in rates of growth of population and migrations, in discoveries of new lands and resources, and finally in scientific and technological discoveries and innovations.

The internal theories look for mechanisms *within* the economic system itself which will give rise to self-generating business cycles, so that every expansion will breed recession and contraction, and every contraction will in turn breed revival and expansion, in an irregular, repeating, never-ending chain.

If you believe in the sunspot theory of the business cycle, then the distinction between external and internal is a fairly easy one to draw; although even here, when you come to explain how and why disturbances on the surface of the sun give rise to the business cycle, you begin to get involved in the internal nature of the economic system. But at least no one can seriously argue that the direction of causation is in doubt, or that the economic system causes the sunspots to fluctuate, instead of vice versa. However, when it comes to such other external factors as wars and politics, or even births and gold discoveries, there is always some doubt as to whether the economic system does not at least react back on the so-called "external" factors, making the distinction between external and internal not such a hard and fast one. However, no one will deny that any such "feedback" effects take us outside the traditional boundaries of economics, and this is the justification for maintaining the distinction between external and internal theories.

SUNSPOTS AND RELATED PURELY EXTERNAL THEORIES

Few professional economists today put much stock in these physical theories. Not infrequently an amateur economist, often a scientist in some other field, will argue that sunspots, which have an average periodicity of some 11 to 13 years, have important effects upon the weather. This affects crops. Good crops cause low incomes and bad business. Or else it is the other way around, and good crops are supposed to mean prosperity. The sunspot theorists cannot always make up their minds just which. In other versions, it is said that sunspots affect the intensity of solar radiation. Everyone knows that vitamin D depends on sunshine, and that people near the North Pole become despondent during the long winter nights. Hence, sunspots affect business by affecting pessimism, optimism, or health in general. One ingenious writer, dropping sunspots because they did not give an 8-year cycle, set forth the belief that whenever the planet Venus came between the sun and the earth, this caused magnetic absorptions and an 8-year business cycle.

Unfortunately, the field of economics has not the classic simplicity of physics or mathematics. In those fields a crank who thinks he can square the circle or build a perpetual-motion machine can be shown up, if not to his own satisfaction, at least to that of every competent observer. In economics, it is not quite so easy to demonstrate that sunspot theories of the cycle are all moonshine, especially if their proponents are willing to spend a lifetime manipulating statistics until they produce agreement. This sad fact is important not because we find it difficult to disprove the sunspot theory—no one really cares much today about sunspot theories—but rather because our cockiness about what we think are better and truer theories must always be subject to liberal reservations in view of the complexity of economic observations and data which makes it difficult to disprove a bad theory or verify a good one.

PURELY INTERNAL THEORIES

As against the crude external sunspot theory, we may describe a simple example of a possible crude internal theory. If machinery and other durable goods all had the same length of life, say 8 or 10 years, then we might try to explain a business cycle of the same length by this fact. If once a boom got started—never mind how—then there would be a bunching of new capital goods all of the same age. A few years later before these goods had worn out, there would be little need for replacement. This would cause a depression.

But after 8 or 10 years all the capital equipment would suddenly wear out and would all have to be replaced, giving rise to an inflationary boom. This in turn would give rise to another complete cycle, with a new cycle of depression and boom every decade. Thus, as a result of self-generating "replacement waves," we might have a purely internal business-cycle theory.

Actually, not all equipment has the same length of life; and not even all identical automobiles produced on the same day are in need of being replaced at the same time. Therefore, any bunching of equipment expenditures will tend over time to spread itself out, at most giving rise to weaker and weaker replacement peaks. Twenty-five years after the Civil War one might have observed a deficit of births because of that conflict. But another generation later and the dip would be hardly noticeable, while today it is just as if there had never been that particular violent disturbance of population. Replacement waves, therefore, are like a plucked violin string. They tend to dampen down and die away unless there is a new disturbance.

The laws of physics guarantee that friction will lessen any purely autonomous physical fluctuations. In social science, there is no law like that of the conservation of energy preventing the creation of purchasing power. Therefore, a much better example than replacement waves of a self-generating cycle would be the case where people became alternately optimistic and pessimistic, each stage leading as inevitably into the next just as the manic stage of an insane person leads eventually to the depressive stage. We cannot rule out such an internal theory. But neither can we be satisfied with it as it stands, for it does not explain a great deal.

COMBINING EXTERNAL AND INTERNAL ELEMENTS INTO A SYNTHESIS

Everyone has observed how a window or a tuning fork may be brought into pronounced vibration when a certain note is sounded. Is this vibration externally or internally caused? The answer is both. The sounded note is certainly an external cause. But the window or tuning fork responds according to its own internal nature, coming into strong resonance not with any sounded note but only with one of a certain definite pitch. It takes the right kind of trumpets to bring down the walls of Jericho.

Likewise we may look upon the business cycle as not unlike a toy rocking horse which is subjected to occasional outside pushes. The pushes need not be regular; great technical inventions never are. But just as the horse rocks with a frequency and amplitude that depends partly upon its internal nature (its size and weight), so too will the economic system according to its *internal* nature respond to fluctuations in external factors. Both external and internal factors are important, then, in explaining the business cycle.

Most economists today believe in a synthesis or combination of external and internal theories. In explaining the major cycles, they place crucial emphasis on fluctuations in *investment* or *capital* goods. Primary causes of these capricious and volatile investment fluctuations are to be found in such external factors as (1) technological innovation and (2) dynamic growth of population and of territory. With these external factors, we must combine the internal factors that cause any initial change in investment to be amplified in a cumulative, multiplied fashion—as people who are given work in the capital-goods industries respend part of their new income on consumption goods and as an air of optimism begins to pervade the business community, causing firms to go to the banks and the securities market for new credit accommodation.

Also, it is necessary to point out that the general business situation definitely reacts back on investment. If high consumption sales make businessmen optimistic, they are more likely to embark upon venturesome investment programs. Inventions or scientific discoveries may occur independently of the business cycle, but their economic introduction will most certainly depend on business conditions. If national income moves to a new postwar plateau which is some 50 per cent higher than prewar, we should expect that a considerable volume of capital formation (new machines, added inventories, construction) would be induced. Therefore, especially in the short run, investment may be in part an *effect* as well as a cause of the level of income.

In the longer run, no matter how high a plateau of income is maintained, the stock of capital goods will become adjusted at a higher level and new net investment will drop off to zero unless there is (1) a growth of income, (2) a continuing improvement of technology, or (3) a never-ending reduction in interest rates. The first of these processes, showing how investment demand may be induced by *growth* of sales and income, has been given a rather high-sounding name—the "acceleration principle." Almost all writers bring it in as one strand in their final business-cycle theories. Let us examine how this internal cyclical mechanism works itself out and interacts with other factors.

THE ACCELERATION PRINCIPLE

According to this law, society's needed stock of capital, whether inventory or equipment, depends primarily upon the level of income or production. Additions to the stock of capital, or what we customarily call *net* investment, will take place only when income is growing. As a result, a prosperity period may come to an end—not simply because consumption sales have gone down— but simply because sales have *leveled off* at a high level or have continued to grow but at a lower rate than previously.

A simplified arithmetical example will make this clear. Imagine a typical textile-manufacturing firm whose stock of capital equipment is always kept equal to about ten times the value of its yearly sales of cloth.[1] Thus, when its sales have remained at 6 million dollars per year for some time, its balance sheet will show 60 million dollars of capital equipment, consisting of perhaps 20 machines of different ages with one wearing out each year and being replaced. Because replacement just balances depreciation, there is no *net* investment or saving being done by the corporation. *Gross* investment is taking place at the rate of 3 million dollars per year, representing the yearly replacement of one machine. (The other 3 million dollars of sales may be assumed to go for wages and dividends.)

Now let us suppose that, in the fourth year, sales rise by 50 per cent—from

[1] We are ignoring any possible change in interest rates or degree of utilization of capacity in order to keep our discussion simple. This could be remedied. Also the reader may wish to include inventory change as well as equipment change in the analysis.

6 to 9 million dollars. Then the number of machines must also rise by 50 per cent, or from 20 to 30 machines. In the fourth year, 11 machines must be bought, 10 new ones in addition to the replacement of the worn-out one.

Sales have gone up by 50 per cent. How much has machine production gone up? By 1,000 per cent! It is this accelerated effect of a change in consumption on investment levels that gives the acceleration principle its name.

TABLE 1. *Illustration of the Acceleration Principle (In millions of dollars)*

Time	Yearly sales	Stock of capital	Net investment	Gross investment, G. I. (N.I. + replacement)
First phase				
First year.......	$ 6	$ 60	$ 0	1 machine at $3 = $3
Second year.....	6	60	0	1 machine at $3 = $3
Third year......	6	60	0	1 machine at $3 = $3
Second phase				
Fourth year.....	$ 9	$ 90	$30	(1 + 10) machines at $3 = $33
Fifth year.......	12	120	30	(1 + 10) machines at $3 = $33
Sixth year.......	15	150	30	(1 + 10) machines at $3 = $33
Third phase				
Seventh year.....	$15	$150	$ 0	1 machine at $3 = $3
Fourth phase (to be filled in by reader)				
Eighth year......	$14.7	—	—	—

If sales continue to rise in the fifth, sixth, and seventh years by 3 million dollars, then we shall continue to have 11 new machines ordered in every year. This is shown in Table 1.

So far, the acceleration principle has given us no trouble. On the contrary, it has given us a tremendous increase in investment spending as a result of a moderate increase in consumption sales. But now we are riding a tiger. Consumption has to keep increasing in order for investment to stand still! If consumption should stop growing at so rapid a rate—if it should level off in the seventh year even at the high level of 15 million dollars per year—then net investment will fall away to zero, and gross investment will fall back to 1 machine (see the table). In other words, a drop of zero per cent in sales has resulted in a 90 per cent drop in gross investment and a 100 per cent drop in net investment!

The Lord giveth and the Lord taketh away. The acceleration principle is a two-edged sword. If sales should drop below 15 million dollars, gross investment would drop away to nothing; in fact, the firm would want to disinvest by selling off some of its machinery on the used-equipment market. It is now clear that a depression can set in just because consumption has stopped growing so rapidly, even if it has not dropped off absolutely, but only leveled off at a high level.

Needless to say, the curtailment of production in the machine-producing industries will cause them to shut down, will curtail their income and spending on food and clothing, and lead to still further "multiplier" changes in spending. This might ultimately cause textile sales to stop growing altogether, or even to decline. This will cause a further accelerated drop in net investment. Thus, we may be in a vicious circle whereby the acceleration principle and the multiplier interact so as to produce a cumulative deflationary (or inflationary) spiral.

It is easy to see that in the acceleration principle we have a powerful factor making for economic instability. We have all heard of situations where people have to keep running in order to stand still. In the economic world, matters may be still worse: the system may have to keep running at an ever-faster pace just in order to stand still.

If business sales go up and down, the acceleration principle intensifies their fluctuation. It induces net investment on the upswing but causes about the same amount of net *dis*investment on the downswing. In the long run, if the system is growing because of population increase or higher real incomes, then the acceleration principle works primarily as a stimulating factor: growing national income causes extensive growth of capital, which in turn means that investment demand will be brisk and unemployment relatively low.

The important lesson to be learned from this chapter is that the economic system is more or less without a steering wheel. There is no mechanism or automatic governor which keeps purchasing power right at the full-employment level, neither too low nor too high. On the contrary, even if businessmen and workers are doing their best and are acting intelligently and unselfishly, the system may still be in the throes of inflation or deflation, depending upon the chance circumstances of the complex interaction between investment and saving.

SUMMARY

1. The business cycle is a pulse common to almost all sectors of economic life and to all capitalistic countries. Movements in national income, unemployment, production, prices, and profits are not so regular and predictable as the orbits of the planets or the oscillations of a pendulum, and there is no magical method of forecasting the turns of business activity.

2. However, the four phases of expansion-recession-contraction-revival can be separated out for analysis and can be distinguished from seasonal fluctuations or long-term trends. The resulting pattern of 8- to 10-year major cycles, shorter minor cycles, and longer construction cycles has been carefully described by economists, statisticians, and historians.

3. When it comes to theories to explain the cycle, our first clue is to be found in the greater amplitude of fluctuations of investment or durable capital-goods formation. Although most economists agree on this fact, they differ in their emphasis upon external or internal factors. Increasingly the experts are tending toward a synthesis of external and internal factors, where on the one hand importance is attached to fluctuations in inventions, in population and territorial growth, in gold discoveries and political warfare. On the other hand, economists stress also the way that these external changes in investment opportunities are modified by the multiplier reactions of the economic system, the credit practices of banks, waves of optimism and pessimism, replacement cycles, the acceleration principle which brings in dynamic rates of change as well as levels, and still other feedback effects of income upon investment.

We must now turn to the problem of what can be done to moderate the wild contortions of the cycle, not only to calm it down, but to do so at a level of high employment and long-term growing income. This is the challenge to fiscal policy.

QUESTIONS FOR DISCUSSION

1. What is meant by the business cycle? What are some of the steps that you would follow to measure it?
2. Describe the history of business cycles in this country.
3. Describe the different phases of the cycle.
4. Which theory or theories of the cycle do you like best? Why?
5. Write a two-page explanation of the acceleration principle.

Chapter 18: FISCAL POLICY

AND FULL EMPLOYMENT

WITHOUT INFLATION

WE have seen in earlier chapters that the behavior of saving and investment determines the level of national income and employment. We have seen that private investment often fluctuates widely from year to year and that the same is true of foreign lending. History shows how painful and wasteful the business cycle has been in the past; today everyone is in agreement that, unless we succeed in laying the ghost of instability in the future, American free enterprise will be in jeopardy.

What prescription follows from our economic diagnosis? No single answer can be given; there is no single cure-all for the economic ills of society. Business, labor, and agriculture must all attempt to pursue price and wage policies aimed at maintaining a stable, high-employment economy. The Federal reserve system can also do a little, by way of interest and monetary policy, to prevent an aggravation of the business cycle. But, if all these measures have been tried and they still do not succeed in avoiding the perils of heavy unemployment or extreme inflation, then there is still the public weapon of fiscal policy. This is not to say that fiscal policy, alone, is a cure-all, but it is an important part of any economic program.

The reader is warned that the subject matter of this chapter is still in a controversial stage. While stress has been placed on limitations as well as on advantages of different fiscal policies, it is idle to believe that, in the present inadequate state of our scientific economic knowledge, economists are in agreement as to the importance of the pros and cons. No reader should form his opinions upon the basis of a hasty reading of some superficially persuasive argument.

A. *SHORT-RUN AND LONG-RUN FISCAL POLICY*

By a positive fiscal policy, we mean the process of shaping public *taxation* and public *expenditure* so as (1) to help dampen down the swings of the business cycle and (2) to contribute toward the maintenance of a progressive, high-employment economy free from excessive inflation or deflation.

The war years have shown fiscal policy to be a very powerful weapon. Indeed, some would argue that it is like the atomic bomb, too powerful a weapon to let men and governments play with; that it would be better if fiscal policy were never used. However, it is absolutely certain that, just as no nation will sit idly by and let smallpox decimate the population, so too in every country fiscal policy always comes into play whenever depressions gain headway. There is no choice then but to attempt to lead fiscal policy along economically sound rather than destructive channels. Every government always has a fiscal policy whether it realizes it or not. The real issue is whether this shall be a constructive one or an unconscious, bumbling one.

COUNTERCYCLICAL COMPENSATION VERSUS LONG-RANGE FISCAL POLICY

There are two main programs of fiscal policy. The first is the least controversial and involves nothing more than the attempt to dampen down the amplitude of the business cycle. This is called a purely "countercyclical compensatory," or "anticyclical" fiscal policy. It involves a budget that is balanced over the business cycle. The second and more controversial part of fiscal policy involves long-range action designed to lift the average level of purchasing power and employment throughout the business cycle as a whole; or, if the long-range situation is inflationary, it involves continued action designed to reduce the average level of purchasing power over the whole cycle.

COUNTERCYCLICAL COMPENSATORY POLICY

When private investment shoots up too high, it seems natural to ask that the government should try to compensate by curtailing public investment and expenditure and increasing its tax collections. On the other hand, when private investment and consumption go off into a slump, the government is then to compensate by stepping up its previously postponed expenditures and by reducing its tax collections. According to the countercyclical view, the government budget need not be in balance in each and every month or year; on the contrary, during inflationary times, the budget should show a surplus of tax receipts over expenditures so that the public debt can be reduced. But when bad times come, then the budget should show a deficit of taxes over expenditures, with the public debt returning to its previous level. Only over the whole business cycle need the budget be in balance.

In a nutshell, that is all there is to counter-cyclical compensatory fiscal policy. Stated in this way, it is seen to be a rather conservative doctrine—too conservative, some of the present generation of economists would be inclined to argue.

TYPES OF COUNTERCYCLICAL POLICY

Public Works. This principle of countercyclical finance with respect to public works was introduced into the American system by Herbert Hoover, while he was Secretary of Commerce to Republican President Coolidge. Hoover argued, and rightly, that inasmuch as the government finds it necessary to build a certain amount of roads, hospitals, schools, post offices, etc., then surely it would be better if these projects were intelligently planned so as not all to fall at a time when private construction is booming and manpower is scarce. Instead, they should be postponed until the time when private industry releases materials and men.

In consequence, there will result a relative stabilization of total business activity, since the peak of construction will be cut down and since the depression trough of construction will be at least partly filled in. Not only will jobs be created when needed most, but more than that, the government will be getting its necessary public works at lower prices and through efficient production. All this is so obviously sensible that no one was surprised when in 1931 Hoover and a Democratic Congress passed a law requiring the Federal government to set up a "permanent shelf of public-works projects" with long-range plans and blueprints always at hand, drawn up in such a way as to permit the anticyclical timing of public works.

Figure 1 illustrates how a countercyclical compensatory fiscal policy stabilizes business activity by "chopping off the hills and filling in the valleys." The solid line, *ABCD*, shows the business cycle as it would be if the government did nothing about it and pursued a neutral policy. The dotted line, *A'B'C'D'*, shows the government's budget. Note that this is not in balance in every year, but only over the whole cycle. Note too that the government's activity is just *opposite* in phase to the private cycle, so that it can compensate and dampen down the cycle. The shaded areas show how, as a result, the boom is reduced and how the depression is mitigated. Note too that the black areas are greater than the volume of public expenditure or deficit; this is because the familiar multiplier is at work both in boom and in depression. The final resulting pattern of national income, after the government's compensatory policy, is given by *abcd*, which is much more nearly stable than was the original.

The private economy is not unlike a machine without an effective steering wheel or governor. Compensatory fiscal policy tries to introduce such a governor or thermostatic control device. As shown in the figure, compensatory

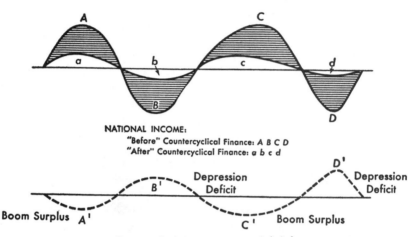

COUNTER CYCLICAL FISCAL POLICY

NATIONAL INCOME:
"Before" Countercyclical Finance: A B C D
"After" Countercyclical Finance: a b c d

Countercyclical PUBLIC FINANCE: A' B' C' D'

FIG. 1. The public budget is supposed to be in balance over the business cycle but not necessarily in every year. Countercyclical finance means reduced spending and higher taxes during boom times to match deficits during depression times.

policy tries to reduce the amplitude of the cycle; it does not necessarily hope to wipe out altogether every bit of fluctuation. Moreover, everyone recognizes that it is very difficult to time our public works exactly as we should want them. We can't simply throw a switch when we want more purchasing power and reverse the dial when we want less. Time is required to get a project under way, especially if it is a big one. Once under way, it would be difficult and expensive to abandon it. Because of these technical difficulties of starting and stopping public works and because we need time to discover whether we are really in a boom or a depression, our ambition must be less pretentious than that of creating 100 per cent stability of national income.

Welfare and Other Expenditure. Fortunately, these difficulties are not insurmountable. Fortunately, too, public-works planning is only one of a number of anticyclical devices. Even without any planning at all, government expenditures on relief and unemployment automatically rise when people get thrown out of work, and automatically tend to fall when jobs again become plentiful.

In country after country all over the world the Great Depression caused budgets to become automatically unbalanced, in part because of an automatic increase in expenditures. Our own 48 states tend to build up in good times an Unemployment Compensation Reserve Fund, less being paid out in benefits to the unemployed than is being collected in payroll taxes. During bad times,

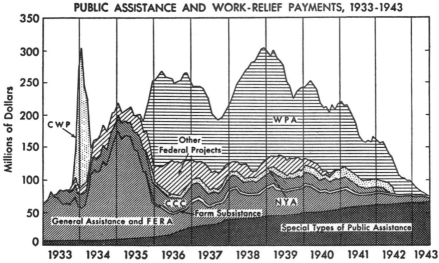

PUBLIC ASSISTANCE AND WORK-RELIEF PAYMENTS, 1933-1943

FIG. 2. SOURCE: *Social Security Bulletin.*

the reverse is true: payments to unemployed workers exceed tax collections, and purchasing power is partly maintained by spending out of the accumulated reserve funds.

During the depressed 1930's, the WPA provided work relief on public projects (schools, swimming pools, road building, writers' and drama projects, etc.). The PWA provided funds for privately contracted Federal and state projects. Home relief was provided for the unemployed and needy. Not all these projects were ideal; some were hastily improvised and unwisely administered. But they did patch up a potentially revolutionary situation and provide for basic human needs, at the same time contributing (with multiplier effects as well) to purchasing power and employment. Figure 2 shows a breakdown of emergency expenditure during the 1930's.

Automatic Changes in Tax Receipts. In addition to public-works expenditure and welfare expenditure, countercyclical compensatory fiscal policy can also rely on cyclically timed tax policies. We have already seen in the earlier chapters on public finance (Chaps. 7 and 8) that our Federal tax system has important income elements in it, so that tax collections tend to vary strongly with national income. Even without Congress or the state legislatures changing any laws, it turns out that governmental tax collections tend to rise automatically when national income rises and to a fall off when national income falls off;[1] and because of the progressive elements in our tax structure, our relative tax collections vary even more sharply than income itself.

A century ago, writers thought that stability of tax revenue was a good thing, and they would have looked with disapproval on the present-day tendency for tax receipts to rise and fall with national income. Today, most believe that the truth is just the reverse. To dampen down a boom, a budgetary surplus is needed. Now there are two ways to produce a surplus: by a reduction in government expenditure, yes; but also by an increase in tax receipts. Indeed, from the standpoint of free private enterprise, tax changes represent the more conservative policy. How lucky we are, therefore, that our present tax system to some degree has "automatic flexibility," with its collections tending to rise in inflationary times and to fall in times of depression. This is a powerful factor stabilizing the whole economy and moderating the business cycle.

Countercyclical Tax-rate Changes. Even this is not all. Congress can also change tax rates. Back before World War I (and still in a few quarters even today), people thought it obviously desirable to balance the budget *in each and every year*. Therefore, they tried to raise tax rates whenever the public was experiencing falling incomes, and to reduce tax rates when incomes were becoming inflated. Once again, the pendulum of expert opinion has swung completely around; today, all but the most conservative students of public finance are opposed to such "preverse flexibility" of tax rates. Those who believe in a countercyclical compensatory fiscal policy argue that the time to reduce tax rates is in depression, when over-all purchasing power is too low; and the time to step up tax rates is during boom times.

Thus taxes as well as expenditures are important for a countercyclical compensatory policy.

LIMITATIONS ON COUNTERCYCLICAL COMPENSATORY POLICY

We have already mentioned (1) some of the difficulties in planning large public-works projects so that they can be quickly got under way or curtailed, and also (2) some of the forecasting difficulties in deciding just exactly when the time has come to step on the gas rather than the brakes. In addition to these

[1] For each 10 billion dollars of change in national income, the collections of our postwar tax system change by more than $2\frac{1}{2}$ billion dollars.

two, there are still other limitations on a perfectly effective countercyclical policy.

Effects on Private Investment.   A third limitation has to do with changes in private investment. For example, some would argue that government expenditure or deficits may not really add much to purchasing power during depressions. If private investment could be assumed constant, then public expenditures would of course have favorable primary effects upon income and employment; more than that, the consumption respending of successive portions of income would give rise to the familiar multiplier chain of favorable secondary effects. What if private investment is frightened off by government expenditure or by the deficit?

This is certainly a possibility. Businessmen may say, "With that man in the White House spending recklessly, we're going to abandon even the little private investment we had planned." Or a private utility company may curtail investment because it fears the threat of public hydroelectric projects. Or when the government spending gives people money to buy in retail stores, the effect in time of deep depression may simply be to permit the merchant to work down his inventory of surplus merchandise; if he does not reorder production goods, the public investment has been just about neutralized by induced private *dis*investment (in inventory) and the multiplier chain is stopped dead in its tracks.

On the other hand, there may be favorable effects on private investment which are just the opposite to these unfavorable repercussions of government finance. When current production is at a low ebb and there is excess plant capacity, no prudent businessman feels like undertaking new capital formation. If the government is able to boost retail sales and the production of consumption goods, then businessmen will have the financial ability and at least some motive to renew equipment and build new plant. (An example of this was provided by the discussion in Chap. 17 of the acceleration principle relating induced investment to the upward change in sales.)

Where there are two such opposing tendencies—favorable and unfavorable effects upon private investment—facts rather than arguments must be our guide. Although economics does not permit us to make controlled experiments to settle the point conclusively, the bulk of the statistical data that have come to the attention of this writer suggests that private investment tends to move on the whole sympathetically with the level of national income. The cash register calls the tune, and in a free-enterprise society, rightly so.

This does not mean that we can neglect unfavorable psychological reactions to deficit financing. But these adverse reactions are of much greater importance in connection with long-range deficit financing than with the purely counter-cyclical case where the budget is balanced over the cycle. We may profitably defer this topic to later sections.

Fiscal Perversity of Local Finance. A fourth limitation on compensatory finance arises from the behavior of state and local governments. Unlike the Federal government, they have a tendency toward a perverse cyclical pattern—borrowing for hospitals and schools in good times and reducing their debts in bad times. This serves to aggravate rather than dampen down the business cycle.

However, it would be unfair to criticize them too harshly for this. The credit of the Federal government actually improves in bad times; also it has the constitutional powers to issue currency and to use the Central Bank to float its loans if Congress deems this necessary. The states and localities, on the other hand, are subject to greater credit difficulties when it comes to borrowing —although in recent years Federal grants-in-aid have been an important source of finance for local public works. Also, states and localities are often hamstrung by constitutional limitations upon their depression borrowing.

On the whole, it is probably too much to expect the states and localities to pursue a militant anticyclical spending policy. But at the very least, we can set for them the goal of being neutral with respect to the cycle rather than aggravating it by buying new fire engines and war monuments during inflation and cutting all services to the bone during depression. Also, it is to be hoped that local governments will avoid *perverse cyclical flexibility* with respect to tax rates, such as introducing deflationary, regressive sales taxes during depression times and cutting income tax rates during prosperity.

The "Pump-priming" Confusion. In addition to the above four criticisms, a number of other limitations upon countercyclical compensatory fiscal policy could be listed. But only one last criticism will be mentioned here. Many people are disappointed to find that *after the government curtails its depression spending, the national income may again fall back to a low level.* Really this is not a criticism of compensatory policy, but rather a case of confusing it with what is popularly called government "pump priming."

When the New Deal was still very new, many people thought that, if the government would only spend a little money, the economy would be lifted from the doldrums and would carry on forever after on its own steam. If only you pour a little water into the pump to prime it, it will repay you with an endless stream of water.

Actually, countercyclical compensatory fiscal policy is as different from pump priming as a gasoline engine is from a perpetual-motion machine. Stop feeding gas and the motor stops; stop eating and you will waste away. So with compensatory finance: public spending may have powerful secondary effects; still, like private investment itself, its effects cease soon after it ceases. In economics, there are few magical ways of getting something for nothing.[1]

So much for the limitations to countercyclical fiscal policy. In conclusion, we may simply note that few people would object in theory to its precepts. What they do occasionally object to is the tendency or danger that what starts out as an innocent-looking countercyclical fiscal policy may turn into a policy of long-range spending. For example, consider the period 1933 to 1938 as a complete cycle. Certainly 1935 and 1937 were in retrospect its best years, and according to the purely countercyclical view should have been years of budgetary surplus. But at the time, with almost 10 million unemployed, putting on the fiscal brakes hardly seemed rational or "political."

LONG-RUN FISCAL POLICY

Let us turn, therefore, to the longer run problem. If we could always be sure of 5 lean years of too small private investment to maintain high employment, followed by 5 fat years in which investments were too large to permit high employment at stable prices, then counter-cyclical finance might be perfect. But what if we move into a postwar era where the years of high boom tend always to *outnumber* those of depression? Then, in such a period of "secular exhilaration," many would argue that the government should not balance the budget over each business cycle. Instead, it should average a "budgetary surplus" (of taxes over expenditure) throughout most of each business cycle and over a long period of years.

This is clearly something quite different from a countercyclical policy aimed at smoothing out fluctuations; it is a policy of *continuous long-run surplus financing* aimed at reducing the average level of purchasing power and inflation.

On the other hand, suppose that the level and fluctuations in private investment were such as to give us a pattern of national income like that shown in Fig. 3. Although our manpower, resources, and know-how are such as to make it possible for the American economy to produce the indicated *potential* pattern of real product, suppose that the balance of saving and investment tends to give the *actual* pattern shown by *ABCDEFG*. The reader can draw in a third line

---

[1] One way of getting a pump-priming situation would be to consider a system where a dollar of expenditure did not create a multiplier chain of $3 = 1 + \frac{2}{3} + (\frac{2}{3})^2 + \cdots$, but rather created a chain of the form: infinity $= 1 + 1 + 1 + 1 + \cdots + 1 + \cdots$. Without any "saving leakages," the pump would give you any amount of water in return for the original amount used for priming.

showing what would be the pattern of income if only a countercyclical smoothing-out policy were pursued. Obviously, there would still be a wastage of resources and product most of the time, even if the contortions of the business cycle were partly ironed out.

Many modern writers would argue for a *long-run policy of full compensation* in such a case. According to them, it would not necessarily be desirable to pull the brakes at *A*, or at *C*, or at *G*. Only at *E* would a strongly contracting spending policy be called for.

PATTERN OF CHRONIC STAGNATION

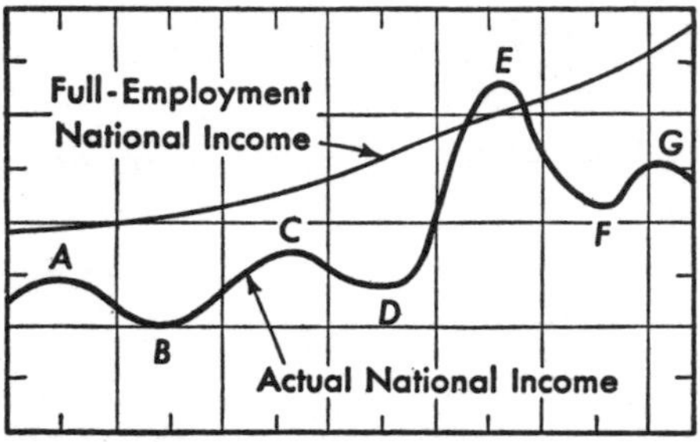

FIG. 3. Hypothetical data to illustrate case where simple countercyclical finance is held inadequate to achieve stable high employment.

According to this new school of fiscal theorists, fiscal policy ought —in such a period of "secular stagnation"—to be expansionary much if not most of the time. Over the business cycle as a whole, the budget might not be in balance, because the lean years would be outnumbering the good ones. As national income grows, so too might the public debt. All this is still controversial, and the reader is warned that many eminent economists are opposed to any policy of continuous deficits.[1]

Long-run surplus financing and long-run deficit financing both differ from a purely countercyclical policy. Which will be appropriate depends upon the happenstance of the long-run balance of saving and investment. Let us first turn to the more pessimistic view of stagnant investment opportunities relative to full-employment saving.

SECULAR STAGNATION?

Countercyclical fiscal policy, with the budget balanced over the cycle, is designed to even out the bumps in business activity, but not to alter the average level of employment very much. Continuous long-run surplus financing is designed to lower the average level of purchasing power in order to curb the inflation that would result from an era of "secular exhilaration" when domestic and foreign investment are tending to run beyond full-employment saving. The third possibility we must now explore: May there not be a tendency in the next few decades for full-employment saving to run ahead of investment

[1] See the lengthy study, "The American Industrial Enterprise System," Vol. II, Chap. XVIII, National Association of Manufacturers, New York, 1946.

opportunities, with the inevitable result of more years of slump than of high employment, of long-lived depressions and brief, anemic recoveries?

Such a view is often called "secular stagnation." It is associated with the name of Prof. Alvin H. Hansen of Harvard University. According to Hansen, dynamic investment is the mainspring of economic fluctuations. As investment shifts to high gear, total demand is high and jobs are plentiful; when the capricious factors making for investment happen to be unfavorable for a long time, the economic system may go through years or decades of considerable unemployment.

So far, almost all economists would agree with Hansen. But a number would get off the band wagon when he goes on to express his opinion that there are a number of long-run factors in the American situation which make it possible or even probable that investment will be a lagging factor relative to full-employment saving. He thinks that a relatively "mature economy" like the United States is especially susceptible to stagnant investment and unemployment. Some of his reasons are as follows:

Investment Prospects.   In the past the principal determinants of investment have been these dynamic—not static!—elements: *rapid population growth, discovery and settlement of new territory*, and *technological innovation*. The geographical frontier is long since gone. Even before World War I the first two of these investment determinants were beginning to slow down. After World War I, and particularly in the decade of the 1930's, almost the full brunt was thrown upon technological innovation. This will be even more true in the decades ahead when immigration and birth rates are sure to be so much less than they were in the nineteenth century.

A full-employment economy, like an airplane, cannot stand still; it must go forward if disaster is to be avoided. An airplane traveling on only one engine instead of three may possibly make out all right, but as a betting proposition the chances of its encountering trouble are increased.

Moreover, Hansen believes that the third dynamic factor behind investment, technological innovation, will go on at a more brilliant pace than ever before in our history, but may to a considerable extent take the form of inventions that *lessen rather than increase the amount of needed investment.* Thus the invention of the airliner may make possible the development of Siberia without billions and billions of dollars of investment in public roads and railroads. The invention of wireless radio or of the multiple-message cable all economize on the tremendous amount of investment needed in capital installations. Atomic energy may minimize the need in many parts of the world for costly hydroelectric reclamation projects. Science gives and takes as far as investment is concerned, and

Hansen thinks there may continue to be—what he believes to have been true of the 1930's—a preponderance of "capital-saving invention."

Personal and Corporate Saving Prospects. Hansen's views with respect to the future of saving round out his theory. He believes that people tend to divide their extra income between consumption and saving. Our incredibly creative scientists and engineers can be expected to increase our full-employment real incomes at a rapid rate. Probably, real wages and productivity will continue to grow at the compound-interest rate of 2 to 3 per cent per year, or even faster than in the past.

If people's tastes and standards of consumption remained the same, this vast increase in income would probably mean an even greater proportionate increase in saving. Fortunately for the prospects of avoiding mass unemployment, people's consumption standards do not remain constant. Their needs and desires are constantly expanding, because of new products invented, because of advertising, because of social custom and imitation.

Throughout all our history the Consumption-income schedule has been shifting upward; the Propensity-to-save schedule has been shifting downward. We now have pretty good statistical records going back more than half a century. These show, rather than an increase in the ratio of saving to income, a remarkable constancy of the proportion which the American people have saved out of past full-employment incomes. Hansen sees no reason why the same should not continue to be true in the years ahead. If rising living standards keep pace with rising productivity, then the percentage of personal saving that has to be offset by investment need not get worse—especially if progressive tax and expenditure policies help to maintain a high consumption economy, and if bold and vigorous attacks on unemployment are effective in forestalling any tendency for people to get frightened into oversaving and to fall behind in their acquiring of higher living standards.

Personal savings are only part of the picture. Increasingly, corporate saving is growing in importance, and here Hansen is less optimistic. It is sound business management for corporations to make full accounting allowances for depreciation and obsolescence; it is sound practice to withhold part of dividends and plow back earnings into a growing business. Hansen thinks that these business savings may be more than enough to finance replacement of capital equipment and new capital formation. And to the extent that corporate investment is completely financed by additional net (or gross) corporate saving, to that extent such investment is not available to offset personal saving and cannot add very much to jobs and purchasing power.

Hansen, who is by nature a confirmed optimist, hopes that the maintenance of continued full employment will cause businessmen to be contented with low unit profits on a high volume of production and with moderate rates of profit and saving.

Some of Hansen's followers are less guarded than he is. Also, there is a sizable body of conservative opinion which is much more pessimistic than he is, in that they agree with him as to the pattern of future and past facts but disagree as to the basic cause of stagnation. They are inclined to attribute the failure of investment in the pre- and postwar to the interference of government with business and to reform legislation. With nations all over the world moving increasingly toward a planned state, and with the American electorate showing a willingness to adjust the minute hand of the clock of history but apparently unwilling to turn the hour hand back toward *laissez faire*, holders of this view naturally tend to be rather despondent.

Before turning to criticisms of the Hansen stagnation thesis, let us beware of one of its common misunderstandings. It is not the growth of our productive potentialities that is believed likely to be stagnant. As Fig. 3 clearly shows, the secular stagnationists believe that our scientists will be more productive than ever—inventing glass neckties and causing 1 man-hour to do the work previously required of 2. As we have seen, Hansen believes that productivity and full-employment production may grow at a compound interest rate, doubling at every generation. The only thing that he thinks is likely to stagnate—if nothing is done about it—is our ability to keep everybody employed so as to realize our potentialities; or to put the matter differently, the level of investment relative to full-employment saving may stagnate in a wealthy, mature economy.

STAGNATION A BOGEY?

By no means are all, or most, economists prepared to regard the stagnation theory as proved or even probable. But surprisingly little vigorous and detailed opposition appeared in print until the Machinery and Allied Products Institute, a federation of trade associations in the industrial equipment field, published a full-size volume entitled "The Bogey of Economic Maturity." This was prepared by George Terborgh, an able economist, and constitutes the fullest reference source for anyone interested in the arguments against the stagnation viewpoint. Without going into details, some of his viewpoints can be briefly mentioned here.

Terborgh believes that the stagnation and mature-economy thesis is a bogey without sound factual or theoretical basis. It is a child of the pessimistic depression period. Prior to 1929, there was little or no evidence of senility of the American economy; and just as one swallow doesn't make a summer, so one depression, even a great one, cannot establish a presumption toward stagnation. Terborgh also believes that the income analysis along saving and investment lines is in itself neutral and establishes no presumption in favor of stagnation. Of course, misuse of the analysis may seem to favor stagnation; *e.g.*, at any time in the past century it would have been difficult to name the industries that would provide us with investment, so that a simple-minded calculator of savings might at any time have come to pessimistic and incorrect conclusions.

Turning to specific facts, Terborgh admits that population growth provides an important quantitative source for investment; but that does not prove that investment would fail to go elsewhere if there were no population growth. Moreover, when population growth slows down, the elderly, retired portion of the population grows in relative importance. Therefore, the slowing down of population growth reduces saving at the same time that it may have diminishing tendencies on investment. Finally, and this is perhaps most important of all, the percentage decline in population has been going on for a century. Why, then, did stagnation not develop years and years ago?

So too with the disappearing frontier. The geographical frontier disappeared in the 1890's. Why no stagnation at that time? Why should new people on new land lead to more investment than new people on old settled land?

Turning to the third source of investment, technological innovation, Terborgh questions the vital importance of a few great and dramatic industries.

The important thing is the total flow of technological development, not its degree of concentration. Given an abundance of rising industries like aviation, mechanical refrigeration, air-conditioning, radio, television, rayon, plastics, quick-freezing, prefabricated housing, light metals, powdered metals, high-octane gasoline, gas turbines, jet propulsion, spun glass, cotton pickers, combined harvesters, electronics—to name only a few at random—the total volume of direct and induced investment can be tremendous. . . . There is . . . no evidence of an increasing proportion of capital-saving innovation.[1]

Terborgh also disbelieves in the bogey of an increase in self-financed business investment. His studies lead him to believe that the Great Depression of the 1930's must be explained in other terms, and that the immediate outlook is a relatively favorable one:

If . . . we suffer from a chronic insufficiency of *consumption and investment combined*, it will not be, in our judgment, because investment opportunity in a physical

[1] GEORGE TERBORGH, "The Bogey of Economic Maturity," pp. 89, 96, Machinery and Allied Products Institute, Chicago, 1945.

and technological sense is persistently inadequate to absorb our unconsumed income; but rather because of political and economic policies that discourage investment justified, under more favorable policies, by these physical factors.[1]

The task of cyclical stabilization is difficult enough without the distraction of stagnationist soothsaying. Even if we renounce the fatuous perfectionism of "sixty million guaranteed jobs," aspiring rather to the more modest immediate goal of relative stability, the task is still difficult. It is not, however, impossible. To its accomplishment, haunted no longer by the demons of economic maturity, we can proceed with courage and resolution.[1]

We shall not attempt here to weigh the relative merits of the stagnation viewpoint. Economic analysis must be prepared to understand the policies called for by stagnation; it must be no less prepared to meet the opposite situation of long-range inflationary conditions. The next section discusses some of these problems and introduces us to some of the important features of our postwar public debt. The final section deals with the problems of an advancing full-employment economy.

SECULAR EXHILARATION, LONG-RUN SURPLUS FINANCING, AND DEBT RETIREMENT

Suppose that private investment demand and the propensity to consume should be so buoyant after the war that the schedules of saving and investment tend to intersect at an income higher than we have the manpower to produce. There would then be a tendency toward "overfull employment." There would be more than a tendency toward inflation, there would be actual inflation. The dollar shrinks in value as prices soar. People want to buy more goods than can be produced; prices are bid up and for the moment may seem to discourage excessive purchases. But the higher prices do not permanently equate supply and demand. The higher prices constitute someone's income—a farmer's, a businessman's, or a worker's. Again demand is excessive, again prices rise, and we have the familiar case of an inflationary spiral which cannot burn itself out so long as the savings and investment schedules fail to intersect at full employment.[2]

There is one thing to do. The government must cut its expenditures in order to reduce purchasing power; it must increase its tax collections so as to produce a surplus. It is not enough to do this for a day or a year; it must continue to run a surplus for as long as total demand remains excessive.

[1] *Ibid.*, pp. 213, 226.
[2] See the earlier discussion of inflation in Chap. 13.

B. *THE PUBLIC DEBT AND POSTWAR FISCAL POLICY*

Under such conditions of secular exhilaration, the Federal debt, which is around 250 billion dollars in 1948, would be gradually retired—not in each and every year, but in all but a few years of depression. If "secular (or long-term) exhilaration" continues for the next few decades, then the debt might be cut at least in half over the next quarter of a century. This is in contrast to a purely countercyclical policy, where the budget is balanced over every cycle and where the debt would dip down every decade to, say, 200 billion dollars and bob back up again to around 250 billion dollars.

Let us analyze the economic process of retiring debt. The government may use its surplus of taxes to retire bonds held by the banks or by the nonbanking public. The second case is the simpler and may be described first.

Retiring Nonbank Debt. Tax collections will reduce people's disposable income, which is just what the doctor orders for inflation. The government could simply let its deposits and cash balances grow at the expense of the rest of the community. More likely, it will use the money to retire bonds and reduce the public debt.

Even if the surplus tax funds are used in this way, the net effect will be deflationary. This is so because the taxes collected directly reduce disposable income and therefore consumption expenditure. But the payment of these taxes to bondholders is a capital rather than a current transaction. They cannot, and ordinarily will not, treat these sums as part of their recurring income to be spent upon consumption, any more than would a man who had sold his house on Wednesday for $15,000 treat that as his day's income.[1]

The public gives up bonds from its lockboxes and mattresses, and in effect it is left with receipted tax bills among its souvenirs. By running the movie camera backward, we see that the disappearance of the debt is an exact reversal of the process by which the war debt was created—out of thin air, so to speak. Instead of taxing the public to pay for battleships and guns, the government in

---

[1] Cashing in of war bonds by relatively poor spenders would, of course, be a different story. Also, using a tax surplus to retire debt may have some downward effects on the interest rate as compared to a policy of letting tax surplus accumulate in the government's bank accounts. Therefore, in an occasional boom period of the type where private investment would respond readily to such an availability of capital funds, the Treasury and the Federal reserve authorities will have to adopt contractionary monetary policies while reducing debt.

effect paid them in government bonds; more precisely, it paid them income which they saved in order to buy bonds.

Retiring Bank Debt. What if the government surplus is used to retire bank-held debt? Then instead of killing off the public's bond assets, we shall be killing off their bank deposits and cash assets. How does this come about? First, I give the government cash or a check to pay my taxes. The government uses its enlarged bank account to buy back a bank-held government bond. The bank loses an asset and at the same time a deposit liability. The public ends up permanently with smaller bank deposits or currency.[1]

In short, retiring bank-held public debt would kill off a substantial part of our supply of money, by exactly reversing the process whereby our wartime expansion of debt vastly increased our supply of deposits and currency. Retiring nonbank government bonds will kill off an important part of the public's holdings of liquid government bonds. Thus, we see how reducing 125 billion dollars, or half of the war debt, would halve the public's liquid wealth (currency, deposits, or government securities).

The Debt and the Propensity to Consume. In fact, after the debt had been dropping for a long time, people might finally begin to feel so poor as to cause the propensity to consume to fall far enough to end secular exhilaration—at which point large surplus tax collections would cease to be defensible.

Nobody knows how important would be the depressing effects upon consumption of a reduction in people's assets of financial wealth, or how significant upon consumption spending has been the great wartime growth of the public debt. The answer depends in part upon whether poor people who are ready spenders hold appreciable amounts of government bonds. It also depends upon whether people's income rather than their wealth most importantly influences consumption, and upon whether people tend to save more or less once they have accumulated a certain amount of saving. It is a little ironical that some writers who were most critical of deficit financing before the war are now the most ardent champions of the notion that the individual postwar holding of government bonds will increase consumption and prosperity.

Debt Retirement and Interest. As another effect of debt retirement, the 5 billion dollars of interest, which the government must now annually pay out to

---

[1] For every 5 billion dollars of bonds bought from the commercial banks, the Treasury will have to buy 1 billion dollars from the 12 Federal Reserve Banks. This is in order to reduce commercial-bank reserve balances in step with their reduced deposits and to keep "excess reserves" from coming into being. The reader is referred to the discussion of central banking in Chap. 15 to refresh his memory on this exact reversal of the wartime pattern.

bondholders, might be considerably reduced. It is true that in 1947 this transfer payment amounted to less than 3 per cent of the national income, but nevertheless every dollar of government expense saved makes possible just that much lower taxes or increased expenditure elsewhere.

Even if the debt were cut in half over the next 25 years, the interest charges on the debt would not have to fall by an equal proportion. The cries of anguish of banks, insurance companies, widows, universities, and other coupon clippers would probably combine with the concomitant brisk demand of business investors to force some upward revision in interest rates. Because of the paradox that the government's credit (as measured by the interest rate that it must pay on its loans) improves in depressed times and deteriorates in good, the average rate of interest on the public debt might increase from today's 2 per cent to 3 or 4 per cent. Thus a halving of the debt could conceivably be fully canceled out by a doubling of the interest rate, with no appreciable change in total interest charge. However, if technological progress and population growth continue to cause our real national product almost to double every generation, then even 5 billion dollars of interest charges would fall to less than 2 per cent of the national income.

THE PUBLIC DEBT AND ITS LIMITATIONS

Now that we have surveyed the effects of retiring the public debt, we are in a good position to analyze some of its economic disadvantages and advantages.

In appraising the burdens involved in a public debt, we must carefully avoid the unscientific practice of making up our minds in advance that whatever is true of one small merchant's debt is also necessarily true of the government's debt. Prejudging the problem in this way might come perilously close to the logical fallacy of composition; and, instead of permitting us to isolate the true— all too real!—burdens of the public debt, might only confuse the issue.

External versus Internal Debt. A large *external* public debt, owed to people outside of the United States, would be a real burden and limitation upon the American economy. This is because as a nation we would be forced to ship valuable goods and services abroad to meet the interest charges on the external debt and possibly to amortize some of its principal. If 10 per cent of the national income had to go abroad in this way, the burden would be—if not an intolerable one—nevertheless a weighty one. The American people would have to work harder and longer, and they would have to do without.

There are also burdens involved in an internally held public debt like our present one, *but the burdens of an internal debt are qualitatively and quantitatively different from those of an external debt.* This is the first and most important lesson to be grasped, without which nobody can go far in understanding the economics of the public debt. The interest on an internal debt is paid by Americans to Americans; there is no *direct* loss of goods and services. When interest on the debt is paid out of taxation, there is no *direct* loss of disposable income; Paul receives what Peter loses, and sometimes—but only sometimes—Paul and Peter are one and the same person.

Borrowing and Shifting Economic Burdens through Time. Still another confusion between an external and internal debt is involved in the often-met statement: "When we borrow rather than tax in order to fight a war, then the true economic burden is really being shifted to the future generations who will have to pay interest and principal on the debt." As applied to an external debt, this shift of burden through time might be true. It is unmistakably false in reference to an internal debt. Why?

To fight a war now, we must hurl present-day munitions at the enemy; not dollar bills and not future goods and services. If we borrow munitions from some neutral country and pledge our children and grandchildren to repay them in goods and services, then it may truly be said that external borrowing permits a shift of economic burden between present and future generations.

But suppose there is no outside nation to lend us goods. Suppose that our direct controls have cut civilian capital formation down to the bone, but still our government needs more resources for the war effort. Suppose that Congress is not willing to vote taxes large enough to permit the government to balance its swollen budget or stringent enough to reduce people's spending to where they will release resources for the war effort and stop bidding up prices. The government will then be running a deficit and will build up a huge debt. (It may also have to pass price-control and rationing laws, but that need not concern us here.)

Can it be truthfully said that "internal borrowing shifts the war burden to future generations while taxing places it on the present generation"? A thousand times no! The present generation must still give up resources to produce the munitions hurled at the enemy. In the future, some of our grandchildren will be giving up goods and services to other grandchildren. That is the nub of the matter. The only way in which we can impose a direct burden on the future nation as a whole is by incurring an external debt or by passing along less capital equipment to our posterity.

This explains why the British are a great deal more worried about their small external debt than they are over their vastly greater internal debt; the former directly impoverishes the British Isles. Fortunately, the United States has come out of the most costly war in all history with little impairment of capital equipment and external debt.

"We All Owe It to Ourselves."   If an internal debt is simultaneously owed and owned by Americans, why do some people think that the wartime creation of 250 billion dollars of government bonds makes the public more wealthy and more ready to spend? If we draw up a consolidated balance sheet for the nation as a whole, we see that the (internal) debt represents a kind of fictitious financial wealth, which cancels out as a liability and asset.

Even purely financial assets have important effects. Every citizen who owns government bonds includes them when drawing up his periodic balance sheet, along with his other assets. But he is a very rare man indeed if he also includes as a present liability the amount of *future* taxes which he may have to pay to finance government interest payments or debt retirement. He does not even have a way of estimating his share of these taxes. The result is that the internal debt, which as a liability should exactly cancel out itself as an asset, tends instead to be counted by people primarily as an asset. Given a nest egg of bonds which they can either sell or cash in, people *feel* richer and more secure and perhaps, therefore, tend to have a higher propensity to consume out of current income.

Debt Management and Monetary Policy.   The existence of a large outstanding public debt may also have an influence on the interest rate and on its use to fight the business cycle. Some writers fear that channeling investment funds into the purchase of government bonds will raise the rate of interest to private borrowers. Alexander Hamilton, the spokesman of the conservative Federalist party, had just the opposite opinion. He felt that, rightly managed and in the right amounts, a public debt would be "a national blessing" because it would provide a secure gilt-edge asset that would give businessmen an income and enable them to trade for smaller profits.

As was shown in Chap. 16 on Central Banking, the Federal reserve authorities have strong powers to regulate rates of interest on government bonds. Therefore, any undue upward or downward pressure of the debt upon interest rates can be offset by open-market purchases and sale of government securities. But, and this is an ironic paradox, the existence of the vast public debt, while it enhances their power, at the same time serves to inhibit the exercise of effective monetary and interest policy by the Federal Reserve Banks.

It will be recalled that monetary policy is supposed to act so as to raise interest rates and tighten credit conditions when over-all demand threatens to be inflationary. But with large amounts of bonds in the hands of banks and the public, the governmental authorities have a strong incentive toward keeping up the selling price of government bonds—in order to keep interest charges on the debt low and prevent financial embarrassment of financial institutions holding government bonds. If government bonds cannot fall in price, then interest rates cannot be tightened; people and banks are always able to convert their bonds into the cash they need for consumption or investment spending. A large debt, therefore, tends to discourage the use of monetary policy to control the business cycle and serves to throw an even larger burden on fiscal policy.[1] It is true that many modern writers do not think that this is much of an evil, since interest rate changes are supposed to have minor influence on consumption and investment expenditure; but still it is an evil.

The True Indirect Burden of Interest Charges. When taxes are used to pay interest charges on the public debt, then money goes from one pocket into another. No direct burden like that of an external debt is involved. But it would be wrong to jump to the hasty conclusion that no burden of any kind is involved. There is an indirect burden which may be very important.

In the first place, although money merely goes out from one pocket and into another, the trousers in question may be worn by different people. The present national debt is very widely held, so that almost every individual has some share, either through outright holdings or through bank deposits and insurance policies. Nevertheless, the statistical evidence suggests that the people who receive bond interest are *on the average* not in the lower income brackets. Thus interest on the public debt constitutes a regressive (Robin Hood in reverse) element in our fiscal system. "Soaking the poor to pay the rich" tends to reduce purchasing power and runs counter to many modern notions of equity. Nevertheless, it is a necessary evil if past commitments with respect to the public debt are to be scrupulously honored, as they must be.

However, with our present public debt this transfer from one income class to another is probably not its single most important indirect burden. More important, *transferring tax money from Peter to pay bond interest to the same Peter will involve a heavy indirect burden on the economy!* This is because taxation always has some distorting effects on people's economic behavior. Centuries ago houses were taxed on their windows, with the result that people built dark houses, even though the government still collected the same revenue by simply raising rates on the few remaining windows. Similarly, taxing people's

---

[1] The effects upon consumption of the large outstanding amount of government bond assets may make matters worse. Consumption becomes less responsive to disposable income and may become more changeable. Fiscal policy then has more work to do and has less leverage to do it.

income may cause them to work too little, or in many cases too hard, in their attempt to maintain the same standard of living. Perhaps of even more importance, high corporation or personal income taxes will often have adverse effects upon people's willingness to venture their capital on risky enterprises. The result: less technological progress and fewer jobs.

At this point, the reader may protest that this is all nonsense and that there is no net tax burden involved in an internal transfer since it is being assumed that we all own bonds in proportion to our share of taxes, and in effect are only paying to ourselves. This reasoning is quite mistaken. *Taxes on each individual matched by exactly equal interest payments to him do not cancel out!*

This is so because what is true of all is not true for each individual. Suppose for simplicity that all Americans earn $4,500 a year in wages. Suppose that each owns $25,000 in government bonds, which at 2 per cent bring in a yield of $500 per year. To pay this interest the government, let us say, adds 10 per cent (in addition to existing taxes) on total income of $5,000 ($4,500 + $500). Previously it just paid me to work an extra bit of overtime to earn the last dollar of my $5,000. But now the government takes another dime out of that dollar. I (and every American like me) may now feel that it doesn't pay to work such long hours. By cutting out, say, one-third of my working hours, my income is now only $3,500. The tax has distorted national effort and production.

The unconvinced reader will say at this point: "What if everybody else does what you do? Then the extra tax rate will have to be raised from 10 per cent to almost 15 per cent if the total of bond interest is to be covered." True enough. But this only proves the point. The final situation may end up with even a greater distortion of effort and risk taking, and with an even higher tax rate. This all happens because, although the nation cannot avoid raising taxes equal to the interest payment, each individual knows that he can affect his taxes by varying his effort, with his own small interest payments going on anyway, regardless of what he or a single small person does.

The above example is oversimplified and undoubtedly exaggerates the harmful effects of internal transfers. Also, different kinds of taxes differ in their harmful effects, but in any case with our taxes already so high, any further burden due to interest on the public debt is just that much more harmful.

Moreover, we have neglected the beneficial effects of interest payments to banks, universities, widows, and other *rentiers*. If there were no public debt or if interest rates were to fall substantially, then (1) charitable institutions would have to be supported by public and private current contributions more than by interest on perpetual endowments, (2) social security and annuities would have to take the place of *rentier* interest, and (3) service charges by banks would have to be increasingly relied upon instead of government bond interest.

THE QUANTITATIVE PROBLEM OF THE DEBT

We may summarize the above section on the economics of a public debt as follows: (1) Our internal debt does not involve the direct burden of an external debt nor the same possibility of shifting real burdens between generations. (2) Although we all owe it to ourselves, people tend to treat bonds as a safe liquid asset which increases their willingness to consume out of current income. The huge volume of outstanding debt hampers an anticyclical interest rate policy because the authorities are loath to see bond prices fluctuate. (3) An internal debt involves an important *indirect* burden whenever new taxes have to be raised to meet interest payments. This would be true even if the typical person was taxed by as much as his own interest payments, but it is further aggravated by the fact that interest receivers appear to be somewhat more wealthy than average taxpayers.

To assess the importance of the public debt, we must turn to the facts. Do interest payments on it swallow up most of the national income? How does the total of all interest payments, public and private, compare with past years and with the experience of other countries? What about foreseeable future trends?

In Chap. 7 (Fig. 1, page 151) the historic growth of our national debt was pictured.[1]

To see how the present quarter of a trillion dollar debt compares with the past and some other countries, Table 1 has been drawn up. It shows for selected times and places the size of national debts and their relationship to size of national income and interest payments. Thus, early in 1947 our national debt of 257 billion dollars represented less than $1\frac{1}{2}$ years of national income, and its interest payments represented less than 3 per cent of national income. Note that England, in 1818, 1923, and 1946 had an internal debt estimated at more than twice national income, and her interest on the debt as a percentage of national income far exceeded anything that we need look forward to. Yet, the

---

[1] The approximate ownership of the total of 257 billion dollars of outstanding Federal debt early in 1947 was as follows (in billions of dollars):

Commercial and mutual savings banks	$84
Federal Reserve Banks	24
Insurance companies	25
Individuals	64
Corporations and miscellaneous	23
Federal, state, and local governments	37

About 51 billion dollars of the total was in the form of familiar United States savings bonds.

century before World War I was England's greatest century—greatest in power and material progress. Nevertheless, as the table shows, her national debt was not substantially reduced; but with the steady growth of her national income, the debt and its interest charges shrank to almost nothing in relative quantitative magnitude.

TABLE 1. *National Debt and Interest Charges Relative to National Income*

Year	National debt	Interest charges on national debt	National income	Size of debt in years of national income	Interest charges as a per cent of national income
				(5) =	(6) ÷ 100 =
(1)	(2)	(3)	(4)	(2) ÷ (4)	(3) ÷ (4)
United States:	(Billions)	(Billions	(Billions)		
1947*	$257	$5	$200	1.3	2.5
1939	34.9	0.97	68.5	0.5	1.4
1932	18.2	0.64	46.7	0.4	1.4
1929	15.1	0.67	79.5	0.2	0.8
1920	23.5	1.06	68.4	0.3	1.5
1916	1.2	0.02	38.7	0.0+	0.0+
1868	2.6	0.13	6.8	3.8	2.0
Britain:	(Millions)	(Millions)	(Millions)		
1946*	£24,500	£500	£8,000	3.1	6.2+
1923	7,700	271	3,800	2.0+	7.1
1913	656	17	2,300	0.3	0.7
1818	840	31	400	2.1	7.7

SOURCE: "Economic Almanac," Department of Commerce, U.S. Treasury; "Colwyn Report," Statistical Abstract of United Kingdom. Data rounded off.
    * Estimated.

In view of these statistics and careful qualitative analysis, it is perhaps fair to conclude that the national debt does not yet constitute a problem of the first magnitude in comparison with the problem of the peace, the atomic bomb, or unemployment. Whether productivity will continue to rise in the future, whether labor and management can learn to bargain collectively without strikes and inflation—all these are more important than the debt itself.

Yet there is a tremendous amount of emotion involved in people's attitudes toward the debt, and this we must not dismiss lightly. Like sex or religion, the public debt is a subject that it does little good to argue about, and yet nobody can help doing so. Many people used to predict the end of the world when the debt reached one-hundredth, one-tenth, and one-fifth of its present level; each year when the dire disaster had not appeared, they renewed their predictions for the following years.

In dispassionately analyzing the growth of the debt, one error we must avoid: *we must not forget that the real national product of the United States is an ever-growing thing.*

Population increase has slowed down some, but for a long time our numbers will continue to grow. As to productivity, there is absolutely no indication that man-hour efficiency and new techniques have begun to slacken off. Upon this, stagnationists and exhilarationists both agree. What seemed like a big debt in 1790 would be nothing today. What our children will come to regard as a big debt, our great grandchildren may consider relatively unimportant.

This explains why England and France, in the crucially formative years of the capitalistic system and industrial revolution, were able to go on—not only decade after decade but almost century after century with their budgets in balance less than half the time. This same factor of growth explains why in the United States, where real national production doubles every generation or so, the public debt might increase by 250 billion dollars in 25 years without its relative percentage burden growing.

This would give the wildest believer in government spending an average deficit of some 10 billion dollars per year before he would have to turn to such even more unorthodox financial expedients as printing money or selling interest-free bonds to the Federal Reserve Banks. Moreover, before turning to such expedients, he would still have open to him the now familiar process of forcing down interest rates on government bonds by a conventional easy-money banking policy.

In short, there is no technical financial reason why a nation fanatically addicted to deficit spending should not pursue such a policy for the rest of our lives, and even beyond. The real question is only whether such a policy will impinge on an economy that is inflationary or deflationary. So long as private and government spending are only enough to offset saving, that is one thing. If a nation or Congress is misguided enough to continue heavy spending and light taxing after total consumption and private investment have become too large, then inflation will be the outcome.

USEFUL VERSUS WASTEFUL FISCAL POLICY

Those who believe in an active fiscal policy set up a perfectionist goal: the maintenance of total effective demand at a level high enough to prevent the wastes of mass unemployment, and low enough so as not to lead to a level of inflationary total spending in excess of total producible goods.

Or, to put the matter in technical terms, they argue that fiscal policy should shape taxes and expenditure, quantitatively and qualitatively, so that the economy's Saving and Investment schedules will intersect neither to the right nor to the left of the region of high (or full) employment. Many equally competent economists insist that there are other goals of equal or greater importance.

It cannot be repeated too often that building pyramids or digging holes and filling them up is indefensible. True, in comparison with a policy of doing nothing about a deep depression, such boondoggling might seem in some ways preferable, because of the favorable responding effects of those who receive government expenditures. But such a policy is surely only the lesser of two evils. Properly planned useful public works have just as favorable secondary effects, and in addition they fill important human needs.

Nor is it necessary or always desirable to fight a depression with useful public works. If the American people feel that private consumption should have a higher social priority, tax reduction or transfer expenditure should be relied upon. The extra income available from the conquest of unemployment will then be going for privately produced and purchased goods.

Which of the alternatives of government expenditure or tax reduction should be followed if private investment and consumption are lacking? The answer should not be given simply in terms of financial orthodoxy: the size of the deficit.[1] It should be given in terms of what the American people consider to be the pressing postwar social priorities. If 10 billion dollars of resources were to be released from investment purposes, the American people would wish to use part of this for extra food, extra clothes, extra leisure, etc. This suggests tax reduction (or increase in transfer expenditure).

But the American people may also want to spend part of their newly available income on education, on public health, on urban redevelopment projects, on roads, etc. This suggests some use of government expenditure in depressed times.

The one way that the American people should not want to spend their

---

[1] The reader is referred to the Appendix to this chapter, which analyzes in quantitative terms four different paths to full employment.

income is upon involuntary unemployment. There should never be any need to indulge in wasteful or inefficient government expenditure; the government should always get something useful for the resources it uses up. If collective consumption projects have a lower social priority than private consumption, then the proper fiscal policy is one of tax reduction and transfer expenditure.

A FUNDAMENTAL DIFFICULTY WITH FULL EMPLOYMENT

One last and important set of qualifications must be made before completing the discussion of fiscal policy and, indeed, of the whole problem of national income determination. In a rough way, we know what is meant by full or high employment; but only in a rough way.

Of course, full employment doesn't mean that every man, woman, and child should be out at work every hour of a 24-hour day. It doesn't mean that I can hold out for a job as pitcher with the New York Yankees, or as a $100-a-day carpenter. But it does mean that reasonably efficient workers, willing to work at the currently prevailing ("fair") wage rates, need not find themselves unemployable as a result of too little general demand. Women who want to do so can work in the home, youths can go to school if they prefer to, and the aged or unwell can retire from the labor force; but none of these are to be forced to do so because of job shortages.

The real difficulty with full employment lies not in its rough definition but in the fact that *wages and prices may begin to soar while there is still considerable unemployment and excess capacity.* An increase in private investment spending or in government spending may be prevented from effectuating full employment, its favorable dollar effects being wasted by a paper rise in prices.

If businessmen and trade-unions react perversely to an increased demand, fiscal policy cannot be relied upon to achieve and maintain full employment. Some pessimists have argued that there is nothing to do but hope for a large enough "army of the unemployed" to keep laborers from making unreasonable wage demands; thus, a reserve army of 10 million jobless hanging around factory gates might keep wages from rising and labor from becoming obstreperous. Still others might see no escape from the dilemma other than to have some degree of inflation most of the time.

Still other writers would then advocate the use of direct price and wage controls to keep prices from spiraling upward at high employment levels. In the present writer's personal opinion, efficient peacetime over-all price controls would involve a degree of planning incompatible with past, and perhaps present, philosophical beliefs of the great majority of the American people. For, as we shall see in Part Three, the problem of setting appropriate social prices is a tremendously complex one—so complex that the whole nature of our economic system would have to be different, once we had decided not to rely upon market forces.

It is hardly too much to say that this price-wage question is the biggest unsolved economic problem of our time: *Can business, labor, and agriculture learn to act in such a way as to avoid inflation whenever private or public spending brings us anywhere near to full employment?* A wage and price policy for full employment—that is America's greatest problem and challenge.

THE EMPLOYMENT ACT OF 1946

Obviously no one has a crystal ball to read the future, particularly the distant future. The case for and against secular stagnation cannot be definitively assessed. But fortunately—and this requires great emphasis—it is not necessary for Congress or the experts to be able to see a decade or more into the future in order to pursue correct economic policies currently.

In the momentous Employment Act of 1946, both political parties in Congress affirmed the responsibility of the government, and of private enterprise, to fight mass unemployment and inflation. This law provided for a Council of Economic Advisers which each year is to keep Congress and the President informed as to the state of "employment, production, and purchasing power"; also a Joint Congressional Committee is set up whose duty it is to study and evaluate the recommendations contained in the President's Annual Economic Report.

By itself, fiscal policy is not enough to create a healthy state of stable high employment with rising productivity and efficient use of economic resources in production. In fact, the eight chapters of Part Three are concerned with the proper relations of prices and different branches of production in a world where the problem of over-all effective demand is nonexistent. If ever the curse of general inflation or deflation has been banished, there will rise to the top of our national policy agenda—and properly so—the true and abiding universal economic problems which every economic society has had to face since the Garden of Eden.

SUMMARY

A. SHORT-RUN AND LONG-RUN FISCAL POLICY

1. Fiscal policies with respect to government spending and taxing fall into two categories: the less controversial problem of countercyclical compensatory spending aimed simply at ironing out the worst swings of the business cycle but not at altering the average level of spending over the whole cycle; and long-run fiscal policy aimed at raising or lowering the average level of income so as to maintain high employment without inflation.

2. Four aspects of a countercyclical policy involve (*a*) careful planning of public-works projects; (*b*) proper timing of welfare and other government spending; (*c*) quasi-automatic changes in tax collections brought about by income changes even with no alterations in tax rates; (*d*) quantitative (and qualitative) changes in tax rates so as to increase tax receipts in prosperity and decrease them in bad times.

The reader should be acquainted with the difficulties of countercyclical finance, and appreciate the difference between it and the special theory of pump priming.

3. We go beyond the realm of countercyclical finance when we argue for a long-run policy of tax surplus and debt retirement if there should turn out to be a postwar era of excessive total demand, *i.e.*, an era of secular exhilaration.

4. If, instead of there being too much demand, there should turn out to be unemployment and too little "offsets to saving," the same reasoning would advocate a long-run increase in the average level of government spending, or decrease in tax collections. It would not insist upon the budget's necessarily being balanced over the cycle, arguing that the public debt will grow with the growth of the whole economy.

B. DEBT AND POSTWAR POLICY

5. The reader should understand the economic effects of debt reduction and also the economics of an internal debt: (*a*) the difference between the direct burden of an external and internal debt, and the ability of a country to shift burdens through time in the two cases; (*b*) the effect of the public debt on people's financial wealth and consumption habits; (*c*) the difficulties created by the debt for a countercyclical interest rate policy because of the desire of government authorities to stabilize bond prices; (*d*) the important indirect

burden of collecting taxes to pay interest on a debt, even if we all owe it to ourselves.

It is important, also, to know roughly what the size of the postwar Federal debt is in relation to national income and interest charges, in order to assess the present, both in terms of the past and in terms of the future. The growth of the debt must be appraised in terms of the growth of the economy as a whole.

6. A full (or high) employment program has as its goal a level of total spending which is neither too little nor too great—so that the Saving and Investment schedules intersect in the region of full employment. The Employment Act of 1946 represents an important innovation in our national government, affirming responsibility of the government for employment opportunities and setting up executive and congressional machinery for policy action.

7. Our economy is still confronted with the dilemma that any approach to full employment—whether brought about publicly or privately—may be followed by wage increases and price rises even before unemployment disappears or idle capacity comes into use. A wage-price policy for full employment provides a fundamental challenge to our mixed system of private enterprise and public responsibility.

QUESTIONS FOR DISCUSSION

1. "No nation can avoid having a fiscal policy. With the government such an important part of the present-day economy, it is almost impossible even to define a 'neutral fiscal policy.' It is even harder to give rational reasons for preferring such a policy to an active fiscal program aimed at preventing inflation and deflation." Subject this statement to critical examination, possibly bringing in some noneconomic considerations.

2. Draw up a list of new college buildings and projects that might be made part of a planned countercyclical program. What would some of the difficulties and disadvantages be in carrying this out?

3. What phase of the business cycle are you now in? What taxation policies would seem appropriate? what expenditure policies?

4. Qualitatively, how would you vary the relative importance of different kinds of taxes (such as income tax rates and exemptions, sales tax rates, or property taxes) so as to compensate for unemployment or inflation?

5. From the early 1870's to the middle 1890's, depressions were deep and prolonged, booms were short-lived and relatively anemic, the price level was declining. What long-run fiscal policy do you think should have been followed in that quarter of a

century? Would your answer be the same for the following 20 years leading up to World War I, a period of rising prices and comparative prosperity?

6. Show step by step how the wartime growth of the public debt caused bank deposits and the public's liquid wealth to expand. Show how contraction of the debt would exactly reverse this process.

7. Comment on the following quotation from the English historian of the last century, Lord Macaulay:

"At every stage in the growth of that debt the nation has set up the same cry of anguish and despair. At every stage in the growth of that debt it has been seriously asserted by wise men that bankruptcy and ruin were at hand. Yet still the debt went on growing; and still bankruptcy and ruin were as remote as ever. . . .

"The prophets of evil were under a double delusion. They erroneously imagined that there was an exact analogy between the case of an individual who is in debt to another individual and the case of a society which is in debt to a part of itself. . . . They made no allowance for the effect produced by the incessant progress of every experimental science, and by the incessant efforts of every man to get on in life. They saw that the debt grew; and they forgot that other things grew as well as the debt."

8. Professor A. P. Lerner has set down the following (abbreviated) principles of "Functional Finance." Criticize:

"There are effective instruments in the hands of the government for maintaining full employment and preventing inflation, but their use is hindered by strong prejudices. The instruments are not available until it is recognized that the size of the national debt is relatively unimportant, that the interest on the debt is not a burden on the nation, and that the nation cannot be made "bankrupt" by internally held debt. Every debt has a corresponding credit. Only external debt is like individual debt and impoverishes the nation. The purpose of taxation is never to raise money but to leave less in the hands of the taxpayer. . . . There is no room for the *principle* of balancing the budget . . . ."

9. "Say what you will, graft keeps money in circulation and gets things done." What do you say?

10. The Council of Economic Advisers to the President, in its first report under the Employment Act of 1946, questions that "we can always create full employment by pumping enough purchasing power into the system," and the doctrine that we have only to "turn the faucet off and cause a contraction." According to the Council Report, " . . . we cannot assume that deficiency of demand in one particular area or of one particular character can be made up just by adding purchasing power in general, for instance through tax relief. . . . If labor is pricing itself out of jobs or manufacturers and farmers are pricing themselves out of a market, or capital is pricing itself out of investment, the basic remedy is the correction of these specific situations, not the injection of some aggregate purchasing power in a dose measured in size to offset an estimated future total of unemployment."

With how much of this would you agree? Why?

APPENDIX TO CHAPTER 18
FOUR QUANTITATIVE PATHS TO FULL
EMPLOYMENT

Concrete numbers often help to illustrate an abstract argument. In this section, four hypothetical quantitative paths to full employment are presented. They are by no means the only ones; but being oversimplified, pure cases, each exemplifies a different portion of the problem.

The first route is the private-enterprise maintenance of high employment: through good luck or policies, it turns out that private consumption and private net investment are just large enough to lead to full employment. This is by all odds the simplest and, to most of us, the best way to have full employment.

But what if private investment is too small? What are other approaches to full employment? The other three paths are designed to illustrate how a given deficiency of private investment may be countered: by an increase in government spending on goods and services alone, by a reduction in net taxes alone, or by a balanced increase in both spending and taxes.

In each of these last three cases, private net investment has been arbitrarily written down by 10 billion dollars, purely for quantitative illustration; this is not intended as a realistic prediction, since there is reason to be more optimistic in the immediate postwar years and since the different fiscal policies might have different effects upon private investment.

Let us turn to Table 2. It has eight lines altogether. Line 1 in every case represents a full-employment *net national product* of 200 billion dollars (at 1947 market prices). Lines 5, 6, and 7 give the breakdown of this NNP into the three components of consumption, private net capital formation or investment, and government expenditure on goods and services (including state and local).

This last government expenditure item definitely excludes all government transfer payments such as relief, veterans' bonuses, and bond interest. These transfer payments which give people money rather than taking it away from them are just like negative taxes. Therefore, all transfer payments have been subtracted from all tax collections to arrive at what is called "net" taxes or withdrawals and are shown in line 3. This means that, in Model I when government expenditure on goods and services is just balanced by "net" taxes or withdrawals at a level of 30 billion dollars, this really corresponds to a combined Federal, state, and local governmental budget of that much plus more than a dozen billion dollars of transfer payments as well.

TABLE 2. *Four Paths to Full Employment* (*In billions of 1947 dollars*)

Line and item	Model I, private investment boom	Model II, deficit spending	Model III, tax-reduction deficit	Model IV, balanced budget
1. Net national product (at 1947 market prices).............	$200	$200	$200	$200
2. Less net corporate saving......	−6	−6	−6	−6
3. Less "net" taxes (total state, local, and Federal taxes and social insurance contributions minus all govt. transfer expenditure).................	**−30**	**−30**	**−17½**	**−80**
4. Disposable income (line 1 − line 2 − line 3).............	164	164	176½	114
5. Consumption expenditure (varies 80 cents for every $1 variation in disposable income)....	$148	$148	$158	$108
6. Private net capital formation (arbitrarily taken as constant).	**22**	**12**	**12**	**12**
7. Government expenditure on goods and services (excludes transfers such as relief and interest)..................	**30**	**40**	**30**	**80**
8. Government deficit (line 7 − line 3)....................	$ 0	$ 10	$ 12½	$ 0

Lines 6, 7, and 3 appear in bold-faced type because investment is assumed to be an arbitrary number in each model and because government spending and taxing are assumed arbitrarily as the definition of each model.

How do we arrive at consumption? Here we must first know what people's disposable income will be and then their propensity to consume out of disposable income. To get disposable income in line 4, we must always subtract from NNP in line 1 the net corporate saving (line 2) and the "net" taxes or withdrawals (line 3). Throughout, net corporate saving (or plowed-back undistributed profits) has been made to depend on NNP and to be equal to 6 billion dollars.

Now that we have disposable income, what about the propensity to consume? A fairly optimistic assumption is made that at 164 billion dollars of disposable income, there will be as much as 148 billion dollars of consumption; and that for every dollar variation of disposable income there will be $\frac{4}{5}$ of a dollar "marginal propensity" for consumption to change. Our assumptions are now complete.

Model I: *Private Enterprise, Full Employment.* In the first path, government expenditure (line 7) and "net" taxes (line 3) are both 30 billion dollars. Disposable income (line 4) is therefore (6 + 30) billion dollars less than the 200 billion dollars of NNP, or 164 billion dollars. According to the propensity to consume, consumption (line 5) is 148 billion dollars. Therefore, private net capital formation to maintain full employment (line 6) must necessarily be 22 billion dollars (200 − 148 − 30). By definition, there is a zero deficit, as can be seen by comparing lines 7 and 3.

If net investment were to fall below 22 billion dollars, say, to fall by as much as 10 billion dollars, then what would happen? If no legislative action were taken, NNP would, of course, fall and, because of the multiplier, by a good deal more than 10 billion dollars.[1] The next three models are designed to show what can be done to prevent this from happening.

Model II: *Deficit-spending Path to Full Employment.* In this model, taxes do not change. Government expenditure on goods and services simply goes up by 10 billion dollars to counter the 10-billion-dollar drop in private investment. Except for lines 6 and 7, the second column of figures is just like the first. But now, of course, there is a 10-billion-dollar deficit.

Model III: *Tax-reduction Path to Full Employment.* Here, taxes are cut (or transfer expenditure increased) until people's disposable income has grown enough to induce them to increase their consumption by as much as the 10-billion-dollar decline in investment. The government's use of resources remains at the 30-billion-dollar level of Model I. But to get people to consume an extra 80 cents, we must change their disposable income by $1; to get them to consume an extra 10 billion dollars, net taxes must be cut by $12\frac{1}{2}$ billion dollars, or in line 3 from 30 down to $17\frac{1}{2}$ billion dollars. This means a $12\frac{1}{2}$-

---

[1] The reader may test his proficiency by filling in a fifth column showing the result of a do-nothing policy. (HINT: Assume that net corporate savings go down 10 cents for every $1 drop in *NNP*, while "net" taxes go down by 25 cents. Show that the final drop in *NNP* is $10\frac{9}{48}$ times the 10-billion-dollar drop in investment.)

billion-dollar deficit (line 8). Note that Model III has a bigger deficit than Model II, that tax reduction or transfer expenditure tends to be weaker dollar for dollar—other things being equal—than extra expenditure on goods and services.[1]

Model IV: *Balanced-budget path to Full Employment.* Because of the slight extra "leverage" of spending over taxing, we can theoretically increase them both together and finally make up for the drop in private investment. But the government's expenditure on resources must now go up by 50 billion dollars to compensate for the 10 billion dollars of net investment! This tremendous expansion of the collective sector of the economy is necessary because insisting upon a balanced budget means that taxes must vastly increase and that private consumption must greatly contract, with government spending having to make up for both the investment and the consumption contractions in the private sector.

This financially orthodox approach is actually most radical from the standpoint of free and individualistic private enterprise. The tax-reduction model, Model III, which is philosophically most consistent with rugged individualism, is financially most heretical. That is why some conservatives are now becoming of the opinion that there are worse things than deficits—*e.g.*, high taxes. And that is why, when investment is for any reason stagnant, only a socialist can afford to be financially orthodox and preach the thrift doctrine of "Poor Richard's Almanac."

[1] There is another way of seeing this. For example, suppose that $1 of expenditure has, counting in all secondary multiplier effects, a $3 effect on income; then a $1 change in taxes is likely—other things being equal—to have less than $3 effect all together, probably only about a $2 total effect. This means that, if we expand both expenditure and taxes by $1 with no deficit at all, there will still be a $1 increase in total national income. The increase of $1 in expenditure gives rise to $3 = 1 + \frac{2}{3} + (\frac{2}{3})^2 + \cdots$. The increase in taxes gives rise to a reduction of $-2 = 0 - \frac{2}{3} - (\frac{2}{3})^2 - \cdots$. The combined effect is $3 - 2 = 1$, the difference being due to the fact that the effect of taxes does not enter into national income on the first round, but affects employment and production only on the successive rounds of respending.

PART THREE

The Composition

and Pricing

of National Output

Chapter 19: DETERMINATION OF

PRICE BY SUPPLY AND DEMAND

IN PART One, there was presented a telescopic picture of the manner in which the price mechanism operates, to make supply equal to demand and price to costs. We must now bring a microscope to bear upon a single market to see just how supply and demand really work. In the first half of this chapter, the equilibrium of supply and demand is worked out in detail; in the second half, various applications are considered.

A. *DETERMINATION OF MARKET PRICE*

THE DEMAND SCHEDULE AND THE DEMAND CURVE

Let us begin with demand. Everyone has observed that the higher the price charged for an article, the fewer will be sold; and the lower its price, the more units people will buy. Thus there exists at any one time a definite relation between the price of a good such as wheat and the amount demanded of that good. The following hypothetical table relating *price* and *quantity demanded* is an example of what economists call a "demand schedule." The student should be able to fill in the blanks of Col. (3).

Let us picture this demand schedule on a diagram, as in Fig. 1. On the vertical axis is a scale representing prices; on the horizontal axis, one representing quantity of wheat.

Just as a city corner is located as soon as you know its street and avenue, so is a ship's position located as soon as you know its latitude and longitude. Similarly, to plot a point on this diagram, we must have two coordinate

TABLE 1. *Demand Schedule Showing Relationship between Price and Quantity of Wheat Sold*

Price of wheat per bu. (1)	Quantity demanded, million bu. per mo. (2)	Value of sales, price × quantity (3) = (1) × (2)
A. $1.40	52	_____
B. 1.20	56	_____
C. 1.00	60	_____
D. 0.80	65	_____
E. 0.60	72	_____
F. 0.40	80	_____
G. 0.20	89	_____

numbers, a price and a quantity. For our first point, *A*, corresponding to $1.40 and 52 million bushels, we move upward 7 20-cent units and then over to the right 52 units. A cross marks the spot, *A*. To get the next cross, at *B*, we go up only 6 20-cent units and over to the right 56 units. The last cross is shown by *G*. Through the crosses we draw a smooth curve.

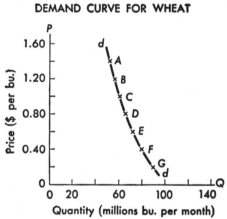

DEMAND CURVE FOR WHEAT

FIG. 1. This shows how much wheat would be bought at each and every possible price.

This picturization of the demand schedule is called the "demand curve." Because quantity and price are inversely related, the curve slopes downward, going from northwest down to southeast. This may presently be given a fancy name: the *law of diminishing consumption*, as price rises. This law is true of almost all commodities: wheat, electric razors, cotton, Ethyl gasoline, and corn flakes. If the price is cut, more will be demanded. To say the same thing in another way, if more is thrown on the market, it can be sold only at a lower price.

A number of obvious reasons can be given for the prevalence of the law of diminishing consumption: (1) At lower prices the consumer's dollar goes farther. He can *afford* to buy more. (2) At lower prices, he will *want* to buy more. Cheap wheat means that people will want to get their calories by substituting bread for potatoes, and white bread for rye bread. (3) Secondary uses of wheat such as for grain alcohol in producing synthetic rubber will be possible only at sufficiently low prices. Each reduction in price will tend to bring in some new buyers and some new uses by old buyers, until finally the price is zero and wheat is used with the lavishness of a free good.

ELASTIC AND INELASTIC DEMANDS

Different goods vary in the *degree* to which their use expands with a reduction in price. In fact, wheat was not a very good example to illustrate our law of diminishing consumption, because its consumption is rather "inelastic." The demand for automobiles, at least in the good old days of the Model T Ford, would have been a better example because it represents an "elastic" demand. A large increase in automobile sales resulted from small cuts in their price. This is illustrated by Table 2.

TABLE 2. *Demand Schedule for Automobiles*

Price per auto (1)	Quantity demanded per year, thousands (2)	Value of sales, or total revenue (3) = (1) × (2)
A. $1,400	3	_____
B. 1,200	15	_____
C. 1,000	30	_____
D. 800	50	_____
E. 600	72	_____
F. 400	100	_____
G. 200	140	_____

Now let us plot the demand curves for autos and for wheat upon the same chart, by a careful juxtaposition of scales (Fig. 2). Immediately we see their difference. The automobile curve is much flatter. On it, the quantity demanded is very *elastic* with respect to price changes. Contrariwise, the wheat curve is steep because its demand is rather *inelastic* even when price changes a great deal. The quantitative degree to which it satisfies the law of diminishing consumption is much smaller.

Now how shall we classify different commodities as having (1) elastic demand, (2) inelastic demand, or (3) so-called "unitary elasticity of demand"? We shall define a coefficient of elasticity of demand that will have a value greater than 1, as, for example, 3.5, when demand is elastic and the demand curve is rather flat. When quantity reacts little to a change in price so that demand is inelastic, then the elasticity coefficient will be less than 1, say, 0.66. The borderline case in between will have a coefficient of exactly 1 and is said to represent unitary elasticity.

To show the important differences characteristic of these three cases, we must turn to Col. (3) of Tables 1 and 2 which were left blank. The value of goods sold, or total dollar revenue, equals the quantity demanded times the price per unit. (For example, 3,000 autos at $600 gives us a total revenue of $1,800,000.) If the student fills in these blank spaces, he will notice an interest-ing difference between the case of wheat and that of autos. When the price of autos is lowered, total rev-enue *increases*, at least up to point *E*. When the price of wheat is lowered, total revenue *decreases*. The quantity of wheat bought goes up when the price falls, but not up by so great a percentage as price falls off.

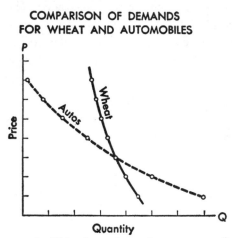

COMPARISON OF DEMANDS FOR WHEAT AND AUTOMOBILES

FIG. 2. This shows how the response of auto sales to price changes is more "elastic" than is the response of wheat sales, which is relatively "inelastic."

Consequently, total revenue, the product of price and quantity, falls off. We say, therefore, that wheat has an inelastic demand.

On the other hand, a 1 per cent reduction in the price of autos results in more than a 1 per cent increase in sales. Consequently total revenue rises when price is slashed. We say, therefore, that autos have an elastic demand.

The borderline case of unitary demand means that a 1 per cent reduction in price causes sales to go up by about 1 per cent so that total revenue remains the same; similarly a doubling of price will cause a halving of output.

In Table 3 the demand for movies is taken to be of unitary elasticity. The student should be able to fill in all the blanks on the basis of the definition given; and also to draw a graph of the resulting demand curve. (This drawing may be superimposed upon the two curves in Fig. 2.)

If one wishes only to know simply whether demand is elastic, inelastic, or unitary, a simple test can be applied. Calculate the ratio: total revenue at lower price ÷ total revenue at higher price. If this ratio is greater than 1, demand is elastic; if it is less than 1, demand is inelastic; if it is exactly equal to 1, we have the borderline case of unitary elasticity of demand. The student should verify that wheat is inelastic, autos elastic, and movies unitary. If, in addition to knowing whether demand is elastic or inelastic, we wish a more exact numerical coefficient, we must use the following relationship:

Elasticity of demand = percentage increase in quantity ÷ percentage reduction in price

This shows us that percentage changes rather than absolute changes are important in reckoning elasticity. Thus it was an oversimplification to have

TABLE 3. *Demand Curve for Movie Seats, as an Illustration of Unitary Elasticity of Demand*

Price per ticket	Quantity demanded per week, total revenue ÷ price	Total revenue or value of sales
(1)	(2) = (3) ÷ (1)	(3)
A. $1.40	308$\frac{4}{7}$	$432
B. 1.20		432
C. 1.00	432	432
D. 0.80		432
E. 0.60	720	432
F. 0.40		432
G. 0.20		432

talked earlier about flatness and steepness. Elasticity and slope should never be confused. They are different. Actually, a straight line, which everywhere has the same steepness, is elastic when it is near the price axis, unitary elastic at the halfway point, and inelastic near the quantity axis; also the demand for movie tickets, which everywhere had the same unitary elasticity, had a steep slope at high prices and a flat slope at large quantities. Since elasticity depends on *percentage changes*, it really depends upon the steepness of the demand curve relative to the ratio P/Q.[1]

---

[1] How do we measure the numerical value of elasticity exactly? The procedure is rather simple. We always compare two different price-quantity situations. The first situation has the upper price, P_u and lower quantity, Q_l. The second situation has the lower price, P_l, and upper quantity, Q_u. For example, suppose that we wish to measure the elasticity of demand for wheat between the points E and F. Then P_u and Q_l are given by $0.60 and 72, while P_l and Q_u are given by $0.40 and 80. Then we always define the elasticity of demand to be: percentage increase in Q ÷ percentage reduction in P.

Now the *absolute* increase in quantity is given by the upper quantity minus the lower

So much for the arithmetic of the problem. The important thing is not to memorize formulas but to understand the common-sense meaning of elasticity, its causes and its effects. A few illustrations may help.

If a monopolist gets control of a very necessary commodity much desired in some circumstances, like penicillin, he can take advantage of its inelasticity of demand and make great profits by jacking up his price. On the other hand, in a highly competitive trade, where patents and consumers' good will are not important, demand for any one firm's output will be very elastic. Why? Because at the slightest raising of price, buyers will go elsewhere and substitute the output of other firms. Thus one small wheat farmer has such a negligible effect upon the price at the Chicago Board of Trade, that the demand for his wheat is infinitely elastic. He can sell 100, 200, 300, or 1,000 bushels of wheat without affecting the price. But at the very slightest increase in price over that of the market, he loses *all* his sales. His demand curve is therefore very flat as in Fig. 3.

In the first chapter we learned that it is a fallacy to think that what is true for each is also true for all together. Here we have an instance as applied to farmers. Although the demand for each competitive farmer's wheat is very elastic, we already know that the demand for all wheat is very inelastic.

---

quantity, $Q_u - Q_l$, or by $80 - 72 = 8$. The *percentage* increase in quantity may be measured by the absolute increase expressed as a fraction of the upper quantity, by $\%_0$, or by $\dfrac{(Q_u - Q_l)}{Q_u}$. The percentage reduction in price is similarly given by the absolute reduction divided by the upper price; by $\dfrac{(0.60 - 0.40)}{0.60} = \dfrac{0.20}{0.60}$, or by $\dfrac{(P_u - P_l)}{P_u}$.

Then according to our formula:

$$\text{Elasticity of demand} = \frac{Q_u - Q_l}{Q_u} \div \frac{P_u - P_l}{P_u}$$

$$= \frac{8}{80} \div \frac{0.20}{0.60} = 0.3$$

This is less than 1, as it should be for wheat. The student can work out the *exact* numerical value of the elasticity of demand for autos and for movies between the points D and E or between any other two points.

Although we say that wheat has an inelastic demand, actually at high enough prices nothing would be bought and total revenue would become zero. Thus above some price level, even wheat would have an elastic demand. Likewise, when automobile prices were reduced to zero, total revenue would fall off and become zero. Thus, at a low enough price even autos would have an inelastic demand; *e.g.*, at all prices lower than that of E in Table 2.

This is the usual rule: At very high prices, all commodities have elastic demands; at low prices, inelastic demands. We call a commodity elastic if at its customary range of prices its demand is elastic. Likewise for the definition of inelastic demand.

The difference results from the great disparity of the horizontal scale of Fig. 3 above and Fig. 1 for wheat. Farmer Brown's piddling few carloads will not move us 1/1,000 inch along the industry's demand curve. Price on the diagram, Fig. 1, will be imperceptibly changed. No wonder that Brown thinks *his* demand is elastic. What if all the millions of Browns, Smiths, and O'Malleys bring a few carloads to market? Then we move a substantial distance along the whole industry's inelastic wheat-demand curve.

In fact, when all farmers are lucky enough to have a large crop, their total revenue actually goes down. Does this mean that farmers pray for drought and bugs? Not necessarily. The more calculating ones pray for bugs on everyone else's field, but none on their own. But since that cannot be expected to happen often, the next best thing is for everyone to have bugs.

Now we begin to understand two things: (1) why farmers wish to restrict crop production to raise their incomes and (2) why they cannot rely on each individual farmer to do his part in restricting, unless government force or bribery is employed. (The student should calculate the gain in farm income in raising the price of wheat from, say, the level in *F* to that in *C*. How large

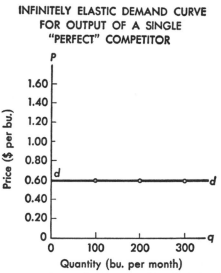

INFINITELY ELASTIC DEMAND CURVE FOR OUTPUT OF A SINGLE "PERFECT" COMPETITOR

FIG. 3. The perfectly competitive individual seller is such a small part of the total market that he can sell all he wishes without depressing the prevailing price.

would the average percentage restriction in output have to be for each individual farmer? Why would each farmer like all others to cut down production, but himself not wish to cut down? Who would be footing the bill? Would there be any other social harm in addition to the extra money paid for wheat?)

One last example. Let us consider the demand schedule for labor; *i.e.*, the number of workers who will be hired at each different wage. If a union can keep outsiders out, if its members have a special skill that cannot be done without, if machinery cannot be substituted for labor, and if the consumers need the employer's product badly, then the demand for union labor will be *inelastic*. The wage can be raised without throwing many people out of work. If the demand for labor is *elastic* because of the absence of one or more of the above conditions, then if the union insists on raising wages, the result will be unemployment for many of its members.

In the construction industry workers are organized into many different craft unions such as carpenters, plasterers, and plumbers. Because a builder's outlay for any one of these skills represents only *a small fraction* of the total cost of building a house, any one union can raise its wage without having its employment react very elastically. This principle is sometimes called "the

TABLE 4. *Supply Schedule for Wheat*

Each possible price per bu.	Quantity that sellers will supply, million bu. per mo.
A. $1.40	130
B. 1.20	122
C. 1.00	115
D. 0.80	100
E. 0.60	72
F. 0.40	45
G. 0.20	10

importance of being unimportant." The result tends to be high wages set by each craft because there is no incentive for them to moderate their demands.

But when all crafts raise their wage rates, the cost of housing goes up markedly and people stop building. Thus the demand for *all* construction labor tends to be *elastic*. Taken together with the technical backwardness and chaos of the construction industries, the result may be much less construction than we need and often unemployment both in the construction industry and elsewhere.

However, one important warning should be sounded. The demand schedule for all labor in the United States, rather than for that of one trade or town, cannot be analyzed by the methods of this chapter. We cannot even be sure that the law of diminishing demand holds generally. An increase in all wages, of those in the industries making machinery along with the others, need not cause *any substitution* of capital for labor. A cut in wage affects people's incomes. It may undermine the demand for business output, so that more labor will not be employed. Its only effect may be to cause prices to fall. If this causes wages to fall farther, we may enter upon a disorganized deflationary spiral with prices, wages, and incomes going downward. Again, this is an illustration of the fallacy of composition: what's valid for the part may be false for the whole.

THE SUPPLY SCHEDULE

Enough has now been said of demand. Let us now turn to the sellers' side or to the supply schedule. The demand schedule related prices and the amounts people wish to buy. *By the supply schedule, we naturally mean the relation between prices and the amounts that people are willing to produce and sell.* Table 4 illustrates the supply schedule for wheat.

Unlike the demand curve, the supply curve in Fig. 4 for wheat rises upward and to the right, from southwest to northeast. At a higher price of wheat, farmers will take acreage out of corn cultivation and put it into wheat. Also they can afford the cost of more fertilizer, more machinery, and poorer land. All these factors increase output with higher prices.[1]

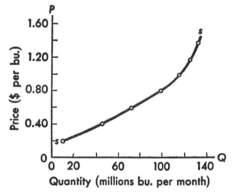

SUPPLY CURVE FOR WHEAT

FIG. 4. This shows how much wheat will be produced at each and every possible price.

EQUILIBRIUM OF SUPPLY AND DEMAND

Let us now combine our analysis of demand and supply to see how competitive market price is determined. This is done in Table 5.

So far we have been considering all prices as possible. We have said, "If price is such and such, sales will be such and such; if price is so and so, sales will be so and so; etc." But to just which level will price *actually* go? How much will then be produced and consumed? The supply schedule alone cannot tell us. Neither can the demand schedule. But both together can.

Let us do what an auctioneer would do, *i.e.*, proceed by trial and error. Can

---

[1] However, later, in Case 4 of the Appendix to this chapter, we shall see that some supply curves can bend backward; that as the wage goes up, workers may feel they can afford to work *fewer* hours. In such cases, the supply curve of labor as a whole would go from southeast to northwest, with high wages being accompanied by a smaller amount supplied. Similarly, if people are trying to save up a certain amount for their old age, a reduction in the interest rate—the "price" offered for saving—may cause them to supply more rather than less savings.

TABLE 5. *Supply and Demand Schedule for Wheat*

Possible prices per bu.	Quantity demanded, million bu. per mo.	Quantity supplied, million bu. per mo.	Pressure on price
(1)	(2)	(3)	(4)
A. $1.40	52	130	↓ Falling
B. 1.20	56	122	↓ Falling
C. 1.00	60	115	↓ Falling
D. 0.80	65	100	↓ Falling
E. 0.60*	72*	72*	↯ Neutral*
F. 0.40	80	45	↑ Rising
G. 0.20	89	10	↑ Rising

* The equilibrium price and output.

situation *A* in the above table, with wheat selling for $1.40 per bushel prevail for any period of time? The answer is a loud and clear "no." At $1.40, the producers will be bringing 130 (million) bushels to the market every month [see Col. (3)]. But the amount demanded by consumers will be only 52 (million) bushels per month [see Col. (2)]. As stocks of wheat begin to pile up, competitive sellers will cut the price just a little. Thus as Col. (4) shows, price will tend to fall. But it will not fall indefinitely down to zero.

To see this, let us try the point *G* with price equal to only 20 cents per bushel. Can that price persist? Again, obviously not. For a comparison of Cols. (2) and (3) shows that consumption will exceed production *at that price*. Storehouses will begin to be emptied; disappointed demanders who cannot get wheat will tend to bid the price up. This

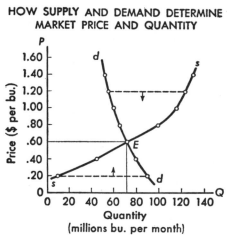

HOW SUPPLY AND DEMAND DETERMINE MARKET PRICE AND QUANTITY

FIG. 5. The "equilibrium" price is at the intersection of the two curves, where the price is such as to make the amounts demanded and supplied exactly equal.

upward pressure on price is indicated in Col. (4) by the rising arrow.

We could go on to try out other prices, but by now the answer is obvious. *The only equilibrium price, i.e., the only price that can last—is that at which the amounts supplied and demanded are equal.* Only at E, with a price of $0.60, will the amount demanded, 72 (million) bushels per month, equal the amount supplied. Price is at equilibrium, just as an olive at the bottom of a cocktail glass is at equilibrium, because there is no tendency for it to rise or fall. Of course, this stationary price may not be reached at once. There may have to be an initial period of trial and error, of oscillation around the right level before price finally settles down and supply balances demand.

Figure 5 shows the same result in pictorial form. The supply and demand curves are superimposed on the same diagram. They cross at one intersection point. This point E represents the equilibrium price and quantity.

At a higher price, the dotted line shows the *excess* of supply over demand. The arrow points downward to show the direction in which price will move because of the competition of *sellers*. At a price lower than the equilibrium price, 60 cents, the dotted line shows that demand overmatches supply. Consequently the eager bidding of *buyers* requires us to point the arrow indicator upward to show the pressure that they are exerting on price. Only at the point E will there be a balancing of forces and a stationary maintainable price.

This is all there is to the doctrine of supply and demand. All that is left to do is to point out some of the cases to which it can be applied and some to which it cannot.

B. *APPLICATIONS OF SUPPLY AND DEMAND*

EFFECTS OF CHANGES IN SUPPLY OR DEMAND

Other things being equal, as economists are fond of saying, there is a unique schedule of supply or demand at any instant of time. But other things will not remain equal. The demand for cotton is declining over the years because of reductions in the price of rayon. The supply schedule of gasoline is increasing because technological progress permits more to be produced at the same cost. As costs and tastes change, as incomes vary, as the prices of rival products (coffee in relation to tea) or cooperating products (sugar in relation to tea) change, our schedules will shift. What will be the effects on consumption, production, and price?

All beginners in the field of economics must beware of a common error. They must take care not to confuse an increase in *demand*—by which is meant a shift of the whole curve to the right and upward, as more is bought at each and every price—with an increase in the *quantity demanded* as a result of moving to a lower price *on the same demand curve*. By "demand" is meant the whole demand curve; by "supply" is meant the whole supply curve; by an "increase" in demand or supply is meant a shift of the whole curve in question to the right. To indicate a single point on a demand curve, we speak of the "quantity bought" or the "quantity demanded" *at a particular price*. A movement *along* the same curve is "a change in the quantity demanded as a result of a price change." It does not represent any change in the demand schedule. The need for this warning will appear in a moment.

Let us suppose that the supply of wheat decreases. This may be for any reason, such as bad weather, or because the price of corn has risen, or perhaps because the producer must pay a sales tax of 20 cents per bushel of wheat to the government.

Let us consider in detail the last example of a 20-cent sales tax on each bushel of wheat. What is the final effect or "incidence" of the tax? Does its burden fall completely on the producer who must in the first instance pay it? Or may it be shifted in part on to consumers? The answer can be derived only by the use of our supply and demand curves.

There is no reason for the demand curve of the consumers to have changed at all. At 60 cents they will still be willing to buy only 72 (million) bushels per month as they neither know nor care that the producers must pay a tax.

But the whole supply curve is shifted leftward and upward: leftward because at each market price the producers will now supply less as a result of the tax; upward because to get the producers to bring any given quantity to market, say 72 (million) units, we must give them a higher market price than before—80 cents rather than 60 cents, or higher by the 20-cent tax.

The student should be able to fill in a new supply column, resembling the Col. (3) in Table 5 but with each price raised by 20 cents. In Fig. 6, the demand curve *dd* is unchanged, but the supply curve *ss* has been shifted everywhere up by 20 cents to a new parallel supply curve *s's'*.

Where will the new equilibrium price be? The answer is found at the intersection of the new demand and supply curves, or at *E'* where *s's'* and *dd* meet. Because supply has decreased, the price is higher. Also the amount bought and the amount sold are less. If we read the graph carefully, we find that the new equilibrium price has risen from 60 to about 75 cents. The new equilibrium output, at which purchases and sales are in equilibrium, has fallen from 72 (million) bushels to about 67 (million) bushels.

Who pays the tax? Well, the wheat farmers do in part because now they receive only 55 cents (75 — 20) rather than 60 cents. But the consumer also shares in the burden, because the price charged by the producer has not fallen by as much as the tax. To the consumer, the wheat costs 55 cents plus the 20 cents tax, or 75 cents all told. Because the consumers need wheat so badly, they pay 15 cents of the tax, or three times as much as the producer. As a final burden, the community is poorer because it is consuming less wheat.

As a check upon his understanding of the above reasoning, the student should consider the case of an opposite shift in supply. Let the government pay producers a subsidy of 20 cents per bushel of wheat instead of taxing them this amount. Draw the new curve $s''s''$. Where is E'', its intersection with dd? What is the new price? the new quantity? How much of the benefit goes to the producer? how much to the consumer?

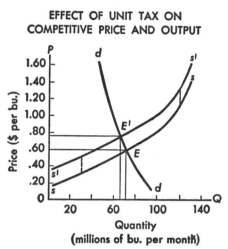

EFFECT OF UNIT TAX ON COMPETITIVE PRICE AND OUTPUT

FIG. 6. A unit tax shifts the supply curve upward by just the amount of the tax and gives rise to a new equilibrium price and quantity.

The student can now probably guess how a change in demand is to be treated. The curve dd shifts rightward or leftward to a new curve $d'd'$. Where this intersects the old supply curve ss, we have the new price and quantity. He should also be able to handle the case where *both* curves shift simultaneously.

At the end of this chapter there are a number of examples to be worked out by the reader. They are designed to do more than test his understanding of the above analysis: They provide an introduction to a number of important economic situations and principles.

A COMMON FALLACY

By now the student has mastered supply and demand. Or has he? He knows that a tax will have the effect of raising the price that the consumer will have to pay. Or does he know this? What about the following argument of a kind often seen in the press and heard from the platform:

The effect of a tax on a commodity might seem at first sight to be an advance in price to the consumer. But an advance in price will diminish the demand. And a reduced demand will send the price down again. It is not certain, therefore, after all, that the tax will really raise the price.[1]

Well, what about it? Will the tax raise the price or not? According to the editor's written word and the Senator's oratory, the answer is "no." Obviously, we have here an example of the treachery of words. One of the four sentences in the quotation is false because the word "demand" is being used in the wrong sense. The student has already been warned against confusing a movement *along* an unchanged curve from a *shift* in the curve.

Actually, the correct answer would be more or less as follows:

A tax will raise the price to the consumer and will lower the price received by the producer, the difference going to the government. At the higher price a smaller quantity will be bought by consumers. This is as it should be because producers are also supplying a smaller quantity at the lower price which they receive. Thus the amounts bought and sold are in balance where the new supply and demand schedules intersect, and there will be no further change in price.

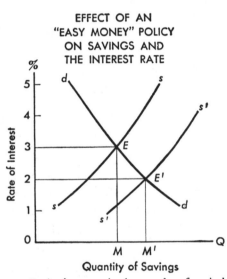

EFFECT OF AN "EASY MONEY" POLICY ON SAVINGS AND THE INTEREST RATE

FIG. 7. An increase in the supply of capital can lower the rate of interest only by making capital funds more abundant.

Any college freshman taking an economics course should be able to see through the above fallacy. But bankers, financial writers, and even professors of economics fall into the same kind of error when discussing the effects of the government's very important "easy-money" policy. Here the commodity bought and sold is the money that is being lent (supplied) and borrowed (demanded); and the price for such transactions is the *rate of interest*.

The demand schedule for loans is provided by the needs of business and

[1] Taken from a quotation in H. D. Henderson, "Supply and Demand," p. 27, Cambridge University Press, London, 1922. The quotation could have been made even more fantastic as follows: "Price goes up and demand falls. This sends price down which makes demand rise. This makes price go up. But the higher price makes demand fall . . . ." And so we have a perpetual oscillation in price, up and down, down and up. The student should spot the error.

government for long-term borrowing. The supply schedule is provided by the willingness of individuals, insurance companies, ordinary commercial banks, and the 12 Federal Reserve Banks to supply funds for this type of investment. All this is shown by *dd* and *ss* of Fig. 7.

Now let us suppose the government adopts a cheap-money or easy-money policy. We have seen in the discussion of Federal reserve open-market purchase policy just what this means, but for the present purpose we may think of it as a shift of the supply curve to the right, to *s's'*, because the Federal Reserve Banks bring new supplies of funds into the capital market.

What is the effect? As we should expect, at the new equilibrium intersection the rate of interest will be lowered to around 2 per cent; thus there is now a cheaper price for savings. The quantity of funds available to big and little business (and the government) has gone up a great deal. How can we reconcile this with the following typical quotation:

The government's easy money policy at first seems to send the interest rate down. This dries up savings and discourages thrift. The reduced *supply* of savings robs business of capital. In fact, capital may be so scarce that the government will find it must pay a higher rather than a lower rate of interest. The country will go to ruin: grass will grow in the streets, ...

Which is the right answer in theory? which in practice?

IS THE LAW OF SUPPLY AND DEMAND IMMUTABLE?

Competitive price and quantity are determined by supply and demand. But do not prices depend on other factors such as the amount of gold production or whether there is a war going on? Actually price does depend on many such factors. However, they are not *in addition* to supply and demand but are included in the numerous forces which determine or *act through* supply and demand. Thus if new gold production gives everyone higher incomes, it will shift demand curves and raise prices. But it is still true that price is determined by supply and demand.

At this point a thoughtful reader should be moved to voice protest. Nothing much has been said about price as being determined by cost of production. Shouldn't this be listed as a third factor in addition to supply and demand? Again our answer is the same. If we exclude perfect or semimonopolies (such as public-utility companies whose rates the state sets on the basis of their accounting costs), *price is affected by cost of production only to the extent that the latter affects supply*. If God sends manna from heaven without cost but in limited supply, then its price will not be zero but will be given by the intersection of the demand and supply curves. On the other hand, if it would cost $50,000 to print the national anthem on the head of a pin, but there is no demand for such a commodity, it simply will not be produced and would not command $50,000 if it were produced. (What the market price of something nonexistent should be called we may leave to the pleasure and imagination of the reader.)

This doesn't mean that cost of production is unimportant for price determination. Under competition it is especially important. But its importance shows itself *through its effects upon supply*. Businessmen do not produce for their health. If they cannot get a price high enough to cover their past costs, then they will not like it. Nevertheless, under competition once the crop is in, so to speak, there is not much they can do about it. But they will not continue *in the future* to supply goods at prices that fail to cover the *extra* costs incurred to produce these goods. Thus supply depends intimately on cost especially on "extra costs" and so too must price.

Moreover, to say that price equals cost does not in itself tell us which is the cause of which. In many cases where an industry uses a productive factor highly specialized to itself (*e.g.*, baseball players, opera singers, vineyard land), *price determines cost rather than vice versa*. Grain land is dear because the price of grain is high. Apartment buildings sell for little because rents are low. This type of relationship was overlooked by the Massachusetts dairy farmers who petitioned during World War II for a higher milk price "because the price of cows is high." If their request had been granted, they would soon have observed the price of cows chasing the milk price upward.[1]

These examples show us that supply and demand are not ultimate explanations of price. They are simply useful catch-all categories for analyzing and describing the multitude of forces, causes, and factors impinging on price. Rather than being final answers, supply and demand simply represent initial questions. Our work is not over but just begun.

This should help to debunk the tendency of neophytes who have just mastered the elements of market price determination to utter sagely, "You can't repeal the law of supply and demand. King Canute could not command the ocean tide to retreat from his throne on the seashore. No more can the government get around or interfere with the workings of supply and demand."

It would be better never to have learned any economics than to be left with this misleading half-baked untruth. Of course the government can affect price.

---

[1] Where a factor of production is inelastic in supply, as in all these cases, its cost is "price-determined" rather than "price-determining" and its return is called an "economic rent." See Case 3 in the Appendix to this chapter.

It can do so by affecting supply or demand, or both. In the previous section we encountered the example of its easy-money policy in which it altered interest rates by enlarging supply. In our earlier discussions of government action to aid farm income, we saw how government plans for restricting production are able to raise price and income by cutting down on supply. Similar programs by government cartels have been pursued all over the world: Brazil has burned coffee to raise its price; Britain during the 1920's pursued the "Stevenson policy" of artificially controlling the price of rubber; sugar is still under international control.

These governments have not violated the law of supply and demand. They have worked through the law of supply and demand. The state has no secret economic weapons or tricks. What is true for the state is also true for individuals. Anyone can affect the price of wheat so long as he has money to throw on the market or wheat to hold off it. Rockefeller, Ford, and Astor could band together to create an easy-money policy if they wished to badly enough. All they would have to do would be to offer to supply enough funds to everyone at a low rate of interest. With this new supply on the market, the rate of interest would have to fall.

Every trade-union influences wages, or tries to, by affecting the supply of labor. Anyone with a somewhat distinctive commodity may try by advertising to increase the demand for his product, and by restricting supply to raise price above his extra costs of production. It should be remembered however that, as soon as individual producers become important enough to affect the price of the things they sell, then they cease to be perfect competitors in the strict sense, and their behavior must be analyzed in terms of a blend of monopoly and competition, i.e., in terms of monopolistic or imperfect competition as described in Chap. 21.

PRICES FIXED BY LAW

There is one important interference with supply and demand whose effects we must analyze. The government sometimes sets a maximum price by law, or a minimum wage. During the war ceilings were placed on items in the cost of living. Even before the war a floor of 40 cents was placed on hourly wages of most factory workers. These interferences by law are quite different from government actions, previously described, which work through supply and demand.

Consider, say, the market for sugar, which has ordinary curves of supply and demand such as we have repeatedly met in this chapter. Suppose that the government through OPA establishes an order prohibiting sugar from rising above 7 cents a pound (retail). Now because of war prosperity and limited shipping, let demand be so high and supply so small that the equilibrium price would have been 20 cents a pound if the government had not intervened. This high price would have contributed to profiteering in that industry, it would have represented a rather heavy "tax" on the poor who could least afford it, and it would only have added fuel to an inflationary spiral in the cost of living,

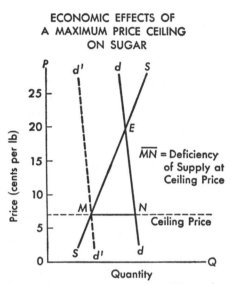

ECONOMIC EFFECTS OF
A MAXIMUM PRICE CEILING
ON SUGAR

with all sorts of inflationary reactions on workers' wage demands, and so forth.

Therefore, the government through Congress and the OPA decided to hold the line on prices. It passed a law putting a maximum price on sugar at the old level of 7 cents a pound. The line MN represents the legal price ceiling. Now what will happen?

At the legal ceiling price supply and demand do not match. Consumers want thousands of pounds of sugar in excess of what producers are willing to supply. This is shown

FIG. 8. Without a legal price ceiling, price would rise to E. At the artificial ceiling price, supply and demand do not balance and some method of rationing, formal or informal, is needed to allocate the short supply and bring the effective demand down to $d'd'$.

by the gap between M and N. This gap is so large that there will not long be enough on grocers' shelves or in the warehouses to make up the difference. Somebody will have to be drinking bitter coffee. If it were not for the maximum price law, that

somebody would gladly bid the price up to 8 or 9 cents or more, rather than do without sugar. As in our earlier discussion (Fig. 5), we could show this by putting an upward pointing arrow perpendicular to MN. The arrow would not stop pointing upward until price had been bid up to the equilibrium level of 20 cents.

It is against the law for the consumer to bid a higher price. Even if she should be so unpatriotic, the seller could not legally take the higher price. There follows a period of frustration and shortage—a sort of game of musical chairs in which somebody is left holding the empty bag when the orchestra stops playing. The inadequate supply of sugar must somehow be rationed. At first, this may be done by "first come, first served" with or without limited sales to each customer. Lines form and women have to spend much of their time on expeditions foraging for food. But this is no solution since somebody must be left at the end of the line when the sugar is gone.

The price mechanism is stymied and blocked. Nonmonetary considerations must determine who will be the lucky buyers and who the unlucky ones: the accident of being in the store when the sugar is unveiled, the warmth of the smile that the customer flashes on the grocer, her previous standing at the store in question, and the amount of other things that the customer is willing to buy.

Nobody is very happy, least of all the harassed grocer. Were it not for the community's elementary sense of fair play, the situation would soon become intolerable. Patriotism is more effective in motivating people to brief acts of intense heroism than to putting up day after day with an uncomfortable situation. So it is no wonder that black markets occasionally develop. The really surprising thing is how infrequently they do occur.

If for political or social reasons market price is not to be permitted to rise high enough to bring demand down to the level of supply, the only solution under these circumstances lies in outright coupon or point rationing.

Once this is adopted most people heave a sigh of relief, because now sellers need not turn people away and buyers can count upon getting their fair quota of the limited supplies. Of course there are always a few women and soapbox orators, who are longer on intuition than brains and who blame their troubles on the mechanism of rationing itself rather than on the shortage. "If only the government could print more coupon points," they sigh. As if that would help rather than hurt the situation! Such people are like the ignorant ancient kings who used to slay the messengers bringing them bad news. They add spice to the human comedy but need not be taken seriously.

Just how do ration coupons work out in terms of supply and demand? Clearly the OPA tries to issue just enough of them to lower the demand curve to *d'd' where supply and the new demand balance at the ceiling price.* If too many coupons are issued, demand is still too far to the right and we encounter the old difficulties, but in lesser degree. If too few coupons are issued, stocks of sugar will pile up. This is the signal for liberalizing the sugar ration.

One goes to an insane asylum to learn to appreciate the normal human behavior. So too, the breakdown of the price mechanism during war gives us a new understanding of its remarkable efficiency in normal times. Goods are always scarce, in the sense that there is never enough to give everyone all he wishes. Price itself is always rationing scarce supplies: rising so as to choke off excessive consumption and in order to expand production; falling to encourage consumption, discourage production, and work off excess inventories. During World War II the price mechanism had to be supplemented by direct controls and rationing, because—as we saw in the analysis of inflation in Part Two—when everything is "short" relative to demand and full-employment capacity, reliance on the price mechanism is inequitable and gives rise to an endless inflationary spiral with grave economic consequences.

It may be left as an exercise, in or out of the classroom, to adapt the above discussion to the problem of a *minimum* wage, or to the problem of government subsidies aimed at keeping the cost of living down while encouraging expanded supplies.

SUMMARY

A. MARKET PRICE DETERMINATION

1. By the demand schedule we mean a table showing the different quantities of a good that can be sold at each different price. The same relationship plotted on a diagram is the demand curve.

2. With but few exceptions, the higher the price, the lower will be the quantity sold; and vice versa. Almost all commodities are subject to this law of diminishing consumption, but in differing degrees.

3. Elasticity of demand measures the degree to which sales expand as price is reduced. Demand is elastic, inelastic, or unitary, depending upon whether a reduction in price increases, decreases, or does not change total revenue. This follows from the definition of elasticity of demand as the percentage change in quantity divided by the percentage change in price.

4. The supply curve or schedule represents the relationship between the prices and the quantities of a good that producers will be willing to sell. Usually, but not always, the supply curve rises upward and to the right, the higher prices calling forth larger supplies.

5. Market equilibrium can take place only at a price where the quantities supplied and demanded are identical. At any price higher than the equilibrium intersection of the supply and demand curves, the quantity supplied will exceed the quantity demanded; there will result a downward pressure on price as some sellers begin to undermine the going price. Similarly, the reader should be able to show why any price lower than the equilibrium price will meet irresistible upward pressure.

B. APPLICATIONS OF SUPPLY AND DEMAND

6. The apparatus of supply and demand enables us to analyze the effects of shifts in either curve or in both simultaneously. Beginners must avoid the pitfalls of confusing the expression "an increase in demand," which means an outward shift of the whole demand curve, with "an increase in quantity demanded" as a result of a reduction in price, which is nothing but a downward movement along an unchanged curve.

7. A thousand forces affect price. But they do so in a free competitive market only by acting through supply and demand. For example, cost of production affects price only to the extent that it affects supply; otherwise not at all.

8. Although the government usually affects price by operating on either supply or demand, occasionally it passes laws that interfere with the workings of the competitive market place. An example is that of a legal maximum price or minimum wage. Under such circumstances, supply and demand need not be equal: some producer or consumer may wish to sell or buy more than he is able to do at the legal price. Unless the discrepancies are parceled out by legislation (rationing, etc.), the results are often most uncomfortable, and illegal black markets may come into existence.

QUESTIONS FOR DISCUSSION

1. List a number of factors that might increase the demand for wheat. Do the same for the supply of wheat.

2. Which of the following do you think has the most inelastic demand: perfume, salt, penicillin, cigarettes, ice cream, chocolate ice cream, Sealtest chocolate ice cream? Try to give reasons for your answer.

3. Comment on the following: "How can price be determined by the equality of supply and demand? After all, the 'amount bought' must be the same in every transaction as the 'amount sold.' How then could they be different at every price but the unique equilibrium price?"

4. Kidneys and livers used to sell for about the same price per pound until science discovered the great nutritive value of liver for building red corpuscles. Just what did this discovery do to their relative prices and how did this come about?

5. What would a cheap mechanical cotton picker do to the price of cotton? to the wages of farm laborers?

6. Cross out the wrong word, and try to justify your discussion in terms of common sense: A tax on the producers of a commodity can be shifted most on to the

consumers when supply is very (elastic, inelastic) and when demand is very (elastic, inelastic).

7. What is an increased demand for cowhides likely to do to the price of beef? (HINT: Ranchers now receive more for a live cow.)

8. Imagine a small competitive market for unskilled labor in a small city. Show how unemployment might be created if the city fathers legislate a very high minimum wage. Why cannot the same analysis be applied to a minimum-wage law for the country as a whole? (HINT: Reread page 454.)

9. How can the demand for plasterers in the building industry be inelastic while the demand for houses is elastic? What factors following World War II have caused the demand for housing to be more inelastic than usual?

10. If the demand for automobiles is elastic, why would not Henry Ford cut the price of his car indefinitely?

11. If price drops from $10 to $9 and sales go up from 100 to 110 units, is demand elastic, inelastic, or unitary? (WARNING: The problem is not so simple as it looks. Examine carefully the exact rule for classifying elasticity given on page 450 and also the exact formula given in the footnote on page 452.) Does your result seem to disagree with the rule given in bold-face type on page 451? How do you account for this?

APPENDIX TO CHAPTER 19
CASES ON SUPPLY AND DEMAND

PROPOSITION 1. (*a*) *As a general rule an increase in demand, supply being constant, will raise price.* (*b*) *Probably also, but less certainly, it will increase the quantity bought and sold.* A decrease in demand has opposite effects.

PROPOSITION 2. *An increase in supply, demand being constant, will almost certainly lower price and increase the quantity bought and sold.* The effects of a decrease in supply are just the opposite.

These two important propositions summarize the qualitative effects of shifts in supply and demand. But the exact quantitative degree of change in price and quantity depends upon the specific shapes of the curves in each instance. A number of cases may be distinguished.

CASE 1. *Constant Cost.* Imagine a manufactured item, like razor blades, whose production can be easily expanded by merely duplicating machinery, plant space, factories, and labor. To produce 100,000 blades per day simply requires us to do the same thing as when we were manufacturing 1,000 per day, except on a hundredfold scale. In this case the supply curve, *ss*, in Fig. 9, is a horizontal line at the constant level of unit costs. An increase in demand will shift the new intersection point, *E'*, to the right, increasing quantity but leaving price unchanged.

What will be the effects of a sales tax of, say, 5 cents per blade, on output and price paid by the consumer? Fill in the diagram.

CASE 2. *Increasing Costs and Diminishing Returns.* Suppose that an industry like wine-grape growing requires a certain kind of soil and location (sunny hillsides, etc.). Such sites are limited in number. The annual output of wine can be increased to some extent by adding more labor and fertilizer to each acre of land and by bidding away more hill sites from other uses. But as we saw in Chap. 2, the law of diminishing returns will begin to operate if variable factors of production, like labor and fertilizer, are added to fixed amounts of a factor like land. Why is that? Because each new variable addition of labor and fertilizer has a *smaller proportion* of land to work with. By the same token, each fixed unit of land has more labor and fertilizer cooperating with it. Therefore land's productivity and earnings are higher. The result: getting extra amounts of wine sends total costs up more than proportionately. Therefore, the cost per unit of wine is rising. The supply curve travels upward from southwest to northeast because at *lower* market prices, *less* will be supplied. At higher prices, *more* will be supplied.

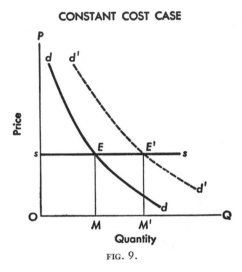

CONSTANT COST CASE

FIG. 9.

Figure 10 shows the supply curve *ss*. What will be the effect on price of an increase in demand? on quantity?

Show by means of a diagram that a tax of 5 cents per ounce of wine will raise price to the consumer by less than a similar tax on razor blades did. Why? What will be the effect on the price received by the producer? If the original demand curves for wine and razors are similar, show that the fall in the output of razors will be *greater* than that of wine. Why?

CASE 3. *Completely Inelastic Supply and Economic Rent.* Some commodities or productive factors are completely fixed in amount, regardless of price, as the following examples show.

There is only one Mona Lisa painting. Nature's original endowment of the "natural and indestructible" qualities of land can also often be taken as fixed in amount. Raising the price offered for land cannot create more than four corners at State and Madison in Chicago. High-paid artists and businessmen who love their work would continue to

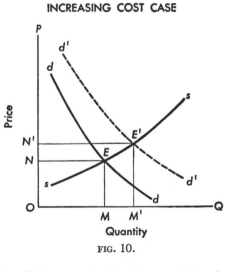

INCREASING COST CASE

FIG. 10.

work at their jobs even if their salaries fell tremendously. Once a bridge is built, it must earn "what the traffic will bear" regardless of its past sunk costs. Numerous other examples could be given.

In all of them the supply curve goes straight up and down, at least in the relevant region. A higher price cannot elicit an increase in supply; nor is the higher price necessary to bring out the existing supply, for even at lower prices the same amount will still be forthcoming. Because it is price-determined rather than price-determining, the return to the factor of production is known as a *pure economic rent or surplus*, which need not be paid to call out the required supply.

If now demand shifts upward, the whole effect is to raise price. Quantity is unchanged. Moreover, the increase in price exactly equals the upward shift in demand.

Likewise if a tax is placed upon the commodity, its whole effect is to reduce the price received by the supplier by exactly the amount of the tax. The tax is shifted completely to the supplier, who absorbs it all out of his economic rent or surplus. The consumer buys exactly as much of the good or service as before and at no extra cost.

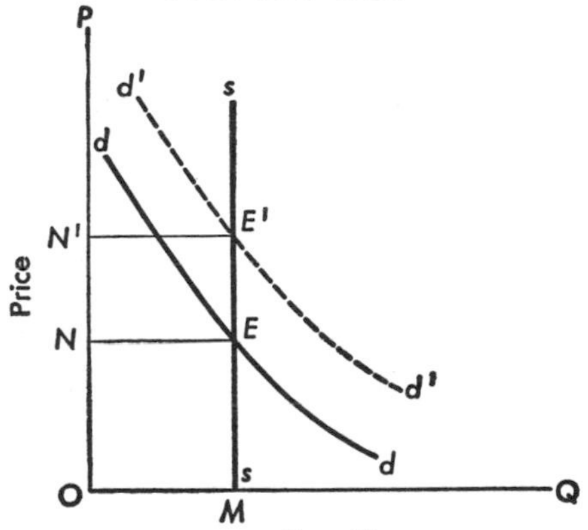

There is much to be said for a tax that falls on *economic surplus*. Especially if you believe that "every acre of land in the world can be

PURE RENT CASE

FIG. 11.

traced back in 'ownership' to the man who first stole it." Or that a too unequal distribution of income is a bad thing. In fact Henry George, observing the great importance of land rent in the nineteenth-century America, attributed most of the ills of society to unearned land rent. In his book, "Progress and Poverty," 1879, which serves as the bible for the "single-tax" movement, he proposed that all government revenue should come from taxes on land rent or "unearned increment." Most economists, including the author, regard this as an extreme position. But they do attach importance to taxes that fall as much as possible on surpluses and disturb individuals' decisions as to the allocation of resources as little as possible.

This raises an important question of social policy. Even if society disapproves of people's earning excessive economic rent (such as Shirley Temple's moving-picture salary or the huge return on a busy city corner), it would be a mistake simply to pass a law limiting the price that they can charge. By charging the highest price that the market will pay, Shirley Temple makes sure that the producer who can put her before the most people gets her services. If her salary were limited to a level within the reach of smaller companies, she might work for them and presumably thereby lessen the total of social satisfaction. Similarly, a rent ceiling on the busiest corner in town might cause it to be leased for an unimportant rather than the most important use.

The moral is to let the maximum of economic rent be collected, even if a majority of the electorate are "hell-bent on soaking the rich." Let the sheep grow as much wool as possible; then fleece them by taxation. In other words, after supply and demand have determined the reward and best use of the factor in question, then by taxation reduce its return down to what is considered a democratically fair level. If the income taxed is really a pure rent, there is no need to worry about the tax's effect on effort or supply. By definition of rent or surplus, the sheep will continue to grow the wool. (Note that the science of economics cannot tell us that rich people should or should not be taxed heavily.)

CASE 4. *A Backward Rising Supply Curve.* Early explorers into new lands often noted that, when they raised the wages of natives, they received less labor rather than more. If wages were doubled, instead of working 6 days a week for their minimum of subsistence, the natives might go fishing for 3 days. The same has been observed among so-called "modern civilized people." As improved technology raises real wages, people feel that they ought to take part of their higher earnings in the form of more leisure and less work. This partly explains why over the decades the average factory working week has dropped from 84 to 40 hours, and why the wives, children, and aged parents of workers do not have to find jobs in such great numbers in order to help make ends meet.[1]

To a lesser degree the same effect has been observed with respect to the supply of savings. Some people, it is true, will save more money if the interest rate is raised. Others are indifferent to the rate of interest; they save money automatically, depending upon their life-insurance commitments, habits, and incomes. But others—and these are the ones of significance in this connection—are trying to put by some certain sum of money for a "rainy day," for their old age, for a trip to Europe, or for their children's college education. If the rate of interest earned on their savings goes up, they no longer need save so much to meet these goals. Likewise, at a lower rate of interest their supply of savings goes up because more is necessary to meet the same goals. Thus, if such people

[1] An attempt to measure this statistically is to be found in Paul H. Douglas, "Theory of Wages," The Macmillan Company, New York, 1934.

are numerically important, we again have a backward-bending supply curve of savings just as we did for labor in the previous paragraph.

Figure 12 indicates the supply curve of labor in this case. At first it rises as higher wages coax out more labor, but beyond the point T higher wages induce more leisure and less work. An increase in demand does increase the price of labor in agreement with Proposition 1 (*a*). But note how lucky we were to have added the words "but less certainly" in 1(*b*)! For the increase in demand has *decreased* rather than increased the quantity of labor.

A partial verification of such a possibility is found in the fact that a decrease in demand for farm products during a depression often causes farmers to work harder in order to restore their incomes. The result: More rather than less is produced in response to a decrease in demand.

CASE 5. *A Possible Exception: Decreasing Cost.* Heretofore our examples have agreed with Proposition of 1(*a*), that an increase in demand raises price. But what about the often observed case where an increase in demand is followed by economies of mass production and decreasing costs? A good theory must make room for all the facts.

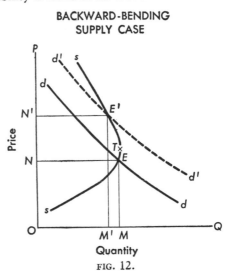

BACKWARD-BENDING
SUPPLY CASE

FIG. 12.

We must frankly admit, therefore, that our first proposition may break down and have exceptions. Of course, we can try to save face a little by pointing out that many of the most important reductions in cost following an increase in demand really represent *permanent downward shifts* in the supply curve rather than movements down a fixed-supply curve.

Let us illustrate this by the case where the government increases its demand for radar sets. The first few sets built must be constructed in the laboratory by experimental methods. They are tailor-made, custom-built, and very expensive per unit. But the know-how gained in the process makes possible the further production of sets for very much less per unit. Even if demand were to go back again to its previous level, price would not return to its previous higher level. In traveling along the arrow EE' marked with a question mark, we are not moving reversibly along the supply curve. Instead, the supply curve has shifted irreversibly downward from *ss* to *s's'*, so that, even when demand is back again at *dd*, the price is now lower at *E''* than it was originally.

The case discussed really does not come under the heading of Proposition 1, but falls under the heading of Proposition 2 dealing with shifts in supply. The final result agrees with the latter's conclusion that an increase in supply will lower price and increase quantity. (Compare *E* and *E''*.) But the present case is still an unusual one because the shift of supply has been induced by a shift in demand.

From the standpoint of economic history, there is tremendous importance in

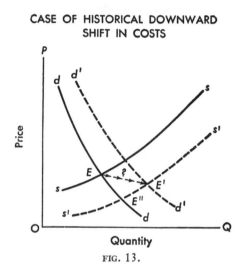

CASE OF HISTORICAL DOWNWARD
SHIFT IN COSTS

FIG. 13.

such cases of reduced cost over time as a result of technological progress partly induced by the expansion of a mass market. Goods are constantly being improved in quality and cheapened in price. The fact that the economist's static-supply curves do not throw much illumination on this phenomenon should not be used to belittle its tremendous significance.

What about the case of genuine *reversible* economies of large-scale production—cases where going back to small-scale production does again send costs up? The alert modern economist will not deny its importance. But he will point out that in a competitive industry each firm will have *already* expanded its output to where the *extra* cost of producing a unit of output has begun to turn up. This is so because each competitive producer will have no fear of spoiling his own market and will have had every incentive to expand his production through and beyond the decreasing cost stage.

The observant critic will not yet be satisfied. Suppose that an industry's demand is so small that one or a few firms working at efficient large-scale production can satisfy all demands. With decreasing costs the firm or firms will expand production and drive other competitors out, since each loss of their markets sends competitors' costs up still farther and lessens their power to compete. "Isn't all this possible?" the critic will ask. The honest economist will answer, "Not only possible, but likely in many industries. Modern technology makes perfect competition of numerous producers out of the question in many lines of activity. In such cases, and they may be the rule rather than the exception, we must replace the analysis of this chapter by the more general analysis of *monopolistic competition.*"[1] This is discussed in detail in Chap. 21.

CASE 6. *Shifts in Supply.* All of the above discussion, with the exception of part of Case 5, dealt with a shift in demand and no shift in supply. To analyze Proposition 2, we must now shift supply, keeping demand constant. This is done in Fig. 14.

If the law of diminishing consumption holds, then increased supply must send us *down* the demand curve, decreasing price and increasing quantity. The student may verify, by drawing diagrams or by comparing automobiles and wheat, the following quantitative corollaries of Proposition 2:

a. An increase in supply will decrease price most when demand is inelastic, and decrease price least when demand is relatively elastic.

b. An increase in supply will increase quantity least when demand is inelastic, most when demand is elastic.

What are the common-sense reasons for these corollaries? Illustrate with automobiles and wheat.

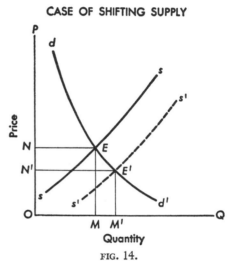

CASE OF SHIFTING SUPPLY

FIG. 14.

In concluding, three rather unimportant exceptions to the universal law of diminishing consumption will be briefly mentioned.

First, items such as diamonds, women's hats, and other goods that are valued not for their intrinsic qualities so much as for their "snob appeal" and expensiveness may fall off in demand if their price is cut. Chic New York shops sometimes take advantage of this fact and find that they do better in

[1] There remains one possibility discussed in advanced economic textbooks. If an increased demand for an industry's product causes each firm's cost curve to *shift downward* (*a*) because cheaper and better trained labor becomes available, (*b*) because better information centers and markets are made possible, or (*c*) because raw materials produced at decreasing costs by other quasi-monpolized industries become cheaper, then this industry may have a truly reversible, competitive, supply curve which is downward sloping. Alfred Marshall, the great English economist of the turn of the century, called this a case of "*external economies*" of production, *i.e.*, economies external to each firm in an industry.

moving a slow-selling item if they raise its price.[1] Customers think, "It really must be good if it costs so much," as if it were universally true that "You only get what you pay for." A penetrating early twentieth-century writer, Thorstein Veblen,[2] coined the phrase "conspicuous consumption" for the phenomena where things are valued because their price tag shows all over them.

There is a second exception to the law of diminishing consumption, which is important especially in the short run. When the price of steel or a share of common stock is first lowered, buyers may not think to themselves, "Ah, this is now cheap. I will buy." Instead they may think, "Aha! Price is falling and will probably fall still more. I'll cut down on my orders and wait until the price falls farther." The same effect (in reverse) is often observed when prices begin to rise: buyers rush to purchase in anticipation of still higher prices. The result: in the short run the amounts demanded may rise rather than fall with increases in price.[3]

The third exception is rather unimportant in practice, but interesting as a curiosity. Certain items, like potatoes, are bought in great quantity by poor people simply because they are cheap and filling. In nineteenth-century Ireland, the peasants were so poor that a good deal of their income was spent in this way. Only in good times when incomes rose could people afford meat and bread and perhaps a few lace curtains. Now what would happen if the price of potatoes should rise? To the despairing housewife this would be just like a cut in her man's income. The family now becomes so poor that, paradoxically, they have to give up all meat and luxuries and fill up even more than before on potatoes. Consequently, the higher the price, the more may potatoes be demanded!

The student may try his hand at finding still other exceptions. But he must not commit the cardinal error of confusing a shift in demand with a movement along the curve. He will receive harsh treatment at the bar of justice if he offers, as a fourth exception, the fact that in prosperity price goes up and so does the quantity demanded. Why?

[1] Similarly, a Boston night club found it paid to advertise itself as the "most expensive place in town."

[2] T. VEBLEN, "The Theory of the Leisure Class," The Macmillan Company, New York, 1899.

[3] This is a dynamic effect hinging not on high or low levels of price but on "the rate of change of price." The destabilizing effects of this are shown in connection with the discussion of stock-market speculation in Chap. 25.

Chapter 20: THE THEORY OF

CONSUMPTION AND DEMAND

WE must now go behind the scenes of the market demand schedule to examine tastes and decisions determining the behavior of families and individuals. Each consumer has a small-scale demand curve relating the quantities that it will buy to the market price of each good. The market demand at any given price is nothing more nor less than the sum total of what each family will buy at that price. This raises the problem of the factors that are important to explain the consumer's demand behavior.

THEORY OF CONSUMER'S CHOICE

A rather fancy theory was developed in the nineteenth century to explain the way a consumer arrives at decisions on what to buy. To begin with, the consumer starts out with a certain amount of income that he—or perhaps we should say "she"—can spend. In addition, he is confronted with a whole array of market prices for all the things he can buy. These prices are quoted to him, and ordinarily they are beyond his power to alter.

Immediately the problem of choice becomes apparent. If goods were free, or if his income were great enough so that he could buy every last thing that suits his fancy, this would not be so. But as things are, the more he buys of one good, the less he can buy of others. Therefore, the advantages of any good must be balanced against the advantages of all the rest. In performing this calculation of comparing goods, it is not enough for him simply to balance the advantage of different goods on an equal basis. A steak may be preferred to a can of pork Spam, but if the steak costs ten times as much, he may decide to buy the Spam. In other words, it is extra satisfaction secured *per unit of money expended* that matters to him. The satisfaction to be derived from different goods is not to be equal if their prices are different; but their extra satisfactions must end up *proportional* to the respective prices of the goods.

The theory being described assumes that the consumer has rather definite opinions about his own (family's) preferences as between different amounts of goods. If a psychologist quizzed him about them, he could probably answer many of the questions. But not necessarily all. Many of these opinions are on the subconscious level because he has become accustomed through repeated experience to make decisions almost automatically. As a matter of fact, most people like to keep deliberate decision making down to as low a level as possible.[1]

In any case, the consumer, possessed of a given income and set of prices of goods, is thereby confronted with a wide range of final batches of goods. Automatically or unconsciously, he can appraise and compare them and finally pick out the best combination, or what is called the "equilibrium combination."

How shall we characterize this equilibrium position? Obviously, it is one from which the consumer will not care to depart. He will be unwilling to give up buying something of one item in order to substitute something of another. Why? Because he has already made his choice of the best combination, and any other combination is inferior.

Or to put the matter another way. He buys more and more units of all commodities until the last little units of each of them yield him satisfactions that are proportional to their respective prices. When the last 10-cent pound of beans yields twice as much satisfaction as does the last 5-cent pound of sugar, then he stops, knowing that he has arrived at the equilibrium point. Notice that the critical satisfactions to be compared concern not the total quantity of each commodity consumed but only the *last* or "marginal" increments. *At this point the extra utility per last cent or nickel is the same in all uses;* this is a necessary condition for equilibrium.

Why? Because if it were not—if the last penny spent on sugar yielded *less* satisfaction than that spent on beans—it would pay him to switch a penny from sugar buying to the purchase of some more beans. When it no longer pays to switch purchases, because the satisfaction per penny from beans has finally

---

[1] The more daring psychologists and economists assume that the consumer experiences a definite quantitative amount of satisfaction or anticipated pleasure when confronted with a given batch of goods. This definite psychological quantity or sensation is given the name "utility." If a first batch of goods and services, A, registers a higher utility score than a second batch, B, and they cost the same, then he will buy A and not B.

The more cautious writers prefer to be agnostic on the question of utility as a magnitude. All they assume is that the consumer can compare A and B and know which he prefers. Whether this is done by giving each some numerical score, these writers do not claim to know; nor do they care since the "facts" of consumer's behavior are the same in either case.

fallen to the level of that from sugar, then he has reached the equilibrium position and will stop.[1] This shows us, by the way, that the equilibrium position in this field, as in other parts of economic life, is usually approached only after a period of trial and error.

The above few pages summarize all that there is to the theory of consumer's behavior. The discussion could be amplified by numerous diagrams and tables, but that is not really necessary. The beginning student of economics need keep firmly in mind only the following three sets of propositions:

1. A consumer with only a finite income, confronted with (nonzero) prices, cannot buy as much as he wants of everything. He must choose and balance, and in doing so must take relative prices into consideration.

2. The consumer is supposed to have a fairly definite set of preferences so that he knows whether a given situation is better, worse, or indifferent as compared to another situation.

3. The consumer is able, therefore, to select out of all possible situations available to him because of (1) the one which is "best" as determined by (2). This is the *equilibrium situation*, characterized by the condition that no further substitution between goods is desirable, because already expenditure has been allocated among goods until *the last penny spent on each commodity gives the same addition of satisfaction as does the last penny spent on every other commodity*.

PRICE AND INCOME CHANGES IN DEMAND

The above theory explains how the amount demanded of each good is determined, once the consumer is given a set of prices and income. Thus it also explains why the amount demanded of a good will change when its price changes, or for that matter when income changes or *the price of some other good* changes.

---

[1] The cautious economists mentioned in the previous footnote, who do not believe in utility as a numerical quantity, would not object to the use of the word "satisfaction" in the above paragraph. This is because the numerical level of this term is not used, but only *comparative* or *relative* levels of utility. Still, the purists in this group would prefer to reformulate the condition of equilibrium so as to avoid all possibility of misunderstanding. They would say, *for the consumer to be in equilibrium, the relative prices (or costs) of each good must be just matched by the rates at which he is just willing to substitute them (in small amounts) for each other; or when relative prices equal relative extra utilities*.

Of course this adds up to exactly the same thing as the other formulation. For example, if the cost ratio of beans to sugar did not match the consumer's relative utility or substitution ratio (as determined by his preferences), it would pay him to substitute one for the other. When would he stop? Only at the equilibrium point where price ratios and substitution ratios are equal.

The first of these three changes, involving the variation in quantity demanded of a good as its own price is raised or lowered, is nothing other than our old friend the demand curve. The second, which relates variations in demand to income changes, is of the greatest importance both in comparing the behavoir of rich and poor and in connection with the effects of ups and downs in national income and employment. The wealth of factual material on this subject has earlier been discussed in terms of family budget behavior, and the propensity to save or consume.

CROSS RELATIONS OF DEMAND

Let us begin by discussing the third case in which the amount demanded of one good changes when the price of another good changes. This rather interesting case of cross interrelationship can be disposed of briefly because its results are in line with general experience. Thus everyone knows that raising the price of tea will decrease the amount demanded of tea. It will also affect the amounts demanded of other commodities. For example, a higher price for tea will lower the demand for a commodity like sugar; *i.e.*, it will shift the whole demand schedule of sugar downward. But it will also increase the amount demanded of coffee. Probably it will have little or no effect on the demand for salt.

We say, therefore, that tea and coffee are *rival*, or *competing*, products, or *substitutes*. Tea and sugar, on the other hand, are *cooperating*, or *complementary* commodities, or *complements*. The in-between pair of tea and salt are said to represent *independent* commodities. The reader will of course be able to classify such pairs as beef and pork, turkey and cranberry sauce, automobiles and gasoline, trucks and railroad freight, oil and coal.

RESPONSE OF QUANTITY TO OWN PRICE

So much for crisscross relationships between goods. Returning now to the relationships between a commodity and its own price, we are in a position to understand why the law of *diminishing consumption* probably holds, or why more will be bought at a lower price.

In the first place, being able to buy a good at a lower price is just like having an increase in your (real) income, particularly if you have been buying a great deal of the commodity. With a higher real income you can afford to buy more of this good, and of every good. And unless the commodity is of the so-called "inferior" variety like oleomargarine or potatoes, you will ordinarily choose to buy something more of it once your real income has been increased. (This is sometimes called an "income effect.")

The second factor explaining diminishing consumption is equally obvious. If the price of wheat goes down while other prices do not, then wheat has become relatively cheaper. It pays therefore to *substitute* some wheat for other goods in order to maintain one's standard of living most cheaply. Thus wheat becomes a relatively cheaper source of calories than before, and more of it will be bought and less of potatoes. Similarly, a cheapening of movies relative to stage plays may cause the consumer to seek his amusement more in the cheaper direction. The consumer is doing here only what every businessman does when cheapening the price of one productive factor causes him to adjust his production methods so as to substitute the cheap input for other kinds of inputs; by this process of substitution, he is able to produce the same output at lower total cost. (This second reason for expanding demand at lower price is sometimes called a "substitution effect.")

Of course, the quantitative importance of each of these effects varies with the good in question and with the consumer. Under some circumstances the resulting demand curve is very *elastic: e.g.*, where the consumer has been spending a good deal on the commodity and where ready substitutes are available; for example, a drunkard's demand for gin. But if the commodity is like salt, which involves only a small fraction of the consumer's budget, which is not easily replaceable by other items, and which is necessary in small amounts to complement more important items, then demand will be *inelastic*.

All this agrees with common-sense notions about economics: that *scarcity* or *rarity* is what gives value to a good in exchange.

Some economists try to "prove" the validity of this generalization by analogy with a fundamental psychological generalization called the Weber-Fechner Law. According to this law, a man who can just perceive a difference in light intensity between a 10- and a 15-watt light bulb will not be able to perceive a difference between a 20-watt bulb and a 25-watt bulb, even though the arithmetic difference in intensity is the same. But he will be able to tell the difference between 20 watts and 30 watts or between 200 watts and 300 watts—because the percentage difference in intensity is what is important. This same effect, a diminution in ability to perceive and recognize minimum differences in stimuli, is claimed by the psychologist to hold with respect to perception of sounds, weights (placed on or in one's hand), and so forth.

The connection of these phenomena with the diminution in desire of an economic consumer for additional units of a commodity is, to say the least, rather far-fetched. The relation is, at best, suggestive rather than conclusive. The validity of the economic law of diminishing consumption must stand or fall on the basis of the economic behavior of consumers. If it should fail, the economist's duty is to modify his theory so as to be consistent with the observable facts.

THE PARADOX OF VALUE

The above analysis helps to explain a famous question that troubled Adam Smith whose book, "The Wealth of Nations" (1776), marks the beginning of modern economics. He asked, "How is it that water, which is so very useful that life is impossible without it, has such a low price—while diamonds, which are quite unnecessary, have such a high price?"

Today even a beginning student can give a correct answer to this problem. "That's simply explained," he will write on an examination, "the supply and demand curves for water are such that they intersect at a very low price. While the supply and demand curves for diamonds are such that they intersect at a high price." This is not an incorrect answer. Adam Smith could not have given it because supply and demand curves as descriptive tools had not yet been invented and were not to be for 75 years or more.

A modern economic neophyte might also attempt to dispose of a similar fundamental question asked by the medieval churchmen: "Is not interest on money unfair usury? Why should there be an interest rate charged for the use of money or capital so long as the principal of the loan is repaid in full?"

After he had read an economic textbook, the student might reply, "Whether or not there is to be a rate of interest is not a philosophical question to be settled by considering the origin of the word in the Latin language; or even by considering what Aristotle had to say about it. No," he will continue, "the problem simply boils down to the question as to whether the supply schedule of the money or capital funds available for investment intersects the demand schedule at a positive rate of interest. If it does—and throughout history it has—then there will be a rate of interest."

Once again, this is not an incorrect argument. But both of these answers are of the sort that would earn a pass rather than high honors on a final examination. For after he had mastered the lingo, old Adam Smith would naturally ask the question, "But *why* do supply and demand for water intersect at such a low price?"

The answer is by now easy to phrase. It consists of two parts. (1) Diamonds are very scarce; the cost of getting extra ones is very great. Water is relatively abundant; the cost of more water in most parts of the world is very low.

These propositions would have seemed reasonable to even the classical economists of more than a century ago, who would probably have let it go at that, and would not have known how to reconcile the above facts about cost with the equally valid fact that the world's water is more *useful* than the world's supply of diamonds. (In fact, Adam Smith never did quite resolve the paradox. He was content simply to point out that the "value in use" of a good—its total contribution to economic welfare—is not the same thing as its "value in exchange"—the total money value or revenue for which it will sell.)

But today, we should add to the cost considerations of (1) the following: (2) the total usefulness of water does not determine its price or demand.

Only the relative usefulness and cost of the *last* little bit of water determine its price. Why? Because people are free to buy or not buy that last little bit. If water is priced higher than its last extra usefulness, then that last unit cannot be sold. Therefore, the price must fall until it reaches exactly the level of usefulness of the last little bit, no more and no less. Moreover, because every unit of water is exactly like any other unit and because there is only one price in a competitive market, *every unit must sell for what the last least useful unit sells for.* (As one student put the matter: The theory of economic value is easy to understand if you just remember that the tail wags the dog.)

Now we know that the more there is of a commodity, the less becomes the relative desirability of its last little unit—even though its total usefulness always grows as we get more of the commodity. Therefore, it is obvious why a large amount of water has a low price. Or even why air is actually a free good despite its vast usefulness. The later units pull down the market value of all units.

This completes the brief excursion behind the supply and demand curves necessary to explain Smith's paradox of value.

CONSUMER'S SURPLUS

The above discussion emphasizes that the accounting system which records the "total economic value" or revenue of a good (price × quantity) differs from that necessary to record "total welfare." The total economic value of air is zero; its contribution to welfare, very great.[1] Similarly, if we increase the quantity produced of a commodity like wheat whose demand is inelastic, we obviously increase the community's welfare, even though we destroy some economic value.

Thus, there is always a gap between total welfare and total economic value. This gap is in the nature of a *surplus*, which the consumer gets because he always "receives more than he pays for."

Nor does he benefit at the expense of the seller. In a swap, one party does

[1] Or, as Smith would say, its value in use is very great; its value in exchange, negligible.

not lose what the other gains. Unlike energy which cannot be created or destroyed, the well-being of all participants is increased by trade.

It is not hard to see how this surplus arises. Every unit of good that the consumer buys costs him only as much as the last unit is worth. But by our fundamental law, the *earlier* units are worth *more* to him than the last. Therefore, he enjoys a surplus on each of these earlier units. When trade stops benefiting him and giving him a surplus, he stops buying.

As final clinching evidence that the consumer always receives a surplus, we may cite the fact that a ruthless seller could present the consumer with an ultimatum: "Either you pay me an extra amount of money for the whole block of the good that you are consuming, or you must go without all the units, from first to last. Take it or leave it!" The consumer would certainly be willing to pay an extra amount rather than do without the good altogether.

Many ingenious ways have been suggested for measuring this consumer's surplus, but they are of no particular significance. The important thing is to see how lucky the citizens of modern efficient communities really are. The *privilege of being able to buy a vast array of goods at low prices cannot be overestimated.*

This is a humbling thought. If ever a person becomes arrogantly proud of *his* economic productivity and *his* level of real earnings, let him pause and reflect. If he were transported with all his skills and energies intact to a primitive desert island, how much would his money earnings buy? Indeed, without capital machinery, without rich resources, without other labor, and above all without the technological knowledge which each generation inherits from society's past, how much could *he* produce? It is only too clear that all of us are reaping the benefits of an economic world we never made.

This basic fact is well stated in the following quotation:

The organizer of industry who thinks that he has "made" himself and his business has found a whole social system ready to his hand in skilled workers, machinery, a market, peace and order—a vast apparatus and a pervasive atmosphere, the joint creation of millions of men and scores of generations. Take away the whole social factor and we have not Robinson Crusoe, with his salvage from the wreck and his acquired knowledge, but the naked savage living on roots, berries, and vermin.[1]

[1] L. T. HOBHOUSE, "The Elements of Social Justice," pp. 162–163, Henry Holt and Company, Incorporated, New York, 1922.

SUMMARY

1. A consumer with a given money income, confronted by finite prices, is limited in what he can buy and so must choose and substitute. To the extent that he is acting rationally, he will consciously or unconsciously substitute one good for another until he has reached the highest level of satisfaction. At this equilibrium point, the last penny spent on each kind of good will yield exactly the same extra satisfaction.

2. The equilibrium amount demanded of any good will change when either income, its own price, or the price of some other good changes. The last change introduces the notion of competing, independent, or complementary goods.

3. The downward response of a good when its price rises—or the relation between scarcity of a good and its price—is the basic economic law of diminishing *consumption*. Together with the important recognition that it is the cost and desirability of the last unit of an article, this law helps to explain Adam Smith's famous paradox of value concerning water and diamonds.

4. Consumer's surplus is a reflection of the fact that the total economic welfare of any good is greater than its total monetary value. This is because all units of a good, being interchangeable, sell for as little as the last is worth. Consequently, the consumer is receiving a surplus on all previous units.

QUESTIONS FOR DISCUSSION

1. "I don't know much about art, but I do know what I like." Is this a correct statement? Do people know what they like in the way of consumption goods? Do they usually like "what is good for them"?

2. Why is it nonsensical to say:

   a. In equilibrium, the satisfaction from the last 5 cents' worth of peas must equal the satisfaction from the last 4 cents' worth of sugar?

   b. In equilibrium, the satisfactions derived from all commodities must be equal?

   c. In equilibrium, the last little bits of satisfaction derived from all commodities must be equal?

   d. In equilibrium, the satisfactions derived from the dollars spent on all commodities must be the same?

Write out a correct fifth statement.

3. Why would your correct condition of equilibrium have to be modified in its application to goods, like automobiles, which are not infinitely divisible like sugar or gasoline? (HINT: Would it be possible to shift 1 penny or $1 from the purchase of automobiles to the purchase of sugar or fountain pens?)

4. Why do farmers work hard when their efforts produce only large crops, low prices, and lower farm incomes? Would anyone benefit from the process?

5. How much would you be willing to pay rather than give up all movies completely? How much do you spend per year on movies?

6. "You only get what you pay for." Is this true?

7. Oscar Wilde said, "What is a cynic? A man who knows the price of everything, and the value of nothing." Could not the same be said of an economist who confined his attention to accounting and statistical dollar data?

APPENDIX TO CHAPTER 20
GEOMETRICAL ANALYSIS OF CONSUMER
EQUILIBRIUM

It is often instructive to show graphically, and without using the language of numerical utility, exactly what the consumer's equilibrium position looks like.

We start out by considering a consumer with a given money income, buying only two commodities, say food and clothing, at definite quoted prices. The consumer is supposed to be able to tell us (1) whether he prefers a given combination of the two goods, say 3 units of food and 2 of clothing, to a second combination, say 2 units of food and 3 of clothing, or (2) whether he is "indifferent" between them, or (3) whether he actually prefers the second batch of goods.

Let us suppose that actually the two batches are equally good as far as the consumer is concerned. Let us go on to list in Table 1 some of the other combinations of goods between which the individual is also just indifferent.

TABLE 1. *Indifference Table Showing Equally Desirable Combinations of Goods*

Food..	1	2	3	4
Clothing.......................................	6	3	2	1.5

This is just one such table. We could have started out with a still higher level of satisfaction or level of indifference, and listed all the different combinations that belonged to it. Thus, we might have filled in a similar indifference table of all combinations indifferent as compared to 3 food and 3 clothing; or still another indifference table for all combinations indifferent to 1 food and 1 clothing.

But if we examine any one of the infinite number of such tables, we shall probably find that it has the same remarkable property as the one indicated above: *the scarcer a good, the greater its relative (substitution) value.*

Thus, the consumer in Table 1 is willing to give up 3 units of clothing—from 6 to 3—in order to get a second unit of food in addition to the first one. But to get a third unit of food, he is now willing to give up only 1 unit of clothing; for still one more unit of food, only $\frac{1}{2}$ unit of clothing.

The above remarks about a consumer's preference or indifference between different commodity situations are summarized in Fig. 1. Each of the indifference tables now becomes an Indifference curve or a contour line of equal utility. Each one of the concave curves represents the locus of all combinations of goods giving equal levels of satisfaction. They are concave in accordance with the fundamental law of scarcity just referred to. Just as there are an infinite number of indifference tables, there are infinitely many of these Indifference curves or isoutility contour lines, each one corresponding to a possible level

CONSUMER EQUILIBRIUM

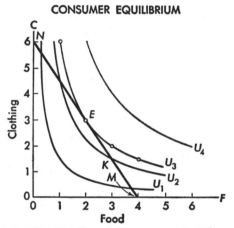

FIG. 1. The curves labeled U_1, U_2, U_3, and U_4 represent Indifference curves or contour lines of equal utility. The straight line MN is the Consumption-possibility curve, upon which the consumer is free to move. Equilibrium is at the point of tangency E, where the Consumption-possibility curve reaches the highest possible level of utility.

of real income or satisfaction. Geometrically they are not unlike contour lines on a topographical map of the earth's surface, or like the lines of equal pressure to be seen on weather maps and in textbooks on thermodynamics. Of course, only a few of the possible Indifference curves or contours are shown in Fig. 1, the lowest corresponding to a level of utility, U_1, the next to U_2, and so forth to the highest, U_4. The curve, U_3, with the clearly marked circular points corresponds to the numerical data of our earlier table.

A consumer has a given income, say $6 per day, and is confronted with fixed prices, say $1.50 for food and $1 for clothing, at which he can convert money into each of the two goods, or each good into the other. Those who like to think geometrically will realize that the Consumption-possibility curve upon which he is constrained to move will be a straight line, as given by NM in the accompanying figure. If he spends all his income on food, he can at most buy the amount of food given at the point M, or 4 units of food; if he spends all on clothing, he can get only the amount of it given by N, or 6 units of clothing; in between he can trade one good for the other at a constant rate, depending upon the relative prices of food and clothing. Therefore, the curve must be a straight line with slope of \$1.50/\$1, or 3 to 2.

Now how can we identify the position of final equilibrium mentioned earlier? Obviously, the consumer will move along the straight line until the highest

EFFECT OF INCOME OR PRICE CHANGE ON EQUILIBRIUM

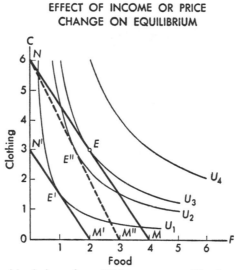

FIG. 2. Confronted with choices along NM, consumer will select the best point, E. If income halves, so that new choice is along $N'M'$, consumer will go to new best point, E'. If instead of an income change, the price of food had increased, then the consumer's choice-line would pivot around N to NM''. The new best point, E'', must be where consumer is tangent to highest level of well-being.

Indifference curve is reached. This cannot be at M, at N, or even at K, because by moving from any of these points the consumer can cross on to higher Indifference curves. Obviously, the equilibrium can be only at the point of tangency, E, where the Consumption-possibility curve touches—but does not cross—the highest Indifference curve.[1] Geometrically, at the point of equilibrium, the slope of the line is just equal to the slope of the Indifference curve.

Or, in terms of our previous words, the price ratio of the two goods (as shown by the slope of the line) is exactly equal in equilibrium to the *relative*

---

[1] If the law of diminishing substitution did not hold, the consumer would still move to the highest Indifference curve. But in this case, he might consume nothing of some commodities. This eventuality should occasion no surprise.

extra utility or substitution ratio at which one good can be given up in small amounts for the other good without losing any satisfaction (as shown by the slope of the Indifference curve).

If the consumer's income were to be halved, the new equilibrium would be in Fig. 2 at E' where the new straight line Consumption-possibility curve—shifted in a parallel fashion half as far in—would just be tangent to a highest Indifference curve.

If only the price of food were to be raised, say to $2, income and clothing prices being unchanged, the total amount of clothing that could be bought (still shown by N) would not be changed. But the amount of food that could be got for each unit of clothing sacrificed would of course be less. Consequently, the new Consumption-possibility line would be rotated downward around N as a pivot and would travel from N to M'', the new point showing how little food (only 3 units) could be bought when all money is spent on food. The new equilibrium point would now be at E'' where there is again tangency with an Indifference curve.

The student should be able to tell what will happen if, say, only the price of clothing is changed, and in a *downward* direction.

Chapter 21: COST AND

THE EQUILIBRIUM OF THE

FIRM UNDER PERFECT AND

IMPERFECT COMPETITION

IN the preceding chapter we went behind the demand curve. Now we must do the same for the supply curve to see just how costs of production in each firm determine the total supply curve of all firms in a competitive market, and the price response of imperfectly competitive markets. The first half of this chapter shows how any individual firm must act in order to maximize its profits. The second applies these principles to a perfectly competitive industry, and to four important patterns of monopolistic or imperfect competition.

A. *THE MAXIMUM PROFIT EQUILIBRIUM POSITION WITHIN THE FIRM*

In these days when "perfect" competition exists only in a few lines of agriculture, we cannot be content to understand perfectly competitive industries alone but must examine the behavior of firms who have some monopoly power and are able to affect the selling prices of their product. Such firms may be very large, very profitable, and in possession of patents or special advantages which effectively exclude other firms from producing the same products. In this case, they may be called a "monopoly." The Bell Telephone System, or the prewar Aluminum Company of America may perhaps qualify for this title.

MONOPOLISTIC COMPETITION

More often a firm has *some* control over price, but only to a limited extent. It has certain peculiar advantages of know-how, location, trade-marks, and reputation; at the same time it has rivals of which the same is true. We may say, therefore, that the firm has some monopoly powers but is also subject to some competition. We do not have perfect competition, nor do we have complete monopoly. Instead we have imperfect competition; a blending of competition and monopoly; or, in short, what may be termed *monopolistic competition.*[1]

One may construct a line, whose one extremity represents "pure" or perfect competition and whose other end represents complete monopoly.

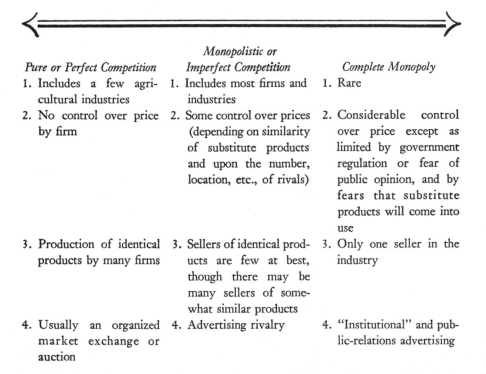

Pure or Perfect Competition	*Monopolistic or Imperfect Competition*	*Complete Monopoly*
1. Includes a few agricultural industries	1. Includes most firms and industries	1. Rare
2. No control over price by firm	2. Some control over prices (depending on similarity of substitute products and upon the number, location, etc., of rivals)	2. Considerable control over price except as limited by government regulation or fear of public opinion, and by fears that substitute products will come into use
3. Production of identical products by many firms	3. Sellers of identical products are few at best, though there may be many sellers of somewhat similar products	3. Only one seller in the industry
4. Usually an organized market exchange or auction	4. Advertising rivalry	4. "Institutional" and public-relations advertising

Most of modern life falls under the heading of monopolistic competition; for example, barber shops, the radio and electrical industry, steel, automobiles,

[1] The interested reader should consult E. H. Chamberlin, "Theory of Monopolistic Competition," especially Chaps. 1 and 4, Harvard University Press, Cambridge, 1946.

retail stores, etc. Exclusive monopolies, like public utilities or telephones, are usually regulated by the government; and even they must take account of the potential competition of alternative products—oil for gas, or cables for telephones. This shows how relatively unimportant complete monopolies are.

The student may easily apply two simple tests to convince himself of how unimportant pure or perfect competition is today:

1. How many firms find it *un*necessary to spend money on advertising, salesmen, and marketing? Obviously, very few except for farmers who produce a homogencous crop.

2. How many firms are unwilling to take on new business at the prevailing price? Obviously, in normal times, only those same farmers mentioned above are unwilling to do so—unwilling because they have already taken to the market all the production that they wish to with no fear of depressing the price. The vast majority of firms normally welcome new buyers.

Both of these answers are incompatible with really perfect competition. The analysis to follow must clearly be general enough to apply to all cases— not just to perfect competition—if it is to throw light on the economic world as it really is, and not as we might wish it to be.

THE FIRM'S DEMAND UNDER PERFECT AND MONOPOLISTIC COMPETITION

For simplicity, let us consider a single firm which produces only a single commodity. It is in business to make as much money as possible. Ideally it would like to charge a very high price and to sell a very large quantity of output. But it knows, or it will soon learn from experience, that these are not independent variables: it cannot set its price very high and at the same time succeed in selling a great deal; to sell a large quantity it must lower its price; and to get a high price, it must keep its commodity scarce.

In other words, the firm is subject to a demand curve, such as was described in Chap. 19 on Supply and Demand; only there we always referred to the demand curve for the industry, whereas now we are speaking of the demand curve for the individual firm. If the firm is in a perfectly competitive field, its demand curve will be very flat, with practically infinite elasticity. If the firm is a complete monopoly, it will be able to raise prices without unduly decreasing sales; and the action of other firms will not be able to shift its curve downward and to the left. Usually, most modern business firms find themselves somewhere in between these conditions, *i.e.*, under monopolistic competition. Their demand curve will have some downward tilt, and it will be shifted downward by the action of rival firms. Two of these three cases are shown in Fig. 1.

PRICE, QUANTITY, AND TOTAL REVENUE

Since imperfect competition includes perfect competition as one very special instance, we may concentrate upon the more general case. Table 1 represents the original demand schedule for the firm under monopolistic or imperfect competition. The reader should fill in the missing figures in the total revenue column of Table 1.

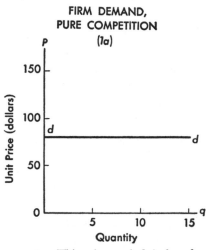

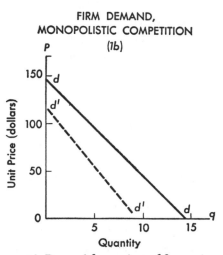

FIG. 1a. This shows infinitely elastic demand for product of firm under "pure" or "perfect" competition.

FIG. 1b. Demand for product of firm under "monopolistic" competition. The broken line d'd' shows a fall in the demand schedule as a result of a cut in rivals' prices.

Clearly, the firm will not charge the highest possible price of $134. Why not? Because then it does not maximize its profits. It is then collecting the highest possible (average) revenue per unit, but it is selling only one unit, and collecting only $134 of total revenue.

How much will the firm produce, and at what price? This question cannot be answered until we know something about its costs of production. For the moment, let us neglect all costs. Clearly, the best quantity for the firm is then around 7 units, and the best price is around $74. This answer is derived from an examination of the total revenue column, $R = P \times q$, where the point of highest total revenue is starred. Price is not at a maximum; neither is quantity. But *total* revenue is being maximized.

TABLE 1. *Demand Schedule for the Individual Firm under Monopolistic Competition*

Quantity q	Price p	Total revenue $R = p \times q$
(1)	(2)	(3)
0	$144 or more	$ 0
1	134	
2	124	248
3	114	
4	104	
5	94	
6	84	504
*7	*74	*518
8	64	512
9	54	—
10	44	—

TOTAL AND MARGINAL COSTS

It is now simple to introduce costs into the picture. Just as the firm had to make a guess at its demand curve, so it must try to estimate the approximate dollar expense that will be incurred in producing different outputs. Although the accounting difficulties in arriving at such a total cost curve are very great and may involve considerable guesswork, the firm's accounting and production departments must endeavor to determine which costs are *fixed*, independently of changes in output, and which are *variable costs* changing with output. Table 2 is an example of such an estimate for a certain firm.

Fixed Costs. Column (1) indicates the different levels of production per unit time, going from 0 up to 10 units. Column (2) indicates that the firm's fixed costs per time period are $256 even if it produces nothing. By definition, fixed costs are fixed; they remain at $256 at all levels of output. They result from past commitments, from costs that are already "sunk," overhead expenses, etc.

Variable Costs. Column (3) lists the estimated amounts of total variable costs per unit time at different levels of production. By definition, variable costs are zero when no output is being produced. But they change with quantity, q. At first as output increases, variable costs seem to grow quite rapidly. But as output increases further, *economies of mass production* come into play and variable costs do not seem to be increasing proportionately with output. Later on, however, as diminishing returns set in, variable costs begin to shoot up more rapidly than output.

Total Cost.   This is given in Col. (4). It is nothing but the sum of fixed and variable costs. It must begin, therefore, even with zero production, at $256 and increase from there on like variable costs. Figure 2 illustrates the three different cost categories pictorially.

TABLE 2. *Fixed, Variable, and Total Costs of Individual Firm*

Quantity q	Fixed cost FC	Variable cost VC	Total cost $TC =$ $FC + VC$	Average cost per unit $AC =$ $TC \div q$	Marginal cost per unit MC
(1)	(2)	(3)	(4)	(5)	(6)
0	$256	$ 0	$256	Infinity	
					$ 64
1	256	64	320	$320	
					20
2	256	84	340	170	
					15
3	256	99	355	118.33	
					13
4	256	112	368	92	
					13
5	256	125	381	76.20	
					19
6	256	144	400	66.67	
					31
7	256	175	431	61.57	
					49
8	256	224	480	60	
					73
9	256	297	553	61.44	
					103
10	256	400	656	65.60	

Average Cost.   Of the three cost schedules discussed, clearly the fundamental one is total cost. The other two are refinements which can easily be calculated from it. Sometimes, however, accountants find it convenient to make still other cost calculations. Thus, in Col. (5) of Table 2, there is listed *average or unit cost* of production. This is easily derived by dividing total cost by the number of units of output in order to get the average cost per unit. (Too much importance should not be attached to average costs because, after all, it is *total* dollar profit and costs that interest any firm.)

Average costs are very high at first because the large fixed costs are saddled on to so few units. In fact, when output is zero, costs per unit have to be infinite. If only one unit were produced, average costs would be $320. But

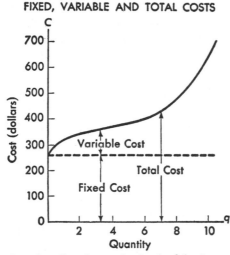

FIG. 2. The horizontal broken line shows the level of fixed cost as given in Table 2. The solid line shows total cost if measured from the q axis, variable cost if measured from the dotted line of fixed cost.

as more units are produced, the $256 of fixed cost is spread over more and more units. This explains the early rapid decline of average costs in Table 2 and in Fig. 3.

After the overhead has been spread thin over many units, fixed costs can no longer have much influence on average costs. Variable costs become important, and as average variable costs begin to rise because of limitations of plant space and management difficulties, average costs finally begin to turn up. Thus, in Table 2, Col. (5), and in Fig. 3, average costs are at their lowest at 8 units, where they are only $60 per unit. Expanding output beyond this point causes average costs to rise. Thus, the average curve is U-shaped: falling at first because of spreading the overhead and economies of mass production, but ultimately rising because of diminishing returns.

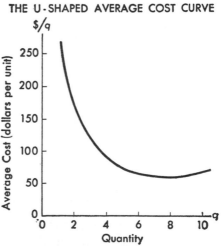

FIG. 3. The average cost curve is computed by dividing total cost by the number of units of production, as given in Table 2.

Marginal Cost. The businessman must decide how much to produce so as to make the greatest profits. He will be more interested, therefore, in the *extra* costs of changing output rather than in over-all average costs.

Column (6) of Table 2 lists the difference in total costs for each extra unit of output. Such extra costs are important enough in economic theory to rate a new and distinctive name: *marginal cost.* Thus, the marginal cost in going from the fifth unit to the sixth unit is derived from Col. (4) by subtracting the total cost of 5 units from the total cost of 6 units. This gives $400 − $381, or $19. (What is the marginal cost in going from the eighth to the ninth unit? Why?)

MARGINAL REVENUE AND PRICE

In a similar way, we define *marginal revenue* as the extra revenue resulting from selling an *extra* unit of goods. Marginal revenue would be derived from the total revenue column of Table 1. This is indicated in Table 3, which repeats Table 1 but has one new column for marginal revenue.

TABLE 3. *Marginal Revenue and Price*

Quantity q (1)	Price p (2)	Total revenue $R = p \times q$ (3)	Marginal revenue MR (4)
0	$144 or higher	$ 0	
			$134
1	134	134	
			114
2	124	248	
			94
3	114	342	
			74
4	104	416	
			54
5	94	470	
			34
6	84	504	
			14
7	74	*518	
			− 6
8	64	512	
			−26
9	54	486	
			−46
10	44	440	

At first, the reader may wonder why there is any difference between price, Col. (2), and marginal revenue, Col. (4). In going from 2 to 3 units of output, why isn't marginal revenue equal to the price at which the third unit is sold? Why isn't it, therefore, $114 instead of the indicated figure of $94?

True, the third unit is sold for $114. But to get it sold, we had to cut the price on the previous 2 units by $10 each (from $124 to $114). This loss on the previous units must be charged up against the third unit in reckoning marginal revenue; thus, the marginal revenue is $114 - (2 \times \$10)$, or $94. Generally speaking, marginal revenue is less than that price, as indicated by the fundamental formula:[1]

Marginal revenue of nth unit = difference in total revenue in going from $(n - 1)$ to n units = price of nth unit − loss in revenue on previous units resulting from price reduction

Only under perfect competition, where the sale of extra units will never depress price at all, is the second term zero. Only then will price and marginal revenue be identical. This explains why a competitive firm need never advertise in order to increase its sales at the existing price, and why it has all the business it wants at the prevailing price.

If elasticity of demand as defined in Chap. 19 falls to less than unity, so that the percentage decrease in price always exceeds the percentage rise in quantity sold, any increase in output will actually *lower* total revenue. In other words, marginal revenue will become negative. Why? Because the second term in our formula—the loss on previous units—will outbalance the first term—the price received on the last unit. From the standpoint of personal profit, the firm would do better under such conditions to burn up extra output rather than let it "spoil the market."

MAXIMIZING PROFITS

We may now bring all our relevant facts together in a supertable, Table 4. Total profit is, of course, the column of greatest interest in this table.

What quantity will maximize total profits, and what price? The simplest way to solve this problem is to compute Col. (5), total profit, which is simply the difference between total revenue and total cost. Running our eyes down this column tells us that the optimal quantity is 6 units, with a price of $84 per unit. No other situation will give us as much profit as the $104 which that situation brings in.

Another way of arriving at the same result is to compare marginal revenue, Col. (6), and marginal cost, Col. (7). So long as a step toward extra output gives us more marginal revenue than marginal cost, we continue to produce more output. But whenever marginal cost exceeds marginal revenue, we con-

[1] The interested reader might check the relationship between price and marginal revenue in Table 3 at some one or more points, by calculating the loss in revenue resulting from the price reduction necessary to get the last unit sold.

tract output. Where is equilibrium? *Where marginal cost and marginal revenue are in balance.* Again we are led to the optimal situation of maximum profits.

TABLE 4. *Summary Table Showing Revenue Cost and Profit Data for the Firm*

Quan-tity q	Price p	Total revenue R = p × q	Total cost TC = FC + VC	Profit Pro	Marginal revenue MR	Marginal cost MC	Marginal profit MR − MC = MPro
(1)	(2)	(3)	(4)	(5)	(6)	(7)	(8)
0	$144 or higher	$ 0	$256	−$256	$134	$ 64	+$ 70
1	134	134	320	− 186	114	20	+ 94
2	124	248	340	− 92	94	15	+ 79
3	114	342	355	− 13	74	13	+ 61
4	104	416	368	+ 48	54	13	+ 41
5	94	470	381	+ 89	34	19	+ 15
*6	*84	504	400	+*104	14	31	−* 17
7	74	518	431	+ 87	− 6	49	− 55
8	64	512	480	+ 32	−26	73	− 99
9	54	486	553	− 67	−46	103	− 149
10	44	440	656	− 216			

This second way of finding the optimum point by comparing marginal cost and revenue is neither better nor worse than the first method of simply examining total profits. They are really exactly the same thing, as is shown by Col. (8), labeled "marginal profit." This is the difference between marginal revenue and marginal cost; or what is the same thing, the *extra* profit from each additional unit of output. So long as marginal profit is positive, we keep expanding quantity. When marginal profit is negative, we contract output. We are at the optimal equilibrium point when marginal costs cancel out marginal revenue; or what is the same thing, where marginal profit passes from + to − as shown by the star in Col.(8).

GRAPHICAL DEPICTION OF FIRM'S OPTIMUM POSITION

The three curves of Fig. 4 illustrate this same procedure. *Total revenue* is a hill whose slope is rising as long as demand is elastic, and falling after the demand has become inelastic. *Total costs* are rising, because you usually can't get extra output for nothing. *Total profit* is the difference between total revenue and cost. It is shown in two places on the diagram: directly by the lowest curve, and also as the vertical distance between the two upper curves. At small outputs, total cost exceeds total revenue and the firm cannot break even; again at very large outputs, price is so low and costs so high that it is again "in the red." Somewhere in between is the optimum point of maximum profit.

This optimum quantity is clearly 6 units. This is where total profit is at a maximum. This is where the vertical difference between the two upper curves is greatest.[1]

It is also the quantity at which the slopes of the total revenue curve and the total cost curve are exactly parallel; and where the slope of the total profit curve is zero and horizontal. At any smaller outputs, such as 4 units, the two slopes are widening out; therefore, the vertical distance between the two curves is increasing and the firm will expand its output.

At any output larger than the optimum, the two slopes are narrowing; by moving backward, we can increase the vertical distance between revenue and cost. Only at the optimum point, where the slopes are exactly parallel, will it pay to move neither to the right nor to the left. This is the firm's equilibrium position of maximum profits.

These respective slopes of the total cost and total revenue curves are nothing

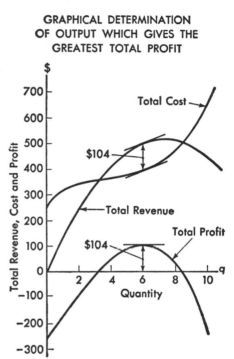

GRAPHICAL DETERMINATION OF OUTPUT WHICH GIVES THE GREATEST TOTAL PROFIT

FIG. 4. The *total profit* curve represents the difference between the *total revenue* and the *total cost* curves. Total profit is at a maximum when that difference is greatest, *i.e.*, where the slopes of the total cost and revenue curves are parallel and equal.

---

[1] The optimum price cannot be immediately indicated on this diagram. However, knowing the quantity to be 6, we can easily determine the price, $84, by consulting the table; or by running up to the demand curve of Fig. 1*b* at a quantity of 6 units, we can read off price.

but our recent acquaintances, marginal cost[1] and marginal revenue. In Fig. 5, the same determination of best output is shown in a new way. The *MC* and *MR* curves are plotted for each output (either from the data of Table 4 or by reading off the numerical slopes from Fig. 4). Where the *MC* curve exactly intersects the *MR* curve, at 6 units, is our most profitable output; at this same output, the

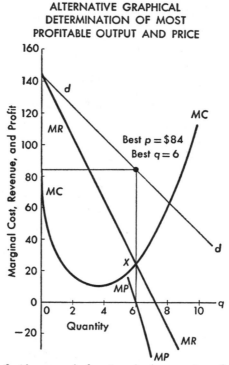

FIG. 5. The most profitable output is found at the intersection of the marginal revenue and marginal cost curves where marginal profit is zero; the price to be charged for the best output is found by going up to the demand curve.

curve of marginal profit, $MPro = MR - MC$, passes from plus to minus and crosses the horizontal axis. Now that we know the best quantity is 6 units, we can run up to the demand curve and find our best price (or average revenue) of $84 per unit.

We are once again led back by the geometry to our fundamental rule: profits are at a maximum when

Marginal cost = marginal revenue

[1] Marginal cost, *MC*, is, after all, nothing more than the rate at which total costs rise

B. *APPLICATIONS OF THE PROFIT MAXI-MIZING PRINCIPLES TO PERFECT COMPETITION AND PATTERNS OF MONOPOLISTIC COMPETITION*

PRICE AND SUPPLY UNDER PERFECT COMPETITION

There is nothing mysterious about the above relations. They simply represent common sense and elementary arithmetic. There is no reason why they should not apply to the competitive wheat farmer as well as to a firm employed in an imperfectly competitive field.

However, one special feature is present in the case of the perfect competitor. At his optimum position, marginal revenue must, of course, equal marginal cost. But as we earlier learned, the pure competitor can sell all he wishes at a given price. Let us repeat this important characteristic of pure or perfect competition. The market price is given to each small, competitive seller.

with small additions of output, as shown by the accompanying diagram.

THE RELATION BETWEEN SLOPE AND MARGINAL COST

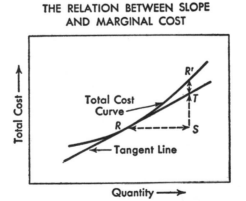

Two slightly different versions of marginal cost are shown on this diagram. The distance from *R* to *S* represents one extra unit of output. The distance from *S* to *R'* represents the resulting increase in total cost, which is the first and simplest definition of marginal cost. The second definition is given by the slope of the total cost curve at the point *R*, or what is the same thing numerically, by the distance from *S* to *T*. In the limit as the size of the extra units becomes small, the discrepancy between the two definitions—or *TR'*—becomes negligible.

Marginal revenue and price then turn out to be identical, there being no loss on previous units to be subtracted from the price received from the extra unit sold.

USE OF MARGINAL COST CURVE TO DETERMINE SUPPLY RESPONSE OF FIRM TO VARYING PRICES

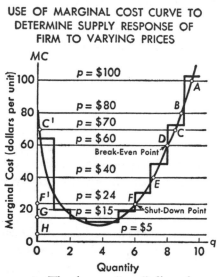

FIG. 6. The heavy "step" line shows marginal cost when the units of production are indivisible. The heavy curved line shows marginal cost when the units are infinitely divisible. Given a market price, as represented by each horizontal line above, a firm will produce up to the point of its intersection with that part of the marginal cost curve which is rising. Thus at a price of $40 a firm would produce about 7.1 units. At any price below $24, the firm will prefer to shut down and produce nothing, rather than fail to recover even its variable costs.

We may combine the above statements, therefore, and say that a perfect competitor, who has no fear of spoiling the market, will always produce up to the point where marginal costs begin to exceed price; or as his equilibrium condition, we have

Marginal cost = price

Now we can predict how much the firm will supply at different prices. If we retain our previous cost data, we may read off from Fig. 6 the supply schedule for the firm in terms of price. Thus, if the price is $100, it will pay to produce 9 units but not 10. This is because the $100 horizontal price line in Fig. 6 intersects the steps of marginal cost at 9 units. Or referring back to the cost data of Col. (6) of Table 2, we see that it pays to produce every additional unit up to the tenth, because that one costs $103 extra and brings in only an additional $100.

This assumes that *fractions* of a unit cannot be produced and sold. Why should we rule out fractions? Of course, a farmer cannot sell one-third of an egg, but he certainly can sell one-third of a carload of eggs. Even if single eggs represent our units of measurement, he can sell eggs at the rate of 1 every 3 hours, which is one-third of an egg per hour. The smooth curve in Fig. 6 shows marginal costs when our units are made indefinitely divisible. It, rather than the irregular steps, enables us to determine the exact quantity response of the firm to different prices.

Thus, when the market price at which the firm can sell is $100 per unit, production will be pushed to the point marked *A*, or to about 9.4 units. Only at that quantity does marginal cost equal price. Only there are its profits at a maximum when price is $100.

As the price drops to $80, the firm will supply only the units shown at point B, or about 8.9 units. This is because the dotted marginal cost curve intersects the $80 price line at that output.

Suppose the price were only $70. What would the firm supply? The $70 price line is seen to intersect the dotted MC curve twice: once at around 8.4 units and again at around 0.2 unit. Our formula, price = MC, is ambiguous. It gives too many answers. Which is the right one?

There is only one final test. We must compute total profit and see where it is larger. The answer is quite obvious. The larger output is the correct one. For if the firm produces only around 1 unit, its revenue is $70 × 1, its cost in Table 2 = $320, and its profits are around −$250. But if it produces about 8 units, its profits are about ($70 × 8) − $480 or about $80. The best output, therefore, is at C, not at C'.

It is not difficult to patch up our price = MC rule so that it will not let us down again and make us recompute profit. When price or marginal revenue equals marginal cost, we can only be sure that profit is standing still. But whether it is leveling off "at the top of the hill of profits," or "at the bottom of the valley," our formula does not tell us. We must, therefore, add to the MR = MC requirement the condition that *marginal cost must be shooting up more rapidly than marginal revenue*. At C this condition was met; at C' the opposite condition held. A little calculation shows that this fact makes C' the worst rather than the best place to be. It pays to move to either the right or the left of that point, because profits are there at a minimum.

DECREASING COSTS AND THE BREAKDOWN OF PERFECT COMPETITION

From now on our rule under perfect competition must take the form

Price = marginal cost, and marginal cost must be rising

Alternatively, we can say that the supply curve of the firm consists of only that part of the U-shaped marginal cost curve (in Fig. 6) which is rising. For, if marginal cost is falling, the firm has every reason to expand its output further, since each new step brings it the same extra revenue but lower extra cost.

This second part of our rule is not just a theoretical refinement. It shows us how and why competition tends to break down! Technology of a given industry often becomes more and more complicated so that efficient production is possible only on a gigantic scale. Until this scale is reached, average and marginal costs tend to fall. Competitive firms tend, therefore, to expand their output. A period of cutthroat or ruinous competition may follow in which all firms have heavy losses. Finally, those few firms which have the most resources or which enjoyed the earliest start will drive the others out of the field, leaving us no longer with perfect competition but with monopolistic competition.

Although other facts than cost were also involved, this seems to be what happened in the automobile industry. Out of a 100-odd American car manufacturers, only a half-dozen of any significance are left. And of these, the "big three," General Motors, Chrysler, and Ford are of predominant importance. The same thing is likely to happen to the "flivver airplane" industry in the next few decades. It does not happen to wheat farming, because each farmer's marginal cost curve turns up long before he becomes sufficiently important to affect the market price. If an invention were discovered which made a million-acre farm the most efficient size, agriculture would cease to be as perfectly competitive as it is.

MINIMIZING LOSSES AND DECIDING WHEN TO SHUT DOWN

Let us return to the supply curve of our hypothetical firm. If price drops to $60, the firm will produce 8 units and will just break even. (This includes wages of managers, and a normal return on invested capital.)

What if price drops down to below $60, the level of lowest average cost? Suppose that times are so hard that the market price is only $40. If the firm produces about 7.1 units, as indicated by the point E where $P = MC$, its total revenue will be around $280 ($40 \times 7$) while its total costs will be about $431 (see Table 2). The firm is "in the red," producing at a loss of some $140 to $150. Our formula of marginal cost and price seems to have led us to ruin.

But has it? If the firm chooses to shut down completely rather than run at a loss, its revenue will be zero and its fixed costs will still be $256. Obviously, its loss would then be $256, an even greater sum than when it is producing 7.1 units. In other words, equating marginal costs to marginal revenue is optimal even when profits are negative, because in that way losses are kept to a minimum.   A perfectly rational businessman will disregard his fixed costs entirely in deciding whether to accept some extra business, for he knows that fixed costs will go on anyway and, therefore, must "cancel out of any decision." As long as he receives total revenue in excess of his variable costs, so that he has something above his out-of-pocket costs, he will be better off to accept the extra business.

What happens if price continues to decrease, down below even $24? At that figure, if the firm produces 6 units, its total revenue will be $144 and its variable cost will be $144. It will be just indifferent between producing or shutting down completely, because in either case it will lose $256.

At any price below $24, say at $15, the firm will not even recover its variable costs. Obviously, therefore, it will choose to shut down. Our marginal cost and price formula is no longer relevant.[1]

We may summarize by saying that any costs that are strictly fixed should be treated as bygones if necessary. "There is no use crying about spilt milk." To make the best of the situation, we minimize our losses by equating marginal cost to price—and marginal cost is unaffected by fixed costs.[2] It is better to earn something above our variable costs which can be applied toward our fixed cost commitments, than to have to pay out fixed costs while receiving nothing.

The above analysis refers to the short run. In the long run our fixed commitments finally expire. Contracts terminate. Buildings wear out, and the decision arises as to whether they should be replaced or contracts renewed. In deciding this question, no costs are (as yet) fixed. In the long run, therefore, the firm is not forced to produce at a loss. It will still produce that output at which marginal cost equals price; but firms will enter or leave the industry until price is just equal to average cost.

Therefore, when there is "free entry," our long-run equilibrium condition for a perfectly competitive firm can be written as

Marginal cost = price = average cost[3]

FIRM AND INDUSTRY

Now that we have the short-run supply response of the competitive firm, we are able to show exactly how the industry's total supply curve is formed. Figure 7 shows the picture of a typical small firm side by side with that of the whole industry. Note the great difference in scale of quantity along the firm's hori-

---

[1] It tells us that producing 5 units is better than producing 4 or 6. But all are worse than producing 0 units.

[2] In Col. (3) of Table 2, the same fixed costs are in the total cost figures for both the tenth and the ninth unit. Therefore, they cancel out of all marginal cost computations. Why?

[3] This point, where $P = MC = AC$, will be at the bottom of the U-shaped average cost curve. Two different reasons for this can be given. First, if the typical firm were producing at any average cost bigger than the minimum, somebody else—under free entry—could come in and make a profit by selling at the existing price. The second reason is more technical: as long as marginal cost is below average cost, the production of a new unit must pull the average down. Similarly, it can be shown that where the marginal cost curve lies above the average cost curve, the average cost curve must be rising. It follows, therefore, that at the intersection of the marginal and the average cost curves, the average curve must be just standing still, at its minimum value.

The reader should be warned against attaching optimal significance to this minimum AC point. The competitive firm is forced there by free entry against its will.

zontal axis as compared to the industry. The picture of the firm can be thought of as representing a thousandfold magnification of a little vertical strip around the equilibrium point of the industry. The industry demand curve *DD* is so stretched horizontally that it appears perfectly flat on the firm's diagram, or as *dd*.

ADDING THE SUPPLY CURVES OF COMPETITIVE FIRMS
TO GET THE SUPPLY CURVE OF THE INDUSTRY

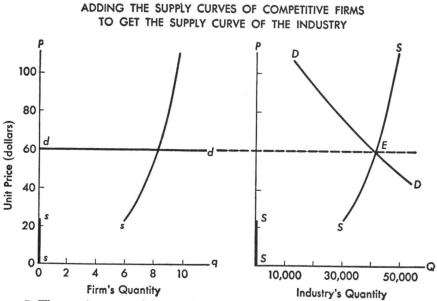

FIG. 7. The supply curve of the individual firm *ss* consists of two parts, corresponding to the price ranges at which the firm will operate and at which it will shut down. This curve is summed horizontally 5,000 times to get the industry supply curve *SS* assuming all 5,000 firms are alike. The demand curve for the firm is *dd*, a horizontal straight line, since the output of one firm has a negligible effect on price. Geometrically, *dd* is the same as a very small segment of *DD* around the point *E*, the segment being stretched out to the scale of the firm diagram.

However, the *firm's* supply curve is not flat, but is as indicated. Also, the industry's supply curve is nothing but the *sum* of the amounts that all the firms will produce at each of the prices. If all the firms were exactly alike and if there were 5,000 firms in the industry, then the industry supply curve *SS* would be a 5,000-fold exaggeration of the *ss* curve of each firm.[1] It would appear infinitely flatter than the firm's supply curve, were it not for the great change of horizontal scale.

[1] If the enterprises are not all alike, and not even two farms in the same county ever are, the industry's supply curve is still the resultant of adding (horizontally) the supply responses of all the individual firms.

This completes the story of the short-run supply conditions of a competitive firm. The long-run supply curve of the industry will tend to be even flatter than SS for a number of related reasons: (1) At prices below full unit cost (including costs that are fixed only in the short run), the quantity supplied will fall off very rapidly. For after all, businesses will not go on producing at a loss indefinitely, if they can help it; and in the long run, they can simply refuse to keep up their investments and to renew their commitments. (2) If high prices are maintained for an indefinitely long period of time, new firms will enter the industry. Thus, the long-run supply curve may become 10,000 or 50,000 times as large as each firm's curve rather than only 5,000 times as large. (3) Each firm's supply and marginal cost curve will be flatter in the long run because it need not confine itself to the same old plants and equipment. It has time to add such new buildings and machines as will enable it to produce more output for less *extra* cost.

For all these reasons, the industry's long-run supply curve would be rather like the short-run SS curve after that curve had rotated clockwise around the equilibrium point as a pivot and had become much more nearly horizontal.[1] The student should draw in such a curve and label it $S'S'$.

The history of agriculture in each past war illustrates how supply is more elastic in the long than in the short run. When food prices fly skyward, output does not at first respond very much. But repeated years of prosperity finally send production greatly upward. After the boom has passed, years and years of painfully low prices may be necessary before downward agricultural readjustments are made.

PRICE AND COST UNDER MONOPOLISTIC COMPETITION

The practical importance of pure competition is not great enough to justify its further discussion. It represents the unusual and rare case where the firm knows its demand curve. The competitive firm need only look at the newspaper price quotations of the Board of Trade to know all there is to know about price, demand, and revenue.

The different cost and revenue concepts developed at the beginning of this chapter can also be applied to imperfectly competitive situations, but with considerably greater difficulty. Not so simple is the task of the ordinary small or large corporation in estimating the demand for its product so as to arrive at the best price to maximize its profits. A railroad can only guess whether a 20 per cent reduction in fares will bring it many more passengers. A radio

[1] In the Appendix to Chap. 19 on Supply and Demand, Cases 1, 2, and 3 illustrated the different degrees of flatness that an industry's supply curve might show.

company has no exact way of judging the elasticity of demand for its many products.

Realistically speaking, we must recognize that modern business firms—even the largest—are unable to calculate their marginal revenue and marginal cost. They cannot determine their optimum price and output with nice exactitude. Yet the day's work must somehow get done. Prices must be set on their products.

This is where unit or average costs enter the picture. In a competitive industry this concept has only limited usefulness. The firm's supply was conditioned only by the *extra* costs, costs of the last units, or marginal costs—not by average costs.[1] Other competing firms might enter or leave the industry so as to drive price toward average costs. But the single competitive firm had no reason to concern itself with average cost. Indeed, as we saw in the chapter on Supply and Demand, the only influence of cost on competitive price is through its indirect influence on supply. Neither the auctioneer nor the stock ticker has any respect for ancient history.

Put yourself in the position of the president of a company producing many products where prices are at its disposal. Your last year's sales are known to you, but your next period's sales can only be guessed even if you leave prices unchanged. Not knowing the extent or elasticity of demand for your products, you will be unable to determine marginal revenue. What will you do?

Probably, you will call in your accountants and sales managers. "Boys," you will say, "what will our volume of output approximately be if we stay on our toes and keep our share of the market?" In making their answers, the sales force will have to guess at the probable level of business activity, consumers' needs, etc.

After they have made their estimates, you will turn to the cost experts and probably ask for the unit cost of producing each product in question at those levels of output. There will be plenty of headaches in aiming at any sort of figure. For example, how shall the administrative and plant overhead costs be allocated between different products? Or if a given process simultaneously creates joint products like meat and hides, how shall the costs be allocated between them? Or if a building will last for many years, how much should be charged against current operations?

Headache or no headache, it is the duty of the accountants to come out with

---

[1] Of course, in determining whether to shut down or not, the firm must calculate its total revenue and total variable cost; but it need not express these in unit terms. Similarly, in determining whether to withdraw from an industry forever or to enter a new field, the firm must consider whether its *total* profits would be positive or negative.

some sort of answer as to unit costs. Management must now decide by how much to mark up price over the cost figure. Depending upon its estimate of the consumers' reaction and the pricing policy of its competitors, the firm may perhaps decide on a 5, 10, or 30 per cent markup.

In bad times when price competition is particularly keen, businessmen may even set prices at less than "full costs" because of the realization that fixed expenses will go on whether or not production is at a low level. But price will never be set below unit *variable* costs unless the item in question is being used as a "loss leader" to attract other business now and in the future, or unless the firm is willing to incur temporary losses in order to crush a rival and drive him out of business completely.

Many investigators of actual business pricing policies have testified that corporations often do follow the above described practice of quoting prices on a "cost and markup" basis, hoping thereby not only to recover their "full cost outlays," but also to make a return on their investments. This theory is therefore realistic, but it is not very informative. It stops tantalizingly short of telling us *why* the average markup is 40 per cent in one industry and 5 per cent in another; or why one large firm in the automobile industry is able to earn 30 per cent on the book value of its invested capital while another firm almost as large has been earning only about $\frac{1}{2}$ of 1 per cent on its capital.

There seems to be nothing to do about this unsatisfactory situation but try to specify a number of different competitive and monopolistic patterns characteristic of various important industrial situations. Four important patterns, intermingling monopoly and competition, are discussed in the remaining pages of this chapter.

ILLUSTRATIVE PATTERNS OF PRICE

1. *Chronically Overcrowded Sick Industries.* Many fields are characterized by an excessive number of firms. Most of these do a small volume of business and remain in the industry only until they have lost their capital. Grocery stores, taverns, restaurants, night clubs, and gasoline stations are typical examples taken from retail trade. But much the same thing is true of the textile industry, the dress trade, and many other industries that require very little initial capital.

Why don't such unprofitable concerns leave the industry? The answer is that they do. But as fast as they leave, new firms enter the industry, leaving the total number unchanged or even growing.

Why do new firms enter the industry in the face of the fact that most existing firms are making losses? Apparently, partly out of ignorance and partly because "hope springs eternal." An old couple putting their lifetime savings of a few thousand dollars into a little retail grocery store do so in the belief that *their* venture will be different, theirs will succeed—and anyway, in the grocery business no one need starve. But alas, with no special business aptitude and with less than the minimum amount of capital necessary for efficient operation, they last in business only until their original capital has gone.

Or in the dress trade, a worker will often save his money in order to become his own boss. He knows that most concerns are not covering their costs, but he also has heard of a few lucky firms whose special "novelty styles" have become a smash hit and have yielded large monetary profits. Even though the odds are heavily weighted against the new entrant, he is willing to buy a ticket in the sweepstake of success.

These chronically overcrowded industries need not be what the economist has called "perfectly competitive"—although in the case of agriculture or "cotton gray goods," they may happen to be so. Too many firms in such a competitive industry is a bad thing, involving as it does wastes of resources and losses. But at least in such a competitive industry the consumer partly gains, through lower prices, what the producers are losing.

Unfortunately, in most chronically overcrowded sick industries market competition is quite imperfect. Being inefficient producers, the small concerns do not sell very cheaply. Instead of competing on a price basis, they tend to charge fairly high prices and simply to divide the business. The resulting economic situation under this form of monopolistic competition may be worse even than under complete monopoly: not only is price excessive, but in addition valuable resources are wasted because each firm has too much idle plant and manpower. The situation is triply bad: producers make losses, resources are wasted, and the prices charged the consumer are too high.

It is to be feared that the liberal credit terms to veterans under the G.I. Bill of Rights may accentuate this problem of injudicious investment by small businessmen into already sick occupations and industries. The only thing that can be said for such small businesses is that they make jobs. But the jobs they make are largely an illusion as far as pay is concerned, and represent boondoggling of as reprehensible and unnecessary a kind as would public-works projects aimed at simply digging holes and filling them in again.

2. *The Case of Few Sellers of Identical Products.* At the other extreme are industries in which there are only two, three, or a few sellers, all producing almost exactly the same products. In such cases, there is always the temptation for each firm to try to undersell the others by the least little bit in the hope of getting a larger share of the total business.

This explains, for example, the railroad price wars of the past century. Customers shipping goods from Chicago to New York will always pick the route that offers even a few pennies of extra cheapness. Thus, each of the three or four trunk lines would intermittently undercut the existing rate schedules, until finally a disastrously low level of rates was reached. At the same time, for short hauls where shippers had no alternative, the railroads would jack up the rates—thus creating an anomalous, discriminatory pattern of charges. The Interstate Commerce Commission was established in 1887 to regulate railroad rates and earnings and prevent such unstable price conditions.

Even without government regulations, in industries characterized by heavy overhead costs and identical products, there usually grows up the realization that competition is ruinous. Formal or informal meetings are held, whose theme song is "We're all in it together." Each firm is taught the lesson that other firms will not stand idly by while it cuts its prices; rather they too will cut their prices, so that everyone will end up worse off.

Therefore, tacitly or explicitly, the firms try to agree on a price that maximizes the profits of all. Trade associations, keeping one eye on the Justice Department lawyers who enforce the Sherman Antitrust Act, may impose penalties on any chiseler in the industry who makes secret price concessions. Occasionally, as new conditions or firms upset the *status quo* in the industry, another price war may break out—to last until everyone has again learned his lesson and the morale of the industry is restored.

In finishing with this second pattern, we must note that the desire of corporations to earn a fair return on their past investments may be at variance with the well-being of the consumer. Too much plant capacity may have been built in the industry in the past; but that isn't justification for continuing high prices and scarce output. Competition, which the businessman regards as destructive, cutthroat, and ruinous may actually be the only way to get the redundant plant capacity into operation or to discourage its maintenance. (Having made the mistake of building the plants, society ought not to add the further error of failing to use them to best advantage.) Losses or subnormal profits is the free-enterprise way of discouraging excess capacity.

The steel and other metal industries are examples of this pattern of imperfect competition. They are naturally very fearful that the additional plant capacity built during the war may make maintenance of an "orderly" price structure difficult in the years following the immediate postwar period.

3. *Monopolies Maintained by Constant Research and Advertising*. Still another common industrial pattern is that of a firm that has considerable control over price by virtue of its technological efficiency, its patents, its trade-marks,

and its slogans. Its monopoly profits are plowed back into further research and advertising, so it is always able to keep abreast or ahead of its rivals. General Motors, duPont, and General Electric are perhaps typical of such companies. In setting prices, a "reasonable" markup over computed unit costs is introduced. Long-run considerations such as the possibility of developing new mass markets keep the firm from "charging all that the traffic will bear" in the immediate future. Moreover, fears of new rivals and aroused public opinion often keep the corporation from being "hoggish" in setting prices.

Because research and advertising are expensive and their results cumulative, success tends to breed success, and profits tend to breed more profits. Therefore, small business cannot always effectively compete with such firms. While admitting the efficiency and progress of some of the monopolists described, critics go on to argue that society would be *still* better off if the full advantages of efficiency were passed on to consumers, or plowed back into research aimed at technological improvements and not simply at profits, if less advertising dollars were spent on "soap operas" and jingles, and if more research dollars went into fundamental science rather than into patentable gadgets. Obviously, this is a controversial subject, upon which each citizen must form his own final judgment.

4. *Publicly Regulated Monopolies.*   As a last case, let us consider a "perfect" monopoly licensed by the state and under government regulation. Such public utilities include gas and light companies, telephone and communication services, railroads and public carriers, etc. Since it is obviously uneconomical to have two local sets of telephone wires, an exclusive franchise is given to a single company. (Why is not the same thing true of milk delivery?)

But having given the utility company a complete monopoly, the state steps in to protect the consumer by setting maximum rates. Usually this is done by public regulating commissions, which specify the maximum prices that can be charged for each kind of service.

In setting such prices it has long been customary to pick prices that will try to give the company a fair return on its capital. Rates such as 5, 6, or 7 per cent are often selected as representing a fair return.

Much more complex is the question of determining the *capital value* base of the company to which this "fair rate" is to be applied. Three measures of fair capital value have been suggested at one time or another: (1) *original cost* (minus depreciation), or the sum of all past prudent investments; (2) *current reproduction cost* (minus depreciation), or the cost of replacing the company's equipment at present prices, corrected for the age and condition of the property; and (3) *capitalized market value* of the public utility's securities or assets.

Of these methods, the third is universally recognized to be nonsensical. As was shown in the earlier discussion of interest and capital (Chap. 3) and good will (Chap. 6), the market value of any income-earning property is given by capitalizing its annual return by the interest rate. For a regulating authority to use capitalized market value as a base for measuring capital would be tantamount to recognizing *any level of earning*, high or low, as fair. Once having been capitalized, excessively high earnings will appear as only moderate interest returns, and the same is true of excessively low earnings. The method of capitalized earnings begs the question that the authorities must answer!

The American courts have, therefore, vacillated between *original* cost and *reproduction* cost. So long as the general price level does not change, the two are not very different. But over a period of decades, when prices may greatly increase, reproduction cost will involve higher earnings and rates than original costs. In periods of declining prices, the reverse discrepancy is to be observed. The use of original cost leads to greater leniency to the nonspeculative investors in public-utility securities. But reproduction cost leads to a more flexible price structure and gives less weight to the dead hand of past costs.[1]

In addition to the case of industry and firm supply under perfect competition, four different imperfectly competitive price patterns have been described here. Numerous others could have been discussed with equal profit had space permitted.

---

[1] From the standpoint of the advanced discussions of "welfare economics," neither method is ideal. Writers in this field have set up a perfectionist formula which would involve pricing of public-utility services at not more than the extra or marginal costs of services. However, this is a radical doctrine which, as a practical matter, few economists would endorse. It could lead to excessive returns to the owners if demand was large in comparison with capacity. But more likely, it would lead to inadequate returns to original investors. Although the state could then, if it wished to, secure by a subsidy justice for investors without interfering with desirable output or price, this would represent a departure from present practice.

The great Federal power projects such as the TVA and Bonneville Dam are from one viewpoint partial approaches toward such a system of pricing. However, the fact that the government can raise capital in larger sums and at lower costs than private industry, and the fact that the same set of dams can simultaneously achieve the ends of national defense, navigation, flood control, and irrigation make any simple yardstick comparison between private and public operations impossible.

SUMMARY

A. MAXIMIZING PROFITS OF THE FIRM

1. In this chapter we have seen how an individual firm must use estimates of its revenue and cost to arrive at the price that yields the greatest profit. This optimum situation can be recognized by the requirement that marginal cost and marginal revenue must be equal, with the former rising more rapidly than the latter, and with total revenue at least in excess of all variable costs.

2. This analysis applied to perfect competitors as well as to firms with some monopoly power. The supply curve of the competitive firm was derived from its marginal cost curve. And the summation of the supply curve of all firms gave us the supply curve of the industry.

B. PATTERNS OF PERFECT AND MONOPOLISTIC COMPETITION

3. Most firms were seen not to be perfect competitors. Price not being given to them, their problem is not that of responding along a supply curve. Instead they must set a best price. Since the typical firm has at best only a hazy notion of the elasticity of demand for its products, it is not in a position to make nice calculations of marginal revenue and marginal cost. Instead it often is content with some sort of calculation of unit or average cost, from which price is determined after the addition of some percentage markup. The peculiar pattern of rivalry and consumer demand characteristic of the industry and the state of general business activity will determine whether the markup is likely to be large or small, or even negative. In an indirect sense, therefore, rough guesses of the firm's demand curve and marginal revenue do influence its behavior, but these influences remain indirect and rough.

4. Finally, four typical market and price patterns were described: chronically overcrowded sick industries; the case of a few firms producing identical products and intermittently tending toward tacit or explicit collusion in setting prices; the case of firms that maintain their monopoly position by scientific research and advertising efficiency; the case of public utilities subject to government regulation.

QUESTIONS FOR DISCUSSION

1. What does it mean to say that a corporation charges what the traffic will bear?

2. How would you divide the various elements of cost as between fixed and variable costs: payrolls, power and light, taxes, depreciation, executives' salaries, raw materials, etc.?

3. What is the numerical value of marginal revenue when the demand curve is of unitary elasticity, as in Table 3 of Chap. 19? Why?

4. "If price is only equal to marginal cost under competition, how can firms ever hope to cover their full costs, including overhead costs?" Discuss.

5. What would average and marginal cost look like if fixed costs were $100, average variable costs were constant at $10 per unit (total variable costs increasing proportionally with output)? Plot marginal cost, average (total) cost, average variable cost, and average fixed cost on the same diagram.

6. "A lump-sum tax on a firm will have no effect on its best output and price, so long as the firm stays in business. Similarly, a 10 per cent tax on a firm's profits will not change its best price or output." Why are these statements true, at least in the short run? Could the same be said of a tax on sales or on each unit of goods produced? Why not?

7. Describe the pattern of competition and monopoly in the automobile industry, the cigarette industry, the aluminum industry, the mousetrap industry, the women's dress trade, the retail grocery trade, the barbershop trade.

8. (a) A perfectly rational entrepreneur will disregard his fixed costs in setting prices. (b) Heavy fixed or overhead costs often make for cutthroat or ruinous competition which leads to monopoly and the death of competition. Are these two statements consistent?

9. "The tragedy of monopolistic competition often has nothing to do with excessive profits. Rather there may be no profits at all, the high price being frittered away in small volume and inefficient production." Discuss.

10. "It is utopian to try to break monopolies up into even a few effectively competing units, because the basic cause of monopoly is the law of decreasing cost with mass production and, in any case, a few competitors are not enough to duplicate the pricing patterns of perfect competition." Discuss both parts of this statement.

Chapter 22: PRODUCTION

EQUILIBRIUM OF THE FIRM AND

THE PROBLEM OF DISTRIBUTION

THE same common-sense principles that guided a firm to the point of optimum output at which profits are maximized apply also to more complicated decisions. Thus, a firm that produces numerous commodities rather than just one will push the production of each to the point where its extra cost just balances the extra revenue it brings in.

Similarly, a firm that is spending money on advertising will push its activities until the last dollar spent upon advertising—in the best way—brings in exactly one extra dollar of revenue. For so long as each new dollar of selling expense brings in more than an extra dollar of net revenue, the firm will continue to expand its advertising budget; and when each new dollar brings in less than a dollar, the firm will contract its expenditure; etc. To take another example, a firm will decide to make its product more durable, more attractive, or more different up to the point where the extra money revenue it derives from the qualitative change is just balanced by its extra cost.[1]

---

[1] These balancing principles explain why a firm selling exactly the same product in different independent markets will find it advantageous to quote different prices in each. Such price discrimination may not be traceable to any legitimate differences in cost, but is introduced purely because it will bring in extra profits to the firm. In allocating a given total of product between the different markets, the firm will charge the lowest prices in those markets where customers react most *elastically* to price.

More specifically, the firm will keep reallocating output between the markets until at the optimal equilibrium allocation the *extra revenue brought in by a unit of output is the same in every market*. Otherwise it would pay to switch output from the markets with low marginal revenue to those with high marginal revenue. Of course, the fact that marginal revenues

These maximizing principles are purely formal. They are rather empty, because they are easier to describe than to use in practice. They are like modern recipes for rabbit stew which omit the traditional beginning, "First catch your rabbit." They are like exhorting a shy man to become the "life of the party" by developing charm. If one had enough information to apply the precepts, one could probably do very well without them.

However, they do throw some light on certain more complex cases of the firm's equilibrium. Thus, they help to explain, in a formal way, the production equilibrium of the firm. This problem constitutes the first part of our chapter, while the second discusses the more general problem of what determines the prices of productive services and the distribution of income.

A. PRODUCTION EQUILIBRIUM OF THE FIRM

FINAL PRODUCTION EQUILIBRIUM: DIRECT APPROACH

Let us examine, then, how a firm determines the equilibrium amount of *inputs* which it will hire. Confronted with market costs of labor, land, machinery, etc., the firm will respond with a definite demand for each. Exactly how are these demands determined?

The answer lies in the desire of the firm to maximize profits. *Each input will be hired up to the point where the extra cost of the last little bit of it as great as the extra revenue it brings in.* The extra revenue brought in by hiring a last man-hour of labor is the result of two things: (1) the extra *physical* output that the factor adds and (2) the dollars of extra *revenue* that the extra output brings in. The extra cost of the productive factor is usually simple to determine: it is the price of the services of land, the wage (or price of labor), the price of machinery, and so forth.[1]

---

are finally equal in every market implies that prices will be *unequal* since the divergence between price and marginal revenue differs with the elasticity of demand.

[1] This statement assumes that the firm is too small a buyer to affect prices of the inputs. If the firm is such an important part of the factor market that it can hire more inputs only by bidding up their price, then the extra cost of the last unit of input is greater than the price paid to it—greater by the increase in price that must be paid to all previous workers. The reader may recall a similar discussion in the previous chapter (p. 498), explaining why marginal revenue falls short of price.

We may write our conditions of production equilibrium between extra input revenue and costs, therefore, in the following form:

Extra physical product of each input × marginal revenue of output = price of each input

There are as many such relations as there are different classes of inputs.

This is simply another application of the fundamental rule that a firm maximizes its profits by changing anything until the extra revenue and extra costs of that "anything" are just in balance. If labor cost $2 an hour and if hiring one extra unit of labor would bring the firm extra output from which it would receive $3 extra revenue, then the firm would certainly decide to hire that extra hour of labor. In fact, it would continue to hire all extra hours of labor whose "marginal-revenue-products" are $2.50, $2.25, or $2.01. But it will not hire extra hours that cost $2 and bring only in $1.99 or less. The same is true for acres of land, bags of fertilizer, and other capital goods.

THE INDIRECT APPROACH TO THE PRODUCTION EQUILIBRIUM

The above formulation makes unnecessary any separate discussion of the cost curve of the firm, and short-circuits the problem of deciding on an optimal output. For, if the firm has wisely selected all inputs, then it has already implicitly decided on the best output, since output is physically determined by inputs.

However, in practice it is often convenient for the firm to subdivide its complete decisions into two stages: (1) to determine the best ways of combining inputs so as to have a total cost curve which is as economical as possible, and then (2) by bringing in demand considerations to supplement the cost analysis, to determine the best output that will maximize profits.

This second problem has already been solved by marginal cost and marginal revenue in the preceding chapter. In this section we propose to solve the first problem—to go behind the cost curve and show what the conditions of equilibrium are in the hiring of inputs so as to keep total expenses down to a minimum.

Of course, when we combine these two steps, we should get an answer identical to that of the direct approach discussed a moment ago; we should find that factors are hired until their extra revenue just matches their extra cost. Let us proceed then to our analysis of the production considerations behind the cost curve.

THE "PRODUCTION FUNCTION"

Up to this point we have accepted the cost curve without raising questions as to its origin. However, the engineer or technical expert cannot alone make the dollars-and-cents decisions that lie back of the cost curve. Such an expert can only pretend to pass judgment on the *physical* relations that exist between output and different productive inputs, such as land, labor, and fertilizer. Any complete economic theory must be able to explain how a firm will decide on the cheapest mode of production; *i.e.*, on the optimal proportions in which the different economic inputs or "factors of production" are to be combined if total dollar expenses are to be kept down to a minimum.

Our technical expert has completed his job when he has handed on to the economist, accountant, or cost engineer the *physical relationship between output and various inputs*. This relationship is called the "production function." The production function tells us how much output we can hope to get if we have so much labor, and so much capital, so much land, etc.

In the simplest case, where there are assumed to be only two inputs, labor, L, and capital, C, and one output, q, the production function is given by a two-way table as in Table 1, which looks very much like a baseball schedule or

TABLE 1. *Production Function Relating the Amount of Output to Varying Combinations of Labor and Capital Inputs*

No. of units of capital							
	6	**346**	490	600	693	775	846
	5	316	448	548	632	705	775
	4	282	400	490	564	632	693
	3	245	**346**	423	490	548	600
	2	200	282	**346**	400	448	490
	1	141	200	245	282	316	**346**
		1	2	3	4	5	6
				No. of units of labor			

like a mileage chart giving the distance between different cities. Along the left-hand side are listed the varying amounts of capital, going from 1 unit up through 6. Along the bottom are listed the amounts of labor, going from 1 through 6. If we are interested in knowing exactly what output there will be when 5 units of capital and 2 units of labor are available, we count up 5 units of capital and then go over 2 units of labor. The answer is seen to be 448 units of product. Similarly, we find that 3 units of capital and 6 of labor will produce 600 units of output. Thus, for any combination of labor and capital, the production function tells us how much product we will have (using, of course, the best methods as decided by the technical engineer).

THE LAW OF DIMINISHING RETURNS ONCE AGAIN

In Chap. 2 we met the law of diminishing returns which told us that adding more and more of a variable factor (like labor) to a fixed factor (like capital) resulted eventually in smaller and smaller additions of product. This can be very nicely illustrated by Table 1.

First let us give the name "marginal product of labor" to the extra production resulting from *one* additional unit of labor. The use of the word "marginal" rather than "extra" is by analogy with such concepts as marginal cost (which we earlier defined to be the extra cost resulting from one additional unit of output). At any point in Table 1 the marginal product of labor can be derived by subtracting the given number (representing product at that point) from the number on its right lying in the same row. Thus, when there are 2 units of capital and 4 units of labor, the marginal product of an additional laborer is 48 (448 − 400).

By the "marginal product of capital" we, of course, mean the extra product resulting from one additional unit of capital, labor being held constant. It involves a comparison of adjacent items in a given column. Thus, when there are 2 units of capital and 4 units of labor, the marginal product of capital is 90 (490 − 400). The reader should be able to compute the marginal product of labor or capital at any point inside the table.

Having defined what we mean by the marginal product of an input, we are now in a position to restate our old friend, the law of diminishing returns:

As we hold a fixed input constant and increase a variable input, the marginal product of the variable input will decline—at least after a point.

To illustrate this, hold capital constant in Table 1 by sticking to a given row —say, that corresponding to capital equal to 2 units. Now let labor increase from 1 to 2 units, from 2 to 3 units, and so forth. What happens to product at each step?

As labor goes from 1 to 2 units, product increases from 200 to 282 units, or by 82 units. But the next dose of labor adds only 64 units (346 − 282). Diminishing returns have set in! Still further additions of a single unit of labor give us respectively only 54 extra units of output, 48 units, and finally only 42 units. The reader should check some other row to verify that the law of diminishing returns holds there too. He should also verify that the same law holds true when labor is held constant and capital is added in a number of steps. (HINT: Examine the changes in product in any *column*.)

At this point, it is well to recall the explanation given for diminishing returns. In Chap. 2, this was attributed to the fact that the fixed factor decreases *in proportion* to the variable factor. Each unit of the variable factor has less and less of the fixed factor to work with, and it is only natural that extra product should begin to fall off.

If this explanation is to hold water, there should be no diminishing returns when both factors are increased in proportion. When labor increases from 1 to 2, and capital *simultaneously* increases from 1 to 2, we should get the same increase in product as when both increase simultaneously from 2 to 3. This can be verified from the table.[1] In the first move we go from 141 to 282, and in the second move product increases from 282 to 423, an equal jump of 141 units.

Also, this explanation of diminishing returns in terms of the proportions of the inputs would lead us to expect that increasing capital will improve the marginal product of labor. Again this can be verified from our table. The fifth unit of labor adds 48 units of product when there are only 2 units of capital. But at 3 units of capital, a fifth unit of labor adds 58 units of product.

COMBINING INPUTS OPTIMALLY IN ORDER TO PRODUCE A GIVEN OUTPUT

The numerical production function shows why the engineer is not able to tell us definitely how any given output is to be produced. There is more than one way to kill a cat. And there is more than one way to produce any given output. Thus, the bold-faced numbers in Table 1 show that the output, $q = 346$, can be produced in any one of the following ways:[2]

TABLE 2. *Alternative Ways of Producing the Output q = 346*

	Labor	Capital
	L	C
A	1	6
B	2	3
C	3	2
D	6	1

[1] Not all production functions met with in real economic life would have these special properties.

[2] The reader can and should make up a similar table for output equal to 490 units or to some other number.

As far as the engineer is concerned, each of these combinations is equally good at producing an output of 346 units. But the accountant, interested in keeping profits of the firm at a maximum and costs at a minimum, knows that only one of these four combinations will give the lowest costs. Just which one will depend, of course, upon the respective prices of the two factors of production.

Let us suppose that the price of labor is $2 and the price of capital $3. Then the sum of the labor and capital costs in situation A will be $20 (1 $\times$ $2 plus 6 $\times$ $3). Similarly, the costs of B, C, and D will be, respectively, $13, $12, $15. At these stated input prices, there is no question that C is the best way of producing the given output.

If either of the prices of the inputs changes, the equilibrium proportion of the inputs will always change so as to use *less* of the input that has gone up most in price. Thus, if labor stays at $2 per unit, but capital falls to $1 per unit, the new optimal combination will be B, where more capital is used and less labor, and where total cost is only $7. The reader should verify this by computing the total expense of each other combination and seeing that they are higher.

Exactly the same sort of thing can be done for any other output; as soon as all input prices are known, we can experiment until we have found the best input combination and the minimum cost of production. (To clinch his understanding of the principles involved, the reader should work out the optimum production decision and cost for output equal to 490 units when price of labor is $2 and price of capital is $3.)

To summarize: The total cost curve, which up until now we have accepted without question, is really the result of some complex economic decisions with respect to the optimal way in which inputs are to be combined to produce any given output—decisions that can be made only when the technical "production function" is known and after the prices of different inputs have been specified.

From our arithmetical examples and from common-sense reasoning, we conclude that the following rule must be followed in making optimum production decisions:

To keep the total cost of a given output down to a minimum, always hire the productive factors until the marginal product of the last dollar is made equal in every use; or until

$$\frac{\textbf{Marginal product of labor}}{\textbf{Price of labor}} = \frac{\text{marginal product of capital}}{\text{price of capital}} = \cdots$$

$$= \text{constant} = \frac{1}{\text{MC}}$$

The constant to which each of these expressions is equal is called the "marginal product of the last dollar spent." In a more advanced discussion, this could be shown to be the reciprocal of our old friend marginal cost (which is defined as the extra dollars per extra unit of product). Therefore, our fundamental condition could be stated in another way: *At a lowest cost position, the price of each input is proportional to its marginal physical product, the factor of proportionality being marginal cost.*

Carefully note that a rational firm will not combine inputs until their marginal products are equal; it would be absurd to expect the marginal product of a man-year of labor to equal that of a kilowatt-hour of electric power or that of a pinch of fertilizer. Only after the marginal products have been rendered comparable by dividing them through by their prices and putting them on a per-dollar basis, will there have to be equality.

To clinch the fact that the marginal product of the last dollar must be equal in every use, the reader should ask himself what he would do if the last dollar spent on capital were yielding him more than the last dollar spent on labor. Would he not benefit by transferring one or more dollars away from labor and on to capital until there was finally an equality? Only then would his costs be at a minimum.

It is important to emphasize that this fundamental equality condition of equilibrium holds everywhere along the cost curve, whatever be the output. This condition does not tell the firm where it should finally produce. It would be astonishing if it did, since nothing at all has been said about the firm's demand curve. Our condition of equality does assure the firm that it has selected its inputs properly so as to keep its total and unit costs at a minimum for each output. That is all it does.

Some readers will wish at this point to turn to the Appendix to this chapter where the common-sense equilibrium condition of this section is explained in graphical terms.

FINAL PRODUCTION EQUILIBRIUM: INDIRECT APPROACH

Let us now add to the above analysis what we already know about the firm's behavior in picking the very best highest profit output. Our two indirect steps should then end up at the same place as did our direct approach.

Chapter 21 told us that the firm would produce up to the point where marginal cost and marginal revenue are just equal. We have just shown that the price of each input must be equal to marginal product multiplied by marginal cost.

At the final complete point of equilibrium, therefore, we may replace marginal cost by marginal revenue. Consequently, in the final equilibrium, it turns out that the price of each input will just equal the result of multiplying its marginal physical output by its marginal revenue.

But this is precisely equivalent to the original result, shown in bold-faced type on page 520. Which is only as it should be. Any way you look at it, we must always be able to say:

> *At the final point of equilibrium, the firm will hire each factor until its extra revenue is just equal to its extra cost, or until its price is just equal to its marginal physical product times marginal revenue of output.*

B. *THE MARGINAL PRODUCTIVITY THEORY AND THE "PROBLEM OF DISTRIBUTION"*[1]

This completes our discussion of the marginal product theory of production. Because the broader significance of this theory has occasionally been exaggerated by economists, a few qualifying remarks may be in order.

First, it is not a theory that explains wages, rents, or interest; on the contrary, it simply explains how factors of production are hired by the firm, once their prices are known.

This fact was not adequately appreciated by the originators of this theory some 50 years ago. Most of them tended to think of national income as one big mass of output which had somehow to be distributed among laborers, landowners, and capitalists. They looked for principles which would govern the distribution of this social product and which would determine "fair wages, fair land rents, and fair interest rates on capital."

One foolish principle, first suggested, said, "Give every input what it produces." In practice this broke down because nobody could decide what each input really produced. Social output is always the joint result of all inputs, just as the area of a rectangle depends on both altitude and base. Consequently this

---

[1] In everyday business parlance, distribution means the process by which factory goods finally get into the hands of consumers; however, the economist more often uses the term to describe the division of the national income among individuals and productive factors, and it is this sense used here. Readers interested only in economic principles may skip this historical discussion and turn directly to the Appendix.

first formula often leads to preposterous results. According to the spokesmen of the workers, "Take away all labor, and capital will produce nothing. Therefore, all our product should go to labor, which 'really' produces all."

The apologist for the capitalist could counter with the assertion, "Set men on a desert island to eke out a living with their bare hands, and they cannot produce one-thousandth part of what can be produced when they have capital. Therefore, almost all of the product should rightfully go to capital. Of course, laborers must be given enough to keep them alive and reproducing themselves, just as must horses. But anything they get above this should be recognized for what it is—*philanthropy* and not justly earned."

Obviously, the debate is only beginning. Along comes the landowner's lobbyist to say, "Even Archimedes couldn't get anywhere without a place to set his lever. Perhaps without labor there would be no product here. But without land there would be no 'here' to be! Therefore, land deserves all."

Each of these arguments is absurd, because the principle of giving each factor what you would lose if you took it all away is absurd. Such a method won't "add up." Instead it tends to give away the total product as many times over as there are factors of production.

CLASSICAL THEORIES OF RENT

It would be out of place here to go beyond brief mention of the rather different attempt of the "classical" economists to define what a given factor really produces by letting it work only with other factors of such poor grade that they are "free." In such a situation, all of the product was thought to be attributable only to the nonfree given factor. Having measured its productive contribution in that one place, the economist thought he had succeeded in measuring it everywhere since identical units of input must receive the same pay and be equally efficient in every place where they continue to work under competition.

Thus, such classical economists would have said that the product of a laborer working on a good farm with good land could be measured by the amount of output produced by his twin brother who was simultaneously working out on the border with land that was just good enough to remain in cultivation and just bad enough to be free for all to use.

This formula was not only supposed to identify the product of labor, but it also identified that of land. The good land's return was said to exceed the zero return of the bad land by the difference between the output produced by labor on it over what similar labor was producing on the poor-grade free land.

How shall we judge this attempt to develop a formula for distributing output by examining differences in the quality of a factor of production? In reality, this approach can be shown to be tantamount to abandoning the search for a principle to identify each input's contribution. Instead it simply examines one (special) aspect of the way in which supply and demand for production services will operate to determine their prices, and it breaks down completely as an explanation if land, labor, and capital were homogeneous.

THE SO-CALLED "MARGINAL PRODUCTIVITY THEORY OF DISTRIBUTION"

All would have been well if at this point economists had recognized the problem of distributing social product by identification of factor shares as a false one, and instead had concentrated upon the complex problem of the interplay of supply and demand for all productive services as well as for consumption goods.

But still pursuing the will-o'-the-wisp, they finally came up, half a century ago, with the marginal productivity theory of distribution, according to which "Each input should be paid the amount of product added by its last small unit."

For example, suppose that adding 1, 2, 3, and finally 4 units of labor to 3 fixed units of capital will result, respectively, in 12, 9, 6, and 5 extra units of output. The believers in this theory said, "Don't give to each of the four units of labor $(12 + 9 + 6 + 5)/4$ or 8 units of product per laborer. That will leave nothing for capital. Instead, since the laborers are all indistinguishable, give them each only as much as the last unit produced, or 5 each. This will leave 12 units $[32 - (4 \times 5)]$ for the 3 units of capital, or 4 units of product per unit of capital."

Their confidence in this formula increased tremendously when some economist discovered that, under certain not too implausible conditions, there was a mathematical law (Euler's theorem) guaranteeing that "what was left over to be divided among each unit of capital would also turn out to be precisely equal to the productive contribution of the last unit of capital." All inputs could, therefore, be treated perfectly symmetrically, as varying or as being held constant.

One catch to this theory was the fact that often product seems to depend upon a joint combination of labor and capital in such a way that increasing one without increasing the other results in *no extra product;* whereas decreasing the one without changing the other often results in a loss of product equal to the *whole productivity* of the combined "dose." The marginal product theory then would set limits on the separate shares of labor and capital which varied between 0 and 100 per cent. Of course, such limits would be quite useless and would make a mockery of the proposed theory of distribution.

It is worth repeating at this point that the marginal product principles developed earlier in this chapter were used only to explain the determination of inputs within a firm and do not pretend to be a theory that determines input prices. Indeed, input prices were assumed to be given to the firm.

If production should depend upon the above-described fixed proportions of labor and capital, no difficulties would be caused for the firm in the theory here expounded. On the contrary, the single firm's decisions would be made simpler, because then at any ratio of factor prices even a dunce would recognize the correct combination of inputs.[1]

Correctly stated, therefore, the marginal product theory is simply a theory of one aspect of the demand for productive services by the firm. The only formally satisfactory theory of determination of factor prices for the economy as a whole is one of "general equilibrium," in which there is a simultaneous interplay of the supplies and demands for *all* economic magnitudes under conditions of either perfect or imperfect competition as the case may be.

Unfortunately, there is little that can be said about this general supply and demand problem which is very useful in understanding the distribution of income between rich and poor, between labor and property owner, between one kind of property owner and another. This is unfortunate and admittedly a deficiency in our economic knowledge. But in any case, the problem of distributing social product is a false one, and the difficulties that arise in its solution are irrelevant ones.

CAN TRADE-UNIONS RAISE WAGES?

What are the institutional forces determining the relative and absolute shares of labor and other factors in the national income? This is one of the most important problems of our age. Yet we must confess that there is no satisfactory body of economic principles that tells us a great deal about this subject—certainly little on the elementary level and not a great deal more on the advanced level.

The old view that artificial interferences with the order of nature cannot affect wages has long been abandoned. The opposite view that the average income of the working class depends only upon the militance and political power of trade-unions is probably equally extreme and unacceptable. Within

---

[1] In terms of the geometry of the Appendix, the Equal-product curve of Fig. 3 would become more and more concavely bent until it looked like a huge L. The lowest Equal-cost line would still be given by a point of intersection where the Equal-product curve touched but did not cross an Equal-cost line. Whatever the ratio of factor prices, this equilibrium point of "generalized tangency" would be at the corner of the Equal-product curve.

limits, real wages can be affected by the process of collective bargaining. But, although no one can define the exact nature of these limits, they are nevertheless real.

Limitation of space precludes any elaborate discussion of this important, thorny question. However, the economic policies of the labor movement fall into main categories which deserve brief description and analysis:

1. *Keeping Down the Total Number of Laborers.* Traditionally American unions have been opposed to wholesale immigration of workers from abroad; they have opposed child labor; they have advocated early retirement of workers; they have observed with mixed feelings the entrance of women into the labor market; they have favored fewer hours of work per week; they have often encouraged "slow-downs" and useless "featherbedding."

Every one of these measures can be interpreted as an attempt of labor to circumvent the law of diminishing returns by keeping labor scarce relative to other factors of production, thereby keeping the average wage rate higher than it would otherwise be. It is not at all clear that such would be the result in the United States. This country is so plentifully endowed with land and supplies of capital that its per capita productivity might be almost as high with 245 million people as it is with 145 million—perhaps higher.

As a matter of fact, there is an alternative plausible explanation for each of these measures. Labor is almost always afraid that there will not be enough jobs to go around—that there is only a certain "lump of work" to be done. If more people come into the labor market or if people work too hard and too efficiently, the result is thought to be unemployment. Certainly no other interpretation can explain the intermittent demand of labor for a working week so short as 30 hours.

2. *Pushing Up Money Wages in Particular Occupations.* Much more important in the opinion of most trade-union members is the effort of unions to push up money rates in particular industries. No one who studies the facts of American labor history, past and present, can doubt that unions usually succeed in this attempt, at least in the short run.

However, their success in doing so is not all gain to the working class for a number of reasons. Wages having been raised, there may follow a reduction in the number of workers who are hired, with the result that some workers are either forced into unemployment or into less-favored nonunion occupations, thereby depressing wages in those lines. This is certainly a theoretical possibility; and yet impartial investigators seem to be often of the opinion that the reverse is true—that high money wages in unionized lines tend to be imitated elsewhere.

There is still another unpleasant possibility, however. Corporations forced to pay higher money wages may pass on these increases to the consumer in the form of higher prices. Because of the higher cost of living, the worker's real wage, what he can buy with his money, may not rise so fast as does his money wage.

Undoubtedly this tendency for price increases to thwart wage increases does happen in some degree. Still, when all is said and done, many observers seem to be left with the feeling that collective bargaining does "squeeze" the profit position of corporations; it does force business to be more efficient; it does often make the worker more efficient by enabling him to be better fed and educated—all these things at least in part.

For good or evil, American labor has declared itself in as a silent partner in every business. With the acquiescence of the public and the government, workers ask for, and usually succeed in getting, some fraction of corporation profits.[1] (The moral for the self-interested laborer is to apprentice himself to a profitable quasi-monopolistic industry which has plenty of gravy to share.)

Modern capitalist society seems so imbued with a feeling of guilt over the existing inequality of income that almost everyone believes in the desirability not only of higher wages, but of much higher wages.[2] Consequently, the demands of workers are literally insatiable. An employer cannot buy them off at any price. All he can buy is a little time; but in a few months, the workers will be back for more.

The above remarks are stated as facts, without any expression of approval or viewing with alarm. It should be said, however, that there is nothing sacred about the traditional fraction of two-thirds of the national income going to wages and salaries. Moreover, with production growing over time, real wages can continue to rise without at all impairing the returns to property. But a reckless labor movement that forces up money wages too rapidly can certainly bring economic ruin upon itself and the economic system as a whole.

---

[1] Whether all this is good or bad depends upon the individual's ethical beliefs, but whether this is factually true or false is an objective problem.

[2] This was not always so. Early nineteenth-century conservative writers were shamelessly frank in attaching greater importance to property than to humanity, and in proclaiming the inevitability and desirability of poverty.

SUMMARY

A. PRODUCTION EQUILIBRIUM OF THE FIRM

1. In final equilibrium every input will be hired up to the point where its extra revenue is just balanced by its cost. This is easily seen by the direct approach.

2. In the indirect approach it is shown that the marginal product of each last dollar must be the same in every use if total costs are at a minimum for all possible outputs. This same condition can be stated in a number of different ways; but they all imply that input prices are proportional to marginal products of the respective inputs, the factor of proportionality being marginal cost.

3. This last condition, when combined with the equality of marginal cost and marginal revenue developed in Chap. 21, leads indirectly but inevitably to the same final conditions of equilibrium as were developed in the direct approach.

B. THE PROBLEM OF DISTRIBUTION

4. The marginal product principles outlined in this previous discussion represent a theory of the reactions of a firm to given factor prices. They do not by themselves constitute a theory of wage rates, of land rent, or of return on capital. Nor do they apply directly to the ill-conceived historical search for principles to determine "how total social product is to be distributed among the different factors of production in accordance with their identifiable productive contributions."

5. At the present time, the science of economics has little to say on the broader question as to the limits within which different groups, such as labor, can increase their real incomes. But it does suggest that there are such limits and that not all increases in money wages that are achieved by collective bargaining can be considered as equivalent additions to the real income of the working population as a whole.

QUESTIONS FOR DISCUSSION

1. If you were a knife manufacturer debating whether to make your products more long-lived by adding more of an alloy, how would you formally decide what to do?

2. What is the extra cost of an input of labor? What does its extra revenue equal? Why?

3. In Table 1, what is the marginal product of the fourth worker (*a*) when capital is equal to 5, (*b*) when capital is equal to 6? Why the difference? What is the marginal product of the sixth unit of capital equal to?

4. Using a row or column of Table 1, illustrate the law of diminishing returns.

5. Draw up a table like Table 2, but for $q = 490$.

6. State in two or more ways the condition for minimizing total expense in producing a given q.

7. Summarize the direct and indirect approaches to final production decisions. Show that they are really equivalent.

8. Robinson Crusoe and Friday produce 100 bushels of corn yearly. How should this be divided between them? What are some of the possibilities? Suppose Crusoe owns the land but does no work. Would your answer be different?

9. "It costs $300 a year to commute from Greenwich, Conn., to New York City. Therefore, land rent in New York City should be at least that much higher than in the suburbs." Discuss.

10. Discuss the problem of the extent to which unions can or cannot raise wages.

11. Sketch the competitive market forces that determine the prices of productive services.

12. Give a graphical presentation of the process of combining factors optimally in order to be on the best possible cost curve.

APPENDIX TO CHAPTER 22
GRAPHICAL DEPICTION OF PRODUCTION
EQUILIBRIUM

The common-sense numerical analysis of the way in which a firm will combine inputs to minimize costs can be made more vivid by the use of diagrams.

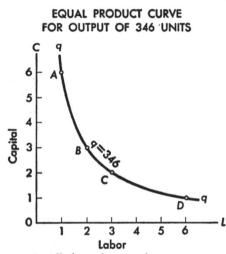

**EQUAL PRODUCT CURVE
FOR OUTPUT OF 346 UNITS**

FIG. 1. All the points on the curve represent the different combinations of capital and labor that can be used to produce 346 units of output.

From the production schedule we can draw a picture of the different input combinations that will produce a given output. Figure 1 is the exact counterpart of Table 2. In it the smooth curve indicates the different combinations of labor and capital that yield an output of 346 units. This could be called a "Production-indifference curve" by analogy with the consumer's Indifference curve of the Appendix to Chap. 20. But a more expressive name would be to call it an "Equal-product" curve. (The reader should be able to draw in on Fig. 1, as a dotted curve, the corresponding Equal-product curve for output equal to 490. He should realize that an infinite number of such Equal-product contour lines could be drawn in, just as a topographical or weather map could be covered with an indefinitely large number of equal-altitude contour lines or equal-barometric-pressure lines.)

Given the price of labor and capital, the firm can evaluate the total cost for points A, B, C, D, or for any other point on the Equal-product curve. Obviously, it will be maximizing its profits only when it has found that optimum point on the Equal-product curve at which total costs are at a minimum. Purely as a graphical trick, the firm might try to save itself much tedious arithmetical computation by evaluating once and for all the total cost of every possible factor combination of capital and labor. This is done in Fig. 2, where the family of parallel straight lines represents all possible Equal-cost curves when the price of labor is \$2 and the price of capital \$3.[1]

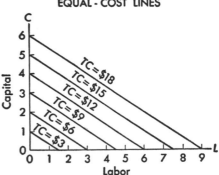

EQUAL - COST LINES

FIG. 2. Every point on a given line represents the same total cost. The lines are straight because of constant factor prices and have a numerical slope equal to the ratio of labor price to capital price.

To find the total cost for any point we simply have to read off the number appended to the Equal-cost line going through that point. The lines are all straight and parallel because the firm is assumed to be able to buy all it wishes of either input at constant prices. The lines are somewhat flatter than 45 degrees because the price of labor, P_L, is somewhat less than the price of capital, P_C. More precisely, we can always say that the arithmetic value of the slope of each Equal-cost line must equal the ratio of the price of labor to that of capital—in this case 2/3.

It is now easy to recognize the optimum equilibrium input position of the firm at which total costs are minimized for the given output. The single Equal-product curve has superimposed upon it the family of Equal-cost lines. This is shown in Fig. 3. The firm will always keep moving along the heavy concave curve of Fig. 3, so long as it is able to cross over to lower cost lines. Its equilibrium will, therefore, not be at A, B, or D. It will be at C, *where the Equal-product curve touches (but does not cross) the lowest Equal-cost line.* This is, of course, a point of tangency, where the slope of the Equal-product curve just matches the slope of an Equal-cost line when the curves are just kissing.

SELECTING INPUTS TO MINIMIZE COST OF PRODUCTION

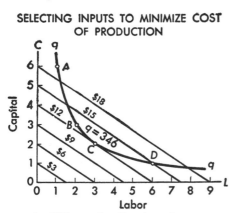

FIG. 3. Where the Equal-product curve touches (but does not cross) the lowest total cost curve is the optimum position. Here factor prices and marginal productivities (or "substitution ratios") are proportional.

We already know that the slope of the Equal-cost curves is P_L/P_C. But

[1] These lines are all straight because $TC = 2L + 3C$.

what is the slope of the Equal-product curve? This slope is a kind of "substitution ratio" between the two factors and depends upon the *relative* marginal products of the two factors of production, just as the rate of substitution between two goods along a consumer's Indifference curve was earlier shown to equal the ratio of the marginal or extra utilities of the two goods (Appendix to Chap. 20).

Thus, our minimum total cost equilibrium can be defined by any of the following equivalent relations:

> *a. The ratio of the marginal productivities of the two inputs equals their price ratio.*

That is,

$$\text{Substitution ratio or } \frac{\textbf{marginal product of labor}}{\textbf{marginal product of capital}} = \frac{\textbf{price of labor}}{\textbf{price of capital}}$$

> *b. The marginal product received from the (last) dollar of expenditure must be the same in every use.*

That is

$$\frac{\textbf{Marginal product of labor}}{\textbf{Price of labor}} = \frac{\textbf{marginal product of capital}}{\textbf{price of capital}} = \cdots$$

This condition holds for any number of inputs; for land as well as for labor and capital, etc. The (*b*) relation is discussed in detail in the main body of the chapter. It could also be derived from (*a*) by transposing terms from one numerator to the other denominator, *i.e.*, by "interchanging means," as is always algebraically permissible.

But the student should not be satisfied with any such abstract explanation. He should always remember the common-sense economic explanation which shows how a firm will redistribute its expenditure on inputs if any one offers a greater return for each last dollar spent on it. Finally, we may state the above relations in the form

> *c. Input prices and their marginal products are proportional, the factor of proportionality being marginal cost.*

That is

Marginal cost of output $\times$ marginal product of labor = price of labor
Marginal cost of output $\times$ marginal product of capital = price of capital

and so on for any number of inputs.[1]

---

[1] A logician would not be satisfied with the earlier proof that the factor of proportionality is really *MC*. There is no simple and rigorous way of making this plausible. It rests on the

The relationships (a), (b), and (c) are all equivalent. Each holds at every point along the total cost curve, *whatever be the output*. They do not tell the firm where it should finally produce. In the main body of the chapter it is shown how they must be supplemented if final equilibrium is to be achieved.

---

fact that for "small" changes, the extra costs of output are the same whether the firm hires only labor, or only capital, or some other combination.

Chapter 23: INTERNATIONAL TRADE AND THE THEORY OF COMPARATIVE ADVANTAGE

AGAIN and again we have seen how specialization increases productivity and standards of living. Now we must show exactly how this works out in the field of international or interregional trade, going behind the façade of international finance. Why did the United States specialize a century ago in the production of agricultural goods and exchange these for the manufacturing output of Europe? Why is she today able to export highly complex mass-produced goods to the far corners of the globe? Why is the agriculture of Australia so different from that of Austria or Belgium? How great would be the costs of complete self-sufficiency to a modern country? How do all countries benefit from trade?

The key to the correct answers to such questions, and many more, is provided by the theory of comparative advantage or comparative cost. Developed more than a century ago by David Ricardo, John Stuart Mill, and other English followers of Adam Smith, the theory of comparative advantage is a closely reasoned doctrine which, when properly stated, is unassailable. With it we are able to separate out gross fallacies in the political propaganda for protective tariffs aimed at limiting imports. At the same time, it helps us to identify the germs of truth that sometimes pop up in the heated claims for protection.

Like much of the reasoning of the classical economists, the theory of comparative advantage can be best understood and defended if we agree in advance to apply it only to a Euclidean world where there is substantially full employment. If this seems objectionable to the reader in view of the grave problem of unemployment, let him be referred to Chap. 16 where the effects of international trade on domestic employment were discussed and where we agreed that a country like the United States must not depend upon beggar-my-neighbor international economic policies to solve her domestic problem of unemployment.

DIVERSITY OF CONDITIONS BETWEEN REGIONS OR COUNTRIES

For simplicity, therefore, let us imagine two countries or continents, each endowed with certain quantities of natural resources, capital goods, kinds of labor, and technical knowledge or know-how. The first link in the comparative-cost chain of reasoning is the *diversity in conditions of production between different countries*. Specifically, this means that the production possibilities of the different countries are very different. Although people could try to produce something of every commodity in any region, it is obvious that they would not succeed; or, if they did succeed, it would be only at a terrific cost. With hot-house procedures and forcing methods, wine grapes could perhaps be grown in Scotland; but the cost in terms of economic resources would be exorbitant, and the resulting product would hardly be fit to drink anyway.

Even if by chance two countries can both produce the same commodities, they will usually find that it pays for each to concentrate its production especially on one of them and to trade it for the other. If we consider trade between, say, the northern temperate zones and the southern tropics, this proposition will seem true and trite. Of course, resources near the equator are more productive in the growing of bananas, and of course northern resources are better designed for wheat growing. Everyone can readily see that in this case specialization and trade will increase the amount of world production of both goods and also each country's consumption of both goods.

It is not so immediately obvious, but it is no less true, that international trade is mutually profitable even when one of the two countries can produce every commodity more cheaply (in terms of all resources) than the other country. One country has an *absolute advantage* in the production of every good; the other country has an absolute disadvantage in the production of every good. But so long as there are differences in the *relative* efficiencies of producing the different goods in the two countries, one can always be sure that even the poor country has a *comparative advantage* in the production of those commodities in which it is relatively most efficient; this same poor country will have a *comparative disadvantage* in those commodities in which it is more than averagely inefficient. Similarly, the rich, efficient country will find that it should specialize in those fields of production where its absolute advantage is comparatively greatest, planning to import those commodities in which the greatly inefficient country has the least absolute disadvantage.

Thus, trade between America and Europe in food and clothing is mutually advantageous even if America should be able to produce both of these items more efficiently (in terms of all economic resources). Moreover, barter between America and Asia is especially advantageous to us even though the Chinese laborer receives only a fraction of the real wages going to productive American labor. We shall see in a moment how this paradoxical situation is possible.

A traditional example used to illustrate this paradox of comparative advantage is the case of the best lawyer in town who is also the best typist in town. Will he not specialize in law and leave typing to a secretary? How can he afford to give up precious time from the legal field, where his comparative advantage is very great, to perform typing activities in which he has an absolute advantage but in which his relative advantage is least? Or look at it from the secretary's point of view. She is at a disadvantage relative to him in both activities; but her relative disadvantage is least in typing. Relatively speaking, she has a comparative advantage in typing.

A SIMPLE CASE: EUROPE AND AMERICA

Let us illustrate these fundamental principles of international trade by a simplified example. Consider America and Europe of a century ago, and concentrate on only two commodities, food and clothing. Now in the Western Hemisphere land and natural resources were then very plentiful relative to labor and capital. Whereas on the Continent, people and capital were plentiful relative to land.

This contrast is best seen if we look at the *intensive* agriculture of a country like Belgium. There, in order to get the greatest possible output, small plots of land have to be cultivated assiduously by many people and much fertilizer. Compare this with the extensive agriculture of the early United States, where one family cultivated many acres and where national product was maximized by each man "spreading himself thin" over the virtually free land. A Belgian farmer would have thought this wasteful. But in view of the relatively high cost of American labor or capital and the low cost of land, it was not. Actually, it was prudent.[1]

Of course, if surplus populations could have all migrated from Belgium to

---

[1] This disregards the practice of burning out the natural fertility of the soil by overuse, and also the destruction of forests, giving rise to floods and soil erosion. From a social point of view, such exhaustion of natural resources undoubtedly represented a tremendous waste. Even today conservation programs in the lumber, oil, and agriculture fields leave much to be desired.

the United States, real wages here would have tended to fall toward equality with rising wages there; and high land rents there would have fallen toward equality with rising rents here. Actually, this would have tended at the same time to increase *total world production*, because the transfer of workers from their poor Belgian farms to rich American farms would entail a gain in their productivity. All this follows from the fundamental law of diminishing returns, discussed earlier in connection with the Malthus population theory.

But let us be selfish and hard-boiled. Let us suppose that immigrants from abroad are to be kept out of the United States in order to keep labor scarce here and wages high. From this same selfish point of view, should the United States also impose a protective tariff designed to keep out imports from abroad? Or should it not? To answer this important social question we must measure carefully the amounts of food and clothing that will be produced and consumed in each country (1) if there is no international trade and (2) if trade is permitted to follow its own course.

AMERICA WITHOUT TRADE

In Chap. 2, we saw that every economy has a Production-possibility (or transformation) schedule indicating how much of one commodity such as food, can be produced if all resources are diverted to it; also how much of the other commodity, clothing, can be produced if all resources are diverted to its production; and how either good can be transformed into the other—not physically, but—by transferring resources from the production of one to the other.

For simplicity, let us suppose that food can always be transformed into units of clothing in America at the *constant ratio* of 10:3. For each 10 units of food sacrificed, we can always secure 3 units of clothing. Let us further assume that, when all resources are diverted to the production of food, America will have altogether 100 (million) units of food.

TABLE 1. *Production-possibility Schedule of America (10:3, Constant-cost Ratio)*

	A	B	C	D	E	F	G	H	I	J	K
Food (millions)	100	90	80	70	60	50	40	*30	20	10	0
Clothing (millions)	0	3	6	9	12	15	18	*21	24	27	30

Then, clearly America can, if she chooses, have 90 (million) units of food and 3 (million) units of clothing, 80 (million) and 6 (million), . . . , or finally 0 (million) of food and 30 (million) of clothing. We may put this in the form of a schedule, as shown in Table 1.

This may be plotted in Fig. 1, just as was done in Chap. 2, Fig. 3. The solid line *AK* is the Production-possibility curve. But something about the diagram looks a little different from those of Chap. 2. Just what? A little remembrance and turning back a few pages will show that this new Possibility curve is a straight line, whereas the previous ones all were rounded and convex.

This is because, in the interest of keeping the argument simple, any tendency toward what is called "increasing costs" has been deliberately assumed away. The returns of food for clothing sacrificed are instead always to be given by the constant cost ratio 10:3, instead of having relative costs rise in a more

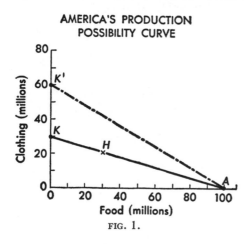

AMERICA'S PRODUCTION
POSSIBILITY CURVE

FIG. 1.

realistic fashion. Constant costs have been assumed only to simplify the argument—to relieve the ·student from having to remember many different cost ratios. As will be seen later, this will not seriously affect the validity of the argument. Where a few qualifications are needed, they are later made in the Appendix to this chapter.

So far we have been talking only about production. However, if the United States is isolated from all trade, what she produces is also what she consumes. Let us suppose, therefore, that the starred quantities, *H*, of Table 1 and Fig. 1 represent the amounts produced and consumed by America in the absence of trade; or in numerical terms America then produces and consumes 30 (million) units of food and 21 (million) units of clothing.

Why was this particular combination decided upon rather than one of the other possibilities? We have seen in Chap. 3 that in a competitive system nobody "decides" upon this, but that the price mechanism, operating through supply and demand for goods and services, determines What shall be produced, How, and For Whom. Well, the starred quantities are the What. Very little need be said here about the How, except for the obvious remark that agricultural food production will require more land relative to labor than will more highly fabricated clothing output. As to the For Whom, we need only repeat that scarcity of labor in the United States will mean rather high wages for workers, while superabundance of land here will mean low rents (per acre) for landlords.

Let us proceed to introduce Europe into the picture. Before doing so, it will pave the way for the later argument to interject a question. What would happen if some American (perhaps Eli Whitney, inventor of the cotton gin, will do as an example) should make a clever invention so that each 10 units of food could be transformed into 6 rather than 3 units of clothing. Would America be potentially better off? The answer is obviously "yes." The Production-possibility curve has shifted outward and upward and is now shown by the broken line, AK', in Fig. 1. Note that America could now go from H to (say) H' and have more of both food and clothing. (It would not be correct to say that she is twice as well off as before, because she will still want some food and there has been no improvement in its production. But clearly she is better off.)

Of course, someone may rise to the floor and ask, "What if the invention throws people out of work? Will America be better off? May not technological unemployment make her worse off?" These are not stupid questions, but they are clearly out of order at this point. They belong to Part Two. Here we have explicitly asserted that we move in a happy, Euclidean, classical world where all resources are fully employed, either as a matter of luck or as a result of sensible public and private domestic policies. Without a doubt, the invention has increased America's *potential* production or her full-employment national income—whatever it does to her realistic chances of attaining or maintaining full employment.

EUROPE WITHOUT TRADE

We can now do for Europe exactly what was done above for America; but with an important difference. Europe's plentiful endowment of labor relative to land would give her a different cost or transformation ratio between food and clothing. She would have less of a comparative advantage in food and more in clothing. For her each 10 units of food may be transformable into, say, 8 units of clothing. She gets 5 more than was true of the United States because of her comparative advantage in clothing. However, in terms of food America gets $1\frac{0}{3}$ or 3.33 units for each unit of clothing sacrificed; while Europe's comparative disadvantage in food production gives her only $1\frac{0}{8}$ or 1.25 units of food for each sacrificed unit of clothing. *The important thing to concentrate upon is the differences in the two cost ratios: 10:3 for America and 10:8 for Europe.*

Let us still keep the two continents isolated from each other. What is Europe's exact Production-possibility schedule? Let us suppose that Europe's

TABLE 2. *Production-possibility Schedule of Europe (10:8 Constant-cost Ratio)*

	A	B	C	D
Food, millions...	—	100	*50	0
Clothing, millions.....................................	0	—	*80	—

population is so large and her land area is such that before trade she was producing and consuming 50 units of food and 80 units of clothing. This fact, plus the constant-cost ratio, 10:8, tells us all we have to know in order to draw up Europe's complete Production-possibility schedule as in Table 2. The student should fill in the blanks. He should check these against the correct Production-possibility line shown in Fig. 2.

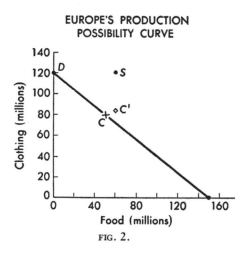

EUROPE'S PRODUCTION POSSIBILITY CURVE

FIG. 2.

THE OPENING UP OF TRADE

Now, for the first time, let us admit the possibility of trade between the two continents. Food can be bartered for clothing at some *terms of trade, i.e.,* at some *price ratio.* To dramatize the process let us suppose that in mid-ocean there stands an impersonal auctioneer, whose business it is to balance supply and demand, offers of clothing, and offers of food. He does this by calling out to both countries an exchange rate or price ratio between food and clothing. Until supplies and demands are balanced, he keeps the bidding going. When he finally hits on the equilibrium price level *at which supply and demand balance,* then he raps his gavel three times and says, "Going, going, *gone!*" But only then.

Probably, he will suspect in advance that Europe is going to specialize on clothing production in which she has a comparative advantage and will wish to export part of her clothing production in exchange for food imports. But he has no idea what the final price ratio or "terms of trade" between clothing and food will be—whether the final food-clothing price ratio will be 10:3, 10:8, 10:5, 10:6, or anything else. For that matter, if the auctioneer is very new at the game, or very stupid, he may think that the final equilibrium exchange level or terms of trade will be 10:1 or 10:12.

Actually, neither of these last two can be the final exchange ratio. He would soon learn this from bitter experience. For let him tell America and Europe that they can get all the clothing they want in exchange for food at the rate of only 1 unit of clothing for every 10 units of food. What will America do? By producing at home, she can get 3 units of clothing for each 10 of food. Clearly she will not be sucked into trading food for clothing on those terms; she would rather remain self-sufficient.

That is only half the story. Why shouldn't America go to the other extreme and export clothing in exchange for food imports? Each 1 unit of clothing gets her 10 units of food from the auctioneer. What will 1 unit of clothing get here at home in domestic food production? Obviously, from Table 1 and Fig. 1 only $1\frac{2}{3}$ or 3.33 units of food. At 10:1, therefore, America should certainly shift all her resources to clothing production; she should export some of her surplus clothing in return for food imports.

Now, what about Europe? At home she gets only $1\frac{2}{8}$ or 1.25 units of food for each unit of clothing. At 10:1, she too will want to trade clothing for food. We see, therefore, what a green hand the auctioneer was. By calling out 10:1, he brings a flood supply of clothing on his head and only demands for food. Since he has no supplies of either good up his sleeve, he must now change his tactics. He must raise the price of food relative to the price of clothing. He had better try the ratio 10:2, or perhaps even 10:9. The student is now in a position to reason out why neither of them will do: why 10:2 will still bring out a tidal wave of clothing; and, on the other hand, why 10:9 represents the opposite error, in which there is a tornado of food.

Clearly, then, *the final exchange ratio cannot be outside the original two-country limits of* 10:3 *and* 10:8! Anywhere in between is a possibility—with America following her comparative advantage and specializing in food, and Europe following her comparative advantage and specializing in the production of clothing.

We are now at a breathing space. Let us summarize exactly what has been proved:

1. If nature endows two regions unequally with factors of production, the *relative* costs of transforming one commodity into another domestically will be different for the two regions.

2. Under international trade, goods will be exchanged for each other at a price ratio somewhere *intermediate* between the domestic cost ratios of the two countries.

3. Each country will specialize in the commodity in which it has a comparative advantage, exporting its surplus of the product for imports from abroad.

4. Each country is made better off by trade and specialization: if America can get, say, 6 units of clothing for each 10 units of food traded, she is certainly better off than when she domestically transforms 10 units of food into only 3 units of clothing; Europe does better when she trades 6 units of clothing for 10 units of food than when she must domestically transform 8 of clothing into 10 of food. The same would be true if we had picked any other trading ratio than 10:6—just so long as it lies between the limits 10:3 and 10:8.

5. Trade is *indirect* production. Trade is efficient production. Efficient production is always better than inefficient production. (The reader should note that the advantage of trade has nothing to do with *relative wage rates*. Under free trade, wages in each country tend to be pulled up to the higher levels of productivity of its export industry and not down to the low efficiency level of the import industry.)

EXACT DETERMINATION OF THE FINAL PRICE RATIO

Just where in between the domestic cost ratios will the terms of trade settle down? David Ricardo, the English economist, to whom the comparative-cost theory is usually attributed,[1] got just up to this point but no further. Some of his immediate followers were foolish enough to say, "We split the difference between the two countries' cost ratios, or in this case pick 10:5½ as the equilibrium rate."[2]

Actually, as John Stuart Mill, the third great classical economist (after Smith and Ricardo) showed a little later, *the exact final level of the terms of trade in between the two cost ratios will depend upon the strength of world supply and demand for each of the two commodities.* If people have an intense desire for food relative to available supplies of food and clothing, the price ratio will settle near the upper level of 10:8; if clothing is much demanded by both countries, it will settle nearer to 10:3.[3]

Mill did what our auctioneer would have to do. He drew up a schedule

---

[1] DAVID RICARDO, "Principals of Political Economy and Taxation," Chap. VII, 1817.

[2] Or would they have said halfway between $1\frac{2}{3}$ and $1\frac{2}{8}$, giving us $11\frac{2}{24}$ or 10:4.5⅚? Both answers are equally foolish.

[3] Also, if America were very small relative to Europe, so that its supplies made hardly a "dent" on the market, then the price ratio might even stay at 10:8. America would then be specializing in food and importing clothing, but all of America's food exports would amount to so little that Europe would still have to produce some food for herself. This is possible only at a price of 10:8. American would in this case get all the gains from international trade. It pays to have a large (different!) neighbor.

showing supply and demand at *each possible price ratio:*[1] how much food America would wish to export and how much food Europe would want to import; and at the same time, how much clothing Europe would be willing to export at each price ratio in comparison with the amount of clothing America expected to import. At one, and (usually) only one, intermediate price ratio, exports and imports will balance. At this equilibrium price, exports and imports will "mesh" (or match), quantitatively as well as qualitatively; the auctioneer

AMERICA AFTER INTERNATIONAL TRADE

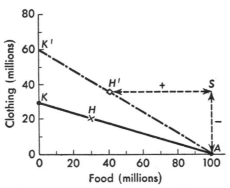

FIG. 3. The heavy line AK represents America's domestic Production-possibility curve; the heavy broken line AK' her new Consumption-possibility curve when she is able to trade freely at the price ratio 10:6, and in consequence has decided to specialize completely in the production of food (at A). The dotted arrows from A to S and S to H' show the amounts exported ($+$) and imported ($-$) by America. As a result of free trade, she finally ends up at H' with more of both goods than before at H.

and Mill will heave a sigh of relief, and trade will continue indefinitely until tastes or technology have changed.

For our numerical problem it has been assumed that the equilibrium terms-of-trade ratio is 10:6, a little nearer to Europe's pretrade ratio than to America's. American concentrates its production completely on food. In Fig. 3, America is production-wise at A. But since she can trade freely at 10:6, America is not limited to her old Production-possibility curve. By trading, she can now move on the dotted line AK' *just exactly as if a fruitful invention had been made.* Is America made potentially better off by trade? Indeed she is.

[1] This schedule would differ from the ordinary supply and demand schedules for wheat, tea, or automobiles observed in Chap. 19 only in the fact that the price of, say, food is not expressed in money terms, but in barter terms, *i.e.*, in terms of clothing. Similarly, it is not money that is offered for food but clothing. We can either say that America supplies food and Europe demands food, or we can just as well say that America demands clothing and Europe supplies clothing.

Just where she will stop on this broken line, which we may call her new *Consumption*-possibility curve, depends upon the workings of her internal price system. It has been assumed that this causes her to stop at the point H', where 40 (million) units of food and 36 (million) units of clothing are consumed. The dotted arrows show America's exports (+) and imports (−).

TABLE 3. *Summary Table Showing Specialization and Gains from Trade According to Comparative Advantage (All data in millions of units)*

	Price ratio of food and clothing	Food produc-tion	Food con-sump-tion	Food exports (+) or imports (−)	Clothing produc-tion	Clothing con-sump-tion	Clothing exports (+) or imports (−)
Situation before trade							
America......	10:3	30	30	0	21	21	0
Europe.......	10:8	50	50	0	80	80	0
World........	None	80	80	0	101	101	0
Situation after trade							
America......	10:6	100	40	+60	0	36	−36
Europe.......	10:6	0	60	−60	120	84	+36
World........	10:6	100	100	0	120	120	0
Gains from trade							
America......	—	—	+10	—	—	+15	—
Europe.......	—	—	+10	—	—	+4	—
World........	—	+20	+20	—	+19	+19	—

All this is summarized in America's rows of Table 3. This important table should be studied very carefully, because to understand it thoroughly is to understand the doctrine of comparative costs.

As a result of specialization and trade, America has become better off; she has more food and more clothing to consume. The same is true of Europe. What is the black magic by which something seems to have been got for nothing? The rows marked World, which represent the sum of the American and European rows give the answer. *World production of both goods has been stepped up by specialization and trade.*

Actually, the second World row gives the data in which the auctioneer would be most interested. He is assured that equilibrium has been reached by two facts shown there: (1) World consumption of each product is identically equal to world production with no goods lost in transit, and (2) the amounts that each country exports are just balanced by the amounts that the other country wishes to import. Thus the price ratio 10:6 is the right one.[1]

This completes our explanation of comparative advantage. The reader might test his full understanding by filling in on Fig. 2 for Europe everything that has already been filled in for America on Fig. 3. Why does Europe's new Consumption-possibility line, made possible by trade, pivot around the point D on the vertical axis? Draw in the arrows to S representing the amounts exported $(+)$ and imported $(-)$ as was done in Fig. 3. Note that Europe's arrows match America's but are opposite in sign. Why is this quantitative meshing of exports and imports necessary at equilibrium?

SUMMARY

1. If two countries have different production conditions so that the costs of converting one commodity into another are different, it is clearly to their separate selfish advantages to trade regardless of whether their wage levels are different. Each country specializes in the commodity in which it is relatively most efficient. The commodity producible at a comparative disadvantage in a country will of course be wanted in some amount by its consumers; but the country in question will find it more efficient to take resources out of *direct* domestic production of that commodity and put them instead into the lines of greatest advantage. Such diverted resources can be thought of as creating the wanted goods *indirectly*, in the sense that exports turned out by them can be more advantageously bartered for the wanted goods in question. A country following comparative advantage is simply acting like any prudent business

---

[1] The auctioneer could have made up a whole book full of such tables, each page corresponding to a different price ratio. But only one page is the right one because at all other prices the algebraic total of exports and imports would not cancel out. Thus, at 10:7, America's desire for clothing imports would surpass Europe's willingness to export clothing. The world as a whole would be trying to consume more clothing than had been produced. Since the auctioneer has no inventories to draw upon, he would have to turn the pages toward a higher price for clothing. On the right page the price ratio would be an equilibrium one, and exports and imports would be in balance.

firm which buys things from outsiders if it cannot produce them as cheaply itself.

2. In international exchange one country does not gain at the expense of another. The benefits from trade are mutual. All countries gain. This is possible because the total of world production is increased by international specialization along the lines of comparative cost.

3. Precisely how these total gains will be split up between the participating nations depends upon the reciprocal supply-demand situation. We can state with confidence that the final terms of trade, or price ratio, will fall somewhere within the divergent domestic cost ratios of the two countries. Whether it will fall near to one's original cost ratio and thereby give most of the benefits to the other, cannot be told in advance.

Moreover, as tastes and technology change, the terms of trade may turn in favor of or against a particular nation. For example, after World War I, surplus agricultural supplies turned the terms of trade against the backward, debtor, agricultural countries of the world. This is typical of depressions, whereas the reverse is usually true in time of prosperity and boom. In the recent postwar period the terms of trade were turned strongly in favor of agriculture, as every food purchaser was bitterly aware.

QUESTIONS FOR DISCUSSION

1. List some products that the United States exports or imports. What other countries are involved?

2. "If a country can buy a good cheaper abroad than it can produce it at home, it is to its advantage to do so." Is this consistent with the theory of comparative advantage?

3. State in a single page the meaning of the theory of comparative advantage.

4. How would you apply that theory to trade between people within a country?

5. Rewrite Table 3 assuming that the new final price or trading ratio is 10:5 rather than 10:6, and that America ends up consuming 35 units of food.

6. Exactly what did John Stuart Mill add to David Ricardo's theory of international trade?

7. "If there are more than two commodities or two countries, the whole theory of comparative advantage has to be scrapped." Discuss.

8. Which of the following two statements is absolutely false?

a. "Even if the United States can produce every product with less labor and capital hours than Czechoslovakia, it may still pay both of us to trade."

b. "Even if the United States can produce every product for fewer *dollars* than they can be imported for from abroad, it will still pay us to trade—provided only that some commodities have relatively higher import prices than others."

How do the statements differ? What are the implications of the valid statement for real wages here and abroad?

9. Compare and evaluate multilateralism and bilateralism.

10. List some qualifications to the simplest theory of comparative advantage.

11. Why shouldn't the United States use international trade to get rid of her unemployment?

APPENDIX TO CHAPTER 23
SOME QUALIFICATIONS TO THE DISCUSSION OF COMPARATIVE ADVANTAGE

Very briefly we must now show what happens when we remove some of the oversimplifications made in the above discussion. The conclusions are not essentially changed, and even the changes in details are usually not too difficult.

MANY COMMODITIES AND COUNTRIES

First note that up until now we have simplified the discussion by considering only two commodities: food and clothing. Obviously, food stands for many different items (beef, milk, etc.), and the same is true of clothing. Moreover, the advantages of exchange are equally great when we consider the thousand and one commodities that can and do enter into international trade.

As is shown in advanced textbooks in international trade,[1] when there are many commodities that are producible in two countries, they can be arranged in order according to their relative advantage or comparative cost. For example, the commodities, automobiles, flax, perfumes, watches, wheat, and woolens might be arranged in the following comparative-advantage sequence:

AMERICA ◄────┼────────┼────────┼────────┼────────┼────────► EUROPE
Wheat, Automobiles, Flax, Watches, Woolens, Perfumes

This means that wheat costs are lowest relative to all other commodities in America; Europe has its greatest comparative advantage in perfumes; its advantage in watches is not quite so great, etc.

From the beginning we can be almost sure of one thing. The introduction of trade will cause America to produce wheat and Europe perfume. But where will the dividing line fall? Between automobiles and flax? Or will America produce flax and Europe confine herself to watches, woolens, and perfumes? Or will the dividing line fall on one of the commodities rather than between them, so that, say, flax might be produced in both places at the same time?

The reader will not be surprised to find that the answer depends upon the comparative strength of international demand for the different goods. If we think of the commodities as beads arranged on a string according to their comparative advantage, the total demand and supply situation will determine where

[1] For example, G. HABERLER, "Theory of International Trade," The Macmillan Company, New York, 1937.

the dividing line between American and European production will fall. Then, an increased demand for automobiles and wheat, for example, may tend to turn the terms of trade in direction of America and make us so prosperous that it will no longer pay us to continue to produce our own flax. Also, there is the possibility that a new scientific discovery permitt'ng America to grow flax on the desert might rearrange the order of the comparative advantages of the different commodities and alter the pattern of specialization and trade.[1]

[1] This ordered array of goods might have arisen from the following numerical data, which are presented only for the curiosity of the more advanced reader and which have nothing to do with the above discussion. As before, it is not necessary to measure costs in terms of money or labor but only in terms of the relative commodities into which any good can be "transformed." Suppose that we choose to measure the costs of every good in both countries in terms of woolens, which is selected arbitrarily because it comes last alphabetically. Then our data might be as arranged alphabetically as in the accompanying table:

Goods	American cost ratio, in terms of woolens	European cost ratio, in terms of woolens	Comparative European costs, in terms of American costs
Automobiles..........	1,000	3,000	$\frac{3,000}{1,000} = 3.0$
Flax...............	0.8	1.6	$\frac{1.6}{0.8} = 2.0$
Perfumes............	5.0	3.0	$\frac{3}{5} = 0.6$
Watches............	50	75	$\frac{75}{50} = 1.5$
Wheat...............	0.2	0.8	$\frac{0.8}{0.2} = 4.0$
Woolens............	1.0	1.0	$\frac{1}{1} = 1.0$

This means that in America one must give up the production of 1,000 units of woolens to get 1 automobile, while in Europe the cost of 1 automobile is the sacrifice of 3,000 units of wool production. Therefore, the comparative cost of automobiles in Europe is three times that in America, and so forth for all the other goods.

Obviously, Europe's relative cost advantage is greatest in perfumes and least in wheat; in between, the commodities are arranged as shown above in the text. The fact that the figures in the last column are predominantly greater than 1 in no way reflects on the efficiency of Europe, but results from the accidental fact that we chose woolens as our common denominator in which to express costs. Had we selected wheat or watches, the opposite would have been the case and yet none of our results would be any different—except for a "scale factor" (such as converts inches to feet or yards).

So much for the complications introduced by many commodities. What about many countries? Europe and America are not the whole world. And even they include many separate so-called sovereign nations.

Introducing many countries need not change our analysis. As far as any one country is concerned, all the other nations with whom she trades can be lumped together into one group as "the rest of the world." The advantages of trade have nothing specially to do with state boundaries. The principles already developed apply between groups of countries and, indeed, between regions within the same country. In fact, were it not for the tariff, they would be more applicable to trade between our Northern and Southern states than to trade between the United States and Canada.

From the standpoint of pure economic welfare, the slogan "Buy American" is as foolish as would be "Buy Wisconsin," or "Buy Oshkosh, Wisconsin," or "Buy South Oshkosh, Wisconsin." Part of the great prosperity of the United States has resulted from the fortunate fact that there have been no restrictive customs duties within our vast 48 states, and we have constituted the world's greatest free-trade area.

THE SYSTEM OF MULTILATERAL TRADE, AS REFLECTED BY THE ORIENTATION OF BALANCES OF MERCHANDISE TRADE IN 1938

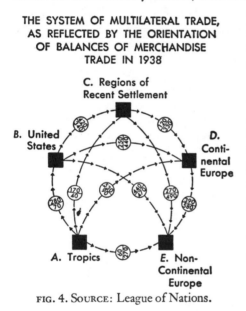

FIG. 4. SOURCE: League of Nations.

There is, however, one new aspect introduced by the existence of many countries. America may find it very profitable to trade indirectly with Europe. America sells Europe much, including finished commodities like automobiles. It buys little from Europe. But it does buy rubber and raw materials from the East Indies. They in turn do not usually buy goods from America. However, they do buy clothing and other goods from England. Thus, we have a very advantageous triangular trade, as shown in the accompanying diagram.

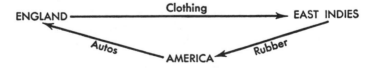

The arrows indicate the predominant direction of exports.

What would happen if all countries tried to sign bilateral trade agreements with each other, so that America could not and would not buy from the Indies unless they bought an equal amount from America? And so forth with every two countries? Very clearly, trade would be cut down severely. Imports would balance exports, but at the level of whichever was the lower. Everyone would be worse off.

Just how tragic to all countries bilateralism would be is indicated by Fig. 4, showing the advantageous international pattern of world multilateral trade.

INCREASING COSTS

Returning again to two countries and two commodities, we must proceed to drop the assumption that costs are constant. The Production-possibility curves of Figs. 1, 2, and 3 should really have been convexly bent, as they were in Chap. 2. It is no longer possible to specify a single cost figure for each country.

Even though America is better endowed on the whole for food production than Europe, still after a great amount of American food is produced, the cost of extra food will begin to exceed that of Europe. Even after American competition has drastically lowered the price of food relative to clothing, a little of the best land in Europe will be able to hold its own in food production. In the same way, that first little bit of American clothing production which can be produced at low costs will continue even after international trade has reached an equilibrium level. However, any attempt to expand American clothing production further would entail higher extra costs and competitive losses.

We may summarize the modifications in international trade made necessary by increasing costs as follows:

> *As a result of international trade, each country will tend to specialize, as before, in the commodity in which it has the greatest comparative advantage; and it will export some of that commodity in exchange for the other country's surplus exports. But because of increasing costs, specialization need not be complete: something of both commodities may still be produced in either country, because even the less favored commodity may have low enough costs to compete when its production is small.*[1]

---

[1] For the geometrically minded, Fig. 5 may be helpful, although most of us will probably do better to skip over it. It shows America's condition before and after trade when increasing costs prevail. The Production-possibility curve is now convex. Before international trade, America is consuming and producing at the starred point, H. The domestic price ratio is 10:3 just equal to the ratio of extra costs of getting (at H) a little more clothing for a little sacrificed food. This is shown by the slope of the AK curve at H.

After trade, when the common price ratio is 10:6, American production shifts to B,

INTERNATIONAL COMMODITY MOVEMENTS AS A PARTIAL SUBSTITUTE FOR LABOR
AND FACTOR MOVEMENTS

Having acknowledged the existence of the law of increasing costs described
in Chap. 2, we must also examine the implications of the law of diminishing
returns within the two countries.

After international trade takes place, resources in Europe flow from food to
clothing production. Because clothing requires relatively much labor and little
land, the pressure of population on the limited land of Europe is relieved. Land
is no longer so relatively dear; rents fall compared to wages. In America the
reverse happens after trade: concentration upon food production in which labor
is economized and land heavily utilized tends to raise rents relative to wages.

In every case the free international movement of goods has effects which are
partly like those following from the free international movement of factors of

---

toward less clothing but not away from clothing altogether. The new production point, B,
will be reached as a result of competition, because the slope of the curve there—*i.e.*, the
ratio of costs of extra clothing for extra food—is $10:6$, or just equal to the common international price ratio. At B, and only there, will the value of America's national product
(weighted by the $10:6$ price ratio) be at a maximum.

INTERNATIONAL TRADE
UNDER DIMINISHING RETURNS
OR INCREASING COSTS

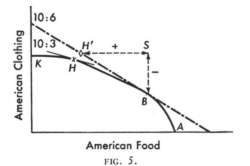

FIG. 5.

The straight line represents the new Consumption-possibility curve to which America
can get as a result of trade. It is straight and not bent because the auctioneer offers to trade
freely, giving America at the $10:6$ ratio as much or little clothing for food as she wishes.
The final levels of consumption, determined by supply and demand, are given by the point
H'. As before, the arrows indicate exports and imports.

There are still gains from trade. But because of diminishing returns and increasing
costs, there is not so much specialization as before and not quite such large gains. Note that
at the equilibrium point, where no further trade is possible, relative (extra or "marginal")
production costs in the two countries are equal, each to the common price ratio $10:6$.

production. Just as the movement of labor from Europe to America would relieve the scarcity of labor in America and of land in Europe, so the movement of clothing from Europe to America and of food from America to Europe tends to make the superabundant factor in each country less abundant, and the scarce factor less rare.

The person who has most clearly emphasized how commodity trade partially relieves the scarcity in all countries of the less abundant factors of production is the Swedish economist and public financier, Ohlin (pronounced O'Lean).[1] He has made the following important addition to the classical doctrine of comparative cost:

> Free movements of labor and capital between countries will tend to equalize wages and factor prices. *However, even without any movements of productive factors across national boundaries, there will result a partial (but not necessarily complete) equalization of factor prices from the free movement of goods in international trade.*

It is clear, therefore, that, although international trade increases national product in England, it may at the same time so reduce the share of particular groups that they are made worse off. Thus, the large British landowners who a century ago constituted the backbone of the Conservative or Tory party may have been selfish in opposing the famous repeal of the English corn law tariffs in 1846, but they were not necessarily unintelligent in making their unsuccessful last-ditch fight to retain protective tariffs on imported grains.

DECREASING COSTS AND INTERNATIONAL TRADE

If economies of mass production are overwhelmingly important, costs may decrease as output expands. This would only strengthen the case for international exchange of goods. In fact, decreasing costs are a second great factor—in addition to differences in comparative costs—which explains why specialization and trade are profitable. For, as was discussed in Chap. 3, large-scale specialization is most fruitful when there is a widely expanded market. In fact, even if there were no differences in comparative cost between two countries, it would pay for them to toss a coin to decide who was to produce each of two goods subject to increasing returns or decreasing costs. Complete specialization would increase world production of both goods.

This may be illustrated by our example in Chap. 3 of the two identical

[1] BERTIL OHLIN, "Interregional and International Trade," Harvard University Press, Cambridge, 1933.

Indian twins who, despite their similarity, still find it advantageous to specialize so that they may reap the efficiencies of mass production.

Moreover, there is one very practical aspect of international trade under decreasing cost. Peculiarly under such conditions is competition likely to break down and be succeeded by monopoly or monopolistic competition. By excluding foreign competition, protective tariffs only serve to consolidate the position of the monopolist. This is recognized in the old slogan: "The tariff is the mother of trusts." Freer international trade is often an effective, and an efficient, way of breaking up such monopoly positions.

DIFFERENCES IN TASTES OR DEMAND AS A REASON FOR TRADE

Two reasons have been given thus far for international trade: (1) differences in comparative costs between regions and (2) decreasing costs. For completeness, a third obvious possible cause for trade may be mentioned. Even if costs were identical in the two countries and increasing, trade might take place as the result of differences in *taste*.

Thus, it might pay both Norway and Sweden to produce fish and meat in about the same amounts. If the Swedes have a relatively great fondness for fish and the Norse for meat, then a mutually profitable export of fish from Norway and meat from Sweden would take place.

Both parties gain from this trade. The sum total of human happiness is increased, just as it is when Jack Spratt trades fat meat for his wife's lean. Both get some "consumer's surplus" from the swap.[1]

TRANSPORTATION COSTS

Up to this point, we have neglected the whole problem of transportation costs. The economic costs of moving bulky and perishable goods lessens the extent of profitable regional specialization. The effects are like those produced by the passage of artificially restrictive tariff legislation. As is discussed in the next chapter, many of these effects are harmful to national economic welfare. In the case of transportation costs, the evil is unavoidable, whereas protective tariffs or artificial barriers to interregional trade within a nation are squarely the responsibility of man.

---

[1] Even two individuals with identical amounts of two goods and the same tastes may in rare instances trade. Two sailors, each with a fifth of rye and a fifth of gin, might toss a coin to decide which is to have 2 fifths of gin and which 2 fifths of rye. The reader should reason out why the same might be true of herring and chocolate, but not of corned beef and cabbage. This fourth cause of trade is primarily only a curio.

Chapter 24: THE ECONOMICS

OF TARIFF PROTECTION

AND FREE TRADE

IT would be absurd to try to decide whether God exists or not by counting on one hand all the arguments in the affirmative, and on the other hand all the arguments in the negative—and then to award the decision to the side with the greater number of points. It would be no less absurd to evaluate the case for tariff protection by a simple numerical counting of unequally important pros and cons.

Indeed, there is essentially only one argument for free or freer trade, but it is an exceedingly powerful one: namely, the fact that *unhampered trade promotes a mutually profitable international division of labor, greatly enhances the potential real national product of all countries, and makes possible higher standards of living all over the globe.* This was elaborated upon in the previous chapter.

The arguments for high protection against the competition of foreign imports take many different forms. They may be divided into three categories: (1) Those which are definitely economically false, some so obviously and palpably so as hardly to merit serious discussion, but some whose falsity can be detected only by subtle economic reasoning. (2) A few arguments for protection which are without validity in a "classical" static full-employment world but which contain some kernels of truth in a world of underemployment and economic development. (3) Finally, certain noneconomic arguments which may make it desirable national policy to sacrifice economic welfare in order to subsidize certain activities admittedly not economically efficient.

559

NONECONOMIC GOALS

Let us begin with the latter for they are most simply disposed of. If you ever are on a debating team and are given the assignment to defend free trade, you will strengthen your case at the beginning by conceding that economic welfare is not the only goal of life. Political considerations are also important. Thus, it may be necessary to become partially self-sufficient in certain lines of activity at great cost because of fear of future wars.

An example is the production of synthetic rubber. Even if the original plant costs are charged off as a military expense of World War II, it is doubtful whether we can as yet produce rubber from petroleum or grain alcohol at less than, say, 15 cents a pound. For the first years after the war, world demand for rubber is so great as to keep its price above the variable unit cost of synthetic production, so that both it and natural rubber will continue to be produced. But if the price should finally fall, what then? During the Great Depression, the price of rubber fell to about 2 or 3 cents a pound in the East Indies, and still supplies were forthcoming. Apparently it is not yet possible for synthetic rubber to beat out natural rubber on a price basis, although the synthetic product will always continue to be used for some special purposes even at a higher price because of its peculiar physical properties.

If, therefore, synthetic rubber capacity is considered necessary for national defense and if the needed amount of capacity is not able to survive under free trade, the economist cannot assert that national policy should be against protection to this industry. But he can insist that a *subsidy* to domestic production would be preferable to a tariff, because this would bring the domestic price down to the international price instead of raising price to the consumer up to the domestic cost. Also the subsidy would show clearly what the total costs of national defense are and would better enable the public to decide whether the game is worth the candle.[1]

The question of a national policy to foster the American mercantile marine is a similar one. Without a doubt the United States does not possess a comparative advantage in building or operating a merchant fleet. As soon as American seamen, through trade-unions or on their own, insist upon living conditions and wages remotely resembling those in Detroit factories, then we cannot compete with English, Dutch, Japanese, and Norwegian ships. If we give no weight to America's "glorious seafaring tradition"—a long way

[1] Also, the economist might question whether a revolving stock pile of rubber would not be cheaper and more effective, and whether relatively small government subsidies to fundamental scientific research and test-pilot plant operation would not be much more effective in terms of long-run national defense than simply keeping inefficient plants in operation.

back!—and consider purely economic welfare, the correct policy is obvious. If America has a comparative advantage in factory production, let men go to Detroit factories where their real productivity is high. American international trade will not suffer by being carried in other countries' bottoms.

However, if national defense makes a large merchant marine necessary, that is another matter. Mail subsidies and complete writing off of the costs of ships built during World War II may then be justified. Still, there is reason to believe that a fraction of such outlays spent in scientifically preserving Liberty ships over the years might be equally effective. And so far as manpower in time of war is concerned, there seems to be no valid reason why merchant seamen should not be recruited and trained by the armed services, just as other sailors and soldiers are.

The problem of deciding how much to spend in peacetime on national defence is always a perplexing question, especially since armament races are both *cause* and effect of international disunity. The economist can claim no special competence to advise on this problem. He can point out that selfish economic interests often wrap themselves in the flag and try to justify uneconomic projects in terms of national defense. With less confidence, the economist can point out that mutually profitable international trade may help to promote international understanding and unity and that political interferences with trade have in the past provided some of the frictions that made war inevitable.

In conclusion, it is well to point out other noneconomic goals that may deserve consideration. Society may feel that there is some special sanctity about farm life, or something worth preserving in the way of life of the "stout agricultural yeoman or happy peasant." (It is to be doubted that most people who rhapsodize in this fashion have ever lived on a farm.) Or some groups may agree with the Soviet Union and the church that rural living is worth fostering because the country has a higher birth rate than the cities. Or the day may arise when decentralization of population will be necessary because of the threat to our concentrated eastern seaboard cities of self-guided atomic bombs. In all such cases subsidies rather than tariffs seem called for. A tariff is simply one rather indirect clumsy form of subsidy which draws attention away from the evil in need of a remedy.

GROSSLY FALLACIOUS ARGUMENTS FOR TARIFF

Keeping Money in the Country. To Abraham Lincoln is sometimes attributed the remark, "I don't know much about the tariff. But I do know that when I buy a coat from England, I have the coat and England has the money.

But when I buy a coat in this country, I have the coat and America has the money."

There is no evidence that he actually ever said this. But it does represent an age-old fallacy typical of the so-called "mercantilistic" writers of the seventeenth and eighteenth centuries who preceded Adam Smith. They considered a country lucky which gave away more goods than it received, because such a "favorable" (!) balance of trade meant that gold would flow into the country in question to pay for its surplus of exports over imports.

In this day and age it should be unnecessary to labor the point that, while an increased amount of money in the hands of one person will make *him* better off, doubling the money in the hands of everybody in a full-employment economy will only serve to raise prices. Unless the single individual is a demented miser like King Midas, the money makes him better off, not for its own sake but for what it will buy or bid away from other individuals. However, for society as a whole, once full employment is reached, new money cannot hope to buy any new goods.[1]

A Tariff for Higher Money Wages.   Today it is agreed that extreme protection can raise prices and attract gold into one country, if all other countries do not retaliate with tariffs. The tariff may even increase *money* wages. But it will tend to increase the cost of living by more than the increase in money wages, so that *real* wages will fall as labor becomes less productive.

One could go on endlessly giving examples of protectionist fallacies which every thoughtful person can explode in a minute by subjecting them to analysis. This does not mean that such crude fallacies can be dismissed as unimportant. Actually, they are most important of all in shaping legislation, the other fancier arguments simply being used as window dressing.

Tariffs for Special-interest Groups.   The single most important motivation for protective tariff is obvious to anyone who has watched the "logrolling" that goes on in Congress when such legislation is on the floor. It is the well-known "give-me." Powerful pressure groups and vested interests know very well that a tariff on their products will help them whatever its effect on total production and consumption. Outright bribery was used in the old days to get the necessary votes; today powerful lobbies are maintained in Washington to drum up enthusiasm for the good old crockery, watch, or buttonhook industry.

---

[1] Of course, the gold might be spent abroad. But this perfectly sensible way of improving welfare by importing was precisely what the mercantilist "bullionists" were arguing against.

SOME LESS OBVIOUS FALLACIES

A Tariff for Revenue.   First, there is the claim that the tariff should be used to raise government tax revenue. Actually, a customs duty on imports is only one form of sales tax, and a peculiarly obnoxious one. The sales tax, itself, is usually regarded as one of the least desirable forms of taxes because of its inequitable and "regressive" burden upon the poor. A custom duty or tariff is especially bad because in addition to its regressive impact, it distorts economic resources away from their best uses. If the people who advance the revenue argument were really sincere, they would advocate a sales tax which would also fall on domestic production. But this would provide no protection at all.

To clinch the point, only remember that a really prohibitively high tariff, which perfectly "protected" us from imports, would collect no revenue at all! Back in 1890, the so-called "billion-dollar Congress" found itself with a surplus of tax revenue over expenditure. Since there was no debt to retire, Congress found the situation embarrassing. It finally solved the problem of excessive tariff revenues not by lowering tariff rates but by raising them so high as to reduce the total of revenue collected.

Tariffs and the Home Market.   A second argument, which by itself is on the whole false but whose fallacy is rather difficult to spot, goes as follows: "Farmers should support a tariff for industry because that will gain them a large home market for their products." Henry Clay, the perennial candidate who turned out to be neither "right" nor "President," often advanced this argument a century or more ago.

Its falsity can be seen from different points of view. First, by cutting down industrial imports we are really at the same time indirectly tending to cut down our farm exports. Thus the farmer is hurt directly. "But," Clay might remonstrate, "what about the extra home market for farm produce?"

Well, what about it? Our detailed example of comparative cost showed that isolation from international trade decreases the total of national product or real income. The total domestic demand for farm products will certainly be less at a low level of real income than at a high level. So unless it can be buttressed by one of the quite different arguments for protection to be discussed later, the slogan about "creating a home market" is seen once again to be fallacious.

Competition from Cheap Foreign Labor.   A third argument for protection has been the most popular of all in American history because it appealed to the large number of labor votes. According to its usual version, "If we let in goods produced by cheap pauper foreign labor—by Chinese coolies who live on a few cents' worth of rice per day or by low-paid Czechoslovakian shoe workers

—then the higher standard of living of American workers cannot be maintained." So stated, the argument cannot stand up under analysis.

We have seen that trade is mutually profitable even if one country can produce every good more cheaply in terms of resources than the other. The important thing is comparative advantage, not absolute advantage. In the last analysis, trade boils down to two-sided barter. One country cannot indefinitely undersell the other in every line of merchandise.

Earlier we have shown that full employment at home does not, or at least should not, depend in the long run on foreign trade. If then everyone in this country remains fully employed at his most suitable occupation, is it not to *our selfish advantage* for the workers of other countries to be willing to work for very little? Or to put the matter another way, the comparative-cost doctrine shows that we benefit most by trading with countries like China or the tropics which are very different from ourselves, rather than with countries like England or Germany which are like our own industrial economy.[1] As a further criticism of the pauper-labor argument, there is the remarkable fact that the analysis of comparative advantage, summarized in Table 3 of Chap. 23, did not concern itself at all with the wage rates in either country. They had nothing to do with the increase in national income that resulted from trade.

So much from a theoretical point of view. If we turn to the real world, we find the argument to be even more incorrect. In Europe and in China the workers beg for tariffs saying, "Protect us from the 'unfair competition' of high paid, efficient American workers who have skill and machinery far better than our own." The rest of the world lives in mortal fear of competition from American mass-production industries. The English protectionist claims that the American worker in Bridgeport, Conn. who is paid $1.50 per hour is more than three times as efficient as the English worker who gets paid 60 cents an hour. This is perhaps an overstatement but it is near to the important truth: high American real wages come from high efficiency and do not handicap us in competing with foreign workers.

Thus far we have had nothing but adverse criticism for the "cheap pauper foreign labor" tariff argument. To be perfectly honest, and without honesty there can be no science, we must admit that it may have an iota of possible truth in it. The Ohlin proposition of the Appendix to Chap. 23 suggested that

[1] This argument must be qualified and amplified. Backward countries, so poor that they have little real purchasing power with which to import, at best can export little to us. Most trade today is between industrialized countries. As a backward country advances industrially, it buys more from industrial countries, and not less; but perhaps not proportionally more, and perhaps there is less surplus per dollar of trade accruing to both parties.

free trade in goods may serve as a partial substitute for immigration of labor into the United States. This implies that labor scarcity in the United States could be alleviated by our international specialization on labor-economizing products and that real wages might actually fall under free trade. Real national product would go up, but the relative and absolute share of labor might go down.[1]

Although admitting this as a slight theoretical possibility, most economists are still inclined to think that its grain of truth is outweighed by other more realistic considerations. Of course, particular laborers such as Waltham watchmakers might be hurt by removing a tariff. Nobody denies that. But since labor is such an important and flexible factor of production with many alternative uses, it seems likely that other laborers would gain more than they lose and that labor as a whole would share in the increased national product resulting from trade.[2]

A Tariff for Retaliation.   Some people admit that a world of free trade would be preferable to a world of tariffs. But they say that so long as other countries are so foolish or so wicked as to pass restrictive tariff legislation, there is nothing that we can do but follow suit in self-defense. Actually, however, a tariff is like an increase in transportation costs. If other countries were foolish enough to let their roads go to ruin, would it pay us to chop holes in ours? The answer is "no." Similarly, if other countries hurt us and themselves by passing tariffs, we should not add to our own hurt by passing a tariff.

To make sure that he grasps the point that our tariff harms us as well as the foreigner, the student should realize that there are four gains when the Hull trade-agreements program succeeds in getting another country and ourselves to lower tariffs reciprocally. The other country's tariff reduction bestows gains (1) on us and (2) on them. Our tariff reduction adds two more gains, (3) upon ourselves and (4) upon them.

The only possible sense in the argument, therefore, that we should retaliate when a foreign country raises tariffs, is that our threat of retaliation may deter

---

[1] The advanced student may be referred to the paper by W. Stolper and P. A. Samuelson, Protection and Real Wages, *Review of Economic Studies*, Vol. 9, November, 1941, pp. 58–74.

[2] It would be inappropriate to discuss in an elementary textbook the theoretically valid argument that by *limited* protection a country may turn the "terms of trade" in her own favor, and so to speak "make the foreigner pay the duty." The reader is referred to G. Haberler, "Theory of International Trade," p. 290, Hodge and Company, London, 1936, for a discussion of this theoretical possibility. Even if we grant it practical importance, we must consider it a beggar-my-neighbor policy which will invite retaliation and which cannot be simultaneously *adopted by everybody with profit.*

them from raising tariffs; and our promise to reduce tariffs may persuade them to reduce theirs. This would justify our passing an occasional tariff as a bluff; but whenever our bluffs do not seem to cause foreigners to reduce their tariffs, we should give them up.

Most realistic students of political science believe from their studies of history that retaliatory tariffs usually cause other countries to raise theirs still higher, and rarely provide an effective bargaining weapon for multilateral tariff reduction.

The "Scientific" Tariff. This is one of the most vicious arguments for a tariff; vicious because it often sounds plausible and moderate, but if taken literally, it would mean the end to all trade. According to the usual form of this argument, tariffs should be passed to "equalize the cost of production at home and abroad." We saw in the preceding chapter that all of the advantage from trade rests upon *differences* in cost or advantage. If tariffs were passed raising the costs of imports to that of the highest American producer, no goods could come in at all.[1]

There is nothing scientific about such a tariff. It is a grave reflection on the economic literacy of the American people that this least desirable of all protectionist arguments has had tremendous political importance in our history, and has even been written into law upon occasion.

ARGUMENTS FOR PROTECTION UNDER DYNAMIC CONDITIONS

At last we are arriving at a point in the protection versus free trade debate where those in favor of tariffs can begin to score some weighty points. Two important arguments fall in this category: (1) that a tariff may help to reduce unemployment and (2) that temporary tariff protection for an "infant industry" with growth potentialities may be desirable.

Tariffs and Unemployment. The first of these arguments need not be discussed in this chapter, because we are here assessing the effects of international trade on a country's potential or full-employment income. This does not mean that the "tariff to aid unemployment" argument is unimportant. Actually the main theme of this book is the problem of full employment. We can no more neglect the influence of international trade on total purchasing power or effective demand than we can ignore the possibility of "technological unemployment." For international trade, like scientific discovery, can conceivably

---

[1] With nonconstant cost the scientific tariff formula is indeterminate. No tariff at all may equalize foreign costs and those of a very few of Americas's most efficient producers. Where should the line be drawn?

increase a nation's *potential* level of total product and at the same time tend to lower the *actual* level of production, consumption, and employment attained. Such a gap between actual and potential production would represent the frittering away of our gains in the form of unemployment and overcapacity. We cannot shirk the task of devising policy measures aimed at closing the gap between actual production and attainable full-employment production.

But beggar-my-neighbor international policies are not the proper methods. In Chap. 16, the favorable multiplier effects of exports on jobs and the unfavorable "leakage" effects of imports were discussed. However, the shortsighted character of such beggar-my-neighbor tactics, which invite retaliation and leave everyone worse off, was also stressed.

Tariffs for "Infant Industries." There is, however, no better time than the present to discuss the "infant-industry" argument for protection. Alexander Hamilton in his famous "Report on Manufactures" stated it very clearly; it is also associated with the name of a nineteenth-century German economist, Friedrich List; and it has received the cautious blessing of John Stuart Mill, Alfred Marshall, Frank W. Taussig, and other orthodox economists.

According to this doctrine, there are many lines of activity in which a country would really have a comparative advantage, *if only it could get them started.* If confronted with foreign competition, such infantile industries are not able to weather the initial period of experimentation and financial stress. But given a breathing space, they can be expected to develop economies of mass production and the technological efficiency typical of many modern processes. Although protection will at first raise prices to the consumer, once the industry grows up, it will be so efficient that costs and prices will actually have fallen.

There is certainly something to this, at least as a theoretical possibility. The late Prof. F. W. Taussig in a careful historical study[1] came to the tentative conclusion that the American silk-manufacturing industry represented a successful case of the infant-industry argument. That is, silk manufacturing finally developed a comparative advantage; it finally grew up so that it could stand on its own feet even were the tariff to be removed. But the same could not be said about the woolen worsted industry. This industry came into being because of tariff protection; but seemingly it never did reach the point where it could utilize our so-called "Yankee mechanical ingenuity" as effectively as other industries. It represented, therefore, a baby that never grew up.

Unfortunately for the practical importance of this argument, even promising

[1] F. W. Taussig, "Some Aspects of the Tariff Question," rev. ed., Harvard University Press, Cambridge, 1931.

baby industries cannot swing many votes. It is not they who tend to receive protection from Congress but rather the old and powerful vested interests who have never shed their diapers for, lo, these many years.[1]

The "Young-economy" Argument.   Probably, the infant-industry argument had more validity for America a century ago than it does today, and has more validity for present-day backward nations than for those which have already experienced the transition from an agricultural to an industrial way of life. In a sense such nations are still asleep; they cannot be said to be truly in equilibrium. All over the world, farmers seem to earn less than industrial workers. Consequently, there is everywhere a relative growth of industry and a decline of agriculture. Populations migrate cityward, but this movement is not rapid enough to achieve an equilibrium of earnings and productivity. A strong case can be made for using moderate protection to accelerate these economically desirable long-run trends. Such a defense of protection might more appropriately be called a "young-economy" argument rather than an infant-industry one.

One final word. Please note that the infant-industry or young-economy arguments are not contradictory to the principle of comparative advantage. On the contrary, their validity rests upon the presumption of an induced, dynamical shift of the Production-possibility curve outward and in the direction of a new comparative advantage in the lines requiring temporary protection.

This completes our discussion of the tariff controversy except for its implications with respect to unemployment which were already discussed in Part Two. No fair-minded reader who takes the trouble to think the matter through can fail to see how shallow are most of the economic arguments for tariff protection. The only serious exception is the infant-industry or young-economy argument. It is not surprising therefore that economists—who are supposed to agree on almost nothing—were unanimously opposed to the extreme tariff rates in the Smoot-Hawley Tariff of the early thirties and have been overwhelmingly in favor of the Hull Reciprocal Trade Agreements and the postwar ITO (International Trade Organization) aimed at lowering trade barriers.

---

[1] Perhaps an exception to this rather cynical view is provided by certain war industries such as chemicals and optics which got a start when World War I cut off German competition. After the war these "war babies" demanded and received protection even though American scientific progress in these fundamental fields was clearly inferior to that of Germany. However, now that Germany has driven out her best scientists, it is likely that we enjoy a comparative advantage in these fields. Even if we didn't, military security might make subsidies to them necessary.

SUMMARY

1. The case for freer trade rests upon the increased productivity which international specialization according to the law of comparative advantage makes possible. Higher world production is made possible, and all countries can have higher standards of living. Trade between countries with different standards of living is likely to be especially mutually profitable.

2. Most of the arguments for tariff protection are simply rationalizations for special benefits to particular pressure groups and will not stand up under analysis.

3. An important exception is provided by the need to favor certain uneconomical lines of activity for reasons of national defense. Perhaps an outright government subsidy would be preferable in such cases.

4. The only other exception of any practical importance, aside from the argument for a tariff to relieve unemployment, is provided by the case of infant industries or young economies which need some temporary protection in order to realize their true long-run comparative advantages.

QUESTIONS FOR DISCUSSION

1. What do you think is the single most favorable argument for a tariff?

2. Make a list of fallacious tariff arguments. How would you outline the various arguments for and against tariffs?

3. Briefly describe the tariff history of the United States.

4. "Import quotas are much like tariffs." Discuss.

5. Comment critically on the infant-industry and young-economy arguments. What is their relation to comparative advantage?

6. Mention some noneconomic considerations relevant to tariffs.

Chapter 25: THE DYNAMICS

OF SPECULATION AND RISK

IN a well-organized competitive market, there tends to be at any one time and place a single prevailing price. This is because of the action of professional speculators or *arbitragers* who keep their ear to the market and, as soon as they learn of any price differences, buy at the cheaper price and sell at the dearer price, thereby making a profit for themselves—at the same time tending to equalize the price.[1]

Two markets at a considerable distance from each other may tend to have different prices. Wheat in Chicago may sell for a few cents more per hundred than in Kansas City, because of the shipping, insurance, and interest charges involved in transportation. But if ever the price in Chicago should rise by more than the few cents of shipping costs, speculators will buy in Kansas City and ship to Chicago, thereby bringing the price up in Kansas City and down in Chicago to the normal differential charge.[2]

SPECULATION AND PRICE BEHAVIOR OVER TIME

In an ideal competitive market there tends to be a definite pattern of prices *over time* just as there is over space. But the difficulties of predicting the future make this pattern a less perfect one, so that we have an equilibrium that is constantly being disturbed but is always in the process of reforming itself—not unlike the surface of the ocean.

Let us consider the simplest case of a grain that is harvested at one period of

[1] On the floor of the Chicago Board of Trade, the important market for grain, some half a hundred important "pit scalpers," or dealers, are said to make all their profits on price changes within each day, closing out all their transactions every night and sleeping peacefully until the next day.

[2] Wheat in Chicago can fall down to the Kansas City price, but then no grain will be flowing between the two cities. Commodities always follow a "reverse law of gravity"—they always flow *up* a rising price hill, whose gradient depends on transport cost.

the year. This crop must be made to last all the year if privation is to be avoided. Since no one passes a law regulating the storage of grain, how is this desirable state of affairs brought about? The answer is through the attempts of speculators to make a profit. A well-informed speculator who is a specialist in this grain realizes that, if all of the grain is thrown on the market in the autumn, it will fetch a very low price because of the glutting of the market. On the other hand, some months later with almost no grain coming on the market, the price will tend to skyrocket upward.

This is what would tend to happen were it not for the action of speculators. They realize that by (1) purchasing some of the autumn crop while it is cheap, (2) withholding it in storage, and (3) selling it later when the price has risen, they can make a profit. This they do. But in doing so, they increase the autumn demand for grain and raise its autumn price; and they increase the spring supply of grain and lower its price at that time. At the same time that they are equalizing the price over the year, they are equalizing the supply coming on the market in each month—which is as it should be. Moreover, if there is brisk competition among speculators,

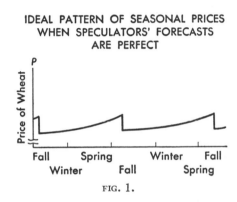

IDEAL PATTERN OF SEASONAL PRICES
WHEN SPECULATORS' FORECASTS
ARE PERFECT

FIG. 1.

none will make an excessive profit over the costs that he incurs (including of course the wages necessary to keep him in this line of activity). Actually the speculator himself may never touch a grain of wheat or a bale of cotton, nor need he know anything about storage, warehouses, or delivery. He merely buys and sells bits of paper, but the effect is exactly as described above.

Now there is one and only one monthly price pattern which will result in neither profits nor losses. A little thought will show that it will not be a pattern of constant prices, but rather one with lowest prices in the autumn and then gradually rising prices until the peak is reached just before the new wheat comes in. The price must rise from month to month to compensate for the storage and interest costs of carrying the crop in storage, in exactly the same way that the price must rise over space from one mile to the next to compensate for the cost of transportation. Figure 1 shows the behavior of prices over an ideal yearly cycle. The increase in price from month to month is not constant, because of the accelerated growth of compound interest on the money tied up in the stored crop.

Not all fluctuations in activity can be so accurately forecast as the seasonal harvesting of a crop. No one can predict with confidence next year's weather or whether a depression will develop in the near future. But to the extent that speculators can form any accurate guesses today about the future *scarcity* of a commodity, they will tend to buy it now for *future* delivery, thereby causing (1) a withdrawal of present supply, (2) an increase of present price, (3) an increase in amount stored, (4) an increase in future supply, (5) a reduction in future price, or in all a relative stabilization of price and consumption over time. The student should trace through the opposite process by which speculators stabilize prices when they correctly foresee an exceptionally large future crop and a low future price: how they then begin to "sell short"[1] for future delivery, tending to depress current prices, increase present consumption, decrease carry-over of stocks, and so forth.

Aside from their possible influence toward stabilizing prices, speculators have another important function. By being willing to take risks on their own shoulders, they enable others to avoid risk. For example, a miller must carry large inventories of grain in the course of his business. If the price of grain goes up, he makes a windfall capital gain; if down, he makes a windfall loss. But let us suppose that he is content to earn his living by milling flour and wishes to forego all risk taking. This he can do by a process called "hedging." This complicated procedure is rather like a man who bets on Army to win the Army-Navy game, and then washes out this transaction, or covers it, by placing an equal bet on the Navy. Whichever side wins, he comes out the same, his left hand winning what his right hand loses.[2]

---

[1] There is really nothing mysterious about selling short. I simply put in an order to my broker in which I agree, in return for a certain price *now*, to deliver *at some later date* (usually but not always exactly specified) an amount of grain. Usually at the time of putting in the order, I do not have on hand the grain. But I legally fulfill my contract by later "covering"; *i.e.*, buying the grain and making delivery. If I later have to pay a higher price in covering than I now receive when selling short, then I make a loss. But if I have guessed right and prices do fall in the intervening period, then I "buy in" for less than I have received and make a profit. Selling short in the stock market works out similarly, except that I am free to cover and make future delivery of the stock at any time I please. In the meantime, the man who has bought the stock receives his stock shares. How? As a result of the fact that my broker, obligingly, lends me the stock certificates to make delivery. Later when I cover, I buy in the stock and turn over the certificates to my obliging broker.

[2] Likewise the miller, in quoting his present price for flour, will do so only after having bought a "future contract" for delivery of wheat to replace his used-up inventory of grain. If the price of wheat should go up a month from now, then the miller will have made a loss by selling his flour too cheap. But the gain he makes on his future purchase just cancels out his loss, and so he is "hedged" against risk.

To the extent that speculators forecast accurately, they provide a definite social service. To the extent that they forecast badly, they tend to aggravate the variability of prices. Were it not for the detailed statistical information provided by the Department of Agriculture and private agencies, the 150-odd main traders of the Chicago Board of Trade would find themselves at the mercy of every idle rumor, hope, and fear. For speculation is essentially a mass contagion, like the inexplicable dancing crazes that swept medieval villages, the Dutch tulip mania that sent the price of a single bulb higher than that of a house, the South Sea Bubble in which companies sold stock at fabulous prices for enterprises which would "later be revealed."

THE GREAT STOCK-MARKET CRASH

This was illustrated more recently in the United States during the fabulous stock market boom of the "roaring twenties." Housewives, Pullman porters, college students between classes—all bought and sold (but mostly bought!) common and preferred stocks. Most purchases in this wild "bull" market were "on margin"; *i.e.*, the buyer of $10,000 worth of stocks had to put up only $2,500 or less in cash, borrowing the difference by pledging his newly bought stocks. What matter that he had to pay his broker 5, 6, or 7 per cent per year on his borrowings when in one day Auburn Motors or Bethlehem Steel might jump 10 per cent in value!

The most wonderful thing about a bull market is that it creates its own hopes. If people buy because they think stocks will rise, their act of buying sends up the price of stocks. This causes them to buy still further, and sends the dizzy dance off on another round. And unlike a game of cards or dice, no one loses what the winners gain. Everybody gets a prize! Of course, the prizes are all on paper and would disappear if everyone tried to cash them in. But why should anyone wish to sell such lucrative securities?

When the whole world is mad, 'tis folly to be sane. Suppose one were so wise or so naïve as to believe that the public-utilities holding companies were paper pyramids on cardboard foundations; or that Florida dream real-estate developments were midway between pine thicket and swamp; or that private foreign loans to South America and Europe were being frittered away in roads to nowhere or on public swimming pools? What could such a social misfit do? He would soon learn the first rule of property values: "A thing is worth what people *think* it is worth." Unfortunately, to be successful this has to be applied in connection with the second rule, which is as hard to follow in practice as belling the cat or catching birds by putting salt on their tails: "Don't be the sucker left holding the bag."

When the black October crash of 1929 came, everyone was caught, the big-league professionals and the piddling amateurs—Andrew Mellon, John D. Rockefeller, the engineer in the White House, and the economics professor from Yale. The bottom fell out of the market. Brokers had to sell out the "margin" accounts of investors who could no longer pony up extra funds to cover the depleted value of their collateral,[1] sending the market down still further. Even those who did not buy on margin lost one-third of their capital by the end of the year, and five-sixths by 1932.

The bull market was over and the bear market had taken its place. And, as the former had lived on its dreams, so the latter was consumed by its own nightmares. Billions of dollars of security values were wiped out every month, taking with them not only the capital of gamblers out for speculative gains, but also the widow's mite supposedly invested for steady income. A "blue chip" stock like United States Steel fell from a 1929 high of 261 to a 1932 low of 21 while less respectable securities dropped off the Board completely. Even though President Hoover and his administration were friendly toward business, in vain did they try to restore confidence by predicting that "prosperity is just around the corner" and "stocks are excellent buys at their present levels."

Finally, after the great banking crisis of 1933 and the NRA, the stock market began to follow general business recovery. Figure 2 shows the movements of stock market values over the whole period. Although stocks were bullish in 1936–1937 and again during World War II, they have never at any time returned to anything like the peak levels of 1929.

To the age-old question, does the market follow business activity or business activity the market, no simple answer can be given. It is reasonably clear that business activity, national income, and corporate earnings determine stock prices and not vice versa; and also that the psychological effects of market movements no longer have primary importance, but are in the nature of a grim national side show. But still the market can occasionally *anticipate* changes in national income and total purchasing power. It then appears to be leading them when really it is following what it thinks they will be later.

There are no simply stated foolproof rules for making money out of the stock market. Anyone who can accurately predict the future course of business activity will prosper, but there is no such person. At least four main classes of investors and speculators can be distinguished:

[1] Frederick Lewis Allen's amusing and interesting chronicle of the 1920's, "Only Yesterday," gives a detailed account of the role of the stock-market boom in American life. This is now a 25-cent Bantam reprint.

1. The group who simply buy and hold. If the national economy has a long-time upward trend, they fare reasonably well over the long run. They might do even better if they would follow the statistical advice of investment services as to how to switch to companies of more favorable growth prospects.

The effect of this group is neither to stabilize nor destabilize prices; except, to the extent that they freeze shares off the market and limit the number of

COMPOSITE AVERAGE 100 STOCKS

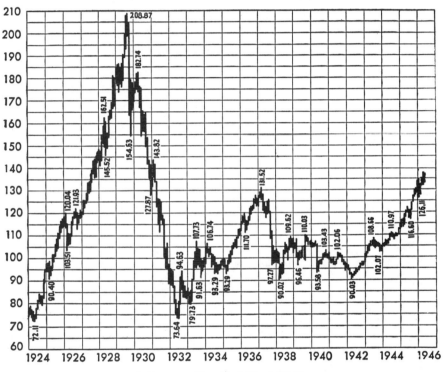

FIG. 2. SOURCE: *New York Herald Tribune*.

tradings, they tend to make the market more "thin." In a thin market there are so few transactions that the attempt to buy a few hundred shares may send its price up a few points because of the absence of ready sellers around the ruling market price. An attempt to sell may depress the price a few points.

2. At the other extreme are the hour-to-hour, day-to-day ticker watchers, to be seen in every brokerage office. Generally speaking, they buy and sell, sell and buy. By and large, they make money only for their brokers.

This group has the effect of making the market less thin. Because of them, any investor can expect to be able to liquidate his market holdings at any time at some price, although not at a price predictable in advance nor necessarily at the price that he would like. Still even this restricted "liquidity" enhances the attractiveness of securities traded on organized exchanges over and above the unlisted issues of smaller companies bought and sold by brokers over the counter.

3. In between are those speculators who play intermediate swings of many months or years. The least successful of these are the amateurs whose entrance into the market at the top when it is too late is the signal for the "smart money" to leave. The most successful speculators are those who are able to avoid the extremes of enthusiasm of the mob and to discern underlying business conditions. This does not mean that they simply buy because a stock looks low and sell when it looks high. On the contrary, they buy when stocks look as if they will continue to rise. When a drop seems imminent, they sell short or, more conservatively, they simply go into cash or high-grade bonds. It takes cool nerves to sell short because on the whole the market is overoptimistic. But if a single individual does it cleverly, he will achieve success in avoiding the losses of a bear market—which by the way is the only time that widespread losses are incurred; more than that, he converts such losses into actual gains.

The behavior of this group of speculators is often destabilizing to prices. They "pile on" to a price rise and send it farther; they similarly *accentuate* any decline.

4. Finally, there are individuals who study special situations. From public or inside sources, they learn in advance of changes in the fortunes of particular companies: of rumored bankruptcies, of special stock dividends, split-ups, or mergers, of likely earnings and dividend announcements, etc. When combined with the successful characteristics of the third group, members of this group, such as the elder statesman of two wars, Bernard Baruch, make the largest profit from the market. During World War II it was not unheard of for a few alert operators to run $1,000 up to $1,000,000 at the same time keeping profits in the form of less heavily taxed capital gains.

But the investor must take to heart Baruch's caution:

If you are ready to give up everything else—to study the whole history and background of the market and all the principal companies whose stocks are on the board as carefully as a medical student studies anatomy—if you can do all that, and, in addition, you have the cool nerves of a great gambler, the sixth sense of a kind of clairvoyant, and the courage of a lion, you have a ghost of a chance.

GAMBLING AND DIMINISHING UTILITY

The defenders of speculation resent the charge that it represents simply another form of gambling, like betting on the horse races or buying a lottery ticket. They emphasize that an uncertain world necessarily involves risk and that someone must bear risks. They claim that the knowledge and the venturesomeness of the speculator are chained to a socially useful purpose, thereby reducing fluctuations and risks to others. We have seen that this is not always the case and that speculation may be destabilizing; but certainly no one can deny all validity to the above claims.

Why is gambling considered such a bad thing? Part of the reason, perhaps the most important part, lies in the field of morals, ethics, and religion; upon these the economist is not qualified to pass exact judgment. There is, however, a substantial economic case to be made against gambling.

First, it involves simply *sterile transfers of money* between individuals, creating no new value.[1] While creating no value, gambling does nevertheless absorb time and resources. When pursued beyond the limits of recreation, where the main purpose after all is to "kill" time, gambling subtracts from the national income.

The second economic disadvantage of gambling is the fact that it tends to promote *inequality* and *instability of incomes*. People who sit down to the gaming table with the same amount of money go away with widely different amounts. A gambler (and his family) must expect to be on the top of the world one day, and when luck changes—which is the only predictable thing about it —he may almost starve.

But why is inequality of income over time and between persons considered such a bad thing? One answer is to be found in the widely held belief that the gain in well-being achieved by an *extra* $1,000 of income is not so great as the loss in well-being of foregoing $1,000 of income. Therefore, a bet at fair odds involves an economic loss: the money you stand to win balances the money you may lose, but the satisfaction you stand to win is less than the satisfaction you stand to lose.

Similarly, if it can be assumed that individuals are all "roughly the same" and are ethically comparable, then the dollars gained by the rich do not create

---

[1] Actually in all professional gambling arrangements, the participants lose out on balance. The leakage comes from the fact that the odds are always rigged in favor of the "house" so that even an "honest" house will win in the long run. Moderate gambling among friends may be considered as a form of consumption or recreation activity whose cost to the group as a whole is zero.

so much welfare as the dollars lost by the poor. This has been used not only as a criticism of gambling, but as a positive argument in favor of "progressive" taxation aimed at lowering the inequality of the distribution of income.

Just as the law of diminishing returns was seen to underlie the Malthusian theory of population, so is the "law of diminishing (marginal or extra) utility" used by many economists to condemn professional gambling. According to this law, as money income increases, each new dollar adds something to well-being, but less and less. In the same way, each extra unit of any good that can be bought with money contributes less and less satisfaction or utility. When we get as much of a food as we wish (*e.g.*, water), it becomes a "free good" because still further units add nothing new to our utility.

As an example of this law, consider the utility or satisfaction to be derived from consuming more or less sugar per week. The accompanying hypothetical table shows how many units of utility are associated with an individual's consumption of different amounts of sugar per week.

TABLE 1. *Utility Schedule of Sugar*

Pounds of sugar per week	Amount of total utility	Extra utility due to last lb.
0	0	
		4
1	4	
		3
2	7	
		2
3	9	
		1
4	10	
		0
5	10	

The first part of Fig. 3 shows how *total utility* grows with the amount of sugar consumed; the second, how much *extra utility* is added with each new pound of sugar consumption. The first set of blocks is increasing, but the law of diminishing utility causes the second set to be decreasing; *i.e.*, the steps go downhill. Note that the sum of all the blocks in the second diagram is equal to the last pillar of blocks in the first diagram. This corresponds to the fact that total utility is the sum of the extra utility added by each of the units.

ECONOMICS OF INSURANCE

We are now in a position to see why insurance, which appears to be just another form of gambling, actually has exactly opposite effects. For the same reasons that gambling is bad, insurance is economically advantageous.

In buying fire insurance on his house, the owner seems to be betting with the insurance company that his house will burn down. If it does not, and the odds are heavily in favor of its not burning, the owner forfeits the small premium charge. If it does burn down, the company loses the bet and must reimburse the owner to the tune of the face value of the policy agreed upon. (For the obvious reason of removing temptation from hard-up home owners who like fire engines, the face value of the policy tends to be something less than the money value of the property insured.)

What is true of fire insurance is equally true of life, accident, automobile, or any other kind of insurance. Actually the famous Lloyd's of London, which is not a corporation but simply a place for insurance brokers to come together, will insure a ball team against rain, dancers against infantile paralysis, a hotel keeper against a damage suit from the widow of a man killed in a fight with another man who bought a drink in the hotel's cocktail lounge, and will write numerous other bizarre policies. But by the common law, Lloyd's cannot bet $10,000 with me that it will not snow on Christmas, since I do not have an "insurable interest" of that amount. But a ski resort owner, who stands to lose that much if it does not snow, would have such an insurable interest and could buy such a policy.

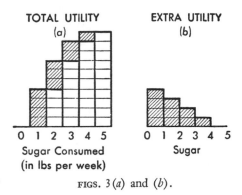

FIGS. 3 (*a*) and (*b*).

Insurance is the opposite of gambling because what is unpredictable and subject to chance *for the individual* is highly predictable and uniform *in the mass*. Whether John C. Smith, age twenty and in good health, will live for 30 more years is a matter of chance, but the famous *law of large numbers* guarantees that out of 100,000-odd twenty-year-olds in good health only a definite proportion will still be alive at the end of such a period of time. The life-insurance company can easily set a life policy premium rate at which it will never lose money. Certainly therefore, the company is not gambling. What about the buyer of life insurance, is he gambling? Actually it is not hard to show the reverse to be true: the man who does not insure his house is doing the gambling. He is risking the whole value of his house against the small premium saved. If his house does not burn down in any year, he has won his bet; if it does, as occasionally must happen, he loses his bet and incurs a tremendous penalty.

At this point, a sporting man will say, "So what? Of course, a man gambles when he doesn't buy insurance. But the odds on such a bet are not unfavorable.

In fact, they are favorable, because we know that the insurance company is not in business for its health. It must keep records, it must support insurance salesmen in the style to which they are accustomed, and so forth. All this costs money and must be 'loaded' on to the insurance premium, detracting from the perfect mathematical odds of the buyer and making the odds for the nonbuyer a little better."

To which a rational man will reply, "When I am among friends, I don't mind a small game of chance for relaxation even at slightly unfavorable odds. But when a big bet is involved, even if the odds are favorable, then I pass. I insure my house because I hardly miss the premium each year, and if it should burn down without being covered, I would feel the loss an awful lot. When I insure, my living standards over time and income are always the same, come what may. When I don't, I may be up for a while, but I risk going way down."

Obviously, although it has been left unsaid, the law of diminishing utility—which makes the satisfaction from wins less important than the privation from losses—is one way of justifying the above reasoning. *This law of diminishing utility tells us that a steady income, equitably divided among individuals instead of arbitrarily apportioned between the lucky or unlucky people whose house did or did not burn down, is economically advantageous.*[1] Also, when a family chooses to buy hospital and medical insurance, there is also the belief that this will be a relatively painless way of making itself "save against a rainy day." This self-imposed compulsory saving feature is another beneficial characteristic of insurance.

WHAT CAN BE INSURED?

Undoubtedly then, insurance is a highly important way of spreading risks. Why then can we not insure ourselves against all the risks of life? The answer lies in the indisputable fact that certain definite mathematical conditions are necessary before sufficiently exact actuarial probabilities can be determined. What are these?

First, we must have a *large number of events*. Only then will there be possible a pooling of risks and a "cancellation of averages." The bank at Monte Carlo knows there is safety in numbers. The lucky streak of a dissolute Hungarian nobleman will be canceled by the losings of a fake Ukrainian countess or else by her next night's losings. Once in a blue moon someone may "break the bank" but in a few more lunar cycles the "house" will more than break even.

---

[1] As was mentioned in Chap. 20 in connection with the discussion of consumer behavior, not all economists are willing to make assumptions about "utility." There, such an attitude made no difference; here, it might.

But large numbers are not enough. No prudent fire-insurance company would confine itself to the island of Manhattan even though there are thousands of buildings there. *The uncertain events must be relatively independent.* Each throw of the dice, each chance of loss by fire, should stand relatively by itself. Obviously, a great fire like that of Chicago in 1871 or in San Francisco after the earthquake, would subject all the buildings in the same locality to the same risk. The company would be making a bet on one event, not on thousands of independent events. Instead, it must diversify its risks. Private companies cannot write atomic bomb insurance for obvious reasons. This explains why it is not possible to buy unemployment insurance from a private company. Depressions are great plagues which hit all sections and all classes at one and the same time, with a probability that cannot be computed in advance with any precision. Therefore only the government, whose business it is to take losses, can take the responsibility of providing unemployment compensation benefit payments. As we have seen in our earlier discussions of Social Security, the government usually does make its benefit payments increase with the size of the worker's or his employer's contribution into the Unemployment Compensation Reserve Fund; nevertheless, the government does not follow the actuarial principles appropriate to private insurance. The lowest paid workers usually stand to receive more benefits than they are called upon to pay for. This is in accord with the fundamental principles of social security or social insurance, which always places a deservedly large emphasis upon the human needs of the recipients.

An ever larger number of life's uncertainties are being banished by insurance. In addition to life, automobile, accident, fire and theft, employee bonding, and other traditional forms of insurance, we are beginning to see the great growth of private old-age annuities, hospital insurance (*e.g.*, Blue Cross), medical insurance (*e.g.*, White Cross, Blue Shield), and so forth. In addition, as we have seen, the possibility of hedging permits those of us who wish to be safe to throw part of the risks of life upon speculators who wish to take risks.

But there still remain, and probably always will, numerous risks of personal and business life. No one can insure the success of a new beauty shop, a new mousetrap, or a hopeful opera singer. Without error there cannot be trial; and without trial, there cannot be progress.

JOINT PUBLIC AND PRIVATE RESPONSIBILITIES

It would not be appropriate to leave the subject of risk taking without indicating the important role of collective group action in this sphere. At best, organized markets and speculation cover only a small part of economic life, and even then largely serve only to *share and transfer* risks. At worst, as we have seen in connection with the stock market, certain types of individual speculation may destabilize the economy and intensify risk.

One of the advantages of monopoly, but one that should not be thought to overshadow its disadvantages, is its ability to avoid the uncertainties of uncoordinated swarms of competitors. Also the government, by means of an "ever-normal granary" program in which a store of wheat is always maintained against the vagaries of the weather and crop yield, may not simply share and transfer risks but actually control and reduce them. Unfortunately, in practice, the ever-normal granary proposals as well as the many highly desirable programs for soil conservation, flood control, and reforestation often become stalking-horses behind which are hidden the attempts of special farmer pressure groups to restrict production so as to raise income by taking advantage of inelasticity of demand.

Also, it is the democratic will of the people that the SEC and the self-imposed edicts of the organized stock exchanges should protect the ordinary stockholder and investor against such abuses as fraud, rigging of the market, false rumors, "concerning" of a crop or security, and "insider" speculation. When a company wishes to sell a new security, it must list it in advance with the SEC to be sure that no false claims are made. A broker is barred from giving advice and tips whose purpose is simply to make a sale. Holding companies whose only function is to "pyramid" tremendous empires of control have been dissolved. In 1946 "margin" requirements were raised to 100 per cent in order to curb the ardor and effectiveness of would-be speculative plungers; a year later they were returned to their former 75 per cent.

SUMMARY

1. The intelligent profit-seeking action of speculators and *arbitragers* tends to create certain definite equilibrium patterns of price over space and time. To the extent that speculators moderate price and consumption instability, they are performing a socially useful purpose. To the extent that they provide a market and permit others to hedge against risk, they are performing a further socially useful function.

2. But to the extent that speculators pile on to price changes and cause great fluctuations in stock prices, commodities, and foreign exchange rates, their function is a harmful one.

3. The economic principle of diminishing (marginal) utility is one way of showing why gambling is economically unsound and insurance sound. There are, of course, necessarily fundamental and important differences between private and social insurance or social security.

QUESTIONS FOR DISCUSSION

1. If the complete shipping costs per bushel of wheat between Kansas City and Chicago are exactly 2 cents, then only one of the following statements is true:

   a. Wheat must sell for 2 cents more in Chicago than in Kansas City.
   b. Wheat must sell for 2 cents more in Kansas City than in Chicago.
   c. Wheat in Chicago can continue to sell for more than 2 cents above the Kansas City price.
   d. Chicago and Kansas City wheat can never sell for the same price, or for within 1 cent of each other.
   e. If wheat is flowing between the two cities, the difference in price will tend to be neither more, nor less, than 2 cents; if wheat is not flowing between them, the price difference can be anything less than 2 cents.

Which is true?

2. Pretend that you are engaging in some stock or commodity transactions. Start out with $10,000 and follow the newspapers to see how you make out.

3. "I can't afford to sell my United States Steel stock today (1937) because if I do I'll take such a great loss over what I paid for it in 1929." Is this good reasoning?

4. Should doctors' services be made subject to private insurance principles?

5. "I love the thrill of gambling, of risking all on the turn of a card. What do I care for odds or economic principles?" Can economic science pass judgment on whether such a person should gamble or not?

6. List some important differences between private insurance and social security. Are they rivals?

Chapter 26: SOCIAL MOVEMENTS

AND ECONOMIC WELFARE

A *FASCISM, COMMUNISM, AND SOCIALISM*

THE CRISIS OF CAPITALISM

After World War I, democratic governments were set up all over Europe. By 1927 the future of the capitalistic way of life appeared serene and assured.

After World War II, the outlook is radically changed. Socialist governments are in power in England, in France, in all of Scandinavia, in Italy, in all the Balkans and eastern Europe. Russia with its communistic government appears to be on the march. Fascism lingers on in Spain. In our own hemisphere, dictatorships are to be found in numerous countries of Latin America.

Only the United States remains as an island of capitalism in our increasingly totalitarian and collectivized world. Even here, the scene is drastically changed in the direction of strengthened powers of government over economic activities.

The capitalistic way of life is on trial. Not only must it perform adequately —more than that, it is required to perform superlatively. A decade of unemployment here at home would have disastrous repercussions upon our prestige abroad, to say nothing of the internal political unrest that a slump would involve.

A BOUQUET OF ISMS

Men have always had visions of a more perfect society. Plato's Republic, Sir Thomas More's Utopia, Marx's Dictatorship of the Proletariat, and so on without number. It is only too easy to contrast concrete present-day imperfections with the ideal features of a vaguely defined utopia. Beyond agreeing on the faults of the present order, different schools of reform have very little in common.

At the one extreme, we have the anarchists who believe in no government at all; at the other, the apologists for an all-powerful collectivized, totalitarian, communistic social order, where the first person singular is all but replaced by the first person plural. Within the field of socialism itself, we find many subdivisions: Christian socialism, state and Marxian socialism, guild socialism, Fabian (or evolutionary) socialism, and many others. In the popular mind, socialists are characters who meet in a cellar lit by a candle thrust in an empty wine bottle to plot a bloody revolution, or at least to brew bombs sent in laundry parcels to government officials and capitalists. Or the term "socialist" is frequently used as a disparaging stereotype to discredit anyone who believes in social security, progressive taxation, bank deposit insurance, some other social improvement, or free love.

Whatever the strength of radical parties abroad, in America before 1948 no third party has ever been able to develop in any strength. The American Socialist party runs a candidate for the presidency every election—along with the Prohibition party—but gains only a negligible fraction of the vote. The Communist party, which is more hated by the Socialists than are the other two parties, has never yet been able to get one of its nominees elected to Congress.[1]

If we look at the picture in Europe, we find the names of almost all the parties have the word "socialism" in them. But this does not mean much: a party like France's Radical Socialists turns out to be anything but radical, being one of the extreme conservative parties. Even Hitler's fascistic party took the name of "National Socialism." Often, however, the leading European "liberal" parties can be characterized as "social democrats." For example, the Labor party in Britain, the pre-Hitler German Social Democratic party, the presently ruling parties in Sweden and Denmark—all of these claim to be in favor of gradual, nonrevolutionary extension of socialism by peaceful and democratic methods. In France, Italy, and the Balkans there are Communist movements of considerable strength. These are invariably pro-Russian and are usually frank in proclaiming that once in power they will not tolerate "reactionary" political movements.

It is clear, therefore, that we do not have to master all of the thousand and one different "isms" in order to understand the world today. It is enough to understand something of (1) relative *laissez faire* or private enterprise, (2)

[1] Theodore Roosevelt's 1912 Bull Moose party was primarily an offshoot of the Republican party. Old Bob LaFollette's 1924 Progressive party was by far the most successful third-party effort, and yet he was able to carry only his home state, Wisconsin. It remains to be seen whether the 1948 Henry Wallace third party will be able to develop more than minor strength.

socialism, (3) communism, and (4) fascism. There is no hard and fast boundary between these; it is all a matter of degree. Moreover, we cannot even range these along a line, with fascism at the extreme right wing and communism at the extreme left wing. In some ways—although neither would admit it— communism and fascism have much in common.

Most of this book has been concerned with describing the capitalistic system, so we may turn to the others.

FASCISM

This is easier to characterize politically then economically. Whether in Hitler's Germany, Mussolini's Italy, Franco's Spain, Salazar's Portugal, or Péron's Argentina, fascism is usually characterized by a one-man dictatorship, by one political party with all others abolished, by the disappearance of civil liberties of the type granted in our Bill of Rights. Fascistic movements are always highly nationalistic, often with the emphasis placed upon a vaguely defined "master race" by whom all minorities are exploited and persecuted. In the words of Mussolini, Fascists are urged to "live dangerously"—to value war and national power as ends in themselves. The individual is to be secondary to the state.

On the economic side, Mussolini's fascism happened to toy with the notion of a "syndicalist" or "corporate state"; each industry and group of workers was organized in a syndicate, and these were to meet and bargain and plan how the economy should be run. However, this syndicalism has not been especially characteristic of other fascist regimes.

Almost all of them are against militant trade unionism; almost all give the central government great regulatory power over every sphere of economic life. Some work hand in glove with religious authorities; others are antichurch. Often capitalists and the lower middle classes contribute to the initial strength of fascist movements; but later when the fascist movement begins to take on— as they sometimes do—revolutionary aspects, the capitalists may regret the Frankenstein's monster that they have helped to create. Their only consolation lies in the fact that one of the earmarks of a fascist regime is opposition to communism; often it sails into power by exaggerating the immediate likelihood of a bolshevik revolution, and after coming into power the threat of communism is used as an excuse for the suppression of all democratic processes.

MARXIAN COMMUNISM AND SOVIET RUSSIA

Travel eastward from New York, and if you continue long enough, you will return to it from the west. Move far enough to the right and you will round the circle and encounter the extreme left-wing communist movement. For three quarters of a century after Karl Marx and Friedrich Engels issued their 1848 Communist Manifesto, numerous international socialist conferences were held; but outside the British Museum, not much was accomplished.

In 1917, the big moment arrived. Czarist Russia was knocked out of the war by the Germans. Nikolai Lenin, a follower of Marx, was transported in a sealed railroad car across Germany and into Russia. Aided by Leon Trotsky, a one-time New York inhabitant, Lenin's Bolsheviks snatched power from the more moderate regime that had overthrown the monarchy. Preaching peace, promising land for the peasants, and a dictatorship to the proletariat, the followers of the red hammer and sickle forcibly took power and gained adherents in the navy and army.

There then followed what Harvard's John Reed (later buried in the Kremlin) called "100 days that shook the world." The meeting of the democratic Constituent Assembly, only few of whose elected representatives were pro-communist, was forbidden. An army was organized and trained by Trotsky, and successive towns were won over to the revolutionary forces—often by strategic capture of the water and power supply alone. Subsequently there followed a great civil war between the Red and White armies, the latter aided by Poland and Western powers. In the end, the officers of the White army ended up chiefly in Paris, driving taxicabs and drinking vodka to the memory of Czar Nicholas II.

The world expected a Russian collapse. In Wall Street, the bookmakers had quoted favorable odds on this event for a number of years running. The communist regime persisted—not without experiencing horrible famines, in which literally millions perished. Aristocrats and bourgeoisie were ruthlessly "purged" and "liquidated"—new words for age-old processes. The Communist party was the only permitted political party; it elected the members of local "soviets" of factories and farms. These soviets elected representatives to still higher soviets, until at the very top over all the 17 autonomous federated Union Republics, there is the Council of People's Commissars of the Supreme Soviet of the USSR (Union of Socialist Soviet Republics).

The Soviet leaders had no blueprint to guide them. Marx had confined himself largely to the faults of capitalism, revealing very little of what the promised land was going to be like. It was not even on the timetable that backward Russia, which had hardly emerged from feudalism into capitalism, should experience its revolution before the downfall of the top-heavy industrialized nations. During the 1920's, Lenin compromised with capitalistic enterprise in the NEP (New Economic Policy). But in 1928–1929, the first Five-year Plan for industrialization of factories and collectivization of agriculture was introduced. This was followed by a second Five-year Plan.

Because of the rapid pace of capital formation, war preparedness, and the state of Russian technology, consumption was severely rationed throughout these years. Workers had ration cards that were honored at specific stores, but money continued to be used. Excess money income could be spent only upon special goods at higher prices than the basic ration. Real and money wages differed between occupations, with piece rates and incentive pay for higher productivity becoming more and more dominant.

Joseph Stalin, one among many of Lenin's lieutenants, finally won out in the struggle for power after Lenin's death in the early 1920's. Trotsky and other old-line revolutionaries were accused of plotting with foreign powers against the Soviet Union, and in the middle 1930's a tremendous purge o generals and officials culminated in the sensational Moscow trials—sensational because all the defendants vied with each other in beating their breasts and avowing their own guilt. After the Chamberlain-Hitler Munich appeasement pact, Nazi Germany and Soviet Russia signed a nonaggression pact, which lasted until Hitler—flushed with his victory over Poland, Scandinavia, and France—attacked Russia.

With the aid of fanatical patriotism and United States lend-lease, the Russians traded their blood for the Germans' until few Germans were left. After the defeat of the Axis, the short-lived comradeship with the Western powers flickered out, and the world now stands in the shadow of the atomic bomb with Russia trying to spread her influence over Europe, and with Britain and ourselves bent on stopping her.

So much for this thumbnail historical sketch of political development. Economically, the Communist regime is far removed from a profit system of individualism. Generally speaking, a central planning committee determines the three basic economic problems: What shall be produced, How, and For Whom. There is, however, some possibility for consumers to express preferences. Factories, land, and capital equipment are owned by state enterprise; individuals are permitted private possession and limited amounts of money saving. Inequality of money, wealth, and inheritance is reduced.

The Russians claim that they have "industrial democracy." This is clearly a different commodity from political democracy as we know it. Even defenders of the Soviet Union will admit that expression of opinion against the government or communist party will not be tolerated. Free press—in our sense—is forbidden. Possibly the Russian people on the whole prefer their form of government, but no one should blind himself to its great differences from our own concepts of democracy and freedom.

SOCIALISM

In defining fascism or communism, we were able to point to Nazi Germany or Soviet Russia. Socialism cannot be so easily described. Of course, we can describe the Swedish socialist government or the British Labor party's program, but these do not have such dramatic contrasts with our system. They represent a middle way.

Nevertheless, there are at least a few elements that seem to characterize socialist philosophy:

1. *Government Ownership of Productive Resources.* The role of private property is gradually to be lessened as key industries such as railroads, coal, and even steel are gradually nationalized. Unearned profits from increases in land value are also limited.

2. *Planning.* Instead of permitting the free play of profit motives in a laissez-faire market economy, coordinated planning is to be introduced. Sometimes the program of "production for use rather than profit" is advocated; advertising expenditure on gadgets is to be wiped out; workers and professional people are to develop instincts of craftsmanship and social service so that they will be guided by other motives than those of our "acquisitive society."

3. *Redistribution of Income.* Through government taxing powers, inherited wealth and swollen incomes are to be reduced. Social security benefits and welfare services provided by the collective purse are to increase the well-being of the less privileged classes.

4. *Peaceful and Democratic Evolution.* As distinct from communism, socialism often advocates the peaceful and gradual extension of government ownership. Revolution by ballot rather than by bullet. This is often more than a tactical move; rather a deep philosophical tenet of faith.

In Britain, the owners of industries that are to be nationalized are given compensation.[1] Anyone who opposes the Labor party's government—and most English newspapers do—is free to express his opinion and organize politically. Even communists are granted full civil rights and liberties as of 1948.

POLITICAL FREEDOM AND ECONOMIC CONTROL

Degree of government centralization is a trait that ranges from a laissez-faire society through a collectivist communist regime. But a survey of history shows that this classification must not be confused with the degree of political freedom and democratic civil liberties. Fascist regimes have often passed

---

[1] Coal, electric power, the Bank of England, the British Broadcasting Company—all these are already publicly owned. Steel and other industries are waiting for their number to be called up.

socialistic measures, and communist bureaus have suppressed personal freedom. On the other hand, socialist Britain (1948) has more civil liberties than did the United States in the 1920 era of rugged individualism, when Attorney General Palmer imprisoned and released hundreds of people alleged to be "reds."

It is one thing to tell a corporation what it may charge for electric power and quite another thing to tell a man what he can say, what he can believe, how he must worship. It will not do to confuse the two.

B. THE USE OF AN OVER-ALL PRICING SYSTEM UNDER SOCIALISM AND CAPITALISM

This is an introduction to economics rather than a book on social movements and comparative political systems. Let us turn, therefore, to see how our economic analysis of pricing can be applied to a noncapitalistic system.

In analyzing the problem of pricing in a planned socialist state, we kill three birds with one stone:

1. We get one of the best possible reviews of the over-all working of an ideal capitalistic price system.

2. We discover a possible method of attacking the almost unbelievably complex problem of socialist economic planning.

3. Finally, we gain an introduction to problems of "welfare economics," *i.e.*, to the study of what is wrong with any economic system. This depends, of course, upon ethical points of view, which are themselves a-scientific. But the economist, as a disinterested observer, may help to throw light upon how successfully an economic system realizes any suggested ethical *goals*.[1]

REVIEW OF FREE COMPETITIVE PRICING

At the beginning of this book we saw that every economic society must somehow solve the three fundamental problems of economic organization: What, How, and For Whom shall economic goods be produced. We saw too that in a free-enterprise, competitive, individualistic, profit-and-loss, market system the unconscious pricing mechanism more or less automatically solves these problems of organization. We also saw that the present economic order is

---

[1] For example, he may be personally opposed to an equal distribution of income, but that doesn't prevent him from measuring the degree of success in reaching this ethical goal.

a mixed one in which monopolistic elements are blended with competition, and public action with private.

In a moment we shall see that there is nothing sacred about the results achieved by a free market system; no, not even if it worked completely without friction and under the most perfectly competitive conditions imaginable. We shall also see, what is less obvious, that a socialist state might, if it wished to, use many of the mechanisms of a pricing system in its own planning. Let us now review the workings of the pricing system from the vantage point of the increased knowledge of economics gained since the early chapter of the book.

Even in a rich modern state, resources are scarce, technology is imperfect, and human wants and needs are far from being sated. This would be true even if society had already solved all the problems of unemployment and purchasing power described in Part Two of this book. With no resources being wasted in unemployment, any economic system must still determine how resources are best used to satisfy human wants as between different commodities and in cooperation with the optimal factors of production.

Part Three, of which this is the concluding chapter, is primarily concerned with the economic forces governing the use of economic resources at high employment; with the problems of market price and consumer's behavior; with cost analysis of industry and firm under perfect competition and monopolistic competition; with production equilibrium and the problem of distribution; with international specialization and trade; and with speculation and dynamic price behavior over time. All these processes remain important problems even when there is no business cycle and no trace of unemployment. A few years ago an economics textbook would have concerned itself with little else; and if ever the business cycle is brought under control by intelligent social action, these will again become the main concern of economics. As we shall soon show, with appropriate modification, the same principles will have relevance for a completely socialized state.

Economic analysis shows that the problems of What, How, and For Whom are not independent but interrelated in the most complex fashion. Suppose that people suddenly begin to change their tastes away from food and in favor of clothing. The first effects seem to be in the field of What shall be produced. By spending (or voting) more money for clothing and less for food, they raise the demand for clothing relative to its supply and do the opposite with respect to food. From the detailed supply and demand analysis in Chap. 19, we know that this will tend to increase the price of clothing and decrease the price of food. But after clothing has risen sufficiently in price, so that profits can be earned in that line, new resources will be rushed into clothing production and new quantities will come on the market; also the higher price for clothing will discourage its consumption. In the long run, there will be a new equilibrium price where the Supply schedule intersects the new Demand curve, and where more clothing and less food are produced. (The reader will be able to go through the reasoning necessary to show how food producers will incur losses until a new equilibrium position is realized in those markets.)

Very well, we have come out with the conclusion that What will be produced is determined by people's buying power and tastes. A change in tastes will affect prices so as to alter the quantities that will be produced.

But this is not all the story. Unfortunately, the process does not end there. A change in tastes will also affect For Whom things are to be produced.

It will affect the supply and demand for land and labor, and this in turn affects the distribution of income between laborers and landowners. How? Because higher prices and production of clothing relative to food means a relatively greater demand for labor and a relatively smaller demand for land; therefore, higher wages and lower land rents. Therefore, a new distribution of personal income.

Even the How is affected. At the old ratio of wage costs to land costs, it paid to combine land and labor in one way. With the new higher costs of labor, it will pay in producing any given output to *substitute* land for labor wherever possible. Under competition, woe to the businessman who doesn't recognize the dawn of a new day and carefully readjust his production methods so as to realize once again the optimal and most efficient production position combination.[1] In the new setup, the cost of clothing, which uses much of the now expensive labor factor, will increase relative to the cost of food. This is not a new fact, but simply another way of looking at the fact mentioned earlier, that the new supply and demand situation dictates a relatively higher price for clothing.

The process is not really at an end even yet. The changed distribution of income between farmers and workers may, if these groups have different spending habits and tastes, cause a further shift in demand and in What shall be produced. But this is just where we first came in, and we need not follow another whirl of the economic circuit.

No wonder our economic system is said to be a "closed circle," made up of interdependent parts. Actually, it's worse than that. It is more like a vast and intricate telephone switchboard, in which everything is connected with every-

---

[1] He must substitute the now cheaper land for labor until the marginal product of the last dollar spent on labor and on land is again equal—in terms of the new price setup. See Chap. 22.

thing else. The student can nowhere find a place in the interdependent system that represents the beginning, nor one that represents the end. He must somehow cut the Gordian knot by breaking in at any convenient point. But when he does so, he must necessarily run the risk of having to admit, "In order to understand Chap. A, I must first have understood Chap. Z; but I can't understand that perfectly until I have already mastered A!"

Regrettable, but true. The only help for the situation is to proceed just as the competitive economic system does itself—by successive approximation. Just as the market price sneaks up on the final complete equilibrium set of prices, the student of economics spirals upward in his general understanding of our complex system, always returning to the same fundamentals, but with new insights.

THE CONCEPT OF GENERAL EQUILIBRIUM

A mathematician might describe the process of price determination as follows:

The correct (equilibrium) set of prices of consumption goods and of productive services, the market quantities of outputs and inputs—all these are "unknowns" whose numerical values are determined by a vast set of "simultaneous equations": the condition that all prices be equal to producers' "marginal costs," and to consumers' relative "extra utilities"; that wages equal "marginal revenue productivities"; that profits be at a maximum, etc.

Given such noneconomic facts as (1) population, (2) technology, (3) tastes, and (4) distribution of ownership of property, there are just enough individual and market relations or equations to determine a unique economic solution. Everything depends on everything else, but all together determine each other in just the way that stationary balls in a bowl mutually determine each other's position.

Who solves the complex equations of economic life? Certainly not mathematicians. Certainly not government bureaucrats or congressmen. Every person—whether a businessman, housewife, farmer, or wage earner—is helping to solve them every time he decides to use one kind of labor and not another, or decides to buy butter and not oleomargarine, or decides to plant more or less intensively so much corn and so much wheat, or decides to quit glass blowing for type setting. We don't have to use slide rules, and we don't have to understand the pricing system to contribute to the solution of "general equilibrium"—any more than the ticker tape in the stock market or the grain market has to understand why price goes up when demand increases and falls when it decreases.

Prices keep moving as a result of our readjustments of behavior. If outside factors such as inventions, wars, or tastes were to remain constant long enough, then we might finally approach the "general equilibrium set of prices," at which all the forces of supply and demand, value and costs, might just be in balance, without any tendency to further change. Of course, in the real world, outside factors never stand still, so that as fast as equilibrium tends to be attained it is disturbed. Still, there is always a tendency—at least in a "perfect" competitive system—for the equilibrium to reestablish itself, or at least to chase after its true position.

(To test his knowledge of the interdependence of our economic system, the reader should show that a new invention affects more than the How: that it may also affect the For Whom and the What. Similarly, a change in the distribution of wealth and income will affect not only the For Whom but also the What and the How.)

PRICING IN A SOCIALIST STATE: CONSUMPTION GOODS PRICES

After this brief review of capitalist pricing, we are ready to tackle the problem of using a price mechanism to help lessen the terrific burden upon a centralized planning authority which has to make millions and millions of economic decisions concerning production and consumption.

Many socialists have insisted that, in their new society, the consumer should still have *freedom of choice* and will not have dictated to him the relative amounts of different commodities which he is to "enjoy." As in the capitalist system each person will receive a sum of money or abstract purchasing power which he can spend among different commodities as he wishes. Thus, vegetarians will not have to eat meat, and those who most prefer meat will be able to exert their preference.

How will relative prices between salmon and Spam or any other consumers' goods be set by the socialist state? Generally speaking, they will be set with the same double purpose as in a capitalist society: (1) just high enough to ration around the existing supplies of consumers' goods, so that none are left over and none are short; and also (2) just high enough to cover the socially necessary extra costs of producing the goods in question—or, in technical terms, prices are to be set equal to relative "marginal utilities" and "marginal costs."

THE DISTRIBUTION OF INCOME

So far the process has worked much like the capitalistic system. However, socialism, almost by definition, means a society in which most land and capital goods or nonhuman resources of all kinds are owned collectively by society and not individually by people. In our society an Astor who owns 500 parcels of New York City land which each produce $2,000 of net rents per year will receive an income of 1 million dollars per year—which may be 1,000 times what a night watchman is able to earn, and 200 times what the average skilled engineer can earn. With most property owned collectively and not distributed with great inequality among different individuals, an important source of inequality of the distribution of income would be removed.

Many people profess to hold the ethical and philosophical belief that different individuals' wants and needs are very much alike and that the present market mechanism works inadequately because the rich are given so many more votes in the control of production than the poor as to make the market demand for goods a poor indication of their true social worth. Such people with a relatively equalitarian philosophy will welcome the great reduction in the spread of incomes between the lowest 90 per cent of all families and the highest 10 per cent. They will argue that taking away $1,000 from a man with an income of $100,000 and giving it to a man with an income of $2,000 will add to social well-being. After the distribution of income between families has been determined correctly, according to society's fundamental (a-scientific) value judgments, then and only then will it be true that the dollars coming on the market will be valid indicators of the value of goods and services; and only then will they be serving to direct production into the proper channels and goods into the right hands.

How is the proper, ethical distribution of income to be achieved aside from the negative act of wiping out unduly high property incomes? The socialist has two answers: (1) in part by letting people get some of their income in the form of wages; but (2) in large part by having these wages supplemented by receipt of a lump-sum *social dividend payment*. This cash payment would presumably be pretty nearly the same for most average families; but even in an equalitarian society, there might be differences to compensate for different numbers of children, different age and health status, and so forth.

It is an ethical rather than a scientific question as to just how large each person's final income ought to be. As a science, economics can concern itself only with the best means of attaining given ends; it cannot prescribe the ends themselves. Indeed, if someone decided that he preferred a feudal-fascistic kind of society, in which all people with little black moustaches were to be given especially high incomes, the economist could set up the pricing rules for him to follow to achieve his strange design best. He would be told to determine his social dividend payments so as to achieve the required optimal distribution of income, after which each dollar coming on the market could be regarded by the economist as correctly representing (that eccentric person's) true social values.

The social dividend differs from a wage because it is to be given to each individual *regardless of his own efforts*. That is why it is called a "lump-sum" dividend. Any bonus based upon productivity or effort is to be treated as a wage. We have not yet seen how wages are to be determined. But before doing so let us first turn to another important problem.

PRICING OF NONHUMAN PRODUCTIVE RESOURCES AND INTERMEDIATE GOODS

What should be the role of land and other nonhuman productive resources as an element of cost in an ideal socialist state? Some people would say that such nonhuman resources should not enter into cost at all; that only human sweat and skill is the true source of all value; and that any extra charges based upon the cost of land or machinery represent a capitalistic surplus which the owners of property are able to squeeze out of the exploited laboring masses by virtue of the private monopoly of ownership of the means of production. This view is sometimes loosely spoken of as the "labor theory of value," and it is usually attributed to Karl Marx, the intellectual father of communistic socialism. Learned scholars dispute over just what Marx meant by the "labor theory of value," and whether he intended it to be applied to a socialistic economy in the short or long run.

We need not enter into this dispute. However, it is important to note that, in its simple form, the labor theory of value will lead to incorrect and inefficient use of both labor and nonlabor resources in even the most perfect socialist society. So long as any economic resource is limited in quantity—*i.e.*, scarce rather than free—the socialist planners must give it a price and charge a rent for its use. This price need not, as in the case of the Astor millionaire under the capitalistic system, determine any individual's income. It can be a purely bookkeeping or accounting price set up by the planners, rather than being a market price. But there must be a price put upon the use of every such resource.

Why? First, we must price nonhuman resources to insure that society is deciding *how* goods shall be produced in the best way, so that we really end up out on the true Production-possibility curve of society and not somewhere inside it. It would be absurd to get rid of the capitalistic system with its alleged wastes due to unemployment, and then by stupid planning end up far inside of society's true production potentialities.

Related to the above point is the second need for all resources to be given a value if correct prices are to be charged to consumers for final goods that use up a great deal of scarce resources. In other words, for society to find itself in the best of all possible positions along the Production-possibility curve, we must price such consumption goods as food and clothing so as to reflect their true relative (extra or marginal) costs of using up scarce resources. Otherwise, the free choice exerted by consumers on their dollar spending will not truly reflect their own or society's best preferences.

THE EXAMPLE OF LAND RENT

These two reasons are difficult to grasp. However, let us try to make the necessity for land pricing clear by considering a single example. Suppose there are two identical twins in a farming utopia. What if one were to produce wheat on an acre of good land, and the other to produce less wheat by the same year's work on an acre of bad land. If they are identical twins, working equally hard, we would certainly have to say that their wage rates should be the same. Now, if wages were to be treated as the only cost, in accord with the labor theory of value, then the same price could not be charged for the two different outputs of wheat, even though the kernels of wheat were identical. The good-land wheat would have involved low labor costs and will have to sell for less than the poor-land wheat.

This, of course, is absurd. A well-wishing social planner might try to get around the dilemma by charging the same price for both, perhaps losing money on the poor-land wheat and gaining on the other. Or what is almost the same thing, he might say "Let us pay the twin on bad land lower wages than his brother, so as to keep the costs of the two wheats the same; but then let us make the richer brother share his wages with the poorer."

Such a solution is not absurd, but it falls short of achieving the desired best results: maximum production and equal pay for equal human effort. In particular, it fails to shift more labor on to the more productive land.

The only correct procedure is to put an accounting price tag on land, the good land having the higher tag. The prices of both kinds of wheat will be equal, because the land cost of the good-land wheat will be just enough higher than that of the poor-land wheat to make up the difference. Most important of all, the socialist production manager must try to minimize the combined labor and land cost of producing each kind of wheat. If he does so according to the marginal product principles discussed in Chap. 22 on Production, he will accomplish something new and important and undreamed of by the simple believer in the labor theory of value.

He will find it pays to work the good land more intensively, perhaps with the time of $1\frac{1}{2}$ men until the extra product there has been lowered by the law of diminishing returns so as to be just equal to the extra product of the $\frac{1}{2}$ man's time on the poor land. Only by putting a price upon inert sweatless land are we using it, and sweating breathing labor, most productively! The price or rent of land rises so as to ration its limited supply among the *best* uses.

Note too that the most finicky humanitarian will have nothing to complain of concerning our solution. By transferring labor from one plot of land to the other until its marginal productivity has been made equal, we get the largest possible total production of wheat.[1]

The two brothers are paid the same wages because they have worked equally hard. But their wages are not high enough to buy all the wheat since part of the cost of the wheat has come from (bookkeeping) land charges. However, the people through their government own the land equally. The land's return does not go to any property owner, but is available to be distributed as a lump-sum dividend to both brothers according to their ethical deserts. By putting a proper accounting price or rent on land, society has more consumption than was otherwise possible.

If we turn now to the production of more than one consumers' good, it will be obvious that their cost prices must be made to reflect the amount of socially limited land and machinery which they each use up. A field crop like potatoes requires little labor and much land as compared to an intensive garden crop like tomatoes. If each commodity were priced on the basis of labor costs alone, potatoes would sell for too little and too much land would be forced out of tomato production. Everyone would end up worse off.

One last point concerning the final determination of a product's cost and price. After the costs of all necessary factors of production have been added together to arrive at total cost, the planning authorities must set their prices at the extra or marginal cost of new units of production. Or more accurately, the socialist managers of a plant must behave like a perfect competitor: they must disregard any influence that their own production might have on market price, and must continue to produce extra units up to the point where the last little unit costs just as much as its selling price. For many industries, such as railroads where unit costs are constantly falling, setting marginal costs equal to price will imply that *full* average costs are not covered. In a noncapitalistic society the difference would be made up by a (accounting) grant from the

---

[1] As the discussions of marginal productivity in an earlier chapter have shown, *total product will be at a maximum only when labor has been transferred from the poor land* (where its marginal product is low) *to the good land* (where its marginal product is high). Every such transfer must necessarily yield us extra product, until finally no further increases in output can result when the marginal products have been equalized in the two uses.

state. For if a railroad system is worth building, it is worth being utilized to the full.[1]

To summarize: Correct social planning requires that all scarce resources, whether human labor or not, be given accounting prices at least. The final costs of consumers' goods should include the sum total of *all* extra costs necessary to produce each good; or, in short, should equal *marginal cost*. The demand for consumers' goods is really an indirect demand for all productive resources, a demand which can be kept in proper check only by putting appropriate valuations on productive resources.

Otherwise, society's valuable nonhuman—and human!—resources will be incorrectly allocated, and the market pricing of finished goods will not lead to maximum consumers' satisfaction. It is to be emphasized that the accounting prices of land and other nonhuman resources need not, in a socialist state, be part of the incomes of anyone. In the language of the visionary critic of private enterprise: no one is "exploited" by having a property owner skim off part of the final product. Instead, the contribution of capital and land to production is given to people in the form of the *social dividend*.

THE ROLE OF THE INTEREST RATE IN A SOCIALIST STATE

In the earlier chapters of this book, we encountered the interest rate in two main forms: (1) as a (discount) factor necessary to convert flows of income into a capitalized present value, or as a yield factor to determine people's income from bonds and other capital assets, and (2) as a necessary premium to get people to give up hoarding of money and instead to hold their wealth in the form of securities.

Neither of these functions of interest would have an important role in a socialist state, because no one would have the opportunity of buying and selling a corner lot or other assets, and presumably the socialist planners would not let people generate a business cycle by varying their desires to hoard money.

However, we have also seen that there is a third important function of the interest rate in a capitalistic, socialistic, or any other kind of economic system.

---

[1] The long-run question as to whether to build a railroad in the first place may involve an "all-or-none decision," which cannot be made step by step. In such a case, there must still be a balancing of the extra (or marginal) advantage and extra cost to society of the enterprise. But for such a big step, price is no longer a good indicator of total welfare, since—as we saw in Chap. 20—there is always an element of consumer's surplus on the total amount of goods that a person consumes, over what he has paid for them. Welfare may go up as price and total value go down.

Capital goods have a "net productivity." So long as resources can be invested for the present or the future, it will be necessary to make important decisions with respect to capital. Shall we apply present land and labor to the production of a corn crop this year or to apples 15 years from now? Shall we have grape juice today or wine 10 years hence? Shall we replace a worn-out printing press by a new expensive one which yields its services over a period of 20 years, or buy a cheap one that will only last 14 years? Every one of these questions can be answered only by using an interest rate to relate future and present economic values. Without such an interest rate, the existing stock of fixed and circulating capital cannot be devoted to its best uses; and whatever amount of national income society has decided to invest in capital formation cannot be embodied in the best form without such an interest rate.

The interest rate acts as a sieve or rationing device: all projects that can yield 6 per cent over time are undertaken before any that yield only 5 per cent are started.

It should be added that most economic writers on socialism do not think that the rate of interest should also determine—as it does in our economy, to some degree—the rate at which capital growth is to take place at the expense of current consumption. The decision as to how much should be saved would be determined by the state "in the light of national and social needs" and not by the "haphazard" notions of individuals with respect to the future. But the level of social saving and capital growth once having been determined, the interest rate must be used to allocate scarce "capital supplies" optimally and to determine the order of priority of alternative projects. Needless to say, in a slowly growing rich country with much capital already accumulated and with few recent capital-using inventions, the rate of interest will be a very low one. Diminishing returns is one law that the Socialist Comissars will not be able to repeal by a plebiscite or a bloody revolution.

WAGE RATES AND INCENTIVE PRICING

We must now return to the problem of how the socialist planners would set wage rates, and then we are done. If the amounts of labor of all kinds and of all skills were perfectly fixed, there would be no reason why labor should not be given accounting prices just like any other productive factor. Workers would receive no wages at all. They would then receive all the national income in the form of an enlarged *social dividend*.

However, if people are to be free to choose their own occupation and if they are to be given a choice between working a little harder and longer in return for extra consumption goods, then it will be necessary to set up a system of *actual market wages* at which people can sell their services. These rates may differ depending upon the irksomeness and unpleasantness of the job; and unlike in our system, the pleasanter jobs may be the lower paid, and the ditch-diggers or garbage collectors may have to be higher paid to attract people into their jobs. Occupations that require much training and skill will receive high pay, but much of that pay may be spent by the state in providing the education necessary to acquire those skills. Piece rates may often be used under socialism, and a worker with a 10 per cent higher productivity may receive higher wages. Workers will in every case be offered wages equal to their marginal or extra productivity.

Therefore, it is not necessarily true that all incomes will be at a dead level in the socialist state. They will differ somewhat as a result of two distinct factors: (1) society's appraisal of the "needs and worth" of different individuals—as reflected primarily in the size of the individuals' lump-sum *social dividends*, and (2) the need for wages to differ to provide incentives and to compensate people for extra disutility and effort. Incomes would not differ, however, because of inequality in the ownership and inheritance of property.

SUMMARY OF SOCIALIST PRICING

1. A socialist system could make use of four different kinds of pricing: (1) consumer-goods prices, (2) wage and incentive rates, (3) accounting prices of intermediate goods, and (4) final lump-sum dividends (when positive, subsidies; when negative, taxes).

2. To give people free choice between consumers' goods, market prices will be set for such goods. Similarly, to provide freedom of choice of occupation, to give people incentives, and to provide compensation for differences between occupations, wage rates will have to be set to correspond to (marginal) productivities and disutilities.

3. Accounting prices will have to be set on all nonhuman productive resources to ration them in their best uses where their (relative) marginal productivities are equal and highest. Similarly, there will have to be a rate of interest to ration the existing and growing stock of capital among its best uses. Any consumption good will have to be produced up to the point where the full marginal cost of production (necessary to attract all resources from other uses and from leisure) is just equal to the price.

4. Lastly, the final distribution of income will be made to correspond to what society regards as the ideal distribution pattern by means of a payment of a lump-sum social dividend to people, depending upon "need and wants" but never—like a wage—on effort or performance. Presumably in a socialist

society, it will be felt that a much more nearly equal distribution of income will be necessary before the dollar votes of consumers can be expected to reflect true social preferences. However, this is a nonscientific, ethical question.

5. None of these processes except the last requires detailed comprehensive planning by a central agency. Mathematicians will not have to be called in to solve thousands and thousands of simultaneous equations. Instead, the decentralized planners would proceed by successive approximation, by trial and error—setting provisional market and accounting prices and cutting them or raising them depending upon whether available supplies are piling up or running short.

WELFARE ECONOMICS IN A FREE-ENTERPRISE ECONOMY

On the basis of the above general principles of pricing, we are in a position to see what is wrong, or not necessarily right from various ethical viewpoints in our present system. The possible deviations from the social optimum may be briefly listed as follows:

1. The existing distribution of property, income, education, and economic opportunity is the result of past history and does not necessarily represent a perfect optimum according to the ethical philosophies of Christianity, Buddhism, paganism, or what may be loosely spoken of as the American creed as expressed by tongue and pen. In part, such deviations from the optimum distribution of income can be corrected by appropriate tax policies. There are always, however, some costs to be incurred in our capitalistic system from such policies because of effects upon incentives, risk taking, effort, and productivity.

2. The widespread presence of monopoly elements in our system and the very limited appearance of perfect competition mean that production is rarely being pushed to the optimum point of equality of marginal cost to price; because the elasticity of demand is not infinite under imperfect competition, production is pushed only to the point of equality of marginal cost to marginal revenue. Because of the fear of "spoiling the market," monopoly price is too high and monopoly output is too low.

Nor are these the only evils of monopoly. Wasteful competitive advertising, needless insignificant differentiation of products, distortion of consumers' tastes and beliefs by selling campaigns and propaganda—all these are in some degree extra evils when pushed beyond the useful informative functions of "legitimate" advertising. They are related to a further evil under monopolistic competition when entry of new firms into an industry is very easy. There will then tend to be an inefficient division of production among too many firms; the price charged is too high, but because of wasteful use of resources, no one is making any profits.[1]

3. Finally, of course, as shown in Part Two, under a laissez-faire system, there are great wastes due to unemployment and the business cycle. Consumers, labor, farmers, and business together with public fiscal and monetary policy must be mobilized in a never-ending war against this greatest of modern scourges—this poverty that has no real cause but stems only from our intricate monetary society.

These imperfections can be ameliorated within the framework of our traditions. In any case, many—perhaps most—Americans will feel that the dynamic vitality of our mixed-enterprise system outweighs its disadvantages.

SUMMARY

A. FASCISM, COMMUNISM, AND SOCIALISM

1. Out of the multiplicity of social movements and philosophies, these three constitute the important challenge to our present order. Perhaps most significant are the noneconomic issues involved in a comparison of capitalism and alternative systems. We have not more than touched upon the question of the extent to which a socialist society might, or might not, be able to develop among its people new attitudes to replace capitalistic incentives, such as instincts of professional good craftsmanship and social service, which put emphasis upon production for use rather than for profit. Nor have we been able to set down final answers to the crucial problems of the relationship between individual freedom and social control in different economic systems.

Can a socialist society preserve the civil rights and political freedoms for the individual? What is the importance of political democracy without economic

---

[1] Another evil, discussed in more advanced economic writings, is the fact that individual firms, in making their decisions, never take into account the possible effects of their production decisions on other firms or industries. In digging his oil well, Pat doesn't realize that he may be robbing Mike's oil pool; and the same with Mike—with the result that less oil is obtained in the end, and with more cost. Because of such so-called "external diseconomies" (or occasionally, "external economies") apparent "private marginal costs" do not reflect true "social marginal costs"; and certain lines of activity deserve to be contracted and others to be expanded. Compare A. C. PIGOU, "Economics of Welfare," The Macmillan Company, New York, 1932.

democracy? How can capitalism be made to function better? A number of references are suggested below for those interested in further readings.[1]

B. PRICING IN SOCIALISM AND CAPITALISM

2. In a pure unmixed competitive society, the economic problems of What shall be produced, How, and For Whom are solved in an intricate, interdependent manner by the impersonal workings of the profit-and-loss market system. Every economic variable depends upon every other, but all tend to be simultaneously determined at their general equilibrium values by a process of successive approximations involving adjustment and readjustment.

3. Unless a socialist economy were uninterested in efficiency and economizing, or in freedom of choice of goods and jobs, it would have to institute a system of pricing. However, some prices would be purely accounting or bookkeeping figures; in addition, the final determination of the distribution of income would involve an outright social dividend, given to everyone by the explicit a-scientific decision of government and society.

4. From the standpoint of welfare economics, it is seen that our own capitalistic system may depart from a social optimum in three main ways: through improper distribution of income, through monopoly, and through fluctuations in unemployment. It is the present writer's belief as exemplified throughout the book, that all these evils can be ameliorated by appropriate policies, within the framework of the capitalist system.

It is too easy to compare the obvious imperfection of our known system with the ideal perfections of an unknown planned order. And it is only too easy to gloss over the tremendous dynamic vitality of our mixed free-enterprise system, which, with all its faults, has given the world a century of progress such as an actual socialized order might find it impossible to equal.

[1] R. H. TAWNEY, "The Acquisitive Society," Harcourt, Brace & Company, Inc., New York, 1920; F. A. HAYEK, "The Road to Serfdom," University of Chicago Press, Chicago, 1944; JOHN ISE, "Economics," Parts VI and VII, Harper & Brothers, New York, 1946; H. C. SIMONS, A Positive Program for Laissez Faire, *Public Policy Pamphlet* 15, University of Chicago Press, Chicago, 1934; A. C. PIGOU, "Socialism versus Capitalism," The Macmillan Company, New York, 1939. For further information on welfare economics, see J. E. MEADE and C. H. HITCH, "An Introduction to Economic Analysis and Policy," Oxford University Press, New York, 1938.

QUESTIONS FOR DISCUSSION

1. Make a list of a number of isms, describing each and outlining its history.

2. Describe your own vision of Utopia. Does it differ from the present order?

3. Compare and contrast fascism and communism. What is the relation of socialism and capitalism to each?

4. Discuss the development of the Labor party in England, and its postwar activities.

5. "I'd rather starve in free America than live off the fat of the land under totalitarian communism." Are these your sentiments? Why?

6. "For all its talk of planning and production for use, Soviet Russia employs its resources less efficiently than the United States and has a slower rate of progress than we do." Discuss.

7. Summarize how a pricing system works to solve the three fundamental economic problems. Illustrate the interdependence of these three problems.

8. Describe what is meant by general equilibrium.

9. Discuss the four kinds of prices in a planned, socialist state.

10. List what you consider to be economic imperfections in the present economic order. What are its virtues?

Chapter 27: EPILOGUE

In 1929, a distinguished committee, called together by President Herbert Hoover, issued a report on "Recent Economic Changes."[1] After much careful research it concluded in these words, "Our situation is fortunate, our momentum is remarkable."

Yet despite their confident expectation that the American economy would remain in an excellent state of "balance" and "dynamic equilibrium," this Committee stood unknowingly on the edge of an abyss. Within 6 months the greatest depression on record had set in, a depression that was to alter profoundly American institutions and economic life.

In 1939, another government investigation conducted by the congressional Temporary National Economic Committee had changed its tune completely. From volume after volume of its hearings, from monograph after thick monograph, came the plaintive chant of stagnation of the American economy.

Yet, within a few years the United States was engaged in a large-scale defense and war program that changed the economic scene completely. Since 1939 another decade has passed—a decade of conversion and reconversion, of shortages and prosperity, of price controls and inflation.

If an introduction to economics enables readers to understand—not necessarily, predict—the exciting events of recent years, it will have fulfilled its purpose. It will be better still if it helps to make clear the rich promise of America's future economic development. This promise can be assured only if there is adequate total demand to maintain full production and technological progress and if the pressure politics of special interests—agriculture, labor, and business—can be kept from distorting the efficient response of the economic system to human wants.

Figure 1 summarizes our economic past and future. The average hours of work per week have dropped from 70 to 40 within the past century. Total

[1] "Recent Economic Changes in the United States," McGraw-Hill Book Company, Inc., New York, 1929.

man-hours have continued to increase because of population growth, but at a very slow rate after the turn of the century. Yet real national income has doubled every generation and gives promise of continuing to do so in the future.

This amazing increase in output has been the result of the steady growth of productivity, measured in the chart by "net output per man-hour (in cents of constant purchasing power)."

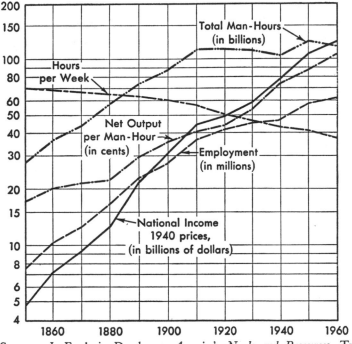

AMERICA'S PAST AND FUTURE

FIG. 1. Source: J. Frederic Dewhurst, *America's Needs and Resources*, Twentieth Century Fund, New York, 1947.

As the Twentieth Century Foundation says in concluding its gigantic investigation, "America's Needs and Resources:"[1]

Whatever may be our accomplishments in the future, the lesson of the past is clear: the only way to raise the ultimate ceiling on production, which is manpower, is through further increases in output per worker and per man-hour. Productivity is the key to future welfare. Within the past century we have achieved almost a fivefold increase

[1] J. Frederic Dewhurst and Associates, "America's Needs and Resources," p. 680, The Twentieth Century Fund, Inc., New York, 1947.

in net output per man-hour. . . . These vast gains in human welfare have lessened human toil.

To this emphasis on productivity, we need add one further reminder: the importance of preventing mass unemployment of men and machines.

The pictured rate of progress means more than an increase in gadgets and luxury goods. It means that fewer and fewer of the population will fall below the poverty line—the line of minimum nutrition, minimum health care, minimum educational opportunities, minimum security, and minimum material enjoyments of life.

All this we can look forward to with confidence, if intelligence can be found to understand our modern economic system and to keep it functioning well.

Index

A

Abilities, distribution of, 81
Absolute advantage, 539
Acceleration principle, 405–407
Acceptances, 345
Accounting, elements of, 134–149
    balance sheet, 134–139
    depreciation, 138–141
        estimating, two methods for, 139
    good will, 148–149
    income statement, 137–138
    intangible assets, 147
    inventories, 136
    profit and loss, statement of, 137–138
    reserves and funds, 145–147
Advertising, 513
Aged, job opportunities for, 83
Agricultural Adjustment Act, 78
Agriculture (*see* Farming)
Allen, Frederick Lewis, 574*n*.
American Federation of Labor (AFL), 71, 185–189
    case study of member of, 188–190
    history of, 186
    membership in, 185
    organization of, 187–188
Annuity, 74
Arbitrager, 57*n*., 570, 582
Assets (*see* Accounting, elements of)
Atomic energy, 17
Ayres, Leonard P., 289

B

Bagehot, W., 401*n*.
Baker, John C., 92*n*.

Balance, of current items, 360–364, 382
    of international payments, 360–364
    of trade, 360, 382
Balance sheet, use of, in accounting, 134–139
Bank of England, 313*n*., 337
Bank deposits, considered as money, 287–288
    insurance of, 311, 322–323
    multiple, contraction of, 331
        creation of, 323–329
            qualifications concerning, 331–333
Banking, branch, 311
    as a business, 313–315
    development of, 315–319
    functions of, 311–312
    modern fractional reserve banking, 317–319
    monopoly, 330
    multiple-deposit contraction, 331
    multiple-deposit creation, 323–329
    safety measures for, 322–323
Baruch, Bernard, 576
Bear and bull market, 573
Beggar-my-neighbor policies, 539, 567
Beney, M. Ada, 88
Bergson, Abram, 81*n*.
Berle, A. A., Jr., 128
Beveridge, William, 400*n*.
Beveridge plan, 222
Bilateralism versus multilateralism, 554–555
Black, J. D., 79*n*.
Black markets, 465
Bonds, corporate, 122
    government, 215–216
    (*See also* Securities)
Budgets, family expenditure, patterns of, 201–203

Budgets, family expenditures, minimum, 64
Bull markets, 573
Bureau of Agricultural Economics (BAE), 212
Bureau of the Census, 176, 178
Bureau of Internal Revenue, 171
Bureau of Labor Statistics (BLS), construction of cost-of-living index by, 204
Business cycle, acceleration principle of, 405–407
    capital formation as key to, 400–401
    length of, 399–400
    measurement of, 394–397
    monetary control of, inadequacies of, 353–354
    phases of, 397–399
    theories of, 401–410
        external, 402–403
        internal, 402, 403–404
        long wave, 399–400
        synthesis, 404–405
Business enterprise, big, 109, 124–126
    infinitesimal and small, 109–111
    organization of, 108–132
        corporate, 118–124
        individual proprietorship, 109–114
        partnership, 114–118
        population of, 108–110
Businessman, family background of, 106
    social position of, 91

C

Capital, circulating, 44–45
    equity, 114–115
    fixed, 44–45
    formation of, 236–238
    and private property, 49–51
    productivity of, real net, 49
    roundabout character of, 42
    supply of, and "easy-money" policy, 460–461
    and time, 42–44
    venture, 113
    working, 45, 112
Capitalism, 42
    crisis of, 584, 603
Capitalist, philanthropic, case study of, 193–194
Capitalization of income, 45–48

Carlyle, Thomas, 152
Case study, of AFL carpenter, 188–190
    of CIO unionist, 190–191
    of Congressman dealing with labor problems, 194–196
    of economist looking at labor problems, 196–199
    of forms of business organization, 111–124
    of labor lawyer, 191–193
    of philanthropic capitalist, 193–194
    of tooth-paste company, 111–124, 135–149
Chamberlin, E. H., 492n.
Chase, Stuart, 206n.
Chicago Board of Trade, 570n.
Children, cost of, 205
Ching, Cyrus S., 197n.
Civil rights, 589–590
Clark, Colin, 69n.
Clark, H. F., 94
Class struggle, 70, 73
Clayton Antitrust Act (1914), 191
College education, cost and value of, 102–105
Commercial Credit Corporation, 116, 311
Committee for Economic Development (CED), 92
Common stocks, 123
Commons, J. R., 52n.
Communism, growth and threat of, 586–588
Communist Manifesto, 67
Comparative advantage, 538–550
    in contrast to absolute advantage, 539
    gains from, 548–549
    Mill's theory of international demand, 546–549
    qualifications on theory of, owing to, increasing and decreasing costs, 555, 557
        multiple products and regions, 552–555
        transportation costs, 558
    Ricardian limits on price ratio under, 544–545
Competition, impure (or imperfect or monopolistic), 38, 492–494
    monopoly mistakes of, 39
    pure (or perfect or atomistic), 36–38, 40, 452–453, 492
    tests for, 493

Competition, ruinous, 39
Complements and substitutes, 480
Conant, James B., 95
Congress of Industrial Organizations (CIO), 71, 185–199
  case study of member of, 190–191
  history of, 186–187
  organization of, 187–188
Conservation of resources, 540*n.*
Consumer, and advertising, 207
  and art of spending money, 206–207
  expenditure at different income levels, 202–203
Consumer's surplus, 483–484, 599*n.*
Consumption, and capital formation, 42–44
  diminishing (*see* Diminishing Consumption)
  graphical treatment of, 487–490
  standards of, 16
  theory of, 477–485
Consumption-possibility curve, 488–490, 547–548
Consumption schedule (*see* Propensity to consume)
Cooke, M. L., 197*n.*
Coolidge, Calvin, 91
Corporation, excess profits tax, 170*n.*
  Federal taxation of, 121–122
  as form of business organization, 118*ff.*
    advantages of, 120–121
    disadvantages of, 121
    financing of, 122–123
    formation of, 118–120
    legal status of, 120–121
  giant or large, 124–126
    achievements of, 132
    amplification of control through holding companies, 128–129
    divorce of ownership and control in, 128–129
    interest groups of, 126
    management of, 129–131
  income tax, 170
Cost, constant, 469
  decreasing, 21, 473–474
    and international trade, 557
  full, 509–511
  increasing, 21, 469–470
  and monopoly competition, 474–475
  total, variable, and fixed, 495–496

Cost, unit or average, 496–497
  (*See also* Marginal cost)
Cost of living, family differences in, 205–206
  index of, construction of, 204
  regional differences in, 203–205
Council of Economic Advisers to the President, 436, 439
Crash, stock-market, 573–574
Credit, pyramid of, 348–350
  small loans and loan sharks, 213–215
Cross relations of demand, 480
Crum, W. L., 110*n.*, 125*n.*
Currency devaluation, and depreciation, 385–387
  and full employment, 373

D

Darwin, Charles, 24
Declaration of Independence, 72
Decreasing costs and international trade, 557
Defense Plant Corporation, 51
Deflation, 280–282
Demand, cross relations of, 480
  and supply (*see* Supply and demand)
Demand curve, 447–455
  elasticity of, 449–454, 481
  under monopolistic or imperfect competition, 493–494
Demand schedule, 447–455
Department of Commerce, 225, 230, 231, 241, 245–249
Department of Labor, 208
Depopulation, 26–27
Depreciation (*see* Accounting, elements of)
Dewhurst, J. Frederic, 607*n.*
Diminishing consumption, law of, 448–449, 480
  exceptions to, 475–476
  reasons for, 480–482
Diminishing returns, law of, 22–23, 522–523, 530
  and international trade, 555*n.*
Diminishing (marginal) substitution, law of, 487, 489*n.*
Diminishing (marginal or extra) utility, law of, 577–580, 583
Discriminatory monopoly, pricing of, 518*n.*
Diseconomies or external economies, 475*n.*, 603*n.*

Disposable income, 242, 248
Distribution, classical theories of, 527
    false problem of, 526–529, 532
    and marginal productivity, 528–529
    meaning of, in economics, 526n.
    "normal," 81
    of savings, by family, 212–213
    (See also Income, distribution of)
Division of labor, 42, 51–53
Domestic system, 67
Douglas, Major, 233n.
Douglas, Paul H., 472n.
Dubinsky, David, 187n.
Dublin, L. I., 26n.

E

"Easy-money" policy, 304–306
    and supply of capital, 460–461
Economic Advisers to the President, Council
    of, 436, 439
Economic development of United States,
    four stages of, 364–366
Economic interpretation of history, 70–71
Economic organization, basic problems of,
    12–17
        solved by a free-enterprise price
        system, 35–41
    technological choices affecting, 17–23
    underlying population basis of, 24–31
Economic policy, 5
Economic systems and historical perspec-
    tive, 154
Economics, boundaries and limits of, 14–16
    and common sense, 6
    and controlled experimentation, 7
    and idealized applications, 8
    and modern preoccupation with unem-
        ployment, depression, and inflation, 3
    and objective approach, 5
    objectives of study of, 3–4
    as political economy, 15
    and semantics, 6–7
    theory versus practice in, 7–8
    welfare, 590, 602–603
Education, college, cost and value of, 102–
    105
    Federal aid to, 95, 104
Edwards, George, 69n.
Elasticity of demand, 449–454, 481

Elasticity of demand, definition of, 451
    exact numerical value of, 451n.
    infinite value of, under pure competition,
        453, 492–494
    for labor, 453–454
    and price discrimination, 518
    test of, 450
Employment Act of 1946, 436
Engels, Friedrich, 67
Engel's Laws, 201n.
English corn law, 557
Equal-cost curves, 534–536
Equal-output curve, 523–524, 534–537
Equilibrium, general, concept of, 593–594
Estates tax, 180
Euclidean or full-employment world, 9–10,
    538, 559
    (See also Social versus private virtues and
    folly)
European Recovery Program (ERP), 358,
    376–377, 381
Ever-normal granary program, 582
Evolutionary versus revolutionary improve-
    ment of society, 71
Excess profits tax, corporate, 170n.
Exchange control, and full employment, 373
Exchange Equalization Fund, 348
Exchange rates, 359–360, 379–381, 385–391
    (See also Finance, international)
Excise tax, 169
Executives, incomes of, 92–93
    and taxation, 93
    leadership of, in modern society, 91
External economies or diseconomies, 475n.,
    603n.
Extra cost (see Marginal cost)
Extra product (see Marginal product)
Extra revenue (see Marginal revenue)
Extra utility (see Marginal utility)

F

Fair Employment Practice Commission
    (FEPC), 83
Fair Labor Standards Act (1938), 88, 192
Fallacy of composition, 8–9, 270, 324, 426,
    452
Farming, income from, 76–79
    on family farms, 76

Farming, income from, instability of, 78–79
  and price-raising programs, 78
  and quest for parity, 78–79
  to laborers, 77
  to sharecroppers, 77
  to tenant farmers, 77
Fascism, 586
Featherbedding, 530
Federal Deposit Insurance Corporation
  (FDIC), 153, 311, 323
Federal government, efficiency and waste in,
  157–158
  expenditures of, 155–157
  financing of, 161–166
  transfer, 160–161
  fiscal policy of, during boom and depres-
    sion, 165–166
  (*See also* Fiscal policy)
  grants-in-aid to states, 182–183
  taxation by (*see* Taxes, Federal)
  and war finance, 164–165
Federal Reserve Act (1913), 312–313
  amendments to, 345
Federal Reserve Banks, assets of, 339–342
  gold certificates, 340–341
  government-securities, 341–342
  balance sheet of, 339–340
  control of quantity of money by, 337–340
  and credit pyramid, 348–350
  excess reserves and, 346–347
  and interest rates, 342–356
  loan and rediscount policy of, 343–345
  and monetary policy, 337–355
  "open-market" operations of, 342–343
  and public debt, 354–355
  reserve requirements of, 345–346
  wartime finance policy of, 351–352
Federal reserve credit, 341–342
Federal reserve system, 152, 310–313
  board of governors of, 175, 176, 178, 212,
    312
  creation of, 312
  legal reserves for member banks, 319–320
  member banks versus reserve banks, 312–
    313
  organization of, 313
Federal Savings and Loan Insurance Corporation, 153
Federal Trade Commission (FTC), 207
Females, discrimination against, 82

Females, earnings of, 82–84
Finance, international, balance of payments
  in, 360–364
  capital movements, 361–364
    monetary versus real aspects of,
      366–368
    significance of, 366–370
  current items (trade balance and
    invisible items), 360–364
  specie movements, 361–364
  exchange rates in, 359–360
    and International Monetary Fund,
      379–381
    freely flexible exchange rates, 385–
      387
      determinants of supply and de-
        mand, 386–387
      disadvantages of, 387
    stable exchange rates, 379–381, 388
      and gold standard, 388–389
      and multiplier analysis of foreign
        trade, 391–392
      and specie-flow-price mechanism,
        389
Fiscal policy, controversial character of,
  409–410, 414–415, 417–418, 421, 426,
  431–432, 434, 436
  four alternative models of, 440–443
  and full employment, 435–436
  limitations of, 412, 414–417, 426–431,
    436
  significance of, 410
  two programs of, 410
    countercyclical, 410–411
      limitations on, 414–417
      types of, 411–414
    long-run, 417–418
  wasteful versus useful, 434–435
Five-year Plans, U.S.S.R., 587–588
Foster and Catchings, 401*n.*
Franklin, Benjamin, 24
Friedman, M., 104*n.*
Full employment, 15, 538
  and fiscal policy, 435–436
  four quantitative paths to, 440–443
  government's role in, 41
  and import quotas, 373
  and international trade, 373
  and long-term price behavior, 284
  and protective tariffs, 373

Full-employment or Euclidean world, 9–10, 538, 559
    (*See also* Social versus private virtues and folly)

G

Gambling, economics of, 577–581
Gaps, inflationary and deflationary, 272–274
General equilibrium, concept of, 593–594
Gold, and value of money, 55, 287, 348
Gold certificates, 340–341, 349
Gold standard, 388–389
Goldsmiths and early banking, 315–317
Gompers, Samuel, 71, 186
Good will, or capitalized earning power, 47–48, 148–149, 515
Goods, economic, 16
    free, 16
Gordon, R. A., 92n., 110n., 128n.
Government, collective services provided by, 40
    coordination of different levels of, 181–183
    economic role of, 40
    national real capital owned by, 51
    taxation and expenditure in income analysis, 274–276
    (*See also* Federal government; Fiscal policy; Local government; State government)
Government bonds, 215–216
Government expenditure, distribution of, by level of government, 154–155
    quantitative growth of, 150–152
    (*See also* Federal government)
G.I. Bill of Rights, 113–114
Government ownership (*see* Socialism)
Government regulation, growth of, 152–154
    (*See also* Labor legislation; Monopoly)
Great Britain, balance of payments problem of, 377
    incomes in, distribution of, 67n.
    taxation in, progressive, 67n.
    working-class conditions in, in mid-nineteenth century, 68
Gresham's law, 56n.
Gross national product (GNP), 240, 242
    measured by major components, 1929–1947, 241, 246, 247

H

Haberler, G., 401n., 552n., 565n.
Hamilton, Alexander, 152, 428, 567
Hansen, Alvin H., 399–400, 401n., 419–421
    secular stagnation, theory of, 419–421
Hawley-Smoot tariff, 568
Hawtrey, R. G., 401n.
Hayek, F. A., 401n., 604n.
Hedging, 572
Highway user tax, 177–178
Hillman, Sidney, 186
Hitch, C. H., 604n.
Hitler, Adolf, 586
Hobhouse, L. T., 484n.
Hobson, J., 401n.
Home Owners' Loan Corporation (HOLC), 345
Home ownership as form of savings, 217–218
Hoover, Herbert, 91, 411, 606
Hull Reciprocal Trade Agreements, 568
Hume, David, 389–391

I

Import quotas and full employment, 373
Income, capitalization of, 45–48
    classified into labor, land, and capital, 73
    consumption expenditure at different levels of, 201–203
    disposable, 242, 248
    distribution of, 61–64
        and distribution of abilities, 81
        frequency, 62–63
        in Great Britain, 67n.
        and inflation, 280–282
        in 1945, 70
        perfect equality in, 65
        and propensity to consume, 257
        (*See also* Distribution)
    family, 61
    from farming (*see* Farming)
    individual, 61
    inequality of, 64–67
    minimum budgets of, 64–67
    national (*see* National income)
    patterns of saving and consumption of, 207–213
        in urban families, 208

Income, per capita U.S., 62
  personal, 242, 247–248
  professional, 93–105
  from property, 72
  unearned versus earned, 72
  and war prosperity, 70
  from work, 72
Income analysis, theory of (*see* Income determination)
Income determination, as affected by government expenditure, 274–275
  as affected by taxation, 274–276
  by consumption and investment, 259–264, 277–278
  numerical example of, 261
  qualifications to theory of, 276–278
  restatement of, 263–264
  by saving and investment, 258–259, 261–264, 277
  theory of, 253–277
    applications of, 265–276, 278
    essentials of, 253–264
    limitations to, 276–278
Income effect, 480
Income statement, 137–138
Income tax, corporation, 170
  personal, 82, 171–174, 180
Index number of prices, statistical construction of, 204, 229–230, 289–290
Indifference curves, 487–490
Industrial revolution, 67
Inferior goods, 202, 480
Inflation, 280–283, 295–296
Inheritance tax, 180
Insurance, of bank deposits, 311, 323
  economics of, 578–581
  life, 218–221
    endowment plan, 220
    industrial, 218
    limited payment, 219
    straight, 219
    term, 219
  private, contrasted with social, 581
  unemployment compensation, 179
Interest, indirect burden of, on public debt, 429–430
Interest rate, 46–47, 301*ff.*, 599
  decline in, 74
  as a discount factor, 48
  history of, since 1932, 304–306

Interest rate, and liquidity preference, theory of, 303–304
  and money, 303–304
  and net productivity of capital, 49, 366–367, 600
  role of, in a socialist state, 599–600
  on small loans, 213–215
International Bank for Reconstruction and Development, 358, 377–379
International Monetary Fund, 358, 378, 379–381
International trade (*see* Trade, international)
International Trade Organization (ITO), 382, 568
Interstate Commerce Commission (ICC) (1887), 152
Inventories, 136
Investment, and acceleration principle, 405–407
  dependence of, on dynamics, 255, 419
  effects of public expenditure on, 415
  foreign, 239
  in government bonds, 215–216
  gross and net, 238–239
  induced by income changes, 269–270
  life insurance, 218–221
  multiplier effects of, 265–270
  and saving (*see* Saving and investment)
  securities, 216
  short-term, 300
  variability of, 255–256
Invisible items in balance of payments, 360–361
Ise, John, 604*n.*

J

Jefferson, Thomas, 152
Jevons, W. S., 401*n.*
Job opportunities, for the aged, 83
  for the Negro, 84, 87
Joslyn, C. S., 106

K

Kallet, A., 206*n.*
Keynes, John Maynard, 253, 303
Knights of Labor, 186
Kuczynski, R. R., 31*n.*
Kuznets, S., 104*n.*, 225*n.*

L

Labor, division of, 42, 51–53
  elasticity of demand for, 453–454
  (*See also* Labor force; Labor legislation; Labor movement; Labor unions; Laborer)
Labor force, 79
  self-employed, 79
  total in United States, 1940–1947, 249
  wage earners, 79
Labor legislation, 153, 189–199
  case study of a labor lawyer, 191–193
  Clayton Antitrust Act (1914), 191
  Fair Labor Standards Act (1938), 88, 192
  Norris-LaGuardia Act (1932), 191
  Sherman Antitrust Act (1890), 191
  Taft-Hartley Labor Relations Act (1947), 189, 192, 194–196
  Wagner National Labor Relations Act (1935), 189, 190, 192
Labor movement, 185–189
  growth of, 185
  history of American, 185–187
  and labor legislation, 189–199
  structure of, 187–188
"Labor theory of value," 596
Labor unions, 185–199
  and ability to pay, 531
  case studies concerning, 188–193
    AFL carpenter, 188–190
    CIO unionist, 190–191
    labor lawyer, 191–193
  craft versus industrial, 186–187
  and labor legislation, 189–199
  structure of, 187–188
  and Taft-Hartley Act, 195–196
  and wages, 529–531
Laborer, domestic, 86–87
  semiskilled, 73, 88
  skilled, 73, 89–90
  unskilled, 73, 88
  white-collar worker, 73
Laissez faire, 34, 585
Law of large numbers, 579
Law of scarcity, 16–17
Lenin, N., 587
Lerner, A. P., 439
Lester, R. A., 56*n*.
Lewis, John L., 186, 187*n*.

Liabilities (*see* Accounting, elements of)
Life insurance (*see* Insurance, life)
Liquidity preference, definition of, 304
  theory of, 297–308
List, Friedrich, 567
Loan financing of government expenditure, 163–164
Loans, commercial, 113
  from Commercial Credit Corporation, 116
  under G.I. Bill of Rights, 113–114
  mortgage, 113, 116
  personal, 213–215
  from Reconstruction Finance Corporation (RFC), 116–117
  term, 113, 116
Local government, borrowing and debt repayment by, 180–181
  expenditures of, 174–176
  fiscal perversity of, 416
  state aid to, 182–183
  taxation by, 175–180
    miscellaneous, 180
    payroll and business tax, 179
    property tax, 175–77
    sales tax, 179
Lorenz curve, 65, 66, 99, 173, 174
Lotka, A. J., 26*n*.
"Lump-of-labor" notion, 530

M

Macaulay, F. R., 66*n*.
Macaulay, T. B., 439
Machinery and Allied Products Institute, 421
Malthus, T. R., 24–26, 31
Malthusian theory of population, 24–26
Margin requirements, 582
  for stock-market purchasing, 348
Marginal (extra) cost, and average cost, 507
  and competitive price, 504
  definitions of, 498, 503*n*.
  equality of, with marginal revenue, 499–502
  and firm's supply, 504
  and production equilibrium, 524–525, 536
  relation to slope, 503*n*.
Marginal (extra) product, 519–520
  definition of, 522
  of last dollar, 524–525
  multiplied by marginal revenue, 520, 526

Marginal propensity to consume, 256–258
  definition of, 209
  of families, 209–211
  and the multiplier, 266
Marginal propensity to save, 256–258
  definition of, 209
  of families, 209–211
  as reciprocal of the multiplier, 266
Marginal (extra) revenue, 498
  and marginal cost, 500–502
  and price, 499
  under price discrimination, 518n.
  in production equilibrium, 519–520, 526, 532
Marginal (extra) utility, 577–579, 583
  relative (see Diminishing substitution law of)
Marriages, and cost of food, 4
Marshall, Alfred, 475n., 567
Marx, Karl, 67, 70, 90, 587, 596
Mass production, economies of, 21–22
Maximization of profits, 494–502
Meade, J. E., 604n.
Means, Gardner C., 128
Mercantile Marine, 560–561
Mill, John Stuart, 538, 546, 567
Minorities, economic problems of, 82–84
Mises, L., 401n.
Mitchell, Wesley C., 398
Mixed enterprise system, 34
  governmental admixture, 36, 40–41
  monopoly admixture, 36, 38–40
Monetary Fund, International, 358, 378, 379–381
Monetary policy, of Federal Reserve Banks, 337–355
  inadequacy of, 353–354
  and public debt management, 354–355
  in wartime, 351–352
Money, categories of, 285–288
    bank deposits, 56, 287–288
    paper currency, 55–56, 285–287
    small coin, 285
  commodity, 54–55
  demands for, 297–299
    investment, 298–299
    precautionary, 298
    transaction, 297
  and determination of interest rates, 303–306

Money, increased supply of, as source of government expenditure, 162–163
  and law of supply and demand, 290
  as long-term asset, 300–303
  as medium of exchange, 57–58
  quantity of U.S. money in circulation, 288
  quantity theory of, 290–294
  relation to saving, investment, and prices, 295–296
  as temporary form of holding wealth, 299
  as unit of account, 57–58
  as unit of reckoning over time, 58–59
  use of, versus barter, 53–54
  value of, as reciprocal of price level, 288–289
Monopolistic competition, 492
  four patterns of, 511–517
  and full-cost pricing, 509–511
Monopoly, 39, 126–128
  and decreasing cost, 40
  discriminatory, pricing of, 518n.
  good will and, 148–149
  holding companies, 128–129
  interest groups, 126
  limiting case of, 492
  monopolistic devices, 127
  and public regulation, 514–516
Moore, H. L., 401n.
Multilateralism versus bilateralism, 381–382, 554–555
Multiplier, 265–267
  as chain of spending, 266
  definition of, 265
  foreign trade, 391–392
  graphic picture of, 267
  and marginal propensities, 266
Murray, Philip, 197n.
Murray-Dingle-Wagner Bill, 223n.
Mussolini, Benito, 586
Myrdal, Gunnar, 84n.

N

National Association of Manufacturers (NAM), 418n.
National Bureau of Economic Research, 225, 398
National Housing Agency (NHA), 217
National income, 225–249
  concepts of, summary of, 242–244

National income, problems introduced by government, 234–235
real versus money, 229–231
sources of estimates of, 225
statistics of, 225, 229, 232–234, 236, 238–239
and transfer payments, 228
two views of, 226–232
as income earned by factors of production, 226–231
as net national product, 231–239
U.S., selected years 1929–1947, 245–248
wages as traditional fraction of, 531
(*See also* Income)
National Industrial Conference Board, 110*n.*, 151, 225
National Labor Relations Board (NLRB), 190, 192, 193
under the Taft-Hartley Act, 196
National Recovery Administration (NRA), 574
National Research Council, 206
National Resources Committee, 28, 62*n.*, 127, 202
National Resources Planning Board, 110*n.*
Natural rights, 73
Negro, job opportunities for, 84, 87
per capita earnings of, 82
Net National Product (NNP), 231–239, 240–242
Net productivity of capital goods, 49, 366–367, 600
Net reproduction rate, 27–29
Net worth (*see* Accounting, elements of)
New Deal, 158–160
New Economic Policy (NEP), 587
"Normal" distribution, 81
Norris-LaGuardia Act (1932), 191
Northrop, H. R., 84*n.*
Notestein, Frank W., 30

O

Office of Price Administration (OPA), 207
(*See also* Price controls)
Ohlin, Bertil, 557*n.*, 564
One hundred per cent reserve plan, 316–317
Open-market operations, 342–343
Overcapacity of sick industries, 511–512

P

Paradox of international charity, 373
Paradox of thrift, 269–272
qualifications to, 272
Paradox of value, 482–483
Pareto, Vilfredo, 66
Pareto's Law, 66–67, 82
Parity, agricultural, 78–79
purchasing-power, doctrine of, 386
Partnership, disadvantages of, 117–118
financing of, 115–117
formation of, 114
unlimited liability of, 117
Patents, as intangible assets, 147
Pay, "take-home," 79–82
Payroll tax, 170, 179
Personal income, 242, 247, 248
Peterson, Florence, 185, 188
Pigou, A. C. 401*n.*, 603*n.*, 604*n.*
Population, 24–31
age distribution of, 28
future, estimated, 30
Malthusian, theory of, 24–25
net reproduction rate of, 27–29
preventive and positive checks to, 25
world, estimated, 26
Poverty, decline of, 67
Preferred stocks, 123
Price control, maximum ceilings, economic effects of, 463–466
minimum-wage laws, 463
and rationing, 465
wartime action of OPA, 466
Price level, long-term goals of, 284
and value of money, 288–290
Prices, 280–284
behavior of, over time, 570–573
and distance between markets, 570
and employment, 282
index number of, statistical construction of, 204, 229–230, 289–290
and limitation of quantity of money, 290
and price ratios, 56–57
and real income, 281
Pricing system, 590
under capitalism, review of, 593–594
economic functions of, 36–38
under socialism, 594–604

Production, direct approach to, 519–520, 526
  equilibrium of, 518–526
  indirect approach to, 520–526
    graphical depiction of, 534–537
Production function, 521–522
Production-possibility curve, 17–22, 542–545
Productivity, increases in, due to technological change and growth of American output, 69, 606
  net, of capital goods, 49, 366–367, 600
Professions, cost and value of training for, 102–105
  education for, 95
  growth of earnings from, with age, 100–101
  incomes from, 93–105
  regional earnings of
  restriction of members in, 94
Profit, and loss, statement of, 137–138
  maximization of, 494–502
Propensity to consume, as affected by government taxes and spending, 274–276
  as approach to income determination, 259–264, 274–276
  of community, 256–258
  and distribution of income, 257
  of families, 201–213
  and liquid wealth, 425
  marginal, 208–211, 266
  shifts of, with time, 420
  table or schedule of, 208–211
Propensity to save, as approach to various determination, 257–278
  of community, 256–258
  of families, 201–213
  marginal, 208–211, 266
  table or schedule of, 208–211
Property rights, individual, 51
Property tax, 175–177
Proprietorship, single, 109–114
  financing of, 112–114
  liability of, 112
  management by, 112
Protection and full employment, 373ff.
Public debt, 212
  external versus internal, 426–427
  indirect burden of interest charges on, 429–430

Public debt, internal borrowing through time and, 427–428
  and monetary policy, 428
  ownership of, 431n.
  quantitative relation to national income, 431–433
  retirement of, effects of, 426
  and secular exhilaration, 423–424
Public utilities, original versus U.S. reproduction cost of, 519–525
Public Utility Holding Company Act (1935), 129
Public works, as type of countercyclical fiscal policy, 411
Public Works Administration (PWA), 183 413
Purchasing-power parity doctrine, 386
"Putting-out" system, 67

Q

Quantity theory of money, 290–294
  and equation of exchange, 293–294
  inadequacies of, 292–294
  in relation to saving, investment, 295–296

R

Rationing, 465
"Recent Economic Changes," 606
Reconstruction Finance Corporation (RFC), 51, 116
Rediscount rate, 343–344
Reed, John, 587
Regional differences in cost of living, 203–205
Relative marginal utility (see Diminishing substitution, law of)
Rent, classical theories of, 527–528
  economic, 462, 470–472
  and proper pricing, 597–599
Rentier, 74, 84
Reproduction rate, net, 27–29
Reserves, in accounting, 145–147
  excess, 342, 346–348
  of Federal Reserve Banks, 348–350
  legal requirements for, 345–346
Resources, allocation of, 10
  conservation of, 540n.
Revenue, marginal (see Marginal revenue)

Revenue, total and average, (or price), 494–495

Revolutionary versus evolutionary improvement of society, 71

Ricardo, David, 70, 538, 546n.

Robinson-Patman Act (1936), 127

Roosevelt, F. D., 64, 93, 153

Roosevelt, Theodore, 153, 585n.

Rubber, natural and synthetic, 560

Ruggles, Richard, 242

Ruinous competition, 513

Rural problem areas, 68

Russell Sage Foundation, 213

Russia, 587

S

Sales tax, 169, 179

Satisfaction (see Utility)

Saving, attempted versus realized, 271
  distribution of, by family, 212–213
  government bonds as form of, 215–216
  home ownership as form of, 217–218
  and investment, 279
    cleavage between, 254–255
    deflationary and inflationary gaps between, 272–274
    determination of income by, 258–259
    qualification to analysis of, 276–277
    (See also income determination)
    measurable identity of, 267–269
    separate motive for 254–255
  life insurance as form of, 218
  securities as form of, 216
  wartime accumulation of, 211–213

Saving schedule (see Propensity to save)

Scarcity, law of, 16–17

Schedule, consumption (see Propensity to consume)
  demand (447–455)
  saving (see Propensity to save)
  supply (see Supply schedule)

Schlink, F. J., 206n.

Schumpeter, J. A., 132n., 400n., 401n.

Scientific management, and piece rates, 89

Secular stagnation, 17, 418–423
  as a bogey, 421–423
  versus secular exhilaration, 423

Securities, bonds, corporate, 122
  government, 215–216

Securities, common stocks, 123
  dividends and earnings of, 143–144, 301, 303
  preferred stocks, 123
  relative advantages of different types of, 124

Securities and Exchange Commission (SEC), 92, 153, 582

Security (see Social security)

Shaw, G. B., 36

Sherman Antitrust Act (1890), 126, 152, 191

Short selling, 572

Sick industry, overcapacity of, 511–512

Simons, H. C., 604n.

Sinclair, Upton, 207

Slope, relation to marginal cost, 503n.
  relation to marginal propensity to consume and to save, 210–211, 267

Smith, Adam, 36, 52n., 70, 482, 538

Social dividend payment, 595–596

Social ends of economic activity, 12–15
  unemployment as an evil, 15

Social sciences, contrasted with physical sciences, 4

Social security, 76, 201–223
  "cradle-to-grave" security, 76
  family allowances, 30, 205
  growth of, 222–223
  and health, 221–222

Social Security Act (1935), 96, 179, 183, 221
  old-age assistance and public welfare, 183, 222
  old-age retirement, 221
  payroll tax under, 170
  unemployment compensation, 221–222

Social Security Bulletin, 413

Social versus private virtues and folly, 270–271

Socialism, 71
  British form of, 589
  elements of, 589
  pricing under, 590–604
  varieties of, 585

Society, modern, capitalistic character of, 42–50
  economic stratification of, 105
  interdependence of, 53

Specialization, 42, 51–53

Speculation, destabilizing effects of, 573, 582
  stabilizing effects of, 571–573, 582
Stalin, Joseph, 588
Standard of living, American, 61–64
Stagnation, secular (*see* Secular stagnation)
State government, borrowing and debt repayment, 68, 180–181
  expenditures of, 174–176
  Federal aid to, 182–183
  fiscal perversity of, 416
  taxation by, 175–180
    highway user tax, 177–178
    inheritance and estates tax, 180
    payroll and business tax, 179
    personal income tax, 180
    property tax, 175–177
    sales tax, 179
Stock-market crash, 573–574
Stocks, common, 123
  margin requirements for market purchase of, 348
  preferred, 123
  prices of, 575
  (*See also* Securities)
Stolper, W. F., 565n.
Substitutes and complements, 480
Substitution, diminishing (marginal), law of, 487, 489n.
Substitution effect, 481
Sunspots, 402–403
Supply and demand, 544
  applications of, 457–466
  effects of governments on, 462–466
  equilibrium of, 455–457
Supply schedule, 454–455
  effects of shifts in, in five cases, 469–473
  of firm and industry, 507–509
  of firm and marginal cost, 503–504
Surplus Property Administration, 116
Survey of Current Business, 97

T

Taft-Hartley Labor Relations Act (1947), 189, 192, 194–196
Tariffs, protective, and full employment, 373ff.
Taussig, F. W., 106, 567
Tawney, R. H., 603n.

Taxation, automatic flexibility of, 413
  changes in, as type of countercyclical fiscal policy, 414
  corporate, 121–122
  in Great Britain, 67n.
  incidence of, 458–459
  progressive versus regressive, 168–174, 175–180
  as source for government expenditure, 162
Taxes, Federal, 168–174
  corporation income, 170
  excess profits, 170n.
  inheritance and estates, 180
  personal income, 82, 171–174
  sales and excise, 169
  social security, payroll and employment, 170
  state and local, 175–180
  highway user, 177–178
  inheritance and estates, 180
  miscellaneous, 180
  payroll and business, 179
  personal income, 180
  property, 175–177
  sales, 179
Taylor, Frederick, 89
Technological unemployment, 9, 17, 543
Temporary National Economic Committee (TNEC), 110n., 218, 606
Tennessee Valley Authority (TVA), 159n., 515
Terborgh, George, 421–423
  theory of stagnation a bogey, 421–423
Terms of (international) trade, 544
Thompson, W. S., 26, 30, 31n.
Thrift, paradox of, 269–272
Tooth-paste company, case study of, 111–124, 135–149
Trade, international, balance of, 360, 382
  beggar-my-neighbor policies in, 373–375
  and decreasing costs, 577
  and diminishing returns, 555n.
  expansion of exports relative to imports, devices for, 373–374
  and full employment, 370–376
  multiplier analysis of, 391–392
  postwar problems, of 375–382
  terms of, 544

Transformation curve, 17–22
Treasury Department, 377, 341
Trotsky, Leon, 588
Trusts, trend toward, 36
Twentieth Century Foundation, 607

U

Unemployment, as an evil, 15
technological, 9, 17, 543
(*See also* Labor legislation; Labor
movement; Labor unions)
Unemployment compensation, 221–222, 581
(*See also* Social security)
Union of Soviet Socialist Republics (USSR),
587
Unions (*see* Labor movement; Labor unions)
United Kingdom (U.K.) (*see* Great Britain)
United Nations, 358, 382
United Nations Relief and Rehabilitation
Administration (UNRRA), 376
United States government (*see* Federal
government)
Utility (or satisfaction), 477–479
equilibrium condition of, 478
marginal (*See* Marginal utility)
nonnumerical character of, 478n.

V

Value, paradox of, 482–483
Value added, 233, 243
Veblen, T., 476n.

W

Wages, differences in, 80–82
geographic pattern of, 88
by hour or piece rates, 88–89
and labor unions, 529–531
male and female, 82–84
Negro and white, 82
as share of national income, 531
Wagner National Labor Relations Act
(1935), 189, 190, 192, 195
Wallace, Henry, 585n.
Walsh, J. R., 102n.
War Labor Board (WLB), 194, 197
"Wealth of Nations," 36
Weber-Fechner Law, 481
Welfare economics, 590, 602–603
Welfare expenditure, as type of counter-
cyclical fiscal policy, 412
Works Progress Administration (WPA),
183, 413
Woytinsky, W. S., 79n.